AMERICAN HISTORY
A Survey
Volume II: Since 1865

American History

SIXTH EDITION

A SURVEY

VOLUME II: SINCE 1865

Richard N. Current
University of North Carolina at Greensboro

T. Harry Williams
late of Louisiana State University

Frank Freidel
University of Washington

Alan Brinkley
Harvard University

 ALFRED A. KNOPF NEW YORK

THIS IS A BORZOI BOOK
PUBLISHED BY ALFRED A. KNOPF, INC.

Sixth Edition
98765432
Copyright © 1959, 1961, 1964, 1966, 1971, 1975,
1979 by Richard N. Current, T. Harry Williams,
Frank Freidel
Copyright © 1983 by Richard N. Current,
T. Harry Williams, Frank Freidel, Alan Brinkley

Library of Congress Cataloging in
Publication Data

Main entry under title:
American history: a survey.
    Rev. ed. of: American history / Richard N. Cur-
rent, T. Harry Williams, Frank Freidel. 5th ed.
c1979.
    Includes bibliographies and index.
    1. United States—History.   I. Current, Richard
Nelson.   II. Current, Richard Nelson. American
History.
E178.1.A492   1983b   973   82-17291
ISBN 0-394-33079-X (pbk.: v. 1)
ISBN 0-394-33080-3 (pbk.: v. 2)

Manufactured in the United States of America

Published 1961; reprinted five times
Second edition, 1966; reprinted three times
Third edition, 1971; reprinted four times
Fourth edition, 1975; reprinted four times
Fifth edition, 1979; reprinted three times

Color essay "The American Landscape": Photo
section—photo selection and text by Paula Franklin. Map section—cartographic research and text
by Michael Conzen, University of Chicago; maps
by David Lindroth.

Cover design and construction by Jack Ribik

Cover photograph by James McGuire

Text design by Leon Bolognese

PREFACE

This book attempts to tell a remarkable story: the story of the American people, from their first settlements in the wilderness many centuries ago to the present day. It is a story in part of triumph, of the creation with startling speed of the wealthiest and most powerful society in the history of the world. It is also a story of travail and injustice, of the oppression of the powerless by the powerful, of the careless exploitation of resources, and of the frustrations of international power. And it is, as well, the story of striving, of a people suffused with ideals and struggling constantly—sometimes successfully, sometimes not—to shape a nation and a world that would embody their dreams.

No single work can hope to tell the full story of any nation. In the case of the United States, a country of almost unparalleled diversity, in which change has occurred with such constant and dizzying speed as to make historical time seem to accelerate, that task is particularly difficult. The authors of this volume, therefore, have chosen to emphasize those themes that seem best to embody the heart of the American experience. First, we have recounted in detail the public life of the United States: the creation of the nation's political institutions, the changing expectations of the people involved in those institutions, and the continually evolving role the institutions have played in shaping the fabric of national life. Second, we have examined the development of America's role in the world, from its position as a weak dependency of the British Empire, through its years as a generally isolated nation with little influence in world affairs, to its rise to international preeminence. Third, we have examined the story of the development of the American economy from its simple agrarian beginnings, through its triumphant rise to industrial greatness, to its present troubled condition. And fourth, we have described the way in which the American people have lived: the cultural and social arrangements they have developed for themselves, the impact of political and economic changes upon those arrangements, and the efforts of diverse and often antagonistic groups to find ways of living together within a single society.

It is in this last effort that this sixth edition of *American History: A Survey* differs most significantly from that of its five predecessors. For in the more than twenty years since the first publication of this book, American historical scholarship has undergone something approaching a revolution: the rise of a new social history. Issues that in earlier eras remained obscure adjuncts to the dominant political and diplomatic history of the nation have now emerged as central themes in the writing of American history: the lives and habits of ordinary people; the plight of the majority of the American people who are women and of the substantial minorities who are black, Hispanic, Indian, and otherwise; the process by which America was settled by successive waves of immigrants, and the process by which those immigrants adapted to their new surroundings; the rise and transformation of the city; and the wrenching changes in the nature of agrarian society. This new edition, which represents the most thorough revision since the initial publication of this book, has attempted to incorporate the important new scholarship in all these fields into its pages, while retaining its thorough and careful coverage of the political and diplomatic history of the United States.

The two decades since the initial publication of this book have seen other changes in historical scholarship. They have, for one thing, produced a history of their own; and in this edition we have greatly expanded and deepened our coverage of the recent past. They have, in addition, called into question many of the assumptions that had guided the writing of American history in the past. So while we have in this book avoided taking a particular political or ideological stance, we have also made an effort to reexamine our earlier accounts of major developments in light of newer interpretations. Our coverage of the twentieth century, in particular, has been almost entirely recast and rewritten; but we have made major changes as well in our treatment of the colonial period of American life, of the late nineteenth century, and of many other subjects.

Those familiar with earlier editions of this work will notice other differences as well: the thorough reworking and expansion of the essays entitled "Where Historians Disagree"; completely new bibliographical essays, with critical commentary; changes in our selection of pictures, maps, charts, and other graphics; the addition of a vivid new cartographic essay illustrating the social and demographic evolution of the United States; and a new color art essay highlighting the many facets of the changing American landscape. The result of these, and other, revisions in this sixth edition is, we hope, a study of the American past that will convey more of the richness and complexity of our national life and that will illuminate more clearly how the study of history can enhance our understanding of our own time.

As always, we are deeply grateful to the many people who have contributed to the work on this new edition. In particular, we appreciate the careful, detailed critiques of the text by the scholars who generously agreed to assist us. Because some of these critics have asked not to be identified to us by name, we have chosen not to identify any of them specifically here. But we hope they will know of our gratitude for their invaluable efforts. We thank as well those students and teachers who have used this book over the past several years and who have offered us their comments, criticisms, and corrections—often unsolicited. We hope they will continue to inform us of their reactions to this book in the future, by sending their comments to us in care of the College Department, Alfred A. Knopf, 201 East 50th Street, New York, N.Y. 10022. Finally, we are grateful to the many people at Alfred A. Knopf who have worked to make this book the success it has been for more than two decades, and to those who have worked to make this new edition possible. In particular, we appreciate the efforts of David Follmer, James Kwalwasser, John Sturman, Liz Israel, June Smith, Lynn Goldberg, and Evelyn Katrak, whose indefatigable copy editing of this vast manuscript has removed many inelegancies and inconsistencies.

RICHARD N. CURRENT
Greensboro, North Carolina

FRANK FREIDEL
Seattle, Washington

ALAN BRINKLEY
Cambridge, Massachusetts

AUGUST 1982

CONTENTS

Appendices

WHERE HISTORIANS DISAGREE

ILLUSTRATIONS

MAPS

CHARTS

The American Landscape

Artistic Perspectives

PLATE 1. Short Bull. *Sun Dance*. Courtesy of American Museum of Natural History, New York.

"Our mother the earth" was how Indians typically described the land that nourished them. "The two-leggeds and the four-leggeds lived together like relatives," said a Plains holy man, "and there was plenty for them and for us." Among all the varied Indian peoples of America, rituals celebrated the unity of nature and humankind. One of these ceremonies was the sun dance of the Dakota Sioux, depicted on canvas in Plate 1. Although it is a late example of Indian art—earlier versions would have been done on hide and omitted horses, which were unknown in the New World until the arrival of the Europeans—it symbolizes an old culture whose attitude toward nature clashed with that of the Europeans who first arrived in the seventeenth century.

PLATE 2. Anonymous. *A New York Farm, with the Catskills in the Background.* New York State Historical Association.

One of the first colonists from the Old World, William Bradford, described America as "a hideous and desolate wilderness" that had to be tamed by cultivation. Prosperous farms displayed not only their owners' industry but also their triumph over hostile surroundings. Few colonial artists depicted the look of the American countryside. Those who did—including the painters of an upstate New York farm scene (Plate 2) and a South Carolina plantation (Plate 3)—showed the natural setting of hills and woods purely as a backdrop for the human settlements that were changing the face of the continent.

Not until the nineteenth century did American artists begin to paint the land for its own sake, to see it as landscape. Their work is typified by Asher B. Durand's *Kindred Spirits* (Plate 4). Durand (1796–1886)

PLATE 3. Thomas Coram. *View of Mulberry (House and Street).* Oil on paper, 10 x 17.6 cm. (visible). Carolina Art Association/Gibbes Art Gallery, Charleston, South Carolina.

PLATE 4. Asher Brown Durand. *Kindred Spirits.* Oil on canvas, 44¼ x 36¼". New York Public Library.

PLATE 5. George Inness. *The Lackawanna Valley* (1855). Oil on canvas, 33⅞ x 50¼″. Gift of Mrs. Huttleston Rogers, 1945, National Gallery of Art, Washington, D.C.

PLATE 7. Albert Bierstadt. *The Rocky Mountains* (1863). Oil on canvas, 73½ x 120¾″. The Metropolitan Museum of Art, Rogers Fund, 1907.

PLATE 6. Fitz Hugh Lane. *The Fort and Ten Pound Island, Gloucester, Massachusetts* (1847). Courtesy, The Kennedy Galleries, Inc.

and his fellows, working primarily in the mountains of New York and New England, belonged to a movement that was dubbed the Hudson River school. They were strongly influenced by Ralph Waldo Emerson, who wrote in his essay *Nature* (1836) that humanity may learn to worship God by contemplating natural beauty. By depicting the wonders of their own country, the Hudson River artists made the American wilderness a symbol of national pride in an intensely nationalistic period. Fittingly, *Kindred Spirits* shows nature poet William Cullen Bryant and Thomas Cole, leader of the Hudson River school, in a setting at once impressive and benign.

The nineteenth century thus emerged as the heyday of landscape painting in America, and gifted artists recorded many facets of the American scene. George Inness (1825–1894) is noted for his sweeping views of the spacious, fertile countryside of the agricultural Northeast. *The Lackawanna Valley*

(Plate 5) also reflects the growing role of railroads, which had begun to alter the landscape of the United States.

The New England coast attracted a number of painters, among them Fitz Hugh Lane (1804–1865). His harbor scene at Gloucester, Massachusetts (Plate 6), indicates the continuing importance of commerce and fishing in this region. Lane and others of the so-called luminist school (including Martin Johnson Heade and Frederick Church) were particularly interested in the dramatic contrasts in light that occur where sky, sea, and shore meet.

For drama, however, nothing could match the splendid vistas of the Far West. As the American frontier moved toward the Pacific coast, the magnificent scenery of the Rockies and other Western peaks seemed appropriate symbols of American achievement. In their day, the vast canvases of Albert Bierstadt (1830–1902), such as *The Rocky Mountains* (Plate 7), were extremely

PLATE 8. Thomas Eakins. *Max Schmitt in a Single Scull* (1871). Oil on canvas, 32¼ x 46¼". The Metropolitan Museum of Art, Purchase, 1934, Alfred N. Punnett Fund and Gift of George D. Pratt.

popular and sold for unprecedented sums (see pp. 499–500).

By the late nineteenth century, the United States had produced two painters of first-rate stature. Thomas Eakins (1844–1916) studied in Europe, like most American artists of his time, but returned to America to live. Known particularly for his unsparing portraits of fellow Philadelphians, he devoted the same scrutiny and technical skill to his outdoor scenes. The clarity of early spring light lends a special quality to his painting of his friend Max Schmitt rowing on the Schuylkill River (Plate 8). Eakins,

PLATE 9. Winslow Homer. *Palm Trees, St. John's River, Florida* (1890). Watercolor. The Kennedy Galleries, Inc.

also a keen sportsman—he was the first serious American artist to depict the world of sports—painted himself sculling in the middle distance. The bridges in the background are a reminder of the industrialization and increasingly complex transportation networks that were transforming much of the nation.

The other master of this period was Winslow Homer (1836–1910), whose subjects ranged from rural scenes to spectacular seascapes. One of the few American painters of the time who did not study abroad, he served his apprenticeship as a staff artist for *Harper's Weekly*, sketching at the front during the Civil War. In Homer's later years, he became fascinated by more exotic, tropical settings. His watercolor of shimmering water and feathery palms in Florida (Plate 9) was done in a loose, free style not unlike the impressionism then flourishing in France.

Impressionism had a number of American followers, most notably James Abbott McNeill Whistler and Mary Cassatt, expatriates who spent most of their lives in Europe. Another, J. Alden Weir (1852–1919), preferred the United States. In *U.S. Thread Company Mills, Willimantic, Connecticut* (Plate 10), Weir lends a New England factory town a gentle, almost pastoral beauty.

The 1920 census revealed that, for the first time, more Americans lived in urban areas than in rural ones. Thus the American landscape was increasingly a cityscape, to be recorded in myriad ways.

One group of painters, formed in the 1890s, aimed at portraying city life, especially that of New York, with objectivity and immediacy. These artists—who in-

PLATE 10. Julian Alden Weir. *U.S. Thread Company Mills, Willimantic, Connecticut.* Oil on canvas, 20 x 24″. The Metropolitan Museum of Art, Collection of Mr. and Mrs. Raymond J. Horowitz.

PLATE 11. John Sloan. *The City from Greenwich Village* (1922). Oil on canvas, 26 x 33¾″. The National Gallery of Art, Washington, D.C.

cluded Robert Henri, William Glackens, George Luks, and John Sloan—called themselves The Eight but were derisively nicknamed the Ashcan school because of their stress on the commonplace. In *The City from Greenwich Village* (Plate 11), Sloan (1871–1951) views the metropolis from an immigrant section that had recently become a favored quarter for artists, writers, and bohemian hangers-on. In its dramatic use of darkness and pinpoints of light, Sloan's work shows that the Ashcan painters could both present the prosaic and the journalistic and achieve a kind of urban poetry.

But Ashcan realism enjoyed only a brief vogue. As early as 1913, at the famous Armory show in New York City, Americans were exposed to the innovations of such post-impressionists as Cézanne, Gauguin, Picasso, Matisse, and Léger. Many critics

and most of the general public reacted with dismay, if not downright hostility: the exhibition was reviled as "a lunatic asylum" whose gospel was "stupid license and self-assertion" (see p. 560).

(see p. 560).

For some artists, however, the new styles were a revelation. Among them was John Marin (1870–1953), who had already come under the influence of the post-impressionists. While the Ashcan painters worked very much in the realistic tradition, Marin became one of the most successful of all American abstractionists. For example, when Brooklyn Bridge officially opened in 1883, its great towers and steel cables symbolized the nation's industrial strength. And in Marin's painting of the bridge (Plate 12), its actual appearance is less important than the feelings it engendered. The jumbled colors and broken forms of his spontaneous watercolor—a medium that Marin gave new power—seem to explode with energy.

The modernism exemplified by Marin had many detractors. It seemed, among other things, too private and too far removed from everyday reality. It was often linked to city sophistication and thus deemed out of touch with the "real" America. A number of painters who reacted against it are grouped together as regionalists, although they had no formal unity. Their goal was the realistic depiction of the American land and its people. Regionalism is associated primarily with the agricultural Midwest of the 1930s. During the trauma of the Great Depression, a restatement of traditional values in the context of rural life offered welcome reassurance to many people. Favorite subjects included farm activi-

ties, folk legends, and American history, particularly the winning of the West.

While all the regionalists tried to rediscover America in picturesque depictions of grass-roots culture, their subject matter varied, and so did their styles. Grant Wood (1892–1942), in scenes of his native Iowa, used smooth, conventionalized forms that tend to make the real world of fields and humble farms take on the aspect of a toy universe. No wind disturbs the trees in *Stone City, Iowa* (Plate 13), and a timeless calm immobilizes the people and animals.

Baptism in Kansas (Plate 14), by John Steuart Curry (1897–1946), shows regionalism in a different mode. Here style is secondary to narrative and sincerity of feeling. The religious fervor of the participants, rather than being diminished by the bleak

PLATE 12. John Marin. *Brooklyn Bridge* (1910). Watercolor, 18½ x 15⅛". The Metropolitan Museum of Art, Alfred Stieglitz Collection, 1949.

PLATE 13. Grant Wood. *Stone City, Iowa* (1930). Oil on wood panel, 30¼ x 40". Joslyn Art Museum, Omaha, Nebraska.

PLATE 14. John Steuart Curry. *Baptism in Kansas* (1928). Oil on canvas, 40 x 50". Collection of the Whitney Museum of American Art, New York.

PLATE 15. Thomas Hart Benton. *Boom Town* (1928). Oil on canvas, 45 x 54″. Memorial Art Gallery of the University of Rochester, Marion Stratton Gould Fund.

Plains setting, is heightened by bright clouds (and a pair of improbable birds).

Still another approach to regionalism was that of Thomas Hart Benton (1889–1975), whose many farm scenes, whether of rice harvesting in Louisiana or plowing in Missouri, emphasize the dignity of labor and the joy of life lived outdoors. *Boom Town* (Plate 15) shows the other side of the coin—the pollution and congestion that followed industrialization and new forms of transportation into the heartland.

PLATE 16. Georgia O'Keeffe. *Ranchos Church* (c. 1930). Oil on canvas, 24 x 36″. The Phillips Collection, Washington, D.C.

PLATE 17. Charles Sheeler. *Western Industrial* (1954). Tempera on plexiglass. Corcoran Gallery of Art, Museum Purchase, William A. Clark Fund.

Although associated with the Southwest, Georgia O'Keeffe (1887–   ) is not considered a regionalist, for she is more interested in the interrelationship of forms as forms than in rendering a particular place at a particular time. Even so, her *Ranchos Church* (Plate 16) seems firmly rooted in the sands of New Mexico.

Despite the regionalists' emphasis on the nation's rural charms, the United States of the mid-twentieth century had become an industrial giant, its horizons bristling with

PLATE 18. Edward Hopper. *Gas* (1940). Oil on canvas, 26¼ x 40¼". Collection, The Museum of Modern Art, New York, Mrs. Simon Guggenheim Fund.

PLATE 19. Horace Pippin. *Cabin in the Cotton, III.* Collection, Roy N. Neuberger.

PLATE 20. Marsden Hartley. *Smelt Brook Falls* (1937). Oil on board, 71.1 x 55.9 cm. The St. Louis Art Museum, Elizabeth McMillan Fund.

factories, refineries, and high-tension wires. Charles Sheeler (1883–1965) turned to these complex forms for his inspiration, rendering them with a sharp, almost antiseptic, purity. (Indeed, he and O'Keeffe are sometimes referred to as precisionists.) Like most of his works, *Western Industrial* (Plate 17) is devoid of human reference.

For several artists of this period, landscape served to express personal feelings and inner moods. Loneliness pervades the paintings of Edward Hopper (1882–1967). His isolated figures, as in *Gas* (Plate 18), seem weighed down by brooding silence. Horace Pippin (1888–1946), the grandson of slaves, depicted various aspects of the black experience (as in Plate 19) with the straightforwardness and lack of sentimentality characteristic of naive painting. For Mars-

PLATE 21. Willem de Kooning. *Door to the River* (1960). Oil on canvas, 80 x 70''. Collection of Whitney Museum of American Art. Gift of the Friends of the Whitney Museum of American Art. Photograph by Geoffrey Clements.

den Hartley (1877–1943), nature symbolized the tragedy of the human condition. *Smelt Brook Falls* (Plate 20), a scene in his native Maine, conveys a sense of the blunt, almost crude, power of natural forces.

Landscape as we know it seemed to disappear almost entirely in the work of the abstract expressionists, who, in the late 1940s, abandoned representation in favor of dramatic daubs and dribbles of color. Their huge, emotionally intense canvases made the United States the leader of the art world for the first time. In spite of the highly personal nature of their paintings, several abstract expressionists hinted at landscapes in their titles, such as *Door to the River* (Plate 21) by Dutch-born Willem de Kooning (1904–   ). The sweeping brushstrokes and the rhythmic movement of its painted surface characterize de Kooning's work.

The immediate environment of the modern world was not to be ignored, however. The artifacts of the affluent consumer society, from soup cans to automobiles, gave rise in the late 1950s to a playful movement known as Pop Art. The work of Roy Lichtenstein (1923–   ) echoes mass-production printing techniques by employing in exaggerated form the dots characteristic of commercial photography. In his hands, even a mountain range (Plate 22) takes on the flatness of a comic strip.

In the 1970s, some artists returned to realism with a vengeance, depicting everyday aspects of contemporary life with a heightened naturalism, known as photorealism, superrealism, or sharp-focus realism. *The Magic Chef* (Plate 23), by John Baeder (1938–   ), typifies this movement's meticulous attention to banal subjects, in this case a stretch of the highway culture that has come to clutter the outskirts of many

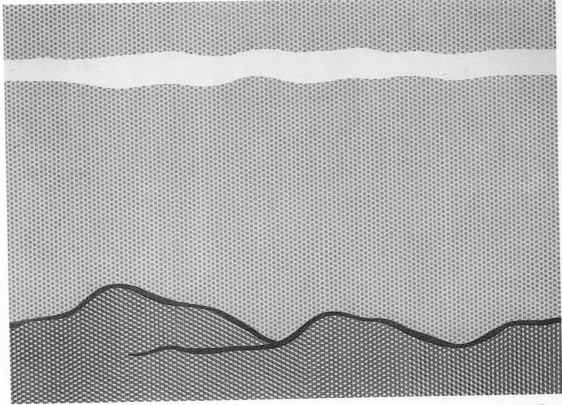

PLATE 22. Roy Lichtenstein. *Purple Range* (1966). Oil and magna on canvas, 36 x 48". Courtesy, Leo Castelli Gallery, New York. Private collection.

PLATE 23. John Baeder. *Magic Chef Cafe* (1975). Oil on canvas, 48 x 72". Collection, Denver Art Museum, Denver, Colorado.

PLATE 24. Eliot Porter. *Colorful Trees. Newfound Gap Road, Great Smoky Mountains Park, Tennessee* (October 1967). Dye transfer photograph. The Metropolitan Museum of Art. Gift of Eliot Porter in honor of David H. McAlpin, 1979.

American towns. The perfection of detail creates an eerie effect.

Clearly, the American landscape has undergone sweeping changes as the United States has grown from a sparsely populated wilderness into a highly urbanized, industrial society. But, despite the defacement or destruction of much that was beautiful, the United States has not lost its visual splendors. Few record them with such fidelity as contemporary nature photographers, who might well be termed the true landscape artists of today.

Photography became respected as an art form in America with the work of Alfred Stieglitz early in the twentieth century (see p. 543). And several painters—including Charles Sheeler, himself a fine photographer—were strongly influenced by the tonalities of black-and-white photography. Like painting, photography lends itself to varied treatments, including romantic impressionism and studio abstractions. A highly developed pictorial imagination informs the work of such modern masters as Eliot Porter (1901–   ). His *Colorful Trees* (Plate 24), capturing the glow of a Tennessee hillside in autumn, is a powerful reminder that natural beauty is still a vital component of the American landscape.

The American Landscape
Geographical Perspectives

Map 1

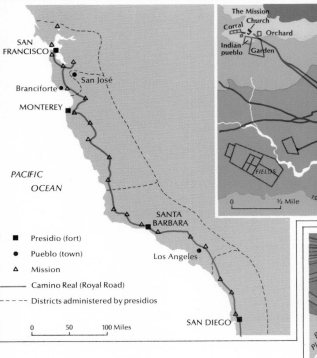

SPANISH COLONIAL SETTLEMENT PATTERNS IN CALIFORNIA

SAN FRANCISCO

Branciforte

San José

MONTEREY

PACIFIC OCEAN

SANTA BARBARA

Los Angeles

SAN DIEGO

■ Presidio (fort)
● Pueblo (town)
△ Mission
— Camino Real (Royal Road)
--- Districts administered by presidios

0   50   100 Miles

The Mission
Church
Corral
Orchard
Indian pueblo
Garden

450
300
150

SANTA BARBARA

The Presidio

El Estero

FIELDS

150

PACIFIC OCEAN

0   ½ Mile

FRENCH LONG LOT LANDSCAPE IN IBERVILLE PARISH, LOUISIANA

 French long lots, as divided by 1858. (Many had plantation houses fronting on the river.)

Swampy areas   — Road

 Town (Plaquemine)   △ Church

0   5 Miles

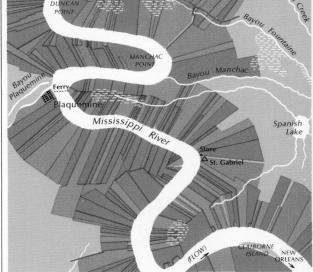

BATON ROUGE
DUNCAN POINT
Wards Creek
Bayou Fountaine
MANCHAC POINT
Bayou Manchac
Bayou Plaquemine
Ferry
Plaquemine
Mississippi River
Spanish Lake
Store
△ St. Gabriel
(FLOW)
CLAIBORNE ISLAND
NEW ORLEANS

Map 2

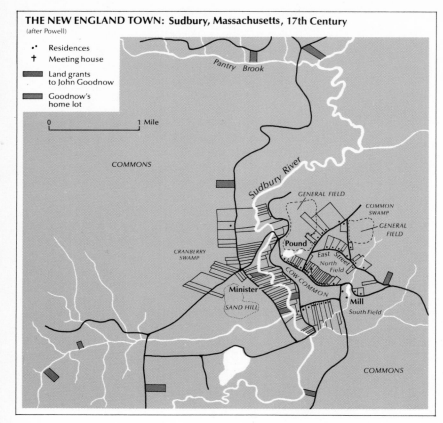

THE NEW ENGLAND TOWN: Sudbury, Massachusetts, 17th Century
(after Powell)

- •˙ Residences
- † Meeting house
- ▬ Land grants to John Goodnow
- ▬ Goodnow's home lot

0   1 Mile

Pantry Brook

COMMONS

Sudbury River

GENERAL FIELD

COMMON SWAMP

GENERAL FIELD

CRANBERRY SWAMP

Pound

East Street

North Field

COW COMMON

Minister

(SAND HILL)

Mill

South Field

COMMONS

MAP 3

The area that now forms the United States contains a rich array of contrasting regions—each with distinctive climate, landforms, and vegetation. And these regional differences have been compounded by the fact that the land was settled by groups of people from many different countries and cultures. Thus, the way in which the American landscape has developed is a reflection of varied goals and backgrounds, in addition to diverse natural conditions.

Despite the speed and scope of social change in modern times, many features discernible today, especially along the Atlantic coast and in parts of the Southwest, owe their distinctiveness to early colonization ventures. In the continental interior, the mixing of population streams and the diffusion of technology have not masked the divergent cultural landscapes that resulted from distinct resource environments. The westward movement of the nation and the progressive industrialization of its economy led to profound changes in population patterns, both in settled farming regions and in urban areas. More recently, settlement patterns have continued to evolve as a result of the enlarged scale of government, population movements, business organization, and social control.

Colonial Beginnings

Of all the major European colonization strategies in what later became the United States, Spain's was the most centralized, politically integrated, and geographically systematized—though often imperfectly realized. California exemplified the Spanish scheme for frontier settlement (Map 1): a string of missions and their surrounding Indian agricultural colonies with a few towns (*pueblos*) of Mexican settlers, all bound together under the protection of four military centers (*presidios*) that served an administrative function. The Spanish colonial network was far-flung, and its population was sparse. Even Santa Barbara, which had both a presidio and a mission, was quite a small settlement.

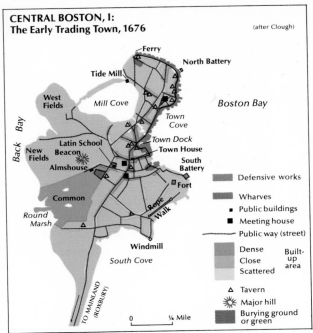

CENTRAL BOSTON, I:
The Early Trading Town, 1676

(after Clough)

Ferry
North Battery
Tide Mill
West Fields
Mill Cove
Boston Bay
Back Bay
Town Cove
Latin School
Town Dock
Beacon
Town House
New Fields
South Battery
Almshouse
Fort
Common
Rope Walk
Round Marsh
Windmill
South Cove

TO MAINLAND (ROXBURY)

Defensive works
Wharves
■ Public buildings
■ Meeting house
Public way (street)
Dense
Close   Built-up
Scattered area
△ Tavern
✳ Major hill
Burying ground or green

0   ¼ Mile

MAP 4

The French colonial network was also thin on a continental scale, but the French were able to create some larger and more autonomous pockets of colonization. Their land-grant system of individual "long lots," which were oriented to major rivers, has left an indelible mark on the cultural landscape of several parts of the United States, most notably the Mississippi bottomlands south of Baton Rouge, Louisiana (Map 2).

English colonizers arrived in North America with several different formulas for settlement. The Puritans produced the social and geographical unit called the New England town (Map 3; see also pp. 74–76). Adapted from the agricultural villages of England, it was distinguished by its system of local, communal government and by its expectations of economic self-sufficiency.

MAP 5

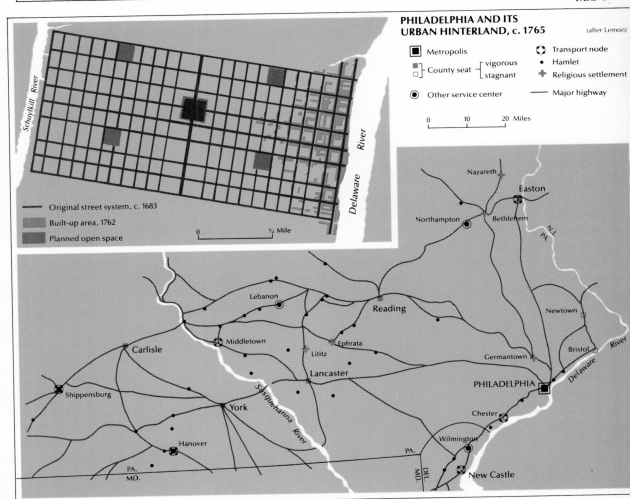

PHILADELPHIA AND ITS
URBAN HINTERLAND, c. 1765

(after Lemon)

■ Metropolis
County seat ⌐ vigorous ⌐ stagnant
◉ Other service center
◖ Transport node
● Hamlet
✚ Religious settlement
Major highway

0   10   20 Miles

Original street system, c. 1683
Built-up area, 1762
Planned open space

0   ½ Mile

Schuylkill River
Delaware River

Nazareth
Easton
Northampton
Bethlehem
N.J. PA.
Lebanon
Reading
Newtown
Carlisle
Middletown
Ephrata
Lititz
Germantown
Bristol
Shippensburg
Lancaster
Delaware River
York
Susquehanna River
PHILADELPHIA
Chester
Hanover
Wilmington
PA.
PA. MD.
DEL. MD.
New Castle

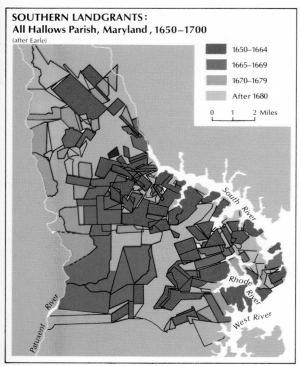

SOUTHERN LANDGRANTS:
All Hallows Parish, Maryland, 1650–1700
(after Earle)

▨	1650–1664
▨	1665–1669
▨	1670–1679
▨	After 1680

0   1   2 Miles

South River

Rhode River

West River

Patuxent River

MAP 6

Because New England lacked a major agricultural staple, trade soon became vital to the region, and Boston developed early as an international port and commercial center (Map 4). Docks, craft industries, and urban institutions soon gave the town a unique aspect, although the agricultural basis of its land and road communication patterns persisted for some time.

In the Middle Colonies, town founding by great proprietors such as William Penn was more centralized. Penn's intentions for Philadelphia were as prescriptive as Boston's experience had been haphazard (Map 5). Prior to the Revolution, Philadelphia's actual built-up area involved only the few city blocks near the Delaware River, but Penn's original plan was kept in mind as the city expanded further. So dominant was Philadelphia's urban growth that settlements in its shadow failed to grow during the colonial period. Nevertheless, a fertile

MAP 7

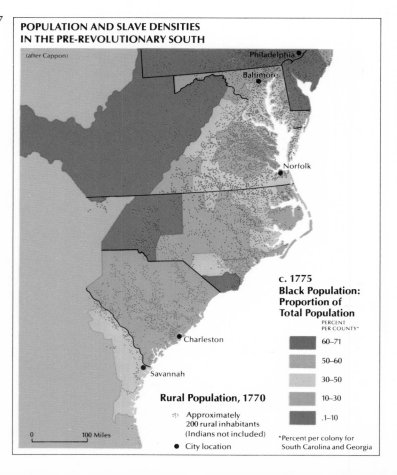

POPULATION AND SLAVE DENSITIES
IN THE PRE-REVOLUTIONARY SOUTH

(after Cappon)

Philadelphia •

Baltimore •

Norfolk •

Charleston •

Savannah •

c. 1775
Black Population:
Proportion of
Total Population
PERCENT
PER COUNTY*

▨	60–71
▨	50–60
▨	30–50
▨	10–30
▨	.1–10

Rural Population, 1770

::: Approximately
     200 rural inhabitants
     (Indians not included)
• City location

0   100 Miles

*Percent per colony for
South Carolina and Georgia

EVOLUTION OF THE MAJOR COMMODITY BELTS

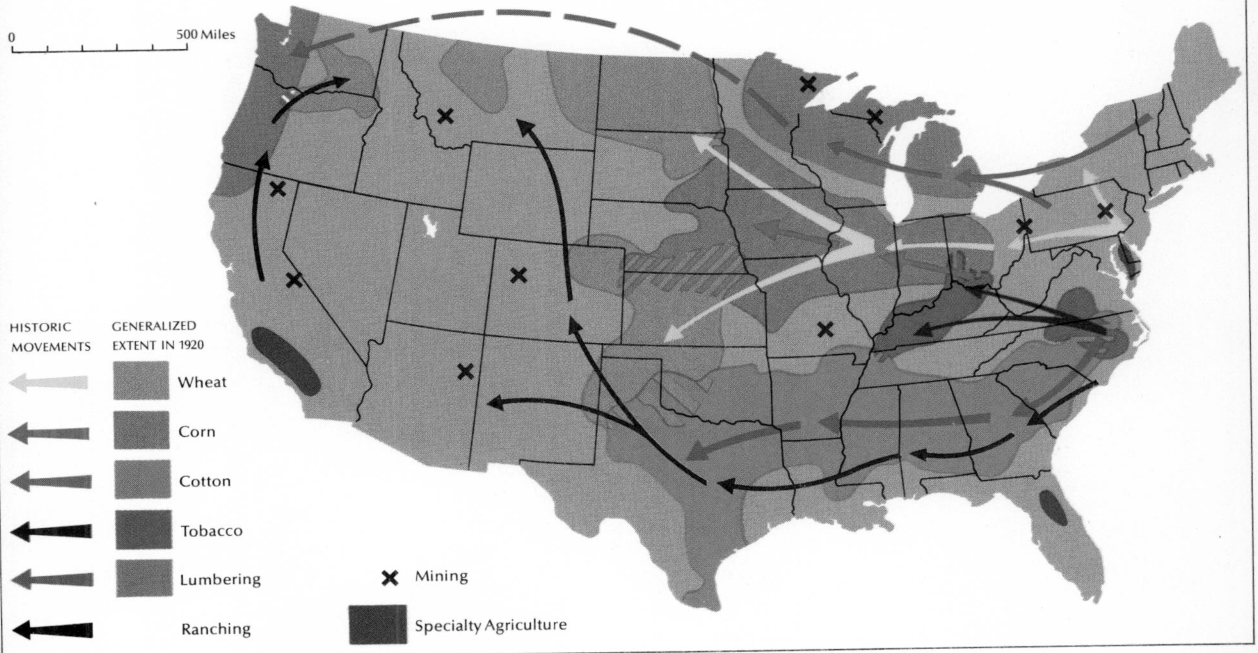

0   500 Miles

HISTORIC MOVEMENTS

GENERALIZED EXTENT IN 1920

Wheat

Corn

Cotton

Tobacco

Lumbering

Ranching

✕ Mining

Specialty Agriculture

MAP 8

hinterland stimulated the early emergence of a regional system of towns with a variety of urban functions.

In the South, circumstances were less favorable to town growth. Instead, the emphasis on a few staple crops such as tobacco led to the rise of a plantation economy (see pp. 72–74). Characteristic of early tidewater settlement was the pattern of land grants in All Hallows Parish, Maryland, where most farms had direct access to water transport (Map 6). Metes-and-bounds surveys, which use natural landmarks rather than a rectilinear system, produced irregular, individualistic, and sometimes overlapping ownership tracts that contrasted markedly with the orderly structure of New England towns. Another distinct characteristic of the South was its increasing reliance on slave labor, especially in the most densely settled districts of Virginia and the Carolinas (Map 7; see also pp. 42–43).

Resource Frontiers

The regional agricultural specializations that had emerged during the colonial period intensified as settlers took grains, tobacco, cotton, and other crops across the Appalachian Mountains (Map 8). During the nineteenth century, wheat, corn, and cotton belts developed and extended westward as population, climate, and market prices determined the zones of optimum planting. Some regions passed through several phases of specialization, such as northern Illinois, with first cattle, then wheat, and then corn; others saw but one, such as northern Wisconsin, with lumbering only.

The settlements produced by these specializations were equally varied. Areas of grain and livestock farming quickly became thickly settled: small and medium-sized holdings, owned mainly by independent farmers, were set in landscapes of road and rail networks, towns of all sizes, and nu-

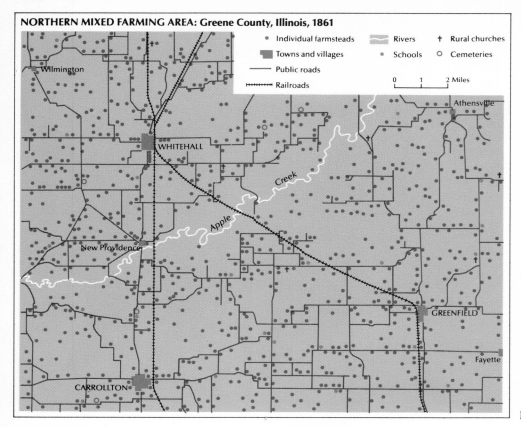

NORTHERN MIXED FARMING AREA: Greene County, Illinois, 1861

Legend:
- Individual farmsteads
- Towns and villages
- Public roads
- Railroads
- Rivers
- Schools
- Rural churches
- Cemeteries

0   1   2 Miles

Wilmington
WHITEHALL
Athensville
Creek
Apple
New Providence
GREENFIELD
Fayette
CARROLLTON

MAP 9

MAP 10

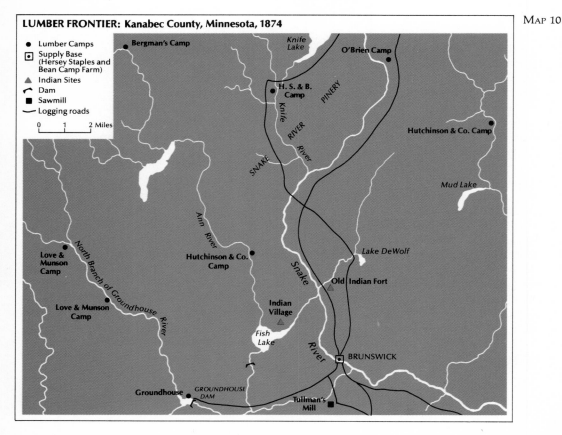

LUMBER FRONTIER: Kanabec County, Minnesota, 1874

Legend:
- Lumber Camps
- Supply Base (Hersey Staples and Bean Camp Farm)
- Indian Sites
- Dam
- Sawmill
- Logging roads

0   1   2 Miles

Bergman's Camp
Knife Lake
O'Brien Camp
H. S. & B. Camp
PINERY
Knife River
SNAKE RIVER
Hutchinson & Co. Camp
Mud Lake
Ann River
North Branch of Groundhouse River
Love & Munson Camp
Hutchinson & Co. Camp
Lake DeWolf
Snake
Old Indian Fort
Love & Munson Camp
Indian Village
Fish Lake
River
BRUNSWICK
Groundhouse
GROUNDHOUSE DAM
Tuilman's Mill

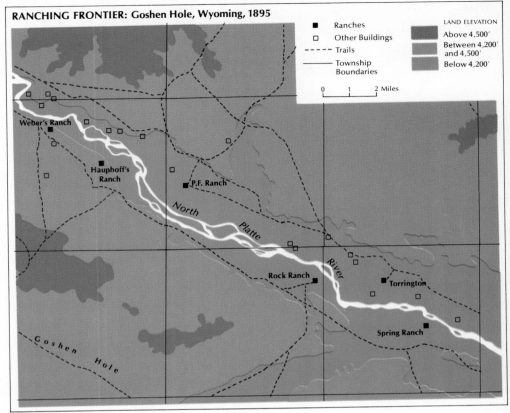

RANCHING FRONTIER: Goshen Hole, Wyoming, 1895

■ Ranches
□ Other Buildings
- - - Trails
—— Township Boundaries

LAND ELEVATION
Above 4,500'
Between 4,200' and 4,500'
Below 4,200'

0   1   2 Miles

Weber's Ranch
Hauphoff's Ranch
P.F. Ranch
North Platte River
Rock Ranch
Torrington
Spring Ranch
Goshen Hole

MAP 11

MAP 12

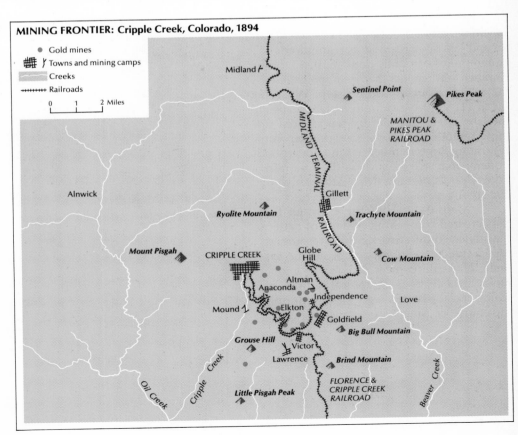

MINING FRONTIER: Cripple Creek, Colorado, 1894

● Gold mines
▦ ⅄ Towns and mining camps
Creeks
++++++ Railroads

0   1   2 Miles

Midland
Sentinel Point
Pikes Peak
MANITOU & PIKES PEAK RAILROAD
Alnwick
MIDLAND TERMINAL RAILROAD
Gillett
Ryolite Mountain
Trachyte Mountain
Mount Pisgah
Globe Hill
Cow Mountain
CRIPPLE CREEK
Altman
Anaconda
Independence
Love
Mound
Elkton
Goldfield
Big Bull Mountain
Grouse Hill
Victor
Brind Mountain
Lawrence
FLORENCE & CRIPPLE CREEK RAILROAD
Oil Creek
Cripple Creek
Little Pisgah Peak
Beaver Creek

MAP 13

RURAL DEPOPULATION IN NORTHERN NEW ENGLAND: Lyme, New Hampshire, 1830–1925

(after Goldthwait)

Land above 1,000 feet elevation

0   1   2 Miles

	ROADS	HOUSES	
		•ˆ	Abandoned 1830–1860
		•.	Abandoned 1860–1892
		••	Abandoned 1892–1925
		o	Summer only } 1925
		⌇	Still in use

Connecticut River

Lyme Plain

Lyme Center

Agrarian Change in Settled Areas

As the frontier pushed westward, older regions of the United States continued to undergo change. One cause of change was the new territory itself: cheap land and virgin soil to the west drew farm youths out of northern New England (as did new factory jobs to the south), resulting in considerable population loss in that region (Map 13; see also pp. 266–267, 321). In the South, the agents of rural change were the dislocations of the Civil War and Reconstruction and the abolition of slavery (pp. 466–467). Many once-profitable, compactly organized plantations were transformed into decentralized operations in which physically dispersed small farms were held together by ties such as sharecropping agreements (Map 14).

merous rural social-service institutions (Map 9). On the extensive lumber frontier, in contrast, isolated camps were connected by streams and logging roads to a few supply towns in a vast sea of forests. Kanabec County, Minnesota, was a good example (Map 10). Even more extensive was the ranching frontier of the Far West. Here cattle and cowboys roamed over hundreds of square miles of public domain, tied loosely to ranch settlements that monopolized major watercourses, as in eastern Wyoming (Map 11). And typical mining landscapes in the late nineteenth century represented still more remote conditions, though often concentrating large numbers of miners around mineral-rich strikes, such as the area near Pikes Peak, Colorado (Map 12; see also pp. 495–496).

As Maps 9–12 show, these various frontiers created contrasting settlement patterns that reflected differing kinds of resources, topographic conditions, and economic systems. These differences fostered an enormous diversity of geographical settings in which social patterns were shaped during the course of American expansion.

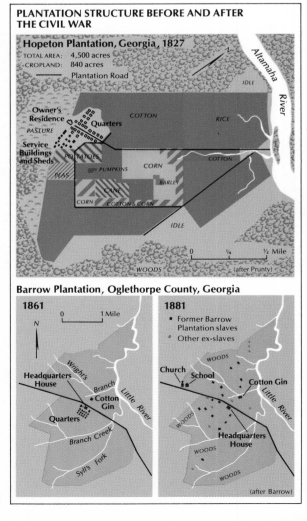

PLANTATION STRUCTURE BEFORE AND AFTER THE CIVIL WAR

Hopeton Plantation, Georgia, 1827

TOTAL AREA: 4,500 acres
CROPLAND: 840 acres
Plantation Road

Altamaha River

IDLE

Owner's Residence   Quarters   COTTON   RICE

PASTURE

Service Buildings and Sheds   POTATOES   COTTON

PEAS   PUMPKINS   CORN

CORN   CANE   BARLEY

CORN   COTTON & CORN

IDLE

WOODS   0   ¼   ½ Mile   (after Prunty)

Barrow Plantation, Oglethorpe County, Georgia

1861

0   1 Mile

N

Wright's Branch

Headquarters House

Cotton Gin

Little River

Quarters

Branch Creek

Syll's Fork

1881

■ Former Barrow Plantation slaves
• Other ex-slaves

WOODS

Church   School

Cotton Gin

Little River

WOODS

Headquarters House

WOODS

WOODS

(after Barrow)

MAP 14

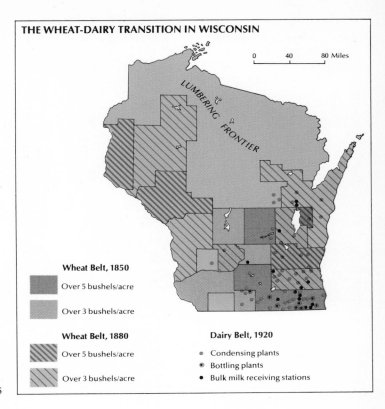

THE WHEAT-DAIRY TRANSITION IN WISCONSIN

0   40   80 Miles

LUMBERING FRONTIER

Wheat Belt, 1850

Over 5 bushels/acre

Over 3 bushels/acre

Wheat Belt, 1880

Over 5 bushels/acre

Over 3 bushels/acre

Dairy Belt, 1920

● Condensing plants

◉ Bottling plants

• Bulk milk receiving stations

MAP 15

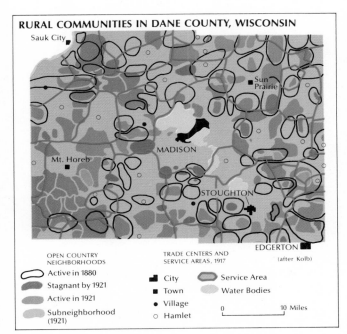

RURAL COMMUNITIES IN DANE COUNTY, WISCONSIN

Sauk City

Sun Prairie

MADISON

Mt. Horeb

STOUGHTON

EDGERTON

(after Kolb)

OPEN COUNTRY
NEIGHBORHOODS

Active in 1880

Stagnant by 1921

Active in 1921

Subneighborhood
(1921)

TRADE CENTERS AND
SERVICE AREAS, 1917

◼ City   Service Area

■ Town   Water Bodies

• Village

○ Hamlet   0   10 Miles

Even in newer states like Wisconsin, the passing of the highly prosperous wheat frontier left many people searching for a new agricultural specialization. Between the 1880s and 1920, eastern and southern parts of the state developed an emphasis on dairying, which required intensive labor and a complex marketing network that linked local farms to the nearby cities of Chicago and Milwaukee (Map 15). As a result, the fabric of rural society changed, too. Farm families that had lived in longstanding country neighborhoods now felt the pull of small towns, which offered an increasing number of institutions and services (Map 16).

MAP 16

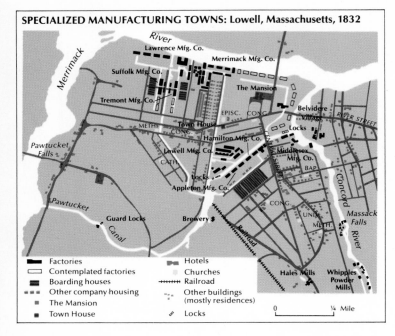

SPECIALIZED MANUFACTURING TOWNS: Lowell, Massachusetts, 1832

Legend:
- Factories
- Contemplated factories
- Boarding houses
- Other company housing
- The Mansion
- Town House
- Hotels
- Churches
- Railroad
- Other buildings (mostly residences)
- Locks

0 ¼ Mile

MAP 17

Urban Developments During Industrialization

While new towns were changing the face of the countryside during the later part of the nineteenth century, major American cities were evolving as well. The potent forces behind urban change were industrialization and the associated transportation revolution. As early as the 1820s, specialized manufacturing cities like Lowell, Massachusetts, were created from nothing to accommodate huge factory-scale production (Map 17; see also pp. 267–268). Lowell's design reflected the supremacy of its textile mills; civic and cultural institutions were little more than afterthoughts. In larger and more diversified centers, the demands of both growth and new commercial functions created a distinctive new land-use zone—the multifunctional central business district, which became more efficient with the evolution of specialized subdistricts for finance, markets, ware-

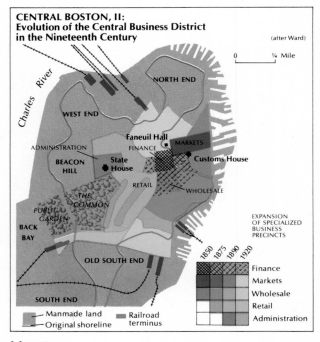

CENTRAL BOSTON, II:
Evolution of the Central Business District in the Nineteenth Century

(after Ward)

0 ¼ Mile

EXPANSION OF SPECIALIZED BUSINESS PRECINCTS

1850 1875 1890 1920

- Finance
- Markets
- Wholesale
- Retail
- Administration

Manmade land
Original shoreline
Railroad terminus

MAP 18

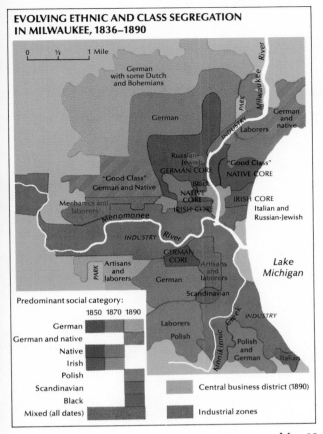

EVOLVING ETHNIC AND CLASS SEGREGATION IN MILWAUKEE, 1836–1890

German with some Dutch and Bohemians

German

INDUSTRY PARK

Milwaukee River

German and native

Laborers

Russian-Jewish

GERMAN CORE

"Good Class"
NATIVE CORE

"Good Class"
German and Native

Black
NATIVE
CORE

IRISH CORE

IRISH CORE

Italian and
Russian-Jewish

Mechanics and laborers

Menomonee River

INDUSTRY River

GERMAN CORE

PARK

Artisans and laborers

German

Artisans and laborers

Scandinavian

Lake Michigan

INDUSTRY

Kinnikinnic Creek

Laborers

Polish

Polish and German

Italian

Predominant social category:

	1850	1870	1890
German			
German and native			
Native			
Irish			
Polish			
Scandinavian			
Black			
Mixed (all dates)			

Central business district (1890)

Industrial zones

MAP 19

housing, and so on (Map 18). This central district became even more important with the advent of railroads, which began to link cities together in the years before the Civil War.

The growth of central business districts was just one manifestation of the urban transformation. Another was the segregation of neighborhoods by ethnic group and social class. Partly because of streetcars, first horse-drawn and later electrified, which opened up new areas to daily commuting, cities developed many residential districts where one or more social group predominated; movement in and out of these districts mirrored ethnic assimilation and class mobility (Map 19). Especially noteworthy were the new districts of middle-class suburban housing, like the Garden District of New Orleans, that were made possible by the rapid growth of streetcar service (Map 20).

In the West, railroads were at once the promoters, predictors, and managers of growth. In the Dakotas, for example, whole networks of towns were planted and nurtured by the Chicago, Milwaukee and St.

MAP 20

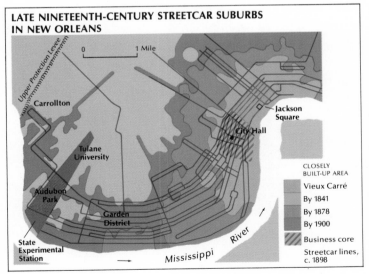

LATE NINETEENTH-CENTURY STREETCAR SUBURBS IN NEW ORLEANS

Upper Protection Levee

Carrollton

Jackson Square

City Hall

Tulane University

Audubon Park

Garden District

State Experimental Station

Mississippi River

CLOSELY BUILT-UP AREA

Vieux Carré

By 1841

By 1878

By 1900

Business core

Streetcar lines, c. 1898

Paul Railway Company, with different localities earmarked for different levels of future urban development (Map 21).

Modern Transformations

By World War I, as a result of such developments, the national urban system was complex and extensive. Almost every area of the country had a well-defined city system (Map 22). The pattern of major cities reflected the continued dominance of the older Eastern seaport cities, the maturation of Midwestern commercial and industrial cities (to form the nation's traditional Northeastern manufacturing belt), and the rise of Southern and Western centers of regional service and long-distance trade.

One of the most vexing consequences of urbanization has been political fragmentation at the local level. Chicago's growth, for example, has been frustrated by suburban resistance to annexation by the metropolis (Map 23). As a result, the efforts to solve

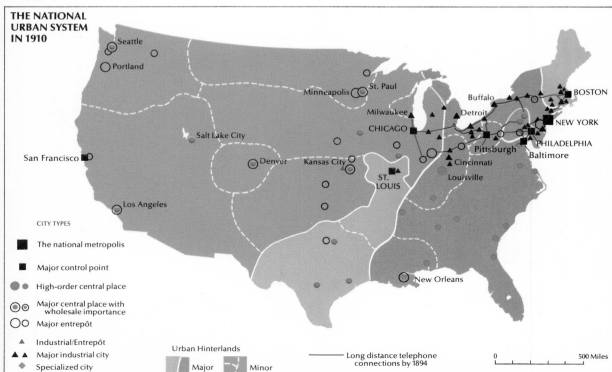

MAP 21

MAP 22

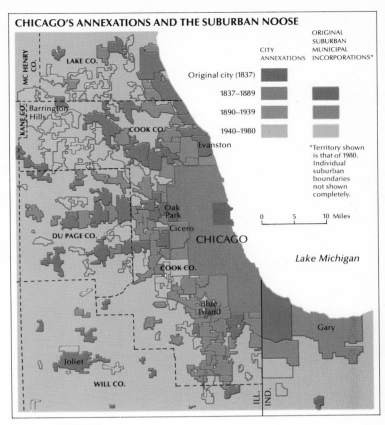

CHICAGO'S ANNEXATIONS AND THE SUBURBAN NOOSE

CITY ANNEXATIONS / ORIGINAL SUBURBAN MUNICIPAL INCORPORATIONS*

Original city (1837)
1837–1889
1890–1939
1940–1980

*Territory shown is that of 1980. Individual suburban boundaries not shown completely.

0   5   10 Miles

MAP 23

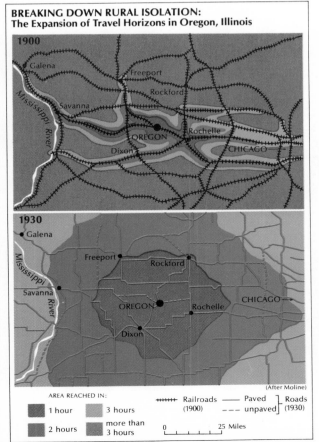

BREAKING DOWN RURAL ISOLATION:
The Expansion of Travel Horizons in Oregon, Illinois

1900

1930

(After Moline)

AREA REACHED IN:

1 hour
2 hours
3 hours
more than 3 hours

Railroads (1900)   Paved — Roads
                     unpaved --- (1930)

0   25 Miles

MAP 24

problems that affect entire metropolitan areas have led to both inefficiency and conflict, although many suburban dwellers have maintained a controlling voice in their immediate local environments.

The transportation revolution that spurred urban growth also transformed the rural scene. In the nineteenth century, railroads had strengthened the links between rural settlements and the outside world, and within decades, these bonds were vastly intensified by the automobile. For example, in 1900, travel to and from the town of Oregon, Illinois, was heavily dependent on train routes and schedules. By 1930, though, the car had brought a far greater territory within the same potential travel time at the convenience of the family (Map 24). Auto travel had become so widespread by 1950 that large cities developed not only huge commuting regions but also outer, exurban rings. By 1970, the urban centers of the Eastern seaboard were well on the way toward complete physical merger in one long

MEGALOPOLIS MATURES, 1950–1970

(after Browning)

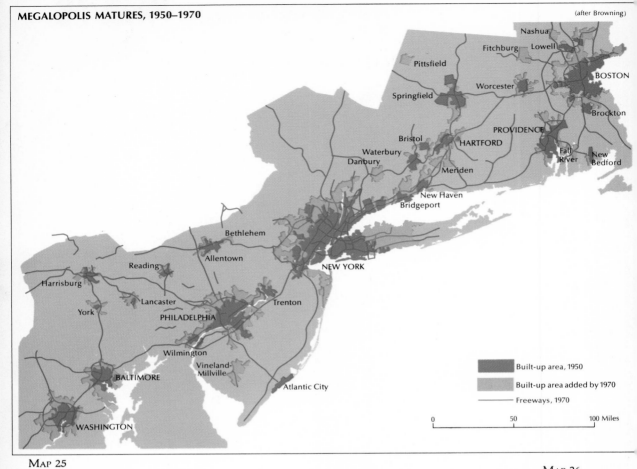

Nashua
Fitchburg
Lowell
Pittsfield
Worcester
BOSTON
Springfield
Brockton
Bristol
HARTFORD
PROVIDENCE
Waterbury
Fall
River
Danbury
Meriden
New
Bedford
New Haven
Bridgeport
Bethlehem
Allentown
Reading
NEW YORK
Harrisburg
Lancaster
Trenton
York
PHILADELPHIA
Wilmington
Vineland-
Millville
BALTIMORE
Atlantic City

WASHINGTON

Built-up area, 1950

Built-up area added by 1970

Freeways, 1970

0   50   100 Miles

MAP 25

MAP 26

RISE OF CORPORATE FARMING AND IRRIGATION DEPENDENCY

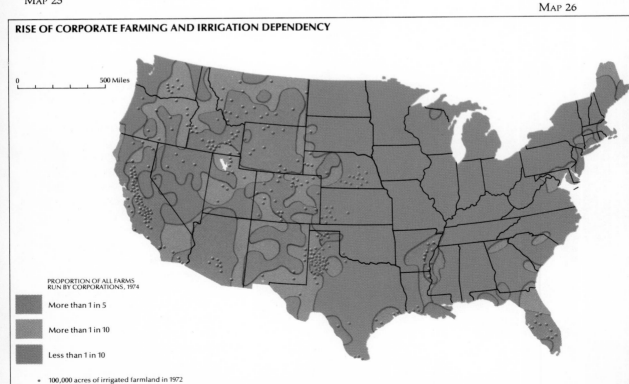

0   500 Miles

PROPORTION OF ALL FARMS
RUN BY CORPORATIONS, 1974

More than 1 in 5

More than 1 in 10

Less than 1 in 10

• 100,000 acres of irrigated farmland in 1972

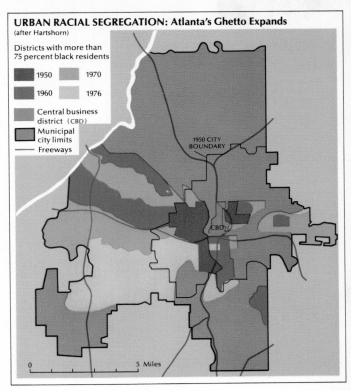

URBAN RACIAL SEGREGATION: Atlanta's Ghetto Expands
(after Hartshorn)

Districts with more than
75 percent black residents

1950	1970
1960	1976

Central business
district (CBD)

Municipal
city limits

Freeways

1950 CITY
BOUNDARY

CBD

0   5 Miles

MAP 27

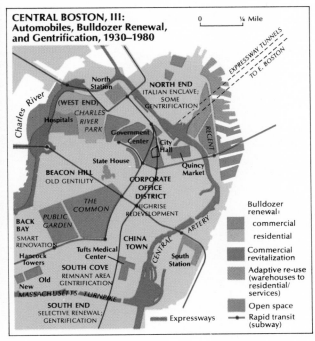

CENTRAL BOSTON, III:
Automobiles, Bulldozer Renewal,
and Gentrification, 1930–1980

0   ¼ Mile

EXPRESSWAY TUNNELS
TO E. BOSTON

Charles River

North
Station

NORTH END
ITALIAN ENCLAVE;
SOME
GENTRIFICATION

(WEST END)
Hospitals

CHARLES
RIVER
PARK

Government
Center

City
Hall

Quincy
Market

State House

BEACON HILL
OLD GENTILITY

CORPORATE
OFFICE
DISTRICT

HIGHRISE
REDEVELOPMENT

THE
COMMON

BACK
BAY

PUBLIC
GARDEN

SMART
RENOVATION

CHINA
TOWN

South
Station

Hancock
Towers

Tufts Medical
Center

SOUTH COVE
REMNANT AREA
GENTRIFICATION

Old
New

MASSACHUSETTS TURNPIKE

SOUTH END
SELECTIVE RENEWAL;
GENTRIFICATION

CENTRAL ARTERY

Bulldozer
renewal:

commercial

residential

Commercial
revitalization

Adaptive re-use
(warehouses to
residential/
services)

Open space

Expressways

Rapid transit
(subway)

MAP 28

belt that has been called Megalopolis (Map 25).

Another trend that has affected many agricultural communities is the application of industrial methods to farming. In the West, for example, large-scale irrigation has extended crop production to regions that were previously too dry—and has heightened problems of overall water supply (Map 26). And the heavy capitalization needs of modern farming have resulted in the rise of corporate farming (agribusiness), heavily concentrated in the irrigated West, the cotton and sugar areas of the lower Mississippi basin, and the specialty crop areas of Florida and the Eastern seaboard.

Since World War II, no social problem in urban America has been more pressing than persistent residential segregation by race. Complex forces (see p. 863), including the movement of middle-class whites to suburban and exurban areas, have encouraged the growth of black and Hispanic ghettoes to the point that they constitute significant portions of the central cities (Map 27). And the inner cities have undergone other important changes in this same

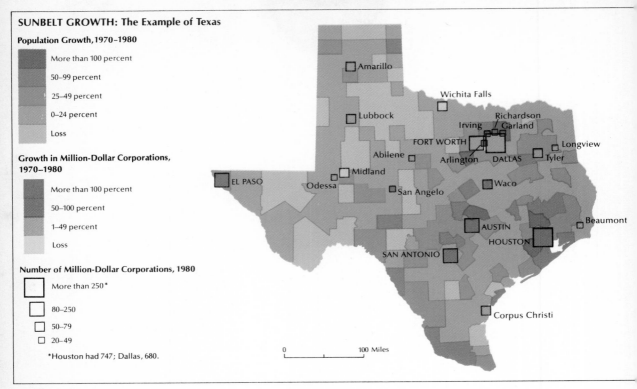

SUNBELT GROWTH: The Example of Texas

Population Growth, 1970–1980

- More than 100 percent
- 50–99 percent
- 25–49 percent
- 0–24 percent
- Loss

Growth in Million-Dollar Corporations, 1970–1980

- More than 100 percent
- 50–100 percent
- 1–49 percent
- Loss

Number of Million-Dollar Corporations, 1980

- More than 250*
- 80–250
- 50–79
- 20–49

*Houston had 747; Dallas, 680.

0   100 Miles

Amarillo
Wichita Falls
Lubbock
Richardson
Irving   Garland
FORT WORTH
Abilene
Arlington   DALLAS   Tyler   Longview
Midland
EL PASO   Odessa   San Angelo   Waco
Beaumont
AUSTIN
HOUSTON
SAN ANTONIO
Corpus Christi

Map 29

period—urban renewal, expressway construction, and, most recently, commercial revitalization and gentrification (Map 28; see also p. 970). In Boston, for example, major redevelopments since the 1930s have dramatically changed what was the nineteenth-century city center; little more than the street system remains from the colonial period. But such vitality will be difficult for cities like Boston to maintain in the face of population shifts not only to the suburbs but also to more economically healthy regions; much urban-regional growth since 1970 has favored the "Sunbelt" (Map 29; see also pp. 969–970).

Today, then, the American landscape is in a state of flux. Will the older Northeastern cities regain their former economic buoyancy? Are the booming cities of the Sunbelt destined to suffer problems associated with speedy growth and equally rapid decline? Whatever the answers, there is little doubt that contrasts in American settlement patterns will remain as a legacy of geographical diversity, historical background, and many agents of change.

Reconstructing the Nation

15

Charleston, 1865 Throughout most of the Civil War, the fighting and destruction were restricted largely to isolated battlefields. In the last year or so of the war, however, as Northern armies began to sweep through large areas of the crumbling Confederacy in an effort to cow the seceded states into surrendering, the war came home to the Southern people as a whole. It was not only cities such as Richmond, Atlanta, and Charleston that were ruined by the Northern onslaught, but large areas of agricultural production as well. And the Northern invasion further disrupted Southern society by provoking tens of thousands of former slaves to leave the plantations on which they had lived and follow the Union armies in search of freedom and security. (Library of Congress)

Few periods in the history of the United States have produced as much bitterness or created such enduring controversy as the era of Reconstruction—the years following the Civil War during which Americans attempted to reunite their shattered nation. Those who lived through the experience viewed it in sharply different ways. To white Southerners, Reconstruction was a vicious and destructive experience—a period of low, unscrupulous politics, a time when vindictive Northerners inflicted humiliation and revenge on the prostrate South and unnecessarily delayed a genuine reunion of the sections. Northern defenders of Reconstruction, by contrast, argued that their policies were the only way to prevent unrepentant Confederates from restoring Southern society as it had been before the war; without forceful federal intervention, there would be no way to forestall the reemergence of a backward aristocracy and the continued subjugation of blacks—no way, in other words, to prevent the same sectional problems that had produced the Civil War in the first place.

To most black Americans at the time, and to many people of all races since, Reconstruction was notable for other reasons. Not a vicious tyranny, as white Southerners charged, nor a drastic and necessary reform, as many Northerners claimed, it was, rather, an essentially moderate, even conservative program that fell far short of providing the newly freed slaves with the protection they needed. Reconstruction, in other words, was significant less for what it did, than for what it failed to do. And when it came to an end, finally, in 1877—as a result of exhaustion and disillusionment among the white leaders of both sections, and of a series of complex bargains in the aftermath of the election of 1876—black Americans found themselves once again abandoned. Although they had, with the help of federal protection, won some important gains during Reconstruction, those gains were limited; and after 1877 there would be nothing to prevent black people from being consigned to a system of economic peonage and legal subordination. The nation's racial problem, which had done so much to produce the Civil War, was left unresolved—to arise again and again in future generations.

THE PROBLEMS OF PEACEMAKING

In 1865, when the Confederate states finally surrendered to the North, no one knew quite what to do in response. Abraham Lincoln could not negotiate a treaty with the defeated government; he continued to insist that that government had no legal right to exist. Yet neither could he simply readmit the Southern states into the Union as if nothing had happened. The South had been devastated by the war, both socially and economically. And there was now an enormous population of freed slaves, many of them wandering aimless and bewildered through the shattered land. Clearly the federal government had to act.

The Aftermath of War

In the North, the wartime prosperity continued into the postwar years; but Northerners who visited the South were appalled when they gazed on the desolation left in the wake of the war—gutted towns, wrecked plantations, neglected fields, collapsed bridges, and ruined railroads. Much of the personal property of white Southerners had been lost with the lost cause. Confederate bonds and currency were now worthless, and capital that had been invested in them was gone forever. With the emancipation of the slaves, Southern whites were deprived of property worth an estimated $2 billion. And Southern blacks were left with no property at all.

Matching the shattered economy of the South was the disorganization of its social system. In the months that followed the end of the war, when thousands of soldiers were drifting back to their homes—258,000 never returned and other thousands went back wounded or sick—life was seriously deranged. To many people the problem of keeping alive, of securing food and shelter, seemed the only thing that mattered.

If conditions were bad for Southern whites, they were generally worse for Southern blacks—the 4 million who were emerging from the bondage that had held them and their ancestors for two and a half centuries. Many of these people, too, had seen service of one kind or another during the war. Some had served as body servants for Confederate officers or as teamsters and laborers for the Confederate armies. Tens of thousands had fought as combat troops in the Union ranks, and more than 38,000 had given their lives for the Union cause. Countless other blacks, who never wore a uniform or drew army pay, assisted the Union forces as spies or scouts. Still others ran off from the plantations and flocked into the Union lines, often to be put to work for the Union armies.

As the war ended, freedom appeared to be on the way, but the date of its arrival was uncertain. The Thirteenth Amendment, which would make slavery unconstitutional, had yet to be ratified by the requisite number of states (it had passed Congress on February 1, 1865, and was not to be proclaimed in effect until December 18, 1865). On many plantations, blacks were still being detained and forced to work. Most planters agreed with a former Confederate leader who was saying (in June 1865) that slavery had been "the best system of labor that could be devised for the Negro race" and that the wise thing to do now would be to "provide a substitute for it."

To get away from their old masters, thousands of blacks continued to leave the plantations. Old and young, many of them feeble and ill, they trudged to the nearest town or city or they roamed the countryside, camping at night on the bare ground. Few had any possessions except the rags on their backs. Somehow they managed to stay alive.

What blacks wanted was, first of all, to be assured of their freedom—to feel it, to exercise it, and to know it was not going to be taken from them. Next, they needed immediate relief from the threat of starvation. Then, looking ahead, they desired land, farms of their own, a bit of economic independence. The blacks longed also for schooling, for their children if not for themselves. Finally, a number of blacks were beginning to demand political rights. "The only salvation for us besides the power of the Government is in the *possession of the ballot*," a convention of the black people of Virginia resolved in the summer of 1865. "All we ask is an *equal chance*."

The federal government, besides keeping troops (many of them black) in the South to preserve order and protect the freedmen, was doing something to assist them in the transition from slavery to freedom. Congress had set up (in March 1865) the Bureau of Freedmen, Refugees, and Abandoned Lands as an agency of the army. This Freedmen's Bureau was empowered to provide food, transportation, assistance in getting jobs and fair wages, and schools for former slaves, and also to settle them on abandoned or confiscated lands. Under the able direction of General Oliver O. Howard, the bureau undertook to perform its allotted functions and more. Its agents soon distributed 20 million rations in the South, to hungry whites as well as blacks. Cooperating with the bureau, especially in its educational work, were missionaries and teachers who had been sent to the South by Freedmen's Aid Societies and other private and church groups in the North. (The bureau also provided considerable assistance to poor whites—many of whom were left homeless and destitute by the war.)

Nevertheless, the future of the blacks remained in doubt. The Freedmen's Bureau, according to the law creating it, was to last for only one year after the end of the war. Meanwhile, most Southern whites resented the activities of the bureau and its agents. These outsiders stood in the way of the desire to set up a substitute for slavery, a substitute that would serve both as a cheap labor system and as a white-supremacy device.

The Issues of Reconstruction

The word "Reconstruction," as contemporaries used it, referred to the process by which states of the defeated Confederacy were to be brought back to their former places in the Union. One possibility would be to grant easy terms, permitting the states to return promptly and with little internal change except for the elimination of slavery.

Another possibility would be to delay the readmission in such a way as to reduce the power of the rebel leaders.

A quick and easy restoration of the Union would be to the advantage of the former Confederates and the Democratic party, North and South. Ironically, the abolition of slavery would increase the power of the Southern states in national politics. In the past, under the "three-fifths clause" of the Constitution, only three-fifths of the slaves had been counted in determining a state's representation in Congress and its electoral votes in presidential elections. In the future, *all* the former slaves would be counted, whether or not they themselves were given political rights.

Freedmen Receiving Rations
The Freedmen's Bureau, established by Congress in March 1865, was designed to assist the former slaves through their passage from servitude to freedom. As the states of the defeated Confederacy began late in 1865 to pass new Black Codes, whose intent was to restore many of the conditions of slavery to the black population of the South, the bureau attempted to expand its functions to protect its clients from oppression. Although Congress never permitted the bureau to proceed beyond a few tentative first steps with its most ambitious aim— redistribution of land to the freedmen—it continued through Reconstruction to provide desperately needed assistance to the former slaves. Most of all, perhaps, the bureau was responsible for establishing the first important system of schools for blacks. (Library of Congress)

The consequences of any easy peace, by the same token, could be disastrous for the Republican party. The Republicans had gained control of the federal government in 1860–1861 only because of the split in the Democratic party and the secession of the Southern states. Once these states had been restored and the Democratic party had been reunited, the Republicans would face the uncomfortable prospect of being reduced to a minority group once again. The outlook was disturbing also for Northern businessmen who during the war had obtained favors from the federal government—a high tariff, railroad subsidies, the national banking system—which might be ended if the Democrats returned to power.

For the men and women emerging from slavery, a quick restoration of the Southern states would be catastrophic. The master class, which had dominated the state governments before and during the war, would continue to do so. Blacks then could expect to be kept in a position that, at best, would be somewhere between slavery and freedom.

Thus the issues of Reconstruction were very similar to those of the war itself. So far as the Southern leaders were concerned, the war had been fought for the independence of the South and for the preservation of slavery. After the war, these leaders hoped to maintain a considerable degree of Southern autonomy through the assertion of states' rights, and they hoped to retain much of the essence of slavery by finding some substitute for it.

The issues were often obscured and complicated by the emotionalism of the controversy over Reconstruction. In the North there was the memory of sacrifice, suffering, and personal loss; in the South there was the added bitterness of defeat. In the North there was a widespread feeling that Southerners ought to be required to acknowledge their defeat by some gesture of submission, and that at least a few of them ought to be punished. Moreover, there was a general conviction that the former slaves ought to be protected in their freedom and assured of justice. And there was a growing belief that Reconstruction offered a heaven-sent opportunity to recast the South in the image of the North—to take that supposedly backward, feudal, undemocratic section and civilize and modernize it.

Even among the majority in Congress—the Republicans—there was disagreement as to the kind of peace that should be imposed on the South. The same factions of the party (the Conservatives and the Radicals) that had clashed on wartime emancipation now confronted each other on the issue of Reconstruction. The Conservatives advocated a mild peace and the rapid restoration of the defeated states to the Union; beyond insisting that the South accept the abolition of slavery, they would not interfere with race relations or attempt to alter the social system of the South. The Radicals, directed by such leaders as Thaddeus Stevens of Pennsylvania and Charles Sumner of Massachusetts, stood for a harder peace; they urged that the civil and military chieftains of the late Confederacy be subjected to severe punishment, that large numbers of Southern whites be disfranchised, that the legal rights of blacks be protected, and that the property of rich Southerners who had aided the Confederacy be confiscated and distributed among the freedmen. From the first, some Radicals favored granting suffrage to the former slaves, as a matter of right or as a means of creating a Republican electorate in the South. Other Radicals hesitated to state a position for fear of public opinion—few Northern states permitted blacks to vote.

Between the Radicals and the Conservatives stood a faction of uncommitted Republicans, the Moderates. They would go further than the Conservatives in demanding concessions of the South, particularly in regard to rights for blacks, but they rejected the punitive goals of the Radicals.

Lincoln's Plan

The process of Reconstruction began while the war was still going on, under a plan presented by President Lincoln. He believed there were a considerable number of actual or potential Unionists in the South. These people, most of them former Whigs, could possibly be encouraged to rejoin the old Whigs of the North and thus strengthen the

Republican party, once the Union had been restored. More immediately, these men could serve as the nucleus for setting up new and loyal state governments in the South and thereby hastening reunion. Above all, Lincoln wanted to restore the Union as soon as possible. Consequently, he proposed a relatively easy mode of Reconstruction. He would subordinate to his larger goal such questions as punishment of the defeated side or determination of the status of the freedmen. The question of whether the defeated states were in or out of the Union he dismissed as a "merely pernicious abstraction." They were only out of their proper relationship to the Union, he said, and they should be restored to that relationship as soon as possible.

Specifically, Lincoln's plan, which he announced to the public in a proclamation of December 1863, offered a general amnesty to all who would take an oath pledging future loyalty to the government. Temporarily excluded from the right to swear the oath were high civil and military officials of the Confederacy. Whenever in any state 10 percent of the number of voters in 1860 took the oath, those loyal voters could proceed to set up a state government. The oath required acceptance of the wartime acts and proclamations of Congress and the president concerning slavery. Lincoln also urged them to give the ballot to at least a few blacks—to those who were educated, owned property, and had served in the Union army. In three Southern states—Louisiana, Arkansas, and Tennessee—loyal governments were reestablished under the Lincoln formula in 1864.

The Radical Republicans were angered and astonished at the mildness of Lincoln's program, and they were able to induce Congress to repudiate his governments. Representatives from the Lincoln states were not admitted to Congress, and the electoral vote of those states was not counted in the election of 1864. The Radicals could not stop, however, with a rejection of Lincoln's plan. The requirements of politics dictated that they produce a plan of their own. But at the moment the Radicals were not agreed as to how "hard" a peace they should enforce on the South, and they were not certain that

Northern opinion would support the ideas of their more extreme leaders.

Under pressure, they prepared and passed (in July 1864) the Wade-Davis Bill, the first Radical plan of Reconstruction. By its provisions, the president was to appoint for each conquered state a provisional governor who would take a census of all adult white males. If a majority of those enrolled—instead of Lincoln's 10 percent—swore an oath of allegiance, the governor was to call an election for a state constitutional convention. The privilege of voting for delegates to this meeting was limited to those who could swear that they had never borne arms against the United States, the so-called ironclad oath. The convention was required to put provisions into the new constitution abolishing slavery, disfranchising Confederate civil and military leaders, and repudiating war debts. After these conditions had been met, Congress would readmit the state to the Union. The Wade-Davis Bill was more drastic in almost every respect than the Lincoln plan, and it assumed that the seceded states were out of the Union and hence under the dictation of Congress. But the bill, like the president's proposal, left up to the states the question of political rights for blacks.

The Wade-Davis Bill was passed a few days before Congress adjourned, which enabled Lincoln to dispose of it with a pocket veto. His action enraged the authors of the measure, Benjamin F. Wade and Henry Winter Davis, who issued a blistering denunciation of the veto, the Wade-Davis Manifesto, warning the president not to interfere with the powers of Congress to control Reconstruction. Lincoln could not ignore the bitterness and the strength of the Radical opposition. Practical as always, he realized that he would have to accept some of the objections of the Radicals. He began to move toward a new approach to Reconstruction.

What plan he might have produced no one can say. On the night of April 14, 1865, Lincoln and his wife attended a play at Ford's Theater in Washington. As they sat in the presidential box, John Wilkes Booth, an unsuccessful actor obsessed with aiding the Southern cause, shot Lincoln in the head. Then he leaped from the box to the stage

Abraham Lincoln and Tad
This famous photograph of Lincoln in 1864, posing with his son Tad, was the work of Mathew Brady, the most celebrated photographer of the Civil War era. (Library of Congress)

(breaking his leg in the process), shouted "Sic, semper tyrannis!" ("Thus always to tyrants!"), and disappeared into the night. The president was carried unconscious to a house across the street, where early the next morning—surrounded by family, friends, and political associates (including a tearful Charles Sumner)—he died.

The circumstances of Lincoln's death—the heroic war leader, the Great Emancipator, struck down in the hour of victory—earned him immediate martyrdom. It also produced wild fears and antagonisms throughout the North. There were widespread accusations that Booth had acted as part of a great conspiracy—accusations that rested on at least a grain of truth. Booth did indeed have associates, one of whom shot and wounded Secretary of State Seward the night of the assassi-

nation, another of whom set out to murder Vice President Johnson but abandoned the scheme at the last moment. Booth himself escaped on horseback into the Maryland countryside, where, on April 26, he was cornered by Union troops and shot to death in a blazing barn. Eight other conspirators were convicted by a military tribunal of participating in the conspiracy (two of them, at least, on the basis of virtually no evidence). Four were hanged.

To many Northerners, however, the murder of the president seemed evidence of an even greater conspiracy—one masterminded and directed by the unrepentant leaders of the defeated South. (There was never any conclusive evidence to support this—and many other—theory of the assassination; but questions continued to be raised about the event well into the twentieth century.) Militant Republicans exploited such suspicions relentlessly in the ensuing months, ensuring that Lincoln's death would—ironically—help doom his plans for a relatively generous peace.

Johnson and "Restoration"

The conservative leadership in the controversy over Reconstruction fell upon Lincoln's successor, Andrew Johnson. Of all the men who have accidentally inherited the presidency, Johnson was undoubtedly the most unfortunate. A Southerner and former slaveholder, he became president as a bloody war against the South was drawing to a close. A Democrat before he had been placed on the Union ticket with Lincoln in 1864, he became the head of a Republican administration at a time when partisan passions, held in some restraint during the war, were about to rule the government. As if these handicaps of background were not enough, Johnson was intemperate in language and tactless in manner.

Johnson revealed his plan of Reconstruction—or "Restoration," as he preferred to call it—soon after he took office, and he proceeded to execute it during the summer of 1865 when Congress was not in session. He applied it to the seven states of the late Confederacy that had not come under the Lincoln plan; and he recognized as legal organizations the Lincoln governments in Louisiana, Arkansas, Tennessee, and Virginia.

In some ways Johnson's scheme resembled Lincoln's; in others it was similar to the Wade-Davis Bill. Like his predecessor, Johnson assumed that the seceded states were still in the Union; and, also like Lincoln, he announced his design in a proclamation of amnesty that extended pardon for past conduct to all who would take an oath of allegiance. Denied the privilege of taking the oath until they received individual pardons from the president were high-ranking Confederate officials and also men with land worth $20,000 or more: Johnson excluded a larger number of leaders than Lincoln had. (Himself a self-made man, Johnson harbored deep resent-

Andrew Johnson
Born in North Carolina, Johnson moved to Tennessee as a young man and worked as a tailor before going into politics. He had a dark complexion and piercing black eyes. A powerful orator on the stump, he easily lost his temper when heckled and used crude and intemperate language. (Library of Congress)

ments toward the old Southern aristocracy and apparently relished the prospect of these Confederate leaders humbling themselves before him to ask for pardons.) For each state, the president appointed a provisional governor, who was to invite the qualified voters to elect delegates to a constitutional convention. Johnson did not specify that a minimum number of voters had to take the oath, as had the Lincoln and Wade-Davis proposals, but the implication was plain that he would require a majority. As conditions of readmittance, a state had to revoke the ordinance of secession, abolish slavery and ratify the Thirteenth Amendment, and repudiate the Confederate and state war debts—essentially the same stipulations that had been laid down in the Wade-Davis Bill. The final procedure before restoration was for a state to elect a state government and send representatives to Congress.

By the end of 1865, the states affected by

Johnson's plan had complied with its requirements. Indeed, if the Lincoln governments are included, all of the seceded states had been reconstructed and were ready to resume their places in the Union—if Congress chose to recognize them when it met in December 1865. Recognition of the Johnson governments was exactly what the Radicals were determined to prevent. And many people in the North agreed with them that Reconstruction was being rushed too fast and accomplished too easily.

This initial phase of Reconstruction—often known as "presidential Reconstruction"—lasted only until the reconvening of Congress in December 1865. At that point, Republican leaders looked over Andrew Johnson's handiwork and expressed their displeasure. Congress immediately refused to seat the senators and representatives of the states the president had "restored." Instead, Radical leaders insisted, Congress needed to learn more about conditions in the postwar South. There must be assurances that the former Confederates had accepted their defeat and that emancipated blacks and loyal whites would be protected. Accordingly, Congress set up the new Joint Committee on Reconstruction to investigate conditions in the South and to advise Congress in laying down a Reconstruction policy of its own. The period of "congressional" or "Radical" Reconstruction had begun.

Congress Takes Over

During the next few months, the Radicals advanced toward a more severe program than their first plan, the Wade-Davis Bill of 1864, which had left to the states the question of what rights the freed slaves should have. The Radicals gained the support of Moderate Republicans because of Johnson's intransigent attitude. Johnson insisted that Congress had no right even to consider a policy for the South until his own plan had been accepted and the Southern congressmen and senators had been admitted.

Northerners were disturbed by the seeming reluctance of some members of the Southern conventions to abolish slavery and by the refusal of all the conventions to grant suffrage to even a few blacks. They were astounded that states claiming to be "loyal" should elect as state officials and representatives to Congress prominent leaders of the recent Confederacy. Particularly hard to understand was Georgia's choice of Alexander H. Stephens, former vice president of the Confederacy, as a United States senator.

RADICAL RECONSTRUCTION

Thaddeus Stevens
Stern, uncompromising, and severe, Thaddeus Stevens of Pennsylvania was the incarnation of Northern evil in the eyes of many Southerners during Reconstruction. To American blacks, however, he was one of the few white leaders who remained firmly committed to racial equality. He served in the House of Representatives from 1849 to 1853 and again, far more prominently, from 1859 until his death in 1868. He spent much of the last year of his life organizing and managing the impeachment trial of Andrew Johnson.
(Library of Congress)

In the meantime, Northerners were learning more about what was happening in the defeated South; and what they learned persuaded many of them—including most of the important leaders in Congress—that far more drastic measures were necessary than the president had contemplated. For throughout the South in 1865 and early 1866, state legislatures were enacting sets of laws known as the Black Codes. These measures were the white South's solution to the problem of the free black laborer, and they were modeled in many ways on the codes that had regulated free blacks in the prewar South. As such, they created a new set of devices to guarantee white supremacy. Economically, the codes were intended to regulate the labor of a race that, in the opinion of the whites, would not work except under some kind of compulsion. Although there were variations from state to state, all codes authorized local officials to apprehend unemployed blacks, fine them for vagrancy, and hire them out to private employers to satisfy the fine. Some of the codes tried to force blacks to work on the plantations by forbidding them to own or lease farms or to take other jobs except as domestic servants. Socially, the codes were designed to invest blacks with a legal although subordinate status. To the South, the Black Codes were a realistic approach to a great social problem. To the North, they seemed to herald a return to slavery.

An appropriate agency for offsetting the Black Codes was the Freedmen's Bureau, but its scheduled year of existence was about to end. In February 1866, Congress passed a bill to prolong the life of the bureau and to widen its powers by authorizing special courts for settling labor disputes. Thus the bureau could set aside work agreements that might be forced on freedmen under the Black Codes. Johnson vetoed the bill, denouncing it as unconstitutional. Efforts to override him fell just short of the necessary two-thirds majority.

In April, Congress struck again at the Black Codes by passing the Civil Rights Bill, which made blacks United States citizens and empowered the federal government to intervene in state affairs when necessary to protect the rights of citizens. Johnson vetoed this

The Black Code of Louisiana

*The sections in the Black Codes regulating black labor angered
Northern opinion and turned many people in favor of Radical Reconstruction. The Louisiana Code had this to say:*

Sec. 1. Be it enacted by the Senate and House of Representatives of the State of Louisiana in general assembly convened, That all persons employed as laborers in agricultural pursuits shall be required, during the first ten days of the month of January of each year, to make contracts for labor for the then ensuing year, or for the year next ensuing the termination of their present contracts. All contracts for labor for agricultural purposes shall be made in writing, signed by the employer, and shall be made in the presence of a Justice of the Peace and two disinterested witnesses, in whose presence the contract shall be read to the laborer, and when assented to and signed by the latter, shall be considered as binding for the time prescribed. . . .

Sec. 2. Every laborer shall have full and perfect liberty to choose his employer, but, when once chosen, he shall not be allowed to leave his place of employment until the fulfillment of his contract . . . and if they do so leave, without cause or permission, they shall forfeit all wages earned to the time of abandonment. . . .

bill, too. With Moderates and Radicals acting together, Congress promptly overrode the veto. Then, despite another veto, Congress repassed the Freedmen's Bureau Bill.

Emboldened by their evident support in Congress, the Radicals now struck again. The Joint Committee on Reconstruction submitted to Congress, in April 1866, a proposed amendment to the Constitution, the Fourteenth, which constituted the second Radical plan of Reconstruction. The amendment was adopted by Congress and sent to the states for approval in the early summer.

Section 1 of the amendment declared that all persons born or naturalized in the United States were citizens of the United States and of the state of their residence. This clause, which set up for the first time a national definition of citizenship, was followed by a statement that no state could abridge the rights of citizens of the United States or deprive any person of life, liberty, or property without due process of law or deny to any person within its jurisdiction the equal protection of the laws.

Section 2 provided that if a state denied the suffrage to any of its adult male inhabitants, its representation in the House of Representatives and the electoral college should suffer a proportionate reduction.

Section 3 disqualified from any state or federal office persons who had previously taken an oath to support the Constitution and later had aided the Confederacy—until Congress by a two-thirds vote of each house should remove their disability.

The Southern legislatures knew that if they ratified the amendment their states would be readmitted and Reconstruction probably would be ended. But they could not bring themselves to approve the measure, mainly because of Section 3, which put a stigma on their late leaders. Johnson himself advised Southerners to defeat the amendment. Only Tennessee, of the former Confederate states, ratified it, thus winning readmittance. The other ten, joined by Kentucky and Delaware, voted it down.

The amendment thus failed to receive the required approval of three-fourths of the states and was defeated—but only temporarily. When the time was more propitious, the Radicals would bring it up again. Meanwhile, its rejection by the South strengthened the Radical cause. To many people in the North, the amendment had seemed to be a reasonable and moderate proposal.

Public acceptance of the Radical program was strikingly manifested in the elections of 1866. This was essentially a contest for popular support between Johnson and the Radicals. The Radicals could point to recent events in the South—bloody race riots in New Orleans and other Southern cities in which blacks were the victims—as further evidence of the inadequacy of Johnson's policy. Johnson harmed his own cause by the intemperate, brawling (and, some believed, drunken) speeches he made on a stumping tour (a "swing around the circle," as it was called) from Washington to Chicago and back. The voters returned to Congress an overwhelming majority of Republicans, most of them Radicals. In the Senate, there were to be 42 Republicans to 11 Democrats; in the House, 143 Republicans to 49 Democrats. Now the Republicans could enact any kind of Reconstruction plan they could themselves agree on. Confidently they looked forward to the struggle with Johnson that would ensue when Congress assembled in December 1866—and to their final victory over the president.

The Congressional Plan

After compromising differences among themselves and with the Moderates, the Radicals formulated their third plan of Reconstruction in three bills that passed Congress in the early months of 1867. All three were vetoed by Johnson and repassed. Together, they constituted a single program.

This plan was based squarely on the principle that the seceded states had lost their political identity. The Lincoln-Johnson governments were declared to have no legal standing, and the ten seceded states (Tennessee was now out of the Reconstruction process) were combined into five military districts. Each district was to be put in the charge of a military commander, supported by troops, who was to prepare his provinces for readmission as states. To this end, he was to institute a registration of voters, which was to include all adult black males and those white males who were not disqualified by participation in rebellion.

After the registration was completed in each province, the commanding general was to call the voters to elect a convention to prepare a new state constitution, which had to provide for black suffrage. If this document were ratified by the voters, elections for a state government could be held. Finally, if Congress approved the constitution, if the state legislature ratified the Fourteenth Amendment, and if this amendment were adopted by the required number of states and became a part of the Constitution—then the state was to be restored to the Union.

By 1868, six of the former Confederate states—Arkansas, North Carolina, South Carolina, Louisiana, Alabama, and Florida—had complied with the process of restoration outlined in the Reconstruction Acts and were readmitted to the Union. Delaying tactics by whites held up the return of Mississippi, Virginia, Georgia, and Texas until 1870. These four laggard states had to meet an additional requirement, which with the existing requirements constituted the fourth and final congressional plan of Reconstruction. They had to ratify another constitutional amendment, the Fifteenth, which forbade the states and the federal government to deny the suffrage to any citizen on account of "race, color, or previous condition of servitude."

Sponsors of the Fifteenth Amendent were motivated by both idealistic and practical considerations. They wished to be consistent in extending to blacks in the North a right they had already given to them elsewhere. The great majority of the Northern states still denied the suffrage to blacks at the time when the Reconstruction Acts granted it to blacks in the Southern states. At the same time they would be putting into the Constitution, where it would be safe from congressional repeal, the basis of Republican strength in the South. They were also concerned with the party's future in the North. A warning of trouble ahead had appeared in the state elections of 1867 in Pennsylvania, Ohio, and Indiana, all of which went Democratic that year. "We must establish the doctrine of national jurisdiction over all the states in state matters of the franchise," the Radical leader Thaddeus Stevens now concluded. "We must thus bridle Pennsylvania, Ohio, Indiana et cetera, or the South *being in*, we shall drift into Democracy." In several of the Northern states the black vote, though proportionally small, would be large enough to decide close elections in favor of the Republicans.

A number of the Northern and border states refused to approve the Fifteenth Amendment, and it was adopted only with the support of the four Southern states that had to ratify it in order to be readmitted to the Union. In the case of both the Fourteenth and Fifteenth amendments, the Southern states were deemed capable of ratifying even while they were not otherwise recognized as states and had no representation in Congress.

Congressional Supremacy

The Radicals saw themselves as architects of a revolution, and they did not intend to let the executive or the judiciary get in their way. They were prepared, if necessary, to establish a kind of congressional dictatorship.

To curb the president, and also to facilitate Radical administration of the acts of 1867, Congress passed two remarkable laws. One, the Tenure of Office Act (1867), forbade the president to remove civil officials, including members of his cabinet, without the consent of the Senate. Its principal purpose was to protect the job of Secretary of War Edwin M. Stanton, who was cooperating with the Radicals. The other law, the Command of the Army Act (1867), prohibited the president from issuing military orders except through the commanding general of the army (General Grant), whose headquarters were to be in Washington and who could not be relieved or assigned elsewhere without the consent of the Senate.

The Supreme Court, under Chief Justice Salmon P. Chase, declared in *Ex parte Milligan* (1866) that military tribunals were unconstitutional in places where civil courts were functioning. Although the decision was applied to a case originating in the war, it seemed to threaten the system of military government that the Radicals were planning for the South. Radical anger at the Court was instant and intense. In Congress, proposals were made to require a two-thirds majority of the justices to overrule a law of Congress, to deny the Court jurisdiction in Reconstruction cases, to reduce its membership to three, and even to abolish it. The judges apparently took the hint. When the state of Mississippi in 1867 asked for an injunction restraining Johnson from enforcing the Reconstruction Acts, the Court refused to accept jurisdiction (*Mississippi* v. *Johnson*). But the next year, the Court agreed to hear arguments in a case involving military courts in Mississippi (*Ex parte McCardle*) and by implication involving the legality of the Reconstruction Acts. The Radicals rushed through Congress a law denying the Court appellate jurisdiction in cases concerning habeas corpus. The Court bowed by refusing to hear the case.

The Impeachment of the President

The most aggressive move of Congress against another branch of government was the effort of the Radicals to remove Andrew Johnson from office. Although the president had long since ceased to be a serious obstacle to the passage of Radical legislation, he was still the official charged with administering the Reconstruction programs; and as such, the Radicals believed, he was a serious impediment to their plans. Early in 1867, therefore, they began searching for evidence that Johnson had committed crimes or misdemeanors in office, the only legal grounds for impeachment; but they could find nothing on

which to base charges. Then he gave them a plausible reason for action by deliberately violating the Tenure of Office Act. He suspended Secretary of War Stanton, who had worked with the Radicals against Johnson, and named General Grant as his successor. Johnson hoped in this manner to secure a Court test case of the tenure law, which he believed to be unconstitutional. But when the Senate refused to concur in the suspension, Grant relinquished the office to Stanton. Johnson then dismissed Stanton.

In the House of Representatives the elated Radicals presented to the Senate eleven charges against the president. The first nine accusations dealt with the violation of the Tenure of Office Act. The tenth and eleventh charged Johnson with making speeches calculated to bring Congress into disrespect and with not faithfully enforcing the various Reconstruction Acts. In the trial before the Senate (March 25 to May 26, 1868) Johnson's lawyers maintained that he was justified in technically violating a law in order to force a test case and that the measure did not apply to Stanton anyway: it gave tenure to cabinet members for the term of the president by whom they had been appointed, and Stanton had been appointed by Lincoln. The House managers of the impeachment stressed the theme that Johnson had opposed the will of Congress. They implied that in doing so he was guilty of crimes and misdemeanors. They brought terrific pressure on all the Republican senators, but seven Republicans joined the twelve Democrats to vote for acquittal. On three of the charges the vote was identical, 35 to 19, one short of the required two-thirds majority. Thereupon the Radicals called off the proceedings.

THE SOUTH IN RECONSTRUCTION

When white Southerners spoke bitterly in later years of the effects of Reconstruction, they referred most frequently to the governments Congress imposed on them—governments, they claimed, that were both incompetent and corrupt, that saddled the region

with enormous debts, and that trampled on the rights of citizens. When black Southerners and their defenders condemned Reconstruction, by contrast, they spoke of its failure to guarantee to freedmen even the most elemental rights of citizenship—a fail-

Reconstruction

Debate over the nature of Reconstruction—not only among historians, but among the public at large—has created so much controversy over the decades that one scholar, writing in 1959, described the issue as a "dark and bloody ground." Among historians, the passions of the debate have to some extent subsided since then; but in the popular mind, Reconstruction continues to raise "dark and bloody" images.

For many years, a relatively uniform view of Reconstruction prevailed among historians, a reflection of broad currents in popular thought. By the late nineteenth century, most white Americans in both the North and the South had come to believe that few real differences any longer divided the sections, that the nation should strive for a genuine reconciliation. And most white Americans believed as well in the superiority of their race, in the inherent unfitness of blacks for political or social equality. In this spirit was born the first major historical interpretation of Reconstruction, through the work of William A. Dunning. In his *Reconstruction, Political and Economic* (1907), Dunning portrayed Reconstruction as a corrupt outrage perpetrated on the prostrate South by a vicious and vindictive cabal of Northern Republican radicals. Reconstruction governments were based on "bayonet rule." Unscrupulous and self-aggrandizing carpetbaggers flooded the South to profit from the misery of the defeated region. Ignorant, illiterate blacks were thrust into positions of power for which they were entirely unfit. The Reconstruction experiment, a moral abomination from its first moments, survived only because of the determination of the Republican party to keep itself in power. (Some later writers, notably Howard K. Beale, added an economic motive—to protect Northern business interests.) Dunning and his many students (who together formed what became known as the "Dunning school") compiled evidence to show that the legacy of Reconstruction was corruption, ruinous taxation, and astronomical increases in the public debt.

The Dunning school not only shaped the views of several generations of historians. It also reflected and helped to shape the views of much of the public. Popular depictions of Reconstruction for years to come (as the book and movie *Gone with the Wind* suggested) portrayed the era as one of tragic exploitation of the South by the North. Even today, many white Southerners in particular continue to accept the basic premises of the Dunning interpretation. Among historians, however, the old view of Reconstruction has gradually lost its credibility. W. E. B. Du Bois, the great black scholar, was among the first to challenge the Dunning view in a 1910 article and, later, in a 1935 book, *Black Reconstruction*. To him, Reconstruction politics in the Southern states had been an effort on the part of the masses, black and white, to create a true democratic society. The misdeeds of the Reconstruction governments had, he claimed, been greatly exaggerated and their

ure that resulted in a new and cruel system of economic subordination. Controversy has raged for more than a century over which viewpoint is more nearly correct (see "Where Historians Disagree"). Most students of Reconstruction tend now to agree, however, that the complaints of Southern whites, although in some respects accurate, greatly exaggerated the real nature of the postwar governments; while the complaints of blacks, although occasionally overstated, were to a large extent justified.

The Reconstruction Governments

In the ten states of the South that were reorganized under the congressional plan, approximately one-fourth of the white men were at first excluded from voting or holding office. The voter registration of 1867 enrolled a total of 703,000 black and 627,000 white voters. The black voters constituted a majority in half of the states—Alabama, Florida, South Carolina, Mississippi, and Louisiana—although only in the last three of these states

achievements overlooked. The governments had been expensive, he insisted, because they had tried to provide public education and other public services on a scale never before attempted in the South. But Du Bois's use of Marxist theory in his work caused many historians who did not share his philosophy to dismiss his argument; and it remained for a group of less radical white historians to shatter the Dunning image of Reconstruction for good.

In the 1940s, historians such as C. Vann Woodward, David Herbert Donald, Thomas B. Alexander, and others began to reexamine the record of the Reconstruction governments in the South and to suggest that their record was not nearly as bad as had previously been assumed. They looked, too, at the Radical Republicans in Congress and suggested that they had not been motivated by vindictiveness and partisanship alone. By the early 1960s, a new view of Reconstruction had emerged from these efforts, summarized finally by John Hope Franklin in *Reconstruction After the Civil War* (1961) and Kenneth Stampp in *The Era of Reconstruction* (1965), which claimed that the postwar Republicans had been engaged in a genuine, if flawed, effort to solve the problem of race in the South by providing much-needed protection to the freedmen. The Reconstruction governments, for all their faults, had been bold experiments in interracial politics; and the congressional Radicals, while far from being saints, had displayed a genuine concern for the rights of

slaves. There had been no such thing as "bayonet rule" or "Negro rule" in the South. Blacks had played only a small part in Reconstruction governments and had acquitted themselves well. Corruption in the South had been no worse than corruption in the North at that time. What was tragic about Reconstruction, the revisionist view claimed, was not what it did to Southern whites but what it did not do for Southern blacks. By stopping short of the reforms necessary to ensure blacks genuine equality, Reconstruction had consigned them to more than a century of injustice and discrimination.

Where historians now tend to disagree is on why Reconstruction fell as short as it did of guaranteeing racial justice. Some scholars claim that conservative obstacles to change were so great that the Radicals, despite their good intentions, simply could not overcome them. Others claim that the Radicals themselves were not sufficiently committed to the principle of racial justice, that they abandoned the cause quickly when it became clear to them that the battle would not easily be won. Still others—for example, Herman Belz, in *A New Birth of Freedom* (1976)—emphasize the positive achievements of Reconstruction. By enacting the Fourteenth and Fifteenth amendments, he argues, the United States took a vital step toward transferring from the states to the federal government the responsibility for protecting the rights of citizenship.

did the blacks outnumber the whites in the population as a whole. But once new constitutions had been framed and new governments launched, most of them permitted nearly all whites to vote (although for several years the Fourteenth Amendment continued to keep the leading ex-Confederates from holding office). This meant that in most of the Southern states the Republicans could maintain control only with the support of a great many Southern whites.

These Southern white Republicans, whom their opponents derisively called "scalawags," consisted in part of former Whigs who, after the breakup of the Whig organization in the 1850s, had acted with the Southern Democrats but had never felt completely at home with them. Some of the scalawag leaders were wealthy (or once wealthy) planters or businessmen. Such men, having long controlled the blacks as slaves, expected to control them also as voters. Many other Southern whites who joined the Republican party were farmers living in areas where slavery had been unimportant or nonexistent. These men, many of whom had been wartime Unionists, favored the Republican program of internal improvements, which would help them get their crops to market.

White men from the North also served as Republican leaders in the South. Opponents of Reconstruction referred to them as "carpetbaggers," thus giving the impression that they were penniless adventurers who had arrived with all their possessions in a carpetbag (a then common kind of valise covered with carpeting material) in order to take advantage of the black vote for their own power and profit. In fact, the majority of the so-called carpetbaggers were veterans of the Union army who had looked on the South as a new frontier, more promising than the West, and at the war's end had settled in it as hopeful planters or business or professional men.

The most numerous Republicans in the South were the freedmen, the vast majority of whom had no formal education and no previous experience in the management of affairs. Among the black leaders, however, were well-educated men, most of whom had never been slaves and many of whom had been brought up in the North or abroad. The blacks quickly became politically self-conscious. In various states they held their own "colored conventions," the one in Alabama announcing (1867): "We claim exactly *the same rights, privileges and immunities as are enjoyed by white men*—we ask nothing more and will be content with nothing less." Blacks were organized, often with the assistance of Freedmen's Bureau agents and other Northern whites, in chapters of the Union League, which had been founded originally as a Republican electioneering agency in the North during the war. Another organization that gave unity and self-confidence to black people was their church. Once they were emancipated, they had begun to withdraw from the white churches and form their own—institutions based on the elaborate religious practices they had developed (occasionally surreptitiously) under slavery. "The colored preachers are *the great power* in controlling and uniting the colored vote," a carpetbagger observed in 1868.

Blacks served as delegates to the conventions that, under the congressional plan, drew up new state constitutions in the South. Then, in the reconstructed states, blacks were elected to public offices of practically every kind. Altogether (between 1869 and 1901) twenty blacks were sent to the House of Representatives in Washington. Two went to the United States Senate, both of them from Mississippi. Hiram R. Revels, an ordained minister and a former North Carolina free black who had been educated at Knox College in Illinois, took in 1870 the Senate seat that Jefferson Davis once had occupied. Blanche K. Bruce, who had escaped from slavery in Virginia and studied in the North, became a senator in 1874.

Hiram R. Revels
Revels was one of the few blacks to attain high office during Reconstruction, acting as United States senator from Mississippi from 1870 to 1871. Born in North Carolina of free parents, Revels became a Methodist minister, and during the Civil War he served as an army chaplain in Mississippi. Returning to the state after the war, he resumed his ministerial duties and entered politics. He was a moderate Republican and, in 1875, joined with the Democrats to overthrow the Republican state regime. For years, he was president of Alcorn College, a black institution. (Library of Congress)

Yet no such thing as "Negro rule" ever existed in any of the states—despite the claims (and complaints) of many Southern whites. No black was elected governor, though Lieutenant Governor P. B. S. Pinchback briefly occupied the governor's chair in Louisiana. Blacks never controlled any of the state legislatures, though for a time they held a majority in the lower house of South Carolina. In the South as a whole the number of black officeholders was less than proportionate to the number of blacks in the population. Nor did the state governments show much if any favoritism toward blacks as a group. Constitutions or statutes prohibited, on paper, discrimination on the basis of color, but segregation remained the common practice.

The record of the Reconstruction governments is many-sided. The financial programs they instituted were a compound of blatant corruption and well-designed, if sometimes impractical, social legislation. The corruption and extravagance are familiar aspects of the Reconstruction story. State budgets expanded to hitherto unknown totals, and state debts soared to previously undreamed-of heights. In South Carolina, for example, the public debt increased from $7 million to $29 million in eight years.

In large measure, the corruption in the South was part of a national phenomenon, with the same social force—an expanding capitalism eager to secure quick results—acting as the corrupting agent in all sections of the country. That much of the alleged corruption was a product of deep forces in contemporary society is demonstrated by the continuance of dishonesty in state government after Republican rule was overthrown.

The state expenditures of the Reconstruction years seem huge only in comparison with the niggardly budgets of the conservative governments of the prewar era; they do not appear large when measured against the sums appropriated by later legislatures. The reconstructed governments represented the poor blacks, who demanded public education, public-works programs, poor relief, and other costly services. Despite theft and foolish spending, there were also positive and permanent accomplishments.

Education

Perhaps the most important of those accomplishments was a dramatic improvement in Southern education—an improvement that benefited both whites and blacks. In the first years of Reconstruction, much of the impetus for educational reform in the South came from outside groups—from the Freedmen's Bureau and from Northern private philanthropic organizations—and from blacks themselves. Over the opposition of many Southern whites, who feared that education would give blacks "false notions of equality," these reformers established a large network of schools for former slaves—4,000 schools by 1870, staffed by 9,000 teachers (half of them black), and teaching 200,000 students (about 12 percent of the total school-age population of the freedmen). In the course of the 1870s, moreover, the Reconstruction governments of the states assumed the initiative and began to build a comprehensive public school system in the South. By 1876, more than half of all white children and about 40 percent of all black children were being educated in Southern schools. A number of black "academies" were also beginning to operate—institutions that were, perhaps, not yet genuine colleges but that were offering more advanced education to freedmen than the public schools provided. Gradually, these academies grew into an important network of black colleges and universities, which would form the basis of black higher education in the South for nearly a century. Among the early institutions, for example, were schools that later became Fisk and Atlanta Universities and Morehouse College.

Already, however, Southern education was becoming divided into two separate systems—one black and one white. Early efforts to integrate the schools of the region were a dismal failure. The Freedmen's Bureau schools, for example, were open to students of all races, but almost no whites attended them. New Orleans set up an integrated school system under the Reconstruction government; again, whites almost universally stayed away. The one federal effort to mandate school integration—the Civil Rights Act

Teachers of the Freedmen
For a few brief years, the Freedmen's Bureau,
established by Congress in 1865, served as a
visible force for racial equality and for an interracial society in the South. This photograph shows the integrated faculty of a
school established by the bureau near Norfolk, Virginia. Hampered by limited funding
and local white hostility, the bureau was able
to achieve only limited results. But the educational institutions it established helped to
create the basis for the important network of
black institutes and colleges in the South.
(Massachusetts Commandery Military Order of the Loyal
Legion and the U.S. Army Military History Institute)

---

of 1875—had its provisions for educational
desegregation removed before it was passed.
And as soon as the Republican governments
of Reconstruction were replaced, the new
Southern Democratic regimes quickly abandoned all efforts to promote integration.

Land Ownership

The most ambitious goal of the Freedmen's
Bureau, and of some Republican Radicals in

Congress, was to make Reconstruction the
occasion for a fundamental reform of land
ownership in the South. The effort failed. In
the last years of the war and the first years of
Reconstruction, the Freedmen's Bureau did
oversee the redistribution of substantial
amounts of land to freedmen in some
areas—notably the Sea Islands off South
Carolina and Georgia and areas of Mississippi that had once belonged to the Davis
family. By June 1865, the bureau had settled
nearly 10,000 black families on their own
land—most of it drawn from abandoned
plantations. Blacks throughout the South
were growing excited at the prospect of
achieving a real economic stake in their region—the vision of "forty acres and a mule."
By the end of that year, however, the experiment was already collapsing. Southern plantation owners were returning and demanding
the restoration of their property. And Andrew Johnson was supporting their demands.
Despite the resistance of General Oliver O.
Howard and other officials of the Freedmen's
Bureau, most of the confiscated land was
eventually returned to the original white
owners. Congress, moreover, never exhibited
much stomach for the idea of land redistribution. Despite the pleas of such Radicals as
Thaddeus Stevens, very few Northern Republicans believed that the federal government had the right to confiscate property.
Land reform did not become a part of Reconstruction.

Nevertheless, there was a substantial
change in the distribution of land ownership
in the South in the postwar years—a result of
many factors. Among whites, there was a
striking decline in ownership of land.
Whereas before the war more than 80 percent of Southern whites had lived on their
own land, by the end of Reconstruction that
proportion had dropped to about 67 percent.
Some whites had fallen into debt and been
forced to sell; some had fallen victim to increased taxes; some had chosen to leave the
marginal lands they had owned to move to
more fertile areas, where they rented. Among
blacks, during the same period, the proportion who owned land rose from virtually
none to more than 20 percent. Black landowners acquired their property through hard

work, through luck, and at times through the assistance of such agencies as the Freedman's Bank, established in 1865 by antislavery whites in an effort to promote land ownership among blacks. (The bank failed in 1874, after a combination of internal corruption and a nationwide financial panic had destroyed its reserves.)

Despite these impressive achievements, however, the vast majority of blacks (and a growing minority of whites) did not own their own land during Reconstruction, and some of those who acquired land in the 1860s lost it in the 1890s. These nonlandowners worked for others, through a great variety of systems. Many black agricultural laborers—perhaps 25 percent of the total—simply worked for wages. Most, however, became tenants of white landowners—that is, they acquired control of their own plots of land, working them on their own and paying their landlord either a fixed rent or a share of their crop (hence the term "sharecropping"). The new system represented a breakdown of the traditional plantation system, in which blacks had lived together and worked together under the direction of a master. As tenants and sharecroppers, blacks enjoyed at least a physical independence from their landlords and had the sense of working their own lands, even if in most cases they could never hope to buy them.

Incomes and Credit

The economic effect of Reconstruction on the freedmen, to the extent that it can be calculated, was mixed. In some respects, the postwar years were a period of remarkable economic progress for blacks. If the food, clothing, shelter, and other material benefits they had received under slavery are considered as income, then prewar blacks had earned about a 22 percent share of the profits of the plantation system. By the end of Reconstruction, they were earning 56 percent of the return on investment in Southern agriculture. Measured another way, the per capita income of blacks rose 46 percent between 1857 and 1879, while the per capita income of whites declined 35 percent. This repre-

sented one of the most significant redistributions of income in American history.

Nevertheless, the economic status of blacks did not improve as much as such figures suggest. For one thing, while their share of the profits was increasing, the total profits of Southern agriculture were declining: a result of the dislocations of the war and of a reduction in the world market for cotton. For another thing, while blacks were earning a greater return on their labor than they had under slavery, they were working less. Women and children were less likely to labor in the fields than in the past; and adult men tended to work shorter days. In all, the black labor force worked about one-third fewer hours during Reconstruction than they had under slavery—a reduction that brought their working schedule roughly into accord with that of white farm laborers. The income redistribution of the postwar years raised both the absolute and the relative economic status of blacks in the South substantially. It did not, however, lift many blacks out of poverty. Black per capita income rose quickly after the war, from about one-quarter of white per capita income to about one-half. But after this initial increase, it rose virtually not at all.

For blacks and poor whites alike, whatever gains there might have been as a result of land and income redistribution were often overshadowed by the ravages of another economic burden: the crop lien system. In the postwar South, the traditional credit structure—based on "factors" (see pp. 336–337) and banks—was unable to reassert its former control. In its stead emerged a new system of credit, centered in large part around local country stores—some of them owned by planters, others owned by independent merchants. Blacks and whites, landowners and tenants: all depended on these stores for such necessities as food, clothing, seed, farm implements, and the like. And since the agricultural sector does not enjoy the same steady cash flow as other sectors of the economy, Southern farmers often had to rely on credit from these merchants in order to purchase what they needed. The credit came at high cost. Interest rates were, in effect, as high as 50 or 60 percent. Suppliers held liens (claims) on the crops of debtor farmers as collateral on the loans. If a farmer suffered a few bad years in a row, as often happened in the troubled agricultural markets of the 1870s, he could become trapped in a cycle of debt from which he could never escape.

This burdensome credit system had a number of effects on the South. One was that some blacks who had acquired land during the early years of Reconstruction gradually lost it as they fell into debt. (So, to a lesser extent, did small white landowners.) Another was that Southern farmers became utterly dependent on cash crops—and most of all on cotton—because only such marketable com-modities seemed to offer any possibility of an escape from debt. Thus Southern agriculture, never sufficiently diversified even in the best of times, became more one-dimensional than ever. Before the war, the South had grown most of its own food. By the end of Recon-struction, the region was importing a large proportion—in some areas more than 50 percent—of what it needed to feed itself. The relentless planting of cotton, moreover, was contributing to an exhaustion of the soil. The crop lien system, in other words, was not only helping to impoverish small farmers; it was also contributing to a general decline in the Southern agricultural economy.

THE GRANT ADMINISTRATION

Exhausted by the political turmoil of the Johnson administration, American voters in 1868 yearned for a strong, stable figure to guide them through the troubled years of Reconstruction. They did not find one. In-stead, they turned trustingly to General Ulysses S. Grant, the conquering hero of the war and, by 1868, a widely revered national idol. An inspired general, Grant was a disas-trous president. During his two terms in of-fice, he faced problems that would have taxed the abilities of a master of statecraft. Grant, whatever his qualities, was no such leader. He was, rather, a generally dull and unimaginative man with few political skills and little real vision.

The Soldier President

At the end of the war both parties had angled to make Grant their candidate, and he could have had the nomination of either party. As he watched the congressional Radicals tri-umph over President Johnson, he concluded that the Radical Reconstruction policy ex-pressed the real wishes of the people. He was receptive when the Radical leaders ap-proached him with offers of the Republican nomination, and virtually without opposi-tion, he received the endorsement of the party convention. The Democrats, spurned by Grant, nominated Horace Seymour of New York.

After a bitter campaign revolving around Reconstruction and Seymour's war record as governor of New York (he had been a Peace Democrat), Grant carried twenty-six states and Seymour only eight. But Grant received only 3,012,000 popular votes to Seymour's 2,703,000, a scant majority of 309,000, and this majority was due to black votes in the reconstructed states of the South.

Ulysses S. Grant was the second profes-sional soldier to be elected to the presidency (Zachary Taylor having been the first). After graduating from West Point with no particu-lar distinction, Grant had entered the regular army, from which after years of service he resigned under something of a cloud. In civil-ian life he undertook several dismal ventures that barely yielded him a living. His career before 1861 could be characterized as forty years of failure. Then came the Civil War, and Grant found at last the one setting, the one vocation for which he was supremely equipped—war.

His political naïveté as president was dis-played in many of his appointments. For the important office of secretary of state he chose an old friend, the former Illinois con-gressman Elihu B. Washburne. By agree-ment, Washburne was to hold the position only a week before resigning to become minister to France, the purpose being to en-able him to brag in Paris that he had headed the foreign office. After offering the appointment to another man, who declined it on the grounds of expense, Grant then named Hamilton Fish of New York.

In choosing his official family, Grant proceeded as if he were creating a military staff. He sent several appointments to the Senate for confirmation without asking the recipients if they would serve; they first heard the news in the papers. Fish, who had been out of politics for twenty years, wired Grant that he could not accept, but his name was already being acted on in the Senate and he was persuaded to let it go through. During his two administrations, Grant named a total of twenty-five men to the cabinet. Most of his later appointments went to men who were, at best, average, and some to men who were incompetent or corrupt or both. Increasingly, in dispensing cabinet and executive patronage, Grant came to rely on the machine leaders in the party—the groups most ardently devoted to the spoils system.

Diplomatic Successes

The Grant administration, like the Johnson administration before it, achieved its greatest success in foreign affairs. These were the accomplishments not of the presidents themselves, who displayed little aptitude for diplomacy, but of two outstanding secretaries of state: William H. Seward, who had served Lincoln during the Civil War and remained in office until 1869; and Hamilton Fish, who served throughout the two terms of the Grant administration.

An ardent expansionist and advocate of a vigorous foreign policy, Seward acted with as much daring as the demands of Reconstruction politics and the Republican hatred of President Johnson would permit. When Russia let it be known that it would like to sell Alaska to the United States, the two nations long having been on friendly terms, Seward readily agreed to pay the asking price of $7.2 million. Only by strenuous efforts was he able to induce the Senate to ratify the treaty and the House to appropriate the money (1867–1868). Critics jeered that the secretary had bought a useless frozen wasteland—

Hamilton Fish
Although he served in an administration best remembered for its corruption and ineptitude, Hamilton Fish earned a reputation as one of the most talented and effective secretaries of state in American history. Faced with a series of extraordinarily difficult diplomatic problems in the aftermath of the Civil War, he managed to resolve most of them with skill and tact. He began his career as a member of Congress from New York, becoming the first of many generations of his family—extending into the 1980s—to serve in the House of Representatives. (The Granger Collection)

"Seward's Icebox" and "Walrussia" were some of the terms employed to describe it—but Alaska, a center for the fishing industry in the North Pacific and potentially rich in such resources as gold (and, as the nation would discover much later, oil), was a bargain. Seward was not content with expansion in continental North America. In 1867, he engineered the annexation of the tiny Midway Islands west of Hawaii.

In contrast with its sometimes shambling course in domestic politics, the performance of the Grant administration in the area of foreign affairs was generally decisive and firm, yet showing a wise moderation. For this, Secretary Fish, to whom President Grant gave almost a free hand, deserves the major credit. A number of delicate and potentially dangerous situations confronted Fish from the beginning, but the most serious one arose out of strained relations with Great Britain.

The United States had a burning grievance against England that had originated during the Civil War. At that time the British government, according to the American interpretation, had violated the laws of neutrality by permitting Confederate cruisers, the *Alabama* and others, to be built and armed in English shipyards and let loose to prey on Northern commerce. American demands that England pay for the damages committed by these vessels became known as the "Alabama claims." Although the British government realized its diplomatic error in condoning construction of the cruisers (in a future war American-built *Alabamas* might operate against Britain), it at first hesitated to submit the issue to arbitration.

Seward tried earnestly to settle the Alabama claims before leaving office. The American minister to England, Reverdy Johnson, negotiated an agreement, the Johnson-Clarendon Convention (1869), providing that all claims on both sides since 1853 be submitted to arbitration. The pact was distasteful to Americans because it embraced so many issues and contained no expression of British regret for the escape of the *Alabama*. Coming before the Senate immediately after Grant took office, it was rejected 54 to 1. The debate featured a speech by Charles Sumner, chairman of the Committee on Foreign Relations, denouncing Britain for its course in the Civil War and arguing that its conduct had prolonged the war by two years. Therefore, said Sumner, England owed the United States for "direct damages" committed by the cruisers and "indirect damages" for the cost of the war for two years—which would have reached the staggering total of some $2 billion.

England naturally would have nothing to do with any arrangement involving indirect claims, and settlement of the problem was temporarily stalled. Secretary Fish, however, continued to work for a solution, and finally, in 1871, the two countries agreed to the Treaty of Washington, one of the great landmarks in international pacification, providing for arbitration of the cruiser issue and other pending controversies. The Alabama claims were to be laid before a five-member tribunal whose members were to be appointed by the governments of the United States, England, Italy, Switzerland, and Brazil. In the covenant, Britain expressed regret for the escape of the *Alabama* and agreed to a set of rules governing neutral obligations that virtually gave the British case away. In effect, this meant that the tribunal would have only to fix the sum to be paid by Britain. Convening at Geneva in Switzerland, the arbitrators awarded $15.5 million to the United States.

The Defection of the Liberals

Through both his foreign and his domestic policies, President Grant antagonized and alienated a number of prominent Republicans, among them the famous Radical Charles Sumner. Senator Sumner's extravagant demand for damages from Great Britain embarrassed Secretary Fish in the latter's diplomacy. Still worse, from the president's point of view, Sumner blocked a treaty for the annexation of Santo Domingo, a project in which Grant took a deep personal interest—indeed, it was a kind of monomania with him. The angry president got revenge by inducing his Senate friends to remove Sumner from the chairmanship of the Committee on Foreign Relations.

Sumner and other Republican leaders joined with civil service reformers to criticize Grant for his use of the spoils system, his reliance on ruthless machine politicians. Such scholarly journalists as E. L. Godkin of *The Nation* and George William Curtis of *Harper's Weekly* were arguing that the government ought to base its appointments not on services to the party but on fitness for office as determined by competitive examinations, as the British government already was doing. Grant yielded to the extent of recommending the establishment of a civil service commission, which Congress authorized in 1871, to devise a system of hiring based on merit. This agency, under the direction of Curtis, proposed a set of rules that seemed to meet with Grant's approval. But Grant was not really much interested in reform, and even if he had been he could not have persuaded his followers to accept a new system that would undermine the very basis of party loyalty—the patronage. Congress, by neglecting to renew the commission's appropriation, soon ended its existence.

Nevertheless, controversy over civil service reform continued, becoming one of the leading political issues of the next three decades of American life. The debate involved more than simply an argument over patronage and corruption. It reflected, too, basic differences of opinion over who was fit to serve in public life. Middle-class reformers were saying, implicitly, that only educated, middle-class people should be permitted access to government office. Those opposing them—not simply party leaders, but immigrant and labor groups, some farmers, and others—argued that the establishment of an elite corps of civil servants would exclude these groups from participation in government and restrict power to the upper classes. The controversy clearly echoed the debate in the Jacksonian era, when the "spoils system" was first introduced and was widely hailed as a "democratic" reform.

Republican critics of the president also denounced him for his support of Radical Reconstruction. He continued to station federal troops in the South, and on many occasions he sent them to support Republican governments that were on the point of collapse. To growing numbers in the North this seemed like dangerous militarism, and they were more and more disgusted by the stories of governmental corruption and extravagance that came up from the South. Some Republicans were beginning to suspect that there was corruption not only in the Southern state governments but also in the federal government. Still others criticized Grant because he had declined to speak out in favor of a reduction of the tariff. The high wartime duties remained substantially unchanged even though the justification for them was past.

Thus, before the end of Grant's first term, members of his own party had begun to oppose him for a variety of reasons—his foreign policies, his use of the patronage, his resort to military force in the South, his high-tariff stand, and his suspected taint of corruption—all of which added up to what the critics called "Grantism." In 1872, hoping to prevent Grant's reelection, his opponents bolted the party. Referring to themselves as Liberal Republicans, they proceeded to set up their own organization for running presidential and vice-presidential candidates.

They named Horace Greeley, veteran editor and publisher of the New York *Tribune* to head their ticket. The Democratic convention, seeing in his candidacy (and in the alliance with the Liberals it would achieve) the only chance to unseat the Republicans, endorsed him with no great enthusiasm. Despite his recent attacks on Radical Reconstruction, many Southerners, remembering Greeley's own Radical past, prepared to stay at home on Election Day. The Republicans, with Grant as their standard-bearer and a platform justifying Reconstruction and calling for a high tariff, moved into the campaign with confidence. In November, Grant polled 286 electoral votes and 3,597,000 popular votes to Greeley's 62 and 2,834,000. The optimistic editor carried only two Southern and four border states. Three weeks later Greeley, apparently crushed by his defeat, died.

During the campaign the first of a series of political scandals had come to light. Although the wrongdoing had occurred before Grant took office, it involved his party, and the onus for it fell on his administration. This scandal originated with the Crédit Mobilier construction company, which helped build the Union Pacific Railroad. In reality, the Crédit Mobilier was controlled by a few Union Pacific stockholders who awarded huge and fraudulent contracts to the construction company, thus milking the Union Pacific, a company of which they owned a minor share, of money that in part came from government subsidies. To avert a congressional inquiry into the deal, the directors, using Oakes Ames, a Massachusetts representative, as their agent, sold at a discount (in effect gave) Crédit Mobilier stock to key members of Congress. A congressional investigation was held, and it revealed that some high-placed Republicans—including Schuyler Colfax, now Grant's vice president—had accepted stock.

One dreary episode followed another in Grant's second term. Benjamin H. Bristow, Grant's third secretary of the treasury, discovered that some of his officials and a group of distillers operating as a "whiskey ring" were cheating the government out of taxes by means of false reports. Among the prominent Republicans involved was the president's private secretary, Orville E. Babcock. Grant defended Babcock, appointed him to another office, and eased Bristow out of the cabinet. A House investigation revealed that William W. Belknap, secretary of war, had accepted bribes to retain an Indian-post trader in office. Belknap resigned with Grant's blessing before the Senate could act on impeachment charges brought by the House. (In fact, Belknap's actions were not much different from the usual methods of administering Indian reservations. Administrations both before and after Grant's made casual use of these important appointments to satisfy their political backers.) Lesser scandals involved the Navy Department, which was suspected of selling business to contractors, and the Treasury, where John D. Sanborn, a special agent appointed to handle overdue taxes, collected $427,000 and retained a 50 percent commission for himself and the Republican bigwigs who had placed him in the job.

The Greenback Question

Meanwhile, the Grant administration and the nation at large suffered another blow: the Panic of 1873. It began with the failure of a leading investment banking firm, Jay Cooke and Company. Cooke, the "financier of the Civil War," had done well in handling government war bonds, but he had sunk excessive amounts into postwar railroad building. Depressions had come before with almost rhythmic regularity—in 1819, 1837, and 1857—but this was the worst one yet. It lasted four years, during which unemployment rose to 3 million and agricultural prices fell so far that thousands of farmers, unable to meet mortgage payments, went more deeply into debt or lost their farms.

Debtors hoped the government would follow an inflationary easy-money policy, which would have made it easier for them to pay their debts and would have helped to stimulate recovery from the depression. But President Grant and most Republicans preferred what they called a "sound" currency, which was to the advantage of the banks, moneylenders, and other creditors.

The money question had confronted Grant and the Republicans in Congress from the beginning of his administration. The question was twofold: How should interest and principal of the war bonds be paid, and what should be the permanent place of greenbacks in the national currency? Representatives of the debtor interests argued that the bonds had been purchased in greenbacks of depreciated value and should, unless stipulated otherwise by law, by redeemed in the same currency. The president favored payment in gold, and the Republican Congress moved speedily to promise redemption in "coin or its equivalent" and to enact a refunding act providing for long-term refinancing of the debt (1869–1870).

Approximately $450 million in greenbacks had been issued during the Civil War, and $400 million of them were still in circulation at the end of the conflict. During the Johnson administration, Congress had authorized the Treasury to reduce their quantity, but protests by farmers and some business groups had halted further action. When Grant entered the White House, the greenback circulation was some $356 million and the gold value of a greenback dollar was 73 cents.

After the Supreme Court, in *Knox* v. *Lee* (1871), reversed an earlier decision and affirmed the legality of greenbacks, the Treasury moved, in 1873, to increase the amount in circulation in response to the panic. For the same reason Congress, in the following year, voted to raise the total further. Grant, responding to pressures from Eastern financial interests, vetoed the measure—over the loud objections of many members of his own party.

With the greenback issue becoming more and more heated and divisive, and with an election year approaching, Republican leaders in Congress began searching for some way to settle the controversy. Their solu-

The Specter of Inflation
The greenback contro-
versy of the 1870s inspired
dire warnings of disaster
from both supporters and
opponents of paper cur-
rency. This cartoon con-
veys the warnings of the
foes of greenbacks of the
catastrophic inflation that
would result from a fail-
ure to return to a "sound"
(specie-backed) currency.
(Culver Pictures)

AN INFLATION LOOK AHEAD.
Boy. "Mother wants Three Cents' worth of Paregoric."
Druggist. "Where is your money?"
Boy. "In the wheel-barrow, of course. Expect me to carry Three Cents' worth of Greenbacks in my Pocket?"

tion—introduced initially by Senator John Sherman of Ohio—was the Specie Resumption Act of 1875. This law provided that after January 1, 1879, the government would redeem greenback dollars at par with gold; that is, the present greenbacks, whose value constantly fluctuated, could be exchanged for new paper currency, whose value would be firmly pegged to the price of gold. The law served several of its intended purposes. It healed many of the divisions within the Republican Party. It protected the interests of the creditor classes, who had worried that debts would be repaid in debased paper currency and were now assured that debtors would pay them with stable dollars. Other groups, however, were less satisfied. In theory, the new law protected the interests of debtor groups as well; by directing the gov-

ernment to increase its gold reserve, the bill presumably would permit an increase in the amount of specie-backed currency in circulation. In fact, "resumption" did not satisfy those who had been clamoring for an increase in greenbacks, because the gold-based money supply was never able to expand as much as they believed was necessary.

Thus the greenback issue survived after 1875, and the question of the proper composition of the currency now emerged as one of the most controversial and enduring issues in American politics. Creditors and established financial interests continued to insist on a "sound" currency based on gold. Debtor groups—farmers, laborers, and some manufacturers—and debtor regions—the South and the West—continued to clamor for a currency based not on gold reserves but on the productive capacity of the nation. Otherwise, they claimed, they would continue to be strangled by an overvalued dollar circulating in insufficient quantities. But the question of greenbacks, and the many other currency controversies that followed, also became symbols of much deeper concerns. Agrarian dissidents and others came to see in the maintenance of the gold standard a conspiracy by entrenched financiers to keep them in economic bondage. Southerners and Westerners saw in the currency policies evidence of their subordination to the Northeast. Because in accepting the gold standard the United States was following the example of Great Britain and other European nations, many Americans came to view the policy as part of a dire international plot to enslave the American people. The greenbackers, as they were called, expressed their displeasure in 1875 by forming their own political organization: the National Greenback party. Active in the next three presidential elections, it failed to gain widespread support. But it did keep the money issue alive. And in the 1880s, the greenback forces began to merge with another, more powerful group of currency reformers—those who favored silver as the basis of currency—to help produce a political movement that would ultimately attain enormous strength.

THE ABANDONMENT OF RECONSTRUCTION

As the North grew increasingly preoccupied with its own political and economic problems, interest in Reconstruction began to wane. The Grant administration continued to protect Republican governments in the South, but less because of any interest in ensuring the position of freedmen than because of a desire to prevent the reemergence of a strong Democratic party in the region. But even the presence of federal troops was not enough to prevent white Southerners from working to overturn the Republican governments that they believed had been so ruthlessly thrust upon them. In a few states, the Democrats (or Conservatives) returned to power almost as soon as civilian government was restored. In Virginia, North Carolina, and Georgia, Republican rule came to an end in 1870. In other states, the Democrats gradually regained control over several years. Texas was "redeemed," as Southerners liked to call the restoration of Democratic rule, in 1873; Alabama and Arkansas in 1874; and Mississippi in 1875. For three other states—South Carolina, Louisiana, and Florida—the end of Reconstruction had to wait for the withdrawal of the last federal troops in 1877, a withdrawal that was the result of a long process of political bargaining and compromise at the national level.

The Southern States "Redeemed"

In the states where the whites constituted a majority—the upper South states—overthrow of Republican control was a relatively simple matter. The whites had only to organize and win the elections. Their success was facilitated by the early restoration of the suffrage to those whites who had been deprived of it by national or state action. Presidential and congressional pardons returned the privilege to numerous individuals; and in 1872, Congress, responding to public demands to remove penalties imposed on many Southerners after the war, enacted the Amnesty Act, which restored political rights to 150,000 ex-Confederates and left only 500 excluded from political life.

In other states, where blacks were in the majority or the population of the two races was almost equal, the whites resorted to intimidation and violence. Frankly terroristic were the secret societies that appeared in many parts of the South—the Ku Klux Klan, the Knights of the White Camellia, and others—which attempted to frighten or physically prevent blacks from voting. Although the societies were effective, their influence has been exaggerated by writers intrigued by their hooded and robed apparel and their elaborate ritual. Moving quickly to stamp out these societies, Congress passed two bills— termed "force acts" by white Southerners— in 1870 and 1871 and the Ku Klux Klan Act (also in 1871), which authorized the president to use military force and martial law in areas where the orders were active.

More potent than the secret orders were the open semimilitary organizations that operated under such names as rifle clubs, Red Shirts, and White Leagues. After the first such society was founded in Mississippi, the idea spread to other states, and the procedure employed by the clubs was called the Mississippi Plan. Briefly stated, the plan called for the whites in each community to organize and arm, and to be prepared, if necessary, to resort to force to win elections. But the heart of the scheme was in the phrase "drawing the color line." By one method or another, legal or illegal, every white man was to be forced to join the Democratic party or leave the community. By similar methods, every black male was to be excluded from political activity; in a few states blacks were to be permitted to vote—if they voted Democratic.

Perhaps an even stronger influence than the techniques practiced by the armed bands was the simple and unromantic weapon of economic pressure. The war had freed the black man, but he was still a laborer—a hired worker or a tenant—dependent on the whites for his livelihood. The whites readily discovered that this dependence placed blacks in their power. Planters refused to rent land to Republican blacks, storekeepers refused to extend them credit, employers refused to give them work. Economic pressure was a force that the blacks could not fight. If the Radicals, in bringing blacks to political power, had accomplished a revolution, it was a superficial one. They failed to provide black people with economic power, as they might have done by giving them possession of confiscated land. Hence their political rights had no lasting basis.

Certainly the blacks' political position was hopeless without the continued backing of the Republican party and the federal government. But they were losing the support of people in the North, even of many humani-tarian reformers who had worked for emancipation and equal rights. After the adoption of the Fifteenth Amendment (1870), most of the reformers convinced themselves that their long campaign in behalf of black people at last was over, that with the vote blacks ought to be able to take care of themselves. Republican disillusionment with the corruption and disorders in the Southern states helped to bring about the party split of 1872, which in turn weakened the Republicans in the South still further. They beheld the discouraging spectacle of such former Radical leaders as Charles Sumner and Horace Greeley now calling themselves Liberals, cooperating with the Democrats, and outdoing even them in denunciations of what they viewed as black-and-carpetbag misgovernment. Most of the white Republicans of the South, including some of those who had come from the North, joined the Liberal movement and went over to the Democrats. Friction between the remaining carpetbaggers and the black Republicans grew because of a well-justified feeling on the part of the blacks that they were not receiving a fair share of the power and the jobs.

When the depression came in 1873, the hard times aggravated political discontent both North and South. In the congressional elections of 1874, the Democrats gained a majority of the seats in the national House of Representatives. After 1875, when the new House met, the Republicans no longer controlled the whole Congress, as they had done since the beginning of the war. And President Grant, in view of the changing temper of the North, no longer was willing to use military force to save from violent overthrow the Republican regimes that were still standing in the South. In 1875, when the Mississippi governor, Adelbert Ames (originally from Maine), appealed to Washington for troops to protect blacks from the terrorism of the Democrats, he received in reply a telegram that quoted Grant as saying: "The whole public are tired out with these annual autumnal outbreaks in the South, and the great majority are now ready to condemn any interference on the part of the government."

After the Democrats had taken Mississippi, only three states were left in the hands of the Republicans—South Carolina, Louisiana, and Florida. In the elections of 1876, again using terrorist tactics, the Democrats claimed victory in all three. But the Republicans maintained that they themselves had won, and they were able to continue holding office because federal troops happened to be on the scene. If the troops should be withdrawn, the last of the Republican regimes would fall. The future was to depend on the settlement of the presidential election of 1876, which was disputed in consequence of the electoral disputes in the South.

The Compromise of 1877

Ulysses S. Grant was eager to run for another term in 1876, and his friends among the Republican bosses tried to secure the nomination for him. But the majority of the Republican leaders ruled Grant out. Impressed by the recent upsurge of Democratic strength, which had delivered the House of Representatives and a number of state governments to the opposition party, and fearful of the third-term issue, they searched for a candidate who was not associated with the scandals of the past eight years and could entice the Liberals back into the fold and unite the party until after the election.

Senator James G. Blaine of Maine offered himself, but he had recently been involved in an allegedly crooked railroad deal. The Republican convention passed over Blaine and other hopefuls and named as the standard-bearer Rutherford B. Hayes, a former Union army officer and congressman, three times governor of Ohio, and a champion of civil service reform.

No personal rivalries divided the Democrats. Only one aspirant commanded serious attention, and with him as their candidate the Democrats were confident of returning to power. The bearer of the party's hopes was Governor Samuel J. Tilden of New York, whose name had become synonymous with governmental reform. A corporation lawyer and a millionaire, Tilden had long been a power in the Democratic organization of his state, but he had not hesitated to turn against

the corrupt Tweed Ring of New York City's Tammany Hall and aid in its overthrow. His fight against Tweed brought him national fame and the governorship, in which position he increased his reputation for honest administration.

Despite the fury of the charges flung at each other by the parties in the canvass, there were almost no differences of principle between the candidates. Hayes was on record as favoring withdrawal of troops from the South, he advocated civil service, and his record for probity was equal to Tilden's. Although the New York governor, reflecting Eastern importing interests, was amenable to some kind of tariff reduction, on other economic issues he was at least as conservative as his rival. He was a gold or "sound-money" man, and he believed that government had no business interfering with economic interests. He looked on himself as a modern counterpart of Thomas Jefferson.

The November election revealed an apparent Democratic victory. In addition to the South, Tilden carried several large Northern states, and his popular vote was 4,300,000 to 4,036,000 for Hayes. But the situation was complicated by the disputed returns from Louisiana, South Carolina, and Florida, whose total electoral vote was 19. Both parties claimed to have won these states, and double sets of returns were presented to Congress. Adding to the confusion was a contested vote in Oregon, where one of the three successful Republican electors was declared ineligible because he held a federal office. The Democrats contended that the place should go to the Democratic elector with the highest number of votes, but the Republicans insisted that according to state law the remaining electors were to select someone to fill the vacancy. The dual and disputed returns threw the outcome of the election into doubt. As tension and excitement gripped the country, two clear facts emerged from the welter of conflicting claims. Tilden had for certain 184 electoral votes, only one short of the majority. The 20 votes in controversy would determine who would be president, and Hayes needed all of them to secure the prize.

With surprise and consternation, the nation now learned that no measure or method existed to determine the validity of disputed returns. The Constitution stated: "The President of the Senate shall, in the presence of the Senate and House of Representatives, open all the certificates and the votes shall then be counted." The question was, how and by whom? The Senate was Republican and so, of course, was its president and the House was Democratic. Constitutional ambiguity and congressional division rendered a fair and satisfactory solution of the crisis impossible. If the president of the Senate counted the votes, Hayes would be the victor. If the Senate and House judged the returns separately, they would reach opposite decisions and checkmate each other. And if the houses voted jointly, the Democrats, with a numerical majority, would decide the result. Resort to any one of these lines of action promised to divide the country and possibly result in chaos.

Not until the last days of January 1877 did Congress act to break the deadlock. Then it created a special electoral commission to pass on all the disputed votes. The commission was to be composed of five senators, five representatives, and five justices of the Supreme Court. Because of the party line-up, the congressional delegation would consist of five Republicans and five Democrats. The creating law named four of the judicial commissioners, two Republicans and two Democrats. The four were to select their fifth colleague, and it was understood that they would choose David Davis, an independent Republican, thus ensuring that the deciding vote would be wielded by a relatively unbiased judge. But at this stage Davis was elected to the Senate from Illinois and suddenly resigned his seat. His place on the commission fell to a more partisan Republican. Sitting throughout February, the commission by a straight party vote of 8 to 7 decided every disputed vote for Hayes. Congress accepted the final verdict of the commission on March 2, only two days before the inauguration of the new president.

Ratification of the commission's findings was not accomplished, however, without some complicated compromising among the politicians. Behind the dealing, and partially directing it, were certain powerful economic forces with a stake in the outcome. A decision by the commission was not final until approved by Congress, and the Democrats could have prevented action by filibustering. The success of a filibuster, however, depended on concert between Northern and Southern Democrats, and this the Republicans disrupted by offering the Southerners sufficient inducement to accept the commission's findings. According to the traditional account, certain Republicans and Southern Democrats met at Washington's Wormley Hotel, and the Republicans pledged that Hayes, after becoming president, would withdraw the troops from the South. As withdrawal would mean the downfall of the last carpetbag governments, the Southerners, convinced they were getting as much from Hayes as they could get from Tilden, abandoned the filibuster.

Actually, the story behind the "Compromise of 1877" is somewhat more complex. Hayes was on record before the election as favoring withdrawal of the troops, and in any event the Democrats in the House could have forced withdrawal simply by cutting out appropriations for the army in the Reconstruction process. The real agreement, the one that brought the Southern Democrats over, was reached before the Wormley meeting. As the price for their cooperation, the Southern Democrats (among them some old Whigs) exacted from the Republicans the following pledges: the appointment of at least one Southerner to the Hayes cabinet, control of federal patronage in their sections, generous internal improvements, national aid for the Texas and Pacific Railroad, and, finally, withdrawal of the troops. The Conservatives who were running the redeemed Southern states were primarily interested in economics—in industrializing the South—and they believed that the Republican program of federal aid to business would be more beneficial for their region than the archaic states'-rights policy of the Democrats.

The End of Reconstruction

In his inaugural address, Hayes stressed the Southern problem. While he took care to say that the rights of the blacks must be preserved, he announced that the most pressing need of the South was the restoration of "wise, honest, and peaceful local self-government"—which meant that he was going to withdraw the troops and let the whites take over control of the state governments. Hayes laid down this policy knowing that his action would lend weight to current charges that he was paying off the South for acquiescing in his election and would strengthen those critics who referred to him as "his Fraudulency."

The president hoped to build up a "new Republican" party in the South composed of whatever conservative white groups could be weaned away from the Democrats and committed to some acceptance of black rights. But his efforts, which included a tour of Southern cities and even the decoration of a memorial to the Confederate war dead, failed to produce any positive results. Although many Southern leaders sympathized with the economic credo of the Republicans, they could not advise their people to support the party that had imposed Reconstruction. Nor were Southerners pleased by Hayes's bestowal of federal offices on carpetbaggers or by his vetoes of Democratic attempts to repeal the "force acts." The "solid South," although not yet fully formed, was beginning to take shape. Neither Hayes nor any other Republican could reverse the trend—particularly since no one was willing to use federal power to protect black voting rights, which alone held promise of giving the Republicans lasting strength in the region.

The withdrawal of the troops was a signal that the national government was giving up its attempt to control Southern politics and to determine the place of blacks in Southern society. The surrender, it is to be noted, was made by the Republicans. They could yield with good grace because after 1877 they had no particular need for the support of the reconstructed South. The economic legislation of the war and postwar years was safe from repeal; industry was securely entrenched in the national economy; and Republican domination of national politics could be maintained without Southern votes.

The Tragedy of Reconstruction

The record of the Reconstruction years is not one of complete failure, as many have charged. That slavery would be abolished was clear well before the end of the war; but Reconstruction worked other changes upon Southern society as well. There was a significant redistribution of income, from which blacks benefited. There was a more limited, but not unimportant redistribution of land ownership, which enabled some former slaves to acquire property for the first time. There was both a relative and an absolute improvement in the economic circumstances of most blacks.

Nor was Reconstruction as disastrous an experience for Southern whites as most believed at the time. The region had emerged from a prolonged and bloody war defeated and devastated; and yet within a decade, the South had regained control of its own institutions and, to a great extent, restored its traditional ruling class to power. No harsh punishments were meted out to former Confederate leaders. No drastic program of economic reform was imposed on the region. Few lasting political changes were forced on the South. Not many conquered nations fare as well.

Yet for all that, Americans of the twentieth century cannot but look back on Reconstruction as a tragic era. For in those years the United States made its first serious effort to resolve its oldest and deepest social problem—the problem of race. And it failed in the effort. What was more, the experience so disappointed, disillusioned, and embittered the nation that it would be many years before an attempt would be made again.

Why did this great assault on racial injustice—an assault that had emerged over a period of more than fifty years—end so badly? In part, of course, it was because of the weaknesses and errors of the people who directed it. But in greater part, it was because the resolution of the racial problem required a far more fundamental reform of society than Americans of the time were willing to make. One after another, attempts to produce solutions ran up against conservative obstacles so deeply embedded in the nation's life that they could not be dislodged. Veneration of the Constitution sharply limited the willingness of national leaders to infringe on the rights of states and individuals in creating social change. A profound respect for private property and free enterprise prevented any real assault on economic privilege in the South, ensuring that blacks would not win title to the land and wealth they believed they deserved. Above all, perhaps, a pervasive belief among even the most liberal whites that the black race was inherently inferior served as an obstacle to the full equality of the freedmen. Given the context within which Americans of the 1860s and 1870s were working, what is surprising, perhaps, is not that Reconstruction did so little,

but that it did even as much as it did. The era was tragic not so much because it was a failure—the failure may have been inevitable from the beginning—but because it revealed how great, even insuperable, were the barriers to racial justice in the United States.

Given the odds confronting them, therefore, black Americans had reason for pride in the limited gains they were able to make during Reconstruction. And the nation at large had reason for gratitude that, if nothing else, the postwar era produced two great charters of freedom—the Fourteenth and Fifteenth amendments to the Constitution—which, although largely ignored at the time, would one day serve as the basis for a Second Reconstruction, one that would renew the drive to bring freedom and equality to all Americans.

SUGGESTED READINGS

The studies by McPherson and by Randall and Donald cited in the readings for the previous two chapters are likewise valuable for the Reconstruction period, both for their narratives of the era and for their bibliographies. William A. Dunning, *Reconstruction, Political and Economic, 1865–1977* (1907), long the standard study of Reconstruction, is now widely conceded to be marred by deep prejudices. More recent overviews of the period, better in tune with contemporary values, are Kenneth Stampp, *The Era of Reconstruction* (1965), and John Hope Franklin, *Reconstruction After the Civil War* (1961). W. E. B. Du Bois, *Black Reconstruction* (1935), is an early challenge to the pro-Southern orthodoxy about the period; while E. Merton Coulter, *The South During Reconstruction* (1947), adheres strictly to traditional views of the period as a time of Northern vindictiveness and Southern suffering. Rembert Patrick, *The Reconstruction of the Nation* (1967), is a modern overview that provides more detail than the relatively brief studies by Stampp and Franklin.

Herman Belz, *Reconstructing the Union* (1969), examines the theoretical basis of the Reconstruction problem. William B. Hesseltine, *Lincoln's Plan of Reconstruction* (1960), considers the first presidential plan; and Willie Lee Rose, *Rehearsal for Reconstruction: The Port Royal Experiment* (1964), describes wartime reconstruction policies in an area of South Carolina captured early by the Union. Louis S. Gerteis, *From Contraband to Freedman* (1973), examines federal pol-

icy toward blacks during the war itself. There are several valuable studies of the political battles that accompanied the switch from presidential to congressional Reconstruction. William R. Brock, *An American Crisis* (1963), is a particularly judicious work. Howard K. Beale, *The Critical Year: A Study of Andrew Johnson and Reconstruction* (1930), is a traditional approach to the subject; while Eric McKitrick, *Andrew Johnson and Reconstruction* (1960), is far more hostile toward Johnson. Two works by Michael Les Benedict, *A Compromise of Principle: Congressional Republicans and Reconstruction, 1863–1869* and *The Impeachment and Trial of Andrew Johnson* (1973), consider congressional politics and antagonisms toward the president. Hans L. Trefousse, *The Radical Republicans* (1963), and David Donald, *The Politics of Reconstruction* (1965), also examine congressional Radicals. Hans Trefousse is the author of another study of the impeachment proceedings, *The Impeachment of a President* (1975). La Wanda Cox and John H. Cox, *Politics, Principles, and Prejudice, 1865–1867* (1963), is an early work that was important in revising previous views of Reconstruction politics. Also useful for the politics of the era are biographies of leading Reconstruction figures. Richard N. Current, *Old Thad Stevens* (1942), is a hostile view; while Fawn Brodie, *Thaddeus Stevens* (1959), is more sympathetic. David Donald, *Charles Sumner and the Rights of Man* (1970), is also important. Harold Hyman, *A More Perfect Union* (1973), and Stanley Kutler, *The Judicial Power and Reconstruction*

Politics (1968), examine the constitutional problems that Reconstruction posed. Charles Fairman, *Reconstruction and Reunion* (1971), considers the Supreme Court in the postwar years. See also Herman Belz, *A New Birth of Freedom* (1976) and *Emancipation and Equal Rights* (1978). William Gilette, *The Right to Vote* (1965), is a study of the framing of the Fifteenth Amendment.

The South in Reconstruction is the subject of a growing literature. Joel Perman, *Reunion Without Compromise* (1973), is a good study of Southern resistance to Reconstruction policies. Valuable works on individual states include Joel G. Taylor, *Louisiana Reconstructed* (1974); Vernon Wharton, *The Negro in Mississippi, 1865–1890* (1965); Peyton McCrary, *Abraham Lincoln and Reconstruction* (1978), on policies toward Louisiana; Joel Williamson, *After Slavery: The Negro in South Carolina During Reconstruction* (1965); Thomas Holt, *Black over White* (1977), on South Carolina; C. Peter Ripley, *Slaves and Freedmen in Civil War Louisiana* (1976); and William Gilette, *Retreat from Reconstruction* (1980), on the end of Reconstruction. A valuable study of the economic impact of Reconstruction on the South is Roger Ransom and Richard Sutch, *One Kind of Freedom* (1977). Leon Litwack, *Been in the Storm So Long* (1979), is an important examination of the effects of Reconstruction on blacks, which should be supplemented by Robert Higgs, *Competition and Coercion* (1977). Allen Trelease, *White Terror* (1967), discusses the Ku Klux Klan. William S. McFeely portrays the head of the Freedmen's Bureau in *Yankee Stepfather: General O. O. Howard and the Freedmen* (1968); and George Bentley, *A History of the Freedmen's Bureau* (1955), examines the institution itself. On carpetbaggers, see Otto Olsen, *Carpetbagger's Crusade: Albion Winegar Tourgée* (1965); L. N. Powell, *New Masters: Northern Planters During the Civil War and Reconstruction* (1980); William Harris, *Day of the Carpetbagger* (1979); and Elizabeth Jacoway, *Yankee Missionaries in the South* (1979). Sarah Wiggins, *The Scalawag in Alabama Politics, 1865–1881* (1977), examines Southern "collaborationists." Likewise valuable are Jacqueline Jones, *Soldiers of Light and Love* (1980), and James Sefton, *The United States Army and Reconstruction* (1967).

On the Grant administration, see William McFeely, *Grant* (1981), for a biography of the president. Allan Nevins, *Hamilton Fish* (1936), is a biography of the secretary of state that provides a portrait of the administration as a whole. William B. Hesseltine, *U. S. Grant, Politician* (1935), is another study of the Grant presidency. On the scandals of the era, see David Loth, *Public Plunder* (1938). John G. Sproat, *"The Best Men"* (1968), examines the role of liberal reformers during the period. Specific political controversies of the time are considered in Ari Hoogenboom, *Outlawing the Spoils* (1961), on civil service reform, and Irwin Unger, *The Greenback Era* (1964), on monetary controversies. Two views of the compromise of 1877 are C. Vann Woodward, *Reunion and Reaction* (1951), and K. I. Polakoff, *The Politics of Inertia* (1973). Edwin C. Rozwenc (ed.), *Reconstruction in the South*, rev. ed. (1952), is a valuable collection of essays on the subject.

PART FIVE

Progress and Its Discontents, 1877-1920

America's industrial revolution had begun well before the Civil War, and by the end of Reconstruction it was already far advanced. But it was in the last thirty years of the nineteenth century that the revolution came of age. During these decades, the United States transformed itself from a predominantly rural, agrarian society into a highly industrialized, urbanized one. It moved from a position of relative unimportance in world affairs to that of a major international power. It changed from a fragmented, largely provincial society into an increasingly centralized and consolidated one. It became a modern nation.

It became, too, a nation with a sharply divided view of itself and its future. On the one hand, Americans took pride in their country's remarkable economic growth, in its great technological advances, in its enhanced world power. They had good reason to do so. The United States by 1900 was the leading industrial nation on earth, and the potential of its economy seemed virtually unlimited. Its natural resources were plentiful. Its labor supply was large and growing. Its technological and administrative capacities were becoming more and more sophisticated. The nation was, its people sensed, on the eve of an era of unbounded prosperity.

But the last years of the nineteenth century also gave Americans reason for alarm. For along with the undoubted benefits of economic growth had come great costs: crowded cities, oppressed minorities, concentrations of power, disparities of wealth, political corruption, and general instability. Large segments of the population—blacks, Indians, many members of the industrial work force, important immigrant groups, women—were finding themselves excluded from the fruits of industrial progress. Entire regions of the country—the South and much of the West, both of which remained primarily agricultural—similarly did not much share in the nation's prosperity and at times seethed with discontent. These and other problems combined in the 1890s to produce a series of wrenching social and economic crises that seemed to confirm what many Americans had been saying for years: that modernization had brought not only progress but chaos and injustice; that the nation must reshape itself to deal with the problems its new economy had created.

Out of this perceived need for reform emerged a wide-ranging effort to produce new institutions and procedures that might bring order to American society—an effort that won for the first years of the twentieth century the label "the progressive era." Progressivism was perhaps most clearly visible in the dramatic political battles of the period, which produced far-reaching changes in the nature of government at every level and elevated the federal government to a position of new importance. But the reform impulse touched far more than politics. It reached out into virtually every area of society: business, the professions, the arts, education, racial minorities, women, and others. By the time the nation entered World War I, the effects of progressivism had become so pervasive, many of its impulses so absorbed into the fabric of national life, that it was no longer a movement so much as a description of the social outlook of vast numbers of Americans. And while the war took its toll on some strands of progressive thought, it helped others to survive and grow stronger. In the years following the fighting, the United States would embark on a series of new experiments in reform that would rest in large part on the progressive legacy.

The New South and the Last West

16

Completing the Trans-continental Railroad
Officials of the Union Pacific and Central Pacific railroads shake hands as the two lines are joined at Promontory, Utah, on May 10, 1869, thus completing the nation's first transcontinental railroad. The Union Pacific line had begun in Nebraska (at the terminus of the existing railroad connections to the East), and the Central Pacific had built eastward from California. Under the Pacific Railroad Act of 1852, both companies had received land grants of ten alternate sections of land on each side of the tracks for the entire length of the route, thus ensuring that the railroads would continue to be an important economic force in the American West.
(Union Pacific Railroad Museum Collection)

Much of the United States in the years following Reconstruction was preoccupied with the expansion and development of an already advanced urban-industrial society. In two regions of America, however, the experience was quite different. In the South, the first region of the country to have been settled by Europeans, and in the West, the last such region, the late nineteenth century was a time of new beginnings. It also became a period of decline relative to the rest of the nation—a decline that would ultimately produce in both regions major social and political upheavals.

The South, recovering from a disastrous war and confronting once again the reality of an economy far less developed than that of the North, faced several choices in the years after Reconstruction. It could attempt to transform itself into a modern, industrial region able to compete effectively with its former enemy. Or it could attempt to rebuild its agrarian economy and restore some semblance of the comfortable stability that white Southerners had so valued in their civilization before the Civil War. In fact, the South attempted to do both. Substantial groups of Southerners set out to promote modern economic development of their region, to imitate Northern ways, even at times to elevate the status of blacks—to build what they liked to call a New South. Their efforts were not without result. But despite substantial progress in certain areas, the South remained at the end of the century what it had long been: an impoverished, primarily agricultural region, far behind the North in the development of commerce and industry. The failure was a result in part of economic obstacles over which the region had little control; but it was a result, too, of the determination of the vast majority of white Southerners to protect the supremacy of their race—a determination that often came to overshadow all efforts at reform.

For the new West—the areas beyond the Mississippi River, most of which had remained unsettled or sparsely settled by white Americans in the years before the Civil War—the late nineteenth century was a time of dramatic growth and development. White settlers now poured into the region—a region larger than all the previously settled area of America combined. And they established there a new civilization of farms, ranches, mining operations, and more. It was a civilization that had much in common with the older regions of the United States, but one that took on a distinctive character of its own. The conquest of the West was in part the story of a courageous struggle against imposing natural obstacles. It was also the story of a brutal assault against the Indian tribes of the region, who were once again disrupted and ultimately displaced by the onward march of white society.

THE SOUTH IN TRANSITION

The Compromise of 1877—the agreement between Southern Democrats and Northern Republicans that helped settle the disputed election of 1876—was supposed to be the first step toward developing a stable, permanent Republican party in the South. In that respect, at least, it failed. In the years following the end of Reconstruction, white Southerners began to establish the Democratic party as the only viable political organization for the region's whites. And they created a social system that, for all its differences from the system of the antebellum period, concentrated most political and economic power in the hands of a powerful white aristocracy. Slowly but systematically, the white leadership excluded black Southerners from any meaningful access to power or influence in the region. The New South was indeed new in some respects; but in others, it was distinctly familiar.

The "Redeemers"

By the end of 1877—after the last withdrawal of federal troops—every Southern state government had been "redeemed." That is, political power had been restored to white Democrats. Many Southerners rejoiced at the restoration of what they liked to call "home rule." In fact, political power in the region was soon more restricted than at any time since the Civil War. Once again, the South had fallen under the control of a powerful, conservative oligarchy, whose members were known variously as the "Redeemers" or the "Bourbons."

This post-Reconstruction ruling class was in some areas of the South much the same as the ruling class of the antebellum period. In Alabama, for example, the old planter elite—despite challenges from new merchant and industrial forces—retained much of its former power and continued largely to dominate the state for decades. In other areas, however, the "Redeemers" constituted a genuinely new class. Merchants, industrialists, railroad developers, financiers—some of them former planters, some of them Northern immigrants who had become absorbed into the region's life, some of them ambitious, upwardly mobile white Southerners from the region's lower social tiers—combined a commitment to "home rule" and social conservatism with a commitment to economic development.

Whatever their differences, the various Bourbon governments of the New South behaved in many respects quite similarly. Although one of the most heated conservative criticisms of the Reconstruction governments had been that they had fostered widespread corruption, the Redeemer regimes were, if anything, even more awash in graft, fraud, and waste. (In this, they were little different from governments in every region of the country.) Virtually all the new Democratic regimes, moreover, adopted policies of lowered taxation, reduced spending, and drastically diminished state services. The "carpetbag" governments of Reconstruction, they complained, had saddled the South with huge debts. (In fact, much of the debt predated the Civil War.) It was the duty of the new leaders, therefore, to put the region back on a sound financial footing. Many of the most valuable accomplishments of Reconstruction were now dismantled. In one state after another, for example, state support for public school systems was reduced or eliminated. "Schools are not a necessity," commented a governor of Virginia.

The power of the Bourbon oligarchies was not unchallenged. By the late 1870s, powerful dissenting groups were protesting the cuts in services. Even more, they were denouncing the commitment of their present governments of paying off the prewar and Reconstruction debts in full, at the original (usually high) rates of interest. In Virginia, for example, a powerful "Readjuster" movement emerged demanding that the state revise its debt payment procedures so as to make more money available for state services. In 1879, the Readjusters won control of the legislature; and in the next few years they captured the governorship and a United States Senate seat. In other states, similar protests emerged. There were demands for greenbacks and for other economic reforms, as well as for debt readjustments (Some such independent movements included significant numbers of blacks in their ranks, but all consisted primarily of lower-income whites.) For a moment, at least, it seemed as though Southern politics was to become genuinely competitive. But the dissident uprising proved only temporary. By the mid-1880s, conservative Southerners—largely by exploiting racial prejudice—had effectively destroyed the Readjusters and other such movements. It would be several years before a new challenge to the power of the Bourbons would arise.

Whites and the New South

The fondest dream of some Southern leaders in the post-Reconstruction era was to see their region become the home of a vigorous industrial economy. The South had lost the war, many now argued, because its economy had been unable to compete with the modernized manufacturing capacity of the North. The region's task, therefore, must now be to "out-Yankee the Yankees." Influential spokesmen—most prominent among them Henry Grady, editor of the *Atlanta Constitution*—espoused a new Southern "creed," that preached the virtues of thrift, industry, and progress: the same qualities that prewar Southerners had so often denounced in Northern society. "We have sown towns and cities in the place of theories," Grady boasted to a New England audience in the 1880s, "and put business above politics. . . . We have fallen in love with work."

Such boasts were not without merit. Southern industry expanded dramatically in the years after Reconstruction and became a more important part of the region's economy than ever before. Most visible was the growth in textile manufacturing. In the past, Southern cotton had usually been shipped out of the region to manufacturers in the North or in Europe. Now, textile factories appeared in the South itself. The number of spindles in the region increased 900 percent in the last twenty years of the century. The tobacco industry, similarly, established an important foothold in the region—largely through the work of James B. Duke of North Carolina, whose American Tobacco Company became for a time a virtual monopoly in the processing of raw tobacco into marketable smoking materials. In the lower South—and particularly in Alabama—the iron (and, later, steel) industry grew rapidly. The city of Birmingham grew within a decade from modest beginnings to become a major center of pig iron processing. The Southern iron and steel industry represented by 1890 nearly a fifth of the nation's total capacity.

And the South made important progress as well toward remedying one of its greatest economic problems: its obsolete transportation system. Railroad development increased substantially in the post-Reconstruction years—at a rate far greater than that of the nation at large. Between 1880 and 1890, the total miles of track in the region more than doubled. And the South took a giant step toward integrating its transportation system with that of the rest of the country when, in 1886, it changed the gauge (width) of its trackage to correspond with the standards of the North. No longer would it be necessary for cargoes heading into the South to be transferred from one train to another at the borders of the region.

Yet Southern industry developed within strict limits, and its effects on the region were never even remotely comparable to the effects of industrialization on the North. Southern wages remained far below the Northern equivalent; indeed one of the greatest attractions of the South to industrialists was that employers were able to pay workers there as little as one half what Northern workers received. Some industries, textiles for example, offered no opportunities at all to black workers. Others—tobacco, iron, and lumber, among others—did provide some employment for blacks but usually only the least desirable and lowest-paid positions. At times, industrialization proceeded on the basis of no wage-paying employment at all. Through the notorious "convict-lease" system, Southern states leased gangs of convicted criminals to private interests as a cheap labor supply. The system not only exposed the convicts to brutal and often fatal mistreatment without pay (the leasing fees went to the states, not the workers); it also denied employment in railroad construction and other projects to the free labor force.

Nor were the dimensions of Southern industrial development as impressive as many Southerners liked to claim, particularly when compared with the rest of the nation. The Southern share of national manufacturing doubled in the last twenty years of the century—to 10 percent of the total. But that percentage was the same the South had claimed in 1860. The region's per capita income increased 21 percent in the same period. But at the end of the century, average income in the South was only 40 percent of that in the North; in 1860 it had been more than 60 percent. And even in those areas where development had been most rapid—textiles, iron, railroads—much, if not most, of the capital had come from the North. Once again, the South was developing a colonial economy.

The major reason for this economic sluggishness was the impoverished state of Southern agriculture, which continued to dominate the region. The post-Reconstruction years saw an acceleration of the process that had begun in the immediate postwar years: the imposition of systems of tenantry and debt peonage on much of the region; the reliance on a few cash crops rather than on a diversified agricultural system; and an increasing absentee ownership of valuable farmlands (many of them purchased by merchants and industrialists, who paid little attention to whether the land was being properly used). During Reconstruction, perhaps a third or more of the farmers in the South were tenants; by 1900 the figure had increased to 70 percent. It was remarkable, perhaps, that despite all this more than 121,000 blacks owned their own land in 1890. But that figure still represented a tiny percentage of the black population as a whole.

That the white South was not yet entirely willing to break with its past was evident, too, in the popular literature of the region. At the same time that Southern writers were extolling the virtues of industrialization in newspaper editorials and speeches, they were painting nostalgic portraits of the Old South in their literature. Few Southerners advocated a literal return to the old ways; but most whites eagerly embraced romantic talk of the "lost cause." And they responded warmly to the local-color fiction of such writers as Joel Chandler Harris, whose folk tales—the most famous being *Uncle Remus* (1880)—presented the slave society of the antebellum years as a harmonious world, marked by engaging dialect and by close emotional bonds between the races. Thomas Nelson Page similarly extolled the old Virginia aristocracy. The New South, in short, faced its future with one foot still in the past.

Blacks and the New South

The spirit of the New South was not the property of whites alone. Many blacks became enchanted by the vision of progress and self-improvement as well. Some blacks succeeded in elevating themselves into a distinct middle class—one economically far inferior to the white middle class, but nevertheless significant. These were former slaves (and, as the decades passed, their offspring) who managed to acquire property, establish small businesses, enter professions. A few blacks accumulated substantial fortunes by

The Black Middle Class
To their white neighbors, the new middle-class blacks of the South were evidence of how Reconstruction was elevating blacks "above their station." In fact, many newly prosperous blacks were achieving their success less because of "artificial" assistance from carpetbaggers and scalawags than because of their own entrepreneurial skills. The free black community suddenly presented enterprising people of both races with new opportunities for profit. (Library of Congress)

establishing banks and insurance companies for their race; most middle-class blacks, however, experienced only modest gains.

A cardinal tenet of this rising group of blacks was that education was vital to the future of their race. With the support of Northern missionary societies and, to a far lesser extent, a few Southern state governments, they expanded the network of black colleges and institutes that had taken root during Reconstruction into an important educational system. The chief spokesman for this commitment to education, and ultimately the major spokesman for his race as a whole, was Booker T. Washington, founder and president of the Tuskegee Institute in Alabama. Born into slavery, Washington had worked his own way out of poverty by virtue of having acquired an education (at Virginia's famous Hampton Institute). Once established, he urged other blacks to follow the same road to self-improvement.

Washington's message was both cautious and hopeful. The "great leap from slavery to freedom," he warned, should not permit blacks to forget how to work with their hands. They should attend school, learn skills, and establish a solid footing in agriculture and the trades. Industrial, not classical, education should be their goal. Blacks should, moreover, refine their speech, im-

prove their dress, and adopt habits of thrift and personal cleanliness; they should, in short, adopt the standards of the white middle class. Only thus, he claimed, could they win the respect of the white population, the prerequisite for any larger social gains. In a famous speech in Georgia in 1895, Washington outlined a philosophy of race relations that became widely known as the Atlanta Compromise. "The wisest among my race understand," he said, "that the agitation of questions of social equality is the extremest folly." Blacks should, rather, engage in "severe and constant struggle" for economic gains; for, as he explained, "no race that has anything to contribute to the markets of the world is long in any degree ostracized." If blacks were ever to win the rights and privileges of citizenship, they must first show that they were "prepared for the exercise of these privileges."

In the context of his time, Washington's message was not as timid and conservative as it would later sound. As the first black leader to acquire a wide audience among members of his race, he offered a powerful challenge to those whites who strove to discourage blacks from acquiring an education or winning any economic gains. He helped to awaken the interest of a new generation to the possibilities for self-advancement.

Booker T. Washington on Black Education [1895]

Washington rose from slavery to the leadership of his people. Founding Tuskegee Institute in Alabama, he advocated that blacks improve their economic status before reaching for political rights. To that end Washington, in a speech in 1895, advocated a vocational type of education, which prompted some blacks to accuse him of subordinating the race's struggle for equal rights:

Our greatest danger is that in the great leap from slavery to freedom we may overlook the fact that the masses of us are to live by the productions of our hands, and fail to keep in mind that we shall prosper in proportion as we learn to dignify and glorify common labour and put brains and skill into the common occupations of life; shall prosper in proportion as we learn to draw the line between the superficial and the substantial, the ornamental gewgaws of life and the useful. No race can prosper till it learns that there is as much dignity in tilling a field as in writing a poem. It is at the bottom of life we must begin, and not at the top. Nor should we permit our grievances to overshadow our opportunities.

But Washington's message was comforting to Southern whites as well. For in it was an implicit promise that blacks would not challenge the system of segregation that they were then in the process of erecting.

The Birth of Jim Crow

Most white Southerners had never accepted the idea of blacks as equal citizens of their region. That the former slaves acquired any legal and political rights at all after emancipation was in large part the result of federal support. That support all but vanished after 1877. Federal troops were no longer available to police the polls and prevent whites from excluding black voters. Congress was no longer taking an interest in the condition of blacks. And the courts were signaling a retreat as well. In a series of decisions in the 1880s and 1890s, the Supreme Court effectively emasculated the Fourteenth and Fifteenth amendments of much of their significance. In deciding the so-called civil-rights cases of 1883, the Court held that the Fourteenth Amendment prohibited state governments from discriminating against people because of race but did not so restrict private organizations or individuals. Thus railroads, hotels, theaters, and the like could legally practice segregation. Eventually, the Court also validated state legislation that discriminated against blacks. In *Plessy* v. *Ferguson* (1896), a case involving a law that required separate seating arrangements for the races on railroads, the Court held that separate accommodations did not deprive blacks of equal rights if the accommodations were equal, a decision that survived for years as part of the legal basis of segregated schools. In *Cumming* v. *County Board of Education* (1899), the Court went even further: laws establishing separate schools for whites, the justices ruled, were valid even if they provided no comparable schools for blacks.

Even before these decisions, white Southerners were at work ensuring their supremacy and, gradually, their separation to the extent possible from contact with the black race. This progression from subordination to segregation was clearly illustrated in the case

of black voting rights. In some states—particularly those such as South Carolina and the Deep South cotton states, where blacks constituted close to a majority of the population—disfranchisement began almost as soon as Reconstruction ended. South Carolina, for example, effectively reduced the black vote beginning early in the 1880s by introducing a complicated system of ballot boxes that illiterate voters could not decipher. Georgia required payment of a poll tax, which blacks generally could not afford. In some areas, however, black voting continued for some time after Reconstruction—largely because conservative whites believed they could use the black electorate to maintain their own power. Bourbon leaders often paid or intimidated blacks to vote for their candidates; thus they managed to beat down the attempts of poor white farmers to take control of the Democratic party.

The relative laxness of these franchise restrictions enabled blacks to continue through the 1880s and much of the 1890s to exercise some political influence—far less than that to which their numbers entitled them, but far more than they would later have. Until the end of the century, Republican candidates in some Southern states continued to receive as much as 40 percent of the vote—most of it from black voters. At least one Southern black served in every session of Congress until 1901. By the late 1890s, however, franchise restrictions were becoming much more rigid. During those years, some small white farmers began to demand complete black disfranchisement—both because of racial animosity and because they objected to the black vote being used against them by the Bourbons. Many members of the conservative elite, at the same time, began to fear that poor whites might unite politically with poor blacks to challenge their hegemony. They too began to support further franchise restrictions. The prospect of whites competing for the black vote—of blacks conceivably becoming the balance of power in the region—frightened whites at all economic levels. The time had come, they believed, to close ranks if white supremacy was to be maintained.

In devising laws to disfranchise blacks, the Southern states had to find ways to evade the intent of the Fifteenth Amendment. That measure had not *guaranteed* suffrage to blacks; it had simply prohibited states from denying anyone the right to vote because of color. The Southern problem, then, was to exclude blacks from the franchise without seeming to base the exclusion on race. Two devices emerged before 1900 to accomplish this goal. One was the poll tax, or some form of property qualification; few blacks were prosperous enough to meet such requirements. Another was the "literacy" or "understanding" test, which required voters to demonstrate the ability to read and to interpret the Constitution. The laws permitted local registrars to administer impossibly difficult reading tests to would-be voters or to rule that their interpretation of the Constitution was inadequate.

Such restrictions affected poor white voters as well as blacks. By the late 1890s, the black vote had decreased by 62 percent, the white vote by 26 percent. One result was that some states passed so-called grandfather laws, which permitted men who could not meet the literacy and property qualifications to be admitted to the suffrage if their ancestors had voted before Reconstruction began, thus barring the descendants of slaves from the polls while allowing poor whites access to them.

The Supreme Court proved as compliant in ruling on the disfranchising laws as it was in dealing with the civil-rights cases. The Court eventually voided the grandfather laws, but it validated the literacy tests (*Williams* v. *Mississippi*, 1898) and manifested a general willingness to let the Southern states define their own suffrage standards as long as evasions of the Fifteenth Amendment were not too glaring.

Laws restricting the franchise and segregating schools were only part of a network of state statutes—known as the Jim Crow laws—that had by the first years of the twentieth century established an elaborate system of segregation reaching into almost every area of Southern life. Blacks and whites could not ride together in the same railroad cars, sit in the same waiting rooms, use the same washrooms, eat in the same restaurants, or sit in the same theaters. Blacks were de-nied access to parks, beaches, and picnic areas; they were barred from many hospitals. Much of the new legal structure did no more than confirm what had already been widespread social practice in the South since well before the end of Reconstruction. But the Jim Crow laws also served to strip many blacks of the social, economic, and political gains they had made in the more fluid atmosphere of the late nineteenth century. Segregation was now rigid and unyielding; and it was to survive without serious challenge for decades.

More than legal efforts were involved in this process. The 1890s witnessed a wave of white violence against blacks that also served to inhibit black agitation for equal rights. The worst such violence—lynching of blacks by white mobs, either because the victim was accused of a crime or because he had seemed somehow to violate his proper station—reached appalling levels. In the nation as a whole in the 1890s, there was an average of 187 lynchings each year, more than 80 percent of them in the South and the vast majority of those inflicted on blacks.

Blacks, of course, suffered by far the most from the violence, the Jim Crow laws, and the whole climate of racial oppression in the South. But many white Southerners suffered as well. Just as in the antebellum period, the shared commitment to white supremacy helped to dilute the class animosities between poorer whites and the Bourbon oligarchies that might otherwise have emerged. Economic issues tended to take a subordinate role to race in Southern politics, distracting the gaze of the region from the glaring social inequalities that afflicted blacks and whites alike. Even when such issues did arise—as they did in the 1890s—the racial question ultimately proved an effective vehicle for dampening their impact.

The Origins of Protest

Black Americans faced enormous obstacles—legal, economic, social, and political—to an effective challenge of their oppressed status. Thus it was not surprising, perhaps, that so many embraced the message of

A Lynch Mob, 1893
A large, almost festive crowd of whites gathered to watch the lynching of a black man accused
of the murder of a three-year-old white girl. The white South used many techniques to reim-
pose its supremacy over the black population of the region in the late nineteenth and early
twentieth centuries. But the most brutal and terrifying instrument of control was the frequent
lynching of blacks suspected of crimes. (Library of Congress)

Booker T. Washington in the late nineteenth
century: a message that urged them to "put
down your bucket where you are," to work
for immediate self-improvement rather than
long-range social change. Not all blacks,
however, were content with this approach.
And by the turn of the century a powerful challenge was emerging—to the philosophy of Washington and, more important, to
the entire structure of race relations. The
chief spokesman for this new approach was
W. E. B. Du Bois.

Du Bois, unlike Washington, had never
known slavery. Born in Massachusetts and
educated at Harvard, he grew to maturity
with a far more expansive view than Washington of the goals of his race and the responsibilities of white society to eliminate
prejudice and injustice. In *The Souls of Black*

Folk (1903), he launched an open attack on
the philosophy of the Atlanta Compromise,
accusing Washington of encouraging white
efforts to impose segregation and of unnecessarily limiting the aspirations of his race. "Is
it possible and probable," he asked,

that nine millions of men can make effective
progress in economic lines if they are deprived of
political rights, made a servile caste, and allowed
only the most meagre chance for developing their
exceptional men? If history and reason give any
distinct answer to these questions, it is an emphatic *No.*

Rather than content themselves with education at the trade and agricultural schools,
Washington advocated, talented blacks
should accept nothing less than a full univer-

sity education. They should aspire to the professions. They should, above all, fight for the immediate restoration of their civil rights, not simply wait for them to be granted as a reward for patient striving.

In 1905, Du Bois and a group of his supporters met in Niagara Falls, Ontario, Canada (no hotel on the American side of the Falls would have them), and launched what became known as the Niagara Movement. Four years later, after a race riot in Springfield, Illinois, they joined with white progressives sympathetic to their cause to form the National Association for the Advancement of Colored People (NAACP). White men held most of the offices; but Du Bois, its director of publicity and research, was the guiding spirit. In the ensuing years, the new organization led the drive for equal rights, using as its principal weapon lawsuits in the federal courts.

Within less than a decade, the NAACP had begun to win some important victories. In *Guinn* v. *United States* (1915), the Supreme Court supported their position that the grandfather clause in an Oklahoma law was unconstitutional. (The statute denied the vote to any citizen whose ancestors had not been enfranchised in 1860.) In *Buchanan* v. *Worley* (1917), the Court struck down a Louisville, Kentucky, law requiring residential segregation. Disfranchisement and segregation would survive through other methods for many decades to come, but the NAACP had

---

The Souls of Black Folk [1903]

William E. Burghardt Du Bois, born in Great Barrington, Massachusetts (1868), was teaching at Atlanta University when he wrote The Souls of Black Folk (1903). *At that time the problem of race relationships was largely, though by no means entirely, a regional one, since the vast majority of black Americans were still concentrated in the South. Of their position, Du Bois observed:*

The dangerously clear logic of the Negro's position will more and more loudly assert itself in that day when increasing wealth and more intricate social organization preclude the South from being, as it so largely is, simply an armed camp for intimidating black folk. Such waste of energy cannot be spared if the South is to catch up with civilization. And as the black third of the land grows in thrift and skill, unless skilfully guided in its larger philosophy, it must more and more brood over the red past and the creeping, crooked present, until it grasps a gospel of revolt and revenge and throws its new-found energies athwart the current of advance. Even to-day the masses of the Negroes see all too clearly the anomalies of their position and the moral crookedness of yours. You may marshal strong indictments against them, but their counter-cries lacking though they may be in formal logic, have burning truths within them which you may not wholly ignore, O Southern Gentlemen! If you deplore their presence here, they ask, Who brought us? When you cry, Deliver us from the vision of intermarriage, they answer that legal marriage is infinitely better than systematic concubinage and prostitution. And if in just fury you accuse their vagabonds of violating women, they also in fury quite as just may reply: The wrong which your gentlemen have done against helpless black women in defiance of your own laws is written on the foreheads of two millions of mulattoes, and written in ineffaceable blood. And finally, when you fasten crime upon this race as its peculiar trait, they answer that slavery was the archcrime, and lynching and lawlessness its twin abortion; that color and race are not crimes, and yet they it is which in this land receive most unceasing condemnation, North, East, South, and West.

established a pattern of black resistance that would ultimately bear important fruits. It had also established itself, particularly after Booker T. Washington's death in 1915, as one of the nation's leading black organizations, a position it would maintain for over fifty years.

The NAACP was not a radical, or even an egalitarian, organization. It relied, rather, on the efforts of the most intelligent and educated members of the black race, the "talented tenth" as Du Bois called them. And it stressed not so much the elevation of all blacks from poverty and oppression as the opportunity for exceptional blacks to gain positions of full equality. Ultimately, its members believed, such efforts would redound to the benefit of all blacks. In the meantime, however, the NAACP remained largely a force of and for the middle class.

THE CLOSING OF THE FRONTIER

By the time of the Civil War, the western rim of English-speaking settlement had already moved far beyond what it had been even twenty years before. American civilization had crossed the Mississippi and established a permanent foothold in the next tier of states—Minnesota, Iowa, Missouri, and Arkansas—as well as in the eastern parts of Nebraska, Kansas, and Texas. But vast regions remained largely empty of those who had settled the rest of the United States. Much of the West was the province of nomadic Indian tribes, of wild animals, and of a few scattered immigrants from the East (most of them white, but some—in regions as scattered as Montana, Kansas, and Nebraska—black).

Even in 1860, however, there were clear signs that the United States would not much longer be content to leave these vast Western territories to the Indians. For one thing, important white settlements had already been established on the Pacific coast, in California and Oregon. For another, ambitious men and women continued to press for access to new lands in the West; as one region began to fill up with settlers, such people demanded the right to move on to the next. And so, in the decades following the Civil War, Americans continued their great migration into the interior of their country and finally closed their frontier.

Delayed Settlement

When the westward-pushing pioneers entered upon the Great Plains, they saw an environment utterly different from the fertile prairies behind them. The physical features that in combination distinguish the Great Plains from earlier frontiers are a level surface, a dearth of timber, and a deficiency in rainfall. Early explorers had dubbed this region "the Great American Desert," and in the 1840s settlers had hastened through it on their way to California and Oregon. Its forbidding reputation was largely responsible for the fact that the frontier, after crossing the Mississippi, had jumped 1,500 miles to the Pacific coast.

By the 1860s, however, people had begun to head for the unsettled parts of the West. They were attracted by gold and silver deposits, by the short-grass pasture for cattle and sheep, and finally by the plains' sod and the mountain meadowland that seemed suitable for farming or ranching.

Settlement was encouraged by the great transcontinental railroad lines. These roads and their feeders moved settlers and supplies into the vast interior spaces and furnished access to outside markets; they provided what the region could not have had without them—the basis for a permanent population and a durable economy. In addition, the railroad companies directly excited migration by disposing of their lands to settlers.

Settlement was also encouraged by the land policy of the federal government, although this had less effect than had been intended. According to the Homestead Act of 1862, for a small fee a settler could obtain a plot of 160 acres if he occupied and improved

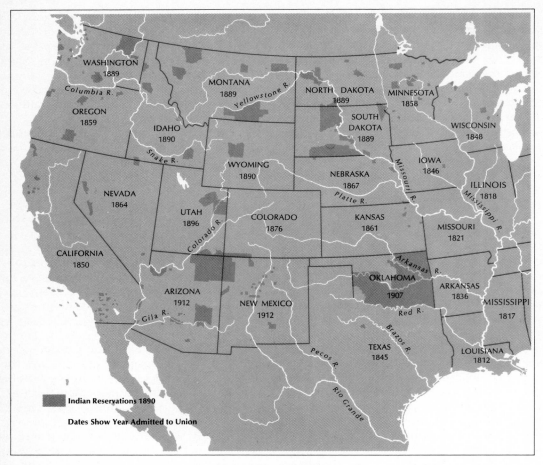

THE LAST FRONTIER

it for five years. A good deal of idealism had gone into the framing of the Homestead Act. It was intended to be a democratic measure, the bestowal of a free farm on any American who needed one, a form of government relief to raise the living standards of the masses. But in practice the act proved a disappointment. Some 400,000 homesteaders became landowners, but a much larger number abandoned the attempt to stake out a farm on the windswept plains.

The defects in the Homestead Act were the result of a series of false premises. The act assumed that mere possession of land was enough to sustain farm life, but this notion ignored the increasing mechanization of agriculture and the rising costs of operation.

Even worse, it was based on Eastern agricultural experiences that were inapplicable to the region west of the Mississippi. A unit of 160 acres was too small for the grazing and grain farming of the Great Plains.

Responding to Western pressures, Congress acted to increase allotments. The Timber Culture Act (1873) permitted a homesteader to receive a grant of 160 additional acres if he planted on it 40 acres of trees. The Desert Land Act (1877) provided that a claimant could buy 640 acres at $1.25 an acre provided he irrigated part of his holding within three years. The Timber and Stone Act (1878), presumably applying to nonarable land, authorized sales of quarter sections at $2.50 an acre.

Through the operation of the various laws, it was possible for an individual to acquire at little cost 1,280 acres. Some enterprising persons got much more. Fraud ran rampant in the administration of the acts. Lumber, mining, and cattle companies, by employing "dummy" registrants and using other tricky devices, grasped millions of acres of the public domain.

Political organization followed on the heels of settlement. After the admission of Kansas as a state in 1861, the remaining territories of Washington, New Mexico, Utah, and Nebraska were divided into smaller and more convenient units. By the close of the sixties, territorial governments were in operation in the new provinces of Nevada, Colorado, Dakota, Arizona, Idaho, Montana, and Wyoming. Statehood rapidly followed. Nevada became a state in 1864, Nebraska in 1867, and Colorado in 1876. In 1889, North and South Dakota, Montana, and Washington won admission; Wyoming and Idaho entered the next year. Utah was denied statehood until its Mormon leaders convinced the government in 1896 that polygamy (the practice of men taking several wives) had been abandoned. At the turn of the century, only three territories remained outside the fold: Arizona and New Mexico, excluded because of their scanty population, their politics (they were predominantly Democratic), and their refusal to accept admission as a single state; and Oklahoma, which was opened to white settlement and granted territorial status in 1889–1890.

The Arrival of the Miners

The first colonists of the last frontier were miners, and the first part of the area to be settled was the mineral-rich region of mountains and plateaus. The life span of the mining frontier was brief. It burst into being around 1860, flourished brilliantly until the 1890s, and then abruptly declined.

News of a gold or silver strike would start a stampede reminiscent of the California gold rush of 1849. Settlement usually followed a pattern of successive stages: (1) individual prospectors exploited the first ores with pan and placer mining; (2) after the shallower deposits were depleted, corporations moved in to engage in lode or quartz mining; (3) commercial mining either disappeared eventually or continued on a restricted basis, and ranchers and farmers appeared on the scene to establish a more permanent economy.

The first great strikes occurred just before the Civil War. In 1858, gold was discovered in the Pike's Peak district of what would soon be the territory of Colorado; and the following year, a mob of 50,000 prospectors stormed in from California and the Mississippi Valley and the East. Denver and other mining camps blossomed into "cities" overnight. Almost as rapidly as it had developed, the boom ended. Eventually, corporations, notably the Guggenheim interests, revived some of the glories and profits of the gold boom, and the discovery of silver near Leadville supplied a new source of mineral wealth.

While the Colorado rush of 1859 was in progress, news of another strike drew miners to Nevada. Gold had been found in the Washoe district, but the most valuable ore in the great Comstock Lode and other veins was silver. The first prospectors to reach the Washoe fields came from California (here the frontier movement was from west to east); and from the beginning, Californians dominated the settlement and development of Nevada. In a remote desert without railroad transportation, the territory produced no supplies of its own, and everything—from food and machinery to whiskey and prostitutes—had to be freighted in from California to Virginia City, Carson City, and other roaring camp towns. When the placer deposits ran out, California capital bought the claims of the pioneer prospectors and installed quartz mining. For a brief span the outside owners reaped tremendous profits; from 1860 to 1880 the Nevada lodes yielded bullion worth $306 million.

No new discoveries agitated the mining frontier until 1874, when gold was found in the Black Hills of southwestern Dakota Territory. Prospectors swarmed into the area, which was then and for years later served only by stagecoach transportation. The town

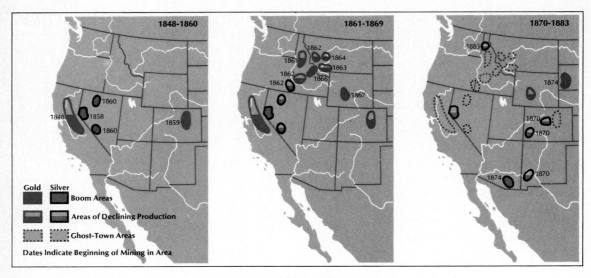

MINING TOWNS, 1848–1883

of Deadwood burst into life as a center of supplies and sin for other camps. For a short time the boom flared, and then came the inevitable fading of resources. Corporations took over from the miners, and one gigantic company, the Homestake, came to dominate the fields. The population declined, and the Dakotas, like other boom areas of the mineral empire, waited for the approach of the agricultural frontier.

Life in the camp towns of the mineral empire had a hectic tempo and a gaudy flavor not to be found in any other part of the last frontier. The speculative spirit, a mood of incredible optimism, gripped everyone and dominated every phase of community activity. The conditions of mine life—the presence of precious minerals, the vagueness of claim boundaries, the cargoes of gold being shipped out—tempted outlaws and "bad men," operating as individuals or gangs, to ply their trade. When the situation became intolerable in a community, those members interested in order set up their own law and enforced it through a vigilance committee, an agency used earlier in California. Sometimes criminals themselves secured control of the committee, and sometimes the vigilantes continued to operate as private

"law" enforcers after the creation of regular governments.

The Day of the Cowboy

The open range—the unclaimed grasslands of the public domain—provided a huge area on the Great Plains where cattlemen could graze their herds free of charge and unrestricted by the boundaries that would have existed in a farming economy. The railroads gave the range-cattle industry access to markets and thus brought it into being; then the same railroads destroyed it by bringing the farmers' frontier to the plains.

In ancestry, the cattle industry was Mexican and Texan. Long before the Americans invaded the Southwest, Mexican ranchers had developed the techniques and tools employed later by the cattlemen and cowboys of the Great Plains: branding (a device known in all frontier areas where stock was common), roundups, roping, and the equipment of the herder—his lariat, saddle, leather chaps, and spurs. All these things and others were taken over by the Americans in Texas and by them transmitted to the northernmost ranges of the cattle kingdom. Also in Texas were found the largest herds of cattle in the country, the animals descended from imported Spanish stock—the famous wiry, hardy longhorns—and allowed to run wild or semiwild. Here, too, were the horses that enabled the caretakers of the herds to control them—the small, muscular broncos or mustangs, sprung from blooded progenitors brought in by the Spanish and ideally adapted to the requirements of the cow country.

At the end of the Civil War, an estimated 5 million cattle roamed the Texas ranges, and Northern markets were offering fat prices for steers in any condition. Early in 1866 some Texas cattlemen started their combined herds, some 260,000 head, north for Sedalia, Missouri, located on the Missouri Pacific Railroad. Traveling over rough country and beset by outlaws, Indians, and property-conscious farmers, the caravan suffered heavy losses, and only a fraction of the animals were delivered to the railroad. But a great experiment had been successfully tested—cattle could be driven to distant markets and pastured along the trail and would gain weight during the journey. The first of the "long drives" prepared the way for the cattle kingdom.

With the precedent established, the next step was to find an easier route leading through more accessible country. Special market facilities were provided at Abilene, Kansas, on the Kansas Pacific Railroad, and for years this town reigned as the railhead of the cattle kingdom. Between 1867 and 1871, 1,460,000 cattle were moved up the Chisholm Trail to Abilene—a town that when filled with rampaging cowboys at the end of a drive, rivaled the mining towns in robust wickedness. But as the farming frontier pushed farther west in Kansas and as the supply of animals increased, the cattlemen had to develop other market outlets and trails. Railroad towns that flourished after Abilene were Dodge City and Wichita in Kansas, Ogallala and Sidney in Nebraska, Cheyenne and Laramie in Wyoming, and Miles City and Glendive in Montana.

From first to last, a long drive was a spectacular episode. It began with the spring, or calf, roundup. The cattlemen of a district met with their cowboys at a specified place to round up the stock of the owners from the open range. As the cattle were driven in, the calves were branded with the marks of their mothers. Stray calves with no identifying symbols, "mavericks," were divided on a pro-rata basis. Then the cows and calves were turned loose to pasture, while the yearling steers were readied for the drive to the north. The combined herds, usually numbering from 2,000 to 5,000 head, moved out, attended by the cowboys of each outfit.

Among the cowboys, the majority (in the early years) were veterans of the Confederate army. The next largest group—more numerous than white Northerners, Mexicans, and other foreigners—consisted of blacks, who usually were assigned such jobs as wrangler (herdsman) or cook. (In other contexts, black men played a role in the West not only as cowboys but also as explorers, trappers, miners, outlaws, and cavalrymen.)

Every cattleman had to have a permanent base from which to operate, and so the ranch emerged. A ranch consisted of the employer's dwelling, quarters for employees, and a tract of grazing land. It might be fenced in or open, owned or leased or held by some quasi-legal claim, but it was definite and durable. Possession of a ranch meant unquestioned access to precious water. As farmers and sheepmen encroached on the open plains, the ranch began to replace the range.

There had always been an element of risk and speculation in the open-range cattle business. At any time the "Texas fever," transmitted by a parasite carried by ticks, might decimate a herd. Rustlers and Indians frequently drove off large numbers of animals. Sheepmen from California and Oregon brought their flocks onto the range to compete for grass and force cattle out (cattle will not graze after sheep); bitter "wars" followed between cattlemen and sheepherders, in which men and stock were killed and equipment destroyed. Farmers ("nesters") threw fences around their claims, blocking trails and breaking up the open range. More wars were fought, bringing losses to both sides.

Accounts of the lofty profits to be made in the cattle business—it was said that an investment of $5,000 would return $45,000 in four years—tempted Eastern, English, and

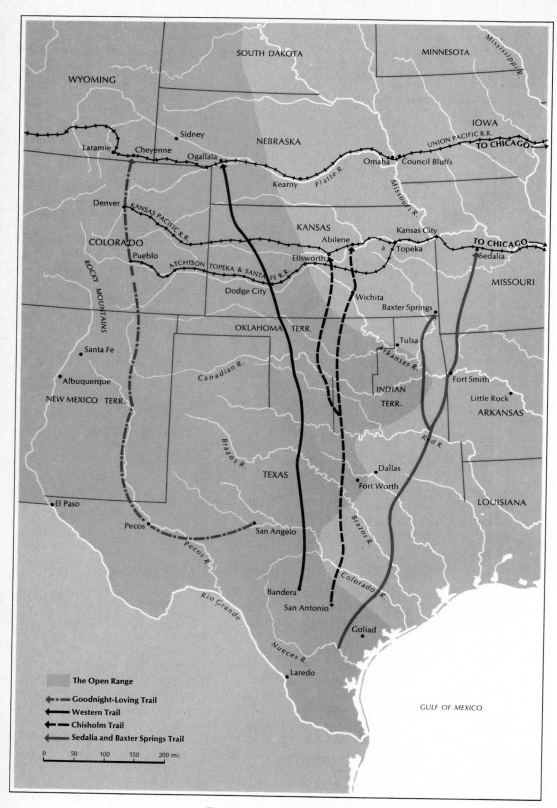

THE CATTLE KINGDOM

Map labels:

WYOMING
SOUTH DAKOTA
MINNESOTA
IOWA
NEBRASKA
Sidney
Laramie
Cheyenne
Ogallala
Kearny
Platte R.
Omaha
Council Bluffs
UNION PACIFIC R.R.
TO CHICAGO
Missouri R.
Mississippi R.
Denver
KANSAS PACIFIC R.R.
KANSAS
Abilene
Kansas City
COLORADO
Pueblo
Ellsworth
Topeka
Sedalia
MISSOURI
ATCHISON TOPEKA & SANTA FE R.R.
TO CHICAGO
Dodge City
Wichita
Baxter Springs
ROCKY MOUNTAINS
Tulsa
Santa Fe
OKLAHOMA TERR.
Arkansas R.
Fort Smith
Albuquerque
Canadian R.
INDIAN TERR.
Little Rock
NEW MEXICO TERR.
ARKANSAS
Brazos R.
Red R.
El Paso
Dallas
Pecos
San Angelo
TEXAS
Fort Worth
LOUISIANA
Pecos R.
Brazos R.
Bandera
Colorado R.
San Antonio
Rio Grande
Goliad
Nueces R.
Laredo
GULF OF MEXICO

Legend:

The Open Range
Goodnight-Loving Trail
Western Trail
Chisholm Trail
Sedalia and Baxter Springs Trail

0   50   100   150   200 mi.

Cowboys Branding Calves
To identify his own herd (which mingled with other herds on the open range), each cattleman had his calves branded with his distinctive mark of ownership. At the spring roundup, cowboys caught the calves, "wrassled" them to the ground, and applied searing hot branding irons. (Western History Research Center, University of Wyoming)

Scottish capital to the plains. Increasingly, the structure of the cattle economy became corporate in form; in one year, twenty corporations with a combined capital of $12 million were chartered in Wyoming. The inevitable result of this frenzied extension was that the ranges, already severed and shrunk by the railroads and the farmers, were overstocked. There was not enough grass to support the crowding herds or sustain the long drives. Overstocking sent prices tumbling downward, and then nature intervened with a destructive finishing blow. Two severe winters, in 1885–1886 and 1886–1887, with a searing summer between them, stung and scorched the plains. Hundreds of thousands of cattle died, streams and grass dried up, princely ranches and costly investments disappeared in a season.

The open-range industry never recovered; the long drive disappeared for good. But the established cattle ranches—with fenced-in grazing land and stocks of hay for winter feed—survived and grew and prospered, eventually producing more beef than ever.

The Romance of the West

The unsettled West had always occupied a special place in the American imagination. But the vast regions of this last frontier had a particularly strong romantic appeal. Some of the reasons were obvious. The Great Plains, the Rocky Mountains, the basin and plateau region beyond the Rockies, and the Sierra Nevada–Cascade ranges beyond that—all constituted a landscape of such brilliant diversity, such spectacular grandeur, so different from anything white Americans had encountered before, it was little wonder that newcomers looked on it with reverence and awe. Painters of the new "Rocky Mountain School"—of whom the best known was Albert Bierstadt—celebrated the new West in grandiose canvases. They emphasized the ruggedness and dramatic variety of the region, exhibiting the same awe toward the land that earlier regional painters had displayed toward the Hudson River Valley and other areas.

Even more appealing than the landscape, perhaps, was the rugged, free-spirited life style that many Americans associated with the frontier—a life style that stood in sharp contrast to the increasingly stable and ordered world of the East. Particular public interest attached to the figure of the cowboy, who was transformed remarkably quickly into a powerful and enduring figure of myth. Admiring Americans seldom thought about the drearier aspects of the cowboy's life: the tedium, the loneliness, the physical discomforts, the relatively few opportunities for advancement. Instead, in Western novels such as Owen Wister's *The Virginian* (1902), they romanticized his freedom from traditional social constraints, his affinity with nature, even his supposed propensity for violence. The cowboy became the last and most powerful symbol of what had long been an important ideal in the American mind—the ideal of the natural man. That symbol survived for more than a century—in popular literature, in song, and later in film and on television.

Yet it was not simply the particular qualities of the new West that made it so important to the nation's imagination. It was also the fact that it was the *last* frontier. Since the earliest moments of European settlement in America, the image of uncharted territory to the west had always been a comforting and inspiring one. Now, with the last of that unsettled land being slowly absorbed into the nation's civilization, that image exercised a stronger pull than ever. Mark Twain, one of the greatest American writers of the nineteenth century, gave voice to this romantic vision of the frontier in a series of brilliant novels and memoirs. In some of his writing—notably *Roughing It* (1872)—he wrote of the Far West itself, and of his own experience as a newspaper reporter in Nevada during the mining boom. His greatest works, however, dealt with life on an earlier frontier: the Mississippi Valley of his boyhood. In *The*

Adventures of Tom Sawyer (1876) and *The Adventures of Huckleberry Finn* (1885), he produced characters who repudiated the constraints of organized society and attempted to escape from it into a more natural world. For Tom Sawyer and Huck Finn, the vehicle of escape might be a small raft on the Mississippi; but their yearning for freedom reflected the larger vision of the West as the last refuge from civilization.

One of the clearest and most influential statements of this romantic vision of the frontier came not from an artist but from the famous historian Frederick Jackson Turner, of the University of Wisconsin. In 1893, Turner delivered a memorable paper to a meeting of the American Historical Association entitled "The Significance of the Frontier in American History." In it, he took note of the findings of the 1890 census that the unsettled area of the West had been "so broken into by isolated bodies of settlement" that a continuous frontier line could no longer be drawn. And he argued that the passing of that line ended an era in the nation's history. For, as Turner explained it, "the existence of an area of free land, its continuous recession, and the advance of settlement westward, explain American development." This experience of expansion into the frontier, by stimulating individualism, nationalism, and democracy, had made Americans the distinctive people that they were. "Now," Turner concluded ominously, "four centuries from the discovery of America, at the end of a hundred years of life under the Constitution, the frontier has gone and with its going has closed the first period of American history."

In fact, Turner's forebodings were somewhat premature. A vast public domain still existed in the 1890s, and during the forty years thereafter the government was to give away many more acres than it had given as homesteads in the past. But in one respect, at least, Turner was correct. Most of the best farming and grazing land was now spoken for. Gone was the chance—always less available than Americans had liked to believe, but available nevertheless—of acquiring a farm for little or nothing, of cultivating it successfully at relatively low cost, of selling it at a profit and moving west to start over again.

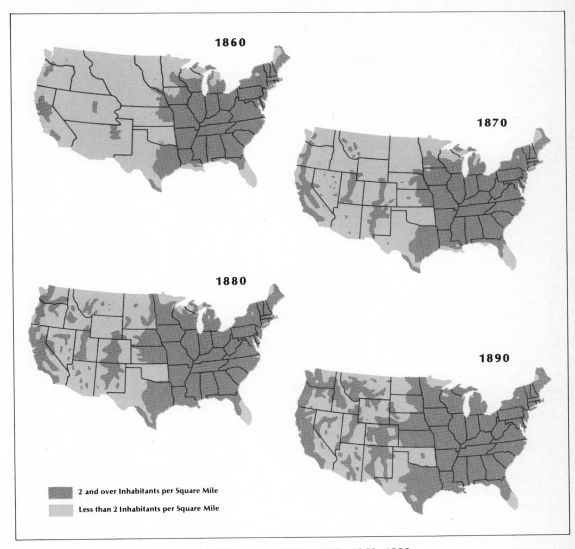

1860

1870

1880

1890

2 and over Inhabitants per Square Mile

Less than 2 Inhabitants per Square Mile

THE RECEDING FRONTIER, 1860–1890

The term "frontier" refers to the line—and to the area bordering that line—that divides the settled part of the country (population two or more per square mile) from the unsettled part (population less than two per square mile).

In the passing of the frontier, perhaps the greatest loss to the American people was a psychological one. As long as the country had remained open at one end, there had seemed to be constantly revitalizing opportunities in American life. Now there was a vague, premonitory sense of being hemmed in. The psychological loss was all the greater because of what the historian Henry Nash Smith in *Virgin Land* (1950) called the "myth of the garden": the once widely held belief that the West was a kind of potential Garden of Eden where life could be begun anew and the ideals of democracy realized. The setting for utopia, once the New World as a whole, had shrunk to the West of the United States. And now even that West was vanishing as a pristine, unconquered land.

In fact, this view of the West rested on illusions. Turner's vision of the frontier as a crucible of freedom and democracy did not reflect the social and political realities of life in the region. More important, the "virgin land" had long ago been replaced as the real symbol of opportunity in America by the new urban-industrial society of the East.

THE DISPERSAL OF THE TRIBES

When the miners and cattlemen began sifting into the last frontier, they came face to face with an obstacle more powerful than anything white Americans had encountered before in their movement westward: the plains Indians. These powerful warriors, stronger and more militant than the woods Indians whom white Americans had dispersed in earlier years, offered determined and sustained resistance to the encroachments upon their tribal lands. And in the prolonged and often vicious wars between the natives and the newcomers, it was the Indians, according to some estimates, who inflicted the greater casualties on their enemy.

In the end, however, the tribes could not effectively resist the superior numbers and technology of the white invaders. Defeated and broken, they were finally forced to accept what meager lands the white man was willing to give them and to adapt themselves to an approximation of the sedentary, agrarian culture of their conquerors.

The Plains Indians

On the rolling, semiarid, treeless plains, the Indians followed a nomadic life. Riding their small but powerful horses, which were descendants of Spanish stock, the tribes roamed the spacious expanses of the grasslands. Permanent abodes were rare; when a band halted, tepees were quickly pitched as temporary dwellings.

The magnet that drew the wanderers and guided their routes was the buffalo, or bison. This huge grazing animal provided the economic basis for the plains Indians' way of life. Its flesh was their principal source of food, and the skin supplied materials for clothing, shoes, tepees, blankets, robes, and utensils. To the Indians, the buffalo was, as someone has said, "a galloping department store." They trailed the herds, estimated to number at least 15 million head in 1865, all over the plains.

The plains Indians were almost uniformly martial, proud, and aggressive. Mounted on their horses, they were a formidable foe, whether armed with bow, spear, or rifle. No Indians previously encountered by whites possessed such mobility, and students of war have ranked them among the best light cavalry in military history.

It was the traditional policy of the federal government to regard the tribes as independent nations (but also as wards of the president in Washington) and to negotiate agreements with them in the shape of treaties that were solemnly ratified by the Senate. This concept of Indian sovereignty was responsible for the attempt of the government before 1860 to erect a permanent frontier between whites and Indians, to reserve the region west of the bend of the Missouri as permanent Indian country. But by the sixties the related principles of tribal independence and a perpetual line of division were breaking down before harsh realities. Administration of Indian matters was divided between the Bureau of Indian Affairs, located in the Department of the Interior, and the army. The bureau was vested with general powers to supervise the disposition of Indian lands, disburse annuities, and, through its agents in Western posts, distribute needed supplies. From top to bottom, the personnel was shot through with the spoils system. Although some agents were conscientious and able men, more were dishonest and incompetent.

The army came into the picture only when trouble developed—when bands of Indians attacked homes or stagecoach lines, or when a tribe went on the warpath. In short, its principal function was to punish, not to police. The army of the frontier was an effective fighting body, and it was led by some able officers. Still, in its "wars" with the Indians the army frequently experienced rugged going. The mobile plains tribesmen were fully a match for cavalrymen armed with carbines. But soon the superior technology of the whites shifted the balance. The Colt repeating revolver gave the army increased fire power, the railroads facilitated quick troop concentrations, and the telegraph reported almost immediately the movements of hostile bands. Even so, the business of suppressing Indians was frightfully expensive (a factor that concerned officials in Washington at least as much as the human cost). Three wars in the sixties cost the government $100 million, and one official estimated that the cost per Indian killed was $1,000.

The subjection of the fierce plains Indians was accomplished by economic as well as orthodox warfare—by the slaughter of the buffalo herds that supported their way of life. After the Civil War the demand for buffalo hides became a national phenomenon. It was partly based on economics—a commercial demand for the hides developing in the East; and it was partly a fad—suddenly everyone east of the Missouri seemed to require a buffalo robe from the romantic West. Gangs of professional hunters swarmed over the plains to shoot the huge animals, divided by the Union Pacific Railroad into southern and northern herds. Some hunters killed merely for the sport of the chase, though the lumbering victims did not present much of a challenge. The southern herd was virtually exterminated by 1875, and within a few years the smaller northern herd had met the same fate. Fewer than a thousand of the magnificent beasts survived. The army and the Indian agents condoned and even encouraged the killing. With the buffalo went the Indians' source of food and supplies and their ability to resist the white advance.

The Warriors' Last Stand

There was almost incessant Indian fighting on the frontier from the sixties to the eighties. During the Civil War, the eastern Sioux in Minnesota, cramped on an inadequate reservation and exploited by corrupt white agents, suddenly took to the warpath. Led by Little Crow, they killed more than 700 whites before being subdued by a force of regulars and militiamen. Thirty-eight of the Indians were hanged, and the tribe was exiled to the Dakotas.

At the same time, trouble flared in Colorado, where the Arapaho and Cheyenne had been restricted to the Sand Creek reservation. Bands of Indians attacked stagecoach lines and settlements, provoking a concentration of territorial militiamen and threats from the army. The governor urged all friendly Indians to congregate at army posts before retribution fell on the hostiles. One Arapaho and Cheyenne band under Black Kettle came into Fort Lyon on Sand Creek and encamped nearby. Although some men just off the warpath were undoubtedly members of the party, Black Kettle understood he was under official protection. Nevertheless, Colonel J. M. Chivington, apparently encouraged by the army commander of the district, led a militia force to the unsuspecting camp and massacred a disputed (but large) number of men, women, and children. The government then forced the Arapaho and Cheyenne to accept an even less desirable reservation, but the Senate neglected to ratify the treaty.

At the end of the war against the southern rebels, wars against the western Indians flared up on several fronts. The most serious and sustained conflict was in Montana, where the army attempted to build a road, the Bozeman Trail, from Fort Laramie, Wyoming, to the mining centers. The western Sioux resented this intrusion into the heart of their buffalo range, and led by one of their great chiefs, Red Cloud, they so harried the soldiers and the construction party that the road could not be completed.

Meanwhile, Congress, shocked by the Chivington massacre and the continued hostilities, appointed a committee to investigate the situation on the scene, and after studying its report, created an Indian Peace Commission, composed of soldiers and civilians, to recommend a permanent Indian policy. The commission called the southern tribes to council at Medicine Lodge Creek in 1867, and the following year it met with the northern tribes at Fort Laramie. At Medicine Lodge, the Arapaho, the Cheyenne, and other tribes agreed to accept reservations in the Indian Territory. At Laramie, the Sioux accepted a reservation in southwestern Dakota, with rights to hunt as far as the Big Horn Mountains in Wyoming; they insisted, however, that the government abandon the Bozeman road, marking probably the only instance in which whites formally yielded to Indians. The minor plains tribes and the mountain tribes consented to smaller reservations. For its part, the government pledged annuity payments and regular supplies. Some of the Arapaho and Cheyenne had another tragic experience before being finally settled on their reserve. Black Kettle, who had escaped the Chivington massacre, and his Cheyennes, some of whom had taken the warpath, were caught on the Washita River, near the Texas border, by Colonel George A. Custer; the chief was killed and his people were slaughtered.

After 1870, the broad outlines of a new Indian policy began to take shape. The tribes were now concentrated in two large reservations, one in Dakota and the other in the Indian Territory. Thus restricted, they found their powers to wage war severely limited. An advisory civilian Board of Indian Commissioners counseled the government to continue the reservation program and to break down the tribal structure with a view to assimilating the Indians to white culture. Congress responded in 1871 by abolishing the practice of treating the tribes as sovereignties, a step calculated to undermine the collective nature of Indian life.

But Indian resistance was far from ended. A source of potential conflict smouldered on the northern plains, where the Sioux roamed from Dakota to Wyoming. It burst into flame in 1875 when many of the tribesmen, angered by the dealings of crooked agents and alarmed by the entrance of miners into the Black Hills, suddenly left the reservation. Commanded to return, they gathered in Montana under Crazy Horse, probably the greatest leader of the plains Indians, and Sitting Bull. Three army columns were sent to round them up. With the expedition, as colonel of the famous Seventh Cavalry, was the colorful and controversial George A. Custer, golden-haired romantic and alleged glory seeker. At the Battle of the Little Bighorn (1876) the Indians surprised Custer with part of his regiment and killed every man. Custer has been accused of rashness, but he seems to have ridden into something that no white man would have believed possible at that time. On this occasion, the chiefs had concentrated at least 2,500 warriors, perhaps 4,000, the largest Indian army ever assembled at one time in the United States.

But the Indians did not have the political organization or the supplies to keep their troops united. Soon the warriors drifted off in bands to elude pursuit or search for food, and the army ran them down singly and returned them to Dakota. The power of the Sioux was now broken. The proud leaders, Crazy Horse and Sitting Bull, accepted defeat and the monotony of agency existence. Both were later killed by reservation police after being tricked or taunted into a last pathetic show of resistance.

In 1877, one of the most dramatic episodes in Indian history occurred in Idaho. Here the Nez Percé, a small and relatively peaceful and civilized tribe, refused to accept a smaller reservation and were, in effect, forced into resistance. When troops converged on them, their able leader, Chief Joseph, attempted to conduct the band to Canada. A remarkable chase ensued. Joseph moved with 200 men and 350 women, children, and old people. Pursued by four columns, he covered 1,321 miles in seventy-five days but was caught just short of the Canadian border. Like so many other crushed tribes, the Nez Percé were shipped to the Indian Territory.

The last Indians to maintain organized resistance against the whites were the Apaches, who fought intermittently from the sixties to the late eighties. The two ablest chiefs of this fierce tribe were Mangas Colo-

Geronimo

Geronimo (*left, mounted*) was not a chief, but he assumed the leadership of one of the Apache bands when, in 1876, the United States government attempted to confine the Apaches on a reservation in Arizona. He established a base in the mountains of Mexico, and from there he led his warriors on raids across the border to terrorize the American countryside. He kept this up for more than ten years. (Culver Pictures)

rados and Cochise. Mangas was murdered during the Civil War, and in 1872 Cochise agreed to peace and a reservation for his followers. But one leader, Geronimo, continued to carry on the fight. When he was finally captured in 1886, formal warfare between Indians and whites may be said to have ended.

A final, tragic encounter in 1890 was hardly a battle. As the Indians saw their culture and their glories fading, and as they suffered near starvation when corrupt government agents reduced their food rations, they turned to an emotional religion that emphasized the coming of a messiah and featured a "ghost dance," which inspired visions. Agents on the Sioux reservation, fearing that the dance might be the preliminary to hostil-

ities, called for troops; and some of the Indians fled to the Badlands. The soldiers caught and tried to disarm them at Wounded Knee. In the shooting that followed, about 40 of the soldiers were killed, and more than 200 of the Indians, including women and children, died at the hands of the troops.

In 1887, Congress had finally moved to destroy forever the tribal structure that was the cornerstone of Indian culture. Although some supporters of the new policy believed they were acting for the good of the Indians, the action was frankly designed to force them to become landowners and farmers, to abandon their collective society and culture, to become, in short, part of white civilization. The Dawes Severalty Act (usually known

A Defender of the Indians

Among the few white voices raised to defend the Indians and criticize the government's policy toward them was that of Helen Hunt Jackson, a writer who lived in Colorado Springs, Colorado. She presented her views in A Century of Dishonor *(1881):*

There is not among these three hundred bands of Indians [in the United States] one which has not suffered cruelly at the hands either of the Government or of white settlers. The poorer, the more insignificant, the more helpless the band, the more certain the cruelty and outrage to which they have been subjected. This is especially true of the bands on the Pacific slope. These Indians found themselves of a sudden surrounded by and caught up in the great influx of gold-seeking settlers, as helpless creatures on a shore are caught up in a tidal wave. There was not time for the Government to make treaties; not even time for communities to make laws. The tale of the wrongs, the oppressions, the murders of the Pacific-slope Indians in the last thirty years would be a volume by itself, and is too monstrous to be believed.

It makes little difference, however, where one opens the record of the history of the Indians; every page and every year has its dark stain. The story of one tribe is the story of all, varied only by differences of time and place; but neither time nor place makes any difference in the main facts. Colorado is as greedy and unjust in 1880 as was Georgia in 1830, and Ohio in 1795; and the United States Government breaks promises now as deftly as then, and with added ingenuity from long practice.

One of its strongest supports in so doing is the wide-spread sentiment among the people of dislike to the Indian, of impatience with his presence as a "barrier to civilization," and distrust of it as a possible danger. The old tales of the frontier life, with its horrors of Indian warfare, have gradually, by two or three generations' telling, produced in the average mind something like an hereditary instinct of unquestioning and unreasoning aversion which it is almost impossible to dislodge or soften.

---

simply as the Dawes Act) provided for the gradual elimination of tribal ownership of land and the allotment of tracts to individual owners: 160 acres to the head of a family, 80 acres to a single adult or orphan, 40 acres to each dependent child. Adult owners were accorded the status of citizenship, but unlike other citizens, they could not gain full title to their property for twenty-five years. The act was hardly a success. The Indians were not prepared for the wrenching change from a collective society to individualism. Congress attempted to facilitate the transition with the Burke Act of 1906. Under its terms, citizenship was deferred until after the completion of the twenty-five-year period contemplated in the Dawes Act, but Indians who proved their adaptability could secure both citizenship and land ownership in a shorter period. Neither then nor later, however, did legislation provide a satisfactory solution to the problem of the Indians—largely because there was no entirely happy solution to be had. The interests of the Indians were not compatible with those of the expanding white civilization. The conflict between the two peoples was, therefore, never truly resolved. White society simply prevailed.

THE DECLINE OF THE FARMER

Hard on the heels of the cattlemen and miners in the new West came the farmers. They poured into the newly opened plains states and beyond, enclosed land that had once been hunting territory for Indians and grazing territory for cowboys, and established a new agricultural region.

For a time in the late 1870s and early 1880s, the new Western farmers flourished—enjoying the fruits of an agricultural economic boom comparable in many ways to the booms that Eastern industry periodically enjoyed. Beginning in the mid-1880s, however, the boom turned to bust. American agriculture—not only in the new West but in the older Middle West and the South as well—was producing more than it ever had. But farmers in some regions, particularly in the plains states, were encountering special difficulties. And farmers everywhere were suffering from declining prices for their goods. Economically and psychologically, the farmer was in decline, often in absolute terms, almost always in relation to the rest of the nation. And those who tried to improve their lot by moving west found that the last frontier no longer provided them with a way out.

Farming on the Plains

Some farmers had drifted into the Great Plains during its first stages of development, but the great rush of settlement came in the late 1870s. In the course of the next decade, the relentless advance of the farming frontier would gradually convert the plains country to an agricultural economy.

Many factors combined to produce this surge of Western settlement, but the most important was undoubtedly the railroads. Before the Civil War, the Great Plains had been virtually inaccessible to all but the most hardy pioneers, who could reach it only through an arduous journey by wagon. But beginning in the 1860s, a vast new network of railroad lines started to develop that would, by the 1870s, open access to huge new areas of settlement. The first step toward this new access was the construction of the great "transcontinental" lines. An 1862 act of Congress (amended in 1864) chartered two railroad corporations, the Union Pacific and the Central Pacific. The Union Pacific was to build westward from Omaha, Nebraska, the

Central Pacific eastward from Sacramento, California, until they met. To provide the new companies with the necessary financial incentive, Congress made use of a practice that would become of vital importance to the future of the West: the land grant. For each mile of track a company laid, it would receive—in addition to the right of way for the track bed itself—twenty square miles of land in alternate sections (laid out in a checkerboard pattern) along the right of way.

The building of the transcontinental line was itself a dramatic and monumental achievement. Thousands of immigrant workers—mostly Irish on the eastern route, Chinese on the western—labored in what were at times unimaginably difficult conditions to penetrate mountain ranges, cross deserts, ward off Indians, and—finally—connect the two lines at Promontory Point in Utah in the spring of 1869. But while this first transcontinental line captured the greatest share of the public imagination, it was the construction of the great network of subsidiary lines in the years which followed that proved of greatest importance to the West. By the end of the century, five transcontinental lines were in operation; and from them were springing more and more spurs, penetrating much of the Great Plains. State governments, imitating Washington, induced railroad development by offering direct financial aid, favorable loans, and more than 50 million acres of land (on top of the 130 million acres the federal government had already offered). In some cases, government aid actually exceeded the cost of construction. Although operated by private corporations, the railroads were essentially public projects.

The construction of the railroad lines helped spur agricultural settlement in several ways. For one thing, it made access to the Great Plains easier—first enabling the farmers to reach the new lands, and later enabling them to ship their crops to market and to receive goods and supplies in return. For another, the railroad companies themselves now had great incentive to promote settlement—both to provide themselves with customers for their services and to add to the value of their vast land holdings. Thus the railroads embarked on a great advertising

Railroad Land Promotion
Railroads were eager to hasten the settlement of the West. They stood to profit from the transportation of migrants, the sale of land to them, and the freight business from settled farmers. This 1867 poster of the Union Pacific is typical of Western railroad advertisements from the 1860s to the 1890s. (Union Pacific Railroad Museum Collection)

campaign to lure settlers into the new region, distributing posters and brochures throughout the East and Midwest with glowing descriptions of the "great fertility," "nutritious grasses," and "numerous streams" to be found in the plains. More than that, the companies set rates so low for settlers that almost anyone could afford the trip West. And it sold much of its land at very low prices, usually between $2 and $5 an acre (which, since the railroads had gotten the land for nothing, was still a significant profit). Some railroad companies even provided liberal credit to prospective settlers to encourage them to move West.

Contributing further to the great surge of expansion was the climate. For years in succession, beginning in the 1870s, rainfall in the plains states was well above average. People now rejected the old idea that the region was the Great American Desert. Some even claimed that cultivation of the plains actually encouraged rainfall. Confident that they faced an era of indefinite prosperity, the new farmers scoffed at those who warned that the climate might change again. They scoffed too at the old cowmen who warned that the light soil of the plains should not be deprived of its protective turf by cultivation.

But even under the most favorable conditions, farming on the plains presented problems not encountered in any previously settled region. First and most critical was the problem of fencing. The farmer had to enclose his land, if for no other reason than to protect it from the herds of the cattlemen. But the traditional wood or stone fences were impossible on the plains. The cost of importing the material was prohibitive, and besides, such barriers were ineffective against range cattle. In the mid-seventies two Illinois farmers, Joseph H. Glidden and I. L. Ellwood, solved this problem by developing and putting on the market barbed wire. Produced in large quantities—40,000 tons a year—it sold cheaply, became standard equipment on the plains, and revolutionized fencing practices all over the country.

The second problem, present even when the rainfall was above average, was water. It became particularly acute after 1887, when a series of dry seasons began. One solution was the use of deep wells and steel wind-mills, which ensured a steady water supply for stock. Another was dry farming—a system of tillage designed to conserve moisture in the soil by covering it with a dust blanket—and the planting of drought-enduring crops. But in many areas of the plains, agriculture could not exist without irrigation. Large-scale irrigation, the only practicable kind, would have to be planned and supported by the government. The national government tried to hand the issue to the states, turning over to them in the Carey Act (1894) several million acres of public land to be reclaimed. The states, however, made little progress, largely because the problems of reclamation cut across state boundaries.

Farming on the plains was always expensive and often risky. The uncertainty of rainfall and the danger of grasshopper plagues and tornadoes made every farm year a speculative experiment. Costs of operation ran high, partly because many supplies had to be imported into the region from distant points, but mainly because of the nature of plains farming. In all the farm areas of the country, machines were playing a larger part in the agricultural process, and they were especially vital on the plains, where grain farming was conducted on large land units.

The last West was not, as has so often been claimed, a refuge for the urban poor or a safety valve for proletarian unrest. The people who settled this area were mostly farmers, and they came from farms in the Middle West, the East, and Europe. In the booming eighties, with land values rising, credit was easy, and the farmers confidently expected to retire their obligations. With the advent of the arid years of the late eighties, the prospect changed with grim suddenness. There followed a reversal of the frontier movement. Many settlers retreated from the Great Plains, sometimes turning once-flourishing communities into desolate "ghost towns." Those who remained gave an unintentional boost to the overproduction that caused farm prices to fall (wheat, which had sold for $1.60 a bushel at the end of the Civil War, dropped to 49 cents in the 1890s) and added to the distress of farmers elsewhere in the country.

Changes in Agriculture

Americans had always liked to talk about the wonderful life of the farmer. According to the popular myth, he was a sturdy yeoman, a simple, honest, happy man who dwelt close to nature and embodied all the virtues. Producing most of the things he and his family required, he was independent, subsisting on his own labor, depending not on the marketplace, and owing no man. The myth may have had some basis in Jefferson's time, but its reality was being destroyed by one of the great agricultural changes of the nineteenth century, the shift from subsistence, or self-sufficient, farming to commercial farming.

In commercial agriculture, the farmer specialized in a cash crop and sold it in a national or world market. He ceased making his household supplies and bought them instead at the town or village store. This kind of farming, when it was successful, raised the farmer's living standards. But now he was dependent on other people and on impersonal factors he could not control: bankers and interest rates, railroads and freight rates, national and European depressions, world supply and demand. In short, he had become a businessman—but with a difference. Unlike the capitalists of the industrial order, he could not regulate his production or influence the prices of what he sold.

Machines came to the aid of the farmer as to the manufacturer. The mechanization of agriculture had accelerated during the Civil War, when the government called thousands of laborers into military service and forced farmers to employ labor-saving devices. For example, approximately 100,000 reapers were in use at the beginning of the war, but 250,000 at its close. The effect of the machines on production and labor was revolutionary. They did not, however, influence all regions equally. Mechanization became a major force in the West long before it did in the South.

Before 1900, farmers were generally hostile to the theories and teachings of scientific agriculture, to what they scornfully termed "book learning." In 1887, Congress passed the Hatch Act, providing for a system of agricultural experiment stations; this was the only major agricultural legislation passed by Congress between 1865 and 1900. But farmers generally spurned the new information. American agriculture before 1900 was, as it always had been, extensive rather than intensive and consequently wasteful.

The period between 1865 and 1900 witnessed a tremendous expansion of agricultural facilities, not only in the United States but all over the world: in Brazil and Argentina in South America, in Canada, in Australia and New Zealand, and in Russia. World production increased at the same time that modern means of communication and transportation—the telephone, telegraph, cable, steam navigation, railroads—were welding the producing nations into one international market. The American commercial farmer, always augmenting his production, produced more than the domestic market could absorb and disposed of his surplus on the world market. Cotton farmers depended on export sales for 70 percent of their annual income, and wheat farmers for 30 to 40 percent; other producers relied on exporting a smaller proportion—it might be 10 to 25 percent—but it was large enough to make the difference between a year of profit and one of loss.

In the forty years after 1860, huge new areas of land were put under cultivation in America, machines became standard equipment on most farms, land values boomed, and production soared to ever higher levels. But while costs of operation increased, prices dropped after 1870. Meanwhile, although the proportion of people living on farms declined in relation to the total population, farm population increased in absolute terms. From 1860 to 1910, the number of farm families rose from 1.5 million to over 6 million. Yet whereas in 1860 agriculture had represented 50 percent of the total wealth of the country, by the early 1900s it represented only 20 percent. Where the farmer had received 30 percent of the national income in 1860, he received only 18 percent by 1910. By the decade of the nineties, 27 percent of the owned farms in the country were under mortgages, and by 1910, 33 percent. In 1880, 25 percent of all farms had been operated by tenants; by 1910, the proportion had grown to 37 percent. The agrarian scene as it presented itself in the 1890s hardly realized Jefferson's dream of sturdy and independent yeomen owning the land they tilled.

The Farmers' Grievances

The farmers were painfully aware that something was wrong. Neither they nor anyone else yet understood, however, the intricate implications of national and world overproduction. Instead, they concentrated their attention and anger on more immediate and more comprehensible problems, problems that were in truth real and important to them, such as freight rates, interest charges, and an adequate currency.

The farmers' first and most burning grievance was that against the railroads. In all sections, and especially in the states west of the Mississippi, farmers depended on the railroads to carry crops to the markets. In many cases, the roads charged higher rates for farm than for other shipments and higher rates in the South and West than in the Northeast. Freight rates sometimes consumed so much of the current price that farmers refused to ship their crops and either let them rot or used them as fuel. Railroads also controlled elevator and warehouse facilities in buying centers and charged arbitrary storage rates.

In the farmers' list of villains, the sources that controlled credit—banks, loan companies, insurance corporations—ranked second only to the railroads. Commercial farming was by its nature expensive, and ambitious producers needed credit to purchase machines or enlarge holdings. Though eager to advance loans during the boom period of rising land values, the lenders insisted on high interest rates. The farmers were in no position to resist, and in the West and the South they had to submit to charges running from 10 to 25 percent. Usually they borrowed money when it was cheap, or abundant, and then had to retire their debts when money had become dear, or scarce. According to one estimate, 1,200 bushels of grain would buy a $1,000 mortgage in the 1860s; twenty years later, it took 2,300 bushels to repay the mortgage. With good reason, the farmers fought for an increase in the volume of currency.

A third grievance of the farmer concerned prices, both the prices he received for his products and the prices he paid for goods he bought. He disposed of his products as an individual in competition with countless other individuals in this and other countries. He possessed little or no advance information on the state of the market and probable price changes; he did not have storage facilities to hold his crop for a favorable price; and he was powerless to regulate his production. Instead of changing his marketing procedures, the farmer blamed his woes on personal villains—grain speculators in distant cities, international bankers, regional and local middlemen. These operators, he became convinced (sometimes with justice), were combining to fix prices so as to benefit themselves while hurting him.

The farmer was also convinced that there was a conspiracy against him in the prices of the goods he purchased. He sold his crops in a competitive market but bought in a domestic market protected by tariffs and dominated by trusts and corporations. According to government reports, more than one hundred articles purchased by farmers—farm machinery, tools, sewing machines, blankets, staple foods, clothing, plowshares, and others—were protected. On these necessary items the tariff added from 33 to 60 percent to the purchase price.

A Sod House on the Plains

Many settlers on the treeless Great Plains lived their first years in sod houses. They built these dwellings by cutting strips of the tough turf into pieces and laying them on top of one another to form walls. In some cases, they first excavated and then erected the walls around the partial dugout. This photograph shows a combined dugout and sod house under construction in Nebraska in 1892. The wagon is bringing a fresh load of turf. (Solomon D. Butcher Collection, The Nebraska State Historical Society)

The Agrarian Malaise

Adding to these economic grievances, and in many ways a direct result of them, was a less tangible but deeply felt resentment. In part, it was an outgrowth of the isolation of farm life in these days before paved roads, automobiles, telephones, and radios. Farm families in some parts of the country—particularly in the prairie and plains regions, where large farms were scattered over vast areas—were virtually cut off from the outside world and human companionship. During the winter months and spells of bad weather, the loneliness could become nearly unbearable.

In addition to the isolation, there was often a general drabness and dullness to farm existence. Many farmers lacked access to adequate education for their children, to proper medical facilities, to recreational or cultural activities, to virtually anything that might give them a sense of being valued members of a community. Older farmers felt the sting of watching their children leave the farm for the city. They felt the humiliation of being ridiculed as "hayseeds" by the new urban culture that was coming to dominate American life. There was, in short, a general feeling of obsolescence, of being left behind by a society that no longer placed much value on the virtues of rural life.

This emerging agrarian malaise found reflection in the growing discontent of many farmers, a discontent that would help to create a great national political movement in the 1890s. It found reflection, too, in the literature that emerged from rural America. Writers in the late nineteenth century might romanticize the rugged life of the cowboy and the Western miner. For the farmer, however, the image was different. Hamlin Garland, perhaps the most celebrated writer to deal with the nature of agrarian life in this period, reflected the growing disillusionment in a series of novels and short stories. In the past, Garland wrote in the introduction to *Jason Edwards* (1891), the agrarian frontier had seemed to be "the Golden West, the land of wealth and freedom and happiness. All of the associations called up by the spoken word, the West, were fabulous, mythic, hopeful." Now, however, the bright promise had faded. In this novel and in other works (including his most famous achievement, a collection of stories entitled *Main-Traveled Roads*, also published in 1891), he showed how the trials of rural life were crushing the human spirit. "So this is the reality of the dream!" a character in *Jason Edwards* exclaims. "A shanty on a barren plain, hot and lone as a desert. My God!" Once, the sturdy yeoman farmer had viewed himself as the backbone of American life. Now, he was becoming painfully aware that his position was declining in relation to the rising urban-industrial society to the east.

SUGGESTED READINGS

Many of the studies of the South during Reconstruction cited at the end of Chapter 15 are of relevance to the New South as well. The classic study of the post-Reconstruction South, from which most other efforts stem, is C. Vann Woodward, *Origins of the New South* (1951). Woodward has also authored two collections of essays valuable to the study of this period: *The Burden of Southern History* (rev., 1968), and *American Counterpoint* (1971). Jonathan Wiener, *Social Origins of the New South: Alabama, 1860–1885* (1978), challenges some of Woodward's conclusions. Paul Buck, *The Road to Reunion* (1937), is an older study of Reconstruction and its aftermath in the South. Paul Gaston, *The New South Creed* (1970), is a valuable examination of the ideology of progress of the post-Reconstruction years. W. J. Cash, *The Mind of the South* (1941),

continues to arouse controversy by its bold interpretation of the Southern psyche.

The impact of national politics on the South is considered in C. Vann Woodward, *Reunion and Reaction* (1951), a study of the Compromise of 1877; Stanley P. Hirshson, *Farewell to the Bloody Shirt: Northern Republicans and the Southern Negro* (1962); Kenneth E. Davison, *The Presidency of Rutherford B. Hayes* (1972); and Vincent P. DeSantis, *Republicans Face the Southern Question: The New Departure Years, 1877–1897* (1959). On politics within the New South, see—in addition to the Woodward works cited above—J. Morgan Kousser, *The Shaping of Southern Politics: Suffrage Restriction and the Establishment of the One-Party South, 1880–1910* (1974); Paul Lewinson, *Race, Class, and Party* (1932); and V. O. Key, Jr., *South-*

ern Politics and the Nation (1949). Francis B. Simkins, *Pitchfork Ben Tillman* (1944); C. Vann Woodward, *Tom Watson: Agrarian Rebel* (1938); and Joseph F. Wall, *Henry Watterson: Reconstructed Rebel* (1956), are biographies of leading Southern political figures. Sheldon Hackney, *Populism to Progressivism in Alabama* (1959), is a valuable study of late nineteenth-century and early twentieth-century political movements in a single state. David Potter, *The South and the Concurrent Majority* (1972), and Carl Degler, *The Other South: Southern Dissenters in the Nineteenth Century* (1974), are also useful.

The post-Reconstruction Southern economy is examined in Melvin Greenhut and W. Tate Whitman (eds.), *Essays in Southern Economic Development* (1964). Roger Ransom and Richard Sutch, *One Kind of Freedom* (1977), examines the origins of the crop lien system. On race relations, see C. Vann Woodward, *The Strange Career of Jim Crow* (rev., 1974); Howard Rabinowitz, *Race Relations in the Urban South, 1865–1890* (1978); James M. McPherson, *The Abolitionist Legacy: From Reconstruction to the NAACP* (1975); Robert Higgs, *Competition and Coercion: Blacks in the American Economy, 1865–1914* (1977); and Joel Williamson, *After Slavery* (1965), which challenges Woodward's view of the origins of segregation. Louis R. Harlan, *Booker T. Washington* (1972), is an excellent study of the preeminent black leader of the New South. See also August Meier, *Negro Thought in America* (1963). Francis Broderick, *W. E. B. DuBois* (1959), and Elliott M. Rudwick, *W. E. B. DuBois: Propagandist of Negro Protest* (rev., 1969), examine the founder of the NAACP.

Ray A. Billington, *Westward Expansion* (1967), and Frederick Merk, *History of the Westward Movement* (1978), both cited earlier, are general studies. Billington and Merk were both disciples of Frederick Jackson Turner. Thomas D. Clark, *Frontier America* (rev., 1969), offers an alternative interpretation. Howard R. Lamar, *The Far Southwest, 1846–1912* (1966), is a more specialized study of the period discussed in this chapter. The arrival of the miners is discussed in Rodman W. Paul, *Mining Frontiers of the Far West,*

1848–1880 (1963); William S. Greever, *Bonanza West: Western Mining Rushes* (1963); and Duane A. Smith, *Rocky Mountain Mining Camps* (1967). The expansion of ranching is the subject of Lewis Atherton, *The Cattle Kings* (1961); Ernest E. Osgood, *The Day of the Cattleman* (1929); Edward E. Dale, *The Range Cattle Industry,* rev. ed. (1969); and J. M. Skaggs, *The Cattle Trailing Industry* (1973). Among books exploring the life of the cowboy, see Andy Adams, *The Log of a Cowboy* (1927), and Joe B. Frantz and Julian Choate, *The American Cowboy: The Myth and the Reality* (1955). Henry Nash Smith, *Virgin Land* (1950), is a brilliant examination of the myth of the West in the American literary imagination. Frederick Jackson Turner, *The Frontier in American History* (1920), presents the influential "frontier hypothesis" of its author. Ray A. Billington, *Frederick Jackson Turner* (1973), is a superb biography.

On the plight of the Indians, see the general account by Wilcomb E. Washburn, *The Indian in America* (1975). Of more specific interest are Ralph K. Andrist, *The Long Death: The Last Days of the Plains Indians* (1964); Francis Paul Prucha, *American Indian Policy in Crisis* (1976); and Robert M. Utley, *Frontier Regulars: The United States Army and the Indian* (1973), and *Last Days of the Sioux Nation* (1963). Robert Mardock, *Reformers and the American Indian* (1971), considers white efforts on behalf of the tribes. Robert F. Berkhofer, Jr., *The White Man's Indian* (1978), examines white images of the Indian.

Walter Prescott Webb, *The Great Plains* (1931), is a classic study of the opening of America's last agricultural frontier. Fred Shannon, *The Farmer's Last Frontier, 1860–1897* (1945), and Gilbert Fite, *The Farmer's Frontier* (1966), are more recent studies. Paul W. Gates, *History of Public Land Development* (1968), examines government policy. Life on the frontier is the subject of Everett Dick, *The Sod-House Frontier* (1937). Allan Bogue, *From Prairie to Corn Belt* (1963), is a broad view of agricultural development. The growth of the agrarian malaise and the emergence of protest are examined in the works on Populism cited after Chapter 19.

Industrial Supremacy

17

On Strike, 1886
The industrial growth of the late nineteenth century was an ambiguous blessing for American workers. It created employment for the large numbers of migrants (both from American farms and from Europe) who were flocking into the factory towns and cities. And, according to most studies, it caused a rise in the average standard of living of workers. But it also subjected men, women, and children to the arduous conditions of factory life, conditions that many of them compared to those of slavery. Labor organization was limited in the nineteenth century, but on occasion workers did manage to stage effective work stoppages. (Culver Pictures)

"With a stride that astonished statisticians, the conquering hosts of business enterprise swept over the continent; twenty-five years after the death of Lincoln, America had become, in the quantity and value of her products, the first manufacturing nation of the world. What England had accomplished in a hundred years, the United States had achieved in half the time." So wrote the historians Charles and Mary Beard in the 1920s, expressing the amazement with which Americans still regarded the remarkable expansion of their economy in the late nineteenth century.

In fact, America's rise to industrial supremacy was not as sudden as some observers believed. The nation had been building a manufacturing economy since early in the nineteenth century; industry was well established before the Civil War. But Americans were clearly correct in observing that the accomplishments of the last three decades of the nineteenth century overshadowed all the earlier progress. Those years witnessed nothing less than the transformation of the nation.

Many factors contributed to this dramatic industrial growth. The United States had an abundance of basic raw materials and energy sources: coal, iron, timber, petroleum, water power, and more. There was a large and growing supply of labor, the result of two great migrations: the movement of American farmers into the cities, and the movement of European peasants across the ocean to the nation's industrial centers. Americans had, moreover, developed a remarkable technological inventive-

ness—widely heralded as "Yankee ingenuity"—capable of creating the necessary machinery for industrial growth.

A talented and energetic group of business organizers, "captains of industry," developed new financial and administrative structures capable of bringing together raw materials, workers, and machines, using them efficiently in the productive process, and distributing goods profitably to a national market. And the market itself, which was growing as a result of population growth, the new railroad network, and a host of new marketing techniques, made possible the mass consumption that is a prerequisite of mass production. Finally, the federal government proved a benign agent for the promotion of economic growth. It refrained from any negative interference with private enterprise, and it worked at the same time to assist and encourage economic growth by turning over public resources for private exploitation, by erecting protective tariff barriers against foreign competition, by establishing a new banking and currency system, and by providing direct subsidies of land and money.

The remarkable growth that resulted from these factors did much to increase the wealth and improve the lives of many Americans. But such benefits were far from equally shared. While the industrial titans and a growing middle class were enjoying a prosperity without precedent in the nation's history, workers, farmers, and others were experiencing an often painful ordeal that slowly edged the United States toward a great economic and political crisis.

SOURCES OF INDUSTRIAL GROWTH

Virtually all the forces that contributed to American economic growth had been in operation in some form before the Civil War.

But there had been other forces at work in those years to inhibit economic development. Perhaps most important, conservative Southern planters, exercising great political power, had served as an obstacle to governmental policies favoring Northern capitalists. The years of war and Reconstruction removed that obstacle, as well as others. And in the 1870s and 1880s, the forces of economic progress took on renewed strength.

Industrial Technology

No one factor can be called the most important prerequisite of industrial growth. Indeed, economic modernization depends above all on the working together of many forces at once. But one of the most important of such forces, certainly, is the emergence of new technologies and the discovery of new materials and productive processes. In the entire history of the United States up to 1860, only 36,000 patents had been granted. For the period from 1860 to 1890, the figure was 440,000.

Many of the postwar inventions and discoveries were in the field of communication. In 1866, Cyrus W. Field succeeded in laying a transatlantic cable to Europe. During the next decade, Alexander Graham Bell developed the first practicable telephone, and by the 1890s, the American Telephone and Telegraph Company, which handled his interests, had installed nearly half a million instruments in American cities. Other inventions that speeded the pace of business organization were the typewriter (by Christopher L. Sholes in 1868), the cash register (by James Ritty in 1879), and the calculating or adding machine (by William S. Burroughs in 1891).

Undoubtedly, the technological innovation that had the most revolutionary effect on industry and on the lives of the urban masses in the industrial centers was the introduction in the 1870s of electricity as a source of light and power. Among the several men who pioneered in developing a commercially practical dynamo were Charles F. Brush, who devised the arc lamp for street illumination, and Thomas A. Edison, who invented, among many other electrical contrivances, the incandescent lamp (or light bulb), which could be used for both street and home lighting.

Edison and others designed improved generators and built central power plants to furnish electricity to office buildings, factories, and dwellings. Before the turn of the century, 2,774 power stations were in operation, and some 2 million electric lights were in use in the country. Already electric power was being employed in street railway systems and in electric elevators in urban skyscrapers, as well as for driving the machines of factories.

The age of steel began in 1865. A process by which iron could be transformed into steel—a much more durable and versatile material—had been discovered simultaneously in the 1850s by an Englishman, Henry Bessemer, and an American, William Kelly. (It consisted of blowing air through molten iron to burn out the impurities.) After the Civil War, the new process transformed the metal industry; and in 1868, another method of making steel—the open-hearth process, introduced from Europe by the New Jersey ironmaster Abram S. Hewitt—made an appearance as well. Together, these techniques enabled the production of steel in great quantities and in large dimensions, enabling the metal to be used for the production of locomotives, steel rails, and, ultimately, heavy girders for the construction of tall buildings.

The steel industry was first concentrated where the iron industry had existed, in western Pennsylvania and eastern Ohio. Here, in a region where iron ore and coal were found in abundance, Pittsburgh reigned as the center of the steel world. But as the industry expanded, new sources of ore had to be tapped, and by the 1870s the mines of the upper peninsula of Michigan were furnishing over half of the supply. Then, in the 1890s, the Eastern steelmasters began to exploit the extensive Mesabi range in Minnesota, which developed into the greatest ore-producing region in the world. Another rich source was discovered around Birmingham, Alabama. Although the Michigan and Minnesota fields were located at a great distance from the Eastern plants, the ore could be transported easily and cheaply by means of railroads and Great Lakes steamers. Eventually new centers of production with ready access to ore

PUBLISHED BY CURRIER & IVES

THE GREAT EAST RIVER BRIDGE.

To Connect the Cities of New York & Brooklyn.

Brooklyn Bridge

As a story of persevering courage, the erection of Brooklyn Bridge by John A. and Washington Roebling can match anything in American military history. In 1866, Manhattan Island was connected with Brooklyn and the rest of Long Island only by ferries. When the East River froze, the tie was sundered. A bridge was needed. John Roebling, engineer and manufacturer of wire cables, proposed a suspension bridge with a central span of 1,600 feet—longer than any that had been built anywhere in the world. Other great engineers said it could not be done. But Roebling's prestige and forcefulness won approval for the idea, and he designed the bridge. Then he unexpectedly died. His son Washington Roebling was stricken by caisson bends. An invalid, he was confined to his bed at Columbia Heights. His wife watched the construction by telescope, and he supervised every detail by letter. In 1883, twelve years after work began, the bridge opened, an object of practical use that also was a thing of beauty. Here was the austere art of the age of steel: the massive granite towers were united in tension with the spidery cables of nineteen wire strands, and the tension held the bridge aloft. The father was dead; the son, paralyzed, growing deaf and blind; but they had shown how straightforward statement of fact could unify industrialism with aesthetics. (Currier & Ives)

---

and coal arose: Cleveland and Lorain in Ohio, Detroit, Chicago, and Birmingham.

The machines of the age of steel could not run without lubrication, and so another vast enterprise came into being in the postwar era: the petroleum industry. (Not until later did oil become important primarily for

its potential as a fuel.) For years before the Civil War, the existence of petroleum had been known, particularly in western Pennsylvania, where it often seeped to the surface of streams and springs. No one was quite sure what it was or what to do with it. Some enterprising individuals peddled it in bottles as a patent medicine. The first person to glimpse its commercial possibilities as an illuminant was George H. Bissell, who sent a sample of oil to Professor Benjamin Silliman of Yale for analysis. Silliman reported in 1855 that the substance could be used for lighting purposes, and that it would also yield such products as paraffin, naphtha, and lubricating oil. Bissell then raised enough money to begin drilling operations; and in 1859, Edwin L. Drake, employed by Bissell, put down the first oil well near Titusville, Pennsylvania. Labeled "Drake's folly" by the skeptical, it was soon producing oil at the rate of 500 barrels a month.

It also started an oil rush, as promoters searched for and found other fields, not only in Pennsylvania but in Ohio and West Virginia as well. By the 1870s nearly 40 million barrels of petroleum had been produced, oil had advanced to fourth place among the nation's exports, and the annual production was approaching 20 million barrels. Because relatively little capital was required for a man to make a start in the oil business, either as a producer or as a refiner, competition at first ran wild. Refineries, which were even more profitable than wells, dotted the Pennsylvania-Ohio region, with Pittsburgh and Cleveland constituting the two principal refining centers.

New technologies and materials similarly transformed other industries. The refrigerated freight car made possible the expansion of the great meat-packing organizations of Gustavus Swift, Philip Armour, and others. New processes of milling flour made possible the emergence of large milling companies in the Midwest (and particularly in Minnesota). New methods of canning foods and condensing milk helped establish the prepared-foods industry under the leadership of Gail Borden and others.

By the beginning of the twentieth century, the new technology was leading to even greater advances. There were early experiments in communication by radio conducted by the Italian inventor Guglielmo Marconi in the 1890s; there were the first steps toward the development of the airplane—the famous flight by the Wright brothers at Kitty Hawk, North Carolina, in 1903. But of more im-

mediate importance was the development of the automobile. In the 1870s, designers in France, Germany, and Austria—inspired by the success of railroad engines—were already beginning to develop engines that might drive independently controlled vehicles. They achieved early successes with an "internal combustion engine," which used the expanding power of burning gas to drive pistons; and with this new engine, they created the first automobiles—essentially traditional carriages fitted with their own source of power, to replace the horse.

Meanwhile, in the United States, such inventors as Charles and Frank Duryea, Elwood Haynes, Ransom Olds, and Henry Ford were designing their own automobiles. The Duryeas built and operated the first gasoline-driven motor vehicle in America in 1903. (Earlier American cars had used other, cruder fuels.) Three years later, Ford produced the first of the famous cars that would bear his name. In 1898, the first automobile advertisement had appeared in *Scientific American*, with the headline: "Dispense With a Horse." The earliest automobile showroom opened in New York in 1901. By 1900, automobile companies were turning out more than 4,000 cars a year. A decade later—when manufacturers were finally able to streamline operations so as to bring the cost down, and when American roads began to be improved to make automobile traffic possible—the industry began to become a major force in the economy. In 1895, there had been only four automobiles on the American highways. By 1917, there were nearly 5 million. The automobile was beginning to remake American life.

Central to the growth of the automobile and other industries were advances in the science of production. Convinced that a modern economy required the modernization of manufacturing processes, industrialists by the turn of the century were turning in growing numbers to the new principles of "scientific management," the leading spokesman for which ultimately was Frederick Winslow Taylor. The new technology, Taylor argued, would be of little use unless workers could be trained to operate the machinery efficiently and effectively. If properly managed,

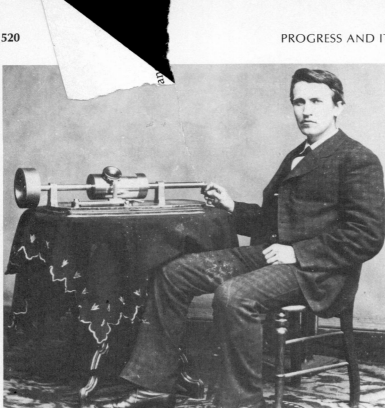

Edison and the Phonograph
Thomas Alva Edison (1847–1931) was one of the most revered Americans of his age—the inventor of the electric light bulb, the phonograph (an early model of which, known as the "talking machine," is depicted here), and hundreds of consumer and industrial devices. His laboratory in Menlo Park, New Jersey, served as a model for the expanding technological efforts of Americans in the late nineteenth century. (UPI)

he argued, fewer and fewer men could perform simpler tasks at infinitely greater speed, increasing productive efficiency manifold. Not until well into the new century—indeed not until the 1920s—did the influence of what became known as "Taylorism" reach its fullest extent. But the impulse behind it—the attempt to bring to the performance of workers the same scientific standards that industrialists were bringing to the creation of new technologies—was affecting industry much earlier than that.

Similarly, manufacturers began placing greater emphasis on industrial research. In part because of the phenomenal success of Thomas Edison's famous industrial laboratory in Menlo Park, New Jersey, dozens of corporations were, by the early years of the twentieth century, establishing laboratories of their own. By 1913, Bell Telephone, Du Pont, General Electric, Eastman Kodak, and about fifty other companies were budgeting hundreds of thousands of dollars each year for research by their own engineers and scientists.

Out of all the new methods and machines emerged the greatest triumph of production technology: mass production, and, above all, the moving assembly line, which Henry Ford introduced in his automobile plants in 1914. This revolutionary technique cut the time for assembling a chassis from twelve and a half hours to one and a half hours. It enabled Ford to raise the wages and lower the hours of his workers while cutting the base price of his Model T from $950 to $290. And it served as an example for many other industries.

Railroad Expansion

At least equally important in promoting industrial growth was the emergence of a modern network of railroads. The railroads not only opened new markets and provided access to new materials. They also helped create new corporate organizations that served as models for other industries.

In 1860, the railroads already constituted the biggest business and the most important single economic interest in the United States. In the years that followed, their importance grew still further. Every decade, the total railroad trackage increased dramatically: from 30,000 miles in 1860, to 52,000 miles in 1870, to 93,000 in 1880, to 163,000 in 1890, and to 193,000 at the turn of the century. Along with the extension of lines came improvements in technology that made railroad travel safer

and more efficient: steel rails, heavier locomotives and cars, uniform track gauge, wider roadbeds, and perhaps most important new braking systems (first introduced by George Westinghouse) that removed much of the danger of pileups and derailments.

Government subsidies—those by the federal government to support the transcontinental lines, and those by federal and local governments to encourage subsidiary routes—were vital to these vast undertakings, which required far more capital than private entrepreneurs could raise by them-

The Ford Assembly Line

In August 1913, at the main Ford plant in the Detroit suburb of Highland Park, it took twelve and one-half man-hours of labor to assemble every Model T chassis. Then the world's first moving assembly line for automobiles was installed; instead of the workers moving to the stationary work, the moving work came to the workers. Within six months, each chassis was being assembled in only one hour and thirty-three minutes. This picture, taken in 1914, shows a portion of the final assembly line, where the radiator and the wheels were placed on the Model T chassis. At this time, the company employed about 12,000 men in making cars, and another 1,000 men in making better tools to use in making cars—a fact that shows how the technical revolution in modern industry had been institutionalized and made continuous. (Ford Motor Company)

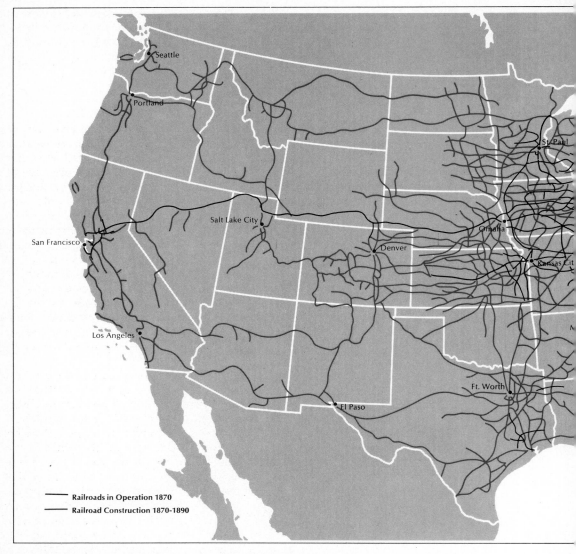

RAILROADS IN OPERATION, 1870; RAILROAD CONSTRUCTION, 1870–1890

selves. Equally important, perhaps, was the emergence of great railroad corporations—the first great economic combinations—which brought a vast proportion of the nation's rails under the control of a very few men. Among the first such combinations was the Pennsylvania Railroad, which not only became one of the first companies to combine a large number of short lines under the direction of a single management but also in-

troduced a new system of administration—staffed by trained managers—that ran the company efficiently. Profits still went to the stockholders; but the actual running of the company was lodged in the hands of men who were not necessarily owners.

Other railroad combinations saw owners continue to play a central role in management: the vast New York Central empire of Cornelius Vanderbilt (a former steamship

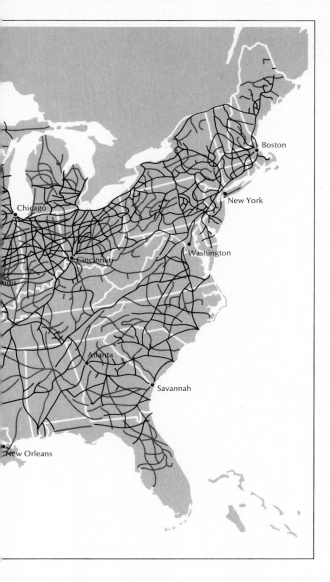

velopment was less significant for its creation of individual barons than for the boost it gave to the development of the modern corporation.

The Corporation

There had been corporations in America since colonial times: organizations chartered by government and charged with running such public facilities as bridges, roads, and banks. But the corporation in the modern sense of the word emerged only after the Civil War, when first railroad magnates and then others realized that with incorporation came the right to sell stock and accumulate capital. Suddenly, a businessman did not need to rely simply on his own money or that of a few friends or relatives to launch a new enterprise. By selling stock to the general public—each purchaser to be held liable only for the amount he or she invested—it was possible to gather vast sums and undertake great ventures.

The new corporation quickly spread beyond the railroad industry to other areas of the economy. In steel, the central figure was Andrew Carnegie, a Scottish immigrant who had worked his way up in the railroad industry. In 1873, he opened his own steelworks in Pittsburgh; and in the following decades, he expanded his company to a place of dominance in the industry. His methods were much like those of other rising industrial titans. He obtained rebates from railroads on his shipments so that he could cut his costs and hence his prices. He bought out rival concerns that could not meet his competition. He set up—in collaboration with his able associate Henry Clay Frick—a carefully integrated system that enabled him to control the processing of steel from mine to market. His company operated a fleet of ore ships on the Great Lakes, acquired railroads and coal mines, and leased part of the Mesabi range. Then, in 1901, he sold out to the banker J. Pierpont Morgan, who merged the Carnegie interests with others to create the giant United States Steel Corporation—a billion-dollar enterprise that controlled almost two-thirds of the nation's steel production.

owner widely known as the "Commodore"), for example; or the Erie Railroad, controlled by the unscrupulous speculators Daniel Drew, Jay Gould, and James Fisk, whose self-serving exploitation of the company ultimately led to disaster. Indeed, these and other railroad tycoons—James J. Hill, Collis P. Huntington, and others—were symbols to much of the nation of great economic power concentrated in a single man. Yet railroad de-

A similar process, although usually on a more modest scale, was at work in other industries. Gustavus Swift developed a relatively small meat-packing company into a great national corporation, in part because of profits earned during the Civil War, in part because of his success in attracting investors in the years after the war. Isaac Singer had patented a sewing machine in 1851 and created—in I. M. Singer and Company—one of the first modern manufacturing corporations.

It was not simply the accumulation of capital that characterized the new organizations. It was also a new approach to management. Large, national business enterprises needed more systematic administrative structures than the limited, local ventures of the past. As a result, corporate leaders introduced a set of managerial techniques—the genesis of modern business administration—that relied on the division of responsibilities, a carefully designed hierarchy of control, modern cost-accounting procedures, and perhaps above all a new breed of business executive: the "middle manager," who formed a layer of command between workers and owners. Beginning in the railroad corporations, these new management techniques moved quickly into virtually every area of large-scale industry.

Efficient administrative capabilities helped make possible another major feature of the modern corporation: consolidation. Railroad companies attempting to create a national network of lines had quickly discovered that combination—the joining of small, local enterprises into huge, national organizations—enabled them to move more quickly and efficiently toward their goals. Other industries attempting to take advantage of the expanding national markets for manufactured goods did likewise, creating giant industrial organizations.

Businessmen created these organizations through two primary methods. One was "horizontal integration"—the combining of a number of firms engaged in the same enterprise into a single corporation. The consolidation of many different railroad lines into one company was an example. The second method, which largely began in the 1890s,

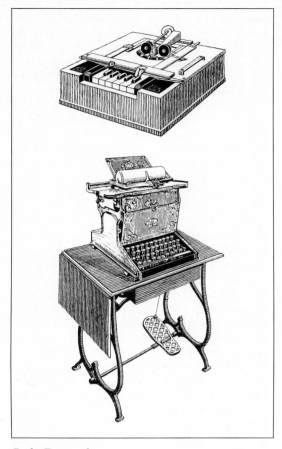

Early Typewriters
The first practical writing machine was developed in Milwaukee, 1867–1873, by Christopher Latham Sholes, James Densmore, and their associates. In 1873, the patent owners made an arrangement with E. Remington & Sons, gunmakers of Ilion, New York, for the manufacture of typewriters on a commercial scale. Not till the late 1880s did the typewriter become standard equipment in business offices. It then began to have revolutionary effects, making possible truly big business and creating new and respectable job opportunities for women. The illustration shows, above, an incomplete model of the first Sholes machine to be patented (1868), and, below, the first Remington-made machine (1874), with a treadle for returning the carriage. (F. E. Compton & Company)

was "vertical integration"—the taking over of businesses on which the company relied for its primary function. Carnegie Steel, which came to control not only steel mills, but mines, railroads, and other enterprises, was an example of vertical integration.

The even more celebrated empire pieced together by the greatest consolidationist of the time, John D. Rockefeller, resulted from the use of both methods. Beginning at the age of nineteen, when he became a partner in a Cleveland produce commission that earned great profits during the Civil War, Rockefeller displayed remarkable talents. Farsighted, acquisitive, and skilled at organization, he decided that his own economic future lay with the oil industry; and shortly after the Civil War, he launched a refining company in Cleveland (which he believed was destined to become a national center of the industry). From the beginning, he sought to eliminate his competition—especially the small-scale companies that he believed were ruining the petroleum industry. Allying himself with other wealthy capitalists, he proceeded methodically to buy out other refineries. In 1870, he formed the Standard Oil Company of Ohio, which in a few years had acquired twenty of the twenty-five refineries in Cleveland, as well as plants in Pittsburgh, Philadelphia, New York, and Baltimore.

So far, Rockefeller had expanded only horizontally. But soon he began expanding vertically as well. He built his own barrel factories and terminal warehouses and a network of pipelines that gave him control over most of the facilities for transporting petroleum. Standard Oil also owned its own freight cars and developed its own marketing organization, thus avoiding commissions to middlemen. By the 1880s, Rockefeller had established such dominance within the petroleum industry that to much of the nation he served as the leading symbol of monopoly.

The rise of "bigness" helped industrialists cope with what many believed was the greatest curse of the modern economy: "cutthroat competition." Businessmen insisted that they believed fervently in free enterprise and a competitive marketplace—but often such beliefs lasted only until they themselves were exposed to competition. Then they realized that the existence of too many competing firms in a single industry could spell instability and ruin for all. Thus, they sought to limit their vulnerability to competition through consolidation. As the movement toward combination accelerated, new vehicles emerged to facilitate it. Again, it was the railroads that moved first. They began with so-called pool arrangements—informal agreements among various companies to stabilize rates and divide markets. But the pools ultimately proved unworkable, especially after the economic panic of the 1890s began to wreak havoc on the railroads and other corporations. And in response there emerged new, more rigorous techniques of consolidation—resting less on cooperation than on centralized control. For the railroads, the solution came through the emergence of great banking empires that took control of many of the failing lines, reorganized them under the control of the bankers themselves, and stabilized their operations. The most prominent of the banking magnates, J. Pierpont Morgan, led the way beginning in the 1880s, when he played a major role in saving the New York Central Railroad from collapse. Other railroads soon looked to Morgan and such other banking firms as Kuhn Loeb and Company for assistance. In the decades that followed, similar systems extended into other industries as well. By 1904, there were 318 major combinations, with a capitalization of more than $7 billion—combinations that reached not only into such primary industries as oil, steel, copper, and railroads, but into such consumer-oriented fields as tobacco, sugar, and whiskey. As a result, 1 percent of the corporations in America were able to control more than 33 percent of manufacturing.

What was emerging, in other words, was a system of economic organization that lodged enormous power in the hands of a very few men—the great bankers of New York, industrial titans such as Rockefeller (who himself gained control of a major bank), and others. These few men directly or indirectly controlled enterprises far beyond their immediate corporate interests.

At the heart of this system was what became known as the "trust." Standard Oil created the first modern trust in the early 1880s, and it soon became the common vehicle for consolidating railroads and other industries as well. Under a trust agreement, stockholders in individual corporations transferred their stocks to a small group of trustees (in the case of the Standard Oil trust, to men chosen and dominated by Rockefeller) in exchange for shares in the "trust" itself. Owners of trust certificates had no direct control over the decisions of the trustees; they simply received shares of the profits of the combination. Thus while John D. Rockefeller officially owned only a few refinery companies, he managed through the mechanism of the trust to extend his reach over a vast range of enterprises. J. P. Morgan, in theory simply a bank president, in reality dominated scores of industrial organizations. Through their trusts, Rockefeller and Morgan between them, a congressional investigation disclosed in 1913, controlled companies valued at more than $22 billion.

These combinations had some success in controlling the chaos of the marketplace. But they themselves often proved to be inefficient and financially precarious. The "oil trust," dominated by Rockefeller, the "steel trust," controlled by Morgan, the "food trusts" of Gustavus Swift and others, the great electrical combinations such as Westinghouse and General Electric—these and other combinations soon became a major source of controversy in American life.

CAPITALISM AND ITS CRITICS

The rise of big business depended not only on technology, transportation, and organization, but on an ideology of growth and progress. Industrialists and financiers in the last decades of the nineteenth century developed a complex and wide-ranging rationale for their methods and power. And while this new set of ideas was in large part meant simply to justify what already existed, it also became a positive force, spurring others to greater efforts at development.

The new business philosophy was not without its critics. Opponents charged that the ideology of free enterprise was a rank hypocrisy—that the American economy in the late nineteenth century was far from free, dominated as it was by great trusts and combinations; that private enterprise was far from private, since it relied on government assistance in countless ways. Others pointed to the injustices and dislocations that modern industry created. Still others charged that big business was not yet sufficiently modernized, that its methods were wasteful and inefficient. Yet despite the criticisms, the business philosophy continued to prevail, not only among the captains of industry but among the majority of the American people.

The Myth of the Self-Made Man

The economic revolution raised up a new ruling class in America. The industrialists and the investment bankers now sat in the seats of power formerly held by Southern planters and Northeastern merchants, by members of the old aristocracy of inherited wealth and the old middle class, by politicians and statesmen of the antebellum Webster-Clay model.

Before the Civil War there had been few millionaires in America; by 1892 there were more than 4,000 of them. Most of the new business tycoons had begun their careers from comfortable and privileged positions on the economic scale. But some—enough to invest the entire group with the aura of the American success story—had emerged from obscurity to riches. Andrew Carnegie had worked as a bobbin boy in a Pittsburgh cotton mill, James J. Hill had been a frontier clerk, John D. Rockefeller had started out as a clerk in a Cleveland commission house, and E. H. Harriman had begun as a broker's office boy. Regardless of economic background, the new millionaires were—or considered themselves to be—self-made men.

Many had gotten ahead through a ruthless disregard for the public welfare. Their attitude was epitomized by Cornelius Vanderbilt's belligerent question: "Can't I do what I want with my own?" and by the much-quoted statement of his son William: "The public be damned." Once, when the elder Vanderbilt's lawyers warned him that a move he contemplated was illegal, he bellowed: "What do I care about the law? Hain't I got the power?" Men like Vanderbilt had the power, indeed. Through their financial contributions to politicians and to parties, by gifts of stock and outright bribes to political personages, they generally managed to get what they wanted from the national and the state governments. It was said that Standard Oil did everything to the Ohio legislature except refine it. On one occasion a member of the Pennsylvania legislature was reported to have said: "Mr. Speaker, I move we adjourn unless the Pennsylvania Railroad has some more business for us to transact."

Wholesale bribery was a weapon in the notorious "Erie war" fought by Cornelius Vanderbilt against Jay Gould and Jim Fisk for control of the Erie Railroad. Vanderbilt attempted to take over the Erie by buying stock, a move his antagonists blocked by the simple expedient of printing more stock than he could purchase. When a bill to legalize the issue of the new stock was introduced in the New York legislature, Gould was present with $500,000, and also on hand was a Vanderbilt agent. Exactly how much money was paid out by both parties before Vander-

The Modern Robber Barons

In this cartoon, the millionaires of business are likened to the "robber barons" of the Middle Ages. As the serfs brought tribute to the feudal lords, so farmers, laborers, and small businessmen had to pay tribute in the form of taxes and interest to the masters of the trusts. The term "robber baron" as a descriptive tag for the big businessmen of the period became popular and even passed into historical usage. From *Puck* (1889).

bilt admitted defeat is not known. The market price of legislators during the fight was $15,000 a head. One influential and imaginative leader collected $75,000 from Vanderbilt and $100,000 from Gould.

Before judgment is passed on the relation of business to government, however, it should be noted that in many cases the politicians deliberately created situations where they had to be bought—in effect, they blackmailed businessmen. And whatever indictments may be brought against the lords of business, these men were emphatically products of their environment; even the most crude and crass of their activities reflected prevailing mores in American society. The big corporations did a quick, if sometimes wasteful and ruthless, job of developing the country's potential economic resources. And the businessmen who headed the corporations ran various risks in whatever they did—the risk of overexpansion, the risk of unscrupulous competition. Not every businessman became a Rockefeller or a Gould.

Even the most ruthless of the tycoons were builders rather than wreckers. They were building, perhaps without realizing what they were doing, the basis of a great economic society. By integrating operations and cutting costs, they were, says Frederick Lewis Allen, opening the way to economical mass production: "In the process of playing remunerative games with the tokens that represented capital, the bankers and the steel men had introduced into America something new: twentieth-century industry, undisciplined still, but full of promise."

Survival of the Fittest

Most tycoons liked to claim that they had attained their wealth by exercising the old American and Protestant virtues of hard work, acquisitiveness, and thrift. They had gotten where they were because they deserved it; people who were not so fortunate were lazy, unintelligent, or profligate. In some way, it was all connected with the moral law and with divine will. "God gave me my money," explained John D. Rockefeller.

To many businessmen, the formula of Social Darwinism seemed to explain both their own success and the nature of the society in which they operated. Social Darwinism was Charles Darwin's law of evolution applied to social organization. As expounded by the Englishman Herbert Spencer, it taught that struggle was a normal human activity, especially in economic life. The weak went down, the strong endured and became stronger, and society was benefited because the unfit were eliminated and the fit survived.

Men who had risen to dominance by crushing their competitors were intrigued and comforted by a doctrine that justified any method that succeeded, and they proclaimed that wealth was a reward for competence. Carnegie, who made himself the leading disciple of Spencer in the United States, contended that the natural law of competition was responsible for the great material growth of the country: "It is here; we can not evade it; no substitutes for it have been found; and while the law may be sometimes hard on the individual, it is best for the race, because it insures the survival of the fittest in every department."

According to Social Darwinism, all attempts by labor to raise its wages by forming unions and all endeavors by government to regulate economic activities would fail, because economic life was controlled by a natural law, the law of competition. This coincided with another supposed "law" that seemed to justify business practices and business dominance: the law of supply and demand as defined by Adam Smith and the classical economists. According to them, the economic system was like a great and delicate machine functioning by natural and automatic rules. The greatest among these rules, the law of supply and demand, determined all economic values—prices, wages, rents, interest rates—at a level that was just to all concerned. Supply and demand worked because human beings were essentially economic creatures who understood and followed their own interests, and because they operated in a free market where competition was open to all.

Businessmen mouthed the clichés of classical economics even though the combinations they were creating were undermining the foundations of the free competitive market and modifying, if not destroying, the validity of the law of supply and demand. Samuel C. T. Dodd, the lawyer who devised the trust organization for Standard Oil, spoke glowingly of the unrestrained right of combination.

Tempering the principle of the survival of the fittest was the "gospel of wealth." If the rich held economic power, they also had responsibilities to exercise their power with Christian magnanimity. If God gave the tycoons their money, as John D. Rockefeller believed, it behooved them to use the money for social purposes.

Carnegie himself elaborated on the idea in his book *The Gospel of Wealth* (1901). The man of wealth, he wrote, ought to consider all revenues in excess of his own needs as "trust funds" that he should administer for the good of the community, "thus becoming the mere trustee and agent for his poorer brethren." Carnegie did not believe in giving directly to the poor, for he feared that such charity would have a pauperizing effect. He preferred to contribute to institutions, notably libraries, that presumably would help the poor to help themselves. He and other men of wealth devoted part of their fortunes to philanthropic works.

The notion of private wealth as a public blessing was spread by numerous popularizers. One of the most persistent was Russell H. Conwell, a Baptist minister, who delivered one lecture on the subject, "Acres of Diamonds," more than 6,000 times. "We ought to get rich if we can by honorable and Christian methods," cried Conwell (who got rich by lecturing), "and those are the only methods that sweep us quickly toward the goal of riches."

Conwell was a champion of another concept that was becoming a part of the American myth: the success story, the notion that any poor boy who was industrious and thrifty could succeed in business. Most of the millionaires in the country, Conwell claimed (inaccurately), had begun on the lowest rung of the economic ladder. Another promotor of the success story was Horatio Alger, a New York minister who wrote more than a hundred novels, of which altogether more than 20 million copies were sold. These books rejoiced in such titles as *Andy Grant's Pluck, Tom the Bootblack,* and *Sink or Swim.* In every volume a poor boy from a small town went to the big city to seek his fortune, and by work, perseverance, and luck he became rich.

It was, perhaps, characteristic of optimistic Americans to combine the Darwinian method with the older idea of progress and come up with a hopeful prognostication. Such an analysis was attempted by Lewis Henry Morgan, a pioneer anthropologist, in his *Ancient Society* (1878), in which he traced human development from its first simple beginnings to the complex but beneficent industrial order of the nineteenth century. The works of such men as Morgan stressed that change was gradual and cumulative and that present society was safely linked with the past. Although such writers foresaw a hopeful future, they rejected the concept of unlimited progress that had marked earlier American thought. They also departed from former notions in insisting that change was evolutionary, instead of revolutionary, and that American development was a phase of a larger European or world scheme and not a unique experiment in a specially favored land. Opposing directions taken by American Darwinians are illustrated by the writings of two pioneers in sociology: William Graham Sumner and Lester Frank Ward.

Sumner, a scholar with a tough mind and a sharp tongue, elaborated his theories in lectures at Yale, in magazine articles, and finally in a famous book, *Folkways* (1906). In contradiction to earlier thinkers who had held that man was a free agent actuated by rational powers, Sumner contended that the human mind was molded by circumstances beyond its control and that human activities consisted of routine behavior determined by mechanistic forces. In short, man had no innate ideas and no power to reform his environment. His freedom was limited to certain narrow areas in which tradition permitted him to operate. But within these areas, Sumner insisted, man must have absolute freedom to struggle, to compete, to gratify his instinct for self-interest. The struggle for survival should be allowed to work itself out and should not be delimited by laws or the state. Sumner's devotion to the principle of the survival of the fittest caused him to be known as the foremost American champion of Social Darwinism. Yet his insistence on the freedom to compete caused him to oppose protective tariffs and thus made him a critic of business policy. Essentially, he was trying to preserve the older America of truly free enterprise by employing the new insights of Darwinism.

Standing in direct opposition to Sumner was Lester Frank Ward, although he was just as much a Darwinian as the Yale sage. Ward expressed his concepts in a number of notable books, beginning with *Dynamic Sociology* (1883). He argued that various forces altered the Darwinian process when applied to complex societies. Desire became subordinate to and controlled by intelligence. Mind thus became the master of nature, and man became capable of devising instruments to direct and improve his evolutionary future. The chief goal of modern society, Ward said, was the greatest good of all its members, and the best instrument to attain the goal was government. In contrast to Sumner, who believed that state intervention to remodel the environment was futile, Ward thought that a positive, planning government was society's only hope.

There came to be widespread acceptance of the principle that institutions should meet social needs and thus be "functional." Even in the churches there was an effort to accommodate functional concepts. Such noted ministers and theologians as Washington Gladden, Walter Rauschenbusch, and Shailer Mathews proclaimed that religion had to concern itself with the material conditions in which Christ's children lived. They advocated such causes as improved working conditions, slum clearance, temperance, and industrial peace; and they would in the early years of the twentieth century play an important role in creating the great movement for progressive reform.

Socialists and Single-Taxers

While some Americans questioned the beneficence of capitalism, others proposed more or less drastic changes in the system, and at least a few thought it should be thrown out entirely.

Americans were less inclined than Europeans to adopt genuinely radical programs such as the "scientific socialism" of Karl Marx (whose *Capital,* the first volume of which appeared in 1867, was one of the most influential books ever written) and the violent anarchism of Mikhail Bakunin. But Marxism and anarchism had some following in America, especially among recent immigrants.

The Socialist Labor party, founded in the 1870s, fell under the leadership of Daniel De Leon, an immigrant from the West Indies; other party chiefs hailed from Eastern Europe. Although De Leon aroused something of a following in the industrial cities, the party never succeeded in polling more than 82,000 votes. De Leon's somewhat theoretical and dogmatic approach pleased intellectuals more than workers. A right-wing faction of his party, desiring to cooperate with organized labor, broke away and in 1901 formed the Socialist party.

Native radicals, with less extreme programs, gained a wider following. One of the most influential was Henry George. His angrily eloquent *Progress and Poverty,* published in 1879, was an immediate success; reprinted in successive editions, it became one of the ten best-selling nonfiction works in American publishing history. George addressed himself to the question of why poverty existed amidst the wealth created by modern industry. "This association of poverty with progress is the great enigma of our times," he wrote. "So long as all the increased wealth which modern progress brings goes but to build up great fortunes, to increase luxury and make sharper the contrast between the House of Have and the House of Want, progress is not real and cannot be permanent."

George blamed all this on monopoly, and he proposed a remedy, a "single tax" on the "unearned increment" in the value of land. An increase in the value of land resulted from the growth of society around it. Hence, George argued, the private owner had not earned the increment, and the community should receive it. A tax taking the whole of this increase would supposedly destroy monopolies, distribute wealth more equally, and eliminate poverty. Single-tax societies sprang up in many cities; and in 1886, George, backed by labor and the Socialists, narrowly missed being elected mayor of New York.

Rivaling George in popularity was Edward Bellamy, whose *Looking Backward*, published in 1888, became a best seller within a few years and eventually topped the million mark. Bellamy's book was a novel, a romance of a socialist utopia. It described the experiences of a young Bostonian who in 1887 went into a hypnotic sleep from which he awakened in the year 2000. He found a new social order, based on universal membership in a workers' army, where want, politics, and vice were unknown, and where people were incredibly happy. All this had come about through a peaceful and evolutionary process: trusts had gone on combining with one another until they formed one big trust, and the government had taken this over. Shortly, more than 160 "Nationalist Clubs" sprang up to propagate Bellamy's ideas, and the author devoted the remainder of his life to championing his brand of socialism.

Thirty-eight similar novels appeared in the nineties, although none of them approached Bellamy's in success. The hundreds of thousands of Americans who read Bellamy and the other utopian authors did not wish to see a socialist system established in the United States. Nor were they merely seeking in literary fantasies an escape from the real problems of their times. The great majority were intrigued by the descriptions of societies that were prosperous and stable because government played a large role, and in their own troubled society they saw the need not for a collective state but for a larger place for government.

The Problem of Monopoly

Relatively few Americans shared the views of those who questioned the entire structure of modern capitalism. But a growing number of people were by the end of the century becoming deeply concerned about a particular, glaring aspect of capitalism: the growth of monopoly.

From the beginning, large segments of the population had looked on the proliferation of trusts and other combinations with mistrust and hostility. The popular description of such men as Rockefeller, Carnegie, and Morgan as "robber barons" suggests the attitude of much of the public. So do the reports of numerous conferences, commissions, and study groups, which pointed with alarm to the effects of consolidation on the marketplace. The United States Industrial Commission reported in 1902 that "in most cases the combination has exerted an appreciable power over prices, and in practically all cases it has increased the margin between raw materials and finished products." Trusts were, in other words, viewed as the cause of artificially inflated prices; the influence of the free market was being restricted by the monopolistic practices of a few men. By the end of the century, a startling range of groups had begun to assail monopoly and economic concentration. Laborers, farmers, consumers, small manufacturers, conservative bankers and financiers, advocates of radical change—all joined the attack.

Defenders and opponents of trusts alike looked with alarm at another problem of the modern economy: its disturbing pattern of instability. Although industrial and agricultural production were expanding rapidly, other areas of the economy could not always keep pace. The nation's banks and financial institutions were neither strong enough nor efficient enough to meet adequately the new demands for their services. The increasingly important stock market was riddled with corruption. Above all, the market for goods was not growing as rapidly as the supply.

The result was that even in the best of times, manufacturers and other businessmen flirted constantly with bankruptcy and battled one another ruthlessly for control of existing markets. It was the fear of this cutthroat competition that drove many industrialists to join the trusts and other combinations. But not even consolidation could remove the underlying problems. Beginning in 1873 and continuing until near the end of the century and beyond, the economy moved in an erratic cycle of booms and busts, with severe recessions creating havoc every five or six years, until finally, in 1893, the system seemed on the verge of total collapse.

Disparities of Wealth

One reason for the economic instability was that the new industries were not passing on enough of their profits to their workers to create an adequate market for the goods they were producing. And this growing disparity in the distribution of wealth was producing not only an imbalance between supply and demand but a deep popular resentment. The standard of living may have been rising for virtually everyone, but the gap between rich and poor was visibly widening into an enormous chasm.

According to one estimate early in the century, 1 percent of the families in America controlled nearly 88 percent of the nation's assets. A small but conspicuous new class had emerged whose wealth almost defied description, whose fortunes were so vast that great feats of imagination were often required to enable them to be spent. Andrew Carnegie earned $23 million from his steel company in 1900 alone, and that was only part of his income (in an era in which there was as yet no income tax). John D. Rockefeller's personal wealth was estimated at one time to exceed a billion dollars.

Some of the wealthy—for example, Carnegie—lived relatively modestly and donated large sums to philanthropic causes. Others, however, lived in a conspicuous luxury that earned the resentment of much of the nation. Like a clan of feudal barons, the Vanderbilts maintained, in addition to many country estates, seven garish mansions on seven blocks of New York City's Fifth Avenue. Other wealthy New Yorkers lavished vast sums on parties. The most notorious, a ball on which Mrs. Bradley Martin spent $368,000, created such a furor that she and her husband fled to England to escape the public abuse.

Observing these flagrant displays of wealth were the four-fifths of the American people who lived precariously, and the one-eighth of the population (10 million people) who lived below the commonly accepted poverty line. To those in difficult economic circumstances, the sense of relative deprivation could be as frustrating and embittering as the poverty itself.

THE ORDEAL OF THE WORKER

For the American worker, the experience of industrialization after the Civil War was similar in many ways to the experience before it. It was a mixed blessing. On the one hand, the average standard of living for laborers—in quantitative terms at least—rose significantly during the last decades of the nineteenth century. On the other hand, workers continued to suffer from the wide disparities in distribution of the nation's new wealth; from working conditions that were often arduous and unsafe; and from the intangible problems of adjusting to the impersonal character of work in the factory. Yet the late nineteenth century was also different for workers from any previous era, if for no other reasons than that their numbers were now vastly larger and the dimensions of both the promise and the problems of industrialization far greater.

The New Working Class

The dramatic expansion in the industrial work force, which was both a cause and a result of economic growth, relied on two primary sources. The first was the continuing flow of rural Americans into factory towns and cities—people disillusioned with or bankrupted by life on the farm and eager for new economic and social opportunities. The second source was the great wave of immigration from abroad (primarily from Europe) in the decades following the Civil War—an influx that all but overshadowed all previous periods of immigration. The 25 million immigrants who arrived in the United States between 1865 and 1915 were more than four times the number who had arrived in the sixty years before. The greatest wave of new arrivals came after 1890; by the end of the first decade of the new century, immigrants were debarking in America at the rate of more than 1 million each year.

In the 1870s and 1880s, most of the immigrants came from the nation's traditional sources: England, Ireland, and Northern Europe. Skilled artisans continued to emigrate from Great Britain to take advantage of the expanding opportunities in America. Economic troubles in European industry in the 1880s induced factory workers from Sweden, Germany, and England to move to the United States. And the declining agricultural economy of Northern Europe (and of Ireland, in particular) pressured still others to journey to America. By the end of the century, however, the major sources of immigrants had shifted, with large numbers of Southern and Eastern Europeans (Italians, Poles, Russians, Greeks, Slavs, and others) pouring into the country and into the industrial work force.

The new immigrants were coming to America not only because economic pressures were pushing them from their native lands. They were coming, too, because they felt the pull of the United States—some of it based on realistic expectations of the opportunities available, some of it on distorted and artificial promises. Railroads, in order to dispose of their Western landholdings, painted an alluring picture of America in advertisements overseas. Industrial employers actively recruited workers under the Labor Contract Law, which—until its repeal in 1885—permitted them to pay for the passage of workers in advance and deduct the amount later from their wages. Even after the repeal of the law, employers continued to encourage the immigration of unskilled laborers, often with the assistance of foreign-born labor brokers, such as the Greek and Italian *padrones* who recruited work gangs of their fellow nationals.

The arrival of these new ethnic groups became a complicating factor in the dynamics of the working class, which were already complicated enough. In addition to concerns about wages, about working conditions, about the declining need for skilled artisans in the face of modern technology, and all the other traditional problems of labor, there were now also serious ethnic tensions. Americans of old stock, as well as ethnics who had arrived in earlier years, often looked on the new immigrants with fear and hostility. Industries that had traditionally been dominated by one national group now began to hire members of others—often at lower wages than the older workers. Poles, Greeks, and others began to displace the British and Irish workers in the textile factories of New England. Italians, Slavs, and Poles began to emerge as a major source of labor for the mining industry, which had traditionally been the province of native workers or Northern European immigrants. Within industries, moreover, workers tended to cluster in particular occupations (and thus, often, at particular income levels) by ethnic group. In industry, at least, the idea of the "melting pot"—of Americans of different ethnic backgrounds melding together into one common culture—was of limited applicability.

Wages and Working Conditions

The average standard of living for workers may have been rising in the years after the Civil War; but for many laborers, the return for their labor remained pitifully small. And it appeared even smaller in relation to the vast fortunes the industrial titans were accumulating and even in comparison with the rising incomes of the middle class. At the turn of the century, the average income of the American worker was $400–$500 a year—below the $600 figure that many believed was the minimum required to maintain a reasonable level of comfort. Nor did most workers enjoy any real job security. The boom-and-bust cycle of the economy made laborers in all industries vulnerable; and in some areas, workers were particularly susceptible to losing their jobs because of technological advances or because of the cyclical or seasonal nature of their work. Even those who were spared unemployment could find their wages suddenly and substantially cut in hard times. Few workers, in other words, were ever very far from the prospect of poverty.

But American laborers faced a wide array

Child Labor and Child Luxury

In the early 1900s, "breaker boys" worked long hours picking slate from coal at Pennsylvania mines. Often the coal dust was so thick that the boys could hardly be seen. At the same time, the children of the rich enjoyed everything that money could buy. Here the children of the American multimillionaire George Jay Gould ride the streets of Paris in "voiturettes," French-made miniature automobiles. (*Top*—Photograph by Lewis Hine, International Museum of Photography, George Eastman House, Rochester, N.Y.; *Bottom*—Culver Pictures)

of other hardships as well. There was, first, the painful adjustment to the nature of modern industrial labor: the performance of routine, repetitive tasks, often requiring little skill, on a strict and monotonous schedule, which in 1900 was usually ten hours a day, six days a week. To rural men and women, accustomed to flexible and changing work patterns, the new routine was harsh and disorienting. To skilled craftsmen, whose once-valued tasks were now performed by machines, the new system was impersonal and demeaning. Factory workers were employed, moreover, in plants free from effective government regulation or inspection. The result was workplaces that were often appallingly unsafe or unhealthy. Industrial accidents were frequent and severe. Compensation to the victims, either from their employers or from the government, was rare.

Particular notoriety attached to the plight of women and children working in factories. One-fifth of American women worked in industry, often for wages as low as $6 to $8 a week, a sum below the minimum necessary for survival. Advocates of a minimum wage law for women created a sensation when they brought several women to a hearing in Chicago to testify that low wages and desperate poverty had driven them to prostitution. (It was not, however, sensational enough for the Illinois legislature, which promptly defeated the bill.)

Child labor, which had always existed in the United States, had by 1900 become a national disgrace. At least 1.7 million children under sixteen were employed in factories and fields; 10 percent of all girls between ten and fifteen, and 20 percent of all boys, held jobs. Under the pressure of outraged public opinion, thirty-eight state legislatures had passed child labor laws; but these laws were painfully insufficient. Sixty percent of child workers were employed in agriculture, which was typically exempt from the laws; such children often worked twelve-hour days picking or hoeing in the fields. The laws were hardly more effective for children employed in factories; they set a minimum age of twelve years and a maximum workday of ten hours, but employers often ignored even these minimal standards. In the cotton mills

of the South, children working at the looms all night were kept awake by having cold water thrown in their faces. In canneries, little girls cut fruits and vegetables sixteen hours a day. Exhausted children were particularly susceptible to injury while working at dangerous machines, and they were maimed and even killed in industrial accidents at an alarming rate.

Yet as much as the appalling conditions of many woman and child workers tugged at the national conscience, conditions for men were often worse. In mills and mines, and on the railroads, the American accident rate was higher than that of any industrial nation in the world. As late as 1907, an average of twelve railroad men a week died on the job. In factories, thousands of workers faced such occupational diseases as lead or phosphorus poisoning, against which employers had taken few precautions.

Emerging Organization

Against such conditions, labor fought back by forming unions to bargain collectively with employers. During the Civil War, twenty craft unions were formed; and by 1870, the industrial states counted thirty such organizations, nearly every one of which represented skilled workers. The first attempt to federate separate unions into a single national organization came in 1866, when, under the leadership of William H. Sylvis, the National Labor Union was founded. Claiming a membership of 640,000, it was a polyglot association that included a variety of reform groups having little direct relationship with labor. After the Panic of 1873 the National Labor Union disintegrated and disappeared.

The trade unions experienced stormy times during the hard years of the 1870s. With their bargaining power weakened by depression conditions, they faced antagonistic employers eager to destroy them, and a hostile public that rejected labor's demand for job security. Several of the disputes with capital were unusually bitter and were marked by violence, some of it labor's fault and some not, but for all of which labor received the blame. Startling to most Americans was the exposure of the activities of the "Molly Maguires" in the anthracite coal region of Pennsylvania. A terrorist group, the Mollies operated within the Ancient Order of Hibernians (that is, Irishmen) and intimidated the coal operators with such direct methods as murder. But excitement over this activity was nothing compared to the near hysteria that gripped the country during the railroad strikes of 1877. The trouble started when the principal Eastern railroads announced a 10 percent slash in wages. Immediately, railroad workers, whether organized or not, went out on strike. Rail service was disrupted from Baltimore to St. Louis, equipment was destroyed, and rioting mobs roamed the streets of Pittsburgh and other cities.

The strikes were America's first major labor conflict and a flaming illustration of a new reality in the American economic system: with business becoming national in its scope, disputes between labor and capital could no longer be localized but would affect the entire nation. State militias were employed against the strikers; and finally—and significantly—federal troops were called on to suppress the disorders. The power of the various railroad unions was seriously sapped by the failure of the strikes, and the prestige of unions in other industries was weakened by similar setbacks.

The Knights of Labor

Meanwhile, another national labor organization had appeared: the Noble Order of the Knights of Labor, founded in 1869 under the leadership of Uriah S. Stephens. Instead of attempting to federate unions, as the National Labor Union had done, the Knights organized their association on the basis of the individual. Membership was open to all who "toiled," and the definition of a toiler was extremely liberal: the only excluded groups were lawyers, bankers, liquor dealers, and professional gamblers. The amorphous masses of members were arranged in local "assemblies" that might consist of the workers in a particular trade or a local union or

simply all the members of the Knights in a particular city or district. Presiding laxly over the entire order was an agency known as the general assembly. Much of the program of the Knights was as vague as the organization. Although they championed an eight-hour day and the abolition of child labor, the leaders were more interested in the long-range reform of the economy than in the immediate objectives of wages and hours that appealed to the trade unions.

Under the leadership of Terence V. Powderly, the order entered on a spectacular period of expansion that culminated in a total membership of 700,000 in 1886. Important factors contributing to the increase in numerical strength were a business recession in 1884 that threw many workers out of jobs, and a renewal of industrial strife that impelled unorganized laborers as well as some trade unions to affiliate with the Knights. Not only was the membership enlarged, but the order now included many militant elements that could not always be controlled by the moderate leadership. Against Powderly's wishes, local unions or assemblies associated with the Knights proceeded to inaugurate a series of strikes. In 1885, striking railway workers forced the Missouri Pacific, a link in the Gould system, to restore wage cuts and recognize their union. Although this victory redounded to the credit of the Knights, it was an ephemeral triumph. In the following year, a strike on another Gould road, the Texas and Pacific, was crushed, and the power of the unions in the Gould system was broken. By 1890, the membership of the Knights had shrunk to 100,000, and within a few years the order would be a thing of the past.

The A.F. of L.

Even before the Knights had entered on their period of decline, a rival organization based on an entirely different organizational concept had appeared. In 1881, representatives of a number of craft unions formed the Federation of Organized Trade and Labor Unions of the United States and Canada. Five years later, this body took the name it has borne ever since, the American Federation of Labor (A.F. of L.). Under the direction of its president and guiding spirit, Samuel Gompers, the Federation soon became the most important labor group in the country. As its name implies, it was a federation or association of national trade unions, each of which enjoyed essential autonomy within the larger organization. Rejecting the idea of individual membership and the corollary of one big union for everybody, the Federation was built on the principle of the organization of skilled workers into craft unions.

The program of the Federation differed as markedly from that of the Knights as did its organizational arrangements. Gompers and his associates accepted the basic concepts of capitalism; their purpose was to secure for labor a greater share of capitalism's material rewards. Repudiating all notions of fundamental alteration of the existing system or long-range reform measures or a separate labor party, the A.F. of L. concentrated on labor's immediate objectives: wages, hours, and working conditions. While it hoped to attain its ends by collective bargaining, the Federation was ready to employ the strike if necessary.

As one of its first objectives, the Federation called for a national eight-hour day, to be attained by May 1, 1886, and to be obtained, if necessary, by a general strike. On the target day, strikes and demonstrations for a shorter workday took place all over the country. Although the national officers of the Knights had refused to cooperate in the movement, some local units joined in the demonstrations. So did a few unions that were dominated by anarchists—European radicals who wanted to destroy "class government" by terroristic methods—and which were affiliated with the so-called Black International. The most sensational demonstrations occurred in Chicago, which was a labor stronghold and an anarchist center.

At the time, a strike was in progress at the McCormick Harvester Company; and when the police harassed the strikers, labor and anarchist leaders called a protest meeting at the Haymarket Square. During the meeting, the police appeared and commanded those present to disperse. Someone—the person's identity was never determined—threw a bomb that resulted in the death of seven policemen and injury to sixty-seven others. The police, who on the previous day had killed four strikers, fired into the crowd and killed four more people. News of the Haymarket affair struck cold fear into Chicago and the business community of the nation. Blinded by hysteria, conservative, property-conscious Americans demanded a victim or victims—to demonstrate to labor that it must cease its course of violence. Chicago officials finally rounded up eight anarchists and charged them with the murder of the policemen on the grounds that they had incited the individual who hurled the bomb. In one of the most injudicious trials in the record of American juridical history, all were found guilty. One was sentenced to prison and seven to death. Of the seven, one cheated his sentence by committing suicide, four were executed, and two had their penalty commuted to life imprisonment.

Although some of the blame for the Haymarket tragedy was unloaded on the A.F. of L., at least as much fell on the Knights, who had had almost nothing to do with the May demonstrations. In the public mind, the Knights were dominated by anarchists and Socialists. The Knights never managed to free themselves from the stigma of radicalism as the A.F. of L. did.

The Homestead Strike

Some of the most violent strikes in American labor history occurred in the economically troubled 1890s. Two of the strikes, the one at the Homestead plant of the Carnegie Steel Company in Pennsylvania and the one against the Pullman Palace Car Company in the Chicago area, took place in companies controlled by men who prided themselves on being among the most advanced of American employers: Andrew Carnegie, who had written magazine articles defending the rights of labor, and George M. Pullman, who had built a "model town" to house his employees.

The Amalgamated Association of Iron and Steel Workers, which was affiliated with the American Federation of Labor, was the most powerful trade union in the country. It

The Haymarket Tragedy
This is a contemporary artist's conception of the bomb exploding among the police. Although eight men were convicted of complicity in the crime, the actual bomb thrower was never discovered. (Library of Congress)

had never been able, however, to organize all the plants of the Carnegie Steel Company, the largest corporation in the industry; of the three major steel mills in the Carnegie system, the union was a force in only one, the Homestead plant. In 1892, when the strike occurred, Carnegie was in Scotland, and the direction of the company was in the hands of Henry Clay Frick, manager of Homestead and chairman of the Carnegie firm. Despite his earlier fine words about labor, Carnegie had decided with Frick before leaving to operate Homestead on a nonunion basis, even if this meant precipitating a clash with the union.

The trouble began when the management announced a new wage scale that would have meant cuts for a small minority of the workers. Frick abruptly shut down the plant and asked the Pinkerton Detective Agency to furnish 300 guards to enable the company to resume operations on its own terms. (The

Pinkerton Agency was in reality a strike-breaking concern.)

The hated Pinkertons, whose mere presence was enough to incite the workers to violence, approached the plant on barges in an adjacent river. Warned of their coming, the strikers met them at the docks with guns and dynamite, and a pitched battle ensued on July 6, 1892. After several hours of fighting, which brought death to three guards and ten strikers and severe injuries to many participants on both sides, the Pinkertons surrendered and were escorted roughly out of town. The company and local law officials then asked for militia protection from the Pennsylvania governor, who responded by sending the entire National Guard contingent, some 8,000 troops, to Homestead. Public opinion, at first sympathetic to the strikers, turned against them when an anarchist made an attempt to assassinate Frick. Slowly workers drifted back to their jobs.

The Pullman Strike

A dispute of greater magnitude and equal bitterness, although involving less loss of life, was the Pullman strike in 1894. The Pullman Palace Car Company leased sleeping and parlor cars to most of the nation's railroads. At its plant near Chicago it manufactured and repaired cars. The company had built the 600-acre town of Pullman, containing dwellings that were rented to the employees. George M. Pullman, inventor of the sleeping car and owner of the company, liked to exhibit his town as a model solution of the industrial problem and to refer to the workers as his "children."

Nearly all of the workers were members of a union, a very militant one, the American Railway Union. This union had recently been organized by Eugene V. Debs, a labor leader formerly active in the Railroad Brotherhoods, an older railworkers' union affiliated with the A.F. of L. Becoming disgusted with the Brotherhoods' lack of interest in the lot of the unskilled workers, he had formed his own union, which soon attained a membership of 150,000, mainly in the Middle West.

The strike at Pullman began during the winter of 1893–1894, when the company slashed wages, through five separate reductions, by an average of 25 percent. With revenues reduced by depression conditions, there was some reason for the company's action; but the cut was drastic, and several workers who served on a committee to protest to the management were discharged. At the same time, Pullman refused to reduce rentals in the model town, even though the charges were 20 to 25 percent higher than for comparable accommodations in surrounding areas. The strikers appealed to the Railway Union for support, and that organization voted to refuse to handle Pullman cars and equipment.

The General Managers' Association, representing twenty-four Chicago railroads, prepared to fight the boycott. Switchmen who refused to handle Pullman cars were discharged. Whenever this happened, the union instructed its members to quit work. Within a few days thousands of railroad workers in twenty-seven states and territories were on strike, and transportation from Chicago to the Pacific coast was paralyzed.

Ordinarily, state governors responded readily to appeals from strike-threatened business, but the governor of Illinois was different. John P. Altgeld had pardoned the Haymarket anarchists remaining in prison. Business was not likely to appeal to such an executive for aid, and Altgeld was not the man to employ militiamen to smash a strike.

Bypassing Altgeld, the railroad operators besought the national government to send regular army troops to Illinois. At the same time, federal postal officials and marshals were bombarding Washington with information that the strike was preventing the movement of mail on the trains. President Grover Cleveland was inclined to gratify the companies, and so was his attorney general, Richard Olney, a former railroad lawyer and a bitter foe of labor. Cleveland and Olney decided that the government could employ the army to keep the mails moving; and in July 1894, the president, over Altgeld's protest, ordered 2,000 troops to the Chicago area.

At Olney's suggestion, government lawyers obtained from a federal court an order restraining Debs and other union officials from interfering with the interstate transportation of the mails. This "blanket injunction" was so broad that it practically forbade Debs and his associates to continue the strike. They ignored the injunction and were arrested, tried for contempt of court (without a jury), and sentenced to six months in prison. With federal troops protecting the hiring of new workers and with the union leaders in a federal jail, the strike quickly collapsed.

It left a bitter heritage. Labor was convinced that the government was not a neutral arbiter representing the common interest, but a supporter of one side alone. Debs emerged from prison a martyr in the eyes of workingmen, a convert to Marxian socialism, and a dedicated enemy of capital.

Despite all the organizations that were formed and all the strikes and demonstrations that were so hopefully launched, labor accomplished relatively little for its cause in the years between 1865 and 1900. Its leaders could point to a few legislative victories: the abolition by Congress in 1885 of the Contract

Labor Law; the establishment by Congress in 1868 of an eight-hour day on public works and in 1892 of the same workday for government employees; and a host of state laws governing hours of labor and safety standards, most of which were not enforced. But an overwhelming majority of employers still regarded labor as a force to be disregarded when possible and crushed when practicable, and the American public in overwhelming numbers considered unions to be alien and dangerous elements in the national economy.

Labor's greatest weakness was that only a small part of its vast strength was organized. The A.F. of L. with its half-million members and the Railroad Brotherhoods (engineers, conductors, firemen, trainmen) represented the skilled workers; but the mass of laborers were not enrolled in any union. All told, only 868,500 workers were union members at the turn of the century. Big business was firmly entrenched; big labor awaited the future.

SUGGESTED READINGS

Several general accounts of the late nineteenth century emphasize industrial development and its consequences. John A. Garraty, *The New Commonwealth* (1968), has a broad focus; while Edward C. Kirkland, *Industry Comes of Age: Business, Labor, and Public Policy, 1860–1897* (1961), lays greater emphasis on industry itself. Samuel P. Hays, *The Response to Industrialism, 1885–1914* (1957), offers a challenging interpretation of the period. Other general studies include Carl Degler, *The Age of the Economic Revolution* (1977), a work of balance and thoroughness; Daniel Boorstin, *The Americans: The Democratic Experience* (1973), a wide-ranging social and cultural history of the era that combines a controversial interpretive stance with valuable examination of cultural institutions; and Thomas C. Cochran and William Miller, *The Age of Enterprise* (1942), a basic study with an economic focus.

Technological advances are considered in Roger Burlingame, *Engines of Democracy: Inventions and Society in Mature America* (1940); Lewis Mumford, *Technics and Civilization* (1934), a provocative interpretive work; George Daniels, *Science and Society in America* (1971); and Nathan Rosenberg, *Technology and American Economic Growth* (1972). Robert W. Bruce, *Bell* (1973), examines the invention (and inventor) of the telephone. Frank E. Hill is the author of *Ford* (1954) and, with Allan Nevins, of *Ford*, 3 vols. (1954–1962), studies of the auto pioneer and his company. Peter Temin, *Steel in Nineteenth Century America* (1964), considers one of the largest of the emerging industries. Frederick A. White, *American Industrial Research Laboratories* (1961), illuminates an important component of industrial growth; and Robert Conot, *A Streak of Luck* (1979), is a biography of Thomas Edison, the head of the most famous of such laboratories. Richard N. Current, *The Typewriter and the Men Who Made It* (1954), discusses the invention of a machine that revolutionized business practices.

Railroad expansion, the key to industrial growth, is examined in George R. Taylor and I. D. Neu, *The American Railroad Network, 1861–1890* (1956). John F. Stover, *The Life and Decline of the American Railroad* (1970), is another good survey. On specific areas of rail development, see Richard C. Overton, *Burlington West* (1941) and *Gulf to Rockies* (1953), for the West; John F. Stover, *The Railroads of the South, 1865–1900* (1955); and Edward C. Kirkland, *Men, Cities, and Transportation*, 2 vols. (1948), for New England. Railroad management is the subject of Thomas C. Cochran, *Railroad Leaders* (1953); and railroad consolidation is examined in Edward G. Campbell, *The Reorganization of the American Railroad System* (1938). Gabriel Kolko, *Railroads and Regulation, 1877–1916* (1965), challenges traditional views of the reasons for reform. See also Lee Benson, *Merchants, Farmers, and Railroads* (1955), and George H. Miller, *Railroads and the Granger Laws* (1971), for more on the subject of regulation. Robert Fogel, *Railroads and American Economic Growth* (1964), questions the centrality of railroads to economic development.

The emergence of the modern corporation is examined in an important book by Alfred P. Chandler, Jr., *The Visible Hand: The Managerial Revolution in American Business* (1977). Other valuable studies include Glenn Porter, *The Rise of Big Business* (1973), a succinct overview; Glenn Porter and H. C. Livesay, *Merchants and Manufacturers* (1971); and Alfred P. Chandler, Jr., *Strategy and Structure: Chapters in the History of American Industrial Enterprise* (1966). Matthew Josephson, *The Robber Barons* (1934), is a classic (and critical) study of the industrial titans. On individual corporate leaders, see Alfred D. Chandler, Jr., *Pierre S. du Pont and the Making of the Modern Corporation* (1971); Harold C. Livesay, *Andrew Carnegie and the Rise of Big Business* (1975); Allan Nevins, *Study in Power: John D. Rockefeller*, 2 vols. (1953), David F. Hawkes, *John D.: The Founding Father of the Rockefellers* (1980); Joseph Wall, *Andrew Carnegie* (1970); and Bernard Weisberger, *The Dream Maker* (1979), on William Durant, the founder of General Motors.

The ideology of late nineteenth-century capitalism is described in Edward C. Kirkland, *Dream and Thought in the Business Community, 1860–1900* (1956); Sidney Fine, *Laissez Faire and the General Welfare State: A Study of Conflict in American Thought, 1865–1901* (1956); and Irvin G. Wylie, *The Self-Made Man in America* (1954). An important study of the work ethic is Daniel T. Rodgers, *The Work Ethic in Industrial America, 1850–1920* (1978). Louis Galambos, *The Public Image of Big Business in America, 1880–1940* (1975), is an examination of attitudes toward business as seen in various popular periodicals. Richard Hofstadter, *Social Darwinism in American Thought* (rev., 1955), is the basic work on the subject. Robert G. McCloskey, *American Conservatism in the Age of Enterprise* (1951), is also valuable. Samuel Chugerman, *Lester F. Ward: The American Aristotle* (1939), and Arthur E. Morgan, *Edward Bellamy* (1944), examine two important social critics. Charles A. Barker, *Henry George* (1955), considers another.

Henry Pelling, *American Labor* (1960), is a useful survey of the subject, with several chapters on this period. A more focused overview is Melvyn Dubofsky, *Industrialism and the American Worker, 1865–1920* (1975). Herbert G. Gutman, *Work, Culture, and Society in Industrializing America* (1976), is a collection of provocative essays about the lives of American workers. David Montgomery, *Beyond Equality* (1975) and *Workers' Control in America: Studies in the History of Work, Technology, and Labor Struggles* (1979), are important social histories. On Gompers and the early A.F. of L., see Stuart Kaufman, *Samuel Gompers and the Origins of the American Federation of Labor* (1978); Philip Taft, *The A.F. of L. in the Time of Gompers*, 2 vols. (1957–1959); and Gompers's autobiography, *Seventy Years of Life and Labor*, 2 vols. (1975). Susan E. Kennedy, *If All We Did Was to Weep at Home* (1979), and Barbara Wertheimer, *We Were There* (1977), examine women workers. Stanley Buder, *Pullman* (1967), is a study of the town and the strike. Henry David, *The Haymarket Affair* (1936), discusses the celebrated incident. J. H. M. Laslett, *Labor and the Left* (1970), studies radical influences on the labor movement. Daniel Nelson, *Managers and Workers: Origins of the New Factory System in the United States, 1880–1920* (1975), examines new forms of interaction. Gerald N. Grob, *Workers and Utopia* (1961), considers labor reform visions.

The Rise of the City

18

The Steerage, by
Alfred Stieglitz
Stieglitz (1864–1946)
was crossing the Atlan-
tic in 1907 when he
photographed these
European immigrants
bound for America
who were crowded
into the cheapest quar-
ters of the ship on
which he was traveling.
Unlike other photogra-
phers of his era (for ex-
ample, Jacob Riis),
Stieglitz chose the im-
migrants as a subject
not to publicize or
document their misery.
He was, rather, trying
to extend the use of
photography as an art
form—as creative ex-
pression in itself, not
simply an imitation of
other arts. Picasso re-
marked of this photo-
graph, "This is exactly
what I have been try-
ing to say in paint."
(Detail from Alfred Stieglitz,
The Steerage [1907]. Photo-
gravure. Collection, The Museum of Modern Art, New
York. Gift of Alfred Stieglitz)

Many Americans—following the lead of the influential historian Frederick Jackson Turner—viewed the closing of the Western frontier as the most profound social development of the late nineteenth century. In fact, the greatest folk movement of the era was not the westward migration, but the shift of population from country to city.

The growth of industry, the expansion of commerce, the discovery of new technologies—all combined to encourage an expansion of the nation's urban population and a transformation of the character of the city. It was there that most of the factories and corporate offices were located, there that the new economic system had its seat. And it was from the city that there emerged a new set of social and cultural values that would ultimately extend to all areas of the nation. The United States, which had throughout its history been a primarily rural nation, was being reshaped in an urban mold.

This change was not without cost.

The rapid growth of the urban population placed an enormous strain on the capacities of most metropolitan communities. Roads, sewers, transportation facilities, housing, social services—all proved inadequate to the new demands being placed on them. Urban political systems fell victim to corruption and ineptitude. And American sensibilities often rebelled at the new and intimidating pace of urban life.

Yet for all the problems, the city continued its rise to dominance in American society—in part because of economic developments over which individuals seemed to have little control, in part because the diversity and excitement of urban life proved alluring to increasing numbers of Americans. Traditional rural values changed slowly in response to the influence of the urban environment, but change they did. By the end of the nineteenth century, the city had clearly emerged as the central focus of American economic, social, and cultural life.

THE NEW URBAN GROWTH

The movement to cities was occurring simultaneously throughout much of the Western world. From countries or regions that were industrializing slowly if at all, people moved to other countries or other regions that were industrializing rapidly. Rural people from both America and Europe, therefore, made their way to the business and industrial centers of the United States in search of opportunity.

The City's Lure

"We cannot all live in cities, yet nearly all seem determined to do so," Horace Greeley wrote soon after the Civil War. " 'Hot and cold water,' baker's bread, gas, the theatre, and the streetcars . . . indicate the tendency of modern taste." The city lured people because of the many conveniences it enjoyed years before such things reached the village or the farm. It drew people because of its institutions of entertainment and culture—not only its theaters and other amusements but also its libraries and museums, its superior schools and colleges. It attracted people, above all, because it offered opportunities for employment at higher pay than the countryside afforded. The lure of the city persisted even though many who came were disappointed and urban life acquired some very unpleasant characteristics.

In the half-century from 1860 to 1910, the rural population almost doubled, but the urban population increased seven times. In

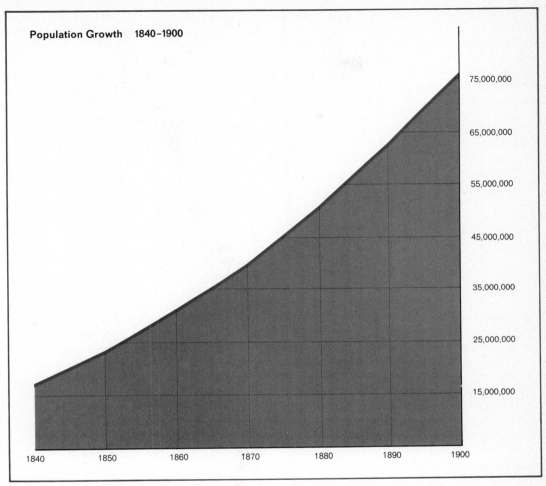

Population Growth   1840–1900

75,000,000

65,000,000

55,000,000

45,000,000

35,000,000

25,000,000

15,000,000

1840   1850   1860   1870   1880   1890   1900

The population of the United States increased significantly during every decade between 1840 and 1900. At the close of the century, there were more than four times the number of Americans as in 1840 and more than twice the number as at the beginning of the Civil War.

1860, approximately one-sixth of the people lived in towns of 8,000 or larger; by 1900, one-third of the people. The number of cities with more than 50,000 inhabitants was 16 in 1860 and 109 in 1910. By 1920, the census revealed that for the first time, a majority of the American people lived in "urban" areas—defined as communities of 2,500 people or more. The population of the New York urban area (the city and its environs) grew from less than 1 million in 1860 to more than 3 million in 1900. Even more spectacular was

the growth of Chicago, which had 100,000 inhabitants in 1860 and more than a million at the end of the century. Towns and cities were getting bigger and more numerous in all sections of the country. And the vast urban-industrial complex that was taking shape was linked in all its parts by rapid railroad transportation and instantaneous telegraphic communication.

While the cities gained, some rural parts of the country were actually losing population (as had happened to a much smaller extent in the early nineteenth century). During the 1880s, for instance, the number of inhabitants was decreasing in two-fifths of Pennsylvania's total area, three-fifths of Connecticut's, more than half of Ohio's and Illinois's, and five-sixths of New York's. People seldom moved directly to a city from the farms. As the historian Arthur M. Schlesinger has observed, "the tendency was to move from the countryside to the nearest hamlet, from the hamlet to the town, and from the town to the city." So for a time the country town retained some importance as a market and a cultural center, but more and more the city overshadowed it. The city was the ultimate goal of restless farm and village folk. They and the immigrants, most of whom had also come from rural areas, made up the great majority of urban dwellers.

The New Immigration

The arrival of great numbers of new immigrants from Europe and elsewhere, which had done so much to transform the nature of the industrial work force, helped to transform the character of the nation's cities as well. The immigration had a profound effect, first, on the sheer size of the urban population. But it changed the social fabric of the city, too, in countless ways, particularly after 1880, when the flow of new arrivals began to include large numbers of people from Southern and Eastern Europe. By the 1890s, about 52 percent of all immigrants came from these new regions, as opposed to fewer than 2 percent in the 1860s.

In earlier stages of immigration, the majority of the new arrivals had headed west. Most Germans, for example, moved to the farming regions of the Midwest; and those who chose urban life settled not on the East Coast, but in such Midwestern cities as St. Louis, Cincinnati, and Milwaukee. Nearly all of the Scandinavians took up land in the Middle West or on the Great Plains. Those who settled in cities were usually relatively well educated and upwardly mobile people: businessmen, professionals, and skilled workers. The one exception had been the Irish, who had tended to congregate in Eastern cities as unskilled workers. Even they, however, had by the late nineteenth century achieved new and enhanced social and economic levels.

The new immigrants of the late nineteenth century, by contrast, settled almost without exception in industrial cities, where they occupied largely unskilled jobs. They lacked the capital to buy land and begin farming in the West. They needed immediate employment. And only the city—with its factories, stockyards, railroads, and other industries—could provide it. The city had another appeal for them as well. As strangers in an alien land, they could in the city find refuge in communities of their fellow nationals.

Most of the new European immigrants were people from rural backgrounds, and the adjustment to city life was often a painful one. To help ease the transition therefore, national groups usually formed close-knit ethnic communities within the cities: Italian, Polish, Jewish, Slavic, and other neighborhoods (often known as "immigrant ghettoes") that attempted to re-create in the New World many of the features of the Old. It was impossible, of course, to reproduce in the modern city the social fabric of the farm villages from which many immigrants came—the seasonal work patterns, the intimate communal ties passed on from generation to generation, the strength of family life based on common economic activities. But the ethnic neighborhoods did provide immigrants with a sense of belonging to a coherent community. The newcomers could find newspapers and theaters in their native languages, stores selling their native foods, church and fraternal organizations that provided links with their national pasts. And they could move through large areas of the city surrounded by their fellow countrymen, an experience that helped cushion them against the loneliness of being in a new land. The immigrants also maintained close ties with their native countries. They kept in contact with relatives who had remained behind. Some returned to Europe after a few years; far more attempted to help bring the rest of their families to America.

The cultural cohesiveness of the ethnic communities clearly eased the pain of separation from the immigrant's native land. Whether it helped immigrants to become absorbed into the economic life of America is a more difficult question to answer. It is clear that some ethnic groups (Jews and Germans in particular) advanced economically more rapidly than others (for example, the Irish). Why that was so is a matter of considerable controversy. But one explanation is that, by huddling together in ethnic neighborhoods, immigrant groups tended to reinforce the cultural values of their previous societies. When those values were particularly well suited to American life—as was, for example, the high value that Jews placed on education—then this ethnic identification helped members of a group to advance. When other values predominated—maintenance of community solidarity, strengthening of family ties, preservation of order—progress was often less rapid.

In virtually all immigrant communities, however, the strength of ethnic ties had to compete against another powerful force: the desire for assimilation. Most of the new arrivals had come to America with romantic visions of the New World. And however disillusioning they might find their first contact with the United States, they usually retained the dream of becoming true "Americans." Even many first-generation immigrants worked hard to rid themselves of all vestiges of their old cultures, to become thoroughly Americanized. Second-generation immigrants were even more likely to attempt to break with the old ways, to assimilate themselves completely into what they believed was a genuinely American culture. Some even looked with contempt on parents who continued to value traditional ethnic habits and values. The tension between the desire to become assimilated and the strength of ethnic ties was one that countless immigrants and their children wrestled with for years.

The arrival of these vast numbers of new immigrants, and the conspicuousness with which many of them clung to old ways and created culturally distinctive communities, provoked fear and resentment among many native Americans, in much the same way earlier arrivals had done. Some people reacted against the immigrants out of simple prejudice, while others honestly wondered if they could be absorbed into national life. Laborers, fighting to raise their incomes and improve their working conditions, were incensed by the willingness of the immigrants to accept lower wages and to take over the jobs of strikers.

With the mounting of the alien tide, the first demands for immigration restrictions rose in the land. Congress acted in 1882 to exclude the Chinese. In the same year, it passed a general immigration law denying entry to certain undesirables—convicts, paupers, idiots—and placed a tax of 50 cents on every person admitted. Later legislation of the 1890s enlarged the proscriptive list and increased the tax. These measures reflected a rising fear that continuing unlimited immigration would exhaust the resources of the nation and endanger its social institutions. They kept out only a small number of aliens, however, and were far from fulfilling the purposes of the extreme exclusionists. The latter group worked for a literacy test, a device intended to exclude immigrants from Eastern and Southern Europe. Congress passed a literacy law in 1897, but President Grover Cleveland vetoed it. Powerful business interests, the employers of cheap labor, continued to oppose restrictions.

The Urban Landscape

The city was a place of remarkable contrasts. It had homes of almost unimaginable size and grandeur, and hovels of indescribable squalor. It had conveniences unknown to earlier generations, and problems that seemed beyond the capacity of society to solve. Both the attractions and the problems were a result of one central fact: the stunning pace with which cities were growing. The demands of (and the potential for profit from) the urban population helped to spur important new technological and industrial developments. But the rapid expansion also produced misgovernment, poverty, overcrowding, traffic jams, filth, epidemics, and conflagrations. The pace of growth was simply too fast for planning and building to keep pace. "The problem in America," one muni-

Tenement Street
The teeming life of a tenement district and something of its squalor are suggested in this late nineteenth-century view of Mulberry Street in New York City. (Library of Congress)

cipal reformer said, "has been to make a great city in a few years out of nothing."

One of the greatest problems of this precipitous growth was that of finding housing for the thousands of new urban residents who were pouring into the cities every day. For the wealthy, housing was seldom a worry. The availability of cheap labor, and the increasing accessibility of tools and materials, reduced the cost of building in the late nineteenth century and permitted anyone with even a moderate income to afford a house. The richest urban residents often lived in palatial mansions in the heart of the city. Others of the rich, and many of the moderately well-to-do, took advantage of the

less expensive land on the edges of the city and settled in new suburbs. Chicago, for example, boasted in the 1870s of having nearly one hundred residential suburbs connected with the city by railroad and offering the joys of "pure air, peacefulness, quietude, and natural scenery." Boston, too, saw the development of some of the earliest "streetcar suburbs"—Dorchester, Brookline, and others—which catered to both the wealthy and the middle class. New Yorkers of moderate means settled in the new suburb of Harlem, on the northern fringes of Manhattan, and commuted downtown by trolley or riverboat.

The majority of urban residents, how-

The Mixed Crowd [1890]

In his famous book How the Other Half Lives *(1890) the Danish-born newspaper reporter Jacob A. Riis had this to say about what he called "the mixed crowd" as it developed in New York City during the 1880s:*

When once I asked the agent of a notorious Fourth Ward alley how many people might be living in it I was told: one hundred and forty families, one hundred Irish, thirty-eight Italian, and two that spoke the German tongue. Barring the agent herself, there was not a native-born individual in the court. The answer was characteristic of the cosmopolitan character of lower New York, very nearly so of the whole of it, wherever it runs to alleys and courts. One may find for the asking an Italian, a German, a French, African, Spanish, Bohemian, Russian, Scandinavian, Jewish, and Chinese colony. Even the Arab, who peddles "holy earth" from the Battery as a direct importation from Jerusalem, has his exclusive preserves at the lower end of Washington Street. The one thing you shall vainly ask for in the chief city of America is a distinctively American community. There is none; certainly not among the tenements. . . .

The once unwelcome Irishman has been followed in his turn by the Italian, the Russian Jew, and the Chinaman, and has himself taken a hand at opposition, quite as bitter and quite as ineffectual, against these later hordes. Wherever these have gone they have crowded him out, possessing the block, the street, the ward with their denser swarms. . . .

A map of the city, colored to designate nationalities, would show more stripes than the skin of a zebra, and more colors than any rainbow.

---

ever, could not afford to move to the suburbs or own their own housing. Instead, they stayed in the city centers and rented. And because demand was so high and space so scarce, they had little power with which to exact high standards. Landowners, to maximize their rental incomes, tried to squeeze as many residents as possible into the smallest available space. In Manhattan, for example, the average population density in 1894 was 143 people per acre—a rate higher than that of some of the most crowded cities of Europe (Paris had 127 per acre, Berlin 101) and far higher than any other American city. More than a million poor New Yorkers were jammed into "tenements"—a term that had originally referred simply to a multiple-family rental building, but that had by the late nineteenth century come to be applied to slum dwellings only. The first tenements, built in 1850, had been hailed as a great improvement in housing for the poor. "It is built with the design of supplying the laboring people with cheap lodgings," a local newspaper commented, "and will have many advantages over the cellars and other miserable abodes which too many are forced to inhabit." But tenements themselves became miserable abodes. The typical structure was three to five stories high, with many windowless rooms, little or no plumbing or central heating, and perhaps a row of privies in the basement. A New York state law of 1879 required a window in every bedroom of tenements built thereafter, but developers complied by providing openings onto dank and sunless airshafts. Jacob Riis, a Danish immigrant and New York newspaper reporter, shocked many middle-class Americans in 1890 with his sensational (and some would say sensationalized) descriptions of tenement life in *How the Other Half Lives*. Slum dwellings, he said, were almost universally sunless, practically airless, and "poisoned" by "summer stenches." "The hall is dark and you might stumble over the children pitching pennies back there."

Urban growth posed monumental challenges to the transportation systems of the nation's cities. Old downtown streets were often too narrow for the heavy traffic that was beginning to move over them. Some were paved with cobblestones, but most lacked a hard surface and were a sea either of mud or of dust—depending on the weather. In the last decades of the century, more and more streets were paved, usually with wooden blocks, bricks, or asphalt; but paving could not keep up with the laying out of new thoroughfares. By 1890, Chicago had surfaced only about 600 of its more than 2,000 miles of streets.

It was not simply the conditions of the streets, however, that impeded urban transportation. It was the numbers of people who needed to move every day from one part of the city to another—back and forth between their homes and their workplaces, churches, stores, and schools. Private vehicles could not answer the need; the solution lay in the development of mass transportation. Streetcars drawn on tracks by horses had been introduced into some cities even before the Civil War. New York had 16 lines by 1866, using 800 cars and nearly 8,000 horses. But the horsecars, while faster than the omnibuses and other smaller vehicles that had served as public transportation in the past, were still not fast enough. As a result, cities embarked on new efforts to improve their mass transit. New York in 1870 opened its first elevated railway, whose steam-powered trains moved rapidly above the city streets on massive iron structures; but they inflicted noise, filth, and often dangerously hot embers on the pedestrians below. New York, Chicago, San Francisco, and other cities experimented with cable cars, towed by continuously moving underground cables. Richmond, Virginia, introduced the first electric trolley line in 1888, and by 1895 such systems were operating in 850 towns and cities, with a total of 10,000 miles of track. Boston in 1897 opened the first American subway when it put a mile and a half of its trolley lines underground.

Cities were growing upward as well as outward—a result of the convergence of technological discoveries and the need for new space in the increasingly crowded downtown areas. The first modern "skyscraper"—a relatively modest (by later standards) ten-story building in Chicago constructed in 1884—inaugurated a new era in urban architecture. Once builders perfected the technique of constructing tall buildings with cast-iron and then steel beams, and once other inventors produced the electric elevator to make possible quick and safe vertical movement, no obstacle remained to even higher buildings. The greatest figure in the early development of the skyscraper was the Chicago architect Louis Sullivan, who introduced many of the modern, functional elements to the genre—large windows, sheer lines, limited ornamentation—in an attempt to emphasize the soaring height of the building as its most distinctive feature. Sullivan's students—among them Frank Lloyd Wright—expanded the influence of these innovations still further, and applied them to low buildings as well as tall ones.

The increasing congestion of the city, and the slow response to that congestion in terms of new services, produced a number of serious health and safety hazards. One was fires. In one major city after another, major conflagrations in the late nineteenth century swept through downtowns, destroying blocks of buildings (many of them still constructed of wood) and forcing the almost total reconstruction of large areas. Chicago suffered its "great fire" in 1871, and Boston a disastrous fire the same year. Other cities—Baltimore, for example, and San Francisco, where a tremendous earthquake produced a catastrophic fire in 1906—experienced similar disasters. The great fires were terrible experiences for those who lived through (or died in) them. But they were also important events in the development of the cities involved. Not only did they induce new strategies to prevent or limit future fires—the construction of fireproof buildings, the development of professional fire departments, and more; they also forced cities to rebuild at a time when new technological and architectural innovations were available. Many of the modern, high-rise downtowns of American cities arose out of the rubble of great fires.

An even greater hazard than fire was disease, especially in poor neighborhoods with inadequate sanitation facilities. But while slums suffered the worst from disease, the entire city was vulnerable. An epidemic that began in a poor neighborhood could (and often did) spread easily into other neighborhoods as well. Even though the germ theory of disease was known to public health experts, few municipal officials recognized the relationship of sewage disposal and water contamination to such epidemic diseases as typhoid fever and cholera. As late as the turn of the century, most city dwellers relied on private vaults and cesspools for the disposal of human wastes. Flush toilets and public sewer systems began to appear in the 1870s, but for many years they failed to solve the problem—largely because such systems emptied their sewage into open ditches within the city limits or into streams nearby, often polluting the city's own water supply in the process.

Urbanization brought more than new conveniences and new insecurities. It also

Chicago, 1910

Stunning growth in the late nineteenth and early twentieth centuries taxed American cities up to, and often beyond, their limits. This view looking south on Dearborn Avenue in Chicago illustrates one of the characteristic problems of metropolitan America during that era: remarkable traffic congestion, as horse-drawn vehicles jostled with electric streetcars and swarms of pedestrians on the streets. (Courtesy, the Chicago Historical Society)

brought a new concept of time and organization. "The complex interrelationship of life in the modern city called for unprecedented precision," writes the historian Oscar Handlin. "The arrival of all those integers who worked together, from whatever part of the city they inhabited, had to be coordinated to the moment. There was no natural span for such labor; arbitrary beginnings and endings had to be set and adhered to. The dictatorship of the clock and the schedule became absolute." Thus the modern city forced the rural people who were increasingly flowing into it to shift their notions of time—which traditionally had been a matter of human whim and of such natural phenomena as the rising and setting of the sun—to reflect the importance of precise scheduling.

Rural Americans and Europeans alike reacted to the city, therefore, with marked ambivalence. It was a place of strong allure and great excitement. Yet it also was a place of alienating impersonality, of a new feeling of anonymity, of a different kind of work with which the individual could feel only limited identification. To many, moreover, it was a place of poverty and sin. Native migrants in particular looked with alarm on the foreigners with their strange customs, on the saloons, dance halls, prostitutes, and other features of urban life that confronted them when they arrived. Yet however ambivalent country people may have felt about the city, urban influence grew steadily in the late nineteenth century. Not only those who lived in the city but many who remained outside it found themselves affected by urban customs and values. More and more, the city was setting the pattern for American character and culture.

Boss Rule

New arrivals to the cities, and foreign immigrants in particular, faced severe obstacles. Many could not speak English. Few knew how to deal with the laws and customs of the new land. Large numbers found themselves indigent for long periods after their arrival before they could find work. There was, in short, an enormous demand for institutions to help immigrants adjust to American urban life.

Private charitable societies answered part of this need. But generally these organizations were run by middle-class humanitarians who insisted on middle-class standards of morality and had little understanding or appreciation of immigrant cultures. Many such societies operated on the assumption that poverty was more commonly a result of laziness and vice than of misfortune, and they confined their help to what they called the "deserving poor"—those who truly could not help themselves (at least according to the standards of the organizations themselves, which conducted elaborate "investigations" to separate the "deserving" from the "undeserving"). Other charitable societies—for example, the Salvation Army, which began operating in America in 1879, one year after it was founded in London—concentrated more on religious revivalism than on the relief of the homeless and hungry.

The limits of these private charitable organizations forced many immigrants to look elsewhere for assistance. They could not look to the government. It would be many years before government at any level—local, state, or federal—would assume any substantial responsibility for welfare work. Instead, the main welfare agency was often the urban machine—one of America's most distinctive and remarkable political institutions. The machine owed its existence to the potential voting power of the large immigrant communities. Any politician who could mobilize that power stood to gain enormous influence or public office. And so there emerged a group of urban "bosses," most themselves of foreign birth or parentage, many of them Irish (they had the advantage of English as a native language). The major function of the boss was to win votes for his organization. And to do so, he engaged in a wide array of activities. To win the loyalty of his constituents, a boss might provide them with occasional relief—a basket of groceries or a bag of coal. He might step in to save from jail those arrested for petty crimes. When he could, he found work for the unemployed. Above all, he rewarded many of his followers with political jobs and with opportunities to rise in the political organization.

Yet machines were not simply mechanisms for maintaining political power. They were also vehicles for making money. Machine politicians enriched themselves and their allies through various forms of graft and corruption. Some of it might be fairly open—what the outspoken Tammany politician George Washington Plunkitt called "honest graft." For example, a politician might discover in advance where a new road or streetcar line was to be built, buy an interest in the land near it, and profit when the city had to buy the land from him or when property values rose as a result of the construction. But there was also a great deal of covert graft. A politician awarded contracts for the construction of streets, sewers, public buildings, and other projects to contractors (usually at prices well above the real cost) on condition that he himself receive a portion of the contract money—that is, a "kickback." In addition to awarding contracts, a municipal official could sell franchises for the operation of such public utilities as street railways, waterworks, and electric light and power systems. Few city bosses were as expansively corrupt as William M. Tweed, boss of New York City's Tammany Hall. Tweed's notorious "ring" once spent $11 million of city funds to build a modest courthouse. And at times, apparently, Tammany officials raided the public treasury in even more direct and blatant ways. But if Tweed was not entirely typical of the urban boss, his exuberant excesses set a pattern that many other machine politicians attempted to emulate in the years following his demise in 1872.

Several factors made the continuation of boss rule possible despite the abuses and corruption. One, of course, was the power of immigrant voters, who were less concerned with political morality than with obtaining desperately needed services. The machines provided services; reformers usually did not. Another was the link between the political organizations and some of the wealthiest and most prominent citizens of many cities—businessmen who profited from their dealings with bosses and resisted efforts to overthrow them. Still another was the structural weakness of many city governments. Within the municipal government, no single official usually had decisive power or responsibility. Instead, authority was generally

Thomas Nast on Boss Tweed

Nast, the most famous political cartoonist of the late nineteenth century, made his reputation through his savage—and effective—caricatures of Boss William M. Tweed of New York's Tammany Hall. Here, he lampoons Tweed's predicament after the 1871 election that swept his "Ring" out of power. Tweed is pictured as Marius in defeat among the ruins of Carthage. (The Bettmann Archive)

"WHAT ARE YOU LAUGHING AT? TO THE VICTOR BELONG THE SPOILS."

divided among many officeholders—the mayor, the aldermen, and others—and was limited by the state legislature, which often had the ultimate authority over municipal affairs. There was, in other words, a vacuum where strong, centralized leadership was needed. The boss, by virtue of his control over his machine, formed a sort of "invisible government" that made up for the inadequacy of the regular government. He might not hold an official position himself. (Leaders of Tammany Hall, for example, seldom held public office.) But through his organization, on which the politicians of his party depended for election, he often controlled a majority of those who were in office.

The urban machine was not without competition. Reform groups frequently mobilized public outrage at the corruption of the bosses and often succeeded in driving machine politicians from office. Tammany, for example, saw its candidates for mayor and other high city offices lose almost as often as they won in the last decades of the nineteenth century. But the reform organizations typically lacked the permanence of the machine; and more often than not, their power faded after a few years. Only basic, permanent, structural change in the institutions of government, many critics of the machine were by 1900 beginning to argue, could effectively rescue the city from "boss rule."

KNOWLEDGE FOR A NEW SOCIETY

The rise of the city affected more than just the material and political circumstances of urban Americans. It had a profound influence on the American mind. Basic changes in old assumptions, most of them emerging first in cities and then radiating outward into the nation at large, transformed American culture. The demands of urban, industrial life forced the nation's educational system to assume new roles. Not all these changes were directly related to the nature of urban life; but most of them owed, if not their origins, then at least their influence to the growing importance of the city—which created a fluid, intellectual environment in which new ideas and systems could flourish.

The New Theorists

The single most profound change in the intellectual life of the United States—and indeed of the whole Western world—in the late nineteenth century was the widespread acceptance of the theory of evolution. The doctrine, associated most prominently with the English scientist Charles Darwin, although it was in fact the result of many years of theorizing by many men, taught that mankind had evolved to its present state from earlier forms of life (and most immediately

from apes). The various species had resulted from a process of natural selection. Here, in other words, was a theory that challenged almost every tenet of traditional American faith. If Darwin and the scientists who were spreading his message were right, then man was not necessarily innately endowed by God with a higher nature. He was only a biological organism, another form of animal life—the highest form, it was true, but still like the other animals that had had their day in past ages. Instead of history being the working out of a divine plan, as many Americans had believed, it was a random process dominated by the fiercest or luckiest competitors.

At first, the theories of Darwinism met widespread resistance from educators, theologians, and even many scientists. By the end of the century, however, the evolutionists had converted most members of the urban professional and educated classes to their point of view. Even most middle-class Protestant theologians had accepted the doctrine, making subtle alterations in theology to accommodate it. Evolution had become enshrined as an irrefutable theory in schools and universities; virtually no serious scientist any longer questioned its basic validity—although there remained disagreement over the details of its application.

Unseen by most urban Americans at the time, however, the rise of Darwinism was contributing to a deep schism between the new, cosmopolitan culture of the city—which was receptive to new ideas such as evolution—and the more traditional, provincial culture of the rural areas—which remained wedded to fundamentalist religious beliefs and older values. Urban Americans smugly assumed that Darwinism had become as basic a scientific truth as the idea that the earth revolved around the sun, that challenges to it were now restricted to only a few superstitious people. In fact, opposition to the theory of evolution remained strong and deep among vast numbers of Americans—as the country would discover in the 1920s and even in the 1980s, when fundamentalist groups began to organize to challenge the doctrine.

Out of the controversy over Darwinism emerged a wide range of new intellectual currents. There was the Social Darwinism of William Graham Sumner and others, which industrialists used so enthusiastically to justify their favored position in American life. But there were also more sophisticated philosophies—among them the doctrine that became known as "pragmatism" and that seemed to many to be peculiarly the product of Americans and peculiarly suited to the nation's changing material civilization. William James, a famous Harvard psychologist (and brother of the novelist Henry James), was the most prominent publicist of the new theory, although earlier intellectuals such as Charles S. Peirce, and later ones such as John Dewey, were at least equally important in its development and dissemination. According to the pragmatists, who accepted the idea of organic evolution, modern society should rely for guidance not on inherited ideals and moral principles but on the test of scientific inquiry. No idea or institution was valid, they claimed, unless it worked. Even religious beliefs, James insisted, were subject to the test of experience. If faith helped an individual understand his world, then it was valid for that person; if it did not, then it was not. "The ultimate test for us of what a truth means," James wrote, "is the conduct it dictates or inspires."

An expanding network of social scientists soon brought this same concern for scientific inquiry into areas of thought long dominated by traditional orthodoxies. New economists, such as Richard T. Ely and Simon Patten, challenged old economic assumptions and argued for a more active and pragmatic use of the discipline. Sociologists such as Edward A. Ross and Lester Frank Ward urged the adaptation of scientific method to the solution of social and political problems. Historians such as Frederick Jackson Turner and Charles Beard challenged prevailing assumptions by arguing that economic factors more than spiritual ideals had been the governing force in historical development. John Dewey, for many decades one of the most influential of all American intellectuals, proposed a new approach to education that placed less emphasis on the rote learning of traditional knowledge and more on a flexible, democratic approach to schooling, one that enabled students to acquire knowledge that would help them deal with the realities of their society. The scientific method, he believed, would be the governing principle of this new, "instrumental" education.

Toward Universal Schooling

A society that was coming to depend increasingly on specialized skills and scientific knowledge was, of course, a society with a fundamental need for effective systems of education. The late nineteenth century, therefore, was a time of rapid expansion and reform of American schools and universities.

Most influential, perhaps, was the spread of universal free public education. That had long been an ideal of American society, but only after the Civil War did it truly begin to become a reality. In 1860, for example, there were only 100 public high schools in the entire United States. By 1900, the number had reached 6,000. And by 1914, that number had doubled—and along with it the number of students attending the high schools. Even more spectacular was the expansion of elementary and grade-school education. By 1900, compulsory attendance laws were in effect in thirty-one states and territories.

Most of this expansion occurred in urban areas. Regions with few major cities—such as the South and parts of the Middle West—trailed far behind the urban-industrial areas in providing public education to their citizens. And in the South in particular, what educational facilities there were were commonly unavailable to blacks.

Although opportunities for education above the high-school level did not expand to nearly the same degree as those below it, colleges and universities were proliferating rapidly in the late nineteenth century. They benefited particularly from great new resources made available by the national government. The federal government, by the Morrill Land Grant Act of the Civil War era, had donated land to states for the establishment of colleges to teach, among other things, agriculture and the mechanical arts. After 1865, particularly in the South and West, states began to take advantage of the law to strengthen existing institutions or to found new ones. In all, sixty-nine "land-grant" institutions came into existence in the last decades of the century—among them the state university systems of California, Illinois, Minnesota, and Wisconsin.

Supplementing the resources of the government were the millions of dollars contributed by business and financial tycoons, who endowed private institutions. The motives of the magnates were various: they were influenced by the gospel of wealth; they believed that education would blunt class differences; they realized that the demands of an industrial society called for specialized knowledge—or they were simply vain. Men such as Rockefeller and Carnegie gave generously to such schools as Harvard, Chicago, Northwestern, Syracuse, Yale, Princeton, and Columbia. Other philanthropists founded new universities and thereby perpetuated their family names—Vanderbilt, Johns Hopkins, Cornell, Tulane, and Stanford.

Taking over as president of Harvard in 1869 at the age of thirty-five, Charles W. Eliot pioneered a break with the traditional curriculum. The usual course of studies at American universities emphasized classical and humanistic courses; and each institution prescribed a rigid program of required courses. Under Eliot's leadership. Harvard dropped most of its required courses in favor of an elective system and increased its course offerings to stress the physical and social sciences, the fine arts, and modern languages. Soon other institutions in all sections of the country were following Harvard's lead.

Eliot also renovated the Harvard medical and law schools, raising the requirements and lengthening the residence period, and again the Harvard model affected other schools. Improved technical training in other professions accompanied the advances in medicine and law. Both state and private universities hastened to establish schools of architecture, engineering, education, journalism, and business. The leading center for graduate study, based on the German system with the Ph.D. degree as its highest award, was Johns Hopkins University (founded in 1876). In 1875, there were only 399 graduate students in the United States. By 1900, the number had risen to more than 5,000.

The post–Civil War era saw, too, an important expansion of educational opportunities for women—although such opportunities continued to lag far behind those available to men (and were almost without exception denied to black women). At the end of the Civil War, women wishing to pursue a higher education had to choose among a very few women's colleges (such as Mount Holyoke) and even fewer coeducational institutions—three, to be exact (including Oberlin). But in the years after the war, an important network of women's colleges developed—most of them as the result of donations from philanthropists. Among them were Vassar, Wellesley, Smith, Bryn Mawr, Wells, and Goucher. Some of the larger private universities created on their campuses separate colleges for women. But the greatest educational gains for women—and the ones that most clearly augured the pattern of education in the future—came in the Middle West, where the new state universities began to admit women along with men.

Publishing and Journalism

America's urban society required not only educational institutions, but new vehicles for

Smith Students in Art Class
Smith College, in Northampton, Massachusetts, was one of a number of institutions founded in the late nineteenth century to fulfill what educators saw as a special mission: the education of young women for their proper roles in society. The new women's colleges represented an important advance for American women, providing them with opportunities not just to learn, but to prepare for careers outside the home. However, the curriculum of these colleges was also designed to reinforce the prevailing assumptions that women occupied a "special sphere" in society, that they were not to think of themselves as candidates for conventionally male careers. (Smith College Archives)

transmitting news and information. As a result, the nature of the country's publishing and journalism was transformed in the decades following the Civil War. Between 1870 and 1910, the circulation of daily newspapers increased nearly ninefold (from under 3 million to more than 24 million), a rate three times as great as the rate of population increase. In the process, the character of journalism changed in several ways: (1) Newspapers became predominantly news organs, while editorial opinion and the editorial page declined in importance. (2) The nature of news changed. Politics received less attention, and there was an increasing emphasis on what was called the human interest story. (3) Journalism became a recognized and respected profession. Salaries of reporters doubled. Able and educated men were attracted to the profession, and schools of journalism were begun on university campuses. (4) Newspapers became corporations, impersonal business organizations similar to those emerging in industry, their worth often reckoned in millions of dollars. At the same time, they tended to become standardized. The press services furnished the same news to all their subscribing papers, and syndicates came into existence to provide their customers with identical features, columns, editorials, and pictures. By the turn of the century there were several newspaper chains, the most powerful being William Randolph Hearst's, which by 1914 numbered nine newspapers and two magazines. Thus the newspapers conformed to and reinforced the trend toward uniformity that characterized American society as a whole.

Another major change occurred in the nature of American magazines. In the past, mostly weekly and monthly periodicals had been literary journals. Now, beginning in the 1880s, there appeared a new kind of magazine, designed to appeal to the masses and achieve a mass circulation. One of the important pioneers of the popular magazine was Edward W. Bok, who took over the *Ladies' Home Journal* in 1899 and, by employing writers who aimed their material at a mass female audience, built the circulation of the journal to over 700,000. By the end of the century, there was a large array of popular magazines, priced at 5 to 15 cents, some of them with circulations of up to a million.

CULTURE IN A METROPOLITAN SOCIETY

Foreign observers and even some American intellectuals in the late nineteenth century often viewed the culture of the United States with contempt. "There is little to nourish and delight the sense of beauty there," wrote the English critic Matthew Arnold in 1888. Mark Twain, a more knowledgeable critic, expressed an equally dismissive view of American culture in 1873, when, with Charles Dudley Warner, he published a novel satirizing the new urban-industrial society. The book's title suggests its message: *The Gilded Age.* To Twain, Warner, and others, American life, despite its glittering surface, was essentially acquisitive and corrupt, with little cultural depth.

Whatever the quality of culture and society in late nineteenth-century America, it was clear that the growth of industry and the rise of the city were having profound effects on them. Some writers and artists—the local-color writers of the South, for example; even Mark Twain, in such novels as *Huckleberry Finn*—responded to the new civilization by evoking an older, more natural world. But others grappled directly with the modern order, exposing its problems and offering solutions.

The Literature of Reality

One of the strongest impulses in late nineteenth- and early twentieth-century American literature was the quest for the re-creation of social reality. There were, of course, many writers who continued to produce novels and poetry of adventure and romance; indeed it was such books that generally attracted the greatest popular audiences. But the nation's most serious writers began to probe more compelling issues: the oppression and suffering that they believed the urban-industrial society had created. The trend toward urban realism found an early voice in Stephen Crane, who—although best known for his novel of the Civil War, *The Red Badge of Courage* (1895)—was the author of a powerful indictment of the plight of the working class. In *Maggie: A Girl of the Streets* (1893), Crane created a sensation with his glum descriptions of urban poverty and slum life. Even more influential in encouraging writers to abandon the genteel traditions of earlier times and turn to the social dislocations of the present was Theodore Dreiser. In 1900, he published the startling *Sister Carrie,* the story of a poor young woman caught in and corrupted by the maelstrom of modern urban life. He dealt so frankly with sex—showing how poverty left women open to exploitation by men—that his publisher suppressed the book for a time.

Many of Dreiser's contemporaries joined him in chronicling the oppression of America's poor. Frank Norris published *The Octopus* in 1901, an account of a struggle between oppressed wheat ranchers and powerful railroad interests in California. Another novel, *The Pit* (1903), attacked exploitation in the grain markets of Chicago. Upton Sinclair's *The Jungle* (1906) exposed abuses in the American meat-packing industry and helped to inspire legislative action to deal with the problem. One of the greatest, and certainly one of the most prolific of the literary realists was William Dean Howells. Unlike the writers who focused on extremes of poverty and

The Sausages [1906]

From Upton Sinclair, The Jungle *(Garden City, N.Y.: Doubleday, 1906):*

There was never the least attention paid to what was cut up for sausage; there would come all the way back from Europe old sausage that had been rejected, and that was mouldy and white—it would be dosed with borax and glycerine, and dumped into the hoppers, and made over again for home consumption. There would be meat that had tumbled out on the floor, in the dirt and sawdust, where the workers had tramped and spit uncounted billions of [tuberculosis] germs. There would be meat stored in great piles in rooms; and the water from leaky roofs would drip over it, and thousands of rats would race about on it. It was too dark in these storage places to see well, but a man could run his hand over these piles of meat and sweep off handfuls of the dried dung of rats. These rats were nuisances, and the packers would put poisoned bread out for them; they would die, and then rats, bread, and meat would go into the hoppers together.

injustice, Howells described the common and the average, exposing the shallowness and corruption in ordinary American life styles. In *The Rise of Silas Lapham* (1884), he offered an unflattering portrait of the self-made businessman. His later novels, written during the more turbulent years of the 1890s and the early twentieth century, dealt more explicitly with social problems and injustices.

Other critics of American society responded to the new civilization not by attacking it but by withdrawing from it. Some, such as Henry Adams, effected an intellectual withdrawal. His great autobiography, *The Education of Henry Adams* (1906), portrayed a man disillusioned with and unable to relate to his society, even though he continued to live in it. Others retreated physically from the United States. Henry James, one of the preeminent writers of the era, lived the major part of his adult life in England and Europe and produced a series of complex, coldly realistic novels—*The American* (1877), *Portrait of a Lady* (1881), *The Ambassadors* (1903), and many others—that showed the impact of Europe on Americans, and his own ambivalence about the merits of the two civilizations.

Art and Social Realism

American art through most of the late nineteenth century remained as it had always been: undernourished and overshadowed by Europe. Almost all major American artists received their education overseas, painted in a European style (although many chose American subjects), and exhibited—if they exhibited at all—in foreign galleries. By 1900, however, important changes were already well under way. Now, nearly every major American city had a museum or gallery of at least modest proportions in which native artists could display their work and in which European masterpieces—many of them purchased by the great industrial titans—could be seen. And a number of American artists, although they continued to study and even at times to live in Europe, broke from the Old World traditions and experimented with new styles. John La Farge, for example, made use of light and color in ways that anticipated the French impressionists. Winslow Homer, perhaps the greatest American artist of the era, was vigorously and almost blatantly American in his paintings of New England maritime life and other native subjects. James McNeil Whistler was one of the first Western artists to appreciate the beauty of Japanese color prints and to introduce Oriental concepts into American and European art.

By the first years of the new century, however, some American artists were turning even more decisively from the traditional academic style (a style perhaps best exemplified in America by the brilliant portraitist

The Armory Show, 1913
The 1913 art exhibition at the New York City Armory shocked traditionalists by displaying the work of such European "moderns" as Cézanne and Matisse. The Armory show, however, inspired many young American artists, helping to move them beyond the Ashcan revolt—which for all its social significance had broken little new artistic ground—and into new, often nonrepresentational fields: into modernism. (Museum of Modern Art)

John Singer Sargent). Instead, younger painters were exploring the same grim aspects of modern life that were becoming the subject of American literature. Influenced by the work of the French impressionists but shaped, too, by the tenor of American urban life, members of the so-called Ashcan School produced work startling in its naturalism and stark in its portrayal of the social realities of the era. John Sloan, for example, attempted to capture the dreariness of American urban slums in his paintings; George Bellows caught the vigor and violence of his time in paintings and drawings of prize fights; Edward Hopper chose as his theme the starkness (and often the loneliness) of the modern city. Ultimately, many of these young artists would move beyond the Ashcan revolt to explore the fields of expressionism and abstraction; for example, they showed their interest in new forms when, in 1913, they helped stage the famous "Armory Show" in New York City, which displayed the works of the French postimpressionists and some American moderns. For a time, however, their work closely paralleled that of the naturalist writers of the era. Bewailed one critic in 1902: "[The prevailing theme of American art] is

sadness, heart-searching, misgiving, melancholy—now spiritual, now sensuous—revolt against surrounding circumstance."

Use of Leisure

Many Americans, especially members of the urban middle and professional classes, found by the late nineteenth century that they had more leisure time than ever before, and incomes sufficient to enable them to gratify their demands for pleasure. Workers, too, had more free time. Farming had been a virtually full-time occupation; now, with the rise of a large class of factory workers, many Americans found their lives neatly compartmentalized, with a rigid distinction between work and leisure that had not existed in the past. The search for forms of recreation and entertainment that resulted from these changes produced, among other things, the rise of organized spectator sports.

Most popular of all the organized sports and well on its way to becoming the national game was baseball. Its origins stretched back to 1839, when Abner Doubleday, a civil engineering student, laid out a diamond-shaped field at Cooperstown, New York, and attempted to standardize the rules governing the playing of such games as town ball and four old cat, the ancestors of baseball. By the end of the Civil War, interest in the game had grown rapidly. More than 200 teams or clubs existed, some of which toured the country playing rivals; they belonged to a national association of "Baseball Players" that had proclaimed a set of standard rules. These teams were amateurs or semiprofessionals; but as the game waxed in popularity, it offered opportunities for profit, and the first professional team, the Cincinnati Red Stockings, appeared in 1869. Other cities soon fielded professional teams, and in 1876 the present National League was organized, chiefly by Albert Spalding. Soon a rival league appeared, the American Association. Competition between the two was intense, and in 1883 they played a postseason contest, the first "world's series." The American Association eventually collapsed, but in 1900 the American League was organized.

The second most popular game, football, arose in the colleges and universities. At first football had been played by rival student groups at the same school. Then, in 1869, occurred the first intercollegiate game in America, between Princeton and Rutgers, with twenty-five men on each team. Soon other Eastern schools fielded teams, organized a conference, the American Intercollegiate Football Association, and attempted to standardize the rules.

As football grew in popularity, it spread to other sections, notably to the Middle Western state universities, soon destined to overthrow the Eastern schools as the powers of the game. It also began to exhibit those taints of professionalism that have marked it

An Early Football Game
Here, in an 1889 contest between Cornell and Rochester, the ball is being put into play by a "scrum," similar to that of rugby. The ball was placed on the ground and a circle of players tried to kick it out to their respective teammates. The "father of American football," one-time Yale star Walter Camp, led in modernizing the game. He persuaded the rule-makers to reduce the number of players to eleven on each side, to permit the offensive team to put the ball into play from a line of scrimmage, with a quarterback, and to require the team to advance the ball five yards in three plays (and then, later, ten yards in four plays) or give it up to the opposing team. Camp also helped to eliminate excessive roughness from what had been a remarkably brutal sport. He selected the first "All-American" eleven. (Library of Congress)

ever since. Some schools employed as players "ringers," tramp athletes who were not even registered as students. In an effort to eliminate such abuses, Amos A. Stagg, athletic director and coach at the University of Chicago, led in forming the Western Conference, or Big Ten, in 1896.

A wide range of other sports also emerged, both as entertainment for spectators and as recreation for large groups of participants. Basketball, the only major sport completely American in origin, was invented in 1891 at Springfield, Massachusetts, by Dr. James A. Naismith. Boxing, which had long been a disreputable activity popular primarily among the urban lower classes, became by the 1880s a more respectable and highly popular sport—particularly after the adoption of the Marquis of Queensbury rules (by which fighters were required to wear padded gloves and to fight in rounds limited to three minutes) and the emergence of the first modern boxing hero, John L. Sullivan, who became heavyweight champion of the world in 1882. Golf and tennis, still primarily participatory rather than spectator sports, experienced a rapid increase in popularity among relatively wealthy Americans—usually the only people who could afford to join the exclusive clubs where facilities for the sports were available.

The new leisure, like the new art and literature, displayed one of the characteristic and troubling features of American life in the industrial era: the inequitable distribution of wealth and opportunity. In small towns and rural areas, the new spectator sports and other forms of entertainment were, at best, a distant vision—brought enticingly into view through newspapers and magazines, but still frustratingly out of reach. Even within cities, there were sharp divisions between the way the middle classes and the working classes spent their leisure time. The growth of industry and the rise of the city may have produced great new wealth and diversity in American life, but it also had created social divisions and cultural tensions that would, in the course of the 1890s, produce the nation's greatest crisis since the Civil War.

SUGGESTED READINGS

General studies of the rise of the city in American life include Blake McKelvey, *The Urbanization of America* (1963); Constance M. Green, *The Rise of Urban America* (1965); Charles N. Glaab and Andrew T. Brown, *A History of Urban America* (1967); and Arthur M. Schlesinger, *The Rise of the City, 1878–1898* (1933). Sam Bass Warner, Jr., *The Urban Wilderness* (1972), examines the physical landscape of the city, while his *Streetcar Suburbs* (1962) describes urban expansion. Lewis Mumford, *The Culture of the Cities* (1938) and *The City in History* (1961), are broad, historical views of the city. A number of works examine the issue of social mobility in urban society. Two of the most important are by Stephan Thernstrom: *Poverty and Progress* (1964) and *The Other Bostonians* (1973). Michael Frisch, *Town into City* (1972); Richard Sennett, *Families Against the City* (1970); and Clyde Griffen and Sally Griffen, *Natives and Newcomers* (1977), also examine the issue. Howard Chudacoff, *Mobile Americans* (1972), considers geographical mobility as well. Stephan Thernstrom and Richard Sennett (eds.), *Nineteenth Century Cities* (1969), is a valuable collection of essays.

Oscar Handlin, *The Uprooted*, rev. ed. (1973), has long been a standard work on the subject of immigration but has come under criticism from other historians of the subject. See, for example, Thomas Kessner, *The Golden Door: Italian and Jewish Immigrant Mobility* (1977); Josef Barton, *Peasants and Strangers: Italians, Rumanians, and Slovaks in an American City* (1975); Virginia Yans-McLaughlin, *Family and Community: Italian Immigrants in Buffalo, 1880–1930* (1977); John W. Briggs, *An Italian Passage* (1978); John B. Duff, *The Irish in the United States* (1971); and Victor Greene, *For God and Country: The Rise of Polish and Lithuanian Ethnic Consciousness in America* (1975). Other useful studies of immigration in general include John Bodnar, *Immigration and Industrialization* (1977); Marcus Hansen, *The Immigrant in American History* (1940); Maldwyn A. Jones, *American Immigration* (1960); David Ward, *Cities and Immigrants* (1965); and Barbara Solomon, *Ancestors and Immigrants* (1965). For specific immigrant groups, see Francis L. K. Hsu, *The Challenge of the American Dream* (1971), on the Chinese; Moses Rischin, *The Promised City: New York's Jews* (1962); and Humbert S. Nelli, *The Italians of Chicago* (1970). Nathan Glazer and Daniel P. Moynihan, *Beyond the Melting Pot* (1963), is a controversial study of the process of assimilation. Leonard Dinnerstein and David Reimers, *Ethnic Americans: A*

History of Immigration and Assimilation (1975), and Milton M. Gordon, *Assimilation in American Life* (1964), offer different perspectives. Thomas Sowell, *Ethnic America* (1981), is a controversial interpretation. Robert D. Cross, *The Church and the City* (1967), examines immigrant religion. John Higham, *Strangers in the Land* (1955), is a superb study of nativism, while his *Send These to Me* (1975) is a valuable collection of essays on immigration and related issues.

Robert H. Bremner, *From the Depths* (1956), is an important study of urban poverty. James T. Patterson, *America's Struggle Against Poverty* (1981), examines poverty (rural as well as urban) in the twentieth century. Thomas L. Philpott, *The Slum and the Ghetto* (1978), examines poor urban neighborhoods. The most prominent contemporary studies of the ghetto are those of Jacob Riis: *How the Other Half Lives* (1890), *Children of the Poor* (1892), and *The Battle with the Slum* (1902). For a general account of reform efforts, see Allen F. Davis, *Spearheads for Reform* (1967). For more specific reform issues, see Marvin Lazerson, *Origins of the Urban School* (1971); Selwyn K. Troen, *The Public and the Schools* (1975); David B. Tyack, *The One Best System: A History of American Urban Education* (1974); Barbara Rosencrantz, *Public Health and the State* (1972); James H. Cassedy, *Charles V. Chapin and the Public Health Movement* (1962); and James F. Richardson, *The New York Police* (1970).

John M. Allswang, *Bosses, Machines and Urban Voters* (1977), is a good introduction to the machine.

On Tammany Hall in New York, see Alexander B. Callow, *The Tweed Ring* (1966), and Seymour Mandelbaum, *Boss Tweed's New York* (1965). Lyle Dorsett, *The Pendergast Machine* (1968), examines Kansas City's organization. Zane Miller, *Boss Cox's Cincinnati* (1968), is a study of machine rule in that city. On urban political reformers, see John Sproat, *The Best Men* (1968).

General studies of social thought in the late nineteenth century include Morton White, *Social Thought in America* (1949); D. W. Marcell, *Progress and Pragmatism* (1974); and Charles Forcey, *The Crossroads of Liberalism* (1961), which traces the origins of early twentieth-century progressive ideals. Lawrence Cremin, *The Transformation of the School* (1961), is a broad study of changes in education, which should supplement the more specific works on urban schools cited above. Frank Luther Mott, *American Journalism*, rev. ed. (1962), is a standard work. Larzer Ziff, *The American 1890s: Life and Times of a Lost Generation* (1966), examines the literary life of the era. See also Jay Martin, *Harvests of Change* (1967). Gunther Barth, *City People* (1980), examines urban leisure activities; while John A. Lucas and Ronald Smith, *Saga of American Sport* (1978), is a general study of the subject. Dale Somers, *The Rise of Sports in New Orleans* (1972), is a local study. Lewis Mumford, *The Brown Decades* (1931), examines art in the late nineteenth century; while Christopher Tunnard and H. H. Reed, *American Skyline* (1955), consider architecture.

From Stalemate to Crisis

19

The Tariff Battle
This June 1889 cartoon in *Puck,* the satirical political journal, illustrates the importance that the issue of the tariff had assumed in late nineteenth-century American politics. Critics of protection (among them the cartoonist whose work is shown here) argued that tariffs raised the price of manufactured goods for farmers; that they choked up American markets, leading to overproduction, surpluses, and unemployment; and that they represented the power of a few influential manufacturers arrayed against the combined will of the people. In fact, the economic problems that so many politicians were blaming on the tariff were the result of far more complicated issues—issues that were all but ignored in public life until the critical years of the 1890s. (Library of Congress)

The United States in the late nineteenth century was changing as rapidly and decisively as in any period of its history. Its economy was expanding; its cities were growing; its entire society was becoming far more diverse and complex. Many of these changes brought tremendous benefits to the American people; others produced enormous and perplexing problems. But all of these developments put new strains upon the nation's traditional social arrangements and political institutions. Growth and change brought not only progress but disorder; and it was to government, gradually, that Americans would begin to look for leadership in the search for stability.

Yet American government during much of this period seemed peculiarly ill-equipped to deal with the challenges confronting it. In the face of unprecedented dilemmas, it responded with passivity and confusion. Its leaders were, for the most part, political mediocrities. The issues with which it was concerned were generally of minor relevance to the problems at hand. Rather than taking active leadership of the nation's dramatic transformation, the American political system for nearly two decades after the end of Reconstruction was locked in a rigid stalemate—watching the remarkable changes that were occurring in the nation and doing little to affect them.

Many observers pointed to the doldrums of the American party system as the major cause of this inaction. For in many respects, the two parties had by the 1880s come to seem almost identical. "Tenets and policies, points of political doctrine and points of political practice have all but vanished," wrote the English historian James Bryce in 1888. "All has been lost, except office or the hope of it." And indeed there was much in the behavior of both the Democrats and the Republicans to support that view. Both parties strove to avoid taking positions on the great issues of the day: the rise of monopoly, the conflict between labor and management, the decline of the agrarian economy, and the defects of a financial system that produced a major collapse every twenty years or so. They tried, rather, to obscure such issues; and politicians often did appear more concerned, as Bryce had lamented, with government jobs than governmental principles.

But the torpor of the party system was more a symptom than the cause of the political stalemate of the late nineteenth century. The retreat from ideology may have been more pronounced during this period than usual, but seldom do American parties take sharply defined stands on major issues. The real problem in American politics in the 1880s and 1890s was that social and economic conditions were changing more rapidly than were ideas about public policy. Most people recognized that there were problems; few people had any idea what to do about them. And as a result, there was little in American political life to counteract the influence of conservative assumptions and powerful private interests.

The result was a political system in which problems and grievances could fester and grow without any natural outlet. And it was not surprising, under the circumstances, that by the 1890s the United States was heading into a grave national crisis. Difficulties emerged from all sides. An economic depression, the worst in American history to that point, produced widespread suffering and instability. American labor grew militant and at times violent. Above all, American farmers—building on years of slow, determined political effort—raised a powerful challenge to the established order through what became known as the Populist revolt. By the mid-1890s, many people were beginning to fear that the nation faced revolution or collapse. Virtually everyone was forced to recognize that American society, for all its progress, faced serious maladjustments.

deny confirmation of the men Hayes had named to replace Arthur and Cornell. Stubbornly, the president refused to retreat and kept on transmitting new appointments until finally the Senate ratified his choices.

The Martyrdom of Garfield

Fortunately for the faction-rent Republicans, prosperity had returned by the time of the election of 1880. An increased export trade and an upward spurt in industrial and agricultural production signaled the end of the depression that had plagued the nation in the mid-1870s and the beginning of another boom period. But the Republican leaders knew that not even prosperity could guarantee victory: they had to patch up their dissensions and settle on a nominee who could unite the party for another contest. Grant, backed by Conkling and the Stalwarts, was again a candidate, while the Half-Breeds were divided between Blaine and Sherman. At the Republican convention Grant led for thirty-five ballots but could not reach a majority. Then the anti-Grant forces united to nominate a "dark horse," James A. Garfield, a veteran congressman from Ohio. Since Garfield was known as a Half-Breed, the convention, to conciliate the Stalwarts, gave the second place on the ticket to Chester A. Arthur, the Conkling henchman just dismissed from office by Hayes.

With the ancient and ill Tilden unavailable, the Democrats were without a leader. They acted as though they were also without hope of victory. As their candidate, they selected General Winfield Scott Hancock, who had won some fame as a corps commander in the Union army but was hardly a commanding national figure. Their apparent purpose was to refute the usual Republican charges of Democratic disloyalty in the Civil War. Also, having witnessed the success of the Republicans in running generals, they wanted to try their luck with a Democratic officer against Garfield, who had been a volunteer general. Although the platform called for a revenue tariff, it emphasized the "great fraud" of the election of 1876 as the paramount issue.

During the bitter campaign, which revolved around such questions as Garfield's complicity in the Crédit Mobilier scandal and alleged errors committed by Hancock in the war, the Democratic candidate was pressed for a statement on the tariff. He replied that it was entirely a "local issue." As a description of how tariff schedules were decided in Congress, where every representative fought for the interests of his own particular constituency, his phrase was reasonably accurate; but it constituted a virtual repudiation of the platform and removed the tariff as a campaign issue. In November Garfield piled up a decisive electoral majority of 214 to 155. But his popular vote was only about 10,000 more than his rival's: 4,454,000 to 4,444,000. The Republicans also captured both houses of Congress.

Up to the time of his accession to the presidency, the career of James A. Garfield had been a perfect example of the American success legend. Born in humble Ohio surroundings—in fact, in a log cabin—he had spent his youth and young manhood as a manual laborer, once working as a mule driver on the Ohio Canal. "From the towpath to the White House" was a theme the Republicans emphasized in the 1880 election. He worked his way through college, became a teacher, studied law, and was admitted to the bar. In 1863, he was elected to the House of Representatives, where he served with increasing (although never enormous) distinction until he became the Republican standard-bearer.

During his brief tenure of office, Garfield gave evidence that he intended to conduct a moderate Half-Breed administration. He appointed Blaine as secretary of state, and as postmaster general (the cabinet official having the most to do with patronage) Thomas L. James, a civil-service champion. He provoked a fight with Conkling by naming his own followers to federal positions in New York. When the president appointed a bitter Conkling foe as collector of the port of New York, the senator tried to prevent Senate confirmation. Failing, he and his colleague, Platt, resigned and asked the New York legislature to reelect them. Their purpose was to awe Garfield into submission, but the legislators, in a fine display of perversity, chose two other men.

While the unseemly quarrel was dragging on, the evils of the spoils system were dramatically brought home to the American people. On July 2, 1881, after only four months in office, President Garfield was in the Washington railroad station, about to leave for a holiday trip, when a man in the crowd fired two pistol shots at him. As Garfield fell, the man with the gun shouted: "I am a Stalwart and Arthur is president now!" The assassin, Charles J. Guiteau, held a grudge because Garfield had refused to give him a government job. (Despite his apparent insanity, Guiteau was ultimately hanged.) Actually, Arthur was not yet president; Garfield lingered for nearly three months—receiving medical treatment that actually worsened what was originally an only moderately serious condition—before dying. At his death, people concerned about the menace of machine politics were doubly grieved. Even some Republicans echoed the sentiment of the man who groaned: "Chet Arthur president of the United States! Good God!"

Arthur and Reform

For all of his political lifetime Chester A. Arthur had been a devoted, skilled, and open spoilsman. Before the assassination of Garfield, he had gone to Albany to lobby for the reelection of his benefactor and mentor, Conkling. But on becoming president, he pursued an independent course between the Republican factions; and he worked zealously and with partial success for the cause of reform. Undoubtedly, he had been deeply affected by the grisly circumstances that had brought him to the presidency. It may be that realizing he now stood in the spotlight of history, he guided his actions accordingly.

The revelation of the "new" Arthur dismayed most of the party bosses. Although the president reorganized the cabinet, he left the majority of Garfield's appointees in office. In his first message to Congress he recommended a civil-service law, and he kept prodding the legislators to act. Although the spectacle of the great spoilsman championing reform seemed incongruous, Arthur was apparently sincere. In any case, his course was smart politics. With the public shocked by Garfield's assassination and disgusted by the postal frauds, sentiment for civil service was running high, and some kind of legislation would have been enacted whether Arthur had intervened or not.

Responding to popular as well as presidential pressure, Congress passed in 1883 the first national civil-service measure, the Pendleton Act. By its terms, a limited number of federal jobs were to be "classified": applicants for them were to be chosen on the basis of competitive written examinations. The law also forbade the financial assessment of officeholders for political purposes. To administer the act, a bipartisan Civil Service Commission, headed by reformer Dorman B. Eaton, was established. At first only about 14,000 of some 100,000 offices were placed on the classified list. But the act provided that future presidents might by executive order enlarge the number of positions subject to civil service. Every chief executive thereafter extended the list, primarily to "blanket" his appointees into office and prevent their removal by his successor. By this piecemeal and partisan process, the government finally achieved by the 1940s a system in which the majority of the people working for it were under the merit system.

The Return of the Democrats

The election of 1884, with its absence of issues and its emphasis on the personal qualities of the candidates, epitomized the politics of the era of complacency. Arthur would have accepted the Republican nomination, but his independent course had pleased neither Half-Breeds nor Stalwarts. (He was, in any case, already suffering from an illness that would kill him only two years later.) Ignoring him and other aspirants, the Republican convention nominated its most popular man and most vulnerable candidate, James G. Blaine, known to his adoring admirers as "the plumed knight" but to thousands of other Americans as a symbol of unsavory party politics. His selection split the party badly. To the Stalwarts he was anathema;

James G. Blaine
Blaine had an enthusiastic following among Republicans and was continually a presidential hopeful from the 1870s to the 1890s, but he was handicapped by a reputation for public dishonesty. This cartoon shows him as Narcissus—recalling the Greek myth of the boy who fell in love with his own reflection and was transformed into a flower. Blaine, covered with tattoos such as "corrupt lobby," here says to himself: "The remarkable resemblance to George Washington is what strikes me!" (Culver Pictures)

Conkling, asked if he intended to campaign for Blaine, snapped that he did not engage in criminal practice. The independent reform faction, now called the Mugwumps, announced they were prepared to bolt the party and support an honest Democrat. Rising to the bait, the Democrats nominated Grover Cleveland, the reform governor of New York. The platforms of the two parties were almost identical. Both endorsed a revision of the tariff that would not endanger domestic industries (an essentially meaningless pledge); both approved and claimed credit for civil service; and both, taking account of popular rumblings against big business, spoke vaguely about subjecting corporations to some kind of regulation.

With no real issues between the parties,

the election was essentially a struggle for office; and the campaign developed into a mud-slinging contest involving the personal fitness, or more accurately unfitness, of the candidates. Eagerly the Democrats went to work on the plumed knight's unsavory record. At torchlit rallies the Democrats chanted:

Blaine! Blaine! James G. Blaine!
Continental liar from the state of Maine!

Frantically the Republicans researched Cleveland's brief political career as mayor of Buffalo and governor of New York for evidence of corruption—a politician had to be corrupt, they seemed to assume—but found nothing. They did discover a juicy personal item. As a young man Cleveland had been accused of fathering an illegitimate child; and whether guilty or not, he had agreed to support the infant. He did not specifically deny the imputation when the Republicans brought it into the campaign. Thereafter, at their rallies the Republicans roared out:

Ma! Ma! Where's my pa?
Going to the White House. Ha! Ha! Ha!

In addition to the issue of Cleveland's personal morals the canvass featured the bloody shirt, waved vigorously by Blaine; freedom for Ireland from British rule, held out to the Irish voters by Republican orators; and religion, a last-minute issue that may have decided the election. In the closing days of the campaign a delegation of Protestant ministers called on Blaine in New York City; their spokesman, Dr. Samuel Burchard, in the course of his remarks referred to the Democrats as the party of "rum, Romanism, and rebellion." Apparently Blaine, whose mother was a Catholic, did not catch the statement or notice its linking of elements. Soon the Democrats were spreading the news through New York and other Eastern cities that Blaine had countenanced a slander on the Catholic church, and his denial came too late to counteract the charge. The so-called Burchard incident may have swung New York State to the Democrats, and New York was the pivotal state in what turned out to be an extremely close election. Cleveland had 219 electoral votes to Blaine's 182; the popular vote showed 4,875,000 for Cleveland and 4,852,000 for Blaine, a Democratic plurality of only 23,000.

Grover Cleveland—short and corpulent, brusque in manner, boldly beardless in a hirsute age—was not an altogether appealing figure. Rigid, self-righteous, and haughty, he did not inspire either public or private affection. He did, however, possess character, courage, and integrity. In his brief career in prominent offices—he had been elected mayor of Buffalo in 1881 and governor of New York in 1882—he had fought politicians, grafters, pressure groups, and Tammany Hall. He had become famous as the "veto mayor" and the "veto governor," as an official who was not afraid to say no. This ability to be honestly negative was at once his greatest strength and his most distressing weakness as a political leader. It enabled him to withstand pressure from any quarter, to oppose the spoilsmen, and to uphold high standards of official probity. It also rendered him tragically incapable of understanding the problems of an industrial society or the role of government in a changing economic order.

Cleveland and the Tariff

When Cleveland became president, he was absorbed with plans to improve the administrative machinery of the government, to install business standards in its operations, and to purify its processes. Such issues as the currency and the tariff did not greatly interest him; nor was he much concerned with the problems of the farmer and the laborer. His knowledge of economics was slender, and his economic philosophy almost primitively simple. He was sincerely opposed to a paternalistic and positive government that extended special favors to any group. Let all stand equal, the giant corporation and the worker, he proclaimed, never comprehending that there were vital power differences among contesting economic interests. He summed up his faith in the veto of an appropriation of $10,000 for drought-stricken farmers. The lesson must never be forgotten, he moralized, that "though the people support the Government, the Government should not support the people."

Although Cleveland was known as a civil-service reformer, in dealing with patronage he had to proceed with due partisan caution. After years of wandering in the political wilderness, the Democrats were hungry for offices, and they expected the president to throw the Republican "rascals" out—immediately and in wholesale lots. Instead, the president compromised in a manner that did not completely satisfy either his own party or his Mugwump followers. He added approximately 12,000 offices to the classified list, but of the jobs not under civil service he removed two-thirds of the incumbents and replaced them with deserving Democrats. Determined to check extravagance and congressional raids on the surplus, Cleveland vetoed a river and harbors bill, and attempted to introduce principles of economy and honesty into the awarding of soldier pensions.

As part of his battle against corruption, Cleveland instructed his secretary of the interior to inspect past grants of public lands in the West to railroad, lumber, and cattle interests and, where the lands had been obtained on fraudulent or false grounds, to institute suits to recover them. Eventually some 81 million acres were restored to the government. Although businessmen bellowed that the president was acting like a radical, he was only being consistently conservative: no special favors to any group.

Cleveland himself precipitated one economic issue into the political arena. Always mildly dubious about the high tariff, he concluded after thorough study that the existing rates were responsible for the annual surplus in federal revenues that tempted Congress to reckless legislation. Once convinced, he acted with sudden and startling vigor. In December 1887, he devoted almost all of his annual message to the lawmakers to a discussion of the tariff and a demand for its downward revision. Although he spoke bitingly of the great fortunes that had been built on protective duties and of the inflated living costs of the poor, he rested his case on immediate and practical considerations: the tariff was bringing in an unneeded surplus, and the piling up of this surplus would eventually depress the economy. In a phrase that intrigued the public, he said: "It is a *condition* that confronts us, not a theory." He assured Congress that reductions could be made without endangering the interests of American manufacturers.

Immediately, the Southern and Western Democrats, who had been moving rapidly to a low-tariff position, responded to the president's leadership. They pushed the Mills Bill through the House, incorporating Cleveland's recommendations and providing for moderate reductions. Only four Democrats voted against it, and doubtless some of the Easterners went along in the knowledge that

Grover Cleveland
Cleveland was the first Democrat to be elected president since the Civil War. Honest, courageous, and stubborn, he was extremely conservative and unable to understand some of the new economic problems emerging in his administration. A bachelor when elected, he married while in the White House. (Library of Congress)

the Republican Senate would kill the measure. In the Senate the Republican leaders, believing that they could sell the tariff to the voters, met the issue head-on. As an alternative to the Mills Bill they enacted a protective measure. Action was deadlocked for the moment, and the tariff was squarely before the people as an issue in the election of 1888.

As the tariff fight swirled to a climax, the Democrats again named Cleveland as their standard-bearer, although some machine bosses and some Easterners, disgusted by his stand on civil service and lower duties, would have preferred another candidate. The platform emphasized the tariff question and pledged support to the president's policy of moderate revision. The Republicans had in protection what they were certain was a winning issue, but they were hard put to find an acceptable and available nominee. They finally decided on Benjamin Harrison of Indiana, who was relatively obscure but formidably respectable (the grandson of President William Henry Harrison); and in their platform endorsed protection for American producers and generous pensions for Union veterans.

The campaign of 1888 was the first since the Civil War to be fought out on a definite issue, the first to involve a clear question of economic difference between the parties. It was also one of the most corrupt campaigns in American history. When the votes were counted, it was obvious that the people had not registered a clear decision. Harrison had an electoral majority of 233 to 168, but Cleveland's popular vote exceeded Harrison's, 5.54 million to 5.44 million.

THE FAILURE OF PARTY POLITICS

Leaders of both parties in the late nineteenth century tried their best to avoid confronting the important public issues of their day, and for nearly a decade they succeeded. But the changes in American social and economic life were so profound and troubling that by the late 1880s they could no longer be ignored. Growing pressure from unhappy farmers, workers, and others forced the government to confront a number of important economic issues—as Cleveland's belated concern with the tariff suggested.

Yet nothing better illustrated the failure of party politics in the late nineteenth century than the inability of either Democrats or Republicans to produce any effective response to the nation's economic problems. Both parties talked bravely of dealing with the power of railroads, with the problem of monopoly, with the unstable currency, and with the tariff. Only rarely did either do anything meaningful about any of these issues; and when the government did take action, that action made the problems worse more often than better.

Railroad Regulation

The issue of railroad regulation came before the federal government through no effort of its own. For years Congress had so studiously ignored all public clamor for regulation that proponents of reform had looked instead to the states. Farm organizations in the Midwest (most notably the Grangers) succeeded in persuading several state legislatures to pass regulatory legislation in the early 1870s. The so-called Granger Laws in Illinois, Iowa, Minnesota, and Wisconsin authorized maximum rates for passenger and freight traffic, provided rules and rates for the storing of grain, and prohibited a number of alleged discriminatory practices.

At first, the Granger Laws fared well. The railroad corporations contested them in court, arguing that the statutes preempted Congress's exclusive power to regulate interstate commerce and that they acted to deprive corporations of their property without the "due process" guaranteed under the Fourteenth Amendment. The Supreme Court, in *Munn* v. *Illinois* (1877), rejected such arguments, ruling that a state could under some circumstances regulate interstate commerce affecting it, in the absence of national regulation, and that a corporation was not a "person" within the meaning of the Constitution.

These initial victories, however, proved short-lived. For the corporations continued to test the Granger Laws in court, and gradually they managed to prevail—after new justices friendly to an expanded notion of property rights and willing to strike down states' powers ascended to the Supreme Court. The first step toward the dismantling of the state regulations came nine years after the *Munn* decision, which had seemed to uphold them. That was the so-called Wabash case of 1886 (*Wabash, St. Louis, and Pacific Railway Co.* v. *Illinois*). Involved was a statute prohibiting higher rates for a "short haul" than a "long haul" between points in Illinois and New York City. The Court held that the statute attempted to regulate interstate commerce and infringed on the exclusive power of Congress. Interstate rates were thus removed from state control, but within its own limits a state could still regulate railroads if the regulations did not directly affect interstate commerce. Later, the roads eliminated even this regulatory power of the states by persuading the Court to limit further the regulatory power of the states (*Chicago, Milwaukee and St. Paul Railroad* v. *Minnesota*, 1890, and later rulings). This constant judicial review of state decrees meant, of course, that state regulation had become a mockery.

If there was to be any meaningful regulation of the railroads, it was now clear, it could come only from the federal government. And Congress, subjected to increasing pressure, soon grudgingly and inadequately responded. There had been demands both in and out of the government since the 1870s for some kind of supervisory legislation to prevent such unsavory railroad practices as pooling, rebates, and other discriminatory devices. Even some railway operators, alarmed by the fierce competition in their industry, were eager for some regulation. As a result, Congress responded in 1887 with the Interstate Commerce Act, aptly described by its chief sponsor, Senator Shelby M. Cullom of Illinois, as "conservative legislation."

The Interstate Commerce Act prohibited rebates, pools, long-short haul discriminations, and drawbacks. It required railroads to publish their rate schedules and file them with the government. It provided that all charges in interstate rail transportation should be "reasonable and just" but failed to furnish a standard or method to determine the justness of a rate. To administer the act, a five-man agency, the Interstate Commerce Commission, was created, with powers to hear complaints from shippers, examine witnesses, and inquire into the books and accounts of railroads. The law did not clearly authorize the commission to fix rates. After investigating a complaint, the commission could issue a cease-and-desist order to a carrier to lower its charges. If the road refused, the commission had to take its case to the courts and justify its decree, a cumbersome procedure that militated against effective regulation.

For almost twenty years after its passage, the Interstate Commerce Act—haphazardly enforced and interpreted exceedingly narrowly by the courts—was without practical effect; it did not accomplish widespread rate reduction or eliminate discrimination. No wonder an attorney general of the United States advised a railroad president not to ask for repeal of the act: "It satisfies the popular clamor for government supervision of the railroads at the same time that that supervision is almost entirely nominal."

The Issue of the Trusts

At the same time that the issue of railroad regulation was gaining strength, another, related economic question was confronting the federal government: what to do about the great corporate combinations, the trusts, whose power had come to seem menacing and dangerous. As with the railroads, the government responded with legislation that gave the appearance of dealing with the problem but in practical terms avoided it.

The trust issue arose most prominently during the dreary administration of Benjamin Harrison, the victor in the close and corrupt election of 1888. Unlike his grandfather, who had died only a month after assuming the presidency forty-eight years earlier, Benjamin Harrison lived out his full term of office. Yet his record as president was little more substantial than his grandfather's.

One reason for Harrison's failure was the intellectual drabness of the members of his administration—beginning with the president himself and extending through his cabinet. Another was Harrison's unwillingness to make any effort to influence the Congress. It was public opinion, not the president, that finally forced the government to confront the issue of the trusts. By the mid-1880s, some fifteen Western and Southern states had adopted laws prohibiting combinations that restrained competition. But corporations found it easy to escape limitations by incorporating in states that offered special privileges (New Jersey and Delaware were notorious examples). Any form of state regulation, moreover, was liable to be rejected by the Supreme Court. If antitrust legislation was to be effective, it would obviously have to come from the national government. In 1888, both parties had promised to curb monopolies.

With little debate and by almost unanimous votes in both houses of Congress, the Sherman Antitrust Act became law in July 1890. Its provisions and phraseology were determined by the fact that the only basis for national action against the trusts derived from the power of Congress to regulate interstate commerce. The heart of the measure was in the first two sections: (1) "Every contract, combination in the form of trust or otherwise, or conspiracy, in restraint of trade or commerce among the several States, or with foreign nations, is hereby declared to be illegal"; (2) "Every person who shall monopolize, or attempt to monopolize . . . any part of the trade or commerce among the several States, or with foreign nations, shall be deemed guilty of a misdemeanor. . . ."

Even though the law on paper prohibited all combinations "in restraint of trade," Congress in passing it was making no very serious effort to break up monopolies, as the vague language of the law suggested. As one senator explained, his colleagues merely wanted to get up "some bill headed 'A bill to Punish Trusts' with which to go to the country" and get themselves reelected. Congress was making a gesture to appease popular discontent without changing the realities of contemporary economic life.

For over a decade after its passage, there was little attempt to enforce the Sherman Act. Before 1901, the Justice Department instituted only fourteen suits under the law against business combinations, and it failed to obtain convictions in almost every one. The courts, uniformly hostile to the law, proceeded to emasculate it. The crowning decision came in *United States* v. *E. C. Knight Co.* (1895), a case in which the government charged that the defendants controlled 98 percent of the manufacture of refined sugar in the country. Chief Justice Melville W. Fuller, speaking for the Supreme Court,

threw out the government's case with a curious distinction between manufacturing and commerce. He admitted that the present combination was a trust to monopolize the refining of sugar but denied that it was therefore illegal: the trust was not in interstate commerce but in manufacturing. The Knight decision created a "twilight zone" between state and national powers, an area of economic life outside the authority of any agency of government.

Revising the Tariff

Having made a token effort to dispose of the trust question, the Republicans turned with anticipation to the subject that most interested them and their business backers and that had been the paramount issue in the campaign of 1888, the tariff. William McKinley of Ohio, a rising party luminary and chairman of the House Ways and Means Committee, and Senator Nelson W. Aldrich of Rhode Island framed, with the assistance of the tariff lobbies, the highest protective measure yet offered to a Congress. It became law in October 1890 as the McKinley Tariff Act.

Seldom has a party in power suffered such a stunning reverse as befell the Republicans in the midterm elections of 1890. Their majority in the Senate was slashed to 8, and in the House they could count only 88 seats to 235 for the Democrats and 9 for the Alliance-Populists. (See below, p. 581ff.) Popular revulsion against the McKinley duties, pictured by the Democrats as raising the living costs of the masses, was an undoubted factor in the Republican debacle; McKinley himself was among those who went down to defeat. But the elections registered more than condemnation of a tariff. They reflected the anxieties of millions of Americans who were beginning to question the fundamental justice of the economic order.

In the presidential election of 1892, Benjamin Harrison was again the Republican nominee and Grover Cleveland the Democratic. Once more the platforms of the two parties were almost identical except for the tariff, with the Republicans upholding protection and the Democrats pledging reduction. Both parties in their official pronouncements ignored the pulsing currents of unrest in the country. Only a new third party, the People's party, with James B. Weaver as its candidate, advocated economic reform. Cleveland amassed 277 electoral and 5,557,000 popular votes as compared to Harrison's 145 and 5,176,000 votes. Weaver ran far behind. (See below, p. 583.) For the first time since 1878 the Democrats won a majority of both houses of Congress.

Despite Cleveland's negative record, a large proportion of the people who had voted for him expected him to devise some original approach to the new problems troubling America. His inaugural address rudely disillusioned them, as he reaffirmed his devotion to laissez faire in words that had become tiresomely familiar: "The lessons of paternalism ought to be unlearned and the better lesson taught that while the people should . . . support their Government its functions do not include the support of the people."

Cleveland called on his party to redeem its pledge to lower the existing tariff rates. In the House, William L. Wilson of West Virginia introduced a bill in 1894 designed to accomplish moderate downward revision and yet provide adequate protection for domestic producers. To get agrarian support and to compensate for an anticipated loss in revenues, the bill provided for an income tax, with a 2 percent levy on incomes over $4,000. When the Wilson bill reached the Senate, the customary lobbying and logrolling began. Eastern Democrats, directed by Maryland's Arthur P. Gorman and abetted by Republicans, added 634 amendments, most of them altering Wilson's duties upward. Strong pressure from the Democratic leadership induced the House to accept the Senate version. Cleveland denounced it as a violation of the party's platform but allowed it to become law without his signature.

The Wilson-Gorman Tariff reduced the general scale of duties only 10 percent, and its duties on raw and refined sugar and other items afforded ample protection to the sugar trust and virtually every other trust. Far from the kind of tariff the Democrats had promised the country, the act seemed to confirm the contention of those who claimed that tariff making was a sham battle between the major parties.

Even the one crust thrown to reformers, the income tax, was shortly snatched away by the courts. In *Pollock* v. *The Farmer's Loan and Trust Co.* (1895), the Supreme Court declared in a 5-to-4 decision that a tax on incomes was a "direct" tax and hence had to be apportioned among the states according to population. Since an income tax, by its very nature, would be effective only if applied on a basis of individual wealth and would have no reality if reckoned on the distribution of population, the Court had made it impossible to levy such a tax without a constitutional amendment. (The nation approved such an amendment—the Sixteenth—in 1913.)

THE SWELL OF AGRARIAN PROTEST

No group watched the dismal performance of the federal government in the 1880s with more dismay than American farmers. Isolated from the urban-industrial society that was beginning to dominate national life, suffering from a long, painful economic decline, afflicted with a sense of obsolescence, rural Americans were keenly aware of the problems of the modern economy and particularly eager for government assistance in dealing with them. The result was the emergence of one of the most powerful movements of political protest in American history: what became known as Populism.

Traditionally, farmers had been perhaps the least likely group to mobilize a movement of collective protest. In the face of their mounting problems, however, many attempted to modify their commitment to individualism and explore methods of organization. The first signs of agrarian cooperation emerged as early as the 1860s, with the creation of the Grange. By the 1880s, the Grange was in decline, and agrarian protest began to center around the new Farmers' Alliances, which gradually evolved into the People's party—the cornerstone of the Populist revolt.

The Grangers

The first farm organization to appear after the Civil War took shape in the 1860s, less as a movement of protest than as a social and self-help association. The depression of 1873 turned it into an agency of political change.

On a tour through the South, Oliver H. Kelley, a clerk in the Department of Agriculture at Washington, became impressed with the isolation and drabness of rural life. In 1867, he and other department employees founded the National Grange of the Patrons of Husbandry, to which Kelley devoted years of labor as secretary. Its announced purposes were social, cultural, and educational. By bringing farm men and women together in groups, it aimed to diffuse knowledge of scientific agriculture, machines, and markets, to furnish a community feeling hitherto absent in rural society, and to keep agriculture "in step with the music of the age." Recognizing that human nature is intrigued by secrecy and ceremony, the founders provided for an elaborate system of initiation and ritual.

At first the Grange grew slowly. It filled an obvious rural need, but farmers were not attracted to it in large numbers while times were good. Then the depression of 1873 struck, and suddenly the farmers saw benefits to be achieved through organization. By 1875, the Grange claimed over 800,000 members and 20,000 local lodges. Granges appeared in almost every state but were most numerous in the staple-producing sections of the Middle West and the South.

As membership increased, the lodges in the Middle West turned to economic issues. They stressed the necessity of collective action by farmers to eliminate the middleman—through the organization of cooperatives—and the urgency of political action to curb the monopolistic practices of the railroads and warehouses. All over the midlands on Independence Day 1873, embittered

farmers assembled to hear Granger orators read "The Farmers' Declaration of Independence." The resolutions proclaimed that the time had come for farmers, "suffering from long continued systems of oppression and abuse, to rouse themselves from an apathetic indifference to their own interests." The declaration also vowed that the farmers would use "all lawful and peaceful means to free [themselves] from the tyranny of monopoly."

The Grangers launched the first major cooperative movement in the United States, although successful collective societies had existed earlier in England and other countries. They set up cooperative stores, creameries, elevators, warehouses, insurance companies, and factories that turned out machines, stoves, and other items. Some 400 enterprises were in operation at the height of the movement, but eventually most of them failed because of the inexperience of the operators and the opposition of middlemen. Not all business groups fought the cooperatives; some sought their trade, and one corporation was formed specifically in 1872 to meet the wants of the Grangers: Montgomery Ward and Company, which brought the mail-order business into existence.

The Grangers labored politically to elect to state legislatures candidates pledged to their program. Usually they operated through the existing parties, only occasionally putting up nominees under such party labels as "Antimonopoly" and "Reform." Marshaling their votes in the local lodges, they were able to gain control of the legislatures in most of the Middle Western states. Their purpose, openly and angrily announced, was to subject the railroads to controls.

The Granger Laws of the early 1870s seemed for a time to vindicate the predictions of those farmers who claimed that their new organization augured a permanent change in the political status of agriculture. But the destruction of the new regulations by the courts, combined with the political inexperience of many Grange leaders and, above all, the return of prosperity in the late 1870s, produced a dramatic decline in the power of the association. Some of the Granger cooperatives survived as effective economic vehicles for many years; but the movement as a whole dwindled rapidly. By 1880, its membership had shrunk to 100,000.

The Alliances

The successors to the Granges as the leading vehicles of agrarian protest began to emerge even before the Granger movement had faded. As early as 1875, farmers in parts of the South (most notably in Texas) were banding together in local Farmers' Alliances. Under the leadership of the Texan C. W. Macune and others, the Southern Alliances grew rapidly in the 1880s and by the end of the decade could boast more than 4 million members. In the meantime, a comparable movement was under way in the plains states and in the Midwest. This Northwestern Alliance never achieved the size or militancy of its Southern counterpart, but it became a significant force nevertheless.

Like the Granges, the Alliances began by working for primarily local objectives; but they defined those objectives far more broadly. In addition to forming cooperatives and other marketing mechanisms, Alliances also established stores, banks, processing plants, and other facilities for their members—to free them from dependence on the hated "furnishing merchants" who bound so many farmers into a miserable system of indebtedness. Central to the vision of the Alliance leaders was a restored community, in which individuals could once again control their own economic future. And essential to such communities, they argued, was cooperation—not a rigid collectivism that would suppress individuality, but a sense of mutual, neighborly responsibility that would enable farmers to resist the oppressive outside forces that threatened to enslave them. The Alliances were, in short, not simply social and economic organizations, but also—in the South at least—vehicles of political education. Alliance "lecturers" traveled throughout rural areas exhorting farmers to a new awareness of their political and economic plight. They lambasted the tendency in modern society of more and more power being concentrated in the hands of a few great corporations and financial institutions.

The Kansas Pythoness
One of the leading Populist orators was Mary E. Lease. Although hostile critics said a woman should not be a stump speaker, Mrs. Lease talked frequently and vividly, delivering some 160 speeches in 1890 alone. In one address she recalled that the farmers had been asked to raise a big crop and had done so. What came of their efforts? "Eight-cent corn, ten-cent oats, two-cent beef, and no-price at all for butter and eggs—that's what came of it." On another occasion she advised Kansas farmers to "raise less corn and more hell." (Brown Brothers)

Although the Alliances quickly became far more widespread than the Granges had ever been, they suffered from similar problems. Their cooperatives did not always work well, partly because the market forces operating against them were sometimes too strong to be overcome, partly because the cooperatives themselves were occasionally mismanaged. Some came under the control of unscrupulous local entrepreneurs, who made them as exploitive as the old system of reliance on railroads and local stores. Thus the combination of enormous numerical strength, ideological fervor, and economic failure helped push the Alliances into a new phase of their existence at the end of the 1880s: the creation of a national political organization.

The first step came in 1889, when the Southern and Northwestern Alliances, despite continuing differences between them, agreed to a loose merger. But the decisive moment came in 1890, when the Alliances staged a national convention at Ocala, Florida, and issued the so-called Ocala Demands. Although the Alliancemen were not yet formally proclaiming the existence of a new party, the demands were nothing less than a party platform.

The Alliances played an active role in the 1890 off-year elections and surprised both conservatives and themselves with their success. The farm forces won partial or complete control of the legislatures in twelve states, eight in the South and four in the West. They elected six governors, three senators, and approximately fifty congressmen. The magnitude of the sweep was not, perhaps, as great as it seemed at first glance. Over forty of the successful Alliance candidates for Congress were loyal members of the Democratic party, who benefited—often passively—from the Alliance endorsements. Nevertheless, the dissident farmers drew enough encouragement from the results to contemplate further political action and—as it gradually became clear that neither of the two major parties was likely to respond to their demands—to form a party of their own.

Sentiment for a third party was strongest among the members of the Northwestern Alliance. But several Southern leaders—among them Tom Watson of Georgia, the only Southern congressman elected in 1890 openly to identify with the Alliance, and Leonidas L. Polk of North Carolina, perhaps the ablest mind in the movement—were similarly becoming convinced of the need for a new political organization. Plans for a third party were discussed at meetings in Cincinnati in May 1891 and St. Louis in February

To Arms Against the Populists
In no state did the Populists have greater support than in Kansas. In 1893, however, the Republicans disputed the results of a state election and claimed control of the legislature. For a time the Populists occupied and held the state house. Finally the Republicans armed themselves, drove out the Populists, and took control. (Kansas State Historical Society, Topeka)

1892—meetings attended by many Northern Alliancemen, a smaller but still significant number of Southern Alliance leaders, and representatives of the fading Knights of Labor (see above, p. 583), whom some farm leaders hoped to bring into the coalition. Then, in July 1892, 1,300 excited and exultant delegates poured into Omaha, Nebraska, to proclaim formally the creation of the new party, approve an official set of principles, and nominate candidates for the presidency and vice presidency. By common consent, the party already had a name, one first used by the Kansas agrarians: the People's party. The movement was more commonly referred to, however, by the Latinate version of that name: Populism.

The election of 1892 dispelled whatever doubts may have remained as to the potential power of the new movement. The Populist presidential candidate—James B. Weaver of Iowa, a former Greenbacker—polled more than a million votes, 8.5 percent of the total, and carried six mountain and plains states for 22 electoral votes. Nearly 1,500 Populist candidates won election to seats in state legislatures. The party elected three governors, five senators, and ten congressmen. It could also claim the support of numerous Republicans and Democrats in Congress, who had been elected by appealing to Populist sentiment.

The Populist Constituency

There is no decisive evidence of precisely how many Populists there were, where they came from, and what characteristics they shared. Some generalizations, however, are possible. First, Populism was stronger in some agrarian regions than others. Its greatest influence was in an arc of states extending from the Dakotas southward through Nebraska and Kansas; in a string of Southern states stretching from Texas through northern Louisiana, Alabama, and Mississippi, and into Georgia and the Carolinas; and in the Rocky Mountain states. It was weakest in those areas where the Granges had been most successful, because that was where agriculture had managed to achieve its greatest security and stability.

Populism was also more appealing to certain kinds of farmers than to others. Unsurprisingly, it was most often small farmers with little long-range economic security who flocked to the movement, people whose operations were only minimally mechanized, if at all, who relied on one crop, and who had access only to limited and unsatisfactory mechanisms of credit. Large, diversified, efficient producers were not likely to flock to the Populist banner; smaller, imperiled farmers were. The status of such farmers differed, of course, from region to region. In the Midwest, the Populists were usually family farmers struggling to hang onto their land (or to get it back if they had lost it). In the South, there were many modest landowners too, but in addition there were significant numbers of sharecroppers and tenant farmers. Whatever their differences, however, most Populists had at least one thing in common: they were engaged in a type of farming that was becoming economically obsolete in the face of new, mechanized, diversified, and consolidated commercial agriculture.

The Populist constituency was as notable for the groups it failed to attract as for those it attracted. Leaders of the movement were aware that if they were to have any hope of genuine national influence, small farmers alone would not be enough. They had to reach out to other oppressed groups. Thus there were energetic and continuing efforts to include labor within the coalition. Representatives of the Knights of Labor attended early organizational meetings; the new party added a labor plank to its platform—calling for shorter hours for workers and restrictions on immigration, and denouncing the use of private detective agencies as strikebreakers in labor disputes. Populist spokesmen attempted to generate enthusiasm for the movement within the working class; and Populist publications spoke of the natural connection between oppressed farmers and oppressed industrial workers. But it was all to little avail. One problem was that the labor organizations themselves were too weak to be able to deliver any substantial support. Another problem was a consistent failure to define clearly enough the areas of common interest between the two groups.

In the South in particular, the movement

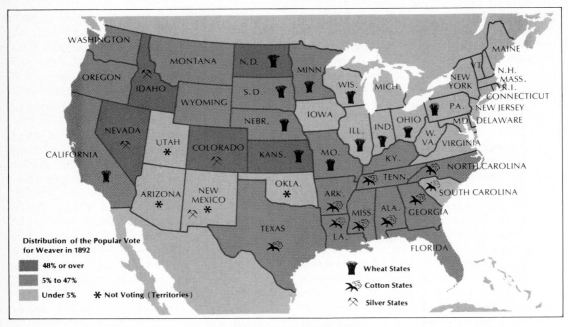

POPULIST STRENGTH, 1892

also considered the desirability of attracting blacks, whose numbers and poverty made them possibly valuable allies. And indeed there was an important black component to the movement—a network of "Colored Alliances" that by 1890 numbered over one and a quarter million members. Many Midwestern Alliancemen advocated a full merger of the Colored Alliances with the national movement. Even some white Southern leaders displayed a notable willingness to foster interracial cooperation. But in the end, the influence of white racism proved stronger than the influence of common economic interests. White Populists on the whole were willing to accept the assistance of blacks only as long as it was clear that whites would remain indisputably in control. When conservatives began to attack the Populists for undermining white supremacy, the interracial character of the movement quickly faded.

Populist leaders, although easier to identify than their constituencies, are nevertheless also difficult to typify. Most were members of the rural middle class: professional men, editors and lawyers, or professional

politicians and agitators. Few were dirt farmers. Almost all leaders were, like their constituents, Protestants. But beyond these basic characteristics, there were wide variations. Some Populist leaders were somber, serious theoreticians; others were semihysterical rabble-rousers. In the South, in particular, Populism produced the first generation of what was to become a distinctive and enduring political breed—the "Southern demagogue." Tom Watson in Georgia, Jeff Davis in Arkansas, and others attracted widespread popular support by arousing the resentment of poor Southerners against the entrenched Bourbon aristocracy. They were the beginning of a line of such figures that stretched well into the twentieth century. There were similarly flamboyant leaders in the Midwest: "Sockless" Jerry Simpson of Kansas, for example, or Ignatius Donnelly of Minnesota. Donnelly, in particular, seemed to exemplify the divided character of the movement: sincere idealism combined with crassness and opportunism. A committed, principled man who spoke eloquently on behalf of Populist ideals and appeared sincerely to believe in them, Donnelly was also at times something of a charlatan. As a member of Congress, he compiled a miserable legislative record marked, among other things, by a series of seamy, secret deals with railroad companies.

The Populist Ideology

The ideology of Populism, like the character of its leadership, was a complex combination of progressive idealism and bewildering rhetorical excess. There were three basic elements of that ideology: a concrete program of reform; a strident and at times almost hysterical denunciation of enemies; and a millennial vision of a just and stable society.

The reform program of the Populists was spelled out first in the Ocala Demands of 1890 and then, even more clearly, in the Omaha platform of 1892. Among the most prominent of the many issues included in these documents was a proposal for a system of "subtreasuries," which would replace and strengthen the cooperatives with which the Grangers and Alliances had been experimenting for years. The government would establish a network of warehouses, where farmers could deposit their crops. Using those crops as collateral, growers could then borrow money from the government at low rates of interest and wait for the price of their goods to go up before selling them. In addition, the Populists called for the abolition of national banks, which they believed were dangerous institutions of concentrated power; the end of absentee ownership of land; the direct election of United States senators (thus weakening the power of conservative state legislatures); and other devices to improve the ability of the people to influence the political process. They called as well for regulation and (after 1892) government ownership of railroads, telephones, and telegraphs. They demanded, too, a system of government-operated postal savings banks, a graduated income tax, the inflation of the currency, and later, the remonetization of silver. Some of the Populist proposals were unrealistic, but the Populist platform was, for the most part, a sound and rational effort to find solutions to difficult problems.

Less sound and rational, at times, were the Populist denunciations of enemies, which often became so strident and hysterical as to border on the irrational. A few Populists were openly anti-Semitic, pointing to the Jews as the leaders of the obscure financial forces attempting to enslave them. Others were anti-intellectual, anti-Eastern, and anti-urban. Some of the leading Populists gave an impression of personal failure, brilliant instability, and brooding communion with mystic forces. Ignatius Donnelly, for example, wrote one book locating the lost isle of Atlantis, another that Bacon had written Shakespeare's plays, and still another—*Caesar's Column* (1891)—with an almost lunatic vision of a bloody revolution and the creation of a Populist Utopia. Tom Watson, once a champion of interracial harmony, ended his career baiting blacks and Jews.

Yet the occasional bigotry of the movement should not be allowed to dominate the image of Populism. The hysterical quality of some Populist "scapegoating" can be explained in part by the condition of many of the members of the movement—people whose personal distress was so great that some excesses were all but inevitable. Much of this denunciation of enemies, moreover, was not as irrational as critics often charged. The rhetoric may have been excessive, but the most frequent targets—banks, railroads, monopolies—were far from irrelevant to the problems of the farmer.

The attacks on these alleged villains, furthermore, was counterbalanced by a well-developed view of a just and stable society. The Populists argued not only for the destruction of monopolistic power but for a new social morality. Society, they claimed, had an obligation to protect the well-being of its individual citizens. The rights of property ownership were, therefore, secondary to the needs of the community. Populists did not reject the idea of private property; most were themselves landowners or aspirants to land ownership. They did, however, emphatically reject the laissez-faire orthodoxies of their time, the idea that the rights of ownership are absolute. They raised, in short, the most overt and powerful challenge to the direction in which American industrial capitalism was

Populism

American history does not offer many examples of successful popular movements operating outside the two major parties. And for that reason Populism, which in its brief, meteoric life became one of the few such phenomena to gain real national influence, has attracted the fascinated attention of many historians—and has produced deep disagreements among them. Scholars have differed on many grounds in their interpretations of Populism, but at the heart of many such disagreements have been disparate views of popular, insurgent politics. Some historians have harbored a basic mistrust of such popular uprisings and have, therefore, viewed the Populists with suspicion and hostility. Others have viewed such insurgency approvingly, as evidence of a healthy resistance to oppression and exploitation; and to them, the Populists have appeared as essentially admirable, democratic activists.

This latter view underlay the first, and for many years the only, general history of Populism: John D. Hicks's *The Populist Revolt* (1931). Rejecting the popular view of the Populists as misguided and unruly radicals, Hicks described them as people reacting rationally and progressively to economic misfortune. They were, he suggested, aware of the harsh, even brutal, impact of industrial growth on rural society; and they were proposing reforms that would limit the oppressive power of the new financial titans and restore a measure of control to the farmers themselves. Populism was, he wrote, "the last phase of a long and perhaps a losing struggle—the struggle to save agricultural America from the devouring jaws of industrial America." A losing struggle, perhaps, but not a vain one; for many of the reforms the Populists advocated, Hicks implied, became the basis of later progressive legislation.

This generally approving view of Populism prevailed among historians for more than two decades. But in the early 1950s—when the memory of European fascism and the uneasiness about contemporary communism combined to create a general hostility among scholars toward mass popular politics—a harsh new attack on the Populist movement appeared in a work by one of the nation's leading historians. Richard Hofstadter, in *The Age of Reform* (1955), admitted in passing that Populism contained some progressive themes. But the bulk of his effort was devoted to exposing both the "soft" and the "dark" sides of the movement. Populism was "soft," he claimed, because it rested on a nostalgic and unrealistic myth, because it romanticized the nation's agrarian past and refused to confront the hard realities of modern life. And it was "dark," he argued, because it was permeated with bigotry and ignorance. Populists showed a strong anti-Semitic tendency, Hofstadter claimed. And they displayed animosity as well toward intellectuals, Easterners, and urbanites. He stopped short of linking Populism directly with fascism, but other scholars—adopting his approach—made such connections explicitly.

Almost immediately, historians more favorably disposed toward mass politics in moving. Populism was not a challenge to industrialization or to capitalism itself, but to what the Populists considered the brutal and chaotic way in which the economy was developing. Progress and growth should continue, they urged, but it should be strictly defined by the needs of individuals and communities.

THE CRISIS OF THE 1890S

The emergence of a powerful movement of agrarian protest was only one of many factors that were combining by the early 1890s to create a national political crisis. There was a severe depression, which began in 1893 and which exaggerated the unhappiness of not only the farmers but other groups as well. There was widespread labor unrest and vio-

general, and Populism in particular, began to challenge what soon became known as the "Hofstadter thesis." Norman Pollack argued in a 1962 study, *The Populist Response to Industrial America*, that the agrarian revolt had rested not on nostalgic, romantic concepts but on a sophisticated and farsighted vision of reform—one that recognized, and even welcomed, the realities of an industrial economy, but one that sought to make that economy more equitable and democratic. Walter T. K. Nugent, in *Tolerant Populists* (1963), argued—as his title implies—that the Populists in Kansas were far from bigoted, that they not only tolerated but welcomed Jews and other minorities into their party, and that they offered a practical, sensible program.

It was not until 1976, however, that a comprehensive study of Populism emerged that could rival Hicks and Hofstadter in its influence. Lawrence Goodwyn, in *Democratic Promise* (and in a briefer version of the same work, *The Populist Moment*, published in 1978), described the Populists as members of a "cooperative crusade," battling against the "coercive potential of the emerging corporate state." Populists were more than the nostalgic bigots Hofstadter described, more even than the progressive reformers portrayed by Hicks. They offered a vision of truly radical change, widely disseminated through what Goodwyn called a "movement culture," and offering an intelligent and, above all, a democratic alternative to the inequities of modern capitalism.

At the same time that historians were debating the question of what Populism meant, they were arguing as well over who the Populists were. Hicks, Hofstadter, and Goodwyn disagreed on many things, but they shared a general view of the Populists as victims of economic distress: usually one-crop farmers in economically marginal agricultural regions victimized by drought and debt. Other scholars, however, have suggested that the problem of identifying the Populists is more complex. Sheldon Hackney, in *Populism to Progressivism in Alabama* (1969), has argued that the Populists were not only economically troubled, but socially rootless, "only tenuously connected to society by economic function, by personal relationships, by stable community membership, by political participation, or by psychological identification with the South's distinctive myths." Peter Argersinger, Stanley Parsons, and others have similarly suggested that Populists were characterized by a form of social and even geographical isolation.

There has, finally, been continuing debate over the legacy of Populism. Historians and politicians alike have argued repeatedly that a Populist tradition has survived throughout the twentieth century, influencing movements as disparate as those led by Huey Long in the 1930s and George Wallace in the 1960s. Others have maintained that the term "Populism" has been used (and misused) so widely as to have become virtually meaningless, that its only real value is in reference to the agrarian insurgents of the 1890s, who first gave meaning to the word.

---

lence, culminating in the tumultuous Pullman strike of 1894. There was the continuing failure of either major party to respond to the growing distress. And there was the rigid conservatism of Grover Cleveland, who took office (for the second time) just at the moment that the economy collapsed.

Out of this growing sense of crisis came some of the most heated political battles in American history, culminating in the dramatic campaign of 1896, which—in the eyes of many Americans—seemed to threaten the future of the nation.

The Panic of 1893

The second Cleveland administration was hardly settled in office when the Panic of 1893 struck the country. There followed the most severe depression the nation had yet experienced. Its causes were various and complicated. The eighties had been a typical boom period, featuring overexpansion and overinvestment in railroads and industrial combinations. Depressed prices in agriculture since 1887 had weakened the purchasing power of a substantial section of the population. Depression conditions that had begun earlier in Europe were resulting in a loss of American markets abroad, a decline in the export trade, and a withdrawal by foreign investors of gold invested in the United States. Whatever the causes of the depression, more than 8,000 business concerns failed in a period of six months, 156 railroads went into receivership, and 400 banks suspended operations. Agricultural prices tumbled to new lows, and perhaps as many as a million workers, 20 percent of the labor force, were thrown out of jobs.

Out of the unrest of the depression emerged new popular demands of government and, when those demands were ignored, new movements of political protest. Jacob S. Coxey, a Massillon, Ohio, businessman and Populist, proposed two lines of government action: (1) Congress should issue $500 million in legal-tender notes to be used in the construction of public highways throughout the country; and (2) local governments wishing to undertake public improvements should be authorized to issue noninterest-bearing bonds that could be exchanged at the federal Treasury for legal-tender notes. Coxey's ideas were derided and dismissed in conservative circles.

Seeking to dramatize his program, Coxey organized a march of the unemployed on Washington to present a petition for work relief to Congress. Only 500 of "Coxey's army" were able to make their way to Washington, and they were barred from the Capitol by armed police. Coxey was arrested on a charge of walking on the grass, and the marchers were herded into camps because their presence supposedly endangered public health.

Coxey's army was only one of several industrial protest movements to stage conspicuous marches and rallies in the 1890s. And there were many other signs of labor unrest as well during the decade—the Homestead and Pullman strikes for example. (See above, pp. 537–540.) To much of the middle class, the worker unrest seemed to augur a dangerous instability, even perhaps a revolution. Labor radicalism—some of it real, much of it imagined by the frightened middle class— was seldom far from the public mind, heightening the general sense of crisis.

The Silver Question

The financial panic deranged the government's monetary system, and in the minds of such people as Cleveland, the silver policy became the primary cause of the depression. This money question—which became the basis for some of the most dramatic political conflicts in American history—had a long history.

From the 1790s on, the United States had been on a bimetallic standard. That is, the monetary unit, the dollar, was based on two metals, gold and silver. Different amounts of each metal could constitute a dollar. Eventually, it was redefined in such a way that the silver dollar contained sixteen times as much silver as the gold dollar did gold. This ratio—16 to 1—was the "mint ratio" between the two metals. But the "market ratio" soon differed. On the market, the amount of silver in a dollar was worth more than the amount of gold in a dollar. Owners of silver could get more by selling it for manufacture into jewelry and other objects than they could by taking it to the mint for conversion into coins. So they stopped taking it to the mint, and the mint stopped coining silver.

In 1873, Congress passed a law that seemed simply to recognize the long-existing situation by officially discontinuing silver coinage. Few objected at the time; but in fact, the measure did much more than confirm the status quo. Silver prices in 1873 had already begun to fall, and it soon became clear that Congress had foreclosed a very real potential method of expanding the currency. Before long many Americans concluded that a conspiracy of big bankers had been responsible for the "demonetization" of silver. Denouncers of the law referred to it as the "Crime of '73."

That very year, 1873, the silver price fell to a point at which the market ratio between silver and gold was the same as the mint ratio. In subsequent years the market value of silver continued to fall, and eventually the silver in a silver dollar came to be worth much less than the gold in a gold dollar. The drop was due simply to changes in demand and supply. The world demand for silver decreased as several European countries abandoned the bimetallic system and went over to the gold standard, defining their currencies only in terms of gold and issuing only gold coins. And the world supply of silver increased as the European governments disposed of their holdings and as huge new deposits of ore were discovered and exploited in Nevada, Colorado, and other Western states.

Two groups of Americans were especially determined to undo the Crime of '73. One consisted of the silver-mine owners, now understandably eager to have the government take their surplus silver and pay them much more than the market price. The other group consisted of the discontented farmers, who wanted an increase in the quantity of money—an inflation of the currency—as a means of raising the prices of farm products and easing the payment of the farmers' debts. In the language of the inflationists, the government ought to return at once to "free silver," that is, to the "free and unlimited coinage of silver" at the old ratio of 16 to 1.

In 1878, a coalition of Democrats and Republicans from the South, Midwest, and Far West attempted to carry a free-silver bill through Congress. They had to settle for a compromise, the Bland-Allison Act, which directed the government to purchase and coin at the old ratio only a limited amount of silver (from $2 million to $4 million worth per month).

Later, in 1890, the Sherman Silver Purchase Act directed the Treasury to buy 4.5 million ounces of silver each month, an amount estimated to be the maximum domestic production, and to pay for the purchased bullion in Treasury notes. The purchased silver was not to be coined, however. The amount of money in circulation did not increase materially, and the price of silver kept on falling. Creditors and conservatives still argued for the adoption of a single metallic standard; debtors and inflationists still agitated for the unlimited coinage of silver at the rate of 16 to 1.

The Populists at first did not emphasize silver. But as the party developed strength, the money question came to overshadow many other issues. The Populists desperately needed money to finance their campaigns. Silver-mine owners were willing to provide it but insisted on an elevation of the money plank and the subordination of other proposals.

The influence of silver on the thinking of Populists, agrarian Democrats, and farmers was graphically illustrated by the enormous popularity of a small and not particularly profound book, *Coin's Financial School*, written by William H. Harvey and published in 1894. "Professor Coin" ran a school, an imaginary institution specializing in finance, and the book reproduced his lectures and his dialogues with his students. The professor's brilliant discourses left even his most vehement opponents dazzled as he persuaded his listeners, with simple logic, of the almost miraculous restorative qualities of free silver: "It means the reopening of closed factories, the relighting of fires in darkened furnaces; it means hope instead of despair; comfort in place of suffering; life instead of death."

Ever since the Resumption Act of 1875 the Treasury had aimed to maintain a minimum gold reserve of $100 million to redeem its paper and silver dollars. During the prosperous eighties the reserve increased, and it reached the figure of $190 million by 1890. But in the last two years of the Harrison administration it fell off sharply. The prohibitive duties of the McKinley Tariff reduced imports and hence revenue; the pension and internal improvements appropriations ate up the surplus; and the Sherman Silver Purchase Act forced the government to buy increased amounts of silver and issue new Treasury notes that the Treasury insisted on redeeming in gold. Holders of greenbacks and silver certificates, jittery at rumors the government might be swept off the gold standard, demanded gold, and when Cleveland assumed office in 1893, the reserve had shrunk to a little over $100 million.

The panic intensified the rush for gold, and soon the reserve sank below the minimum deemed necessary to sustain the gold standard. Cleveland had always disliked the Sherman Silver Purchase Act, and now he was convinced that it was the chief factor draining gold from the Treasury and that, if allowed to stand, it would force the country off the gold standard and impair the government's financial honor. In one of his rare moods of leadership, the president summoned Congress into special session and demanded the repeal of the Sherman Act. He worked his will, but only by swinging the patronage lash hard on recalcitrant Democrats and enlisting the support of Eastern Republicans. Western and Southern Democrats fought repeal to the last, and in defeat were incredibly bitter. A historic party split was in the making.

The president had his victory, but the financial crisis deepened. In 1895, Cleveland approached the big New York bankers for help. A banking syndicate headed by J. P. Morgan agreed to take up a $65 million bond issue and to use the influence of the financial community to check the flow of gold to Europe. As a result, public faith that the government would maintain the gold standard was strengthened. The stampede to redeem notes eased. To agrarian Democrats and Populists, however, it seemed that Cleveland had sold out to Wall Street and concluded a crooked deal with the moneylenders. Actually, there had been no deal and no corruption, although the bankers undoubtedly turned an excessive profit.

The Cleveland administration ended amidst flaming portents of social unrest. The Democratic party was bitterly divided. The president's gold policy had aligned the Southern and Western Democrats in a solid phalanx against him and his Eastern followers.

"A Cross of Gold"

As the election of 1896 approached, Republicans—gloating over the failure of the Democrats to deal effectively with either the economic crisis or the social chaos that seemed to have emerged from it—were confident of success. The only question of importance that appeared to confront them was the identity of the man they would anoint as the next president.

Marcus A. Hanna, boss of the Ohio machine and soon to be national boss of the party, was a wealthy industrialist who aspired to be a president maker. He represented a new type in politics, the businessman who held office and actively manipulated parties instead of remaining in the background and paying out money for services rendered. He had picked out his man and had been grooming him carefully since 1890. The man was William McKinley, governor of Ohio, who as a congressman had been the author of the tariff act of 1890.

By the time the convention met, Hanna had lined up enough Middle Western and Southern delegations to nominate McKinley. Everywhere and on every occasion he presented his candidate as "Bill McKinley, the advance agent of prosperity" and the champion of protection for American producers.

The platform as finally framed endorsed the protective tariff, ignored completely such questions as the income tax, railroad and trust abuses, and labor injunctions, and opposed the free coinage of silver except by international agreement with the leading commercial nations. As other countries, particularly Great Britain, were unlikely to abandon the gold standard, the Republicans were, in effect, supporting gold. Thirty-four delegates from the mountain and plains states walked out when the currency plank was adopted. Their obvious destination was the Democratic party.

The Democrats met amid scenes of drama seldom equaled in American politics. The Southern and Western delegates came to the convention determined to seize control of the party from the Easterners. Alarmed by the rise of Populist strength in their sections, they intended to write free-silver and other planks of the third party into the platform and to nominate a silver candidate.

The resolutions committee presented to the convention two reports. The majority platform demanded tariff reduction, endorsed the principle of the income tax, denounced the issue of currency notes by the national banks, condemned the use of injunctions in industrial disputes, pledged a "stricter control" of trusts and railroads, and—this was the issue that headlined the platform—called for free silver: "We demand the free and unlimited coinage of both silver and gold at the present legal ratio of 16 to 1, without waiting for the aid or consent of any other nation." The minority resolution opposed the free coinage of silver except by international agreement, a stand identical to that of the Republicans.

William Jennings Bryan
The United States has produced many orators who could sway crowds with the magic of their voices, but it is generally agreed that Bryan had no superior in power and persuasiveness. Here he is speaking late in his career. The poster on the platform, in the lower left-hand corner of the picture, shows him as he appeared in 1896, when he was the Boy Orator of the Platte, engaged in the silver crusade. (Library of Congress)

Six speakers debated the resolution, three for gold and three for silver. The defenders of gold had the better of the oratorical tournament—up to the final address. Then from the Nebraska delegation a strikingly handsome young man walked to the platform to close the debate. He was William Jennings Bryan, thirty-six years of age. His political experience was limited to two terms in the House of Representatives; but he was widely known in the plains country as a magnetic orator, and he eagerly hoped for the presidential nomination. Through the farthest reaches of the vast hall now rang his magnificent organlike voice.

He ended with a peroration that brought the delegates and the spectators to their feet in a frenzied tumult of passion and that was declaimed by later generations of schoolboys all over rural America: "If they dare to come out in the open and defend the gold standard as a good thing, we will fight them to the uttermost. Having behind us the producing masses of this nation and the world, supported by the commercial interests, the laboring interests and the toilers everywhere, we will answer their demand for a gold standard by saying to them: 'You shall not press down upon the brow of labor this crown of thorns; you shall not crucify mankind upon a cross of gold.'"

The majority platform was adopted. The agrarians had found their leader. And the following day, Bryan was nominated on the fifth ballot. It is doubtful that he understood the technical implications of the money problem that he had discussed so eloquently before the convention. It is even more dubious that he realized the full import of the protest movement or the Populist program. He seized on one Populist plank, free silver, the most superficial of the various protest proposals, and erected it into a personal and political obsession.

One Republican, Joseph Foraker, when asked if he thought Bryan's title, the Boy Orator of the Platte, was an accurate phrase, replied that it was, because the Platte River was six inches deep and six miles wide at the mouth. More descriptive was another designation applied to Bryan: the Great Commoner. Born in Illinois of typical middle-class stock, he had attended a small sectarian college, had practiced law with only average success, and then, repeating a normal American pattern, had moved to Nebraska, a frontier area, to try his fortune. He served as a potent symbol of rural, Protestant, middle-class America.

The choice of Bryan and the nature of the Democratic platform placed the Populists in a cruel quandary. They had expected both of the major parties to adopt conservative programs and nominate conservative candidates, leaving the Populists to represent the growing forces of protest. But now the Democrats had stolen much of the Populists' thunder. The Populists faced the choice of naming their own candidate and splitting the protest vote or endorsing Bryan and losing their identity as a party. When the party assembled, the convention voted to approve Bryan but nominated its own vice-presidential candidate, Tom Watson, whom the Democrats were expected to adopt but whom they ignored. Many Populists argued fervently that "fusion" with the Democrats—who did not share the most important of the Populists' beliefs—would destroy their party. But the majority seemed to feel that there was no viable alternative.

The Conservative Victory

There has never been another campaign quite like the one of 1896. It had unequaled drama, intense excitement, a clean-cut issue, and a David-and-Goliath theme: the boy orator Bryan contending against the powerful boss Hanna and his hand-picked candidate, McKinley. The boss had the great advantage of ample funds to spend on organization. The business and financial community, frightened beyond reason at the prospect of Bryan's sitting in the White House taking advice from John P. Altgeld and Ignatius Donnelly, pressed contributions on Hanna. Just how much money Hanna had to dispense has been disputed, but the lowest estimate is $3.5 million and the highest is $7 million. The Democrats, by contrast, reported expenditures of only $300,000, a sum only slightly larger than the contribution of one firm, Standard Oil, to the Republican war chest.

Shrewdly, Hanna kept McKinley off the hustings, knowing better than to pit his solemn candidate against the matchless Bryan. From his home at Canton, Ohio, McKinley conducted a dignified "front-porch" campaign before pilgrimages of the Republican faithful, organized and paid for by Hanna. They came every day, but McKinley always had a speech ready for them, and always he stressed one theme: the Republican party was the only agency that could bring prosperity to the country.

No such decorous restraint marked the campaigning of the young and vital Bryan. Joyously bearing the brunt of the battle for his party, he inaugurated techniques never before witnessed in American political contests. Previous candidates had addressed audiences in campaigns and had even toured the country to speak at a few selected points. But Bryan was the first to stump systematically every section, to appear in villages and hamlets, the first, really, to say frankly to the voters that he wanted to be president. He traveled 18,000 miles, speaking several times a day, and addressed an estimated 5 million people.

Some businessmen grew almost hysterical at the thought of a possible Bryan victory. Many a company told its employees that, if Bryan should win, the company would have to go out of business. Employers threatened to fire workers who voted for him. Bankers

The Currency Issue [1896]

The Republican Platform: The Republican party is unreservedly for sound money. It caused the enactment of a law providing for the redemption [resumption] of specie payments in 1879. Since then every dollar has been as good as gold. We are unalterably opposed to every measure calculated to debase our currency or impair the credit of our country. We are therefore opposed to the free coinage of silver, except by international agreement with the leading commercial nations of the earth, which agreement we pledge ourselves to promote, and until such agreement can be obtained the existing gold standard must be maintained.

The Democratic Platform: We demand the free and unlimited coinage of both silver and gold at the present legal ratio of 16 to 1 without waiting for the aid or consent of any other nation. We demand that the standard silver dollar shall be a full legal tender, equally with gold, for all debts, public and private, and we favor such legislation as will prevent for the future the demonetization of any kind of legal-tender money by private contract.

said they could not renew the mortgages of farmers who did so.

Such threats, however, were less important than Bryan's own character in turning Democratic voters away from him. His revivalistic, camp-meeting style was pleasing enough to most Protestant sectarians of old native stock, but it antagonized many of the immigrant Catholics, who normally voted Democratic. Now many of them decided to stay home on election day, if not to go out and vote Republican.

Meanwhile, Bryan attracted fewer Republican farmers than he had hoped for. Again, the reason was not simply a fear of economic reprisals. More important was the fact that shortly before the election the price of wheat suddenly rose, and Western farm discontent just as suddenly fell.

On election day, McKinley polled 271 electoral votes to Bryan's 176. The popular vote was 7,105,000 to 6,503,000. Bryan won the Confederate South plus Missouri, swept the plains and mountain states except North Dakota, but lost California and Oregon on the Pacific coast. In short, he carried only the mining regions and the areas where staple farming was predominant and agricultural

prices were lowest. He went down to defeat in all the Granger states in the Midwest. The Democratic program, like that of the Populists, had been designed to serve the needs of one segment of one class, the most depressed fraction of agriculture, and this appeal was too narrow to win a national election.

Conservative Americans breathed a collective sigh of relief at the results of the 1896 election. What they had perceived as a radical threat to the nation's future had been averted—but only barely. It would be many years before they would forget that the "spirit of revolution" had seized control of one of the two major parties. For the Populists and their allies, the election results were nothing short of a disaster. They had gambled everything on their "fusion" with the Democratic party, and they had lost. The Populist movement stood exposed, it seemed, as a phenomenon too weak to influence national politics. And within months of the election, the People's party began to dissolve. Never again would American farmers unite so militantly to demand economic reform. And never again would any group of Americans raise so forceful a protest against the nature of the industrial economy.

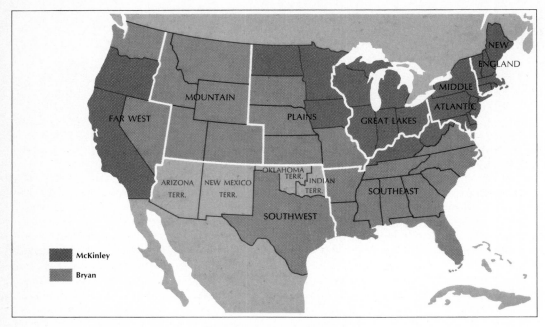

THE ELECTION OF 1896

McKinley and Prosperity

The administration of William McKinley, which began in the aftermath of turmoil, saw the nation return to a relative calm. One reason was simple exhaustion. By 1897, the labor unrest that had so frightened many middle-class Americans and so excited working-class people had subsided, victim of the internal weaknesses of the labor movement and of the strength of the corporate forces opposing it. And with the simultaneous decline of agrarian protest, the greatest destabilizing forces in the nation's politics were— temporarily at least—removed. Another reason was the character of the McKinley administration itself, which was politically shrewd and nothing if not committed to a reassuring stability. Most important, however, was the gradual easing of the economic crisis and the return of prosperity, a change that undercut many of those who were agitating for change.

William McKinley, a shrewd political operator, was the last of the long list of veteran officers of the Union army (beginning with

Grant) to sit in the White House. Friendly, kindly, and lovable, he was inclined to defer to stronger characters such as Hanna and to act in harmony with his party's leaders. He and they realized the dangers inherent in the currency issue. Silver had many adherents, as evidenced by Bryan's huge popular vote, and the Republican party numbered many silverites in its Western wing. Impulsive action might divide the party in its hour of victory.

Postponing action on the money problem until a more propitious time, the administration turned to an issue on which Republicans were agreed, the necessity for higher tariff rates. Immediately after assuming office, McKinley summoned Congress into special session to consider tariff revision. With record brevity, the Republican majority whipped into shape and passed the Dingley Tariff, raising the duties to an average of 57 percent, the highest in history.

On the currency question, the administration proceeded in accordance with the party's platform pronouncement that bimetallism could not be established except by international action. McKinley sent a commission to Europe to explore the possibility of a silver agreement with Great Britain and France. As he and everyone else anticipated, Britain refused to abandon its gold standard, thus effectively ending any hopes for international bimetallism. The administration could now argue that if the United States embarked on a silver program alone it would be economically isolated from the rest of the world, and the argument was hard to refute. Believing that their position was unassailable, the Republicans finally moved to enact currency legislation. The Currency, or Gold Standard, Act of 1900 legalized the gold standard and enlarged the redemption fund, which was to be maintained as a separate and special charge to protect the supply of gold from depletion.

And so the "battle of the standards" ended in victory for the forces of conservatism. Economic developments at the time seemed to prove that the conservatives had been right in the struggle. In 1898 prosperity returned to America. Foreign crop failures enlarged the farmer's market and sent farm prices surging upward. At the same time business entered another cycle of booming expansion. Prosperity and gold had come hand in hand—the lesson seemed obvious.

But it was not quite that simple. Bryan and the silverites were essentially right in demanding currency inflation. In the quarter century before 1900 the countries of Western civilization had experienced a spectacular augmentation of productive facilities and population. Yet the supply of money had not kept pace with economic progress, because the supply was tied to gold and the amount of gold remained practically constant. A committee of the British House of Lords, hardly a radical agency, reported after a careful investigation that the world's economy required a larger money supply.

It so happened that the supply was vastly increased soon after the Republicans took over the government in 1897. A new technique for extracting gold from low-content ores, the cyanide process, made it possible to work mines previously considered marginal or unprofitable. At the same time, huge new gold deposits were discovered in Alaska, South Africa, and Australia. In 1898, two and a half times as much gold was produced as in 1890, and the currency supply soon was inflated far beyond anything proposed by Bryan. The price level, which had been declining since 1865, started on an upward swing.

With McKinley, then, there came a tariff increase, the gold standard, and prosperity. There also came a new departure in foreign policy, as the nation entered upon the path of overseas imperialism and took its place among the "great powers" of the world.

SUGGESTED READINGS

General overviews of the political history of the late nineteenth century include John A. Garraty, *The New Commonwealth* (1969), for the period 1877–1890, and Harold U. Faulkner, *Politics, Reform, and Expansion* (1959), for the turbulent 1890s. Morton Keller, *Affairs of State* (1977), is a more interpretive analysis of public life in the late nineteenth century. Matthew Josephson, *The Politicos* (1963), is a hostile study of late nineteenth-century politicians; while David J. Rothman, *Politics and Power: The United States Senate, 1869–1901* (1966), and Robert D. Marcus, *Grand Old Party* (1971), are more temperate in their judgments. H. Wayne Morgan, *From Hayes to McKinley* (1969), is a basic narrative of the political events of the period; and Leonard D. White, *The Republican Era* (1958), examines the administrative developments of the time.

Several specialized studies examine some of the specific political issues of the "Gilded Age." Ari Hoogenboom, *Outlawing the Spoils* (1961), examines civil-service reform. Walter T. K. Nugent, *Money and American Society* (1968); Allen Weinstein, *Prelude to Populism* (1970); and Irwin Unger, *The Greenback Era* (1964), consider the money issue. John Sproat, *"The Best Men"* (1968), is a fine study of the origins of mugwumpery; while Geoffrey Blodgett, *The Gentle Reformers* (1966), examines reform Democrats in Massachusetts. James Bryce, *The American Commonwealth*, 2 vols. (1888) is a classic contemporary study of American politics by a British observer. Important biographies of leading figures of the era are Thomas C. Reeves, *Gentleman Boss* (1975), on Chester A. Arthur; Harry Barnard, *Rutherford B. Hayes and His America* (1954); Kenneth Davison, *The Presidency of Rutherford B. Hayes* (1972); Allan Peskin, *Garfield*

(1978); David Jordan, *Roscoe Conkling of New York* (1971); Allan Nevins, *Grover Cleveland: A Study in Courage* (1933); Harry J. Sievers, *Benjamin Harrison*, 3 vols. (1952–1968); H. Wayne Morgan, *William McKinley and His America* (1963); and Paolo Coletta, *William Jennings Bryan: Political Evangelist* (1964), the first of three volumes of the most thorough biography of Bryan. C. Vann Woodward, *Tom Watson, Agrarian Rebel* (1938), is a classic biography of the Populist leader; also valuable is Francis B. Simkins, *Pitchfork Ben Tillman* (1944).

The cultural aspects of late nineteenth-century politics are considered in two books by Paul Kleppner: *The Cross of Culture: A Social Analysis of Midwestern Politics, 1850–1900* (1970) and *The Third Electoral System, 1853–1892* (1979); and in Richard Jensen, *The Winning of the Midwest: Social and Political Conflict, 1888–1896* (1971).

The economic problems of the 1890s (and some of their political consequences) are the subject of Samuel McSeveney, *The Politics of Depression* (1972), which focuses on the Northeast. On labor unrest, see Donald McMurray, *Coxey's Army* (1929); Ray Ginger, *The Bending Cross* (1949), on Eugene Debs, the socialist leader; Almot Lindsey, *The Pullman Strike* (1942); and Ray Ginger, *Altgeld's America* (1958).

A large literature has emerged on the issue of Populism, of which the standard work was for many years John D. Hicks, *The Populist Revolt* (1931). Superseding Hicks as the most important single study of Populism is Lawrence Goodwyn, *Democratic Promise* (1976), also published in an abridged paperback version entitled *The Populist Moment* (1978). Norman Pollack, *The Populist Response to Industrial America* (1962), argues that the Populists were forward-looking radicals, thus challenging the view of Richard Hofstadter, *The Age of Reform* (1954), that they were nostalgic and basically conservative. Differing with both Pollack and Hofstadter is Sheldon Hackney, *Populism to Progressivism in Alabama* (1969). C. Vann Woodward, *Origins of the New South* (1972), includes a classic analysis of Southern Populism. Robert McMath, *Populist Vanguard* (1975), is a good study of the Farmers' Alliances that helped create the People's party. Bruce Palmer, *Man over Money* (1980), is an admiring examination of Populist ideology. Other important studies of Populism include Walter T. K. Nugent, *The Tolerant Populists* (1960), a study of Kansas that challenges Hofstadter's view of the Populists as narrow-minded and often bigoted; Theodore Saloutos, *Farmer Movements in the South, 1865–1933* (1960), which places Populism in a larger chronological context; Fred Shannon, *The Farmer's Last Frontier* (1945); and Peter Argersinger, *Populism and Politics: William Alfred Peffer and the People's Party* (1974).

On the important election of 1896, several good studies are available, among them Paul Glad, *McKinley, Bryan, and the People* (1964) and *The Trumpet Soundeth* (1960); Stanley Jones, *The Presidential Election of 1896* (1964); and J. Rogers Hollingsworth, *The Whirligig of Politics: The Democracy of Cleveland and Bryan* (1963). For information on the McKinley administration, see—in addition to the two works by H. Wayne Morgan and the general studies of the era cited above—Margaret Leech, *In the Days of McKinley* (1959), and Herbert Croly, *Marcus Alonzo Hanna* (1912).

The Imperial Republic

20

The Rough Riders
The volunteer cavalry regiment organized by Theodore Roosevelt during the Spanish-American War and known as the Rough Riders was typical of the amateurish way in which the United States engaged in its first overseas conflict. Only because the Spanish military situation was so hopelessly inadequate were the Americans able to prevail quickly. (Culver Pictures)

The American republic had been an expansionist nation since the earliest days of its existence. Throughout the first half of the nineteenth century, as the population of the United States grew and pressed westward, the government continually acquired new territory for its citizens to occupy: the trans-Appalachian West, the Louisiana Territory, Florida, Texas, Oregon, California, New Mexico, Alaska, and more. It was the nation's "Manifest Destiny," so many Americans believed, to expand into new realms.

In the last years of the nineteenth century, however, with the United States having virtually reached its continental limits, expansionism moved into a new phase. In the past, the acquisitions had nearly always been areas contiguous to the existing boundaries of the nation. Land was annexed with the idea of providing new areas of settlement for the American people. The new acquisitions were expected to be organized as territories and, ultimately, admitted to the Union as states. But the expansionism of the 1890s, the new Manifest Destiny, involved acquiring possessions separate from the continental United States: island territories, many of which were already thickly populated, most of which were not suitable for massive settlement from America, few of which could be expected ever to become states of the Union. Like the great colonial powers of Europe at the same time, the United States was acquiring, for largely economic reasons, an empire. It was joining England, France, Germany, and other expanding nations in the great imperial drive that was, by the end of the century, to bring much of the underdeveloped world under the control of the industrial powers of the West.

There had been some agitation in America for overseas expansion as early as the 1850s, agitation that continued after the Civil War and, to some extent, during the ensuing decades. Not until the 1890s, however, was the nation truly ready for the new imperialism. In the wake of a brief, victorious war with Spain, the United States suddenly found itself in possession of a substantial empire. And having emerged as a widely recognized "world power," it pursued three basic foreign policies. In dealing with Europe, Americans sought to promote commerce but avoid diplomatic entanglements (what was often inaccurately called "isolation"). In relations with the Americas, the goal was to defend the hemisphere from overseas incursions and promote "Pan-Americanism"—a hemispheric unity in which the United States would be the dominant force. In regard to Asia, the policy was defined as defense of the "Open Door"—the right of American commerce to operate without restriction in China.

Out of the imperial experience of the late nineteenth century emerged many of the basic premises that would dominate American foreign policy for many decades to come. And out of it, too, would emerge many of the problems that would accompany the nation's position as a "great power."

STIRRINGS OF IMPERIALISM

In the two decades after 1870, the American people seemed to have abandoned the expansionist impulse of the prewar years. They were occupied with things closer to home— reconstructing the South, settling the last frontier, building a network of railroads, and expanding their great industrial system. By the 1890s, however, they were ready—indeed, eager—to resume the course of Manifest Destiny that had impelled their forebears to wrest an empire from Mexico in the expansionist 1840s.

The New Manifest Destiny

Various developments subtly played a part in shifting the attention of Americans from their own country to lands across the seas. The passing of the frontier gave rise to a feeling that resources would soon become scarce and that they must be sought abroad. The depression beginning in 1893 seemed to confirm the fear of certain businessmen that industry had been overbuilt and was producing more goods than customers at home could buy. The bitter social protests of the time—the Populist movement, the free-silver crusade, the bloody labor disputes—led many people to believe that the nation was threatened with internal collapse. Some politicians advocated a more aggressive foreign policy to divert the popular mind from dissensions at home.

The swelling volume of American exports to other countries altered the nature of the nation's trade relations and directed the attention of political leaders to the importance of foreign markets—and to the possible advisability of securing foreign colonies. The value of American exports in 1870 was approximately $392 million; in 1890 the figure was $857 million, and by 1900 it had leaped to $1.394 billion. "Today," Senator Albert J. Beveridge of Indiana cried in 1899, "we are raising more than we can consume. Today, we are making more than we can use. Therefore, we must find new markets for our produce, new occupation for our capital, new work for our labor."

In the century's closing years the powers of Europe partitioned most of Africa among themselves and then turned eager eyes on the Far East and the feeble Chinese Empire. Imperialism was in the air, and a leading American expansionist, Senator Henry Cabot Lodge of Massachusetts, warned that the United States "must not fall out of the line of march."

A philosophic justification for expansionism was provided by historians, professors, clergymen, and other intellectuals, who found a basis for imperialism in their interpretations of Charles Darwin's theories (interpretations that Darwin himself never intended). These thinkers contended that, among nations, or "races," as well as among biological species, there was a struggle for existence, and only the fittest could survive. If the strong dominated the weak, that was in accordance with the law of nature. It was an application to world affairs of the same distortion of Darwinism that industrialists and others had long been applying to domestic economic affairs.

One of the first to argue this proposition was the popular writer John Fiske, who predicted in an article in *Harper's Magazine* (1885) that the English-speaking peoples would eventually control every land that was not already the seat of an established civilization. Support for Fiske's position came from Josiah Strong, a Congregational clergyman and champion of overseas missionary work. In a book entitled *Our Country: Its Possible Future and Its Present Crisis* (1885), Strong declared that the Anglo-Saxon "race," and especially its American branch, represented the great ideas of civil liberty and pure Christianity and was "divinely commissioned" to spread its institutions over the earth. John W. Burgess, founder of Columbia University's School of Political Science, gave the stamp of scholarly approval to imperialism. In his *Political Science and Comparative Law* (1890), he flatly stated that the Anglo-Saxon and Teutonic nations possessed the highest political talents. It was the duty of these nations, he said, to uplift less fortunate peoples, even to force superior institutions on them if necessary: "There is no human right to the status of barbarism."

The ablest and probably the most effective apostle of imperialism was Alfred Thayer Mahan, a captain, and later an admiral, in the navy. Mahan presented his philosophy in three major works: *The Influence of Sea Power upon History, 1660–1783* (1890); *The Influence of Sea Power upon the French Revolution and Empire, 1793–1812* (1892); and *The Interest of America in Sea Power* (1897). His thesis may be briefly stated. The sea-power nations were the great nations of history, and the United States, a huge island, had to build its greatness on sea power. The essential links in sea power were a productive domestic economy, foreign commerce, a merchant marine to monopolize national trade, a navy to defend the trade routes and national interests, and colonies to provide raw materials and markets and to serve as bases for the navy. Specifically, Mahan advocated that the United States construct a canal across the isthmus of Central America to join the oceans, acquire defensive bases on both sides of the canal in the Caribbean and the Pacific, and take possession of Hawaii and other Pacific islands. "Whether they will or no," he proclaimed, "Americans must now begin to look outward."

Mahan doubted that the United States would achieve its destiny, because its navy was not large enough to play the role he envisioned for it. But he did not accurately gauge the progress of the naval construction program launched in the Garfield-Arthur administration and continued by every succeeding administration. By 1898, the United States had advanced to fifth among the world's naval powers; and by 1900, to third.

Hemispheric Hegemony

The most ardent practitioner of the new, assertive diplomacy was Harrison's secretary of state, James G. Blaine, who in 1889 was beginning his second tour of duty in the foreign office. He believed that his country was destined to dominate the Caribbean and the Pacific. His expansionist policy was based largely on his conviction that the United States had to find enlarged foreign markets for its surplus goods. The most likely foreign outlet, he believed, was Latin America, with whose countries he wanted friendly commercial relations.

During his first term of office (1881), Blaine had invited the Latin nations to a Pan-American conference in Washington to discuss trade matters and arbitration of disputes. But after Garfield's death, Blaine left office, and his cautious successor withdrew the invitations. Shortly before the Harrison administration took office, however, Congress authorized the convoking of a conference, and the State Department issued the invitations. With delegates from nineteen American nations in attendance, the first Pan-American Congress assembled in 1889. Blaine (now back in the State Department) tried to persuade the conference to endorse his two principal objectives: (1) to draw the United States and Latin America into a customs union and (2) to create machinery to arbitrate controversies among the hemispheric nations. The Latin delegates rejected both proposals. They preferred to buy in the cheaper European market, and they feared the dominance of the United States in arbitration. Still, the meeting was not entirely a failure. Out of it arose the Pan-American Union, an agency in Washington that became a clearinghouse for distributing information to the member nations; and other congresses would meet in the future to discuss common hemispheric matters.

When, after the election of 1892, the Democrats took over, the change in personnel meant no break in the new self-assertive diplomacy. Indeed, in 1895 President Cleveland and his secretary of state, Richard Olney, in a dispute with Great Britain over the boundary of Venezuela carried the country close to the brink of war.

For years, Britain and Venezuela had argued about the boundary between Venezuela and British Guiana, the dispute assuming new importance when gold was discovered in the disputed area. Both Cleveland and Olney, as well as the American public, were disposed to sympathize with Venezuela as the little underdog country confronting the great power. The president and Congress publicly expressed hopes that Britain would see fit to arbitrate the matter. When the English government took no action, Olney drafted a note to Lord Salisbury of the foreign office protesting that Britain was violating the Monroe Doctrine. Any European interference with hemispheric affairs—and the boundary dispute, he implied, constituted interference—came within the scope of the famous doctrine, said the secretary. In bellicose language designed to make England sit up and listen, he declared: "Today the United States is practically sovereign on this continent, and its fiat is law upon the subjects to which it confines its interposition."

After months of delay, Salisbury replied to Olney. With firm finality and a touch of condescension, he informed the secretary that the Monroe Doctrine did not apply to boundary disputes or the present situation and was not recognized as international law anyway. Britain was not going to arbitrate. Cleveland was enraged. In December 1895, he sent a special message to Congress reviewing the controversy. He asked for authority to create a special commission to determine the boundary line and declared that if Britain resisted the commission's decision the United States should fight.

Enthusiastically Congress voted support for Cleveland's plan, and war talk flamed all over the country. Belatedly, the British government realized that it had stumbled into a genuine diplomatic crisis. The last thing in the world that England wanted or could afford was a war with the United States. Suddenly, the British backed down and agreed to arbitration.

Hawaii and Samoa

The first area into which the United States directed its expansionist impulse after the Civil War was the vast Pacific Ocean region.

The islands of Hawaii in the mid-Pacific had been an important stopover station for American ships in the China trade since the early nineteenth century. The first American settlers to reach Hawaii were New England missionaries, who, like their fellows in Oregon at approximately the same time, advertised the economic possibilities of the islands in the religious press. Soon other Americans arrived to become sugar planters and to found a profitable new industry. Eventually, officers of the growing navy looked longingly on the magnificent natural base of Pearl Harbor on the island of Oahu.

The American residents of Hawaii came to dominate the economic life of the islands and also the political policies of the native ruler. Commercial relations were inexorably pushing Hawaii into the American orbit and making it, as Blaine accurately contended, a part of the American economic system. A treaty signed in 1875 permitted Hawaiian sugar to enter the United States duty-free and bound the Hawaiian kingdom to make no territorial or economic concessions to other powers. The trade arrangement tied the islands to the American economy, and the political clauses meant that, in effect, the United States was guaranteeing Hawaii's independence, and hence was making the islands a protectorate. In 1887, a new treaty renewed the existing arrangements and granted the United States exclusive use of Pearl Harbor as a naval station. The course of events in the Pacific was rendering outright political union almost inevitable.

Sugar production in Hawaii boomed, and prosperity burgeoned for the American planters. Then the McKinley Tariff of 1890 dealt the planters a bad blow; by removing the duty on foreign raw sugar and giving domestic producers a bounty, it deprived Hawaii of its privileged position in the American sugar market. Annexation (which would give Hawaiian planters the same bounty that American planters were receiving) seemed the only alternative to economic strangulation. At the same time there ascended to the throne a new ruler, Queen Liliuokalani, who was determined to eliminate American influence in the government.

The American residents decided to act at once. They started a revolution (1893) and called on the United States for protection. At a critical moment the American minister, John L. Stevens, an ardent annexationist and friend of Blaine, ordered 160 marines from a warship in Honolulu harbor to go ashore to aid the rebels. The queen yielded her authority, and a delegation representing the triumphant provisional government set out for Washington to negotiate a treaty of annexation. They found President Harrison highly receptive, but before the resulting treaty could be acted on by the Senate he was succeeded by Cleveland.

However disposed Cleveland was to upholding American rights under the Monroe Doctrine, his conservative ideas about the sanctity of property ownership made him wary of the proposed annexation. Suspicious of what had happened in Hawaii, he withdrew the treaty and sent a special representative to the islands to investigate. When this agent reported that Americans had engineered the revolution, Cleveland endeavored to restore the queen to her throne. But the Americans were in control of the kingdom and refused to budge. Reluctantly the president had to accord recognition to their government as representing the "republic" of Hawaii. Cleveland had only delayed the inevitable. In 1898, with the Republicans again in power and with the United States constructing a colonial empire in both oceans, Hawaii was annexed by joint resolution of both houses of Congress.

Three thousand miles to the south of Hawaii, the Samoan Islands dominated the sea lanes of the South Pacific and had long served as a way station for American ships in the Pacific trade. As American commerce with Asia increased after the completion of the first transcontinental railroad in 1869 and the extension of a steamship line from San Francisco to New Zealand, certain business groups regarded Samoa with new interest; and the navy eyed the harbor at Pago Pago on the island of Tutuila. In 1872, a naval officer visited the islands and negotiated a treaty granting the United States the use of Pago Pago, but the Senate rejected it. President Grant nevertheless sent a special representative to Samoa to encourage American trading and business interests. The familiar chain of events leading to involvement was being set in motion. In 1878, a native prince was brought to Washington. He signed a treaty, which was approved by the Senate, providing for an American naval station at Pago

Pago and binding the United States to use its "good offices" to adjust any differences between a foreign power and Samoa. This treaty indicated that the American government meant to have a voice in Samoan affairs.

The opportunity to express that voice soon came. Great Britain and Germany were also interested in the islands, and they hastened to secure treaty rights from the native princes. For the next ten years the three powers scrambled and intrigued for dominance in Samoa, playing off one ruler against another and coming dangerously close to war. In 1889, warships of the contending nations appeared in one Samoan harbor, and a clash seemed imminent. But a tropical hurricane dispersed the vessels, and the German government, not wishing to antagonize the United States, suggested a conference of the interested powers in Berlin to settle the dispute. Germany and Britain would have preferred a division of the islands, but Secretary Blaine insisted on preserving native Samoan rule. The result was that the conferees agreed on a tripartite protectorate over Samoa, with the native chiefs exercising only nominal authority.

The three-way arrangement proved unsatisfactory, failing altogether to halt the intrigues and rivalries of the signatory members. It was abrogated in 1899, when the United States and Germany divided the islands between them, with Britain being compensated elsewhere in the Pacific. Germany obtained the two largest islands, but the United States retained Tutuila with its incomparable harbor at Pago Pago. The three colonial powers were finally satisfied—at the expense of the Samoans.

WAR WITH SPAIN

Imperial ambitions had thus begun to stir within the United States well before the late 1890s. Not until the coming of a war with Spain in 1898, however, did those stirrings develop into an overt expansionism.

Controversy over Cuba

The immediate background of the Spanish-American War lay in the Caribbean island of

Cuba, which with nearby Puerto Rico represented nearly all that was left of Spain's once extensive Latin American empire. The Cubans had long resented Spanish rule, and they had engaged in a notable attempt to overthrow it between 1868 and 1878 (the Ten Years' War). During that revolt, the American people were strongly sympathetic to the Cuban cause, but their feelings did not go beyond expressions of support. The govern-

**"And Spain Calls
This War!"**
Joseph Pulitzer's New
York *World* (in which this
1898 cartoon appeared)
and William Randolph
Hearst's New York *Journal*
were the leading
examples of the lurid
"yellow journalism" that
did so much to inflame
American public opinion
in the months preceding
the Spanish-American
War. In cartoons such as
this one, Spain was
portrayed as a vicious
power, imposing tyranny
and starvation upon a
hapless Cuban population
crying out for American
assistance. (Brown Brothers)

AND SPAIN CALLS THIS WAR!

ment maintained a position of strict neutrality, despite a strong provocation offered by Spain. In 1873, the Spanish authorities captured a Cuban-owned arms-running ship, the *Virginius*, and executed fifty-three of its crew. Because the vessel had flown an American flag and some of its seamen were Americans, popular indignation was intense. But Secretary of State Hamilton Fish avoided a crisis by inducing the Spanish government to return the *Virginius* and pay an indemnity to the families of the executed men.

In 1895, the Cubans rose up again. Not only the continuing Spanish misrule but also the American tariff policy created conditions of misery that prepared the way for revolt. Cuba's principal export was sugar, and the bulk of the crop went to the United States. The Wilson-Gorman Tariff in 1894, with its high duties on raw sugar, shut off the island's chief source of wealth and prostrated its economy.

From the beginning, the struggle took on aspects of ferocity that horrified Americans. The Cubans deliberately devastated the island to force the Spaniards to leave. To put down the insurrection, the Spanish resorted to methods equally extreme. General Valeriano Weyler—or "Butcher" Weyler, as he soon came to be known in the American press—confined the entire civilian population of certain areas to hastily prepared concentration camps, where they died by the thousands, victims of disease and malnutrition.

Many of the same savage techniques had been employed earlier in the Ten Years' War without shocking American sensibilities. But in the nineties a wave of anger ran through the American public. The revolt of 1895 was reported more fully and floridly by the American press than the former outbreak—and so reported as to give the impression that all the cruelties were being perpetrated by the Spaniards.

At this time, Joseph Pulitzer with his New

York *World* and William Randolph Hearst with his New York *Journal* were revolutionizing American journalism. The new "yellow press" specialized in lurid and sensational news; when such news did not exist, editors were not above creating it. To Hearst and Pulitzer, engaged in a ruthless circulation war, the struggle in Cuba was a journalist's dream. Both sent batteries of reporters and illustrators to Cuba with orders to provide accounts of Spanish atrocities. "You furnish the pictures," Hearst supposedly told an overly scrupulous artist, "and I'll furnish the war."

The mounting storm of indignation against Spain left President Cleveland unmoved. Convinced that both sides in Cuba were guilty of atrocities and that the United States had no interests justifying involvement in the struggle, he issued a proclamation of neutrality and attempted to stop the numerous filibustering expeditions being organized by a "junta" of Cuban refugees in New York City. When Congress, in a state of excitement, passed a resolution favoring recognition of Cuban belligerency, he ignored the action. His only concession to the demands for intervention was to offer America's good offices to mediate the conflict, a proposal that Spain declined.

When McKinley took over the presidency in 1897, he renewed the American mediation offer, which was again refused. Taking a stronger line than his predecessor, he protested to Spain against its "uncivilized and inhuman" conduct. The Spanish government, alarmed that McKinley's course might forebode American intervention in Cuba, recalled Weyler, modified the concentration policy, and took steps to grant the island a qualified autonomy. At the end of 1897, with the insurrection losing ground, it seemed that war might be averted.

If there was any chance to a peaceful settlement, it was extinguished by two dramatic incidents in February 1898. The first occurred when a Cuban agent in Havana stole a private letter written by Dupuy de Lôme, the Spanish minister in Washington, and thoughtfully turned it over to the American press. Published first in Hearst's New York *Journal*, and later in newspapers across the land, the minister's letter described McKinley as a weak man and "a bidder for the admiration of the crowd." This was no more than many Americans, including some Republicans, were saying about their president—Theodore Roosevelt described McKinley as having "no more backbone than a chocolate éclair"—but because a foreigner had made the remark it was considered a national insult. Popular anger was intense, and Dupuy de Lôme resigned before the outraged McKinley could demand his recall.

While the excitement was still at fever pitch, even more sensational news hit the front pages: the American battleship *Maine* had been blown up in Havana harbor with a loss of more than 260 lives. This vessel had been ordered to Cuban waters in January on a "friendly" visit, but the real reason for its presence was to protect American lives and property against possible attacks by Spanish loyalists. Many Americans jumped to the conclusion that the Spanish had sunk the ship—"an act of dirty treachery," Theodore Roosevelt announced—and the imperialists and the jingoists screamed for war. This opinion seemed confirmed when a naval court of inquiry reported that an external explosion by a submarine mine had caused the disaster. In fact, the real cause of the *Maine* explosion was never determined. Nevertheless, war hysteria swept the country, and Congress unanimously appropriated $50 million for military preparations. "Remember the *Maine*" became a national chant for revenge.

After the *Maine* incident there was little chance that the government could keep the people from war, although McKinley still did not wish to resort to force. In March 1898, he asked Spain to agree to an armistice, with negotiations for a permanent peace to follow, and an immediate ending of the concentration system. After a slight delay, Spain essentially accepted the American demands on April 9. Two days later McKinley asked Congress for authority to use military force to end the hostilities in Cuba—in short, for a declaration of war. After reviewing the reasons that impelled him to recommend war ("in the name of humanity, in the name of civilization, in behalf of endangered Ameri-

Wreck of the *Maine*
During the night after the explosion, the *Maine* settled down into the mud on the harbor bottom, so that only the wrecked superstructure remained visible, as shown here. Soon afterward, divers examined the hull. From their findings and from other evidence a naval court of inquiry concluded that an underwater mine had exploded, setting off explosions in the ship's powder magazines. Years later, in 1911, the wreck was raised so that it could be examined for a second court of inquiry. This court agreed with the first one on the essential point—that there had been both external and internal explosions—but disagreed on certain significant details. Finally, the hulk was towed out to sea and sunk in water too deep to permit another examination. (National Archives)

can interests"), he mentioned only casually, at the end of the message, that Spain was already capitulating to his requests.

By huge majorities, Congress on April 19 passed a joint resolution declaring Cuba free and authorizing the president to employ force to expel the Spanish from the island. There was, as yet, only limited support for territorial expansion as a war aim. Some national leaders were calling openly for imperialism, but a powerful anti-imperialist movement more than counterbalanced them for the time. Evidence of the anti-imperialists' strength was the addition to the congressional resolution of the Teller Amendment, which disclaimed any intention on the part of the United States to annex Cuba.

"A Splendid Little War"

The Spanish-American conflict was, in the words of Roosevelt's friend John Hay, "a splendid little war." Indeed, to virtually all Americans, with the possible exception of the enlisted men who fought it, it seemed almost an ideal conflict. It was the last small, short, individualistic war before the huge, protracted, impersonal struggles of the twentieth century. Declared in April, it was over in August. Newspaper readers easily and eagerly followed the campaigns and the heroic exploits of American soldiers and sailors. Only 460 Americans were killed in battle or died of wounds, but some 5,200 perished of disease: malaria, dysentery, typhoid, and other ills.

Blithely and confidently, the United States embarked on a war it was not prepared to fight. The regular army, numbering only 28,000 troops and officers scattered around the country at various posts, was a tough little force, skilled at quelling Indian outbreaks, but with no experience in large-scale warfare. Hastily Congress directed the president to increase the army to 62,000 and to call for 125,000 volunteers. It was expected that the National Guard, the state militia, would furnish the bulk of the volunteers, and in addition the president was authorized to accept directly into the national service three volunteer cavalry regiments. By far the most colorful of the cavalrymen were the Rough Riders, nominally commanded by Leonard Wood but actually by Theodore Roosevelt, who was about to burst onto the front pages as a war hero. The services of supply, manned by elderly bureaucratic officers, proved incapable of meeting the modest wants of the forces raised during the war. On hand were enough Krag-Jorgensen repeating rifles, using smokeless powder, for the regulars; but the volunteers had to make do with the old black-powder, single-shot Springfields. American soldiers campaigning in tropical regions were clothed in the traditional heavy blue uniforms and fed canned rations that they called "embalmed beef."

The Spanish army numbered almost 130,000 troops, of whom 80,000 were already in Cuba at the beginning of the war. Despite its imposing size, it was not an efficient force; its commanders seemed to be paralyzed by a conviction of certain defeat. The American navy, fifth largest in the world, was far superior to the Spanish in ships, gunnery, and personnel.

The greatest weakness in the American military system was that no agency in it, either in the army or in the navy, was charged with strategic planning. Only the navy had worked out an objective, and its objective had little to do with freeing Cuba.

The assistant secretary of the navy in the McKinley administration was Theodore Roosevelt, ardent imperialist and proponent of war. In consultations with naval officers, Roosevelt prepared to seize Spain's Philippine Islands in the far Pacific. He strengthened the Asiatic squadron and instructed its commander, Commodore George Dewey, to attack the Philippines in the event of war. Immediately after war was declared, Dewey left the China coast and headed for Manila, where a venerable Spanish fleet was stationed. On May 1 he steamed into Manila Bay, and as his ships prepared to pass down the line of anchored enemy vessels he uttered the first slogan of the war: "You may fire when ready, Gridley." When the firing

THE SPANISH-AMERICAN WAR: PACIFIC FRONT

was finished, the Spanish fleet was completely destroyed, one American sailor lay dead—of a heat stroke—and George Dewey, immediately promoted to admiral, had become the first hero of the war.

The Spaniards still held Manila, and Dewey had no troops with which to attack them. While he waited nervously, the government assembled an expeditionary force to relieve him and take the city. Not until August 13 did the Americans receive the surrender of Manila.

In the rejoicing over Dewey's victory, few Americans paused to note that the character of the war was being subtly altered. What had begun as a war to free Cuba was becoming a war to acquire colonies.

But Cuba was not to be left out of the war picture. Late in April it was known in the

United States that a Spanish fleet under Admiral Pascual Cervera had sailed for the west, presumably for a Cuban harbor. Cervera's antique armada was no match for the powerful American Atlantic squadron, as the Spanish government well knew. The Atlantic squadron, commanded by Admiral William T. Sampson, with Commodore W. S. Schley second in command, was expected to intercept and destroy Cervera before he reached his destination. (The squadron was "as strong as Sampson and as Schley as a fox," newspapers happily assured their readers.) But the Spaniard turned out to be the fox. Easily eluding his pursuers, he slipped into the Santiago harbor, on the southern coast of Cuba, where he was not discovered by the Americans until ten days after his arrival. Immediately the Atlantic fleet moved to bottle him up.

While the navy was monopolizing the first phases of the war, the War Department was trying to mobilize and train an army. The volunteer and National Guard units were collected near Chattanooga, Tennessee, while the regulars, plus the Rough Riders,

were assembled at Tampa, Florida, under the command of General William R. Shafter. The entire mobilization process was conducted with remarkable inefficiency. There were appalling shortages of arms, ammunition, food, clothing, and medical supplies.

The army's commanding general, Nelson A. Miles, veteran of the Civil War, had planned to train the troops until autumn, then to occupy Puerto Rico and, in conjunction with the Cuban rebels, attack Havana. But with a Spanish naval force at Santiago, plans were hastily changed. It was decided to send Shafter with his force of 17,000 to take Santiago. So in June the expedition left Tampa. The embarkation was accomplished amid scenes of fantastic incompetence, but it was efficiency itself compared to the landing. Five days were required to put the army ashore, and this with the enemy offering no opposition.

Once landed, Shafter moved his army toward Santiago, planning to surround and capture it. On the way he fought and defeated the Spaniards at two battles, El Caney and San Juan Hill. In both engagements the

THE SPANISH-AMERICAN WAR: CARIBBEAN FRONT

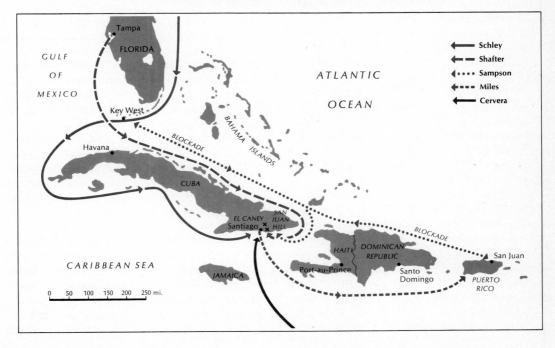

Rough Riders were in the middle of the fighting and on the front pages of the newspapers. Colonel Roosevelt rapidly emerged as a hero of the war. Shafter was now before Santiago, but his army was so weakened by sickness that he feared he might have to abandon his position. When he appealed to Sampson to unite with him in a joint attack on the city, the admiral answered that mines in the harbor made it too dangerous to take his big ships in.

At this point, disaster seemingly confronted the Americans; but unknown to them, the Spanish government had decided that Santiago was lost. On July 3, Cervera, acting under orders from home, broke from the harbor to attempt an escape that he knew was hopeless. The waiting American squadron destroyed his entire fleet. Shafter then pressed the Spanish army commander to surrender, and that official, after bargaining for generous terms, including free transportation back to Spain for his troops, turned over Santiago on July 16. While the Santiago campaign was in its last stages, an American army landed in Puerto Rico and occupied it against virtually no opposition.

Spain was defeated (more as a result of its own weakness and incompetence than because of American strength) and knew it. Through the French ambassador in Washington, the Spanish government asked for peace; and on August 12, an armistice ended the war.

Decision for Imperialism

In agreeing to a preliminary peace, the United States had laid down terms on which a permanent settlement must be based: Spain was to relinquish Cuba, cede Puerto Rico to the United States, cede also to the victor an island in the Ladrones, midway between Hawaii and the Philippines (this turned out to be Guam), and permit the Americans to hold Manila pending the final disposition of the Philippines. The last clause reflected the confusion in the McKinley administration as to what to do about the islands where its forces had won a foothold. The demands for Puerto Rico and Guam showed how quickly the war to free Cuba had assumed an imperialist

character. Aroused by the excitement of military victory and a heady sense of mastery, the American government and people were disposed to keep what American arms had won.

In October 1898, commissioners from the United States and Spain met in Paris to determine a permanent peace. Protesting almost not at all, Spain agreed to recognize Cuba's independence, to assume the Cuban debt, and to cede Puerto Rico and Guam to the victor. Then the American commissioners, acting under instruction from McKinley, startled the conference by demanding the cession of all the Philippines. The president later said that he had arrived at his decision as a result of divine guidance. Probably such mundane factors as the swelling sentiment for annexation in the country and the pressure of the imperialist leaders of his party influenced his thinking more. Stubbornly the Spanish resisted the American demand, although they realized they could retain the islands only by resuming the war. They yielded to the inevitable when the United States offered a money payment of $20 million. The Treaty of Paris was signed on December 10, 1898, and sent to the United States for ratification by the Senate.

When the treaty was submitted to the Senate, it encountered immediate and fierce criticism and occasioned in that body and throughout the country one of those "great debates" that frequently precede a departure in American foreign policy. The chief point at issue was the acquisition of the Philippines, denounced by many, including prominent Republicans, as a repudiation of America's high moral position in the war and a shameful occupation of a land that wanted to be free. Favoring ratification were the imperialists, the big navy lobby, the Protestant clergy—who saw in a colonial empire enlarged fields for missionary enterprise—and most Republicans. Business, which had generally opposed the war, for fear of a disruption of commerce, now swung over to support the treaty, converted by the notion that possession of the Philippines would enable American interests to dominate the Oriental trade. Perhaps the strongest argument in favor of annexation, however, was the apparent ease with which it could be accomplished. The United States, after all, already possessed the islands as a result of its military triumph. In the forces opposing the treaty were more conservative or idealistic Americans who objected to their country's annexing other people against their will, traditionalists who feared that a colonial empire would necessitate large armaments and foreign alliances, a majority of the intellectuals, economic interests such as the sugar growers who foresaw colonial competition, and most Democrats, who saw annexation as a Republican issue.

After weeks of bitter wrangling, the treaty was ratified on February 6, 1899, but only because it received an unexpected assist from William Jennings Bryan, who expected to be his party's candidate again in the election of 1900. Bryan persuaded a number of Democratic senators to vote for ratification. It has been charged that he was looking for a campaign issue, and in his defense it has been said that he thought the question of the Philippines should be decided by a national referendum: if the Democrats won in 1900, they would free the islands.

In 1900, Bryan ran against McKinley again, and this time Bryan went down to a crushing defeat. Although the Republicans claimed a popular mandate for imperialism, other factors had helped to determine the outcome. The victors had again exploited the money and tariff issues; they had harped on the continuing prosperity in the country under a Republican administration; and they had displayed to the voters the colorful personality of their vice-presidential candidate, the hero of San Juan Hill, Colonel Theodore Roosevelt.

THE REPUBLIC AS EMPIRE

The new colonial empire was extensive enough to warm the heart of the most ardent imperialist. Stretching from the Caribbean to the far reaches of the Pacific, it embraced Puerto Rico, Alaska, Hawaii, a part of Samoa, Guam, the Philippines, and a chain of minor Pacific islands.

But with the empire came new problems. Many of the predictions of the anti-imperialists proved accurate. Ultimately, as a colonial power, the United States had to maintain large stockpiles of armaments, concern itself with the complexities of Far Eastern international politics, and modify its traditional policy of holding aloof from alliances.

Governing the Colonies

Immediately, the nation faced the problem of how it was to govern its dependencies, and here a host of perplexing questions arose. Did Congress have to administer the colonies in accordance with the Constitution? Did the inhabitants of the new possessions have the rights of American citizens? Could Congress levy tariff duties on colonial imports? Or, in a phrase that pleased the public fancy, did the Constitution follow the flag? The Supreme Court pointed to a solution in the so-called insular cases (*De Lima* v. *Bidwell*, *Downes* v. *Bidwell*, and others, 1900–1904), involving duties on colonial trade. In a series of decisions the Court distinguished, in extremely technical language, between "incorporated" and "unincorporated" territories. In legislating for the latter—the insular possessions—Congress was not bound by all the limitations in the Constitution applicable to incorporated territories, although some restrictions did apply. What the Court was saying, in effect, was that the Constitution followed the flag only if Congress so decided and that the government could administer its colonies in almost any way it saw fit.

Three of the dependencies—Hawaii, Alaska, and Puerto Rico—were given territorial status as quickly as Congress considered them ready for it. For Hawaii, with its large American population and close economic ties with the United States, a basis for government was provided by an act of 1900. This measure granted American citizenship to all persons who were citizens of the Hawaiian republic, authorized an elective two-house legislature, and vested executive authority in a governor appointed from Washington.

Alaska was being governed by appointed civil officials. The discovery of gold there in 1896 caused the first substantial influx of Americans; and in 1912, Alaska received territorial status and a legislature, and its inhabitants were given the rights of citizenship. In Puerto Rico, the people readily accepted American rule. Military occupation of the island was ended, and civil government was established by the Foraker Act in 1900. The governor and upper house of the legislature were to be appointed from Washington, while only the lower house was to be elected. The act did not declare the Puerto Ricans to be American citizens, this privilege being deferred until 1917.

Smaller possessions in the empire were dealt with more arbitrarily. Such places as Guam and Tutuila were placed under the control of naval officials; and many of the small islands, containing only a handful of inhabitants, experienced no form of American government at all.

American military forces, commanded by General Leonard Wood, remained in Cuba until 1902, the occupation being protracted to enable American administrators to prepare the island for the independence promised in the peace treaty of 1898. The vigorous occupiers built roads, schools, and hospitals, reorganized the legal, financial, and administrative systems, and introduced far-reaching sanitary reforms. They also laid the basis for years of American domination of the island—a domination that ultimately would become as intolerable to the Cuban people as the Spanish rule against which they had first rebelled.

At Wood's urging, a convention assembled to draft a constitution for independent Cuba. The document contained no provisions concerning relations with the nation responsible for Cuba's freedom. Many Americans considered this a significant oversight, for the United States, with its expanding interests in the Caribbean, expected to exercise some kind of control over the island republic. Therefore, in 1901, Congress passed the Platt Amendment, as a rider to an army appropriation bill, and pressured Cuba into incorporating the terms of the amendment into its constitution. The Platt Amendment stated that Cuba should never impair its independence by treaty with a foreign power (this was equivalent to giving the United States a veto over Cuba's diplomatic policy); that the United States had the right to intervene in Cuba to preserve Cuba's independence, life, and property; and that Cuba must sell or lease to the United States lands for naval stations. The amendment left Cuba only nominally independent. With American capital taking over the island's economy— investments jumped from $50 million in 1898 to $220 million by 1914—Cuba was in fact, if not in name, an American appendage.

Americans did not like to think of themselves as imperial rulers in the European mold. Their mission, they believed, was different—to enlighten and reform the societies they had acquired, to improve the lives of their newly subjugated peoples. Yet like other imperial powers, the United States soon discovered that controlling a foreign colony required more than ideals; it required strength as well and often brutality. That, at least, was the lesson of the American experience in the Philippines. The Filipinos had been rebelling against Spanish rule even before 1898, and they had hailed Admiral Dewey and the expeditionary force he sent to Manila as their deliverers from tyranny. When the hard fact sank in that the Americans had come to stay, the Filipinos resolved to expel the new invaders. The result was a cruel and prolonged war (or, as the Americans termed it, rebellion), a conflict far more costly and savage than the Spanish-American War itself. Ably led by Emilio Aguinaldo, the Filipinos began fighting in 1899, and they harried the American army of occupation from island to island for more than two years. In the end, Americans managed to quell the rebellion only by resorting to the same brutal methods for which they had so vehemently condemned the Spaniards in Cuba—among them, the use of concentration camps. The war, which revived intermittently until as late as 1906, cost the United States $170 million and 4,300 American lives. The cost to the people of the Philippines was

An Argument Against Imperialism [1899]

The anti-imperialists included both Democrats and Republicans and men as different as Andrew Carnegie and William Jennings Bryan. Most of them had long supported various political and social reforms. They organized the American Anti-Imperialist League, which in October 1899, in the midst of the Philippine insurrection, drew up a platform that denied the obligation of Americans to support an unjust, undeclared war such as the one the United States was carrying on against the Filipinos. The platform also included the following statements:

We hold that the policy known as imperialism is hostile to liberty and tends toward militarism, an evil from which it has been our glory to be free. We regret that it has become necessary in the land of Washington and Lincoln to reaffirm that all men, of whatever race or color, are entitled to life, liberty, and the pursuit of happiness. We maintain that governments derive their just powers from the consent of the governed. We insist that the subjugation of any people is "criminal aggression" and open disloyalty to the distinctive principles of our Government. . . .

We hold, with Abraham Lincoln, that "no man is good enough to govern another man without that man's consent. When the white man governs himself, that is self-government, but when he governs himself and also governs another man, that is more than self-government—that is despotism. . . . Our reliance is in the love of liberty which God has planted in us. Our defense is in the spirit which prizes liberty as the heritage of all men in all lands. Those who deny freedom to others deserve it not for themselves, and under a just God cannot long retain it."

An Argument for Imperialism [1900]

Senator Albert J. Beveridge of Indiana addressed the Senate on January 9, 1900, after visiting the Philippines, where American troops were fighting to put down the struggle of the Filipinos for independence. He began by saying that the "hurtful" resolutions and speeches of the anti-imperialists were "costing the lives of American soldiers." He continued:

The Philippines are ours forever, "territory belonging to the United States," as the Constitution calls them. And just beyond the Philippines are China's illimitable markets. We will not retreat from either. We will not repudiate our duty in the archipelago. We will not abandon our opportunity in the Orient. We will not renounce our part in the mission of our race, trustee, under God, of the civilization of the world. . . .

Mr. President, this question is deeper than any question of party politics; deeper than any question of the isolated policy of our country even; deeper even than any question of constitutional power. It is elemen-

tal. It is racial. God has not been preparing the English-speaking and Teutonic peoples for a thousand years for nothing but vain and idle self-contemplation and self-admiration. No! He has made us the master organizers of the world to establish system where chaos reigns. He has given us the spirit of progress to overwhelm the forces of reaction throughout the earth. He has made us adepts in government that we may administer government among savage and senile peoples. Were it not for such a force as this the world would relapse into barbarism and night. And of all our race He has marked the American people as His chosen nation to finally lead in the regeneration of the world.

much higher. No accurate figures exist as to the number of Filipino dead in the conflict, but estimates run as high as 300,000 people. Ultimately, the American forces managed to restore order to the islands and establish a civil government. Gradually after 1901, the Filipinos began to adjust to the occupation and to travel the long road that would lead, in 1946, to the independence they had never ceased ardently to desire.

The Open Door

The acquisition of the Philippines made the United States an Asian power. American interest in the Far East, already aroused by the growing trade with China, reached a new intensity immediately after 1898. Other nations more experienced in the ways of empire were casting covetous eyes on China, ancient, enfeebled, and seemingly open to exploitation by stronger countries. By the turn of the century, the great European imperialistic powers—England, France, Germany, and Russia—and one Asian power, Japan, were beginning to partition China into "spheres of influence." One nation would force the Chinese government to grant it "concessions" to develop a particular area; another would use pressure to secure a long-term lease to a specific region. In some cases, the outside powers even asserted ownership of territory. The process, if continued, threatened to de-

The Open Door in China
"Uncle Sam has distanced all competitors in gaining access to the Flowery Kingdom," says the caption of this cartoon. He holds the key to the door while the other powers look on. Obviously, Secretary of State John Hay had aroused much popular enthusiasm by his Open Door notes, though in fact they represented no great diplomatic triumph for the United States. From the Utica, New York, *Saturday Globe*, March 3, 1900. (Culver Pictures)

Defeat of the Anti-Imperialists
This 1899 lithograph, reproduced from *Puck* magazine, pictures Bryan and other members of the "Anti-Expansion Band" leaving Washington in defeat and humiliation, while McKinley smilingly rides the "Expansion Train" toward continued political success. (Culver Pictures)

stroy American hopes for a vast trade with China.

The situation posed a delicate problem for the men directing American foreign policy. Knowing that public opinion would not support any use of force, they had to find a way to protect American interests in China without risking war. McKinley's secretary of state, John Hay, attempted an audacious solution. In September 1899, he addressed identical notes to England, Germany, and Russia, and later to France, Japan, and Italy, asking them to approve a formula that became known as the "Open Door." It embodied three principles: (1) each nation with a sphere of influence was to respect the rights and privileges of other nations in its sphere; (2) Chinese officials were to continue to collect tariff duties in all spheres (the existing tariff favored the United States); and (3) each nation with a sphere was not to discriminate against other nations in levying port dues and railroad rates.

Hay could hardly have expected an enthusiastic response to his notes, and he got none. Russia declined to approve the Open Door, and the remaining powers gave evasive replies. Each one stated in effect that it approved Hay's ideas in principle but could make no commitment until the others had acted. Apparently, the United States had met a humiliating rebuff; but Hay boldly announced that since all the powers had accepted the principle of the Open Door, his government considered their assent to be "final and definitive." Although the American public applauded his diplomacy, Hay had won little more than a theoretical victory. The United States could not prevent any nation that wanted to violate the Open Door from doing so—unless it was willing to resort to war.

No sooner had the diplomatic maneuvering over the Open Door ended than a secret Chinese society known as the Boxers instigated an uprising against foreigners in

China. The movement came to a blazing climax when the Boxers and their supporters besieged the entire foreign diplomatic corps in the British embassy in Peking. At this point, the powers with interests in China decided to send an international expeditionary force to rescue the diplomats. The situation seemed to offer a perfect excuse to those nations with ambitions to dismember China.

The United States contributed 2,500 troops to the rescue force, which in August 1900 fought its way into Peking and broke the siege. McKinley and Hay had decided on American participation in order to secure a voice in the settlement of the uprising and to prevent the partition of China. Again Hay sent a note to the world powers. This time he called for the Open Door not only in the spheres of influence but in "all parts of the Chinese Empire." He also called for the maintenance of China's "territorial and administrative integrity." The "integrity," or independence, of China thus became a corollary of the Open Door policy. Hay persuaded England and Germany to approve his views, and then with their support, he induced the participating powers to accept a money indemnity as satisfaction. The sum allotted to the United States amounted to almost $25 million, which greatly exceeded damages, but later the American government reduced the obligation and even remitted the unpaid balance. China used part of this money to educate Chinese students in the United States.

A Modern Military System

The war with Spain had revealed glaring deficiencies in the American military system. The greatest weakness had appeared in the army, but there had been an absence of coordination in the entire military organization that might have resulted in disaster had the United States been fighting a more powerful nation. The army, now being called upon to police the new colonial possessions, obviously needed a thorough overhauling. To do the job, McKinley appointed Elihu Root, an extremely able administrator, as secretary of war in 1899. Between 1900 and 1903, Root put into effect, by congressional authorization or by executive order, a series of reforms that gave the United States what amounted to a new military system.

The Root reforms, in summary form, were as follows:

1. An enlarged regular army, with a maximum size of 100,000.
2. Federal supervision of the National Guard, provided by the Dick Act of 1903.
3. The creation of a system of officer-training schools, crowned by the Army Staff College (later the Command and General Staff School) at Fort Leavenworth, Kansas, and the Army War College at Washington.
4. The establishment in 1903 of a general staff headed by a chief of staff, who would replace the former commanding general of the army and act as military adviser to the secretary of war.

While Root was intent on improving the professional quality and efficiency of all segments of the army, his primary concern was to provide it with a central planning agency modeled on the example of European staffs. The general staff was charged with many functions (it was to "supervise" and "coordinate" the entire army establishment), but one of its most important branches was to devote its whole work to planning for possible wars. To ensure interservice strategic cooperation, an Army and Navy Board, representing both services, was created.

Whatever the shortcomings of the Root reforms, they invested the army with a new and needed competence. The United States entered the twentieth century with something resembling a modern military system. The country would have need of it, for the coming years would see the American role in the world constantly expanding.

SUGGESTED READINGS

A useful overview of late nineteenth-century American foreign policy is Charles S. Campbell, *The Transformation of American Foreign Relations, 1865–1900* (1976). More succinct is Robert L. Beisner, *From the Old Diplomacy to the New, 1865–1900* (1975). Basic works on the expansionism of the 1890s and the early twentieth century include Julius W. Pratt, *Expansionists of 1898* (1936), long the standard work and still a valuable study; Albert K. Weinberg, *Manifest Destiny: A Study in Nationalist Expansionism in American History* (1935); and Walter LaFeber, *The New Empire* (1963). William Appleman Williams, *The Tragedy of American Diplomacy* (rev., 1972), is a provocative interpretation of American foreign policy that begins with late nineteenth-century imperialism and emphasizes the economic motives for expansionism. Ernest May, *Imperial Democracy* (1961) and *American Imperialism: A Speculative Essay* (1968), offer a more multidimensional view of the problem. Other general studies are David F. Healy, *U.S. Expansionism: Imperialist Urge in the 1890s* (1970); John Dobson, *America's Ascent: The United States Becomes a Great Power, 1880–1914* (1978); H. Wayne Morgan, *America's Road to Empire* (1965); and Milton Plesur, *America's Outward Thrust* (1971).

David F. Trask, *The War with Spain in 1898* (1981), is a study of the conflict that precipitated America's imperial expansion. Other studies of the war include Frank Freidel, *The Splendid Little War* (1958), a pictorial work; Walter Millis, *The Martial Spirit* (1931); and Philip S. Foner, *The Spanish-Cuban-American War and the Birth of American Imperialism*, 2 vols. (1972), a revisionist study. Graham A. Cosmas, *An Army for Empire: The United States Army in the Spanish-American War* (1971), examines army operations; while Richard S. West, Jr., *Admirals of the American Empire* (1948), discusses the role of the navy. Richard Challener, *Admirals, Generals, and American Foreign Policy, 1889–1914* (1973), discusses the role of the military in policymaking. Edmund Morris, *The Rise of Theodore Roosevelt* (1979), includes a colorful account of the future president's celebrated role in the Spanish-American War.

Some of the domestic implications of the war are examined in Gerald F. Linderman, *The Mirror of War: American Society and the Spanish-American War* (1974). The active anti-imperialist movement is the subject of Robert L. Beisner, *Twelve Against Empire* (1968); E. Berkeley Tompkins, *Anti-Imperialism in the United States, 1890–1920* (1970); Sondra Herman, *Eleven Against War* (1968); and Richard E. Welch, Jr., *Response to Imperialism: The United States and the Philippine-American War, 1899–1902* (1979). The Philippine insurrection is examined also in Leon Wolff, *Little Brown Brother* (1961). Frederick Merk, *Manifest Destiny and Mission in American History* (1963), is an important study of the forces in American history that produced the imperialist urge. Julius W. Pratt, *America's Colonial Empire* (1950), considers diplomatic activities at the end of the war and subsequent problems of imperial administration.

America's role in the Far East is considered in several of the general works listed above and also in Marilyn B. Young, *The Rhetoric of Empire* (1968); Warren Cohen, *America's Response to China* (rev., 1980); Akira Iriye, *Across the Pacific* (1967) and *Pacific Estrangement: Japanese and American Expansion* (1972); Robert McClellan, *The Heathen Chinese: A Study of American Attitudes Toward China* (1971); Charles Neu, *The Troubled Encounter* (1975), which examines American relations with Japan; and Paul Varg, *The Making of a Myth: The United States and China, 1897–1912* (1968) and *Missionaries, Chinese, and Diplomats* (1958). Peter Stanley, *A Nation in the Making: The Philippines and the United States* (1974); Daniel B. Schirmer, *Republic or Empire?* (1972); Paul M. Kennedy, *The Samoan Tangle* (1974); Glenn May, *Social Engineering in the Philippines* (1980); and Merze Tate, *The United States and the Hawaiian Kingdom* (1965), examine the experiences of the nation in administering its Pacific conquests. James Thomsen, Jr., Peter Stanley, and John Curtis Perry, *The Sentimental Imperialists* (1981), is an overview of American–East Asian relations.

The Rise of Progressivism

21

Suffragettes
Women played a vital role in the promotion of progressive social reform. In addition to spearheading many of the efforts to aid the urban poor, they launched a major effort on their own behalf: the fight for the right to vote. The crusade finally triumphed in 1920, with the ratification of the Nineteenth Amendment to the Constitution. (Culver Pictures)

The last decades of the nineteenth century—and the tumultuous 1890s in particular—had a profound effect on the nation's political and social outlook. Well before 1900, a large number of Americans had become convinced that the rapid modernization of their nation had created intolerable problems, that new measures would be necessary to impose order on the growing chaos and to curb industrial society's most glaring injustices. In the early years of the new century, that outlook acquired a name: progressivism.

Not even the progressives themselves could always agree on what the word really meant. To some, it suggested simply a broad cultural vision. To others, it meant a cluster of moral and humanitarian goals. To still others, it was a particular set of political reforms (and, later, a particular political party). At times, in fact, it seemed that virtually everyone had become a progressive: middle-class reformers and machine bosses, big businessmen and small entrepreneurs, white segregationists and black activists, industrial workers and farmers, immigrants and immigration restrictionists. More than one historian has suggested that the word *progressive* be dropped from our vocabulary. (See "Where Historians Disagree," pp. 620–621.)

Yet if progressivism was a movement of remarkable scope and diversity, it was also one that had a relatively consistent set of central assumptions, assumptions that reflected both the hopefulness and the concern that were the legacy of the late nineteenth century. It was, first, an optimistic vision. Progressives believed, as their name implies, in the idea of progress. They believed that society was capable of improvement, even of perfection, that continued growth and advancement were the nation's destiny. There was in progressivism a heady, boisterous enthusiasm, a continuing excitement over possibilities.

But progressives believed, too, that growth and progress could not continue to occur recklessly, as they had in the nineteenth century. Order and stability, they claimed, were essential for social betterment. Not all progressives agreed on the best way to create order, but most believed that government could play an important role in the process. Only government could effectively counter the corrupt special interests that were responsible for social disarray. Only government could provide the services and the regulation that were necessary for future progress. It was essential, therefore, to rescue the nation's political institutions from the influence of selfish interest groups; and it was vital that government expand its role in the society and in the economy. Not all progressive efforts required the assistance of government, but the broad reordering of society that most progressives believed necessary would be impossible without it.

THE PROGRESSIVE IMPULSE

Beyond these central goals, progressivism flowed outward in two broad streams, embodying two varieties of reform. One rested on a belief in process, in the importance of the organizations and procedures through which society operated. The other reflected a commitment to humanitarian reform, to the alleviation of social injustice. The two streams were not entirely separate. Technocratic and humanitarian reform were often synonymous. But the distinction was a real one, and in the end the two approaches met different fates.

The Organizational Impulse

The first, and ultimately the stronger, progressive impulse was the one toward process and organization. Americans of the early twentieth century placed much emphasis on the need for rationalizing their society, for making it operate more efficiently and thus more productively. It was natural, therefore, that they should develop a profound concern for the creation of orderly systems and institutions. To many Americans, the process by which a goal was achieved often seemed as important as the goal itself.

Nothing was so valued among many progressives, therefore, as scientific knowledge and expertise. Nothing so characterized their outlook as the belief that even non-scientific problems were subject to scientific analysis. Society could no longer be left in the hands of untrained amateurs. Enlightened experts and scientifically designed bureaucracies must create the order that America so badly needed.

This impulse found expression in innumerable ways, among them the writings of a new group of scholars and intellectuals. Unlike the Social Darwinists of the nineteenth century, these theorists were no longer content with merely justifying the existing industrial system. They spoke instead of the creation of a new civilization, one in which the expertise of scientists and engineers could be brought to bear on the problems of the economy and society. Their most influential spokesman was the social scientist Thorstein Veblen. Harshly critical of the industrial tycoons of the late nineteenth century—the "leisure class" as he satirically described them in his first major work, *A Theory of the Leisure Class* (1899)—Veblen proposed instead a new economic system in which power would reside in the hands of highly trained engineers. Only they, he argued, could fully understand the "machine process" by which modern society must be governed. Only they could provide the effi-

ciency and order necessary for the industrial economy. By the end of his life, he was calling for government by a "soviet of technicians," who would impose on the economy their own instinct for rational process.

In practical terms, the impulse toward expertise and organization helped produce the idea of scientific management, or "Taylorism." It encouraged the development of modern mass-production techniques and, above all, the assembly line. (See above, pp. 519–520). And it produced, too, a new movement toward organization among the expanding new group of middle-class professionals.

The Professions

The late nineteenth century had seen not only a growth of the industrial work force but also a dramatic expansion in the number of Americans engaged in administrative and professional tasks. Industries needed managers, technicians, and accountants as well as workers. Cities required a growing range of commercial, medical, legal, and educational services. The demand for technology required scientists and engineers who, in turn, required institutions and instructors to train them. The industrial state, in short, had produced an enormous new infrastructure of specialized, professional services. And by the turn of the century, those performing these services had come to constitute a distinct social group—a new middle class. Unlike the older middle class, whose status often derived from family background and stature within the local community, the new middle class placed a far higher value on education and accomplishment. Almost 6 million strong by 1910, its members were hard at work creating organizations and standards to secure and stabilize their position in society.

As their vehicle, they created the modern, organized professions. The idea of professionalism had been a frail one in America even as late as 1880. When every patent-medicine salesman could call himself a doctor, when every frustrated politician could proclaim himself a lawyer, when anyone who could read and write could present himself as a teacher, it was clear that a professional

The Progressive Movement

One reason that historians have so often disagreed about what progressivism meant is that they have never been able to agree on just what the movement was. To some, progressivism was a largely political impulse, involving clearly identifiable reformers and a coherent set of legislative reforms. To others, the phenomenon has appeared to be much broader—a wide-ranging effort to reshape American society, not only politically but socially, economically, even intellectually. The differences over this basic question have helped to determine the differences among the leading interpretations of progressivism.

Until about 1950, most historians were in general accord about the nature of the progressive movement. It was, they generally agreed, just what it had said it was: a movement by the "people" to curb the power of the "special interests." In particular, it was a protest by an aroused citizenry against the corruption and excessive power of urban bosses, corporate moguls, and tame elected officials. Progressive reform, scholars argued, was an effort to restore power to the people, to revive political, economic, and social democracy.

In the early 1950s, however, a new interpretation emerged to challenge the traditional view. It retained the earlier view of progressivism as a largely political movement, but it offered a new explanation of who the progressives were and what they were trying to do. George Mowry, in *The California Progressives* (1951), described the reform movement in that state not as a protest by the mass of the people, but as an effort by a relatively small and privileged group of business and professional men to limit the overbearing power of large corporations and labor unions. Viewing themselves as natural social leaders, they resented their loss of political power to these new economic forces and envisioned reform as a way to restore both their economic fortunes and their social importance and self-esteem. Richard Hofstadter expanded on this idea in *The Age of Reform* (1955), in which he described progressives throughout the country as people suffering from "status anxiety"—old, formerly influential, upper-middle-class families seeking to restore their fading prestige by challenging the powerful new institutions that had begun to displace them. Like the Populists, Hofstadter suggested, the progressives were suffering from psychological, not economic, discontent.

The Mowry-Hofstadter thesis was for a time widely influential, but it was not without its critics. In particular, it received strong challenges from historians who disagreed with two of the basic assumptions of the interpretation. First, these scholars maintained, Mowry and Hofstadter were mistaken in examining progressivism purely in terms of its visible political leaders. It was a movement with a far broader social and economic base. Second, they claimed, progressive reformers were not expressing a vague psychological malaise, but a clear recognition of their own self-interest. Beyond that, the new historians of progressivism often disagreed with one another as much as they disagreed with Mowry and Hofstadter.

Perhaps the most strident challenge to earlier interpretations came from the New Left historian Gabriel Kolko, whose influential 1963 study, *The Triumph of Conservatism*, dismissed the supposedly "democratic" features of progressivism as meaningless rhetoric and examined instead the impact of progressive economic reforms. Progressivism was, he agreed, an effort to regulate business. But it was not the people who were responsible for this regulation. It was the businessmen who saw in government supervision

label would by itself carry little weight. There were, of course, skilled and responsible doctors, lawyers, teachers, and others; but they had no way of controlling the charlatans and other incompetents who presumed to practice their trades. As the demand for services increased, so did the pressures, from both within and without, for reform.

Among the first to respond was the medical profession. Throughout the 1890s, doctors who considered themselves true professionals—who had had formal training in medicine, who understood the new scientific

a way to protect themselves from ruinous competition. Regulation, Kolko claimed, was "invariably controlled by the leaders of the regulated industry and directed towards ends they deemed acceptable or desirable"—ends, he suggested, that generally ran counter to the goals of economic democracy, rather than enhancing them.

A somewhat more moderate challenge to the "psychological" interpretation of progressivism came from historians embracing a new "organizational" view of history. Samuel P. Hays was the first to suggest the approach in *The Response to Industrialism, 1885–1914* (1957) and other writings. Hays argued that progressives were indeed businessmen, as Kolko had suggested. But their impulse was not so much naked self-interest as a broad desire to bring order and efficiency to political and, hence, economic life. The most important progressives, he claimed, were members of the upper class, who viewed a restoration of stability as essential to the preservation of their privileged position.

Even more influential was a 1967 study by Robert Wiebe, *The Search for Order, 1877–1920*. Wiebe saw progressivism as a response to the dislocations in American life that had resulted from a rapid change in the nature of the economy without a corresponding change in social and political institutions. Economic power was now lodged in large, national organizations, while social and political life was centered primarily in local communities. The result was widespread disorder and unrest, culminating in the turbulent 1890s. Progressivism, Wiebe argued, was the effort of a "new middle class"—a class tied to the emerging national economy—to stabilize and enhance their position in society. It was, therefore, an attempt to impose order on the chaos of industrial society by replacing antiquated local institutions with modern, na-

tional organizations. Progressivism, in short, went far beyond politics. It was a widespread effort to reshape virtually all of American life.

Yet despite all the challenges to the original view of progressivism as a democratic movement, some historians continued to produce evidence that the reform phenomenon was indeed a movement of the people against the interests. J. Joseph Huthmacher argued in 1962 that much of the force behind progressivism came from members of the working class, especially immigrants, who pressed for such reforms as workmen's compensation and wage and hour laws. And David P. Thelen, in a 1972 study of progressivism in Wisconsin, *The New Citizenship*, offered an even broader challenge to both the "status anxiety" and the "conservatism-organizational" views. Thelen found a real clash between the "public interest" and "corporate privilege" in Wisconsin. The depression of the 1890s had mobilized a broad coalition of citizens of highly diverse backgrounds behind efforts to make both business and government responsible to the popular will. The movement, in short, corresponded quite closely to the progressive rhetoric of the time.

Given the range of disagreement over the nature of the progressive movement, it is hardly surprising that some historians have despaired of finding any coherent definition for the term at all. Peter Filene, for one, suggested in 1970 that the concept of progressivism as a "movement" had outlived its usefulness. "It is time," he suggested, "to tear off the familiar label and, thus liberated from its prejudice, see the history between 1890 and 1920 for what it was—ambiguous, inconsistent, moved by agents and forces more complex than a [single, uniform] progressive movement."

discoveries that were revolutionizing their methods—began forming local associations and societies. In 1901, finally, they reorganized the American Medical Association into a modern, national, professional society. Between 1900 and 1910, membership increased from 8,400 to over 70,000; by 1920, nearly

two-thirds of all American doctors were members. The first major effort of the AMA was to insist on strict, scientific standards for admission to the practice of medicine, with doctors themselves serving as protectors of the standards. State and local governments readily complied, passing new laws that re-

The New Middle Class
The rise of the modern corporation, economic bureaucratization, and sophisticated management structures all aided the growth in the early twentieth century of what some have called a "new middle class"—a large and expanding group of workers engaged in specialized administrative tasks. In this 1920 scene, the bookkeeping department of the Guaranty Trust Company in New York attends to some of the extensive paperwork that modern finance requires. (Culver Pictures)

quired the licensing of all physicians and restricting licenses to those practitioners approved by the profession.

Accompanying the emphasis on strict regulation of the profession came a concern for rigorous scientific training and research. By 1900, medical education at a few medical schools—notably Johns Hopkins in Baltimore (founded in 1893)—compared favorably with that in the leading institutions of Europe. Doctors such as William H. Welch at Hopkins revolutionized the teaching of medicine by moving students out of the classrooms and into laboratories and clinics. New, rigorous standards forced many inadequate medical schools out of existence, and those that remained were obliged to adopt a strict, scientific approach.

There was similar movement in other professions. By 1916, lawyers in all forty-eight states had established professional bar associations; and virtually all of them had succeeded in creating central examining boards, composed of lawyers, to regulate admission to the profession. Increasingly, aspiring lawyers found it necessary to enroll in graduate programs, and the nation's law schools accordingly expanded greatly, both in numbers and in the rigor of their curricula. Teachers made similar efforts to organize

and regulate their profession. They established a vast network of teachers' colleges and schools of education and, in 1905, created the National Education Association, which fought, among other things, for government licensing of teachers. Businessmen supported the creation of schools of business administration and created their own national organizations: the National Association of Manufacturers in 1895 and the United States Chamber of Commerce in 1912. Even farmers, long the symbol of the romantic spirit of individualism, responded to the new order by forming, through the National Farm Bureau Federation, a network of agricultural organizations designed to spread scientific farming methods, teach sound marketing techniques, and lobby for the interests of their members.

The behavior of the professions—in creating organizations, in imposing scientific standards on their members, in stressing technical training and expertise—reflected impulses that were coming to characterize American society as a whole. Modern society was too complex, many people now believed, to be left to individuals or to local institutions. Centralized, scientific management, through efficient organizations staffed by experts, was the key to a successful future.

The Humanitarian Impulse

While many progressives were emphasizing science and organization as the vehicles for bringing order to America, others were turning to the task of humanitarian social reform. The social reformers were not always distinct from the technocratic progressives; often, they brought to their work the same belief in science and organization. The humanitarian efforts, however, were less directly concerned with stabilizing the position of the middle class than with attacking the problems of the poor—in working, as some put it, for "social justice."

Reformers brought to these efforts one of the strongest elements of progressive thought: its belief in the influence of the environment on individual development. Social Darwinists such as William Graham Sumner had argued that a person's fortunes reflected his inherent "fitness" for survival; progressive theorists disagreed. Ignorance, poverty, even criminality, they argued, were not the result of inherent moral or genetic failings or of the workings of divine providence. They were, rather, the effects of an unhealthy environment. To elevate the distressed, therefore, required an improvement of the conditions in which they lived.

Of particular interest to such reformers were the urban immigrant ghettoes, which publicists such as Jacob Riis were exposing through vivid photographs and lurid descriptions. Riis himself adopted a callous approach to the problem; he urged the razing of the most offensive slums without making any provision for the relocation of displaced residents. (Later, he became an advocate of immigration restriction.) Other progressives, however, responded more sensitively. Borrowing ideas from reform movements in Europe, especially England, committed men and women established settlement houses in immigrant neighborhoods. Staffed by members of the middle class, these institutions sought to help immigrant families adapt to the language and customs of their new country. Settlement houses offered educational services, staged community events, built libraries, and in general tried to enhance the lives of their neighborhoods without adopt-

ing the stance of disapproving moral superiority that had hampered the success of earlier philanthropic efforts. Jane Addams's Hull House, founded in Chicago in 1889, became a model for more than 400 similar institutions throughout the nation.

The proliferation of settlement houses helped expose another major change in progressive society: the expanding role of women. Increasingly, middle-class women found themselves not only free from much of the burden of housework—a result both of their own affluence and of technological advances—but aroused to public service by new forms of education. Vassar, founded in 1865, was the first of a growing number of women's colleges that awakened their students to the possibility of a more active social role. The new state universities, particularly in the Midwest, were admitting women as well as men, opening even greater opportunities. It was these educated women who were by the end of the nineteenth century staffing settlement houses, forming clubs to agitate for social reform, and helping to elevate the humanitarian issues of the era to the level of compelling national questions.

The settlement houses also helped to spawn another important institution of reform: the profession of social work. Workers at Hull House, for example, maintained a close relationship with the University of Chicago's pioneering work in the field of sociology; and a growing number of programs for the professional training of social workers began to appear in the nation's leading universities, partly in response to the activities of the settlements. The professional social worker combined a compassion for the poor with a commitment to the values of bureaucratic progressivism: scientific study, efficient organization, reliance on experts. The new profession produced elaborate surveys and reports, collected statistics, and published scholarly tracts on the need for urban reform.

The Social Gospel

The professional social workers combined their sensitivity to human problems with a belief in organization and expertise. Other

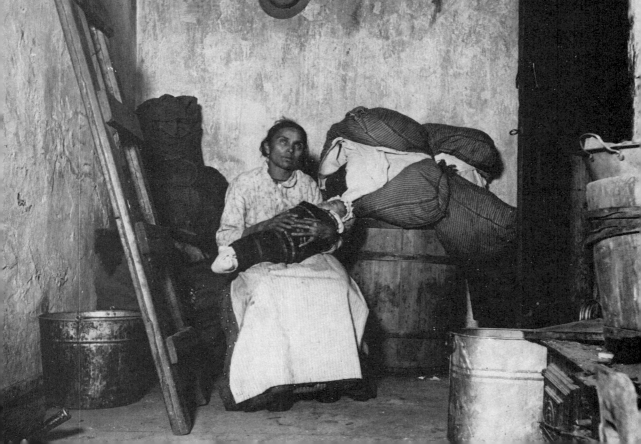

urban reformers emphasized instead the social demands of religion. A powerful movement within American Christianity (and, to some extent, within American Judaism), often known as the Social Gospel, had emerged by the early twentieth century as a vigorous force in the effort to redeem the nation's cities. The Salvation Army, which had come to the United States from England, boasted a corps of 3,000 officers and 20,000 privates by 1900, offering both material aid and spiritual service to the urban poor. Ministers of many denominations, priests, and rabbis left traditional parish work to serve in the troubled cities, and their efforts soon became part of the folklore of their time. Edward Sheldon's *In His Steps* (1898), the story of a young minister who abandoned a comfortable post to work among the needy in Chicago, sold more than 15 million copies and established itself as the most successful novel of the era.

Walter Rauschenbusch, a Protestant theologian from Rochester, New York, published a series of influential discourses on the possibilities for human salvation through Christian reform. To him, the message of Darwinism was not that the individual was engaged in a brutal struggle for survival of the fittest, but that all individuals should work for a humanitarian evolution of the social fabric. "Translate the evolutionary themes into religious faith," he wrote, "and you have the doctrine of the Kingdom of God." American Catholics seized on the 1893 publication of Pope Leo XIII's encyclical *Rerum Novarum* as justification for their own crusade for social justice. Catholic liberals such as Father John A. Ryan took to heart the pope's warning that "a small number of very rich men have been able to lay upon the masses of the poor a yoke little better than slavery itself. . . . No practical solution of this question will ever be found without the assistance of religion and the church." For decades, he worked to expand the scope of Catholic social welfare organizations.

The Social Gospel was never the dominant element in the movement for urban reform. Some of the most influential progressives dismissed it as irrelevant moralization; others viewed it as little more than a useful complement to their own work. But the engagement of religion with reform had a lasting impact, bringing to progressivism a powerful moral component, a belief that society's mission was not simply to cure disorder in the cities but to redeem the lives of even the lowliest residents. Walter Rauschenbusch captured some of both the optimism and the spirituality of the Social Gospel with his proud comment, after a visit to a New York slum known as Hell's Kitchen where Christian reformers were hard at work: "One could hear human virtue cracking and crashing all around."

Chicago's "Ghetto": Jefferson and 12th Streets, 1906
Typical of the residents in this area were a Russian man and his wife who earned $2 a day finishing coats. Their household was thus described: "Three small children and the grandmother constitute the family, the latter dying of a cancer without medical attendance or nursing. Man has been 18 years in this country and owns a populous frame tenement house. He also owns the wretched rear cottage, on the second floor of which his family lives. His work room contains a bed, an upright piano, dining table, sewing machine and the couch on which his mother lies dying. The filth and smell are intolerable. He does only the finest custom work and was making a valuable coat. Most of the year he has been making police uniforms." (Courtesy, Chicago Historical Society)

Life in an Immigrant Slum
An Italian mother holds her baby in what appears to be a basement room in a New York City tenement. This photograph was taken around 1900 by the Danish immigrant, newspaperman, and crusader for housing reform Jacob A. Riis. (The Jacob A. Riis Collection, Museum of the City of New York)

THE CHALLENGE OF POLITICAL REFORM

Sooner or later, most progressive goals required the involvement of government. Social workers wanted laws to protect woman and child workers and to improve conditions in the ghettoes. Professionals advocated legal standards for admission to the practice of law or medicine. Others urged legislative solutions to such problems as the power of trusts or the destructive effects of "cutthroat competition." Only government, progressives agreed, could provide the centralized regulation and control necessary to impose order and justice on modern society.

But American government at the dawn of the new century was, the progressives believed, peculiarly ill-adapted to perform these ambitious tasks. At every level, political institutions were outmoded, inefficient, often corrupt. In other words, before society could be effectively reformed, it would be necessary to reform government itself.

Municipal Reform

It was the cities, many progressives believed, that posed the greatest challenge to American society. And it was city government, therefore, that became the first target of those working for political reform. Settlement houses, social workers, and scholars all attempted to focus attention on urban problems and the need for governmental changes to combat them. But it was a new breed of journalists who were most successful in arousing public outrage at the rampant corruption and incompetence in city government. These muckrakers, as they were often called, leveled harshly polemical and carefully researched attacks on the evils of "boss rule" (as well as on the trusts and corporations). And benefiting from the rise of mass-circulation newspapers and magazines, they attracted wide attention to their cause.

The many young journalists who achieved wide renown through muckraking included Ida Tarbell, Ray Stannard Baker, Samuel Hopkins Adams, William Allen White, and Upton Sinclair. The most influential, however, was Lincoln Steffens, a reporter for *McClure's* magazine, who traveled through much of the country in the first years of the century and produced a series of articles on municipal corruption that aroused a major public outcry. His portraits of "machine government" and "boss rule," his exposures of "boodlers" in cities as diverse as St. Louis, Minneapolis, Cleveland, Cincinnati, Chicago, Philadelphia, and New York, his tone of studied moral outrage (as reflected in the title of his series and of the book that emerged from it, *The Shame of the Cities*)—all combined to persuade urban progressives of the need for a militant response.

Steffens and his fellow muckrakers struck a responsive chord among a powerful group of urban middle-class progressives. For several decades after the Civil War, "respectable" citizens of the nation's large cities had avoided participation in municipal government. Viewing politics as a debased and demeaning activity, they shrank from contact with the "vulgar" elements who were coming to dominate public life. By the end of the century, however, a new generation of activists—some of them members of old aristocratic families, others a part of the new middle class—were taking a renewed interest in government. The nineteenth-century middle class had abdicated control of politics to the urban masses; the twentieth-century middle class, appalled by the abuses and failures that had ensued, would win it back.

They faced a formidable array of opponents. In addition to challenging the powerful city bosses and their entrenched political organizations, they were attacking a large group of special interests: saloon owners, brothel keepers, and, perhaps most significantly, those businessmen who had established cozy and lucrative relationships with the urban machines and viewed reform as a threat to their profits. Allied with these interests were many influential newspapers, which ridiculed the reformers as naïve do-gooders or prigs. Finally, there was the great constituency of city working people, mostly of immigrant origin, to whom the machines were a source of needed services. To them, the progressives often seemed to be middle-class prudes, attempting to impose an alien and unappealing life style. Gradually, however, the reformers gained in political strength—in part because of their own growing numbers, in part because of the conspicuous failures of the existing political leadership. And in the first years of the twentieth century, they began to score some important victories.

One of the first major successes came in Galveston, Texas, where the old city government collapsed in ineffectuality in the wake of a destructive tidal wave in 1900. Capitalizing on public dismay, reformers (many of them local businessmen) won approval of a new city charter. The mayor and council were replaced by a commission whose five members would jointly enact ordinances and individually run the main city departments. In 1907, Des Moines, Iowa, adopted its own version of the commission plan, and other cities soon followed. Another approach to reform was the city-manager plan, by which elected officials hired an outside expert—often a professionally trained business manager or engineer—to take charge of the government. Responsible not to the voters but to the councilors or commissioners who appointed him, the city manager would presumably remain untainted by the corrupting influence of politics. Staunton, Virginia, was one of the first municipalities to hire a city manager, in 1908. Five years later, Dayton, Ohio, attracted wider attention to the device when it adopted the new system after a major flood. By the end of the progressive era, almost 400 cities were operating under commissions, and another 45 employed city managers. Many municipalities adopted even more direct techniques to limit the influence of corrupt party politics on city government. Some employed a nonpartisan ballot in elections for municipal office, thus curbing the power of party organizations in selecting candidates. Others embraced such structural reforms as the initiative, the referendum, and the recall—all designed to lodge as much power as possible directly in the hands of the people.

Some of the most successful reformers, in fact, emerged not from the new commission and city-manager systems but from conventional political structures that progressives had come to control. Tom Johnson, the celebrated reform mayor of Cleveland, waged a long and difficult war against the powerful streetcar interests in his city, fighting to raise the ridiculously low assessments on railroads and utilities properties, to lower streetcar fares to three cents, and ultimately to impose municipal ownership on certain basic utilities. After Johnson's defeat and death, his talented aide Newton D. Baker won election as mayor and helped maintain Cleveland's reputation as the best-governed city in America. Hazen Pingree of Detroit, Samuel "Golden Rule" Jones of Toledo, and other mayors succeeded where advocates of city-manager and commission systems occasionally failed—in creating city governments that were both honest and humane, and in establishing reform as a politically viable force in their communities.

Yet for all the successes of progressives in some cities in limiting the power of traditional party bosses, in other areas the old machines remained nearly as powerful as ever. In large part, this was because the bosses themselves, who were usually intelligent men, recognized that they must change in order to survive. And thus they sometimes allowed their machines to become vehicles of social reform. The best example was New York's Tammany Hall, the nation's oldest and most notorious city machine. Its extraordinarily astute leader, Charles Francis Murphy, began in the early years of the century to fuse the techniques of boss rule with some of the concerns of social reformers. In the process, he ushered his organization into one of the most successful eras in its history.

Murphy did nothing to challenge the fundamental workings of Tammany Hall. The machine continued to mobilize working-class immigrant voters to support its candidates; it continued to offer them favors and services in return; its members continued to use patronage and even graft to strengthen their positions and expand their bank accounts. At the same time, however, Tammany began to take an increased interest in state and national politics, which it had traditionally scorned; and it used its political power on behalf of legislation to improve working conditions, protect child laborers, and eliminate the worst abuses of the industrial economy.

In 1911, a sudden fire swept the factory of the Triangle Shirtwaist Company in New York; 146 workers, most of them women, died. Many of them had been trapped inside the building because management had locked the emergency exits to prevent malingering. It was the worst industrial tragedy in the city's history, and the outrage it produced echoed across the nation. For the next three years, a broad-based state commission studied not only the background of the fire but the general condition of the industrial workplace; and by 1914, it had issued a series of reports calling for major reforms in the conditions of modern labor.

The report itself was a classic progressive document, based on the testimony of experts, replete with statistics and technical data. Yet when its recommendations reached the New York legislature, its most effective supporters were not middle-class progressives but two Tammany Democrats: Senator Robert F. Wagner and Assemblyman Alfred E. Smith. With the support of Murphy and the backing of other Tammany legislators, they steered through a series of pioneering labor laws that imposed strict regulations on factory owners and established effective mechanisms for enforcement. Tammany Hall, the incarnation of evil in the eyes of many progressives, had itself become a potent agent for reform.

Statehouse Progressivism

Often frustrated in their assault on boss rule in the cities, many progressives turned to state government as an agent for reform. Crusading district attorneys such as Hiram Johnson in California and Joseph W. Folk in Missouri left their cities to become reform

The Triangle Fire
The 1911 fire in the Triangle Shirtwaist Factory in New York, in which 146 workers (virtually all of them women) died, aroused the conscience of the nation. To progressive reformers, the fire was evidence of the need for new government regulations to oversee factory safety standards. In the aftermath of the tragedy, the New York legislature enacted some of the most stringent building-code and labor-safety laws in the nation. In this photograph, policemen and investigators stand amid the coffins of some of the victims. (Culver Pictures)

governors. Elsewhere, progressive leaders arrived in the statehouse by other routes. Whatever their backgrounds, however, such reformers agreed that state government must take a leading role in the task of stabilizing American life.

State-level progressives agreed, too, on the unfitness of existing state governments to provide reform. They looked with particular scorn on state legislatures, whose ill-paid, relatively inconspicuous members were, they believed, generally incompetent and often corrupt. Since the legislatures were unfit, they argued, it was necessary to circumvent them, to return power directly to the people.

The result was a wave of reforms in state after state that attempted to "democratize" state government by limiting the authority of elected officials and increasing the influence of the electorate. Two of the most important changes were innovations first proposed by leaders of the Populist movement in the 1890s: the initiative and the referendum. The initiative gave reformers the ability to circumvent their legislatures altogether by submitting legislation directly to the voters in general elections. The referendum provided a method by which actions of the legislature could be returned to the electorate for approval. Oregon, in 1902, became the first state to enact such reforms. By 1918, nineteen other states had followed.

Progressives also attempted to improve the quality of elected officials, and for this purpose they created two more "democratic" devices: the direct primary and the recall. The primary election was an attempt to limit the influence of party machines on the selection of candidates. The recall gave voters the right to remove a public official from office at a special election, which could be called after a sufficient number of citizens had signed a petition. Mississippi adopted the nation's first direct primary in 1902, and by 1915 every state in the nation had instituted primary elections for at least some offices. The recall encountered a more difficult road. No progressive measure so horrified conservatives as this effort to subject officeholders to voter censure before the end of their terms, and they blocked the adoption of the recall more effectively than any other reform.

Just as progressives had emphasized process and order in their creation of commissions and city managers at the municipal level, so at the state level they were emphasizing the creation of systems as the cornerstone of reform. And just as such systems were not always effective in cities, so they often failed in the states. Initiatives and referendums could just as easily become vehicles for conservative changes as for progressive ones. Primaries could be, and often were, dominated by machines, whose ability to mobilize their constituencies far exceeded that of the reformers. The recall proved cumbersome and found only occasional use. Reform efforts proved most effective in states that also elevated vigorous and committed politicians to positions of leadership. In New York, Charles Evans Hughes exploited progressive sentiment to create a commission to regulate public utilities. In California, Hiram Johnson used the new reforms to limit the political power of the Southern Pacific Railroad in the state. In New Jersey, Woodrow Wilson, the Princeton University president elected governor in 1910, used executive leadership to win a substantial array of reforms designed to end New Jersey's widely denounced position as the "mother of trusts." If he did not succeed in making the state a model of progressivism, Wilson did manage to eliminate some of its most glaring political and economic flaws. Like the cities, state governments were finding that men as well as systems were necessary for securing reforms. Perhaps the best evidence of this came from the state that virtually all progressives agreed had become the nation's leading center of reform: Wisconsin, the home of the great progressive hero Robert M. La Follette.

La Follette had begun his career in Wisconsin as a conservative defender of free enterprise against its "radical" challengers. By the end of the 1890s, however, he had become convinced of the need for major reforms to curb the power of bosses, railroads, trusts, and financiers—the special interests that were, he argued, corrupting American life. Elected governor in 1900, he called for a new concept of politics: as the vehicle for enhancing the public interest, rather than as an

Robert M. La Follette Campaigning in Wisconsin
"Battling Bob" La Follette (1855–1925) in the 1880s was a Republican congressman sufficiently regular to help prepare the McKinley Tariff. Although he remained in the party during the 1890s, he began to champion reforms of a Populist nature. In 1901, pledged to fight for a direct primary, tax reform, and railroad control, he was elected governor of Wisconsin. His advice came from experts at the University of Wisconsin, his votes largely from a rural constituency. In 1905, he finally obtained a legislature that would enact his program. Although he had already been elected United States senator, he remained governor until the end of the year, when his proposals had become law. In Washington he advocated a similar national program, especially rigorous regulation of railroads. It brought him into conflict with both the old guard and President Roosevelt; he entitled a chapter of his autobiography "Alone in the Senate." Roosevelt, La Follette wrote, "acted upon the maxim that half a loaf is better than no bread. I believe that half a loaf is fatal whenever it is accepted at the sacrifice of the basic principle sought to be attained." Although nationally La Follette was at times isolated in his advanced agrarian progressive position, in Wisconsin he and his sons commanded so loyal a following that they dominated the state politically for nearly forty years. (State Historical Society of Wisconsin)

---

arena in which special interests contended for favors.

In the years that followed, La Follette and his supporters turned Wisconsin into what reformers across the nation described as a "laboratory of progressivism." The Wisconsin progressives won approval of direct primaries, initiatives, and referendums. They secured the effective regulation of railroads and utilities. They obtained the passage of laws to regulate the workplace and provide compensation for laborers injured on the job. They instituted graduated taxes on inherited fortunes, and they nearly doubled state levies on railroads and other corporate interests.

La Follette brought to progressivism his

own fervent, almost evangelical, commitment to reform; and he used his charismatic leadership to widen public awareness of progressive goals and to mobilize the energies of many previously passive groups. Reform was not simply the responsibility of politicians, he argued, but of newspapers, citizens' groups, educational institutions, and business and professional organizations. Progressivism, he suggested, must become a part of the fabric of American life. Ultimately, La Follette would find himself overshadowed by other national progressive leaders. In the early years of the century, however, few men were as effective in publicizing the message of reform. None was as successful in bending state government to that goal.

Order and Exclusion

The federal government was somewhat slower to respond to the demands of progressive reformers than were state and local governments, but it was hardly immune to their influence. From the beginning, many progressives had viewed national politics as the most important vehicle for reform. And they cited, in particular, a series of highly charged issues that they believed required not state or local but national attention. Some of the causes espoused by reformers seemed to many progressives to be decidedly illiberal, although they represented at least one current of progressive thought. Two such movements were those on behalf of the prohibition of alcoholic beverages and the restriction of immigration.

To some progressives, the elimination of alcohol from American life was a necessary step in the task of restoring order to society. Workers in settlement houses and social agencies (particularly women) abhorred the effects of drinking on working-class families: scarce wages vanished as workers spent hours in the saloons; drunkenness spawned violence, and occasionally murder, within urban families. Employers, too, regarded alcohol as an impediment to industrial efficiency: workers often missed time on the job

because of drunkenness or, worse, came to the factory intoxicated and performed their tasks sloppily and dangerously. Critics of economic privilege denounced the liquor industry as one of the nation's most sinister trusts. And political reformers, who looked on the saloon (correctly) as one of the central institutions of the machine, saw an attack on drinking as part of an attack on the bosses. Out of such sentiments emerged the prohibition movement.

Despite substantial opposition from immigrant and working-class voters, pressure for prohibition grew steadily through the first decades of the new century. The sporadic protests of its opponents could not compete with the disciplined efforts of such organizations as the Woman's Christian Temperance Union and the newer Anti-Saloon League. With the support of rural fundamentalists, who opposed alcohol on moral and religious grounds, progressive advocates of prohibition in 1917 finally steered through Congress a constitutional amendment embodying their demands. Two years later, after ratification by every state in the nation except Connecticut and Rhode Island (bastions of Catholic immigrants) the Eighteenth Amendment became law, to take effect in January 1920. The federal government, many progressives believed, had taken an important step toward eliminating a major source of social instability and inefficiency. Only later did it become clear that prohibition would create far more disorder than it was able to cure.

A similar concern for order fueled the movement demanding the restriction of immigration, which likewise gained force throughout the progressive era. While virtually all reformers agreed that the burgeoning immigrant population had created social problems, there was wide disagreement on how best to respond. Many progressives, convinced that open immigration was one of the nation's most valued traditions, believed that helping the new residents adapt to American society was the proper approach. Others, however, argued that efforts at assimilation had failed and that the only solution was to limit the flow of new arrivals.

The first decades of the century, therefore, saw a steady growth in pressure on the federal government to close the nation's gates. New scholarly theories, designed to appeal to the progressive respect for expertise, argued that the introduction of immigrants into American society was polluting the nation's racial stock. The spurious "science" of eugenics spread the belief that human inequalities were hereditary and that immigration was contributing to the multiplication of the unfit. Skillful publicists such as Madison Grant, whose *The Passing of the Great Race* (1916) established him as the nation's most effective nativist, warned of the dangers of racial "mongrelization" and of the importance of protecting the purity of Anglo-Saxon and other Nordic stock. As on other issues, progressives in Washington established a special commission of "experts," chaired by Senator William P. Dillingham of Vermont, to study the problem of immigration. Supported by elaborate statistics and scholarly testimony, the commission's report argued that the newer immigrant groups—largely southern and eastern Europeans—had proven themselves less assimilable than earlier immigrants. Immigration, the report implied, should be restricted by nationality.

Racial arguments mobilized impressive support behind the restriction movement, but even many who rejected such arguments supported limiting immigration. The continuing influx of foreigners was, they believed, creating unmanageable urban problems: overcrowding, unemployment, strained social services, social unrest. The combination of these concerns gradually won for the nativists the support of some of the nation's leading progressives: Theodore Roosevelt, Henry Cabot Lodge, and others. Powerful opponents—employers who saw immigration as a source of cheap labor, reformers who valued the ethnic culture of immigrant communities, immigrants themselves and their political representatives—managed to block the restriction movement for a time. But by the beginning of World War I (which itself effectively temporarily blocked immigration), the nativist tide was clearly gaining strength. Progressivism, it was apparent, did not always come in a purely liberal guise.

Suffrage for Women

A movement that bore more immediate fruits, and one that reflected a larger spirit, was the effort of women to win the right to vote. If the agitations for prohibition and immigration restriction were attempts to remove dangerous influences from American life, the suffrage movement was an attempt, its supporters believed, to inject into society a healthy new force. Giving women the right to vote, suffrage advocates claimed, was not only a matter of abstract principle; it was a practical measure to strengthen the forces of reform.

The movement for woman suffrage had already experienced a long and often frustrating history as the twentieth century began. Women had played an important role in the crusade for the abolition of slavery in the 1840s and 1850s, and they had included suffrage among their political demands after the Civil War. Spurned by political leaders who insisted that this was "the Negro's hour," suffragists continued their efforts through the last decades of the nineteenth century, winning a few victories in some of the new Western states but lacking sufficient power to change national policy.

It was the merging of the suffrage movement with other reform efforts in the first years of the new century that transformed it from a small interest group into a major national force. As women became active in settlement houses, social work, and other humanitarian activities, they began to argue that their participation in politics would strengthen demands for social welfare reforms. As many of the same women joined the growing prohibition movement, they linked votes for women with elimination of alcohol. Others argued in more general terms: that women would bring to politics a humane and gentle spirit that would help cleanse the nation of selfishness and corruption. As the reform spirit grew, such arguments attracted the support of an increasing number of progressive men.

Women themselves, however, remained the major force in the movement. Under the spirited leadership of Anna Howard Shaw, a

Are Women Human Beings? [1912]

Charlotte Perkins Gilman was probably the greatest intellect among the American feminists of her time. She gained international fame from her book Women and Economics *(1898), in which she analyzed the effects of industrialization on women and argued for their economic independence. In a subsequent magazine article (1912) she raised the question "Are Women Human Beings?" She answered in part:*

As social evolution has never waited for the complete enlightenment of mankind, we find the enfranchisement of women going on in all civilized countries; but since the opposition to it is strong enough to cause years of delay and a continuous outlay of organized effort, it seems worthwhile to point out the main error actuating that opposition. . . .

This error is due to a certain arrested development of thought. It consists in seeing in women only feminine characteristics; and, conversely, seeing in all the complex functions of civilization only masculine characteristics.

Under this conception it is held, quite naturally, that women need do nothing more than fulfill their "womanly duties," i.e., to be wives, mothers, and houseworkers; that for them to desire any other activities in life is to be unwomanly, unnatural, to become some sort of pervert or monster. They are spoken of as "denatured women," as "epicene," as "unsexed," as "seeking to become men." Miss Ida Tarbell in a recent magazine article describes women's professional and industrial advance as "making a Man of Herself. . . ."

As animals, we share in the universal distinction of sex; but as human beings, we alone possess a whole new range of faculties, vitally essential and common to both sexes. . . .

This universal, glaring fact is what these sex-obsessed opponents of the normal progress of women cannot see. They see only the feminine characteristics of women, and fail to see the human ones. . . .

The women of our age in most countries of the same degree of development are outgrowing the artificial restrictions so long placed upon them, and following natural lines of human advance. They are specializing, because they are human. They are organizing, because they are human. They are seeking economic and political independence, because they are human. They are demanding the vote, because they are human.

Boston social worker, and Carrie Chapman Catt, a journalist from Iowa, the National American Woman Suffrage Association grew from a membership of about 13,000 in 1893 to over 2 million in 1917. The involvement of such well-known and widely admired women as Jane Addams brought added attention to the cause. The Triangle fire in New York and other such incidents strengthened the arguments of suffragists that woman laborers needed the protection of woman voters. The movement made steady gains in the first decades of the progressive era. By 1919, thirty-nine states had granted women the right to vote in at least some elections; fifteen had allowed them full participation. In 1920, finally, suffragists won ratification of the Nineteenth Amendment, which guaranteed political rights to women everywhere. Encouraged by that success, many feminists turned their energies to a new goal: enactment of an equal rights amendment to the Constitution that would prohibit all discrimination on the basis of sex, a battle that would continue for more than sixty years.

The suffrage movement may have gained important strength from its identification with humanitarian reform, but the Social Gospel was not the only impulse behind it. The movement was a coalition of diverse elements; while much of its support was based on a broad and humane social outlook, some of its appeal was to a far narrower view. Some women argued that they needed the vote to counteract the political influence of corrupt and illiterate immigrants who were polluting the electorate. Others claimed that women deserved at least the same political rights as black men. While some feminists tried to fuse the movement with efforts to elevate the status of the immigrant and the black, others supported literacy tests for potential voters and insisted that suffrage would not threaten the system of segregation. The demand for the vote united a wide spectrum of feminine opinion (although by no means all of it), but on other issues women were often no more in agreement than men. Once enfranchised, the new voters did little to support the arguments of those suffragists who had claimed that women would operate in politics as a coherent force for reform.

The Dream of Socialism

Prohibition, immigration restriction, woman suffrage—these and other issues attracted large but limited constituencies. Of more general concern to progressives of all backgrounds was the state of the nation's economy. From the beginning, it had been animosity toward the great industrial combinations—the trusts—that had formed the core of progressive sentiment. It was to the task of limiting the power of the giant corporations, therefore, that many reformers devoted their greatest energies.

On how best to deal with the trusts, however, there was wide disagreement. Some reformers believed in the importance of careful government regulation, others in the necessity of destroying the trusts. But others, moving beyond the strictures of progressivism, argued that the problem lay not in the abuses of the economic system but in the system itself—that the solution lay in replacing capitalism with socialism.

At no time in American history to that point, and in a few times after it, did radical critiques of the capitalist system attract more support than in the period between 1900 and 1914. Although never a force to rival, or even seriously threaten, the two major parties, the Socialist party of America grew during the progressive era into a force of considerable strength. In 1900, it had attracted the support of fewer than 100,000 voters; in 1912, its durable leader and perennial presidential candidate, Eugene V. Debs, received nearly 1 million ballots. Strongest in urban immigrant communities (particularly among Germans and Jews in New York, Chicago, Milwaukee, and elsewhere), it won the loyalties, too, of a substantial number of Protestant farmers in the South and Midwest. Socialists won election to over a thousand state and local offices, and they attracted the admiring attention of some journalists and intellectuals as well as of members of the lower class. Lincoln Steffens, the crusader against municipal corruption, ultimately became a defender of socialism. So for a time did Walter Lippmann, the brilliant young journalist who was to become one of the nation's most important social critics.

Virtually all socialists agreed on the need for basic structural changes in the economy, but they differed widely on how drastic those changes should be. Some endorsed the sweepingly radical goals of European Marxists; others envisioned a more moderate reform that would allow small-scale private enterprise to survive but would nationalize the major industries. There was still less agreement on tactics. Militants within the party favored drastic, even violent, action. Most conspicuous was the radical labor union the Industrial Workers of the World (IWW), known to opponents as the "Wobblies." Under the leadership of William ("Big Bill") Haywood, the IWW advocated a single union for all workers and abolition of the "wage slave" system; it rejected political action in favor of strikes and industrial sabo-

Strikers Confront the Militia, 1912
In January 1912, mill workers in Lawrence, Massachusetts, struck in protest against a wage cut.
Organizers from the radical IWW arrived to assist the strikers and win recruits to the union. The
mayor called in the state militia, which threatened the workers with guns. Before the strike
ended, a woman was killed in a clash between strikers and policemen. (Library of Congress)

tage. Although small in numbers, the
"Wobblies" struck terror into the hearts of
the middle class with their inflammatory
rhetoric and their occasional dynamiting of
railroad lines and power stations.

More moderate socialists advocated
peaceful change through political struggle,
and it was they who dominated the party.
They emphasized a gradual education of the
public to the need for change, and patient efforts within the system to enact it. It soon became clear, however, that the period before
World War I was not the first stage of an effective socialist movement but the last. By
the end of the war, socialism was virtually
dead as a significant political force. Party
leaders continued to talk of the need for
change, but hardly anyone was listening.

Decentralization and Regulation

A far more influential debate was raging at
the same time between those who believed in
the essential premises of capitalism but
urged reforms to preserve it. The debate centered around two basic approaches: decentralization and regulation.

To many progressives, the greatest threat
to the nation's economy was excessive centralization and consolidation. The trusts had
made it impossible for the free market to
work as it should; only by restoring the economy to a more human scale could the nation
hope for stability and justice. Few such reformers envisioned a return to a society of
small, local enterprises; some consolidation,

they recognized, was inevitable. They did, however, argue that the federal government should take forceful action to break up the largest combinations, to enforce a balance between the need for bigness and the need for competition. It was a viewpoint often identified with Louis D. Brandeis, the brilliant lawyer and, later, justice of the Supreme Court, who spoke and wrote widely (most notably in his 1913 book *Other People's Money*) about the "curse of bigness."

To other progressives, competition was an overrated commodity. Far more important was efficiency. And since economic concentration tended to enhance efficiency, the government, they believed, should not discourage it. What government should do, however, was to ensure that "bigness" did not bring with it abuses of power. It should stand constant guard against irresponsibility and corruption in the great corporations. It should distinguish between "good trusts" and "bad trusts," encouraging the good while disciplining the bad. Such progressives—for example, Herbert Croly, whose *The Promise of American Life* (1909) became one of the most influential of all progressive documents—argued that America had entered a new era. Economic consolidation, they foresaw, would remain a permanent feature of society, but continuing oversight by a strong, modernized government would be vital.

Whatever their differences, most progressives believed that the federal government was an essential partner in the work of reform. But just as at the state and local levels, the national government seemed at first unable to respond to popular demands, mired as it was in the tired partisan politics of the nineteenth century. There were efforts by progressives in Congress to limit the power of conservative party leaders and make the legislative process more responsive to the popular will. Some reformers, for example, urged an end to the system whereby United States senators were elected by the members of their state legislatures; they proposed instead a direct popular election, which they believed would force the Senate to react to public demands. The Seventeenth Amendment provided for that change; after conservatives had delayed action on it for years, it was finally passed by Congress in 1912 and ratified by the states in 1913.

Even a reformed Congress, however, could not be expected to provide the kind of coherent leadership that the progressive agenda required. If the federal government was truly to fulfill its mission, it would, most reformers agreed, have to do so largely through the executive branch. It would require, above all, strong leadership from the one office capable of providing it: the presidency.

THEODORE ROOSEVELT AND THE PROGRESSIVE PRESIDENCY

"Presidents in general are not lovable," Walter Lippmann, who had known many, said near the end of his life. "They've had to do too much to get where they are. But there was one President who was lovable—Teddy Roosevelt—and I loved him."

He was not alone. To a generation of progressive reformers, Theodore Roosevelt was more than an admired public figure; he was an idol. No president before and few since could match him in attracting attention and devotion. Yet Roosevelt was not the era's most advanced progressive. In many respects he was decidedly conservative. He earned his

extraordinary popularity less because of the extent of the reforms he championed than because of the vigor and dynamism with which he approached them. He brought to his office a broad conception of its powers, and he invested the presidency with something of its modern status as the center of national political life.

The Accidental President

Roosevelt was not intended by his party for the presidency. Republican leaders had nom-

Theodore Roosevelt
Roosevelt's public presence in the first years of the twentieth century was so powerful that hobbies and sports he enjoyed became national crazes, and casual phrases he used, such as "Bully!", became part of everyday language. For generations, the most popular toy in the nation was a stuffed animal named for the president: the teddy bear. A biography for youths, *A Boy's Life of Theodore Roosevelt*, remained one of America's most popular books for decades. And Roosevelt's exhortations on behalf of the outdoors and the "strenuous life" left a lasting imprint upon the values of his society. (Theodore Roosevelt Collection, Harvard University)

inated him to run for vice president with William McKinley in 1900 largely to remove him from the governorship of New York, where he was proving troublesome to party bosses. When President McKinley suddenly died in September 1901, the victim of an assassination, Roosevelt was only forty-two years old, the youngest man ever to assume the presidency. Already, however, he had achieved a notoriety that caused party leaders to feel something close to despair. "I told William McKinley that it was a mistake to nominate that wild man at Philadelphia," Mark Hanna was reported to have exclaimed. "I asked him if he realized what would happen if he should die. Now look, that damned cowboy is President of the United States!"

Roosevelt's reputation as a wild man was, characteristically, a result less of the substance than of the style of his early political career. As a young member of the New York legislature, he had displayed an energy seldom seen in that lethargic body. As a rancher in the Dakota Badlands (where he retired briefly after the sudden death of his first wife), he had helped capture outlaws. As New York City police commissioner, he had been a flamboyant battler against crime and vice. As commander of the "Rough Riders," he had led a heroic, if militarily useless, charge up San Juan Hill in Cuba during the Spanish-American War.

Never, however, had Roosevelt openly rebelled against the leaders of his party; and once in the White House, he continued to balance his personal dynamism against the demands of the political establishment, becoming a champion of cautious, moderate change. Reform was, he believed, less a vehicle for remaking American society than for protecting it against more radical challenges. "I cannot say," he once admitted, "that I entered the presidency with any deliberately planned and far reaching scheme of social betterment." His greatest ambition, it seemed, was to be elected president in his own right.

Managing the Trusts

For all his cautiousness, however, Roosevelt did bring certain assumptions to the presidency that markedly differentiated him from his predecessors. Imbued with progressive ideas about the importance of the efficient, modern management of society, he envisioned the federal government not as the agent of any particular interest but as a mediator of the public good. The president would be the central figure in that mediation.

Such attitudes found open expression in Roosevelt's policies toward the great trusts. Like William McKinley, he was not opposed to the principle of economic concentration. Unlike McKinley, however, he acknowledged that consolidation produced abuses of power that could prove harmful to society. From the beginning, therefore, he allied himself with those progressives who urged regulation (but not destruction) of the trusts.

At the heart of Roosevelt's policy was his desire to win for government the power to investigate the activities of corporations and to publicize the results. The pressure of educated public opinion alone, he believed, would eliminate most corporate abuses. Government could legislate solutions for those that remained. The new Department of Commerce and Labor (later to be divided into two separate departments), established in 1903, was to assist in this task through its investigatory arm, the Bureau of Corporations.

Roosevelt was not above an occasional flamboyant gesture on behalf of a more drastic approach to reform. Although not a trust buster at heart, he engaged in several highly publicized efforts to break up notorious combinations—actions that strengthened his credentials as a progressive without offering any fundamental challenge to the structure of the economy. In 1902, he ordered the Justice Department to invoke the Sherman Antitrust Act against a great new railroad monopoly in the Northwest, the Northern Securities Com-

pany, a $400 million enterprise pieced together by J. P. Morgan, E. H. Harriman, and James J. Hill. To Morgan, accustomed to a warm, supportive relationship with Republican administrations, the action was baffling. Hurrying to the White House with two conservative senators in tow, he told the president, "If we have done anything wrong, send your man to my man and they can fix it up." Roosevelt proceeded with the case nonetheless, and in 1904 the Supreme Court ruled that the Northern Securities Company must be dissolved. At the same time, however, he assured Morgan and others that the suit did not signal a general campaign to dissolve the trusts. Other monopolistic corporations, such as United States Steel, he would challenge only if "they have done something we regard as wrong." Although he filed more than forty additional antitrust suits during the remainder of his presidency, and although he succeeded in dissolving several important combinations, Roosevelt made no serious effort to reverse the prevailing trend toward economic concentration. Regulation, with the government serving as mediator between corporate and public interests, remained his central goal.

Government and Labor

A similar commitment to establishing the government as an impartial regulatory mechanism shaped Roosevelt's policy toward labor. In the past, federal intervention in industrial disputes had almost always meant action on behalf of employers, as in the Pullman strike in 1894. Roosevelt, however, was willing to consider labor's position as well.

He displayed this willingness during a bitter strike in 1902 by members of the United Mine Workers employed in the anthracite coal industry. Miners, under the leadership of John Mitchell, were demanding a 20 percent wage increase, an eight-hour day, and recognition of their union. Management, represented by the truculent George F. Baer, was responding with conspicuous arrogance and contempt. When the strike threatened to drag on long enough to endanger coal supplies for the coming winter, Roose-

Mine Workers
Powder men emerge from the Perrin coal mine, about 1902. Theodore Roosevelt's intervention in the United Mine Workers' strike of that year averted what might have been a disastrous blow to the nation's economy by forcing the resumption of coal production. It resulted, however, in only minor improvements in the position of mine workers. (Harvard University Library)

velt decided to step in—not to assist management but to invite both the operators and the miners to the White House, where he asked them to accept impartial federal arbitration. Mitchell readily agreed. Baer balked.

Furious at the obstinacy of the mine owners (who had already alienated public opinion), Roosevelt threatened drastic action. He would, he told them, order 10,000 federal troops to seize the mines and resume coal production. Under pressure from politicians, the press, and, perhaps most significantly, J. P. Morgan, the operators finally relented. Arbitrators awarded the strikers a 10 percent wage increase and a nine-hour day, but no recognition of the union. It was a meager reward for a long and costly strike, but it was more than the miners might have won without the government's intervention.

Despite such episodes, Roosevelt viewed himself as no more the champion of labor than of management. On several occasions, he ordered federal troops to intervene in strikes on behalf of employers—in Arizona in 1903 and in Colorado in 1904. And although he believed in the right of workers to join a union, he believed, too, in the right of employers to refuse to bargain with it.

The Square Deal

Even if Roosevelt had wished to move more quickly on economic reforms (and there was little evidence that he did), he would have been reluctant to do so during his first term as president. Much of his energy in those years he was devoting to the business of winning reelection. Above all, he was working to ensure that the conservative Republican Old Guard, which bristled at even the most modest of reforms, would not block his nomination in 1904.

It was a legitimate concern, for men such as Nelson Aldrich and Mark Hanna in the Senate and Joseph Cannon in the House were not only influential within the party but suspicious of the new president. Had Roosevelt engaged them in open battle, they might well have destroyed him in 1904. As it was, however, quite the opposite occurred. By skillfully dispensing patronage to conservatives and progressives alike, by reshuffling unstable Republican organizations in the South, by winning the support of northern businessmen while making adroit gestures to reformers, he succeeded in all but neutralizing his opposition within the party and won its presidential nomination with ease. And in the general election, where he faced a pallid conservative Democrat, Alton B. Parker, he stormed to one of the largest victories in the nation's history. Roosevelt captured over 57 percent of the popular vote and lost not one state outside the South. Now, relieved of immediate political concerns, he was free to display the full extent (and the real limits) of his commitment to reform.

During the 1904 campaign, Roosevelt boasted that he had worked in the anthracite coal strike to provide everyone with a "square deal." In his second term, he became noticeably more aggressive in his efforts to extend the square deal even further. He continued to operate from the political center, offending many of the business interests that had contributed to his campaign and, at the same time, offending many Midwestern progressives who subscribed to what he termed "the La Follette type of fool radicalism." But he delighted the great majority of Americans who believed in careful, moderate change.

Among his most important targets was the railroad industry, for nearly half a century one of the most powerful forces in the nation and for much of that time a target of all those who feared unrestrained corporate power. The Interstate Commerce Act of 1887, establishing the Interstate Commerce Commission (ICC), had been an early effort to regulate the industry; but over the years, the courts had virtually nullified its influence. Roosevelt, through a series of intricate maneuvers, pushed a new, more forceful regulatory law through Congress, a law that would give the government considerable power over the setting of railroad rates.

Roosevelt managed to win approval of a particularly strong version of the bill in the House (partly at least because he agreed in return not to push for a tariff reduction). The legislation gave the ICC broad powers to set shipping rates in response to complaints from shippers and to investigate corporate records and supervise accounting methods. In the Senate, however, the Republican Old Guard insisted on amendments to increase the power of the courts to review ICC rulings (an important change given the prevailing conservatism of the judiciary). During the negotiations between the two bodies that followed, Roosevelt finally agreed to the conservative changes, and in June 1906 the Hepburn Railroad Regulation Act became law.

It was a classic example of the cautiousness with which Roosevelt, even after his 1904 mandate, approached reform. At first, he had seemed to support the position of militant progressives such as La Follette, who wanted to give the ICC power to evaluate railroad property as a basis for determining rates. Ultimately, however, he settled for legislation that even many conservatives considered acceptable. La Follette, who believed the president had betrayed him, never forgave Roosevelt.

The Hepburn Act was the most conspicuous reform legislation of Roosevelt's second term, but only one of many new regulatory measures. The president won approval of laws providing for compensation by employers to injured workingmen in the District of Columbia and certain other, limited areas. He pressured Congress to enact the Pure Food and Drug Act, which, despite weaknesses in its enforcement mechanisms, did restrict the sale of some dangerous or ineffective medicines. When Upton Sinclair's powerful novel *The Jungle* appeared in 1906, featuring nauseating descriptions of the preparation of meats in the nation's stockyards (see "The Sausages," p. 559), Roosevelt insisted on passage of the Meat Inspection Act, which, despite a shaky start, ultimately succeeded in eliminating many diseases once transmitted in impure meat.

Starting in 1907, moreover, he seemed to expand his vision of regulation and began to propose even more stringent measures: an eight-hour day for workers, broader compensation for victims of industrial accidents, inheritance and income taxes, regulation of the stock market, railroad property valuation (the La Follette proposal he had previously abandoned), and others. He was openly and self-consciously moving to the left; and in the process he started openly to criticize conservatives in Congress, who were blocking much of this legislation, and to denounce the judiciary, which was striking down many of the measures that did pass. The result was not only a general stalemate in Roosevelt's reform agenda, but a widening gulf between the president and the conservative wing of his party.

Conservation

Nothing contributed more to the creation of that gulf than Roosevelt's aggressive policies on behalf of conservation. An ardent sportsman and naturalist, he had long been concerned about the unregulated exploitation of America's natural resources and the despoiling of what remained of the nation's wilderness. Using executive powers, he began early in his presidency to restrict private development in millions of acres of undeveloped land still controlled by the government, adding them to the hitherto modest system of national forests and parks. When vigorous conservative and Western opposition finally resulted in legislation in 1907 to restrict his authority over public lands, Roosevelt and his chief forester, Gifford Pinchot, worked furiously to seize all the forests and many of the waterpower sites still in the public domain, before the bill became law. By the time he left office, Roosevelt had added about 125 million acres to the national forest system and greatly expanded government holdings of phosphate beds and coal lands.

Roosevelt was the first president to take an active interest in the new and struggling American conservation movement, and his policies had a lasting effect on national environmental policies. More than most public figures, he was sympathetic to the concerns of the naturalists—those within the movement committed to protecting the natural beauty of the land and the health of its wildlife from human intrusion. Early in his presidency, Roosevelt even spent four days camping in the Sierras with John Muir, the nation's leading preservationist and the founder of the Sierra Club. In the end, however, Roosevelt's policy tended to favor less the preservationists than another faction within the conservation movement—those who believed in carefully managed development. The leading conservation figure in government, therefore, was Gifford Pinchot. The first professionally trained forester in the United States, Pinchot supported rational and efficient human use of the wilderness. The Sierra Club might argue for the "aesthetic" value of the forests; Pinchot insisted, in contrast, that "the whole question is a practical one." Trained experts in forestry and resource management, such men as Pinchot himself, should, Roosevelt believed, apply to the landscape the same scientific standards that others were applying to the management of cities and industries. The president did side with the preservationists on certain issues, but the more important legacy of his conservation policy was to establish the government's role as manager of the continuing development of the wilderness.

To much of the Old Guard, the extension of government control over vast new lands smacked of socialism. Even worse, Roosevelt's use of executive powers to achieve that control smacked of dictatorship. Many of these same interests, however, displayed no such scruples in supporting another important aspect of Roosevelt's natural resource policy: public reclamation and irrigation projects. In 1902, the president supported the Newlands Reclamation Act, which provided federal funds for the construction of huge dams, reservoirs, and canals in the West—projects to open new lands for cultivation and provide cheap electric power. By 1915, the government had invested $80 million in twenty-five such projects, the largest of which—a dam on Arizona's Salt River—carried Roosevelt's name. It was the beginning of many years of federal aid for irrigation and power development in the Western states.

The Panic of 1907

The flurry of reforms Roosevelt was able to enact, and the enormous popularity he attracted as a result, made it easy for members of his administration to believe that finally the government had imposed a strong, effective set of regulations on the new industrial economy. The chaos of the late nineteenth century, they began to tell themselves, was becoming a thing of the past. In actuality, the Roosevelt record—although impressive when compared with that of his predecessors—had been a relatively modest one, and the economy at large remained essentially uncontrolled. That truth was harshly brought home to Roosevelt and his allies in 1907, when a serious panic and recession revealed how flawed the nation's economic structure remained. The scenario was eerily familiar to those who remembered 1893. Once again, American industrial production had outrun the capacity of either domestic or foreign markets to absorb it. Once again, the banking system and the stock market had displayed pathetic inadequacies. Once again, irresponsible speculation and rampant financial mismanagement had helped to shatter a prosperity that many had come to believe was now permanent. Banks failed; industries cut or ceased production; workers suffered layoffs and wage cuts.

To many conservatives, Roosevelt's "mad" economic policies were the obvious cause of the disaster. The president, naturally and correctly, disagreed; but the panic was clearly unnerving to him, and he acted quickly to reassure business leaders that he would not interfere with their recovery efforts. J. P. Morgan, in a spectacular display of his awesome financial power, helped construct a pool of the assets of several important New York banks to prop up shaky financial institutions. The key to the arrangement, Morgan told the president, was the purchase by U.S. Steel of the shares of the Tennessee Coal and Iron Company currently held by a threatened New York bank. He would, he insisted, need assurances that no antitrust action would ensue. Roosevelt tacitly agreed, and the Morgan plan proceeded. Partly as a result, the panic soon subsided.

For eight years to come, until the outbreak of war in Europe reinvigorated the economy, the nation continued to stumble through a series of modest booms and partial busts, never fully able to stabilize its financial position. The efficient, scientifically managed economy that so many progressives had advocated and that some had come to believe they had achieved was still far from reality.

THE BIG STICK

At the heart of Roosevelt's domestic policies was a continuing concern for imposing order and stability on the troubled American economy. The same concern dictated his behavior in international affairs. Only by expanding overseas markets for America's industrial products, most progressives believed, could the nation avoid the disastrous economic collapses that had marred the 1890s. And only by acting forcefully to prevent disorder in those regions important to American trade could the markets be secured. For Roosevelt, as for many later presidents, foreign affairs had an additional attraction. There, he could act without fear of a recalcitrant Congress or conservative courts. There, he could free himself from concerns about public opinion; for most of the public thought like Walter Lippmann, who once wrote: "I cannot remember taking any interest whatsoever in foreign affairs until after the outbreak of the First World War." Overseas, the president could exercise power unfettered and alone.

Sea Power and Civilization

Roosevelt was well suited, both by temperament and by ideology, for an activist foreign policy. A vigorous athlete and once an enthusiastic college boxer, he spoke often of the virtues of the "strenuous life" and viewed physical combat as an ennobling, manly challenge. His fondness for battle was not dampened by his famous charge up San Juan Hill, a crucial event in the development of his political career.

Roosevelt believed, moreover, that an important distinction existed between the "civilized" and "uncivilized" nations of the world. "Civilized" nations, as he defined them, were predominantly white and Anglo-Saxon or Teutonic; "uncivilized" nations were generally nonwhite, Latin, or Slavic. But racism was only partly the basis of the distinction. At least as important was economic development. Thus it was that Japan, a rapidly industrializing society, seemed to Roosevelt to have earned admission to the ranks of the civilized.

There was, of course, another important aspect of this global division. Civilized nations were, by Roosevelt's definition, producers of industrial goods; uncivilized nations were suppliers of raw materials and markets. There was, he believed, an economic relationship between the two parts that was vital to both of them; and it was natural, perhaps, that he should come to believe in the right and duty of the civilized societies to intervene in the affairs of "backward" nations to preserve order and stability. The economic health of the globe might depend on the result.

Accordingly, Roosevelt early became an outspoken champion of the development of American sea power. A friend and admirer of Alfred Thayer Mahan, Roosevelt had believed since his days as assistant secretary of the navy in 1897 that the United States must move rapidly to expand the size and power of its fleet. Only thus, he argued, could the nation play an active and important role in world affairs. To Roosevelt, as to many other early twentieth-century internationalists, the concept of sea power soon assumed the same central significance that the concept of air power would assume in later decades. By 1906, Roosevelt's support had enabled the American navy to attain a size and strength surpassed only by that of Great Britain (although Germany was fast gaining ground).

Frustrations in Asia

The new strength was not, however, always enough to enable the president to have his way in global developments, as events in the Pacific soon illustrated. Roosevelt believed that the "Open Door" was vital to maintain American trade in the Pacific and to prevent any single nation from establishing hegemony there. (See above, pp. 612–613.) He looked with alarm, therefore, at the military rivalries involving Japan, Russia, Germany, and France in the region.

He was particularly concerned by Russian efforts to expand southward into Manchuria, a province of China; and when in 1904 the Japanese attacked the Russian fleet at Port Arthur in southern Manchuria, Roosevelt, like most Americans, was inclined to approve. Yet the president was no more eager for Japan to control Manchuria than for Russia to do so. Japanese control might, he believed, "mean a struggle between them and us in the future" over commercial rights in the region. In 1905, therefore, he eagerly agreed to a Japanese request to mediate an end to the conflict. Russia, faring badly in the war—and, as a result, already experiencing a domestic instability that twelve years later would culminate in revolution—had no choice but to agree.

At a peace conference in Portsmouth, New Hampshire, Roosevelt extracted from the embattled Russians a recognition of Japan's territorial gains—control of Korea, South Manchuria, and part of Sakhalin Island, formerly a Russian outpost. Japan, in return, agreed to cease the fighting and expand no further. At the same time, Roosevelt worked to secure American interests by negotiating a secret agreement with the Japanese to ensure that the United States could continue to trade freely in the region.

Roosevelt was pleased with his work at the Portsmouth Conference, particularly when it helped him to win the Nobel Peace Prize in 1906. But his triumph was, in actuality, a hollow one. In the years that followed, relations between the United States and Japan steadily deteriorated, and the careful assurances Roosevelt had won in 1905 proved all but meaningless. Having destroyed the Russian fleet at Port Arthur,

American Naval Power on Display
The "Great White Fleet" sailed around the world in 1908, demonstrating
the new resolve of the United States to behave as an international power.
(U.S. Navy photo)

Japan now emerged as the preeminent naval power in the Pacific and soon began to exclude American trade from many of the territories it controlled.

It did not help matters that in 1906 the school board of San Francisco voted to segregate Oriental schoolchildren in the city in separate schools; or that a year later, the California legislature attempted to pass legislation limiting the immigration of Japanese laborers into the state. Anti-Oriental riots in California and inflammatory stories in the Hearst papers about the "Yellow Peril" further fanned resentment in Japan.

The president did his best to douse the flames. He quietly persuaded the San Francisco school board to rescind its edict in return for a Japanese agreement to stop the flow of agricultural immigrants into California. Then, lest the Japanese government construe his actions as a sign of weakness, he sent sixteen battleships of the new American navy on an unprecedented 45,000-mile voyage around the world that included a call on Japan. Despite fears by some members of Congress that a naval conflict might ensue, the "Great White Fleet," as the flotilla was called, received a warm reception when it arrived in Yokohama. For the moment, Roosevelt's foreign policy—which he once summarized with the African proverb: "Speak softly and carry a big stick"—seemed to have

borne important fruit. But the United States had failed to stop Japanese expansion in Asia, and Roosevelt himself had to admit that the situation in the Pacific posed a grave threat to future peace.

Mediation in Europe

At the same time that Roosevelt was attempting to create a balance of power in the Pacific, he was participating in efforts to maintain a balance in Europe. He was particularly concerned with ensuring that the growth of German power in Europe did not threaten the stability of the Continent or the ability of the British navy to maintain peace in international waters.

When a bitter quarrel arose between Germany and France over control of Morocco in northern Africa, Roosevelt was at first reluctant to involve the United States. But as the dispute grew more heated, he began to feel compelled to do something "to keep matters on an even keel in Europe." When Kaiser Wilhelm of Germany asked him to help mediate an end to the conflict, Roosevelt persuaded France and Great Britain to send delegates to an international conference in Algeciras, Spain, to establish the status of Morocco. At the 1906 Algeciras conference, the American delegates sided from the beginning with the British and the French, although they managed to extract some concessions for Germany from the negotiations. The agreement that ensued maintained French control of Morocco and succeeded, Roosevelt believed, in stabilizing the increasingly precarious balance of power in Europe.

The Iron-Fisted Neighbor

Even before the Algeciras conference, Roosevelt had begun to become concerned, some believed almost obsessed, by the possibility of German penetration into Latin America, which the United States had come to consider its exclusive sphere of influence. Unwilling to share trading rights, let alone military control, with any other nation, Roosevelt embarked on a series of ventures in the Caribbean and South America that established an ominous pattern of American intervention in the region.

Crucial to Roosevelt's thinking was an incident early in his presidency. When the government of Venezuela began in 1902 to renege on debts to European bankers, naval forces of Britain, Italy, and Germany erected a blockade along that country's coast. Roosevelt at first expressed little concern. "If any South American country misbehaves toward any European country," he had written to a friend in Germany, "let the European country spank it." But when that "spanking" expanded to include a German bombardment of a Venezuelan port and rumors that Germany planned to establish a permanent base in the region, Roosevelt changed his mind. In 1903, he warned the Germans (according to his own later account) that Admiral Dewey and his fleet were standing by in the Caribbean and would act against any German effort to acquire new territory. The German navy finally withdrew.

The incident helped to persuade Roosevelt that European intrusions into Latin America could result not only from aggression but from internal instability or irresponsibility (such as defaulting on debts) in Latin American nations. As a result, he imposed a new interpretation on the Monroe Doctrine. In a 1904 message to Congress, he claimed that the United States had the right not only to oppose European intervention in the

Theodore Roosevelt's Latin American Policy [1905]

It cannot be too often and too emphatically asserted that the United States has not the slightest desire for territorial aggrandizement at the expense of any of its southern neighbors, and will not treat the Monroe Doctrine as an excuse for such aggrandizement on its part. . . . Moreover . . . we do not intend to permit the Monroe Doctrine to be used by any nation on this Continent as a shield to protect it from the consequences of its own misdeeds against foreign nations. . . . On the one hand, this country would certainly decline to go to war to prevent a foreign government from collecting a just debt; on the other hand, it is very inadvisable to permit any foreign power to take possession, even temporarily, of the custom houses of an American Republic in order to enforce the payment of its obligations; for such temporary occupation might turn into a permanent occupation. The only escape from these alternatives may at any time be that we must ourselves undertake to bring about some arrangement by which so much as possible of a just obligation shall be paid. . . . The justification for the United States taking this burden and incurring this responsibility is to be found in the fact that it is incompatible with international equity for the United States to refuse to allow other powers to take the only means at their disposal of satisfying the claims of their creditors and yet to refuse, itself, to take any such steps.—Annual Message to Congress, *December 5, 1905.*

Western Hemisphere, but to intervene itself in the domestic affairs of its neighbors if those neighbors proved unable to maintain order on their own.

The immediate motivation for the Roosevelt Corollary (as it became known), and the first opportunity for putting the doctrine into practice, was a crisis in the Dominican Republic. A revolution had toppled the corrupt and bankrupt government of that nation in 1903, but the new regime proved no better able than the old to make good on the country's $22 million of debts to European nations. Both France and Italy were threatening to intervene to recover their losses, and the new Dominican leaders had turned to the United States for help. Using the rationale he had outlined in his address to Congress, Roosevelt established, in effect, an American receivership, assuming control of Dominican customs and distributing 45 percent of the revenues to Santo Domingo and the rest to foreign creditors. This arrangement lasted, in one form or another, for more than three decades.

Two years later, another opportunity for intervention in the Caribbean arose. In 1902, the United States had granted political independence to Cuba, but only after the new government had agreed to the so-called Platt Amendment to its constitution, giving the United States the right to prevent any foreign power from intruding into the new nation. When, in 1906, a series of domestic uprisings seemed to threaten the internal stability of the island, Roosevelt reasoned that America must intervene to "protect" Cuba from disorder. American troops landed in Cuba, quelled the fighting, and remained there for three years.

The Panama Canal

The most celebrated accomplishment of Roosevelt's presidency, and the one that illustrated most clearly his own expansive view of the powers of his office and the role of the United States abroad, was the completion of the Panama Canal. Construction of a channel through Central America linking the Atlantic and the Pacific had been a dream of many nations since the mid-nineteenth century, but somehow the canal had never been built. Roosevelt was determined to do better.

The first step was the removal of an old obstacle. In 1850, the United States and Great Britain had agreed to a treaty under which the two nations would construct, operate, and defend any such canal together. The McKinley administration had already begun negotiations to cancel the agreement; Roosevelt completed the process. In 1901, the Hay-Pauncefote Treaty gave the United States the right to undertake the canal project alone.

The next question was where to locate the canal. At first, the Roosevelt administration (and many congressional leaders) favored a route across Nicaragua, which would permit a sea-level canal requiring no locks. A possible alternative was the Isthmus of Panama in Colombia, the site of an earlier, abortive effort by a French company to construct a channel. The Panama route was shorter (although not at sea level), and construction was already about 40 percent complete. When the French company lowered its price for its holdings from $109 million to $40 million, and when it combined this gesture with skillful lobbying efforts in Washington, the president and Congress changed their minds.

Roosevelt quickly dispatched John Hay, his secretary of state, to negotiate an agreement with Colombian diplomats in Washington that would allow construction to begin without delay. Under heavy American pressure, the Colombian chargé d'affaires, Tomas Herrán, signed an agreement highly unfavorable to his own nation. The United States would gain perpetual rights to a six-mile-wide "canal zone" across Colombia; in return, it would pay Colombia $10 million and an annual rental of $250,000. The treaty produced outrage in the Colombian Senate, whose members angrily pointed out that the defunct French company was to receive four times the amount the government of Colombia was to be paid. The senators refused to ratify the agreement and sent a new representative to the United States with instructions to demand at least $20 million from the Americans plus a share of the payment to the French.

Roosevelt was furious. The Colombians,

he charged, were "inefficient bandits" and "blackmailers"; and he began to contemplate ways to circumvent the Bogotá government. He found a ready ally in the person of Philippe Bunau-Varilla, chief engineer of the French canal project and one of the most effective lobbyists in the campaign to persuade the United States to choose the Isthmus of Panama for its own efforts. Bunau-Varilla watched with dismay as the government of Colombia appeared ready to destroy his efforts, and in November 1903 he helped organize and finance a revolution in Panama. There had been many previous revolts, all of them failures. But this one had an important additional asset: the support of the United States. Using an 1846 American-Colombian treaty as justification, Roosevelt landed troops from the U.S.S. *Nashville* in Panama to "maintain order." Their presence prevented Colombian forces from suppressing the rebellion, and three days later the United States recognized Panama as an independent nation. The new Panamanian government, under the influence of Bunau-Varilla, quickly agreed to a new treaty. It would grant the United States a canal zone ten miles wide; the United States would pay it the $10 million fee and the $250,000 annual rental that the Colombian Senate had rejected. Work on the canal proceeded rapidly, despite the enormous cuts and elaborate locks (which alone cost $375 million) that the construction required. It opened in 1914, three years after Roosevelt had proudly boasted to a university audience, "I took the Canal Zone and let Congress debate!" Few at the time would have disagreed.

The Roosevelt Retirement

Theodore Roosevelt loved being president. He had made that plain during his first moments in office, when, torn between his excitement at his new position and his distress at McKinley's death, he had written, "It is a dreadful thing to come into the Presidency in this way; but it would be a far worse thing to be morbid about it." As his years in office produced increasing political and diplomatic successes, as his public popularity continued to rise, more and more observers began to doubt that he would happily stand aside in 1908.

Events, however, dictated otherwise. The Panic of 1907, combined with Roosevelt's growing "radicalism" during his second term, had deeply alienated conservatives in his own party. He would, he realized, have considerable difficulty winning the Republican nomination for another term. In 1904, moreover, he had made a public promise to step down four years later, a promise that would surely emerge to haunt him if he decided to run again. And so, after nearly eight energetic years in the White House, during which he had transformed the role of the presidency in American government, Theodore Roosevelt, fifty years old, retired from public life—briefly.

SUGGESTED READINGS

Historians have disagreed sharply in their interpretations of progressivism. Among the contending views are Richard Hofstadter, *The Age of Reform* (1955); Robert Wiebe, *The Search for Order* (1967); Gabriel Kolko, *The Triumph of Conservatism* (1963); and James Weinstein, *The Corporate Ideal in the Liberal States, 1900–1918* (1969). Studies of progressive thought include Morton White, *Social Thought in America* (1949); D. W. Marcell, *Progress and Pragmatism: James, Dewey, Beard and the American Idea of Progress* (1974); Charles Forcey, *The Crossroads of Liberalism: Croly, Weyl, Lippmann* (1961); and Richard Abrams, *The Burdens of Progress* (1978). Sudhir Kakar, *Frederick Taylor* (1970), examines the father of "scientific management." Burton Bledstein, *The Culture of Professionalism* (1976), provides a critical view of the rise of the professional ethic. Donald Fleming, *William H. Welch and the Rise of Modern Medicine* (1954), examines changes in the medical profession. The progressive response to the cities is examined in Allen F. Davis, *Spearheads of Reform: The Social Settlements and the Progressive Movement, 1890–1914* (1968); Roy Lubove, *The Progressives and the Slums: Tenement House Reform in New York City* (1962); Sheila M. Rothman, *Woman's Proper Place* (1978); and Henry May, *Protestant Churches and Industrial America* (1949). A useful overview of the progressive era is John W. Chambers, *The Tyranny of Change* (1980).

Louis Harlan, *Booker T. Washington* (1973), examines the career of the preeminent black leader of the era, while Elliott Rudwick, *W. E. B. Du Bois* (1969), chronicles the life of his major challenger. George Fredrickson, *The Black Image in the White Mind* (1968), is an overview of white racial attitudes. For a discussion of literature and the arts in the progressive era, see Alfred Kazin, *On Native Grounds* (1942); Van Wyck Brooks, *The Confident Years* (1952); and Kenneth Lynn, *The Dream of Success* (1955).

Important studies of progressive journalism, and in particular muckraking, include Harold S. Wilson, *McClure's Magazine and the Muckrakers* (1970); C. C. Regier, *The Era of the Muckrakers* (1932); and David Chambers, *The Social and Political Ideas of the Muckrakers* (1964). Studies of individual reporters include Justin Kaplan, *Lincoln Steffens* (1974); and Leon Harris, *Upton Sinclair* (1975). Urban political reform movements receive attention in Zane Miller, *Boss Cox's Cincinnati* (1968); John D. Buenker, *Urban Liberalism and Progressive Reform* (1973); James B. Crooks, *Politics and Progress: The Rise of Urban Progressivism in Baltimore* (1968); Melvin G. Holli, *Reform in Detroit* (1969); J. Joseph Huthmacher, *Senator Robert F. Wagner and the Rise of Urban Liberalism* (1971); and Oscar Handlin, *Al Smith and His America* (1958). For state-level progressive reform, see George E. Mowry, *California Progressives* (1951), a pathbreaking work whose conclusions have been challenged by, among others, David P. Thelen, *The New Citizenship: Origins of Progressivism in Wisconsin* (1972), and Sheldon Hackney, *Populism to Progressivism in Alabama* (1969). See also Robert S. Maxwell, *La Follette and the Rise of Progressivism in Wisconsin* (1944); Russel B. Nye, *Midwestern Progressive Politics* (1951); Richard M. Abrams, *Conservatism in a Progressive Era: Massachusetts* (1964); Robert F. Wesser, *Charles Evans Hughes: Politics and Reform in New York State, 1905–1910* (1967); and David Thelen, *Robert La Follette and the Insurgent Spirit* (1976).

For discussion of national progressive issues, see James T. Timberlake, *Prohibition and the Progressive Movement* (1963); Joseph Gusfield, *Symbolic Crusade: Status Politics and the Temperance Movement* (1963); John Higham, *Strangers in the Land* (1955), an indispensable study of American nativism; Aileen S. Kraditor, *Ideas of the Woman Suffrage Movement* (1965); and Ellen C. Lagemann, *A Generation of Women: Education in the Lives of Progressive Reformers* (1979). James Weinstein, *The Decline of Socialism in America* (1967), examines one approach to economic reform. Robert Wiebe,

Businessmen and Reform (1962), and Sidney Fine, *Laissez Faire and the General Welfare State* (1956), examine other progressive economic beliefs. Melvyn Dubofsky, *We Shall Be All* (1969), is a history of the Industrial Workers of the World (IWW).

An eloquent popular study of the prepresidential life of Theodore Roosevelt is Edmund Morris, *The Rise of Theodore Roosevelt* (1979). Important full-scale biographies include Henry F. Pringle, *Theodore Roosevelt* (1931), a critical study, and William H. Harbaugh, *Power and Responsibility* (1961), published in paperback under the title *The Life and Times of Theodore Roosevelt*. John Morton Blum, *The Republican Roosevelt* (1954), provides a succinct, interpretive account of TR's career. Other works on Roosevelt's presidency and the national politics of his era include George E. Mowry, *The Era of Theodore Roosevelt* (1958), and G. Wallace Chessman, *Theodore Roosevelt and the Politics of Power* (1969). John A. Garraty, *The Life of George W. Perkins* (1960), chronicles the career of one of Roosevelt's most important political allies. Samuel P. Hays has provided the most penetrating study of progressive conservation policies in *The Gospel of Efficiency: The Progressive Conservation Movement, 1890–1920* (1962). See also Elmo P. Richardson, *The Politics of Conservation* (1962). Horace S. Merrill and Marion G. Merrill, *The Republican High Command* (1971), considers party politics.

Howard K. Beale, *Theodore Roosevelt and the Rise of America to World Power* (1956), is the standard work on TR's foreign policy. Other useful studies include Richard Challener, *Admirals, Generals, and American Foreign Policy, 1898–1914* (1973); David H. Burton, *Theodore Roosevelt: Confident Imperialist* (1969); and Julius W. Pratt, *Challenge and Rejection: The United States and World Leadership, 1900–1921* (1967). Richard Leopold, *Elihu Root and the Conservative Tradition* (1954), examines Roosevelt's secretary of war and state. On American policy in Asia, see Akira Iriye, *Pacific Estrangement: Japanese and American Expansion, 1897–1911* (1972); Charles E. Neu, *An Uncertain Friendship: Roosevelt and Japan, 1906–1909* (1967); and Charles Vevier, *United States and China* (1955). For American policy in the Caribbean, see Dana G. Munro, *Intervention and Dollar Diplomacy in the Caribbean, 1900–1921* (1964); Dwight C. Miner, *Fight for the Panama Route* (1966); Walter LaFeber, *The Panama Canal* (1978); and David McCullough *The Path Between the Seas* (1977), a lucid popular history of the building of the canal.

Progressivism Divided and Triumphant

22

Pershing in Mexico
General John J. Pershing leads American troops across the Santa Maria River in Mexico during his ill-fated 1916 intervention in that nation's civil war. The long and fruitless effort to shape the outcome of the Mexican struggle was characteristic of the nation's Latin American policy during the progressive era: a combination of economic self-interest and missionary idealism that persuaded Woodrow Wilson and others that it was the nation's duty to help control its less developed neighbors. (Culver Pictures)

It seemed at first that William Howard Taft, who assumed the presidency in 1909, would be that rare thing among politicians: a leader acceptable to virtually everyone. He had been Theodore Roosevelt's most trusted lieutenant and his hand-picked successor; progressive reformers believed him to be one of their own. He had been one of the first viceroys of the new American empire, serving as governor general of the Philippines, secretary of war, and special envoy to Japan; imperialists trusted him to maintain America's active role in world affairs. He had been a restrained and moderate jurist, a solicitor general of the United States, and a man with a punctilious regard for legal process; conservatives expected him to abandon Roosevelt's aggressive use of presidential powers.

It was perhaps unsurprising, then, that in 1908 Taft won election to the White House with almost ridiculous ease. With the support of both Roosevelt and much of the Republican Old Guard, he received his party's nomination virtually uncontested. His victory in the general election in November was a foregone conclusion. Although his popular margin was smaller than Roosevelt's in 1904, it was nevertheless decisive: 51 percent of the votes as compared to 43 percent for the Democratic candidate, William Jennings Bryan, running forlornly for the third time. His electoral margin was a comfortable 321 to 162. Delighted Republican progressives predicted brilliant new achievements. "Roosevelt has cut enough hay," they proclaimed. "Taft is the man to put it into the barn." Republican conservatives rejoiced that they were rid of the "mad messiah." Taft entered the White House on a wave of good feeling.

It was therefore ironic that four years later, Taft would leave office the most decisively repudiated president of the century, his party deeply, perhaps irrevocably, divided, and the government in the hands of a Democratic administration for the first time in twenty years. It had been his misfortune to bring to the presidency a personality and philosophy of leadership ill-suited to his time, and to preside over an era in which the contending forces of progressivism finally broke into open combat.

Yet out of that combat came not a weakening of progressivism but new strengths. For the election of 1912 brought to the White House a man who would become the most successful reform president of the era. Woodrow Wilson presided for a time over a government in which the ideals of progressive reformers seemed finally to have triumphed—until the approach of a dreaded war finally diverted the attention of Americans away from their internal affairs and toward the rest of the world.

THE TROUBLED SUCCESSION

It had been obvious from the start that Taft and Roosevelt were not at all alike, but it was not until Taft took office that the real extent of the differences became clear. Roosevelt had been the most dynamic public figure of his age; Taft was stolid and respectable and little more. Roosevelt was an ardent sportsman and athlete; Taft was sedentary and obese—he weighed over 300 pounds and required a special, oversized bathtub to be installed in the White House. Most of all, Roosevelt had taken an expansive view of the powers of his office; Taft, by contrast, was slow, cautious, even lethargic, insistent that the president must take pains to observe the strict letter of the law.

Yet even had Taft been the most dynamic of political figures, he would still have had difficulties, for he quickly found himself in the middle of a series of political controversies from which no leader could emerge unscathed. Having come into office as the darling of progressives and conservatives alike, he soon found that he could not please them both. Gradually he found himself, without really intending it, pleasing the conservatives and alienating the progressives.

Congress and the Tariff

The first fiasco occurred in the opening months of the new administration, when Taft called Congress into special session to enact legislation lowering protective tariff rates. Tariff reduction had been a consistent demand of many progressives for nearly a decade. It had reflected less a belief in free trade than a conviction that foreign competition would weaken the power of the great trusts and thus lower domestic prices. Theodore Roosevelt had made several tentative gestures on behalf of tariff reform but had always pulled away from the issue in the end. Taft was determined to do more. "I believe the people are with me," he had written in January 1909, "and before I get through I think I will have downed Cannon and Aldrich too."

But the president was not able to down the Old Guard so easily; often, moreover, he seemed not to be trying to do so. A tariff revision acceptable to most progressives moved relatively easily through the House; but in the Senate, Nelson Aldrich and other conservatives, aided by the relentless efforts of protectionist lobbies, waged a powerful campaign to weaken the bill. For weeks, a spirited battle raged on the Senate floor, conservatives working to amend the bill, progressives (among them La Follette) fighting tirelessly to block them. But the devastating arguments the reformers were able to marshall against the tariff were not enough. They needed help from the White House, and that they never received. Taft agonized, hesitated, made ineffectual efforts to produce a compromise, and ultimately simply withdrew from the controversy. He was, he claimed, reluctant to violate the constitutional doctrine of separation of powers by intervening in legislative matters. Without presidential assistance, the progressive efforts finally failed, with La Follette and his allies embittered by what they considered a betrayal by Taft. On August 5, 1909, the president signed the Payne-Aldrich tariff, passed without the support of the Midwestern reformers.

It was not a good bill. Conservatives had made only the slightest concesssions to progressives, and tariff rates, when they were not actually raised, were scarcely reduced at all. The act seemed, moreover, conspicuously to favor Aldrich's New England at the expense of the rest of the nation. Taft, nevertheless, tried to defend the measure as an important progressive victory, "a sincere effort on the part of the Republican party to make a downward revision." On a speaking tour of the Midwest that fall, he increased progressive resentment by standing in the heart of tariff opposition—Winona, Minnesota—and declaring: "On the whole . . . the Payne bill is the best bill that the Republican party ever passed." The rest of his trip, one reporter wrote, was "a polar dash through the world of ice."

The wedge between Taft and the Republican progressives drove deeper as a result of the president's role in efforts to reform the House of Representatives. The almost dictatorial power of Speaker Cannon had been a thorn in the side of progressives for many years; Taft himself harbored a strong dislike for the aging "Uncle Joe." So when reformers began a campaign during the 1909 special session to limit the Speaker's power, Taft at first expressed cautious approval. He soon found, however, that without Cannon's support, his beloved tariff legislation faced almost certain death, and he backed away from the insurgent revolt. Again, congressional progressives watched their reform efforts collapse; again, they blamed Taft for betraying them. The following year, after a fierce debate that raged for nearly thirty hours, progressive Republicans under the leadership of George W. Norris finally succeeded in stripping Cannon of some of his most im-

"The Easy Umpire"
"He slugs me every chance he gets, and you can't or won't see it," the tiny player labeled "The Plain People" protests to the umpire, President Taft, while pointing at the bully, Senator Aldrich. For years the dominant figure in the Senate, Aldrich furthered the interests of big business. From *Puck*, November 10, 1909.
(Culver Pictures)

portant powers. Even then, however, they acted without the president's support.

Dollar Diplomacy

Many of those who had admired Theodore Roosevelt's vigorous command of American foreign policy and his strenuous efforts to maintain a world balance of power were similarly dismayed by Taft's performance in international affairs. Although the new president made no decisive break with the policies of his predecessor, and while in some areas he actually extended American involvement abroad, he was in general no readier to exert strong leadership internationally than he was domestically. He worked to advance the nation's economic interests overseas, but he seemed to lack Roosevelt's larger vision of world stability. Worst of all, several of his most important foreign policy initiatives were conspicuous failures.

The thrust of Taft's foreign policy was best symbolized by the man he chose to administer it: Secretary of State Philander C. Knox, a corporation lawyer committed to using his position to promote American business interests overseas. Roosevelt, of course, had promoted American economic interests too; but Knox seemed at times to regard the State Department as little more than an agent of the corporate community. He worked aggressively to extend American investments into underdeveloped regions, motivating critics to label his policies "Dollar Diplomacy."

The Taft-Knox foreign policy faced its severest test, and encountered its greatest failure, in the Far East. Ignoring Roosevelt's tacit 1905 agreement with Japan to limit American involvement in Manchuria, the new administration succumbed to the persuasive powers of American bankers, and began to move aggressively to increase America's economic influence in the region. When British, French, and German bankers formed a consortium to finance a vast system of railroads in China, Knox insisted that Americans should also participate; and when in 1911 the Europeans finally agreed to include the United States in their venture, Knox proposed that an international syndicate purchase the South Manchurian Railroad to remove it from Japanese control. Japan responded by signing a treaty of friendship with Russia—a warning to the Europeans—and the entire railroad project quickly collapsed. Having attempted to expand its influence in Asia, America now found the door to Manchuria slammed in its face.

In the Caribbean, the new administration continued and even expanded upon Roosevelt's policies of maintaining order and stability in troubled areas without regard for the national integrity of the nations involved. Limiting European influence in the region meant, they believed, not only preventing disorder but establishing a significant American economic presence there—replacing the investments of European nations with investments from the United States. In 1909, Knox tried to arrange for American bankers to establish a financial receivership in Honduras. Later, he persuaded New York bankers to invest in the National Bank of Haiti. But Dollar Diplomacy was not always so peaceful. When a revolution broke out in Nicaragua in 1909, the administration quickly sided with the insurgents (who had been inspired to revolt by an American mining company) and sent United States troops into the country to seize the customs houses. As soon as peace was restored, Knox encouraged American bankers to move into Nicaragua and offer substantial loans to the new government, thus increasing Washington's financial leverage over the country. Within two years, however, the new pro-American government faced a revolt of its

own; and Taft, following his policy to its logical extreme, again landed American troops in Nicaragua, this time to protect the existing regime. The troops remained there for more than a decade.

Taft did not entirely abandon Roosevelt's commitment to mediating international conflict. He shared his predecessor's faith in the impartial arbitration of disputes, a cardinal tenet of progressivism, and he sought at times to extend the American role as a world mediator. As in so many other areas where he attempted to emulate Roosevelt, however, he encountered only frustration. The Senate time and again blocked agreements that might force the United States itself to submit to arbitration, and Taft lacked the political strength to advance the scheme on his own.

The Pinchot-Ballinger Affair

With Taft's standing among Republican progressives steadily deteriorating and with the party growing more and more deeply divided, a sensational controversy broke out late in 1909 that helped to destroy for good Taft's popularity with admirers of Theodore Roosevelt. Many progressives had been unhappy when Taft replaced Roosevelt's secretary of the interior, James R. Garfield, an aggressive conservationist, with Richard A. Ballinger, a corporate lawyer and a far less fervent environmentalist. Suspicion of Ballinger grew when he attempted to invalidate Roosevelt's actions in removing nearly a million acres of forests and mineral reserves from the public domain. The previous administration had acted illegally, Ballinger insisted; those lands should now be released for private development.

In the midst of this mounting concern, Louis Glavis, an Interior Department investigator, uncovered information that he believed constituted proof that the new secretary had once connived to turn over valuable coal lands in Alaska to a private syndicate in exchange for personal profits. Glavis took the evidence to Gifford Pinchot, who had remained as head of the Forest Service and had been appalled by Ballinger's retreat from Roosevelt's policies. Pinchot took the charges to the president. Taft listened to Pinchot, heard Ballinger's rebuttal, asked Attorney General George Wickersham to investigate, and finally announced his support for his interior secretary. The charges, he insisted, were groundless.

Pinchot, however, was not satisfied. Unhappy that Ballinger remained in office and angry when Taft fired Glavis for his part in the episode, he leaked the story to the press and appealed directly to Congress to investigate the scandal. The president quickly discharged him for insubordination, and the congressional committee appointed to study the controversy, dominated by the Old Guard, exonerated Ballinger. But Taft's victory had come at a high cost. Progressives throughout the country rallied to the support of Pinchot, whom they considered the defender of the public interest against the onslaught of big business. Taft, by contrast, appeared to have capitulated to conservatives and to have repudiated the legacy of Theodore Roosevelt. The controversy aroused as much public passion as any dispute of its time; and when it was over, Taft had alienated the supporters of Theodore Roosevelt as completely as his tariff actions had alienated the followers of La Follette.

The Return of Roosevelt

During most of Taft's first year in office, Theodore Roosevelt was far from the political fray. He embarked first on a long hunting safari in the jungles of Africa; from there he traveled to Europe for visits to the major heads of state. To the American public, however, Roosevelt remained a formidable presence. Reports of his triumphant European tour dominated the front pages of newspapers across the country. Rumors that he would return to retake control of his party abounded. His arrival in New York in the spring of 1910 was a major public event; and progressives noted that, although he turned down an invitation from Taft to visit the White House, he met at once with Gifford Pinchot (who had already traveled to England to see him several months before).

Roosevelt insisted that he had no plans to return to active politics, but his resolve lasted less than a week. Politicians began flocking immediately to his home at Oyster Bay, Long Island, for endless conferences; Roosevelt himself took an active role in several New York political controversies; and within a month, he announced that he would embark on a national speaking tour before the end of the summer. Furious with Taft, who had, he believed, "completely twisted around the policies I advocated and acted upon," he was becoming convinced that he alone was capable of reuniting the Republican party.

The real signal of Roosevelt's return to active leadership of the progressives was a speech on September 1, 1910, in Osawatomie, Kansas, where he outlined a set of principles that he labeled the "New Nationalism." The speech made clear how far Roosevelt had moved from the cautious conservatism that had marked the first years of his presidency. Social justice, he argued, could be attained only through vigorous efforts of a strong federal government whose executive acted as the "steward of the public welfare." Those who thought primarily of property rights and personal profit "must now give way to the advocate of human welfare, who rightly maintains that every man holds his property subject to the general right of the community to regulate its use to whatever degree the public welfare may require it." Such generalizations were frightening enough by themselves to the Republican Old Guard, but Roosevelt went beyond them with a list of "radical" specific proposals: graduated income and inheritance taxes, workers' compensation for industrial accidents, regulation of the labor of women and children, tariff revision, and firm regulation of corporations through a more powerful Bureau of Corporations and ICC. Western progressives were now ready to proclaim him their next presidential candidate; but among his right-wing opponents, his friend Henry Cabot Lodge warned him, he was regarded as "little short of a revolutionist."

Spreading Insurgency

The congressional elections of 1910 provided further evidence of how far the progressive revolt had spread through the Republican party and how damaging it had become. In primary elections, conservative Republicans suffered defeat after defeat at the hands of progressive insurgents—forty in the House of Representatives alone. Incumbent progressives, moreover, won renomination almost without exception. In the general election, the Democrats, who were increasingly offering progressive candidates of their own, won control of the House of Representatives for the first time in sixteen years and greatly strengthened their position in the Senate. Progressive insurgency, it seemed, had become a virtual tidal wave. Still, Roosevelt hesitated to move openly to regain the presidency. For months, he claimed that his real purpose was to pressure Taft to return to progressive policies, that he had no wish to break openly with the president. Two events, however, changed his mind.

The first was a 1911 decision by the Taft administration that became, in Roosevelt's eyes, the final, inexcusable indignity. With his strong respect for the letter of the law, Taft had from the beginning been far more active than Roosevelt in enforcing the provisions of the Sherman Antitrust Act, launching dozens of suits against corporate combinations. To Roosevelt, such actions were troubling by themselves, for they reflected what he believed to be a wholly unrealistic attempt to abolish trusts when the proper course was to regulate them. But what truly outraged him was the announcement on October 27, 1911, that the administration was filing an antitrust suit against the United States Steel Corporation, charging, among other things, that the 1907 acquisition of the Tennessee Coal and Iron Company had been illegal. Roosevelt had approved that acquisition in the midst of the 1907 panic, and he was enraged by the clear implication that he had acted improperly. The episode inspired his most strident attacks on the Taft administration to date.

There remained, however, another obstacle to Roosevelt's pursuit of the presidency. Since January 1911, Robert La Follette had been working through the newly formed National Progressive Republican League to secure the presidential nomination for himself.

Many reformers believed he had established first claim to the leadership of any insurgent revolt, and Roosevelt was at first reluctant to challenge him. But La Follette's candidacy stumbled in February 1912, when, exhausted and plagued by personal worries (including the illness of his daughter), he appeared to suffer a nervous breakdown during a speech in Philadelphia. With almost indecent haste, many of his supporters abandoned him and turned to Roosevelt, who finally announced his candidacy on February 22.

TR Versus Taft

La Follette never forgave Roosevelt for "using" and then "betraying" him, and some diehard loyalists refused to abandon their allegiance to the Wisconsin senator. But for all practical purposes, the campaign for the Republican nomination had now become a battle between Roosevelt, the champion of the progressives, and Taft, the candidate of the conservatives. Roosevelt scored overwhelming victories in every presidential preference primary (there were thirteen in all) and arrived at the convention convinced that he had proved himself the choice of the party rank and file. Taft, however, remained the choice of most party leaders, and in the end it was their preference that proved decisive.

The battle for the nomination at the Chicago convention revolved around an unusually large number of contested delegates: 254 in all. Roosevelt needed about 100 of the disputed seats to clinch the nomination. But the Republican National Committee, which ruled on credentials, was controlled by members of the Old Guard; and it awarded all but 19 of the disputed seats to Taft. The president had secured his victory even before the delegates met. Roosevelt and his followers responded bitterly. The decision to seat the Taft delegates, they claimed, was an example of the same corrupt politics that progressives had been fighting for years; once more the people had been thwarted by the special interests. At a rally the night before the convention opened, Roosevelt addressed 5,000 madly cheering supporters and announced that he would not feel bound by the decision of his party if it refused to seat his delegates, that he would continue to fight for a candidacy that had now, it seemed, become a holy cause. "We stand at Armageddon," he told the roaring crowd, "and we battle for the Lord." As good as his word, Roosevelt the next day led his supporters out of the convention, and out of the party. Taft was then quietly nominated on the first ballot.

With financial support from newspaper magnate Frank Munsey and industrialist George W. Perkins, Roosevelt summoned his supporters back to Chicago in August for another convention, this one to launch the new Progressive party and nominate Roosevelt as its presidential candidate. By now, even Roo-

sevelt was aware that the cause was virtually hopeless, particularly when many of the leading insurgents who had supported him during the primaries refused to follow him out of the Republican party. Nevertheless, he approached the battle feeling, as he put it, "fit as a bull moose" (thus giving his new party an enduring nickname). At the meeting in Chicago, he delivered a resounding "Confession of Faith" in which he castigated both of the traditional parties for representing "government of the needy many by professional politicians in the interests of the rich few"; and he produced a platform that embodied a full array of the most advanced progressive reforms.

THE RISE OF THE NEW FREEDOM

Yet even while Roosevelt was constructing his New Nationalism as a challenge to conservatives within his own party, a more powerful alternative was emerging from the ranks of the Democrats. The contest, it soon became clear, was not simply one between conservatives and reformers; it was also one between two brands of progressivism, expressing two different views of America's future.

Wilson and the New Freedom

For most of the first decade of the century, the Republican party had often seemed the sole home of progressive reform. In fact, however, progressive sentiment had been gaining strength within the Democratic party as well; and by 1912 it was ready to assert its dominance. At the Democratic convention in Baltimore in June, it appeared at first as though nothing could stop Champ Clark, the conservative Speaker of the House, from securing the presidential nomination. From the beginning, he controlled a majority of the delegates; but on ballot after ballot he failed to assemble the two-thirds necessary to win. For days the battle dragged on inconclusively until finally, on the forty-sixth ballot, Wood-

row Wilson, the governor of New Jersey, emerged as the party's nominee. His victory was in part a result of the last-minute support of Senator Oscar Underwood of Alabama, who had himself been one of the leading contenders for the nomination, and of William Jennings Bryan, who was to become Wilson's secretary of state. It was also, however, a result of Wilson's position as the only genuinely progressive candidate in the race.

Born in Virginia and raised in Confederate Georgia and Reconstruction South Carolina, Wilson had risen to political prominence by an unusual path. An 1879 graduate of Princeton University, he attended law school and for a time engaged unhappily in practice in Atlanta. He was, however, far more interested in politics and government, and after a few years he enrolled at Johns Hopkins University, where he earned a doctorate in political science. By virtue of his effective teaching and his lucid if unprofound books on the American political system, he rose steadily through the academic ranks until in 1902 he was promoted from the faculty to the presidency of Princeton. There, he displayed both the strengths and the weaknesses that would characterize his later political career. A champion of academic reform,

Woodrow Wilson and Champ Clark
Speaker Clark seemed an almost certain nominee at the 1912 Democratic convention, at one point receiving well over a majority of the delegates' votes, 556 to 350½, but it took two-thirds to nominate. When finally he lost to Wilson he went to Sea Girt, New Jersey, where Wilson was spending the summer, to demonstrate his party support. (Culver Pictures)

he acted firmly and energetically to place Princeton on the road to becoming a great national university. At the same time, however, he displayed during controversies a self-righteous morality that at times made it nearly impossible for him to compromise.

It was a series of such stalemates that propelled him out of academia and into politics. Elected governor of New Jersey in 1910, he brought to his new office the same commitment to reform that he had displayed in the past; and during his two years in the statehouse, he compiled an impressive record of progressive legislation—one that earned him a wide national reputation. At the same time, however, he was gradually alienating conservative party leaders with his intransigence and self-righteousness, and greatly hampering his ability to govern. His nomination for president in 1912 rescued him from what might well have become a political disaster in New Jersey.

In later years, Wilson's personal characteristics would help polarize the nation. In 1912, however, he sparked controversy by presenting a brand of progressivism that was both forceful and sharply different from Theodore Roosevelt's New Nationalism. His supporters soon began to describe Wilson's program as the "New Freedom"; and although in later years the two phrases began to seem like meaningless slogans, reflecting few important differences, the opposing philosophies—"nationalism" versus "freedom"—were in fact distinct from each other in important ways.

In its narrowest sense, Wilson's New Freedom differed from Roosevelt's New Nationalism in its approach to economic policy, in particular its approach to the trusts. Roosevelt had always believed in accepting economic concentration and using government to regulate and control it. Wilson, by contrast, was a disciple of Louis Brandeis's approach to economic reform. He sided with those who believed that bigness was both unjust and inefficient, that the proper response to monopoly was not to regulate it but to destroy it. The federal government, therefore, should not become the great centralizing force that Roosevelt envisioned. Government should, rather, work to destroy economic privilege and concentration; it should assure small entrepreneurs the chance to prosper and open opportunities for the "man on the make."

The Credit Monopoly [1913]

Advocates of the New Freedom found support for their views in the work of the Pujo Committee, a congressional investigating committee chaired by Representative Arsene Pujo of Louisiana, which examined the problem of economic concentration in America. Its 1913 report, from which the passage below is extracted, was among the most influential of all progressive documents.

Far more dangerous than all that has happened to us in the past in the way of elimination of competition in industry is the control of credit through the domination of these groups over our banks and industries. . . .

Whether under a different currency system the resources in our banks would be greater or less is comparatively immaterial if they continue to be controlled by a small group. . . .

If the arteries of credit now clogged well-nigh to choking by the obstructions created through the control of these groups are opened so that they may be permitted freely to play their important part in the financial system, competition in large enterprises will become possible and business can be conducted on its merits instead of being subject to the tribute and the good will of this handful of self-constituted trustees of the national prosperity.

The Three-Way Contest

Despite the philosophical importance of the issues in 1912, the campaign itself was surprisingly uneventful. Voters seemed generally unaware of the ideological differences between Roosevelt and Wilson, and the election in the end reflected traditional party divisions.

From the beginning, it was a three-candidate election but a two-candidate campaign. William Howard Taft, resigned to defeat, delivered a few desultory, conservative speeches and then lapsed into silence. "There are so many people in the country who don't like me," he sadly explained. Roosevelt campaigned energetically (despite a gunshot wound from a would-be assassin that forced him to the sidelines during the last weeks before the election), and he continued to generate excitement among his Republican followers. He failed, however, to draw any significant numbers of Democratic progressives away from Wilson, who as the campaign wore on was beginning to evoke an enthusiastic national following of his own. The results in November were, therefore, predictable. Roosevelt and Taft split the Republican vote; Wilson held onto the Democratic vote and won. He polled only a plurality of the popular vote: 42 percent, to 27 percent for Roosevelt and a dismal 23 percent for Taft. Eugene Debs, the Socialist candidate, received 6 percent of the vote. In the electoral college, Wilson produced a landslide: 435 of the 531 votes. Roosevelt had carried only six states, Taft only two. It was an impressive mandate for reform. Taft, the only conservative in the race (and even he could make some claim to progressivism), had received less than a quarter of the vote. More than 70 percent of the electorate had supported spokesmen for progressive change. Woodrow Wilson entered the presidency with the forces of reform, which had been gathering strength for almost two decades, at the peak of their power.

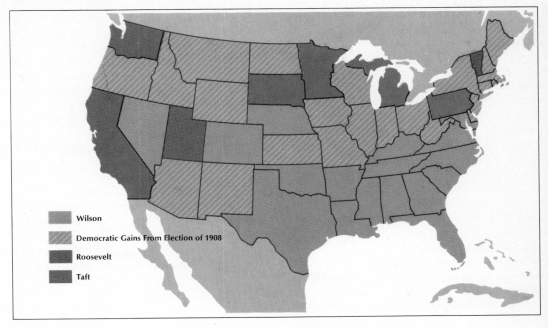

THE ELECTION OF 1912

WOODROW WILSON AND THE MODERN STATE

The administration of Woodrow Wilson ended unhappily, both for the president and for the nation. It began, however, in triumph. For nearly five years, until international problems turned his attention elsewhere, Wilson served as the most successful leader of domestic reform of his era. Because of his political skill, the federal government moved far toward becoming what many reformers had long advocated: a powerful instrument of economic and social control. It was ironic, perhaps, that Wilson, who had campaigned in 1912 in opposition to Theodore Roosevelt's overbearing nationalism, should become the instrument for completing much of Roosevelt's program. In the flush of the moment, however, few progressives noticed the irony. If Wilson had not become precisely the kind of leader he had promised, he had become exactly the sort of leader for whom most reformers had been waiting.

The Scholar as President

Wilson brought to the White House a conception of the presidency based on long years of scholarly study. His first published book, *Congressional Government* (1898), expressed what remained a lifelong admiration for the British parliamentary system and a belief in its adaptability to American institutions. In his later writings, however, he began to display more interest in the possibilities of presidential leadership. "His is the only voice in national affairs," he wrote of the president only four years before he himself assumed the office. His must therefore be the voice of popular aspirations, the hand that guides public demands into legislative realities.

More than William Howard Taft, therefore, more even than Theodore Roosevelt, Wilson concentrated the powers of the executive branch in his own hands. He exerted firm control over his cabinet, and he delegated real authority only to those whose loyalty to him was beyond question. Perhaps the clearest indication of his style of leadership was the identity of the most powerful figure in his administration: Colonel Edward M. House, a man whose only claim to authority was his personal intimacy with the president. Holding no office, attracting little public renown, House nevertheless wielded broad powers on behalf of the president. "He can walk on dead leaves and make no more noise than a tiger," one contemporary noted. That was just what the president wanted. Wilson had little patience with those who attempted to establish an authority within his administration independent of him.

In his dealings with Congress, Wilson viewed himself as the leader of the legislative process. He was not a natural politician, and he often seemed uncomfortable in the presence of those who were. He was, however, unusually adept at using his position as head of his party to pressure and cajole members of Congress into supporting his positions. In his distribution of patronage, he rejected the demands of some reformers that he ignore conservative Democrats and reward progressive ones. Instead, he used his appointive powers to weld together a coalition of conservatives and progressives who would, he believed, support his program. His task was eased, of course, by the existence of Democratic majorities in both houses of Congress and by the realization of many Democrats that the party must enact a progressive program in order to maintain those majorities.

Tariffs and Taxes

Wilson's first triumph as president was the fulfillment of an old Democratic and progressive promise—a substantial lowering of the protective tariff. Roosevelt had avoided the issue; Taft had failed at it. Wilson moved quickly and forcefully to succeed. On the day he took office, he called a special session of Congress. And when it met, he did what no president since Jefferson had done: he appeared before it in person. In a short, graphic message aimed less at the congressmen than

at their constituents, he brought to a blaze the rising public sentiment for genuine tariff reform. With the president's active support, Representative Oscar W. Underwood introduced a bill in the House providing for tariff cuts substantial enough to bring European manufacturers into competition with Americans and thus, progressives hoped, to help break the power of trusts. Like earlier tariff bills, the Underwood-Simmons tariff, as it became known, passed easily in the House. Unlike earlier bills, however, it survived as well the efforts of conservative senators to weaken it. Wilson's forceful exercise of party powers mobilized virtually the entire Democratic majority behind it. The law as Wilson finally signed it lowered tariff rates an average of about 8 percent and added many imports to the free list. The economic upheavals of war came too soon to allow the bill to prove the boasts of its supporters that it would lower the cost of living without damaging business. The measure did, however, demonstrate conclusively that the Democrats could unite to enact against great hazards a significant piece of reform legislation.

To make up for the loss of revenue under the new tariff, Representative Cordell Hull of Tennessee drafted an amendment to the bill providing for a graduated income tax, which the recently adopted Sixteenth Amendment to the Constitution now permitted. Hull cautiously set the rates exceedingly low. To his delight, however, progressive Republican and Democratic senators united to force them substantially higher. This first modern income tax imposed a 1 percent tax on individuals and corporations earning over $4,000, with rates ranging up to 6 percent on incomes over $500,000. It was the beginning of a fundamental change in the American tax structure, which would slowly shift a proportionately greater share of the cost of government to the wealthy.

Banking Reform

Rather than lose momentum, President Wilson held Congress in session through the sweltering summer to begin work on a major reform of the American banking system.

"The great monopoly in this country," he had declared in 1911, "is the money monopoly. So long as that exists, our old variety and freedom and individual energy of development are out of question." Few progressives would have disagreed. Yet there were apparently conflicting explanations of the nature of the problem, and there were wide differences of opinion about how best to attack it. Wilson attempted to construct a compromise that would reconcile the contending camps.

Some legislators, of whom Representative Carter Glass of Virginia was one, wanted to decentralize control of the banking system but leave ultimate authority over it with the bankers themselves. Others, whose hatred of the "money trust" was more intense—for example, William Jennings Bryan and fellow agrarians—wanted firm government control. After consultation with Louis Brandeis, Wilson accepted a plan that would place a central supervisory board, overseeing the entire system, in the hands of the government, while maintaining banker control of boards at the regional level. With Bryan mediating and Wilson brandishing every presidential power in his arsenal, the measure passed both houses of Congress and was signed by the president on December 23, 1913. It was the most important piece of domestic legislation of Wilson's administration and one of the most important in several decades.

The Federal Reserve Act created twelve regional banks, each to serve and to be owned and controlled by the individual banks of its district. The Federal Reserve banks would hold a certain percentage of the assets of their member banks in reserve; they would use those reserves to support loans to private banks at an interest (or "discount") rate that the Federal Reserve system would set; they would issue a new type of paper currency—Federal Reserve notes—which would become the nation's basic medium of trade and be backed by the government. Most importantly, perhaps, they would serve as central institutions able to shift funds quickly to troubled areas, to meet increased demands for credit or to protect imperiled banks. Supervising and regulating the entire system was a Federal Reserve Board, whose members were appointed by the president. All national banks were required to join the system; smaller banks were encouraged to do the same. Within a year, nearly half the nation's banking resources were represented in the system; by the late 1920s, the proportion had swelled to 80 percent. Although the American Bankers' Association had strenuously opposed the legislation (fearing government control of their operations), financiers soon found they had little cause for alarm. The Federal Reserve Board, to which Wilson appointed conservative men sympathetic to the bankers' views, looked, one progressive senator complained, as though the president of the National City Bank had selected its members.

For all its limitations, and there were many, the Federal Reserve Act marked a notable advance in American banking practices, historically among the least stable and efficient in the Western world. The new system provided a more elastic currency, enabling bankers to lend money more easily to farmers and to deal more readily with national financial crises. It contributed to, although it did not approach the completion of, a decentralization of the nation's capital. And it provided the government, through the Federal Reserve Board, with a powerful instrument of economic influence—although it was not until many years later that economists recognized the power that control over the money supply provided. The Great Depression of the 1930s would prove that, despite these changes, the American banking structure remained weak and inadequate; but the Federal Reserve Act was an important first step toward the stabler system that ultimately emerged.

The Problem of the Trusts

The cornerstone of Wilson's campaign for the presidency had been his promise to attack economic concentration, most notably to destroy monopolistic trusts. By the beginning of his second year in office, however, it was becoming clear that his thinking had changed significantly. Increasingly he moved away from his earlier insistence that government dismantle the combinations and toward a commitment to regulating them. On this issue, at least, the New Freedom was giving way to the New Nationalism. Wilson's attitude toward two major pieces of economic legislation symbolized the trend. When in 1914 he began to promote a sweeping plan to deal with the problem of monopoly, two elements emerged at its core. There was a proposal to create a federal agency through which the government would help business police itself—in other words, a regulatory commission of the type Roosevelt had advocated in 1912. There were, in addition, proposals to strengthen the government's power to prosecute and dismantle the trusts—a decentralizing approach more characteristic of Wilson's campaign. The two measures took shape, ultimately, as the Federal Trade Commission Act and the Clayton Antitrust Act.

Wilson fought hard for the Federal Trade Commission Act, which created a regulatory agency of the same name, and he signed it happily when it arrived at the White House. The new commission would, he promised, remove "uncertainty" within the corporate community, allowing businesses to determine in advance whether their actions would be acceptable to the government. It would also have authority to launch prosecutions against "unfair trade practices," which the law did not define, and it would have wide power to investigate corporate behavior. The act, in short, increased the government's regulatory authority significantly. At the same time, Wilson gradually lost interest in the Clayton Antitrust Act and showed a notable lack of vigor in fighting to protect it from conservative assaults. When its opponents in Congress so weakened the bill that progressives complained it lacked enough teeth to masticate milk toast, Wilson did little to strengthen it. When it failed to include any binding guarantees that it would not be used, as earlier antitrust laws had been, as a weapon against unions, Wilson did nothing to change it. Nevertheless, when the emasculated bill finally reached his desk, he lauded it as a major accomplishment. In fact, like the Sherman Antitrust Act before it, this legislation proved to be almost impotent as a weapon against the trusts but a stout club against striking or boycotting unions.

Nor did Wilson act very forcefully within the executive branch to prosecute the trusts. The relative ineffectiveness of the new Federal Trade Commission—to which Wilson appointed men so inept or so sympathetic to the trusts they were supposed to regulate that Brandeis once dismissed them as useless and "stupid"—did nothing to renew his animosity toward monopoly. And the Justice Department remained less than aggressive in its pursuit of illegal combinations. Attorney General James C. McReynolds, who had served in the Roosevelt administration, announced that large corporations doubtful about the legality of their practices could avoid lawsuits if they would straighten their affairs out quietly with the assistance of the government. He managed as a result to win consent decrees from several large combinations, which divested themselves of important acquisitions. But the vigorous legal pursuit of monopoly that Wilson had promised in 1912 never materialized. The future, he had apparently decided, lay with governmental supervision. Economic concentration would survive.

Retreat and Advance

By the fall of 1914, Wilson believed that the program of the New Freedom was essentially complete and that the agitation for reform would now subside. As a result, he himself began a conspicuous retreat from political activism. Citing the doctrine of states' rights, he declined to support the movement for woman suffrage. Accepting the inclinations of the many Southerners in his cabinet, he condoned the reimposition of segregation in the agencies of the federal government (a sharp contrast to Theodore Roosevelt, who had ordered the elimination of many such barriers and even taken the unprecedented step of inviting a black man—Booker T. Washington—to the White House). When congressional reformers attempted to enlist his support for new social legislation, he breezily dismissed their proposals as unconstitutional or unnecessary.

The president's complacency could not, however, long survive the congressional elections of 1914. It was disturbing enough that Democrats suffered major losses in the House of Representatives. But it was even more alarming that voters who had in 1912 supported the Progressive party were returning in droves to the Republicans. Wilson would not be able to rely on a divided opposition when he ran for reeelection in 1916; he would need more than his 1912 total of 42 percent of the vote, and he would need the support of some of Theodore Roosevelt's former constituency to get it.

By the end of 1915, therefore, Wilson had shed his lethargy and begun to support a second flurry of reforms. In January 1916, he appointed Louis Brandeis to the Supreme Court, making him not only the first Jew but the most advanced progressive to be so named; and he weathered a conservative uproar in the Senate to obtain Brandeis's confirmation. Later, he supported a measure to make it easier for farmers to receive credit and one creating a system of workers' compensation for federal employees. But the real significance of this renewed effort at reform was that Wilson seemed now to have capitulated to the New Nationalism almost entirely; indeed, he had moved beyond it. No longer were there appeals for the restoration of a competitive, decentralized economy. No longer were there warnings about excessive federal power. Instead, Wilson was sponsoring measures that expanded the role of the national government in important ways, giving it new instruments by which it could not only regulate the economy but help shape the economic and social structure itself.

In 1916, for example, Wilson supported the Keating-Owen Act, the first federal law regulating child labor. It was important not only for the problem it addressed but for the means it adopted. The measure prohibited the shipment of goods produced by underage children across state lines, thus giving a new and greatly expanded importance to the constitutional clause assigning Congress the task of regulating interstate commerce. (It would be some years before the Supreme Court would uphold this interpretation of the clause—the Court invalidated the Keating-Owen Act in 1918—but an important precedent for future federal efforts had been established.) The president similarly supported measures that used federal taxing authority

Louis Brandeis
Brandeis was one of the most celebrated legal figures of his age. In the early years of the century, he became the leading spokesman for aggressive government efforts to decentralize economic power, helping to stimulate a debate that would rage for decades. Woodrow Wilson, who deeply admired Brandeis, appointed him to the Supreme Court in 1916; he was its first Jewish justice. For the next twenty-five years, Brandeis served as one of the Court's most influential members and as a major force for the protection of civil liberties—all the while lobbying behind the scenes on behalf of the many other political causes to which he was committed. (UPI)

as a vehicle for legislating social change. When the Court struck down Keating-Owen, a new bill attempted to achieve the same goal by imposing a heavy tax on the products of child labor. (The Court later struck it down too, but not before yet another important instrument of federal power, the use of the tax codes to induce social change, had been born.) The government's spending authority likewise became an instrument of social control. The Smith-Lever Act, for example, had as early as 1914 offered matching federal grants to states that agreed to support agricultural extension education, a mechanism that would help undermine the autonomy of state governments. Other measures extended the process further.

Having won a mandate for the New Freedom in 1912, Wilson had by the end of his first term made remarkable strides toward enacting the program of the New Nationalism. He had dramatically expanded the role of the federal government in American society, helping to make it the efficient, centralized regulatory mechanism that Roosevelt and others had long advocated. He had accepted the importance of orderly bureaucratic procedures and enlightened expertise in governing an industrial society, and he had backed away from the vision of a nation liberated from centralized controls. It was not, as one conservative congressman charged, "the first step away from the democracy of Thomas Jefferson . . . to the socialism of Karl Marx." But it was an important step toward the creation of the modern state.

It was also virtually the last step in the long progressive campaign for social and economic reform. By the end of 1916, the nation's attention was turning elsewhere; and it would remain for later generations to deal with the problems that remained. They would discover that the progressive accomplishments, significant as they were, did not include any fundamental restructuring of the nation's economy. The corporate community had been forced to abandon some of its most egregious abuses, but its essential power survived. Laborers had received protection from certain afflictions, but they continued to lack effective bargaining power and to receive far less than their proportional share of the national income. Farmers had received a modicum of additional security, but they remained painfully vulnerable to the fluctuations of a market they could not control. Others had fared even less well. Blacks and other minorities had been all but ignored; in many ways, in fact, their position had deteriorated. Urban immigrants had received only scant benefits; they remained, for the most part, isolated from and mistrusted by the bulk of the populace. For a while, it would be possible for many Americans to believe that the fundamental problems of their society had been solved. But the problems would resurface in agonizing form less than a generation later. Future reformers, at least, would be able to face them with a machinery of government that included some effective instruments of change.

DIPLOMACY AND MORALITY

"It would be the irony of fate," Woodrow Wilson remarked shortly before assuming the presidency, "if my administration had to deal chiefly with foreign affairs." It would also, as it turned out, be a tragedy. Wilson faced international challenges of a scope and gravity unmatched by any president before him; and he brought to his treatment of them not only remarkable vision but an often inflexible, even self-righteous morality that would ultimately destroy both him and many of the goals for which he fought. Although the true ordeal of Wilsonian diplomacy did not occur until after World War I, many of the qualities that would help produce it were evident in his foreign policy from his first moments in office.

Closed Doors

Through much of his administration, Wilson made strenuous but generally unsuccessful efforts to maintain an open door for American trade in China and to resist the expansion of Japanese influence in the Pacific. At the same time, however, the United States was itself working assiduously to close the door to all nations but itself in Latin America. Wilson presided over a foreign policy that not only continued but greatly increased American intervention in the Caribbean and in Latin America, justifying his actions by citing both economic necessity and moral imperative.

The list of American incursions was lengthy and impressive. Having already seized control of the finances of the Dominican Republic in 1905, the United States established a military government there in 1916 when the Dominicans refused to accept a treaty that would have made the country a virtual American protectorate. The military occupation lasted eight years. In Haiti, which shares the island of Hispaniola with the Dominican Republic, Wilson landed the marines in 1915 to quell a revolution in the course of which a mob had murdered an unpopular president. American military forces remained in the country until 1934, and American officers drafted the new Haitian constitution adopted in 1918. When Wilson began to fear that the Danish West Indies might be about to fall into the hands of Germany, he bought the colony from Denmark and renamed it the Virgin Islands. Concerned about the possibility of European influence in Nicaragua, he signed a treaty with that country's government ensuring that no other nation would build a canal there and winning for the United States the right to intervene in Nicaragua's internal affairs to protect American interests. In one case after another, the United States was openly disregarding the national integrity of its neighbors, acting instead in response to what Wilson considered a higher mission: the creation of order and, not coincidentally, the protection of American markets and investments. The president had no doubt that the recipients of his attention would become stabler, more democratic nations as a result. In most cases, he was wrong.

Mission in Mexico

It was in Mexico that Wilson's missionary view of America's role in the Western Hemisphere received its greatest test and suffered its greatest frustrations. For many years, under the benevolent auspices of dictator Porfirio Díaz, American businessmen had been establishing an enormous presence in Mexico, with investments totaling more than $1 billion. In 1910, however, the corrupt and tyrannical Díaz had been overthrown by Francisco Madero, who excited many of his countrymen by promising democratic reform but alarmed many American businessmen by threatening their investments in his country. With the approval of, among others, the American ambassador in Mexico, Madero was himself deposed early in 1913 by a reactionary general, Victoriano Huerta.

A relieved Taft administration prepared, in its last weeks in office, to recognize the new Huerta regime and welcome back a receptive environment for American investments in Mexico. Before it could do so, however, Huerta murdered Madero, producing horror and outrage around the world. Wilson, therefore, inherited a difficult and unresolved dilemma. But he displayed no hesitation in responding. He would never, he insisted, recognize Huerta's "government of butchers." (In so doing, Wilson added a new weapon to his foreign policy arsenal: the withholding of diplomatic recognition to signal disapproval of a regime.)

The problem dragged on for years. At first, Wilson hoped that simply by refusing to recognize Huerta he could help topple the regime and bring to power the opposing Constitutionalists, led by Venustiano Carranza. When Huerta established a full military dictatorship in October 1913, however, the president decided on a more forceful approach. First he pressured the British to stop supporting Huerta. Then he offered to send American troops to assist Carranza. Carranza, aware that such an open alliance with the United States would undermine his popular support in Mexico, declined the offer; but he did request and receive from Wilson the right to buy arms in the United States. Still the stalemate continued.

Finally, a minor naval incident provided the president with an excuse for more open intervention. In April 1914, an officer in Huerta's army briefly arrested several American sailors from the U.S.S. *Dolphin* who had gone ashore in Tampico. Although a superior officer immediately released them and apologized to the ship's commander, the American admiral, chafing from inaction, demanded that the Huerta forces fire a twenty-one-gun salute to the American flag as a public display of penance. The Mexicans refused. Wilson seized on the silly incident as a pretext for sending all available American naval forces into Mexican waters; and a few days later, eager to prevent a German ship from delivering munitions to the Huerta forces, he ordered the navy to seize the Mexican port of Veracruz.

Wilson had envisioned a bloodless action, but he was not to have his way. In a clash with Mexican troops in the city, the Americans killed 126 of the defenders and suffered 19 casualties of their own. With the two nations at the brink of war, Wilson now drew back and began to look for alternative measures to deal with the crisis. His show of force, however, had in the meantime helped strengthen the position of the Carranza faction, which captured Mexico City in August and forced Huerta to flee the country. At last, it seemed, the crisis might find a solution.

It was not to be. Wilson reacted angrily when Carranza refused to accept American guidelines for the creation of a new government, and he briefly considered throwing his support to still another aspirant to leadership: Carranza's erstwhile lieutenant Pancho Villa, who was now leading a rebel army of his own. When Villa's military position deteriorated, however, Wilson abandoned the scheme and finally, in October 1915, granted preliminary recognition to the Carranza government. But by now the president had created yet another crisis. Angry at what he considered an American betrayal, Villa retaliated in January 1916 by taking sixteen Americans from a train in northern Mexico and shooting them. Two months later, he led his soldiers (or bandits, as the United States preferred to call them) across the border into New Mexico, where they murdered nineteen more Americans. His goal, apparently, was to destabilize relations between Wilson and Carranza and provoke a war between them, which might provide him with an opportu-

THE U.S. IN MEXICO, 1914–1917

nity to improve his own declining fortunes. He almost succeeded.

With the permission of the Carranza government, Wilson ordered General John J. Pershing to lead an American expeditionary force across the Mexican border in pursuit of Villa. The American troops, during their 300-mile penetration of Mexico, were never able to manage a clash with Villa. They did, however, engage in two ugly skirmishes with Carranza's army, in which forty Mexicans and twelve Americans died. Again, the United States and Mexico stood at the brink of war. By now, however, Wilson's attention was turning to what he considered matters of greater importance in Europe; and he agreed, therefore, to the face-saving expedient of referring the dispute to an international commission, which debated for six months without agreeing on a solution. In the meantime, Wilson was quietly withdrawing American troops from Mexico; and in March 1917, having spent four years of effort and gained nothing but a lasting Mexican hostility toward the United States, he at last granted formal recognition to the Carranza regime.

THE ROAD TO WAR

The Great War (as it was known to a generation unaware that another, greater war would soon follow) began modestly in August 1914 when Austria invaded the tiny Balkan nation of Serbia. Within weeks, however, it had grown into a widespread conflagration, engaging the armies of all the major nations of Europe and shattering forever the delicate balance of power that had maintained a general peace on the Continent since the early nineteenth century. Americans looked on with horror but also with a conviction that the conflict had little to do with them. They were wrong.

From the beginning, Woodrow Wilson's policy of maintaining American neutrality was based on a false premise. The United States had nothing at stake in this war, he told the nation. In fact, America had a great deal at stake, and as the war dragged on, that stake grew. The nation's economy was critically dependent on trade with Europe; its shipping had long been dependent on the maritime stability that the British navy had always provided; and as Europe's own industrial capabilities declined because of the fighting, the American economy roused itself from a recession by taking up the slack. The nation surely was not unaffected by the war. Neither would it long be able to remain uninvolved.

A False Neutrality

Wilson called on his countrymen in 1914 to remain "impartial in thought as well as deed." He himself, however, soon discovered that his own thoughts were far from neutral. Like many Americans of his background, he was a deep admirer of England—its traditions, its culture, its political system; almost instinctively, therefore, he attributed to the cause of the Allies (Britain, France, Italy, Russia) a moral quality that he denied to the Central Powers (Germany and the Austro-Hungarian Empire). More important, however, he soon recognized that economic realities made it essential for him to adopt one policy toward England and quite another to-

ward Germany. The neutral rights that he so ardently sought to uphold included, among other things, the right of an impartial nation such as the United States to trade freely with both sides in the conflict. The British, whose control of the seas was their most effective weapon, refused to oblige. They clamped a naval blockade on Germany to prevent munitions and supplies—from neutrals as well as belligerents—from reaching the enemy. Wilson had two choices. He could preserve a genuine American neutrality by denouncing the blockade and imposing an embargo on trade with Great Britain; or he could accept the situation and allow trade with England to continue and trade with Germany to cease. Economic realities, combined with his own inclination to support the British, caused him to choose the latter. The United States could survive an interruption of trade with the Central Powers. It could not, however, easily weather an embargo on trade with the Allies as well, particularly when war orders from Britain and France jumped from $824 million in 1914 to $3.2 billion two years later. The war had produced the greatest economic boom in the nation's history, and no president could afford to destroy it for a matter of abstract principle.

By 1915, therefore, the United States had gradually transformed itself into the arsenal of the Allies. In the process, it had replaced its stance of genuine neutrality with something quite different. Americans would acquiesce quietly, or with feeble protests, in violations of their rights by the British, who periodically seized American ships suspected of carrying supplies destined for Germany. When Germany infringed on neutral rights, however, the response of the United States was harsh and unyielding. The Germans intensified that antagonism by resorting to a new and, in American eyes, barbaric tactic: submarine warfare. Unable to challenge British domination on the ocean's surface, Germany began early in 1915 to use the newly improved submarine to try to stem the flow of supplies to England. Enemy vessels, the Germans announced, would be sunk on sight, prompting Wilson to declare that he

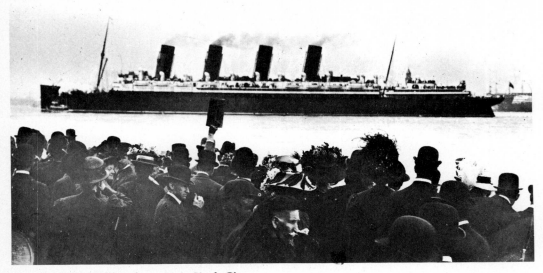

The *Lusitania* Sailing from New York City
On May 1, 1915, newspapers carried both the Cunard advertisement that the *Lusitania* was sailing that day and an unusual German warning: "Vessels flying the flag of Great Britain, or any of her allies, are liable to destruction . . . and . . . travelers sailing in the war zone on ships of Great Britain or her allies do so at their own risk." Passengers and crew discussed the announcement, but the *Lusitania* sailed on time, and by May 6 was proceeding along the coast of Ireland much as in peacetime, at a slow pace and not zigzagging. The commander of the German submarine U-20, seeing a large ship, fired a torpedo. Almost immediately the ship listed so sharply that few lifeboats could be launched; then it sank. As its bow went high in the air, the U-boat commander for the first time read on the ship the name *Lusitania*. (Brown Brothers)

would hold Germany to "strict accountability" for unlawful acts. A test of this pronouncement came only months later, when on May 7, 1915, a German U-boat (short for *Unterseeboot*, undersea boat) sank the British passenger liner *Lusitania* without warning, causing the deaths of 1,198 people, 128 of them Americans. The ship was, it later became clear, carrying not only passengers but munitions; at the time, however, the attack seemed to most Americans to be what Theodore Roosevelt called it: "an act of piracy."

Wilson reacted by initiating an angry exchange of notes with Germany, demanding assurances that such outrages would not reoccur and that the Central Powers would respect the rights of neutral nations, among which, he insisted, was the right of their citizens to travel on the nonmilitary vessels of belligerents. (After one particularly threatening such note, Secretary of State William Jennings Bryan—who argued that equally strenuous protests should be sent to the British in response to their blockade—resigned from office as a matter of principle, one of the few high government officials of the United States ever to do so.) The Germans finally agreed to Wilson's demands, but a pattern of relations had been established that would increasingly bring the two nations into conflict. Early in 1916, American–German relations soured anew when, in response to an announcement that the Allies were now arming merchant ships to sink submarines, Germany proclaimed that it would fire on such vessels without warning. A few weeks later, it did just that, attacking the unarmed French steamer *Sussex* and injuring several American passengers. Again, Wilson demanded that Germany abandon its "unlawful" tactics;

again, the German government relented. Lacking sufficient naval power to enforce an effective blockade against Britain, the Germans decided that the marginal advantages of unrestricted submarine warfare did not yet justify the possibility of drawing America into the war.

Preparedness Versus Pacifism

Despite the president's increasing bellicosity in 1916, he was still far from ready to commit the United States to war. One obstacle was American domestic politics. Facing a difficult battle for reelection, Wilson could not ignore the powerful factions that were continuing to insist on peace. His policies, therefore, represented an effort to satisfy the demands both of those who, like Theodore Roosevelt, insisted that the nation defend its "honor" and economic interests and those who, like Bryan, La Follette, and others, denounced any action that seemed to increase the chance of war. Ranged on one side stood the American military establishment, painfully aware of how unprepared the nation was to fight a major war and adamant that a rapid build-up of its armed forces was essential; American business leaders; insisting that the government act forcefully to ensure that Germany did not interfere with trade with the Allies; and belligerent nationalists, who considered Wilson's policy of neutrality "cowardly" and "dishonorable." On the other side stood German-Americans, who sympathized with their homeland; Irish-Americans, who opposed any assistance to the hated British; large groups of farmers and workers, who saw the war as a battle for commercial and financial supremacy from which they stood to gain little; and a broad, diffuse group who opposed war on moral grounds or viewed the conflict as antithetical to the progressive precepts around which American society had been shaping itself. The United States, they argued, should remain aloof from the "cesspool" of Europe.

The question of whether America should make military and economic preparations for war provided a preliminary issue over which the two coalitions could battle. Wilson at first sided with the antipreparedness forces, denouncing the idea of an American military build-up as needless and provocative. As tensions between the United States and Germany grew, however, he changed his mind. In the fall of 1915, he endorsed an ambitious proposal by American military leaders for a large and rapid increase in the nation's armed forces, to cost more than half a billion dollars; and amid howls of outrage from pacifists in Congress and elsewhere, he worked hard to win approval of it. He even embarked on a national speaking tour early in 1916 to arouse support for the proposal. By midsummer his efforts had in large part succeeded, and rearmament for a possible conflict was well under way.

Still, the peace faction wielded considerable political strength. How much strength became clear to Wilson at the Democratic Convention that met to renominate him in the summer of 1916. The keynote speaker turned his address into a paean of praise for Wilson's efforts to avoid American intervention. He evoked a remarkable response. As he recited a litany of the president's diplomatic accomplishments, the delegates chanted again and again, "What did we do? What did we do?" And the speaker shouted in response, "We didn't go to war! We didn't go to war!" Out of that almost hysterical exchange came one of the most prominent slogans of Wilson's reelection campaign (although one that he himself never used or approved): "He kept us out of war."

In the face of such pressures, therefore, Wilson remained highly cautious. When prowar rhetoric became particularly heated, Wilson spoke defiantly of the nation being "too proud to fight." And when the Republicans chose as their 1916 presidential candidate Charles Evans Hughes, a progressive who attracted the support of the bellicose Theodore Roosevelt, Wilson did nothing to discourage those who argued that Hughes was more likely than he to lead the nation into war. At times, he issued such warnings himself. Wilson's promises of progressivism and peace ultimately combined to give the Democrats, once again a minority party against the reunited Republicans, a narrow victory in November. Wilson won reelection

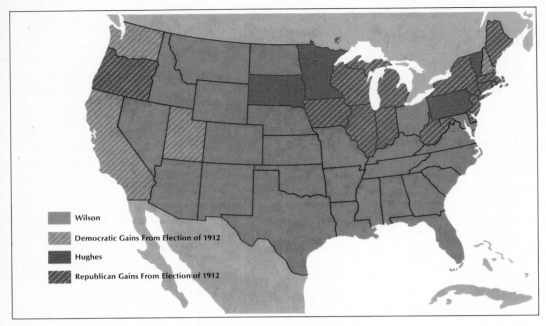

THE ELECTION OF 1916

by one of the smallest margins in American history: fewer than 600,000 popular votes and only 23 electoral votes, with the Democrats retaining a precarious control over Congress.

A War for Democracy

With the election behind him, and with tensions between the United States and Germany unabated, there remained for Woodrow Wilson a final obstacle to involvement in the world war. He required a lofty justification for American intervention, one that would not only unite public opinion but satisfy his own sense of morality. The Germans had gone far toward providing such a justification with their "barbaric" tactics on the seas and their alleged atrocities on land (including, as the American prowar press ardently reported, the use of poison gas and the senseless butchering of women and children). Wilson himself, however, created the most important rationale. The United States, he insisted, had no material aims of its own in the conflict. The nation was, rather, com-

mitted to using the war as a vehicle for constructing a new world order, one based on the same progressive ideals that had motivated reform in America. The United States, he maintained, could serve as a model and a guide to the Old World in building an international community founded on democratic principles and governed by impartial commissions that would arbitrate disputes and prevent future conflicts. In a speech before Congress in January 1917, he presented a plan for a postwar order in which the United States would help maintain peace through a permanent league of nations—a peace that would include self-determination and equality for all nations, a "peace among equals," a "peace without victory." For a time, he hoped that he could achieve these goals by providing mediation to end the conflict. As the war dragged on, however, he became convinced that only by playing an active role in ending the fighting would the United States be able to exert its moral authority to shape the peace.

Thus it was that in the first months of 1917, when new provocations once again inflamed German-American relations, Wilson was at last ready to fight. In January, after months of inconclusive warfare in the trenches of France, the military leaders of Germany decided on one last dramatic gamble to achieve a quick and decisive victory. They would launch a series of major assaults on the enemies' lines in France. At the same time, they would begin unrestricted submarine warfare in an effort to cut off vital supplies from Britain. The Allies would collapse, they hoped, before the United States had time to intervene. Beginning February 1, the German ambassador informed Wilson, U-boats would sink all ships, enemy and neutral alike, in a broad zone around the British Isles. If America chose to continue supplying the Allies, it would have to risk attack.

With that, the president recognized that war was inevitable; the only question remaining was to determine the appropriate time to declare it. Two additional developments helped clear the way. On February 25, the British turned over to him an intercepted telegram from the German foreign minister, Arthur Zimmermann, to the government of Mexico. It proposed that in the event of war between Germany and the United States, the Mexicans should join the struggle against the Americans. In return, they would regain their "lost provinces" to the north when the war was over. Widely publicized by British propagandists and in the American press, the Zimmermann telegram inflamed public opinion and helped build up popular sentiment for war.

A second event, in March, provided Wilson with additional comfort. A revolution in Russia toppled the reactionary czarist regime, which had been tottering ever since the Russo-Japanese War in 1905. A new, republican government took its place. The United States would now be spared the embarrassment of allying itself with a despotic monarchy. The war for a progressive world order could proceed untainted.

On the rainy evening of April 2, two weeks after German submarines had torpedoed three American ships, Wilson appeared before a joint session of Congress and spoke words that brought to an end the years of uncertain waiting:

It is a fearful thing to lead this great peaceful people into war, into the most terrible and disastrous of all wars, civilization itself seeming to be in the balance. But the right is more precious than peace, and we shall fight for the things which we have always carried nearest our hearts—for democracy, for the right of those who submit to authority to have a voice in their own Governments, for the rights and liberties of small nations, for a universal dominion of right by such a concert of free peoples as shall bring peace and safety to all nations and make the world itself at last free.

The audience in the House chamber roared its approval. In Europe, the Allied nations rejoiced at their deliverance. Even some of Wilson's bitterest enemies, men such as Theodore Roosevelt and Henry Cabot Lodge, offered warm words of praise.

The sentiment for war was not, however, unanimous. For four days, amid cries of treason and cowardice, pacifists in Congress carried on their futile struggle. When the declaration of war finally passed on April 6, fifty representatives and six senators had voted against it. America was entering a new era, but it was doing so divided and fearful. And Woodrow Wilson, perhaps aware of the ordeal that lay ahead, returned to the White House after his dramatic war address and, according to one account, broke down and wept.

SUGGESTED READINGS

The standard biography of Taft is Henry F. Pringle, *The Life and Times of William Howard Taft*, 2 vols. (1939), which contrasts its subject favorably with Theodore Roosevelt. Studies of Taft's presidency include Paolo E. Coletta, *The Presidency of Taft* (1973); Norman Wilensky, *Conservatives in the Progressive Era* (1965); and Donald E. Anderson, *William Howard Taft* (1973), which applies a political-science model developed by Richard Neustadt to the Taft administration and finds Taft wanting. The acrimonious Pinchot-Ballinger controversy receives discussion in James L. Penick, *Progressive Politics and Conservation*

(1968), and Harold T. Pinkett, *Gifford Pinchot: Private and Public Forester* (1970). For the foreign policy of the Taft years, consult—in addition to the volumes listed at the end of Chapter 21—Walter Scholes and Marie Scholes, *The Foreign Policies of the Taft Administration* (1970). The Republican rift of 1912 is chronicled in George Mowry, *Theodore Roosevelt and the Progressive Movement* (1946).

Arthur S. Link, long the nation's preeminent Wilson scholar, is the author of by far the most definitive and intelligent biography, not yet complete. The five volumes of his *Woodrow Wilson* (1947–1965) follow Wilson's life from birth to the American entrance into World War I. Link is also the author of *Woodrow Wilson and the Progressive Era, 1910–1917* (1954), a general history of the politics of that era; *Wilson the Diplomatist* (1957), a series of concise essays on his foreign policies; and *Woodrow Wilson: Revolution, War, and Peace* (1979), a major revision of the 1957 essays. Other standard studies of Wilson include John Morton Blum, *Woodrow Wilson and the Politics of Morality* (1956), and Alexander George and Juliette George, *Woodrow Wilson and Colonel House* (1956), a psychoanalytic study of the careers of and the relationship between the two intimate friends. John Morton Blum, *Joseph Tumulty and the Wilson Era*

(1951), explores the events of the Wilson administration through the career of the president's closest White House associate.

Wilson's foreign policy has spawned a particularly large literature. In addition to the Link essays, see Robert Freeman Smith, *The United States and Revolutionary Nationalism in Mexico, 1916–1932* (1972); Kenneth Grieb, *The United States and Huerta* (1969); Robert Quirk, *An Affair of Honor: Woodrow Wilson and the Occupation of Veracruz* (1962) and *The Mexican Revolution, 1914–1915* (1960); David Healy, *Gunboat Diplomacy in the Wilson Era: The U.S. Navy in Haiti, 1915–1916* (1976); and Dana Munro, *Intervention and Dollar Diplomacy in the Caribbean, 1900–1914* (1964). For the story of American entry into World War I, see Ernest R. May, *The World War and American Isolation* (1959), for an excellent account of domestic attitudes. Patrick Devlin, *Too Proud to Fight: Woodrow Wilson's Neutrality* (1974), and John Milton Cooper, Jr., *The Vanity of Power: American Isolation and the First World War* (1969), are also valuable. Ross Gregory, *The Origins of American Intervention in the First World War* (1971), and Daniel Smith, *Robert Lansing and American Neutrality* (1958), examine the diplomatic events leading to intervention.

America and the Great War

23

The American Expeditionary Force Comes Home American soldiers return home from the front in the winter of 1918–1919. The United States military involvement on the side of the Allies in World War I proved decisive in breaking the long stalemate between the Allies and the Central Powers. But there were continuing tensions between the Americans and their European confederates, largely the result of Woodrow Wilson's insistence that the American Expeditionary Force fight as a separate entity in Europe, that it not submit to joint command by the Allies. Wilson was so intent to keep the United States apart from the European belligerents that he refused to allow it to be referred to as one of the Allies; it was, he claimed, an "associated" power. (Culver Pictures)

By its decision of April 1917, the United States had joined the most savage war in history. For two and a half years the fighting had dragged on, inconclusive, almost inconceivably murderous, engaging not only the armies of the contending nations but their civilian populations as well. It was the first truly "total" war, one that pitted entire societies against one another and that had by 1917 left Europe decimated and on the brink of utter collapse. By the time of the armistice, Germany had lost nearly 2 million soldiers in battle, Russia 1.7 million, France 1.4 million, Great Britain 900,000. The civilian toll was impossible even to estimate. An entire generation of European youth was virtually slaughtered; centuries of political, social, and economic traditions were all but eroded and destroyed.

For America, however, the war was the source of a very different experience. As a military struggle, it was brief, decisive, and—in relative terms—without great cost. Only 112,000 American soldiers died in the conflict, half of them from disease rather than combat. Economically, it was the source of a great industrial boom, one that helped spark the years of prosperity that would follow. And the war propelled the United States into a position of almost unquestioned world supremacy.

In other respects, however, World War I was a painful, even traumatic experience for the American people. At home, after joining the fight, the nation became obsessed with not only a search for victory but a search for social unity—a search that continued and even intensified in the troubled years following the armistice, and that helped shatter many of the progressive ideals of the first years of the century. And in the world at large, once the conflict ended, the United States encountered frustration and disillusionment. The "war to end wars," the war "to make the world safe for democracy," became neither. Instead, it led directly to twenty years of international instability that would ultimately generate another great conflict.

WAR WITHOUT STINT

Armies on both sides in Europe were decimated and exhausted by the time of Woodrow Wilson's declaration of war. The German offensives of early 1917 had failed to produce an end to the struggle; French and British counteroffensives had accomplished little beyond adding to the appalling number of casualties. The ghastly stalemate continued, and the Allies looked desperately to the United States to provide them with a chance for victory.

The Americans were eager to oblige. Wilson had called on the nation to wage war "without stint or limit." And in that spirit, the American government proceeded to launch massive campaigns against German submarines in the Atlantic and against German armies in France, and to mobilize the nation's economic resources on a grand scale.

The Naval War

It had been the conflicts at sea that had brought the United States into the war; and it was on the naval struggle that American participation had the most immediate effect. By the spring of 1917, Great Britain was suffering such vast losses from attacks by German submarines—one of every four ships embarking from British ports never returned—that its ability to continue ferrying vital supplies across the Atlantic was coming into serious question. Within weeks of joining the war, the United States had begun to alter the balance. A fleet of American destroyers aided the British navy in its assault on the U-boats; other American warships escorted merchant vessels across the Atlantic; United States assistance was crucial in sowing antisubmarine mines in the North Sea. The results were dramatic. Sinkings of Allied ships had totaled nearly 900,000 tons in the month of April 1917; by December, the figure had dropped to 350,000; by October 1918, it had declined to 112,000. The flow of weapons and supplies from the United States to England and France continued; without it, the Allied cause would have been lost.

The Land War

At first, most Americans believed that this naval assistance was all that would be required of them. It soon became clear, however, that a major commitment of American ground forces would be necessary as well. Britain and France by 1917 had few reserves left from which to draw. Russia was in even direr straits; and after the Bolshevik Revolution in November 1917, the new government, led by Nikolai Lenin, negotiated a hasty and costly peace with the Central Powers. Battalions of German troops were now free to fight on the western front. It would be up to American forces to counterbalance them.

In 1917, however, those forces barely existed. The regular army was almost negligible, and little thought had been given to an effective method for expanding it. Theodore Roosevelt, old and ill, swallowed his personal hatred of President Wilson and visited the White House, offering to raise a regiment to fight in Europe. Others, similarly, urged an entirely voluntary recruitment process. The president, however, decided otherwise. Only a national draft, he insisted, could provide the needed men; and despite the protests of those who agreed with House Speaker Champ Clark that "there is precious little difference between a conscript and a convict," he won passage of the Selective Service Act in mid-May. The draft brought nearly 3 million men into the army; another 2 million joined various branches of the armed services voluntarily.

The engagement of these forces in combat was intense but brief. Not until the end of 1917 did the first members of the American Expeditionary Force (AEF), as it was called, arrive in Europe. Not until the following spring were they there in significant numbers. Eight months later, the war was over. Under the command of General John J. Pershing, whose unhappy experience in Mexico only a year before had not diminished his military reputation, the fresh American troops first joined the existing Allied forces in turning back a series of new German assaults. In May, they assisted the French in repelling a bitter German offensive at Chateau-Thierry, near Paris. Six weeks later, the AEF helped turn away another assault, at Reims, further south. By July 18, the German advance had been halted; and for the first time in what seemed years, the Allies began a successful offensive of their own. On September 26, an enormous American fighting force began to advance against the Germans in the Argonne Forest, part of a grand, 200-mile attack that was to last forty-seven days. Over 1 million American soldiers took part in the assault, using more ammunition than the entire Union army had used in four years of the Civil War; and by the end of October, they had helped push the Germans back to their own border and had cut the enemy's major supply lines to the front.

Faced with an invasion of their own country, German military leaders now began to seek an armistice—an immediate cease-fire that would, they hoped, serve as a prelude to negotiations among the belligerents. Pershing wanted to drive on into Germany itself; but other Allied leaders, after first insisting on terms so stringent as to make the agreement little different in effect from a surrender, accepted the German proposal. On November 11, 1918, the Great War shuddered to a close. And American troops, having fought in it for only about six months of its four years, boasted proudly that it had been they who had won it. Whether or not the claim was militarily accurate, it was already clear that the United States was the only real victor in the conflict.

Captain Edward V. Rickenbacker and Other Pilots of the 94th Pursuit Squadron
The "hat-in-the-ring" squadron, as it was popularly known, was the first American-trained
squadron to engage in combat. It began operations on April 3, 1918. The overall record of
the Americans, who engaged for the most part in individual combat against German aviators flying the superior Fokker planes, was not impressive. At the armistice they constituted only 10 percent of the Allied air power. Individually they were brave to the point of
foolhardiness—they refused to wear parachutes. The exploits of the seventy-one American
aces (those who shot down five or more enemy airplanes) were followed eagerly at home
by newspaper readers hungry for heroes. Captain Rickenbacker (*center*), who shot down
at least twenty-six German planes, became more famous than most generals. (National
Archives)

Financing the War

At home, in the meantime, the war was having profound economic and social effects.
The conflict had begun to transform the
American economy even before the United
States joined the struggle. After the declaration of war, the pace of change quickly accelerated. In the process, the American economy moved far toward becoming the

consolidated, centrally directed instrument
of which many progressives had long
dreamed. At the same time, however, it was
becoming clear that such organization could
lead to results few progressives had foreseen.

Americans encountered many surprises
in 1917. They were surprised when they
learned that substantial American ground
troops would be necessary in Europe. They
were surprised when they discovered that a

draft would be necessary to recruit them. And they were surprised above all when they learned how much the war was going to cost them. Many government officials had scoffed at early predictions that the United States would need to spend $10 billion before the fighting ceased; but it soon became clear that even that figure was preposterously low. Before it was over, the federal government had appropriated $32 billion for expenses directly related to the war.

To raise this sum, which by the standards of the time was astoundingly large, the government relied on two devices. First, it launched a major drive to solicit loans from the American people—"Liberty Bonds" they were called. By 1920, the sale of bonds, which was accompanied by a carefully orchestrated appeal to patriotic fervor, had produced $23 billion. At the same time, new taxes were bringing in an additional sum of nearly $10 billion—some of it from levies on

the "excess profits" of corporations, much of it from new, steeply graduated income and inheritance taxes that ultimately rose as high as 70 percent in some brackets. There was one conspicuous loophole: many corporations stopped paying heavily taxed dividends to their stockholders and distributed shares of tax-exempt stock instead. Nevertheless, the nation financed the war by spreading the burden widely and reasonably efficiently. It was an experience that persuaded many Americans that major government spending could be accomplished without creating economic chaos.

The War Boards

An even greater challenge than raising the necessary funds was the task of organizing the nation's economy to ensure that war needs could be met. It was an undertaking

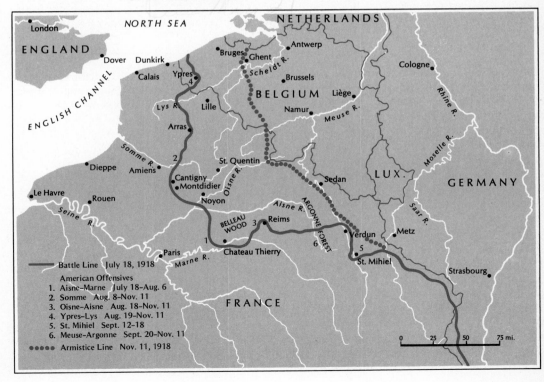

U.S. PARTICIPATION IN ALLIED OFFENSIVES, 1918

Battle Line July 18, 1918
American Offensives
1. Aisne–Marne July 18–Aug. 6
2. Somme Aug. 8–Nov. 11
3. Oisne–Aisne Aug. 18–Nov. 11
4. Ypres–Lys Aug. 19–Nov. 11
5. St. Mihiel Sept. 12–18
6. Meuse–Argonne Sept. 20–Nov. 11
••••• Armistice Line Nov. 11, 1918

Fourth Liberty Loan Parade, New Orleans
In October 1918, shortly before the armistice, the Fourth Liberty Loan drive set out to raise
$6 billion. American heroes, celebrities, and volunteer workers all did their bit; the news from
the western front was encouraging. Again, the loan was oversubscribed. (National Archives)

that required an unprecedented degree of
centralized regulation and control of American life, an undertaking for which neither the
government nor the business sector, despite a
generation of progressive reform, was prepared. As a result, much of the early planning fell almost by default into the hands of a
small group of engineers and scientists. As
early as the summer of 1916, the Civilian
Advisory Commission, an offshoot of the
new Council of National Defense, began to
lay plans and propose techniques for the mobilization of the economy behind the war. Its
members, disciples of the engineering gospel
of Thorstein Veblen and the "scientific management" principles of Frederick Winslow
Taylor, were committed to creating an efficient, rationalized society that reflected their
own technocratic values. They urged organizing a series of planning bodies, each to
supervise a specific sector of the economy.

Thus one agency would control transportation, another agriculture, another manufacturing. Above all, the government would rely
on a systematic, scientific use of statistics,
modern procedures, and efficient administration. One planner said of William E. Coffin,
an engineer influential in the early war efforts, that were he to talk in his sleep, his
only words would be "Standardize! Standardize! Standardize!" The administrative
structure that slowly emerged reflected many
of the technocrats' assumptions, although it
seldom worked as smoothly as they had envisioned. It also elevated one impulse of progressivism—efficiency—at the expense of
another—the curbing of corporate power.

Shortly after the declaration of war, the
Council of National Defense began creating a
series of agencies to supervise those areas of
the economy deemed vital to the war effort.
A Railroad War Board, under the direction of

Treasury Secretary William McAdoo, attempted to run the nation's major transportation resource as a single unified system. Using a half-billion-dollar budget for improving equipment and raising wages, McAdoo succeeded in untangling the flow of rail traffic and dramatically increasing the transport of goods to the East, where they could be shipped on to Europe. A new Fuel Administration was charged with allocating the increasingly scarce supplies of coal among the many contending groups seeking to buy it. By raising the price of coal to high levels, it stimulated increased production in what had earlier been only marginally profitable mines. Even so, the fuel shortage continued to intensify, forcing the agency to adopt even more drastic measures. Eastern industries were forced to endure several coal "holidays" early in 1918; some energy consumers were encouraged to forgo using coal altogether and convert to a newer, cheaper, and more plentiful fuel: oil.

Perhaps the most dramatically effective of all the new war agencies was the Food Administration, established under the Lever Act in August 1917 and headed by the brilliant young engineer and business executive Herbert Hoover. Hoover had supervised a spectacularly successful effort earlier in the war to provide food and relief to Belgium, which had been devastated by the German invasion. He brought the same administrative skills to bear on the far greater task of supervising the feeding of the nation, its armies, and its Allies—all of whom were becoming dependent on the products of American agriculture. At one level, he attempted to increase supplies by encouraging voluntary conservation. Americans should, he announced, plant gardens, observe meatless and wheatless days, substitute plentiful for scarce foods, and cut waste. At the same time, he encouraged increased production of basic foodstuffs such as wheat by arranging for the government to purchase crops at high prices to stimulate farmers to plant as much as possible. Wheat acreage jumped from 45 million in 1917 to 75 million in 1919. Although Hoover avoided rationing and price controls, he worked diligently and effectively to prevent shortages and to keep prices from rising too quickly. Grocers were instructed, for example, to sell no more than two pounds of sugar a month to each customer. To a remarkable degree, these largely voluntary efforts succeeded, partly as a result of Hoover's effective mobilization of public opinion through the use of such slogans as "Food Will Win the War." The nation managed to supply many of the needs of Europe as well as to continue feeding itself; and Hoover emerged from the war as one of the most admired figures in the country.

Government, Industry, and Labor

At the center of the effort to rationalize the economy was the War Industries Board, an agency created in July 1917 to coordinate government purchases of military supplies. It was to become the central mechanism of control over the industrial sector. Casually organized at first, it stumbled badly until March 1918, when Wilson restructured it and placed it under the control of the Wall Street financier Bernard Baruch. From then on, the board wielded powers greater than any governmental agency had ever possessed. Baruch became, in fact, a virtual czar of American industry, using his position not only to coordinate the government's own purchases, but to direct industry itself in many of its most basic decisions. It was Baruch who decided which factories would convert to the production of which war materials; it was he who set prices for the goods that resulted; it was he who imposed standardized production procedures on industries to increase the efficiency of their operations and to promote interchangeability of parts among their products. When materials were scarce, Baruch decided to whom they should go. When corporations were competing for government contracts, he chose among them. He had become, in some senses, the ultimate expression of the progressive ideals of the New Nationalism. He was providing the centralized regulation of the economy that many reformers had long urged.

There was, however, a crucial difference between Baruch's performance and the progressive ideal. Government regulation, as reformers had envisioned it, was to be disinterested. It was to mediate between the interests of the corporate community and those of the public at large. Baruch, in contrast, viewed himself, openly and explicitly, as the partner of business. Indeed, the relationship between the public and private sectors during the war was so warm and mutually supportive that to many people it began to seem as though the line between the two had all but dissolved. Baruch wielded his powers in constant consultation with the leaders of industry. He ensured that manufacturers coordinating their efforts in accord with his goals would be exempt from antitrust laws. He helped major industries earn enormous profits from their efforts. Steel manufacturers, for example, saw their prices rise 300 percent during a single year of the war. Corporate profits as a whole increased threefold between 1914 and 1919. Rather than working to restrict private power and limit corporate profits, as many progressives had urged, the government was working to enhance the private sector through a mutually beneficial alliance. Business itself, once antagonistic to the idea of any government interference, was beginning to see the advantages of having the state control competition and sanction what were, in essence, collusive arrangements.

This growing link between the public and private sectors—the beginning of what would later become known, both in America and in Europe, as corporatism—extended, although in greatly different form, to labor. The National War Labor Board, established in April 1918, served as a kind of supreme court for labor disputes. It pressured industry to grant important concessions to workers: an eight-hour day, the maintenance of minimal living standards, equal pay for women doing equal work, recognition of the right of unions to organize and bargain collectively. In return, it insisted that workers forgo all strikes and that employers not engage in lockouts. Samuel Gompers, president of the American Federation of Labor, sat on the board and supported its decisions; and he watched approvingly as membership in labor unions increased by more than 1.5 million between 1917 and 1919. Yet while labor accomplished more in two years of war than it had been able to do in decades of peacetime, its gains were meager in comparison with those of the corporations. The wage increases workers obtained were almost wiped out by wartime inflation. And many of the organizational gains of the trade unions would not long survive the armistice.

The Results of Organization

Despite the enthusiasm with which government and business alike greeted their new, cooperative relationship, the material results were often disappointing. The proliferation of government agencies at times created more confusion than order. Bureaucracies occasionally contradicted one another in the directives they issued. Lines of authority were never entirely clear. And excessive regulation sometimes slowed, rather than enhanced, production. The federal government, lacking experience in large-scale planning, was finding that bureaucracies were more difficult to control in reality than they were in theory.

Nor did the planned economy always succeed in its ultimate goal: increasing production for war. There were spectacular accomplishments, of course: Hoover's efficient organization of food supplies, McAdoo's success in untangling the railroads, and others. In some areas, however, progress was so slow that the war was over before many of the supplies ordered for it were ready. The Aircraft Production Board, for example, had promised to deliver 22,000 new planes to the western front by July 1918. By the time the armistice was signed, it had managed to produce only 1,185 of them. The Emergency Fleet Corporation, created to oversee production of a vast armada of merchant vessels, took more than a year to overcome the effects of its own incompetent management. By the end of the war, American shipbuilding facilities were beginning to produce new ships at a remarkable rate; but most were not completed in time to contribute to the war effort. Had the fighting continued another year, it is likely that the productive machinery the Wilson administration had so painstakingly constructed would have begun to accomplish great feats. As it was, the eighteen months of war were not enough time for the planned economy to learn to function with real efficiency. They were, however, enough to convince many leaders of both government and industry of the economic advantages of a close, cooperative relationship between the public and private sectors.

THE SEARCH FOR SOCIAL UNITY

The idea of unity—not only in the direction of the economy but in the nation's social purpose—had been the dream of many progressives for decades. To them, the war seemed to offer an unmatched opportunity. At last, America was to close ranks behind a great and common cause. In the process, they hoped, society could achieve a lasting sense of mutual purpose. In fact, however, the search for unity that the progressives had so optimistically foreseen became an experience of ugly hysteria and bitter repression. American society remained divided, both in its attitude toward the war and in its larger political and social goals. And the attempt to impose unity on a diverse and contentious people became a painful exercise.

Selling the War

Government leaders were painfully aware of how deeply divided public opinion had been up to the moment of America's declaration of war. They knew, too, that many pacifists and isolationists remained opposed to United States participation even after that participation had begun. It was easy to argue, therefore, that a crucial prerequisite for victory was the uniting of public opinion behind the war effort. The government approached that task in several ways.

Most conspicuous was a propaganda campaign far greater than any the government had ever undertaken. It was, indeed, almost without precedent. A Committee on Public Information (CPI), under the direction of journalist George Creel, supervised the distribution of innumerable tons of prowar literature (75 million pieces of printed material in all). War posters plastered the walls of offices, shops, theaters, schools, churches, homes. Newspapers dutifully printed official government accounts of the reasons for the war and the prospects for quick victory. Creel encouraged reporters to exercise "self-censorship" when reporting news about the struggle; and although many people in the press resented the suggestion, the veiled threats that accompanied it persuaded most of them to comply. The CPI employed more than 150,000 people to produce prowar propaganda or to disseminate government doctrine. Over 75,000 volunteers served as Public Information speakers, appearing at almost every conceivable public event to proselytize on behalf of the war.

The CPI attempted at first to distribute only the "facts," believing that the truth would speak for itself. As the war continued, however, their tactics became increasingly crude. Government-promoted films, at first relatively mild in tone, were by 1918 becoming vicious portrayals of the savagery of the Germans, bearing such titles as *The Prussian Cur*. CPI-financed advertisements in magazines appealed to citizens to report to the authorities any evidence among their neighbors of disloyalty, pessimism, or yearning for peace. Creel and his associates were not acting cynically or with deliberate viciousness; but their concern for social unity was producing dark and troubling excesses.

Legal Repression

The inflammatory propaganda of the CPI was perhaps the least damaging aspect of the government's campaign to win public support for the war. The Wilson administration soon began not only to encourage public approval but to suppress opposition. The Espionage Act of 1917 imposed heavy fines and stiff jail terms on those convicted of spying, sabotage, or obstruction of the war effort.

The Sedition Act [1918]

Be it enacted.... Whoever, when the United States is at war, shall wilfully make or convey false reports or false statements with intent to interfere with the operation or success of the military or naval forces of the United States ... or ... obstruct the sale by the United States of bonds ... or incite ... insubordination, disloyalty, mutiny, or refusal of duty in the military or naval forces of the United States, or shall wilfully obstruct ... the recruiting or enlistment service ... [or] wilfully utter, print, write, or publish any disloyal, profane, scurrilous, or abusive language about the form of government of the United States, or the Constitution of the United States, or the military or naval forces of the United States, or the flag ... or the uniform of the Army or Navy of the United States ... or shall wilfully ... urge, incite, or advocate any curtailment of production in this country of any thing or things ... necessary or essential to the prosecution of the war ... and whoever shall wilfully advocate, teach, defend, or suggest the doing of any of the acts or things ... enumerated ... shall be punished by a fine of not more than $10,000 or imprisonment for not more than twenty years, or both....

Those crimes were often broadly defined. The law also empowered the postmaster general to ban from the mails any "seditious" material—an authority he exercised enthusiastically and often capriciously. Far more repressive, however, were two measures of 1918: the Sabotage Act of April 20 and the Sedition Act of May 16. These bills expanded the meaning of the Espionage Act to make illegal any public expression of opposition to the war; in practice, it allowed officials to prosecute those who criticized the president or the government in any way at all.

The most frequent target of the new legislation (and one of the reasons for its enactment in the first place) was the Socialist party and its radical offshoot, the Industrial Workers of the World (IWW). Unlike their counterparts in Europe, American socialists had not dropped their opposition to the war after their country had decided to join it; the impact of this decision on them was devastating. Many Americans had favored the repression of socialists and radicals even before the war; now, the new government policies made it possible to move against them with full legal sanction. Eugene V. Debs, the humane leader of the party, a pacifist but no friend of Germany, was sentenced to ten years in prison in 1918. Only a presi-

dential pardon ultimately won his release in 1921. The pursuit of other party leaders followed. Big Bill Haywood and members of the IWW were especially energetically prosecuted. Only by fleeing to the Soviet Union did Haywood avoid long imprisonment. In all, more than 1,500 people were arrested in 1918 for the mere act of criticizing their government.

Popular Repression

The federal government did its share to feed the hysteria of the war years, but it was not alone. State governments, local governments, corporations, universities, and above all the actions of private citizens contributed even more to the climate of repression. So obsessed did many Americans become with the need for uniform loyalty that they adopted heavy-handed, often extralegal, and occasionally violent methods to ensure it. Vigilante mobs seemed to spring up spontaneously to "discipline" those who dared challenge the war. A dissident Protestant clergyman in Cincinnati was pulled from his bed one night by a mob, dragged to a nearby hillside, and whipped "in the name of the women and children of Belgium." An IWW organizer in Montana was seized by a mob and hanged from a railroad bridge. More corrosive than these scattered episodes of brutality, however, were the actions of a cluster of citizens' groups that mobilized "respectable" members of their communities to root out disloyalty. The American Protective League, probably the largest of such groups, enlisted the services of 250,000 people, who served as "agents"—prying into the activities and thoughts of their neighbors, stopping men on the street and demanding to see their draft cards, opening mail, tapping telephones, and in general attempting to impose on their communities the unity of opinion of a police state. Attorney General Thomas W. Gregory described them approvingly as a "patriotic organization." Other vigilante organizations—the National Security League, the Boy Spies of America, the American Defense Society—performed much the same function.

The most frequent victims of such activities were immigrants, who had throughout the early decades of the century been a source of concern to much of American society. Now they became the targets of special abuse. "Loyal" Americans described immigrant communities as spawning grounds for radicalism. Vigilantes devoted special attention to immigrant groups suspected of sympathizing with the enemy. Irish-Americans faced constant accusations because of their historic animosity toward the British and because they had, before 1917, often expressed hopes for a German victory. Jews aroused suspicion because many had expressed opposition to the anti-Semitic policies of the Russian government, until 1917 one of the Allies. Immigrant ghettoes were strictly policed by the "loyalist" citizens' groups. Even settlement workers, many of whom had once championed ethnic diversity, often contributed to their efforts.

The German-Americans

The greatest target, perhaps the inevitable target, of abuse was the German-American community. Its members had unwittingly contributed to their plight; in the first years of the war in Europe, some had openly advocated American assistance to the Central Powers, and many had opposed United States intervention on behalf of the Allies. But while most German-Americans loyally supported the American war effort once it began, public opinion remained hostile. An almost maniacal campaign to purge society of all things German quickly gathered speed, at times assuming ludicrous forms. Sauerkraut was renamed "liberty cabbage." Hamburger became "liberty sausage." More often, however, the hostility took less innocent forms. Performances of German music were frequently banned; German books were removed from the shelves of libraries; courses in the German language were removed from school curricula. For Americans of German descent, moreover, life became a dangerous ordeal. Germans were routinely fired from jobs in war industries, lest they "sabotage" important tasks. Others were fired from positions entirely unrelated to the war; Karl Muck, the brilliant German-born conductor of the Boston Symphony Orchestra, was forced to resign his position and was interned for the last months of the war. Vigilante groups routinely subjected Germans to harassment and beatings; there was even a lynching—in southern Illinois in 1918. Relatively few Americans favored such extremes, but many came to agree with the belief of the eminent psychologist G. Stanley Hall (the man responsible for the first visit of the Austrian Sigmund Freud to America in 1909) that "there is something fundamentally wrong with the Teutonic soul."

PLANNING A NEW WORLD ORDER

It was ironic that in the midst of an unprecedented experience of hysteria and repression at home, the United States should be articulating a vision of a new international order based on lofty democratic principles. Woodrow Wilson had led the nation into war promising a more just and stable peace at its conclusion. Even before the armistice, therefore, he was beginning preparations to lead the fight for a postwar settlement based on principle, not selfish nationalism.

It was, he realized from the beginning, a difficult task. America had barely joined the war when the new Bolshevik government in Russia began disclosing terms of secret treaties negotiated earlier among the Allies. Britain, France, and imperial Russia had already agreed, according to these reports, on how to divide the colonies of their enemies among them. To Wilson, such treaties ran counter to the idealistic vision for which he was exhorting Americans to fight. It was all the more important, he decided as a result, to build strong international support for his own war aims.

The Fourteen Points

On January 8, 1918, therefore, Wilson appeared before a joint session of Congress to present the principles for which he claimed the nation was fighting. The war aims fell under fourteen headings, widely known as the Fourteen Points; but their essential elements clustered in three major categories. First, Wilson's proposals contained a series of specific recommendations for adjusting postwar boundaries and for establishing new nations to replace the defunct Austro-Hungarian and Ottoman empires, all reflecting his belief in the right of every people to self-determination. Second, it contained a set of general principles to govern international conduct in the future: freedom of the seas, open covenants instead of secret treaties, reductions in armaments, free trade, and impartial mediation of colonial claims. Finally,

The Fourteen Points [1918]

I. Open covenants of peace, openly arrived at. . . .

II. Absolute freedom of navigation upon the seas. . . .

III. The removal, so far as possible, of all economic barriers, and the establishment of an equality of trade conditions among all the nations consenting to the peace and associating themselves for its maintenance.

IV. Adequate guarantees given and taken that national armaments will be reduced to the lowest point consistent with domestic safety.

V. A free, open-minded, and absolutely impartial adjustment of all colonial claims. . . .

VI. The evacuation of all Russian territory. . . .

VII. Belgium, the whole world will agree, must be evacuated and restored. . . .

VIII. All French territory should be freed and the invaded portions . . . and . . . Alsace-Lorraine . . . [restored].

IX. A readjustment of the frontiers of Italy should be effected along clearly recognizable lines of nationality.

X. The peoples of Austria-Hungary . . . should be accorded the freest opportunity of autonomous development.

XI. Rumania, Serbia, and Montenegro should be evacuated . . . Serbia accorded free and secure access to the sea. . . .

XII. The Turkish portions of the present Ottoman Empire should be assured a secure sovereignty, but the other nationalities . . . should be assured . . . autonomous development, and the Dardanelles should be permanently opened. . . .

XIII. An independent Polish state should be erected . . . which should be assured free and secure access to the sea. . . .

XIV. A general association of nations must be formed. . . .

and most important of all to Wilson, there was a proposal for a league of nations that would help to implement these new principles and territorial adjustments, and serve to resolve future controversies. It would be, Wilson announced, "a general association of nations . . . formed under specific covenants for the purpose of affording mutual guarantees of political independence and territorial integrity to great and small states alike." Together, Wilson told the members of Congress, the Fourteen Points would help make the world "fit to live in."

There were serious flaws in Wilson's proposals, a result more of what they omitted than of what they contained. He provided no formula for deciding how to implement the "national self-determination" he promised for subjugated peoples. He made no mention of the new Soviet government in Russia, even though its existence had struck fear in the hearts of all Western governments. He said little about economic rivalries and their effect on international relations, even though it had been just such economic rivalries that had been in large part responsible for the war. Nevertheless, Wilson's picture of the postwar world was the clearest and most eloquent expression of an international vision that would enchant not only much of his own generation but members of generations to come. It reflected his belief, strongly rooted in the ideas of progressivism, that the world was as capable of just and efficient government as were individual nations; that once the international community accepted certain basic principles of conduct, and once they constructed modern institutions to implement them, the human race could at last live in peace. The rule of law, he promised, would replace the rule of national passions and self-interested diplomacy.

The Fourteen Points came at a low moment in the war—before American troops had arrived in Europe in substantial numbers, at a time when many among the Allies believed the struggle might still be lost. It was greeted, therefore, with special yearning both in America and in Europe. The Allied leaders might have been cool toward the proposals, but there was an enthusiastic popular response among liberals, working people, and others throughout the world. Many Germans, too, welcomed the Wilsonian principles as a promise of a democratic postwar Germany that could assume a position of equality in the community of nations.

Early Obstacles

Wilson was confident, as the war neared its end, that this popular support would enable him to win Allied approval of his peace plan. He seemed at times to expect virtually to dictate a settlement. There were, however, ominous signs, both at home and abroad, that his path might be more difficult than he expected. In Europe, leaders of the Allied powers were marshaling their energies to resist him even before the armistice was signed. Most of them had resented, since the first days of the war, what they considered his tone of moral superiority. They had reacted unhappily when Wilson refused to make the United States their "ally," but had kept his distance as an "associate" of his European partners. They had been offended by his insistence on keeping American military forces separate from the Allied armies they were joining. Most of all, however, Britain and France, having suffered incalculable losses in their long years of war, and having stored up an enormous reserve of bitterness toward Germany as a result, were in no mood for a benign and generous peace. They were determined to gain something from the struggle to compensate them for the catastrophe they had suffered.

At the same time, Wilson was encountering signs that he might also face problems at home. In 1918, with the war almost won, Wilson unwisely appealed to the American people to show their support for his peace plans by returning Democrats to Congress in the November elections. A Republican victory, he declared, would be "interpreted on the other side of the water as a repudiation of my leadership." Only days later, the Republicans captured majorities in both houses of Congress. Domestic economic troubles, more than international issues, had been the most important factor in the voting; but because of the president's ill-timed appeal, the results were interpreted both at home and abroad just as he had predicted: as a sign of his own political weakness. The election fiasco contributed as well to another dangerous development: Wilson's alienation of the leaders of the Republican party. They had been furious when he attempted to make the 1918 balloting a referendum on his war aims, especially since many Republicans had been loyally supporting the Fourteen Points. They grew angrier in the ensuing weeks at Wilson's implications that only Democrats were committed to a just peace. And whatever ties may have remained between the president and the Republican party were all but severed when Wilson refused to appoint any leading Republicans to the negotiating team that would represent the United States in Paris, where a treaty was to be drafted. Although such men as Elihu Root and William Howard Taft had supported his war aims, Wilson named only one Republican—a little-known diplomat—to the group.

To the president, who was becoming almost obsessed with his own moral mission, such matters were unimportant. There would be only one member of the American negotiating team with any real authority: Wilson himself. And once he had produced a just and moral treaty, the weight of world and American opinion would compel his enemies to support him. Confident of his ability to create a new world, Woodrow Wilson stepped aboard the steamer *George Washington* and on December 3, 1918, sailed for Europe.

THE LOST PEACE

Wilson arrived in Europe in 1919 to a welcome such as few men in history have experienced. To the war-weary people of the Continent, he was nothing less than a savior, the man who would create a new and better world. And when he arrived in Paris on the afternoon of December 13, he saw clear evidence of their adulation in the form of the largest crowd in the history of France. It was the kind of demonstration that Wilson believed would make it impossible for other world leaders to oppose his peace plans. The negotiations themselves, however, proved far less satisfying.

The Versailles Conference

The meeting at the Palace of Versailles to draft a peace treaty was almost without precedent, and it entailed a sizable risk. International negotiations had traditionally been the province of diplomats; kings, presidents, and prime ministers had generally avoided direct encounters. At Versailles, there were four national leaders meeting face to face: David Lloyd George, the prime minister of Great Britain; Georges Clemenceau, the president of France; Vittorio Orlando, the prime minister of Italy; and Wilson, who hoped to dominate them all. Some of Wilson's advisers had warned him that if agreement could not be reached at the "summit," there would be nowhere else to go and that it would therefore be better to begin negotiations at a lower level. Wilson, however, was adamant; he alone would represent the United States.

From the beginning, Wilson's commitment to personal diplomacy encountered difficulties. Heads of state in the glare of world publicity were, he soon found, reluctant to modify their nations' demands. The atmosphere of idealism he had sought to create was, therefore, tinged with a spirit of national aggrandizement. There was, moreover, a pervasive sense of unease about the situation in eastern Europe, where starvation seemed imminent and the threat of communism menacing. Russia, whose new Bolshevik government was still fighting "White" counterrevolutionaries, was unrepresented; but the radical threat it seemed to pose to Western governments was never far from the minds of the delegates.

In this tense and often vindictive atmosphere, the Fourteen Points did not fare well. Wilson was unable to win approval of many

The "Big Four" at Versailles

Surface amiability disguised the tensions among the so-called Big Four, particularly the growing resentment felt by European leaders toward Woodrow Wilson's high (some thought sanctimonious) moral posture in the negotiations. From left to right are David Lloyd George of Great Britain, Vittorio E. Orlando of Italy, Georges Clemenceau of France, and Wilson. (National Archives)

of the broad principles he had espoused: freedom of the seas, which the British refused even to discuss; free trade; "open covenants openly arrived at" (the Versailles negotiations themselves were often conducted in secret). Despite his support for "impartial mediation" of colonial claims, he was forced to accept a transfer of German colonies in the Pacific to Japan, to whom the British had promised them in exchange for Japanese assistance in the war. His pledge of "national self-determination" for all peoples suffered numerous assaults. Italy, for example, obtained new territory in which 200,000 Austrians lived, and then expressed outrage at not also receiving the port of Fiume, which became part of the new nation of Yugoslavia. Poland received a corridor to the sea which ran through territory that was ethnically German. Economic and strategic demands were constantly coming into conflict with the principle of cultural nationalism.

Where the treaty departed most conspicuously from Wilson's ideals was on the question of reparations. As the conference began, the president was staunchly opposed to exacting punitive damages from the defeated Central Powers. The other Allied lead-ers, however, were intransigent, and slowly Wilson gave way. Although he resisted the demand of the French government that Germany be required to pay $200 billion to the Allies, he ultimately bowed to pressure and accepted the principle of reparations, the specific sum to be set later by a commission. The final figure, established in 1921, was $56 billion, supposedly to pay for civilian damages and military pensions. Although lower than some earlier demands, it was still far more than the crippled German economy could absorb. The reparations, combined with other territorial and economic penalties, constituted an effort to keep Germany not only weak but prostrate for the indefinite future. Never again, the Allied leaders believed, should the Germans be allowed to become powerful enough to threaten the peace of Europe.

But Wilson did manage to win some important victories at Versailles. He secured approval of a plan to place many former colonies in "trusteeship" to be supervised by the League of Nations—the so-called mandate system. He blocked a French proposal to break up western Germany into a group of smaller states, although in return he had to concede to France the disputed territory of Alsace-Lorraine and agree to a demilitarization and Allied occupation of the Rhineland. He oversaw the creation of the new nations of Yugoslavia and Czechoslovakia and the strengthening of Poland. Such accomplishments were of secondary importance to Wilson, however, when compared with his most visible triumph: the creation of a permanent international organization to oversee world affairs and prevent future wars. On January 25, 1919, the Allies voted to accept the "covenant" of the League of Nations; and with that, Wilson believed, the Treaty of Versailles was transformed from a disappointment into a success. Whatever mistakes and inequities had emerged from the peace conference, he was convinced, could be corrected later by the League.

The covenant provided for an assembly of nations that would meet regularly to debate means of resolving disputes and protecting the peace. Authority actually to implement League decisions would rest with a nine-member Executive Council; the United States would be one of five permanent members of the council, along with Britain, France, Italy, and Japan. The covenant, like the larger treaty of which it was a part, left many questions unanswered, most notably how the League would enforce its decisions. Wilson, however, was confident that once established, the new organization would find suitable answers. The League of Nations, he believed, would become not only the centerpiece of the Treaty of Versailles, but the cornerstone of a new world order. Like other progressives considering other issues, the president was placing his hopes for the future in the process, rather than the substance, of international relations. If rational institutions could be established, then the actual conduct of world affairs would become rationalized as well.

The Ratification Battle

Wilson was well aware of the political obstacles awaiting him at home. Many Americans, accustomed to their nation's isolation from Europe, questioned the wisdom of this major new commitment to internationalism. Others had serious reservations about the specific features of the treaty and the covenant. On a brief trip to Washington in February 1919, during a recess in the peace conference, the president listened to harsh objections from members of the Senate and others; and although he reacted angrily and haughtily to his critics, he returned to Europe and insisted on certain modifications in the covenent to satisfy them. The amendments provided that a nation need not accept a mandate (responsibility for overseeing a League territory) against its will, that a member could withdraw from the organization with two years' notice, and that the League would not infringe on the Monroe Doctrine. Beyond that, however, Wilson refused to go. When Colonel House, his close friend and trusted adviser, told him he must be prepared to compromise further, the president retorted sharply: "I have found that you get nothing in this world that is worth-while without fighting for it."

How bitter that fight would be soon became clear, for there was ample inflexibility and self-righteousness on both sides of the conflict. Wilson presented the treaty to the Senate on July 10, 1919, asking: "Dare we reject it and break the heart of the world?" In the weeks that followed, he consistently refused to consider even the most innocuous compromise. (His deteriorating physical condition—he was suffering from hardening of the arteries and had apparently experienced something close to a stroke in Paris—may have contributed to his intransigence.) The Senate, in the meantime, was raising a host of objections to the treaty. For the fourteen so-called "irreconcilables"—Western progressives who included Hiram Johnson, William Borah, and Robert La Follette—the Versailles agreement was totally unacceptable. The United States should never become embroiled in the sordid politics of Europe, they argued; not even the most generous compromise could have won their support for the League. Other opponents, with less fervent convictions, were more concerned with constructing a winning issue for the Republicans in 1920 and with embarrassing a president whom they had not yet forgiven for his polit-

A Comment on the Ratification Fight
This savage characterization of the partisan opposition to the Treaty of Versailles may not have been fair to all the Senate Republicans opposing ratification. But personal hatred of Woodrow Wilson was a powerful factor in shaping the course of Senator Henry Cabot Lodge, the most important opposition leader. During the last months of Theodore Roosevelt's life, he and Lodge had met frequently to encourage each other in their deep contempt for Wilson. Lodge reportedly believed that he himself should have been elected president in 1916 and may have resented Wilson even more as a result. (Library of Congress)

ical tactics in 1918. Most notable of these was Senator Henry Cabot Lodge of Massachusetts, the powerful chairman of the Foreign Relations Committee. A man of stunning arrogance and a close friend of Theodore Roosevelt (who had died early in 1919, spouting hatred of Wilson to the end), Lodge loathed the president with genuine, unrestrained passion. "I never thought I could hate a man as I hate Wilson," he once admitted. He used every possible tactic, therefore, to obstruct, delay, and ultimately, he hoped, defeat the treaty. Public sentiment clearly favored ratification, so Lodge at first could do little more than play for time. When the document reached his committee, he spent two weeks reading aloud each word of its 300 pages; then he held six weeks of public hearings to air the complaints of every disgruntled mi-

nority (Irish-Americans, for example, angry that the settlement made no provision for an independent Ireland). Gradually, Lodge's general opposition to the treaty crystallized into a series of "reservations"—amendments to the League covenant limiting American obligations to the organization.

Wilson might still have won approval at this point if he had agreed to some relatively innocuous changes in the language of the treaty. But the president refused to yield. The United States had a moral obligation, he claimed, to respect the terms of the agreement precisely as they stood. When one senator warned him that his position was becoming hopeless, that he would have to accept some of the Lodge reservations to have any hope of victory, Wilson retorted: "Never! Never! . . . I'll appeal to the country!"

Wilson's Ordeal

What followed was a political disaster and a personal tragedy. Against the stern warnings of his physician, Wilson decided to embark on a grueling, cross-country speaking tour to arouse public support for the treaty. For more than three weeks, he traveled by train from city to city, covering more than 8,000 miles, writing his own speeches as he went along, delivering them as often as four times a day, an hour at a time. He received little rest. In the beginning, the crowds were small and the speeches clumsy. As the tour progressed, however, both the size and the enthusiasm of the audiences grew; and Wilson's own eloquence and moral fervor increased. Had it been possible to sway the Senate through public opinion, the tour might have been a success. But it had long ago become plain that the opposition in Washington had little to do with popular sentiment. So the tour was not only an exhausting ordeal for Wilson but a futile one as well.

Finally, the president reached the end of his strength. After speaking at Pueblo, Colorado, on September 25, he collapsed with severe headaches. Canceling the rest of his itinerary, he rushed back to Washington, where, a few days later, he suffered a major stroke. For two weeks, he was close to death; for six weeks more, he was so seriously ill that he could conduct virtually no public business. His wife and his doctor formed an almost impenetrable barrier around him, shielding the president from any official pressures that might impede his recovery, preventing the public from receiving any accurate information about the gravity of his condition.

Wilson ultimately recovered fully enough to resume a limited official schedule, but he was essentially an invalid for the eighteen remaining months of his presidency. His left side was partially paralyzed; more important, his mental and emotional state was precarious and unstable. Like many stroke victims, he found it difficult to control his feelings, often weeping at the slightest provocation. And his condition only intensified what had already been his strong tendency to view public issues in moral terms and to resist any attempts at compromise. When the Senate Foreign Relations Committee finally reported the treaty, recommending nearly fifty amendments and reservations, Wilson refused to consider any of them. When the full Senate voted in November to accept fourteen of the reservations, Wilson gave stern directions to his Democratic allies: they must vote only for a treaty with no changes whatsoever; any other version must be defeated. On November 19, 1919, forty-two Democrats, following the president's instructions, joined with the thirteen Republican "irreconcilables" to reject the amended treaty. When the Senate voted on the original version without any reservations, thirty-eight senators, all but one a Democrat, voted to approve it; fifty-five voted no.

It did not seem so at the time, but the battle was now for all intents and purposes over; Wilson's long and painful struggle for a new world order was lost. There were sporadic efforts to revive the treaty over the next few months; on March 19, 1920, the day of the final vote, the amended version came as close as seven votes short of the necessary two-thirds majority. But Wilson's opposition to anything but the precise settlement he had negotiated in Paris remained too formidable an obstacle to surmount. He was, moreover, becoming convinced that the 1920 national election would serve as a "solemn referendum" on the League, that the force of public opinion could still compel ratification of the treaty. He even spoke, somewhat pathetically, of running for reelection himself. By now, however, public interest in the peace process had begun to fade—partly as a reaction against the tragic bitterness of the ratification fight, but more in response to a series of other crises.

POSTWAR INSTABILITY

Even during the Paris Peace Conference, the attention of many Americans was directed less toward international matters than toward events at home. There were increasing economic problems; there was widespread social unrest and violence; there was a growing fear of revolution. Some of this unease was a legacy of the almost hysterical social atmosphere of the war years; some of it was a response to issues that surfaced after the armistice. Whatever the reasons, however, America was, in the immediate postwar years, a turbulent and often unhappy place.

The Troubled Economy

Citizens of Washington, on the day after the armistice, found it impossible to place long-distance telephone calls. The lines were jammed with officials of the war agencies canceling government contracts. The fighting had ended sooner than anyone had anticipated; and without warning, without planning, the nation was launched into the difficult task of economic reconversion.

At first, to the surprise of almost everyone, the wartime boom continued. But it was a troubled and precarious prosperity, based largely on the lingering effects of the war (government deficit spending continued for some months after the armistice) and on sudden, temporary demands (a booming market for scarce consumer goods at home, a strong European market in the war-ravaged nations). It was accompanied, moreover, by raging inflation, a result in part of the precipitous abandonment of wartime price controls. Through most of 1919 and 1920, prices rose at an average of more than 15 percent a year.

Finally, late in 1920, the economic bubble burst, as many of the temporary forces that had created it disappeared and as inflation began killing the market for consumer goods. Between 1920 and 1921, the gross national product (GNP) declined nearly 10 percent; the index of wholesale prices fell from 227.9 to 150.6; 100,000 businesses went bankrupt; 453,000 farmers lost their land; nearly 5 million Americans lost their jobs. Recovery began quickly, and by 1923 it was complete. But the experience of dizzying inflation followed suddenly by a crushing recession was a frightening and disorienting one at the time.

Labor Unrest

Perhaps the most visible result of the postwar economic problems was a dramatic increase in labor unrest. American workers had refrained from strikes during the war. But with the fighting over, they were willing to be patient no longer. Many factors combined to produce labor discontent: the raging inflation, which wiped out what had been at best modest gains in wages during the war; concern about job security, heightened by the return to the labor force of hundreds of thousands of veterans; arduous working conditions—such as the perpetuation of the twelve-hour day in the steel industry. Employers aggravated the discontent by using the end of the war (and the end of government controls) as an excuse for taking back some of the benefits they had been forced to concede to workers in 1917 and 1918—most notably recognition of unions. Mine owners even reneged on promised wage increases. In such a climate, conflict was inevitable.

The year 1919 saw, therefore, an unprecedented wave of strikes—more than 3,600 in all, involving over 4 million workers. Several of the strikes received wide national attention and raised particular alarm. In January, a walkout by shipyard workers in Seattle, Washington, evolved into a general strike that brought the entire city to a virtual standstill. The mayor requested and received the assistance of United States Marines to keep the city running, and eventually the strike failed. But the incident was widely cited as evidence of the vulnerability of any community to disruption from labor agitation. In September, there was an even more alarming strike by the Boston police force, which was demanding recognition of its union. Seattle had remained generally calm; but with its police off the job, Boston erupted in violence and looting. Efforts by local businessmen, veterans, and college students to patrol the streets proved ineffective; and finally Governor Calvin Coolidge called in the National Guard to restore order. (His public statement at the time that "There is no right to strike against the public safety by anybody, anywhere, any time" attracted national acclaim.) Eventually, Boston officials dismissed the entire police force and hired a new one.

The Steel Strike, 1919
Striking steelworkers demonstrate near a U.S. Steel plant in Chicago in September 1919. The strike, which lasted three and a half months, was a result of the refusal of the chairman of the board of U.S. Steel, Elbert H. Gary, to confer with labor leaders over their grievances. Orchestrated by radical labor organizer William Z. Foster and supported by the A.F. of L., the strike centered around five demands: recognition of the steelworkers' union; the right of workers to bargain collectively, through their union, with management; the abolition of the twelve-hour day; the abolition of company unions; and wage increases. The strike dissolved in failure early in January 1920. (UPI)

Of all the strikes of 1919, the greatest was the one, also in September, by 350,000 steelworkers in several Midwestern cities. They were demanding an eight-hour day and recognition of their union; but Elbert Gary, president of United States Steel, led the industry management in standing firm. The strike was long and bitter, marked by frequent violent conflicts, and climaxed by a riot in Gary, Indiana, in which eighteen strikers were killed. With the assistance of their own armed guards, steel executives managed to keep most plants running with nonunion labor; and by January, the strike had collapsed. Public opinion had turned so decisively against the strikers that the timid A.F.

of L. had finally repudiated them. It was a setback from which organized labor would not recover for more than a decade.

The Red Scare

Viewed objectively, the great wave of strikes, most of which ended in failure, was evidence of the weakness of the labor movement and the strength of the corporate establishment. To much of the public, however, the industrial warfare was a frightening omen of social instability. More than that, it was a sign of a dangerous increase in domestic radicalism. The mayor of Seattle claimed that the general strike was an attempt by revolutionaries "to establish a Soviet government." The leaders of the steel industry insisted that "radical agitators" had stirred up trouble among their employees, who were, they claimed, content with things as they were. That such charges were virtually groundless did not diminish their effectiveness.

This was in part because other evidence emerging at the same time likewise seemed to suggest the existence of a radical menace. The Russian Revolution of November 1917 had been disturbing enough by itself—so disturbing to Woodrow Wilson, in fact, that in 1918 he permitted the landing of American troops in the Soviet Union. They were there, he claimed, to help a group of 60,000 Czech soldiers trapped in Russia escape. But the Americans soon became involved, both directly and indirectly, in assisting the White Russians in their fight against the Bolsheviks. Some American troops remained as late as April 1920. Wilson's actions failed to undermine Lenin's communist regime; they did, however, become the source of lasting Russian-American hostility and mistrust. American concerns about the communist threat grew even more intense in 1919 when the Soviet government announced the formation of the Communist International (or Comintern), whose purpose was to export revolution around the world. No one in the United States seemed to notice that the Russian communists had not yet even secured their own revolution, that they were in no position to begin any overseas adventures.

In America, in the meantime, there was, in addition to the great number of imagined radicals, a modest number of real ones. And when they heard the frightened warnings that a revolution was imminent, they tended to believe them. Some, therefore, engaged in sporadic acts of terrorism to speed the supposed crisis on its way. It was these small bands of radicals, presumably, who were responsible for the series of bombings in the spring of 1919 that produced great national alarm. In April, the Post Office intercepted several dozen parcels addressed to leading businessmen and politicians that were triggered to explode when opened; several reached their destinations, one of them se-verely injuring the servant of a Georgia public official. Two months later, eight bombs exploded in eight cities within minutes of one another, suggesting a nationwide conspiracy. One of them damaged the façade of Attorney General A. Mitchell Palmer's home in Washington.

In response to these and other provocations, the nation embarked on a crusade against radicalism that resembled in many ways its wartime crusade against disloyalty and dissent. Nearly thirty states enacted new peacetime sedition laws imposing harsh penalties on those who promoted revolution; some 300 people went to jail as a result. Citizens in many communities removed "subversive" books from the shelves of libraries; administrators in some universities dismissed "radical" members from their faculties. A mob of off-duty soldiers in New York City ransacked the offices of a socialist newspaper and beat up its staff. Another mob, in Centralia, Washington, dragged an IWW agitator from jail and castrated him before hanging him from a bridge. Perhaps the greatest contribution to the Red Scare, as it later became known, came from the federal government. Attorney General Palmer, angered by the bombing of his home and ambitious for his party's 1920 presidential nomination, ordered the Justice Department to take steps to quell what he later called the "blaze of revolution . . . sweeping over every American institution of law and order." On New Year's Day, 1920, he orchestrated a series of raids on alleged radical centers throughout the country and arrested more than 6,000 people. The Palmer Raids had been intended to uncover huge caches of weapons and explosives; they netted a total of three pistols and no dynamite. Nevertheless, many of those arrested spent days and weeks in jail with no formal charges filed against them. Most were ultimately released, but about 500 who were not American citizens were summarily deported. For these egregious violations of civil liberties, A. Mitchell Palmer received a barrage of favorable publicity and enjoyed a period of intense (if brief) national popularity.

The ferocity of the Red Scare soon abated, but its effects lingered well into the

Sacco and Vanzetti Being Taken into Court, 1927
When Sacco and Vanzetti were brought before Judge Webster Thayer on April 9, 1927, they were allowed to speak. Sacco said: "I never knew, never heard, even read in history anything so cruel as this Court.... I know the sentence will be between two classes, the oppressed class and the rich class, and there will always be collision between one and the other." Vanzetti said: "I am suffering because I am a radical and indeed I am a radical; I have suffered because I was an Italian, and indeed I am an Italian.... but I am so convinced to be right that you can only kill me once but if you could execute me two times, and if I could be reborn two other times, I would live again to do what I have done already." Judge Thayer then sentenced them to death. One of the counsel for the two men, who did not "belong even remotely to [their] school of thought," warned after the execution of "minds that are closed by deep prejudice or transient passion." "If," he declared, "the local hostility was inflamed by foolish words of their sympathizers or wicked deeds of their exploiters, this also is a fact to be recollected." The publisher of the conservative Boston *Herald,* which had called for an impartial commission to review the case, asserted: "The momentum of the established order required the execution of Sacco and Vanzetti, and never in your life or mine, has that momentum acquired such tremendous force."
(Brown Brothers)

1920s, most notably in the celebrated case of Sacco and Vanzetti. In May of 1920, two Italian immigrants, Nicola Sacco and Bartolomeo Vanzetti, were charged with the murder of a paymaster in Braintree, Massachusetts. The evidence against them was at best questionable; but because both men were confessed anarchists, they faced a widespread public presumption of guilt. The judge in their trial, Webster Thayer, was openly prejudiced; and it was perhaps unsurprising under the circumstances that they were convicted and sentenced to death. Over the next several years, however, interest in the case grew in many quarters—among a group of young journalists, among disenchanted progressives, among many intellectuals, and among an increasing number of others who were impressed by the courage and dignity the two condemned men continued to display. Again and again, supporters of Sacco and Vanzetti filed requests for a new trial or a pardon; repeatedly, judges, the governor, and finally a special review board (whose members included the presidents of Harvard and MIT) denied all appeals. After years of frustrating debate, the struggle ended; on August 23, 1927, Sacco and Vanzetti, still proclaiming their innocence, died in the electric chair. All over the world, crowds demonstrated in protest. In the United States, thousands of men and women expressed anger, shame, and sorrow. It was a cause that a generation of Americans never forgot, an episode that kept the bitter legacy of the Red Scare alive for many years.

Racial Unrest

No group suffered more from the inflamed climate of the postwar years than American blacks. To them more than to most, the war seemed to offer a major opportunity for social and economic advancement. Over 400,000 blacks served in the army, half of them in Europe; and they expected to earn the gratitude of the nation in return. Several hundred thousand more migrated from the South to Northern industrial cities in search of the factory jobs that the war was rapidly generating. Almost overnight, the nation's racial demographics were transformed; suddenly there were enormous black communities crowding into the urban North, which had received only a relatively few blacks in the past. Just as black soldiers expected their military service to enhance their social status, so black factory workers regarded their move north as an escape from racial prejudice and an opportunity for economic gain.

Even before the war ended, however, the racial climate had begun to sour; and in 1919, it turned savage and murderous. In the South, there was a sudden increase in lynchings—more than seventy blacks, some of them war veterans, died at the hands of white mobs in 1919 alone. In the North, conditions were even worse. Black veterans were cruelly disillusioned when they returned to find a society still unwilling to grant them any significant social or economic gains; black factory workers were facing layoffs as returning white veterans displaced them from their jobs. These economic difficulties contributed to an already tense situation. The Great Migration that had begun in 1915 had thrown thousands of blacks into close proximity with Northern whites who were unfamiliar with and generally hostile to them. As they jostled together on the streets, trolleys, and subways of the overcrowded cities, tensions escalated; and as whites became convinced that black workers, with their lower wage demands, were hurting them economically, the animosity grew further. The result was a rash of disorder and violence. As early as 1917, there had been serious race riots in cities as diverse as Houston, Philadelphia, and East St. Louis (where forty-nine people, thirty-nine of them blacks, were killed). In 1919, things grew far worse. In Chicago, a black teen-ager swimming in Lake Michigan on a hot July day happened to drift toward a white beach. Whites on shore allegedly stoned him unconscious; he sank and drowned. The incident became the match that ignited already severe racial tensions in the city; and for more than a week, Chicago was virtually at war—black and white mobs roaming through each other's neighborhoods, beating and shooting passersby, destroying homes and properties. In the end, 38 people died— 15 whites and 23 blacks—and 537 were injured; over 1,000 people were left homeless. The Chicago riot was the worst but not the only riot during the so-called red summer of 1919; in all, 120 people died in such racial outbreaks in the space of little more than three months.

Blacks responded to the turmoil in various ways. Some were simply bewildered, deeply disillusioned at the shattering of their hopes, frightened by the savagery to which they were now exposed. Others were defiant. The NAACP urged blacks to fight back, to defend themselves and demand government protection. At the same time, a black Jamaican, Marcus Garvey, began to attract a wide American following with an ideology of black nationalism. Black culture was superior to that of white society, he told supporters; blacks should leave America and return to Africa, where they could create a new society of their own. At the peak of his popularity, Garvey claimed a following of 4 million. In the end, however, most blacks had little choice but to acquiesce in the social and economic subjugation being forced on them. Although they continued to make certain limited gains, it would be more than thirty years before they made any substantial progress toward social or economic equality.

The Retreat from Idealism

The economic problems, the labor unrest, the fear of radicalism, the racial tensions—all combined in the years immediately following the war to produce a general sense of disillusionment. By 1920, the American people were tired: tired of idealism, tired of reform, tired of the controversy and instability they believed these impulses had caused. For decades, they had been living in turbulent times:

through a series of social crises in the 1890s, through a highly charged era of reform in the first decade and a half of the new century, through an intense and savage war, through a troubled and bitter peace. They yearned now for tranquillity.

How deeply they yearned for it became apparent in the election of 1920. Woodrow Wilson wanted the campaign to be a referendum on the League of Nations; instead, in effect, it became a referendum on the future. The Democratic candidates, Ohio Governor James M. Cox and Assistant Secretary of the Navy Franklin D. Roosevelt, worked hard to keep Wilson's ideals alive. The Republican presidential nominee, however, offered a different vision. He was Warren Gamaliel Harding, an obscure Ohio senator whose only real asset seemed to be his pliability; party leaders had settled on him late one night in a "smoke-filled room" in a Chicago hotel, confident that he would do their bidding once in office. In the course of his brief and spiritless campaign, Harding offered no soaring ideals, only a vague and comfortable

THE ELECTION OF 1920

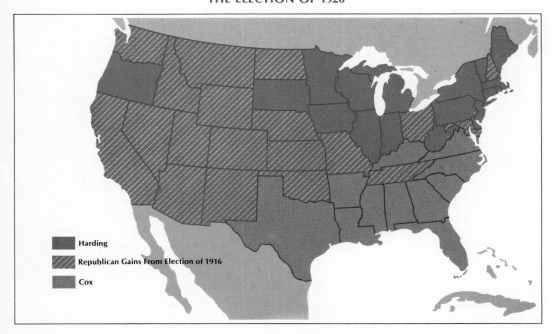

Harding

Republican Gains From Election of 1916

Cox

reassurance of stability, the promise of a return, as he later phrased it, to "normalcy." He won in a landslide. The Republican ticket received 61 percent of the popular vote and carried every state outside the South. The party made major gains in Congress as well.

Woodrow Wilson, for so long a symbol of many of the nation's ideals, stood repudiated. Early in 1921, he retired to a house on S Street in Washington, where for the next three years he lived quietly and inconspicuously. On February 3, 1924, he died.

SUGGESTED READINGS

For the military history of the American experience in World War I, see Edward M. Coffman, *The War to End All Wars* (1969); Harvey A. De Weerd, *President Wilson Fights His War* (1968); A. E. Barbeau and Florette Henri, *The Unknown Soldiers: Black American Troops in World War I* (1974); and Russell Weigley, *The American Way of War* (1973). Frank Freidel, *Over There* (1964), is a pictorial history. On wartime diplomacy, see Arno Mayer, *Political Origins of the New Diplomacy* (1959); George F. Kennan, *Russia Leaves the War* (1956) and *Russia and the West Under Lenin and Stalin* (1961); W. B. Fowler, *British-American Relations, 1917–1918* (1969); and Carl Parrini, *Heir to Empire: United States Economic Diplomacy, 1916–1923* (1969).

David M. Kennedy, *Over Here* (1980), offers the best overview of the general impact of the war on American society. It should be supplemented with Jordan Schwarz, *The Speculator* (1981), a study of Bernard Baruch; Robert D. Cuff, *The War Industries Board: Business–Government Relations During World War I* (1973), an excellent study of wartime industrial mobilization; and Daniel Beaver, *Newton D. Baker and the American War Effort, 1917–1919* (1966). Seward Livermore, *Politics Is Adjourned* (1966), examines relations between Wilson and Congress during the war. See also Charles Gilbert, *American Financing of World War I* (1970). George T. Blakey, *Historians on the Homefront* (1970); J. R. Mock and Cedric Larson, *Words That Won the War* (1939); Stephen Vaughn, *Holding Fast the Inner Lines* (1980); and Zechariah Chaffee, Jr., *Free Speech in the United States* (1941), analyze wartime propaganda and public opinion. H. C. Peterson and Gilbert Fite, *Opponents of War, 1917–1918* (1957), examines dissent and civil liberties. Chapters in John Higham, *Strangers in the Land* (1955), discuss the effects of the war on immigrant communities; while Federick Luebke, *Bonds of Loyalty* (1974), examines the plight of German-Americans.

As an introduction to the vast literature on postwar diplomacy, consult Arthur S. Link, *Wilson the Diplomatist* (1957); N. Gordon Levin, Jr., *Woodrow Wilson and World Politics* (1968); and two works by Thomas A. Bailey, *Woodrow Wilson and the Lost Peace* (1944) and *Woodrow Wilson and the Great Betrayal* (1945). A controversial analysis of the Versailles Conference, emphasizing the influence of anti-communist sentiment on the negotiations, can be found in Arno Mayer, *Wilson vs. Lenin* (1959) and *Politics and Diplomacy of Peacemaking* (1965). See also Peter Filene, *Americans and the Soviet Experiment* (1967). Inga Floto, *Colonel House at Paris* (1980), is a good study of the Versailles negotiations. For the battle over ratification, see, in addition to the above, John A. Garraty, *Henry Cabot Lodge* (1953); Ralph Stone, *The Irreconcilables* (1970); Denna Fleming, *The United States and the League of Nations* (1932); and Arthur Link, *Woodrow Wilson: War, Revolution, and Peace* (1979). Gene Smith, *When the Cheering Stopped* (1964), is a moving popular account of Wilson's last years. George Kennan, *Decision to Intervene* (1958), and John L. Gaddis, *Russia, the Soviet Union, and the United States* (1978), examine American intervention in the Soviet Union during the Revolution.

Postwar economic turmoil is summarized in Burl Noggle, *Into the Twenties* (1974). Stanley Coben, *A. Mitchell Palmer* (1963), and Robert K. Murray, *The Red Scare* (1955), examine the antiradicalism of the postwar years. Roberta Strauss Feuerlicht, *Justice Crucified* (1977), is one of many studies of the Sacco-Vanzetti case. David Brody, *Labor in Crisis* (1965), examines the steel strike of 1919; Francis Russell, *A City in Terror* (1975), considers the Boston police strike; and Robert L. Friedheim, *The Seattle General Strike* (1965), examines another labor uprising. William M. Tuttle, Jr., *Race Riot* (1970), analyzes the Chicago riot of the same year; and Elliott Rudwick, *Race Riot at East St. Louis* (1964), examines an earlier disturbance. On Marcus Garvey and Garveyism, see David Cronon, *Black Moses* (1955), and Amy J. Garvey, *Garvey and Garveyism* (1963). Wesley M. Bagby, Jr., *The Road to Normalcy* (1962), examines the campaign of 1920.

PART SIX

Prosperity, Depression, and War, 1920-1945

In many respects, the period between the end of World War I and the end of World War II was one of sharp discontinuities. Few eras in American history present such vivid contrasts compressed into so short a time.

Politically, the nation experienced what many considered a virtual sea change after the election of 1920. For a full decade, the government remained in the hands of the Republican party and—for eight of those years at least—in the hands of two conservative presidents who rejected most of the liberal assumptions of the progressive era. An age of reform seemed to have given way to an era of reaction. Then, beginning in 1933 with the inauguration of Franklin Delano Roosevelt, the Democratic party—the minority organization for most of the previous seventy-five years—established a dominance that it was not to relinquish for decades. And with it came a new administration and a new Congress that would together produce major reforms and a drastic expansion of the role of government in American life. Finally, after the outbreak of World War II, the nation witnessed a rapid strengthening of conservative forces that brought the march toward liberal reform once again to a virtual halt.

Economically, there were equally profound shifts. Beginning in 1921, the American economy embarked on a period of growth without precedent in the history of the world. The nation's industrial capacity grew exponentially; the income of its citizens soared; America's position in world trade became one of unrivaled supremacy. And the American corporate world, after having been on the defensive for many years, basked in a widespread public popularity that turned once-despised captains of industry into national heroes. Then, starting with a dramatic stock market crash in 1929, the imposing economic edifice collapsed, and the country entered the worst

economic crisis in its history. Industrial production declined; new investment virtually ceased; unemployment reached epic proportions. And although the magnitude of the crisis varied from one year to the next, the
Great Depression, as it soon became known, continued for nearly a full decade. Only the outbreak of World War II and the stimulus that the conflict
gave to the economy brought the misery to an end. By 1942, the United
States was once again embarked on a period of economic growth—one that
from the outset put even the prosperous 1920s to shame.

Culturally, there were equally sharp apparent contrasts. In the 1920s,
a bitter conflict emerged between the forces of modernism associated with
the new urban-industrial society, and the forces of traditionalism associated
with more provincial, usually rural communities. On issues such as prohibition, religion, and race, the tensions between the new society and the old
were vividly displayed. In the 1930s, by contrast, the nation's outlook appeared to shift dramatically. Cultural divisions now seemed less important
than economic ones, and the controversies of the 1930s revolved less
around questions of values than around questions of wealth and power. The
outbreak of World War II, however, dampened the economic conflicts and
helped to produce a new search for national unity.

Yet for all the very real differences between the 1920s and the 1930s,
and between both periods and World War II, there were also important
continuities. For the United States during these years remained involved in a
process that transcended the changing fortunes of the moment: a process of
political, economic, and cultural consolidation. Through prosperity, depression, and war, the nation continued to experience a steady increase in
the influence of government on the lives of its people; it witnessed a continuing movement toward centralization of economic power in great national institutions; and it saw—often despite itself—the emergence of a
social and cultural outlook that helped to overcome local and regional differences and to draw the entire country together into increasingly similar
patterns of thought and behavior.

The late nineteenth and early twentieth centuries had seen great
progress toward the creation of a new industrial society in the United States.
The middle years of the century saw that society approach its full modern
form.

The New Era

24

The Roaring '20s
This 1926 cover of *Judge,* a popular humor magazine of the period, illustrates several aspects of the popular culture of the 1920s: the popularity of jazz music; the glittering night life of the urban middle class; and the uninhibited social activities of many women. Although these changes affected only a relatively small proportion of the population directly, they helped set the tone of the decade as one of rapid social modernization. (Culver Pictures)

"America's present need is not heroics, but healing; not nostrums, but normalcy." The year was 1920, and the speaker was Warren G. Harding, soon to become president of the United States. "The world needs to be reminded," he added, "that all human ills are not curable by legislation."

To many reformers at the time, the 1920s seemed to fulfill Warren Harding's vision of an end to the nation's long involvement with progressivism. An age of governmental activism and social dynamism was, it appeared, giving way to a decade of stagnant, materialistic conservatism. To other Americans, however, the 1920s represented something very different. Progressivism had not died, they believed. It had triumphed. The nation was at last building the stable, prosperous, organized social order of which progressives had long dreamed. The United States

had entered a "New Era" of limitless potential.

There was some truth in both views. Progressivism had always embodied two basic impulses: an idealistic, even humanitarian commitment to correcting social and economic injustices; and a harder, more pragmatic concern with order, efficiency, and process. The 1920s witnessed the debilitation of the former and the strengthening of the latter. The nation retreated noticeably from the progressive commitment to reform, which had become identified with radicalism and disorder. At the same time, however, America was making great strides toward fulfilling the progressive dream of national unity and consolidation. Far from being a stable, passive era, the 1920s were years of crucial political, economic, and cultural changes. As a result, they were also years of social turbulence and conflict.

REPUBLICAN GOVERNMENT

The federal government in the 1920s gave ample evidence of how progressivism had simultaneously increased its influence and narrowed its focus. Beginning in 1921, both the presidency and the Congress rested securely in the hands of the Republican party—a party in which the power of reformers had dwindled to almost nothing, a party with little interest in attacking social injustice and even less in attempting to curb corporate power. Yet the government of the New Era was more than the passive, pliant instrument that critics often described. It was in many respects an active and powerful agent of economic change.

Warren G. Harding

Nothing seemed more clearly to illustrate the death of crusading idealism in the 1920s than

the characters of the two men who served as president during most of the decade: Warren G. Harding and Calvin Coolidge.

Harding was elected to the presidency in 1920 having spent many years in public life doing absolutely nothing of note. He had advanced from the editorship of a newspaper in his hometown of Marion, Ohio, to the state legislature by virtue of his good looks, polished speaking style, and geniality. He had moved from there to the United States Senate as a result of his party regularity. And he had moved from there to the White House as a result of a political agreement among leaders of his party who considered him, as one noted, a "good second-rater."

The new president had few illusions about his own qualifications for office. Awed by his new responsibilities, he made sincere efforts to perform them with distinction. He appointed capable men to the most impor-

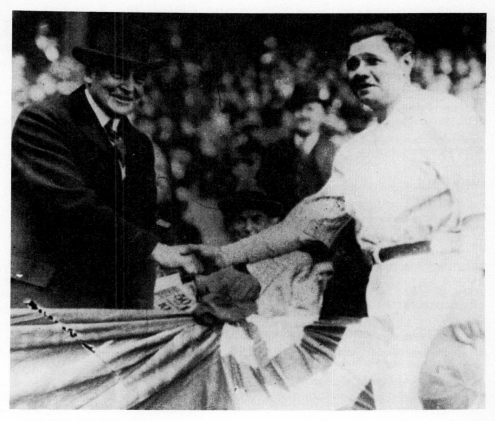

The President and the Babe
Two pleasure-loving heroes of the 1920s: President Warren G. Harding, whose
handsome geniality made him widely beloved until his death in 1923 and the
exposure shortly thereafter of widespread scandal within his administration;
and Babe Ruth, the "Sultan of Swat," whose popularity rested not only on his
record-setting hitting for the New York Yankees, but on his free-spirited life
style as well. (The Bettmann Archive)

tant cabinet offices; he attempted to stabilize
the nation's troubled foreign policy; and he
displayed on occasion a vigorous humanity,
as when he pardoned socialist Eugene V.
Debs in 1921. Even as he attempted to rise
to his office, however, he exhibited a sense of
bafflement about his situation, as if he recognized his own unfitness. "I am a man of limited talents from a small town," he
reportedly told friends on one occasion. "I
don't seem to grasp that I am President." Unsurprisingly, perhaps, Harding soon found
himself delegating much of his authority to
others: to members of his cabinet, to political
cronies, to Congress, to party leaders. In the

meantime, the nation's press, overwhelmingly Republican, was portraying him as a
wise and effective leader.

It was Harding's personal weaknesses
as much as his political naïveté that finally
resulted in his demise. He realized the importance of capable subordinates in an administration in which the president himself
was reluctant to act. At the same time, however, he lacked the strength to abandon the
party hacks who had helped create his political success. One of them, Harry Daugherty,
an Ohio party boss, he appointed attorney
general. Another, Albert B. Fall, he made secretary of the interior. Members of the so-

called Ohio Gang filled important offices throughout the administration. It was widely known within the government that the president's cronies led active, illicit social lives; that they gathered nightly at the famous "House on K Street" to drink illegal alcohol, play poker, and entertain attractive women; and that the president himself often joined in all these activities.

What remained for a time generally unknown was that Daugherty, Fall, and others were engaged in a widespread pattern of fraud and corruption. They sold government offices and favors, bribed congressmen and senators to support legislation favorable to their interests, and plundered the agencies and departments in which they worked of millions.

The most spectacular scandal involved the rich naval oil reserves at Teapot Dome, Wyoming, and Elk Hills, California. At the urging of Albert Fall, Harding transferred control of those reserves from the Navy Department to the Interior Department. Fall then secretly leased them to two wealthy businessmen—Harry F. Sinclair and Edward L. Doheny—and received in return nearly half a million dollars in "loans" to ease his private financial troubles. Fall was ultimately convicted of bribery and sentenced to a year in prison; Harry Daugherty barely avoided a similar fate for his part in another scandal.

For several years, apparently, Harding himself remained generally unaware of the rot infecting his administration. But by the summer of 1923, only months before Senate investigations and press revelations brought the scandals to light, he began to realize how desperate his situation had become. Tired and depressed, the president left Washington for a speaking tour in the West and a visit to Alaska. In Seattle late in July, he suffered severe pain, which his doctors diagnosed as food poisoning. A few days later, he seemed to rally and traveled on to San Francisco. There, on August 2, he died. He had suffered two major heart attacks.

Calvin Coolidge

In many ways, Calvin Coolidge, who succeeded to the presidency on the death of Harding, was utterly different from his predecessor. Where Harding was genial and garrulous, Coolidge was dour and silent. Where Harding adopted a loose, even debauched life style, Coolidge lived soberly and puritanically. And while Harding was, if not personally corrupt, then at least tolerant of corruption in others, Coolidge was honest beyond reproach. The image of stolid respectability that he projected was so unassailable that the Republican party managed to avoid any lasting damage from the Teapot Dome and related scandals. In other ways, however, Harding and Coolidge were similar figures. Both represented no soaring ideals but an unadventurous conservatism. Both took a passive approach to their office.

Like Harding, Coolidge rose to the presidency on the basis of virtually no substantive accomplishments. During his years in Massachusetts politics, he had won a reputation as a safe, trustworthy figure; and largely as a result of that, he had become governor in 1919. His response to the Boston police strike won him national attention and, in 1920, his party's vice-presidential nomination. Three years later, news of Harding's death reached him in Vermont; and there, by the light of a kerosene lamp on a kitchen table, he took the oath of office from his father, a justice of the peace.

If anything, Coolidge was an even less active president than Harding, partly as a result of his conviction that government should interfere as little as possible in the life of the nation and partly as a result of his own personal lassitude. He took long naps every afternoon. He kept official appointments to a minimum and engaged in almost no conversation with those who did manage to see him. He proposed no significant legislation and took little part in the running of the nation's foreign policy. "He aspired," wrote one of his contemporaries, "to become the least President the country ever had. He attained his desire."

In 1924, he received his party's presidential nomination virtually unopposed. Running against Democrat John W. Davis, a wealthy corporate lawyer who had served in the Wilson administration, he won a comfortable victory: 54 percent of the popular

Calvin Coolidge, 1925
Looking typically dour, Calvin Coolidge stands with government officials. Coolidge remained highly popular with the American people throughout the six years of his presidency despite—or perhaps because of—his reputation for silence. A joke famous in the 1920s told of a woman seated next to Coolidge at a dinner party who began her conversation by saying: "Mr. President, I made a bet with my friend that I could get you to say three words." Coolidge looked at her and replied: "You lose." (Culver Pictures)

ative, custodial view of the presidency clearly had the approval of the great majority of the American people. Four years later, it still did. The president could probably have won renomination and reelection easily in 1928. Instead, in characteristically laconic fashion, he walked into a press room one day and handed reporters a slip of paper containing a single sentence: "I do not choose to run." He retired from office a living symbol of the nation's disinterest in idealism and reform.

Government and Business

The story of Harding and Coolidge themselves, however, is only a part—and by no means the most important part—of the story of their administrations. However inert the New Era presidents may have been, much of the federal government was working effectively and efficiently during the 1920s to adapt public policy to the widely accepted goal of the time: helping business and industry to operate with maximum efficiency and productivity. The close relationship between the private sector and the federal government that had been forged during World War I continued. Indeed, government often seemed to have become an agent of private industry.

In the executive branch, the most active efforts came from members of the cabinet. Secretary of the Treasury Andrew Mellon, the extraordinarily wealthy steel and aluminum tycoon who became one of the most influential and respected figures in government, devoted himself to working for substantial reductions in taxes on corporate profits and personal incomes and inheritances. Largely because of his efforts, Congress cut them all by more than half, actions that redounded largely to the benefit of the wealthy. The result, Mellon claimed, would be to stimulate investment and ensure general prosperity. Mellon also worked closely with President Coolidge after 1924 on a series of measures to trim dramatically the already modest federal budget. The administration even managed to retire half of the nation's World War I debt.

The most prominent member of the cabinet was Commerce Secretary Herbert

vote and 382 of the 531 electoral votes. Robert La Follette, the candidate of the reincarnated Progressive party, received only 16 percent of the popular vote and carried only his home state of Wisconsin. Coolidge's neg-

Hoover, a man active in so many areas that he often seemed to be running the entire federal government single-handedly. He used his position to promote a better organized, more efficient national economy. Only thus, he claimed, could the nation hope to fulfill its most important task: the elimination of poverty. During his eight years in the Commerce Department, Hoover constantly encouraged voluntary cooperation in the private sector as the best avenue to stability. But the idea of voluntarism did not require the government to remain passive; on the contrary, public institutions, Hoover believed, had a duty to play an active role in creating the new, cooperative order. Above all, he became the champion of the concept of business associationalism, a concept that envisioned the creation of national organizations of businessmen in particular industries. Through such trade associations, private entrepreneurs could, Hoover believed, stabilize their industries and promote efficiency in production and marketing. Hoover strongly resisted those who urged that the government sanction collusion among manufacturers to fix prices, arguing that competition was essential to a prosperous economy. He did, however, believe that shared information and limited cooperation would keep that competition from becoming destructive and thus improve the strength of the economy as a whole.

This combination of open, unembarrassed enthusiasm for the business community and a sober devotion to the principles of centralized and efficient management found reflection in other areas of government in the 1920s. The regulatory commissions, for example, had in the prewar era made at least token efforts to restrict the power of private enterprise. In the 1920s, particularly as Harding and Coolidge filled them with members of the very businesses they were supposed to regulate, the agencies began to believe that their role was not to regulate industry but to assist it. The Interstate Commerce Commission, for example, openly helped railroad companies to negotiate lucrative contracts with shippers. Meetings to discuss these agreements often took place in the offices of the commissioner himself.

The Supreme Court in the 1920s further confirmed the business orientation of the federal government, particularly after the appointment of William Howard Taft as chief justice in 1921. The Court struck down federal legislation regulating child labor (*Bailey* v. *Drexel Furniture Company*, 1922); it nullified a minimum wage law for women in the District of Columbia (*Adkins* v. *Children's Hospital*, 1923); and it sanctioned the creation of trade associations, ruling in *U.S.* v. *Maple Flooring Association* (1925) that such organizations did not violate antitrust statutes as long as some competition survived within an industry. Five years earlier, in *United States* v. *U.S. Steel*, the Court had applied the same doctrine to the monopolistic United States Steel Corporation; there was no illegal "restraint of trade," it ruled, as long as U.S. Steel continued to face any competition, no matter how slight.

The probusiness policies of the Republican administrations were not without their critics. There survived in Congress throughout the 1920s a large and influential group of progressive reformers of the old school, whose vision of public power as an antidote to private privilege remained very much alive. They continued to criticize the monopolistic practices of big business, to attack government's alliance with the corporate community, to decry social injustices, and to call for economic reform. Occasionally they were able to mobilize enough support to win congressional approval of progressive legislation, most notably an important scheme to assist farmers in marketing their goods (the McNary-Haugen Bill) and an ambitious proposal to use federal funds to develop public power projects on the Tennessee River at Muscle Shoals. But clearly, the progressive reformers were no longer the dominant force in American political life. When the president vetoed the legislation they had promoted, as he almost always did, they lacked the strength to override him. No longer was there a national consensus on behalf of reform.

Critics of American foreign policy in the New Era often used a single word to describe the cause of their disenchantment: isolationism. Having rejected the Wilsonian vision of a new world order, the nation had, many charged, turned its back on the rest of the globe and taken no active role in international affairs. In fact, quite the opposite was the case. The United States did indeed refuse to participate in most efforts to promote international cooperation and collective security. It did so, however, not because it wanted to isolate itself from world affairs but because it wanted to participate in them on its own terms. There would, Americans believed, be a new world order. But it would be one shaped and dominated by the United States.

Replacing the League

It was clear when the Harding administration took office in 1921 that American membership in the League of Nations was no longer a realistic possibility. As if finally to bury the issue, Secretary of State Charles Evans Hughes promptly secured from Congress legislation declaring the war with Germany at an end and then proceeded to negotiate separate peace treaties with the former Central Powers. Through these treaties, American policymakers believed, the United States would receive all the advantages of the Versailles Treaty with none of the burdensome responsibilities. Hughes was, however, committed to finding something to replace the League as a guarantor of world peace and stability. He embarked, therefore, on a series of efforts to build safeguards against future wars—but safeguards that would not hamper American freedom of action in the world.

The most important of such efforts was the Washington Conference of 1921, an attempt to prevent what was promising to become a costly and destabilizing naval armaments race among America, Britain, and Japan. Hughes startled the delegates by proposing in his opening speech a plan for dramatic reductions in the fleets of all three nations and a ten-year moratorium on the construction of large warships. He envisioned the actual scrapping of nearly 2 million tons of existing ships. Even more surprising than the proposal, perhaps, was that the conference ultimately agreed to accept most of its terms. The Five-Power Pact of February 1922 established both the limits for total naval tonnage and a ratio of armaments among the signatories. For every five tons of American and British warships, Japan would maintain three and France and Italy 1.75 each. (Although the treaty seemed to confirm the military inferiority of Japan, in fact it sanctioned Japanese dominance in East Asia. America and Britain had to spread their fleets across the globe; Japan was concerned only with the Pacific.) The Washington Conference also produced two other, related treaties: the Nine-Power Pact, pledging a continuation of the Open Door Policy in China, and the Four-Power Pact, by which the United States, Britain, France, and Japan promised to respect one another's Pacific territories and cooperate to prevent aggression.

The Washington Conference began the New Era effort to protect the peace without accepting active international duties. The Kellogg-Briand Pact of 1928 concluded it. When the French foreign minister, Aristide Briand, asked the United States in 1927 to join an alliance against a resurgent Germany, Secretary of State Frank Kellogg (who had replaced Hughes in 1925) proposed instead a multilateral treaty outlawing war as an instrument of national policy. Fourteen nations signed the agreement in Paris on August 27, 1928, amid great solemnity and wide international acclaim. Forty-eight other nations later joined the pact. It contained no instruments of enforcement but rested, as Kellogg put it, on the "moral force" of world opinion. Some critics would later ridicule it as an "international kiss," but to the American people (and many others) at the time, it was a triumph of peaceful diplomacy.

Business and Diplomacy

The first responsibility of diplomacy, Hughes, Kellogg, and others agreed, was to ensure that American overseas trade faced no obstacles to expansion and that, once established, it would remain free of interference. Preventing a dangerous armaments race and reducing the possibility of war were two steps to that end. So were new financial arrangements that emerged at the same time. Most important to the United States was Europe, upon whose economic health American prosperity in large part depended. Not only were the major industrial powers there suffering from the devastation of war, they were also staggering under a heavy burden of debt. The Allied powers were struggling to repay $11 billion in loans they had contracted with the United States during and shortly after the war, loans that the Republican administrations were unwilling to reduce or forgive. "They hired the money, didn't they?" Calvin Coolidge replied when queried about the debts. At the same time, an even more debilitated Germany was attempting to pay the enormous reparations levied against it by the Allies. With the financial structure of Europe on the brink of collapse as a result, the United States stepped in with a solution.

Charles B. Dawes, an American banker, negotiated an agreement in 1924 among France, Britain, Germany, and the United States under which American banks would provide enormous loans to the Germans, enabling them to meet their reparations payments; in return, Britain and France would agree to reduce the amount of those payments. The Dawes Plan became the centerpiece of a growing American economic presence in Germany. It also became the source of a troubling circular pattern in international finance. America would loan money to Germany, which would use that money to pay reparations to France and England, which would in turn use those funds to repay war debts to the United States. The flow was able to continue only by virtue of the enormous debts Germany was acquiring to American banks and corporations.

Those banks and corporations were doing more than providing loans. They were becoming a daily presence in the economic life of Europe. American automobile manufacturers were opening European factories, capturing a large share of the overseas market. Other industries were establishing in the 1920s subsidiaries worth more than $10 billion throughout the Continent, taking advantage of the devastation of European industry and the inability of domestic corporations to recover. Some groups within the American government warned that the reckless expansion of overseas loans and investments, many in enterprises of dubious value, threatened disaster; that the United States was becoming too dependent on unstable European econmies. The high tariff barriers that the Republican Congress erected (through the Fordney-McCumber Act of 1922) created additional problems, such skeptics warned. European nations unable to export their goods to the United States would find it difficult to earn the money necessary to repay their loans. Such warnings fell, for the most part, on deaf ears; and American economic expansion in Europe continued until disaster struck after 1929.

The federal government felt even fewer reservations about assisting American economic expansion in Latin America. The United States had, after all, long considered that region its exclusive sphere of influence; and its investments there had become large even before World War I. During the 1920s, American military forces maintained a presence in numerous countries in the region, despite Hughes's withdrawal of troops from the Dominican Republic and Nicaragua. United States investments in the region more than doubled between 1924 and 1929; American corporations built roads and other facilities in many areas, partly, they argued, to weaken the appeal of revolutionary forces in the region, but at least equally to assist their own exploitation of Latin America's rich natural resources. American banks were offering large loans to Latin American governments, just as they were in Europe; and just as in Europe, the Latin Americans were having great difficulty earning the money to repay them in the face of the formidable United States tariff barrier. By the end of the 1920s, resentment of "Yankee imperialism" was already reaching alarming proportions; the economic troubles after 1929 would only accentuate such problems.

THE NATIONAL ECONOMY

Both at home and across the globe, the federal government was actively engaged in promoting the interests of American business. The recipients of this attention did much to justify such efforts, for the American economy in the 1920s had become one of the wonders of the world. After the recession of 1921–1922, the United States began a period of almost uninterrupted prosperity and economic growth. At the same time, the nation continued the process of organization and consolidation that was reshaping the structure of American economic life.

Economic Performance

No one could deny the remarkable, some believed miraculous, feats that the American economy was performing in the 1920s. The nation's manufacturing output rose by more than 60 percent during the decade; the gross national product increased at an average of 5 percent a year; output per worker rose by more than 33 percent. Inflation was negligible. Reliable unemployment figures are not available, but most estimates suggest that only a little over 2 percent of the work force was jobless during most of the decade. Per capita income increased from $522 in 1921 to $716 in 1929. A mild recession in 1923 momentarily interrupted the pattern of growth; but when it subsided early in 1924, the economy expanded with even greater vigor than before.

The economic boom was a result of many things. The most obvious cause, perhaps, was the debilitation of Europe after World War I, leaving the United States for a time the only truly healthy industrial power in the world. The economy benefited as well from benign government policies at home and abroad: protective tariffs, favorable tax schedules, the easing of regulatory and antitrust pressures, aggressive policies to open and protect international markets. Most important, however, was the emergence of new industries or the expansion of older ones within the United States itself. The automobile industry, for example, grew from a relatively modest size

in the years before the war to become one of the most important forces in the nation's economy. Americans bought 1.5 million cars in 1921; in 1929 they purchased more than 5 million. Expansion in one industry meant, of course, expansion in others. Auto manufacturers purchased the products of steel, rubber, glass, and tool companies. Auto owners bought gasoline from the oil corporations. Road construction in response to the proliferation of motor vehicles became itself an important industry. The increased mobility that the automobile afforded increased the demand for suburban housing, fueling a boom in the construction industry. Other new industries—electronics, motion pictures, airplanes, home appliances—contributed as well to the economic growth.

Technological advances made possible much of this expansion. The modern assembly line, which Henry Ford had first introduced shortly before the war, was vital not only to the automobile industry but to many others. So were countless other new production techniques, many of them developed during the war. Improved methods of extraction and transportation made greater supplies of more varied raw materials available. Cheap, readily available energy—from newly discovered oil reserves, from the expanded network of electric power, and from the nation's abundant coal fields—further enhanced the ability of industry to produce. Improvements in management techniques also played a role in increasing productivity. More and more industries were subscribing to the "scientific-management" theories of Frederick Winslow Taylor, making deliberate efforts to improve the efficiency of their operations.

Economic Organization

The quest for improved efficiency in industry was only part of a larger trend. American business in the 1920s was making rapid strides toward national organization and consolidation. The process had begun, of course, decades before; but the New Era witnessed

At Work on the Empire State Building Symbolic of the exuberant self-confidence of American business in the 1920s was the rapid construction of huge new skyscrapers to house the offices of modern corporations. This construction worker sits astride a beam of the rising Empire State Building, completed in 1931, which remained the world's tallest building until the late 1960s. (International Center for Photography, George Eastman House)

an acceleration of such trends. By the end of the decade, 8,000 small mining and manufacturing companies had been swallowed up into larger combinations; 5,000 utilities had disappeared, most of them into great holding companies. Local merchants foundered and vanished as national chain stores cornered more than a quarter of the nation's food, apparel, and general merchandise markets. In some industries, power resided in so few firms that competition had all but vanished. U.S. Steel, the nation's largest corporation, controlled its industry almost alone; its dominance was suggested by the widely accepted use of the term "Little Steel" to refer to all of its competitors combined.

The consolidation of the economy was accomplished in various ways. Great cor-

porations, adopting new management structures, expanded to control not only a large proportion of their own industries but many related (and ultimately even unrelated) industries as well. General Motors, which was by 1920 not only the largest automobile manufacturer but the fifth largest American corporation, was a classic example. Under the leadership of Alfred P. Sloan, GM developed a modern administrative system that replaced a chaotic management structure with an efficient divisional organization. With the new management in place, not only was it easier for GM to control its many subsidiaries; it was also a simpler matter for it— and for the many other corporations who adopted similar administrative systems—to expand further. Other industries proved less susceptible or more resistant to domination by a few great corporations. Nevertheless, even those characterized by the survival of a great number of relatively small companies often experienced their own consolidation. An important vehicle was the trade association—a form of national organization promoted by Hoover and others to permit central coordination of an industry.

Labor's Dilemma

The remarkable economic growth was only one side of the American economy in the 1920s. The other was the severe maldistribution of wealth that persisted and in some respects even increased during the decade. New Era prosperity was real enough, but it was restricted to a minority of the population. More than two-thirds of the American people in 1929 lived at no better than what one study described as the "minimum comfort level." Half of those languished at or below the level of "subsistence and poverty." Large segments of the society remained unable to organize, and they found themselves without sufficient power to protect their economic interests.

American labor experienced both the benefits and the deficiencies of the 1920s as much as any other group. On the one hand, most workers saw their standard of living rise during the decade; many enjoyed greatly improved working conditions and other benefits. At the same time, however, laborers received wage increases that were proportionately far below the increases in corporate profits; and they worked in a climate unremittingly hostile to unionization.

The improvements in wages and working conditions were impossible to ignore. Employers in the 1920s, eager to avoid disruptive labor unrest and forestall the growth of unions, adopted paternalistic techniques that came to be known as "welfare capitalism." Industrialists such as Henry Ford shortened the work week for their employees and instituted paid vacations. Manufacturers such as U.S. Steel spent millions of dollars installing safety devices and improving sanitation in the workplace. Most important, perhaps,

many employers offered their workers substantial raises in pay and other financial benefits. Real wages for laborers increased 26 percent between 1919 and 1929. By 1926, nearly 3 million industrial workers were eligible for pensions on retirement. In some companies, employees were permitted to buy stock at below market value. When labor grievances surfaced despite these efforts, workers could voice them through the so-called company unions that were emerging in many industries—workers' councils and shop committees, organized by the corporation itself, through which employees could demand improvements in benefits and working conditions.

Yet for all the undoubted benefits that welfare capitalism provided, American workers remained in the 1920s a relatively impoverished and powerless group. Their wages had risen; but the average annual income of a worker remained below $1,500 a year at a time when $1,800 was considered necessary to maintain a minimally decent standard of living. In some industries, such as coal mining and textiles, hours remained long and wages rose scarcely at all. Company unions may have been psychologically comforting, but they were for the most part feeble vehicles for demanding benefits. In most companies, the workers' councils were forbidden to deal with questions of wages and hours. Nor could workers do very much to counter the effects of technological unemployment. Total factory employment increased hardly at all during the 1920s, even while manufacturing output was soaring.

Some laborers continued to regard an effective union movement as the best hope for improving their position. But the New Era was a bleak time for labor organization. Part of the blame lay with the workers themselves, many of whom were seduced by the benefits of welfare capitalism and displayed no interest in organizing. Even more of the blame rested with the unions, which failed to adapt to the realities of the modern economy. The conservative American Federation of Labor remained wedded to the concept of the craft union, in which workers were organized on the basis of particular skills. In the meantime, a huge new segment of the work force was emerging: unskilled industrial workers, many of them immigrants from southern or eastern Europe. They received little sympathy or attention from the craft unions and found themselves, as a result, with no organizations to join. The A.F. of L., moreover, remained throughout the 1920s painfully timid about supporting strikes—partly in reaction to the disastrous setbacks it had suffered in 1919. William Green, who became president of the organization in 1924, was committed to peaceful cooperation with employers and strident opposition to communism and socialism.

However much the workers and unions themselves contributed to the weakness of the labor movement, corporate and government policies contributed more. If welfare capitalism was the carrot for inducing workers to accept the status quo, the antiunion policies of most industrialists constituted the stick. Corporate leaders worked hard after the turmoil of 1919 to spread the doctrine that unionism was somehow subversive and un-American, that a crucial element of democratic capitalism was the protection of the open shop (a shop in which no worker could be required to join a union). The crusade for the open shop, euphemistically titled the "American Plan," received the endorsement of the National Association of Manufacturers in 1920 and became a pretext for a harsh campaign of union busting across the country. When such tactics proved insufficient to counter union power, government assistance often made the difference. In 1921, the Supreme Court declared picketing illegal and upheld the right of lower courts to issue injunctions against strikers. In 1922, the Justice Department intervened to quell a strike by 400,000 railroad workers. In 1924, legal agencies refused protection to members of the United Mine Workers Union when mine owners launched a violent campaign in western Pennsylvania to drive the union from the coal fields.

The result of all these factors was that union membership suffered a serious decline in the 1920s. Union membership as a whole fell from more than 5 million in 1920 to about 4.3 million in 1929. Not until the mid-

1930s, when a combination of increased labor militancy and active government assistance added strength to the labor movement, would the antiunion syndrome be broken.

The Plight of the Farmer

Despite their other setbacks, many American workers gained at least an increase in income during the 1920s. In contrast, most American farmers of the New Era experienced only decline. Agriculture, like industry, was discovering the advantages of the new technology for increasing production. The number of tractors at work on American farms, for example, quadrupled during the 1920s, helping to open 35 million new acres to cultivation. But while the increases in industrial production were matched by increases in consumer demand, the expansion of agricultural production was not. The European market for American foodstuffs contracted rapidly after the war, when European agriculture began to resume production. At the same time, domestic demand for food rose only slightly. The result was a disastrous decline in food prices and thus a severe drop in income for farmers. The average annual income for Americans not engaged in agriculture in 1929 was $870. For farmers, it was $223. In 1920, farm income had been 15 percent of the national total; by 1929, it was 9 percent. More than 3 million people left agriculture altogether in the course of the decade. Of those who remained, an alarming number were forced into tenancy—losing ownership of their lands and having to rent instead from banks or other landlords.

In response, farmers began to demand government relief. A few gravitated to such vaguely radical organizations as the Nonpartisan League of North Dakota or its successor, the Farmer-Labor party, which established a foothold as well in Minnesota and other Midwestern states. Most farmers, however, adopted a more moderate approach, agitating for a restoration and strengthening of government price supports. Through such organizations as the Farm Bureau Federation, they put increasing pressure on Con-

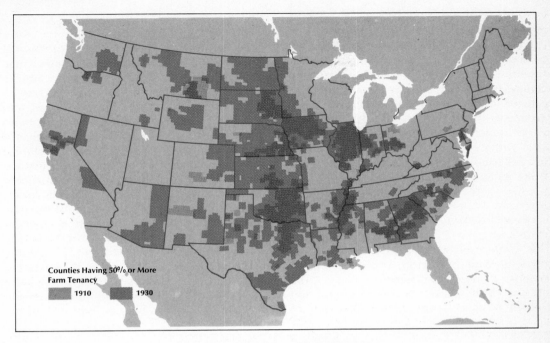

FARM TENANCY, 1910 AND 1930

gress (where farmers continued to enjoy disproportionately high representation); and while reform sentiment in most other areas made little headway in the 1920s, the movement for agrarian reform rapidly gathered strength.

One price-raising scheme in particular came to dominate agrarian demands: the idea of parity. "Parity" referred to a price for crops determined by a complicated formula. The parity price of agricultural goods was to reflect what farmers called a "fair exchange formula," which was based on the average price of the crop during the decade preceding the war as compared with the general average of all prices during the same period. Its purpose was to ensure that farmers would earn back at least their production costs no matter how the national or world agricultural market might fluctuate. The government would guarantee parity to farmers in two ways: first, by maintaining a high tariff barrier against foreign competition, thus ena-

bling American agriculture to sustain high prices at home; second, by buying up any surplus crops at parity and selling them abroad at whatever the world market would bring. An "equalization fee"—that is, a general tax on all crops—would compensate the government for any loss while spreading the burden evenly among all farmers.

The legislative expression of the demand for parity was the McNary-Haugen bill, named after its two principal sponsors in Congress and introduced repeatedly between 1924 and 1928. In 1924, a bill requiring parity only for grain failed in the House. Two years later, with cotton, tobacco, and rice added to win Southern support, the measure passed, only to fall victim to a veto by President Coolidge. In 1928, it won congressional approval again, only to succumb to another presidential veto. Despite the farmers' impressive political strength, as long as agrarian problems did not seem to affect the general prosperity there was little hope for reform.

THE NEW CULTURE

The 1920s were notable not only for prosperity and the triumph of the business civilization but for a series of profound cultural changes: changes in the way people lived and thought. Americans of the New Era were beginning to live their lives and perceive their world in increasingly similar ways; and they were being exposed to a new set of values that reflected the prosperity and complexity of the modern economy.

Consumerism

The United States of the 1920s was for the first time becoming a true consumer society—a society in which not only the affluent but many ordinary men and women bought items not just because of need but for the sheer pleasure of buying. What they bought, moreover, helped change the way they lived. Middle-class families rushed to purchase such new appliances as electric refrigerators, washing machines, and vacuum cleaners. Men wore wristwatches and smoked cigarettes; women purchased cosmetics and mass-produced fashions. Americans in every part of the country ate commercially processed foods distributed nationally through chain stores and supermarkets. The clearest illustration of the new consumerism was the frenzied excitement with which Americans greeted the automobile, which was in the 1920s becoming more widely available and affordable than ever before. By the end of the decade, there were more than 30 million cars on American roads. Automobiles had, in the process, be-

The Automobile Culture
The expanding importance of the automobile, both to the American economy and to the nation's life style, is suggested by this 1925 photo of the parking lot of a Massachusetts beach. (Wide World Photos)

come not just a means of transportation but the first great national consumer obsession.

No group was more aware of the emergence of consumerism (or more responsible for creating it) than a new and growing sector of the economy: the advertising industry. The first advertising and public relations firms (N. W. Ayer and J. Walter Thompson) had appeared well before World War I; but it was in the 1920s, partly as a result of techniques pioneered by wartime propaganda, that advertising truly came of age. Publicists began to see themselves as more than purveyors of information. They viewed themselves, rather, as agents of the growing American economy; and they advertised products by attempting to invest them with glamor and prestige. They also encouraged the public to absorb the values of promotion and salesmanship and to admire those who were effective "boosters" and publicists. One of the most successful books of the 1920s was the work of an advertising executive, Bruce Barton. In *The Man Nobody Knows*, Barton drew a portrait of Jesus Christ, describing him less as a religious prophet than as a "super salesman" who "picked up twelve men from the bottom ranks of business and forged them into an organization that conquered the world." The parables, Barton argued, were "the most powerful advertisements of all time." Perhaps the most telling indication of how clearly Barton's image mirrored popular assumptions was that virtually no one objected to the book as sacrilegious or offensive. Most considered the portrait a flattering one.

National Communications

The advertising industry could never have had the impact it did but for the emergence of new vehicles of communication that made it possible to reach large audiences quickly and easily. Some such vehicles were traditional media in changing guises. Newspapers and magazines, for example, were undergoing an important transformation. The number of local newspapers was shrinking rapidly; and those that survived were often becoming members of great national chains—which meant that readers in widely

scattered cities were reading identical material in their newspapers. There was, as well, a growing number of national, mass-circulation magazines—*Time, Life, Reader's Digest*—aimed at the widest possible audience. Fewer and fewer sources of information were servicing larger and larger groups of people.

Even more influential in shaping the popular culture of the 1920s was the popularity of the movies. They too were not new, but they were expanding greatly. Over 100 million people saw films in 1930, as compared to only 40 million in 1922. The addition of sound to motion pictures, beginning with the first "talkie" in 1927, *The Jazz Singer* with Al Jolson, created nationwide excitement. All across the nation, Americans were watching the same films, idolizing the same screen stars, and absorbing the same set of messages and values.

The most important communications vehicle of all, however, was the only one that was truly new to the 1920s: radio. The first radio station in America, KDKA in Pittsburgh, began broadcasting on election night in 1920; and the first national radio network, the National Broadcasting Company, took form in 1927. By 1923, there were more than 500 radio stations, covering virtually every area of the country; by 1929, more than 12 million families owned radio sets. Broadcasting became, therefore, the ultimate vehicle for linking the nation together, providing Americans everywhere with instant access to a common source of information and entertainment.

One result of the communications revolution was that America became in the 1920s a society in which fads and obsessions could emerge suddenly and powerfully. Radio helped elevate professional sports, and in particular professional baseball, from the level of limited local activities to that of a national craze. Men and women across the country shared a pleasure in popular stunts—flagpole sitting, marathon dancing, goldfish swallowing. They shared an interest in national sensations, such as the tortuous progress of the Sacco-Vanzetti case. It is not surprising that Frederick Lewis Allen, the celebrated chronicler of the 1920s, referred to the decade as the "Ballyhoo Years."

The New Medium
The changing leisure activities of the 1920s are depicted in this picture of two generations of a middle-class family seated in a parlor. While the parents indulge in traditional evening activities—reading a newspaper or book—the children enjoy one of the technological innovations of the New Era as they listen through earphones to an early radio set. (UPI)

Modern Religion

It was not only fads that were engaging the attention of the nation. Americans in the 1920s were being exposed as well to a wide range of new standards of thought and behavior, and their own values and life styles were changing as a result. Such changes affected some of the nation's most basic institutions, among them religion. The scientific advances of the late nineteenth and early twentieth centuries had by the 1920s already produced profound changes in American theology. Protestant clergymen in particular had revised religious doctrine to reconcile traditional faith with the theories of Charles Darwin. Ministers in the progressive era had played an important role in promoting social

issues; churches had become not only centers of worship but agents of reform. After World War I, the increasing secularism of American society worked even further changes on both religious faith and religious behavior. Theological modernists, among them Harry Emerson Fosdick and A. C. McGiffert, taught their followers to abandon many of the traditional trappings of religion (literal interpretation of the Bible, belief in the Trinity, attribution of human traits to the deity) and to accept a faith that many believed was only one step removed from agnosticism.

The extremes of religious modernism found acceptance among only a relatively few people. Changes in popular religious assumptions and patterns were, however, widespread. The sociologists Robert and

Helen Lynd discovered during a study of community life in Muncie, Indiana, for example, that while most people continued to attend church and express a belief in God, they also were experiencing important changes. Fewer people seemed to believe in hell; many admitted that they "think of Heaven less than they used to." "One infers," the Lynds reported in their famous study *Middletown* (1929), "that doubts and uneasiness among individuals may be greater than a generation ago." Religion, which had for centuries been one of the most powerful forces in American life, was beginning to occupy a secondary place in the daily lives of many members of the middle class.

Women and the Family

Even greater changes were occurring in the structure and behavior of the family—changes in the role of women and the concept of marriage. Technological advances had long ago released many middle-class women from some of the burdens of housework; new, more advanced appliances in the 1920s speeded that liberation even further. Other factors produced additional changes. American society in the first years of the twentieth century had placed a high value on the idea of motherhood, on the belief that a woman's mission was to bear and raise children, on the assumption that women were uniquely and instinctively qualified for parenthood. After World War I, however, an influential group of psychologists—the "behaviorists," led by John B. Watson—began to challenge such assumptions. Maternal affection was not, they claimed, sufficient preparation for child rearing. Instead, mothers should rely on the advice and assistance of experts and professionals: doctors, nurses, and trained educators in nursery schools and kindergartens.

For many middle-class women, these changes removed what had been an important and consuming activity. They were no longer required to spend endless hours engaged in housework; now they were finding that motherhood occupied far less time as well. Clearly, women needed to discover new activities, a new role to fill the void. For some, that role became entry into a profession. Women in the 1920s were doing far more than those of any previous generation to win for themselves positions in the economic mainstream; in some professions in particular—fashion, publishing, cosmetics, social work, nursing, education—they were making major inroads.

Most women, however, avoided professional activities, discouraged by the historic prejudice against females entering careers. Instead, they devoted new attention to their roles as wives and companions. A woman's relationship with her husband assumed, therefore, a greatly enhanced importance. Women increasingly shared in their husbands' social lives; they devoted attention to cosmetics and seductive clothing in an effort to please their husbands; they tried to prevent children from interfering with the development of marital relationships. Most of all, perhaps, they were encouraged to think of their sexual relationships with their husbands not simply as a means of procreation, as earlier generations had been taught, but as an important and pleasurable experience in its own right, as the culmination of romantic love. Thus it was that the 1920s saw the emergence of a national birth-control movement, pioneered by Margaret Sanger. Women should, Sanger argued, be free to enjoy the pleasures of sexual activity without relation to the bearing of children.

These changes combined to produce among many women a great sense of liberation. No longer did they feel required to maintain a rigid, Victorian "respectability." They were free to adopt far less inhibited life styles. They could smoke, drink, dance, wear seductive clothes and make-up, and attend lively parties. The popular image of the "flapper"—the modern woman whose liberated life style found expression in dress, hair style, speech, and behavior—became one of the most widely discussed features of the era.

But the changes came, too, at great cost. By placing more and more emphasis on their relationships with men, women were increasing their vulnerability to frustration and unhappiness when those relationships proved unsatisfactory. It was not surprising, perhaps, that the national divorce rate climbed dramatically in the 1920s; nor that many women who remained married experienced boredom and restlessness.

Education and Youth

The growing secularism of American culture and the emphasis on training and expertise were clearly reflected in the changing role of education, which was beginning to occupy an increasingly important role in the lives of American youths. The changes were evident in numerous ways. First, more people were going to school in the 1920s than ever before. High-school attendance more than doubled during the decade: from 2.2 million to over 5 million. Enrollment in colleges and universities increased threefold between 1900 and 1930, with much of that increase occurring after World War I. In 1918, there had been 600,000 college students; in 1930, there were 1.2 million, nearly 20 percent of the college-age population. Attendance was increasing as well at trade and vocational schools and in other institutions providing the specialized training that the modern economy demanded. Schools were, in addition, beginning to perform new and more varied functions. Instead of offering simply the traditional disciplines, they were providing training in modern technical skills: engineering, management, economics.

The growing importance of education was contributing as well to the emergence of a separate youth culture. The idea of adolescence as a distinct period in the life of an individual was for the most part new to the twentieth century. It was a result in some measure of the influence of Freudian psychology. But it was a result, too, of society's recognition that a more extended period of training and preparation was necessary before a young person was ready to move into the workplace. Schools and colleges provided adolescents with a setting in which they could develop their own social patterns, their own hobbies, their own interests and activities. An increasing number of students saw school as a place not just for academic training but for organized athletics, extracurricular activities, clubs, fraternities, and sororities; that is, as an institution that allowed them to define themselves less in terms of their families and more in terms of their peer group.

The Decline of the Self-Made Man

Most of all, however, the increasing importance of education and the changing nature of adolescence underscored one of the most important changes in American society: the gradual disappearance of both the reality and the ideal of the self-made man. The belief that any person could, simply through hard work and innate talent, achieve wealth and renown had always been largely a myth; but it had had enough basis in reality to remain a convincing myth for generations. By the 1920s, however, it was becoming difficult to believe any longer that success was possible without education and training. "The self-made manager in business," wrote *Century Magazine* in 1925, "is nearing the end of his road. He cannot escape the relentless pursuit of the same forces that have eliminated self-made lawyers and doctors and admirals."

The "Doom of the Self-Made Man," as *Century* described it, was a difficult development for Americans to accept. It suggested that individuals were no longer entirely in control of their own destinies, that a person's future depended in large part on factors over which he or she had only limited control. And like many of the other changes of the decade, many Americans greeted this one with marked ambivalence. These mixed feelings were reflected in the identity of three men who became the most widely admired heroes of the New Era: Thomas Edison, the inventor of the electric light bulb and many other technological marvels; Henry Ford, the creator of the assembly line and one of the founders of the automobile industry; and Charles Lindbergh, the first aviator to make a solo flight across the Atlantic Ocean. All received the adulation of much of the American public. Lindbergh, in particular, became a national hero the like of which the country had never seen before. And the reasons for their popularity indicated much about how

Lucky Lindy
Charles A. Lindbergh—
the greatest hero of the
1920s—is shown wear-
ing aviation gear in one
of the most widely
published photographs
in the world. Lind-
bergh's popularity was
such that when, in
1928, he endorsed Her-
bert Hoover for presi-
dent, the Republicans
adopted a campaign
song entitled "If He's
Good Enough for
Lindy, He's Good
Enough for Me." (UPI)

Americans viewed the new epoch in which they were living. On the one hand, all three men represented the triumphs of the modern technological and industrial society. On the other hand, all three had risen to success without the benefit of formal education and largely through their own private efforts. They were, it seemed, genuinely self-made men. Even many Americans who were happily embracing a new society and a new culture were doing so without entirely diverting their gaze from a simpler past.

The Disenchanted

To a generation of artists and intellectuals coming of age in the 1920s, the new society in which they lived was even more disturbing. They were experiencing a disenchantment with modern America so fundamental that they were often able to view it only with contempt. As a result, they adopted a role sharply different from that of most intellectuals of other eras. Rather than involving themselves with their society's popular culture and attempting to influence and reform the mass of their countrymen, they isolated themselves and embarked on a restless search for personal fulfillment. Gertrude Stein once referred to the young Americans emerging from World War I as a "lost generation." For many writers and intellectuals, at least, it was an apt description.

At the heart of the Lost Generation's critique of modern society was a sense of personal alienation, a belief that contemporary America no longer provided the individual with avenues by which he could achieve personal fulfillment. Modern life, they argued, was cold, impersonal, materialistic, and thus meaningless. The sensitive individual could find no happiness in the mainstream of American society.

This disillusionment had its roots in many things, but in nothing so deeply as the experience of World War I. To those who had fought in France and experienced the horror and savagery of modern warfare—and even to those who had not fought but who nevertheless had been aware of the appalling costs of the struggle—the aftermath of the conflict was shattering. Nothing, it seemed, had been gained. The war had been a fraud; the suffering and the dying had been in vain. Ernest Hemingway, one of the most cele-

brated (and most commercially successful) of the new breed of writers, expressed their contempt for the war in his novel *A Farewell to Arms* (1929). Its hero, an American officer fighting in Europe, decides that there is no justification for his participation in the conflict and deserts the army with a nurse with whom he has fallen in love. Hemingway made it clear that he was to be admired for doing so.

At least equally dispiriting was the character of the nation these young intellectuals found on their return home at war's end. It was, they believed, a society utterly lacking in vision or idealism, obsessed with materialism, steeped in outmoded, priggish morality. Worst of all, it was one in which the individual had lost the ability to control his or her own fate. It was a sleek, new, industrialized and professionalized world that was organized in a dehumanizing way.

H. L. Mencken [1933]

As columnist for the Baltimore Sun, *and especially as editor of the* Smart Set *and the* American Mercury, *Mencken exercised great influence for the fifteen years following World War I. Often regarded as an iconoclast whose values were purely negative, Mencken actually used the grace and taste of the eighteenth-century aristocracy as a standard to condemn the "booboisie" he saw around him. Outstanding for his pioneering studies of the American language, for his opposition to censorship and prohibition, and for his championing of such writers as Joseph Conrad, Theodore Dreiser, and Ring Lardner, he wrote a virile and sinewy prose. His wit (and his scorn for American politicians) shows in his obituary for Calvin Coolidge, published in April 1933:*

In what manner he would have performed himself if the holy angels had shoved the Depression forward a couple of years—this we can only guess, and one man's hazard is as good as another's. My own is that he would have responded to bad times precisely as he responded to good ones—that is, by pulling down the blinds, stretching his legs upon his desk, and snoozing away the lazy afternoons. . . . He slept more than any other President, whether by day or by night. Nero fiddled, but Coolidge only snored. . . . Counting out Harding as a cipher only, Dr. Coolidge was preceded by one World Saver and followed by two more. What enlightened American, having to choose between any of them and another Coolidge, would hesitate for an instant? There were no thrills while he reigned, but neither were there any headaches. He had no ideas, and he was not a nuisance.

One result of this alienation was a series of savage critiques of modern society by a wide range of writers, some of whom were often described as the "debunkers." Most influential was the Baltimore journalist H. L. Mencken, a man somewhat older than many of the new intellectuals (he was forty years old in 1920), but one who served as a spokesman for the Lost Generation nevertheless. In the pages of his magazines, first the *Smart Set* and later the *American Mercury*, he delighted in ridiculing everything Americans held dear: religion, politics, the arts, even democracy itself. He found it impossible to believe, he claimed, that "civilized life was possible under a democracy," because it was a form of government that placed power in the hands of the common people, whom he ridiculed as the "booboisie." When someone asked Mencken why he continued to live in a society he found so loathsome, he replied: "Why do people go to the zoo?"

Echoing Mencken's contempt was the novelist Sinclair Lewis, the first American to win a Nobel Prize in literature. In a series of savage novels, he lashed out at one aspect of modern society after another. In *Main Street* (1920), he satirized life in a small Midwestern town (much like the one in which he himself had grown up). In *Babbitt* (1922), he ridiculed life in the modern city. *Arrowsmith* (1925) attacked the medical profession (and by implication professionalism in general). *Elmer Gantry* (1927) satirized popular religion. Lewis's message was one of cynicism, despair, and hopelessness. There was nothing redeeming in American life, he seemed to say, nothing of value.

To those who held the values of their society in such contempt, the standard avenues for advancement held little appeal. Intellectuals of the 1920s turned their backs on the traditional goals of their parents, openly rejecting the "success ethic" that they believed dominated American life. F. Scott Fitzgerald, whose first novel, *This Side of Paradise* (1920), established him as a spokesman for his generation, ridiculed the American obsession with material success in *The Great Gatsby* (1925). The novel's hero, Jay Gatsby, spends his life accumulating wealth and social prestige in order to win the woman he loves. The

The Fitzgeralds
Novelist F. Scott Fitzgerald, his wife, Zelda, and their daughter Scottie in 1927. Fitzgerald had already won fame as the preeminent spokesman for his generation through his novels chronicling the experiences of the "Lost Generation" and his short stories describing life in the "Jazz Age." But by the late 1920s, he was also experiencing many of the personal troubles that would plague him throughout the rest of his life: his wife's mental illness, his own alcoholism, and a life style of conspicuous consumption that left him constantly in debt. (Culver Pictures)

world to which he has aspired, however, turns out to be one of pretension, fraud, and cruelty, and Gatsby is ultimately destroyed by it. Fitzgerald and his intellectual contemporaries claimed to want nothing to do with conventional American society (although Fitzgerald himself seemed at the same time desperately to crave acceptance by it). They chose, instead, to search elsewhere for fulfillment.

A Refuge in Art

Their quest took them in several different directions, often at the same time. Many Lost Generation intellectuals left America to live in France, making Paris for a time a center of American artistic life. Some adopted hedonistic life styles, indulging in conspicuous debauchery: drinking, drugs, casual sex, wild parties, and a generally flamboyant way of life. (The publicity they received helped set the tone for other, less alienated members of their generation, who began to imitate this uninhibited pursuit of pleasure.) Many intellectuals resorted to an outspoken self-absorption, openly repudiating any responsibility for anyone but themselves. For most of these young men and women, however, the only real refuge from the travails of modern society was art—not art for any social purpose, but art for its own sake. Only art, they argued, could allow them full individual expression; only the act of creation could offer them fulfillment.

The result of this quest for fulfillment through art was not, for the most part, personal satisfaction for the writers and artists involved. They remained throughout the 1920s a restless, usually unhappy generation, searching in vain for contentment. They did, however, produce a body of work that made the decade one of the great eras of American art. Most notable were the writers: Hemingway, Fitzgerald, Lewis, as well as others such as Thomas Wolfe, John Dos Passos, Ezra Pound, and Eugene O'Neill—the first great American playwright and the only one ever to win a Nobel Prize. T. S. Eliot, a native of Boston who spent most of his adult life in England, led a generation of poets in breaking with the romanticism of the nineteenth century. His epic work *The Waste Land* (1922) brought to poetry much of the harsh tone of despair that was invading other areas of literature. Yet the writers of the 1920s were notable not only for the effectiveness of their critiques but for their success in pioneering new literary styles and techniques. Some incorporated Freudian psychology into their work, using literature to explore the workings of the psyche as well as the external actions of characters. Others produced innovations in form, structure, and dialogue: Ernest Hemingway, with his spare, clean prose; Sinclair Lewis, with his biting satire; John Dos Passos, with his use of the techniques of journalism as well as of literature. The literature of the 1920s was escapist; but it was also intensely creative, even revolutionary.

Other Visions

Not all intellectuals of the 1920s, however, expressed such total alienation and despair. Some expressed reservations about their society not by withdrawing from it but by advocating reform. Older progressive theorists continued to expound the values they had celebrated in the years before the war. Thorstein Veblen, for example, continued to attract a wide audience with his argument that modern society should adopt the "discipline of the machine" and assign control to engineers and technocratic experts. John Dewey remained influential with his appeals for "practical" education and experimentation in social policy. Charles and Mary Beard, perhaps the most influential historians of their day, promoted "progressive" principles. In their book *The Rise of American Civilization* (1927) they stressed economic factors in tracing the development of modern society and suggested the need for social and economic planning. These progressive intellectuals were often harshly critical of the society of the 1920s; yet they were, indirectly, legitimizing some of its most important features. Society was not, they were saying, excessively routinized and disciplined, as members of the Lost Generation were complaining. If anything, it was not disciplined and organized enough.

The Negro Artist [1926]

Born in Missouri in 1902, Langston Hughes traveled in Mexico, Africa, and Europe before settling in New York City, where he became the most prolific and versatile of the black writers, earning for himself a reputation as "Harlem's Shakespeare." In an article, "The Negro Artist and the Racial Mountain," in The Nation, *June 23, 1926, he wrote:*

One of the most promising of the young Negro poets said to me once, "I want to be a poet—not a Negro poet," meaning, I believe, "I want to write like a white poet"; meaning subconsciously, "I would like to be a white poet"; meaning behind that, "I would like to be white." And I was sorry the young man said that, for no great poet has ever been afraid of being himself. And I doubted then that, with his desire to run away spiritually from his race, this boy would ever be a great poet. But this is the mountain standing in the way of any true Negro art in America— this urge within the race toward whiteness, the desire to pour racial individuality into the mold of American standardization, and to be as little Negro and as much American as possible.

. . . We younger Negro artists who create now intend to express our individual dark-skinned selves without fear or shame. If white people are pleased we are glad. If they are not, it doesn't matter. We know we are beautiful. And ugly too. The tom-tom cries and the tom-tom laughs. If colored people are pleased we are glad. If they are not, their displeasure doesn't matter either. We build our temples for tomorrow, strong as we know how, and we stand on top of the mountain, free within ourselves.

To another group of intellectuals, the solution to contemporary problems lay neither in escapism nor in progressivism, but in an exploration of their own regional or cultural origins. In New York City, a new generation of black intellectuals created a flourishing Afro-American culture widely described as the "Harlem Renaissance." The Harlem poets, novelists, and artists drew heavily from their African roots in an effort to prove the richness of their own racial heritage (and not incidentally to prove to the white race that the black was worthy of respect). The poet Langston Hughes captured much of the spirit of the movement in a single sentence: "I am a Negro—and beautiful." Other black writers—James Weldon Johnson, Countee Cullen, Claude McKay, Alain Locke—as well as emerging black artists and musicians helped to establish a thriving culture rooted in the historical legacy of their race.

A similar effort was under way among an influential group of Southern intellectuals. Known variously as the "Fugitives" and the "Agrarians," these young poets, novelists, and critics sought to counter the depersonalization of industrial society by evoking the strong rural traditions of their own region. In their controversial manifesto *I'll Take My Stand*, a collection of twelve essays by twelve Southern intellectuals, they issued a simultaneously radical and conservative appeal for a rejection of the doctrine of "economic progress" and the spiritual debilitation that had accompanied it. The supposedly "backward" South, they argued, could serve as a model for a nation drunk with visions of limitless growth and modernization.

Perhaps the greatest of all American writers of this era avoided such stridency but expressed nevertheless the Southerner's strong sense of place and of cultural heritage. William Faulkner, in a remarkable series of novels set in the fictional Mississippi county of Yoknapatawpha—*The Sound and the Fury* (1929), *Absalom, Absalom* (1936), and others—was, like many of his contemporaries, concerned with the problems of the individual seeking fulfillment in the modern world. But unlike others, he painstakingly re-created the bonds of region and community, rather than expressing a detachment from society.

A CONFLICT OF CULTURES

The modern, secular culture of the 1920s did not exist alone. It grew up alongside an older, more traditional culture with which it continually and often bitterly competed. One was the society of an affluent, largely urban middle class, committed to a new set of values, adopting a new, increasingly uninhibited life style, linked to a national cultural outlook. The other was a society of less affluent, less urban, far more provincial Americans—men and women who continued to revere traditional values and customs and who feared and resented the modernist threats to their way of life. Beneath the apparent stability of the New Era and its celebrated business civilization, therefore, raged a series of harsh cultural controversies.

Prohibition

When the prohibition of the sale and manufacture of alcohol went into effect in January 1920, it had the support of most members of the middle class and most of those who considered themselves progressives. Within a year, however, it had become clear that the "noble experiment," as its defenders called it, was not working. What had happened, in essence, was that Americans had simply refused to stop drinking.

The first prohibition commissioner promised rigorous enforcement of the new law. But violations were soon so rampant that the resources available to him proved ludicrously insufficient. The government hired only 1,500 agents to do the job. Before long, it was almost as easy to acquire illegal alcohol in much of the country as it had once been to acquire legal alcohol.

More disturbing than the laughable ineffectiveness of the law, however, was the role prohibition played in stimulating organized crime. An enormous, lucrative industry was now barred to legitimate businessmen; underworld figures quickly and decisively took it over. In Chicago, Al Capone built a vast criminal empire based largely on illegal alcohol. He guarded it against interlopers with an army of up to 1,000 gunmen, whose zealousness contributed to the violent deaths of more than 250 people in the city between 1920 and 1927. Other regions produced gangsters and gang wars of their own. Prohibition, in short, became not only a national joke but a national scandal.

Nevertheless, it survived. The growing strength of repeal forces was more than countered by the increasing militance of defenders of the experiment. The reason was simple. The middle-class progressives who had originally supported prohibition may have lost interest; but an enormous constituency of provincial, largely rural, overwhelmingly Protestant Americans continued vehemently to defend it. To them, drinking and the general sinfulness with which they associated it were an assault on their conservative code of morality. More than that, these manifestations represented the encroachments of the new, urban civilization on their traditional way of life. Prohibition had, in short, taken on implications far beyond the issue of drinking itself. It had come to represent the effort of an older America to maintain its dominance in a society that was moving forward in spite of it. As the decade proceeded, opponents of prohibition (or "wets," as they came to be known) gained steadily in influence. Not until 1933, however, when the Great Depression added weight to their appeals, were they finally able to challenge the "drys" and win repeal of the Eighteenth Amendment.

Disposing of Illegal Booze
During the 1920s, federal prohibition agents—like those emptying bottles down a sewer in this photograph—were assigned to confiscate and get rid of bootleg liquor. But the agents could not keep up with the bootleggers. The head of the Prohibition Bureau once estimated that law-enforcement agencies were catching only one-twentieth of the liquor that was being smuggled in from Canada and other countries, to say nothing of the tremendous quantities that were being produced illegally in the United States. (Culver Pictures)

Nativism and the Klan

Hostility to immigrants was not new to the 1920s. Nor was it restricted to the defenders of the traditional, provincial society. Like prohibition, agitation for a curb on immigration had begun in the nineteenth century; and like prohibition, it had gathered strength in the years before the war largely because of the support of middle-class progressives. Such concerns had not been sufficient in the first years of the century to win passage of curbs on immigration; but when in the years immediately following the war immigration began to be associated with radicalism, popular sentiment on behalf of restriction grew rapidly.

In 1921, therefore, Congress passed an emergency immigration act, establishing a quota system by which annual immigration from any country could not exceed 3 percent of the number of persons of that nationality who had been in the United States in 1910. The new law cut immigration from 800,000 to 300,000 in a single year, but the nativists remained unsatisfied. In 1924, Congress enacted an even harsher law: the National Origins Act, which banned immigration from east Asia entirely (deeply angering Japan) and reduced the quota for Europeans from 3 to 2 percent. The quota would be based, moreover, not on the 1910 census, but on the census of 1890, a year in which there had been far fewer southern and eastern Europe-

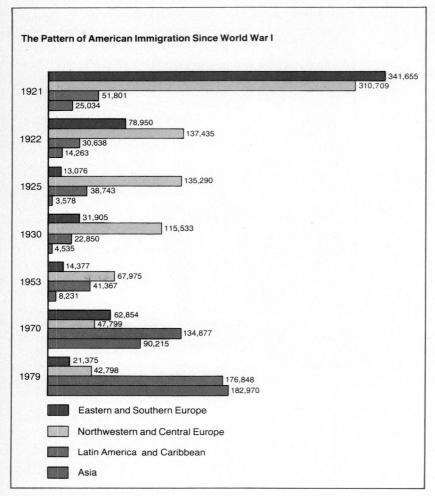

The Pattern of American Immigration Since World War I

1921
- 341,655
- 310,709
- 51,801
- 25,034

1922
- 78,950
- 137,435
- 30,638
- 14,263

1925
- 13,076
- 135,290
- 38,743
- 3,578

1930
- 31,905
- 115,533
- 22,850
- 4,535

1953
- 14,377
- 67,975
- 41,367
- 8,231

1970
- 62,854
- 47,799
- 134,877
- 90,215

1979
- 21,375
- 42,798
- 176,848
- 182,970

- ■ Eastern and Southern Europe
- ▨ Northwestern and Central Europe
- ▨ Latin America and Caribbean
- ■ Asia

This graph illustrates the changing sources of American immigration in the years since World War I. In 1921, before the passage of the first immigration-restriction laws, the main sources of immigrants were the countries of eastern and southern Europe, especially Italy. Beginning in 1922, a series of legal measures altered the pattern to favor immigrants from northwestern and central Europe—a trend that continued into the 1950s. By 1970, after the repeal of some of the quotas, the balance between the two European regions had been more or less restored. But by then, major sources of immigration had shifted away from Europe altogether—to Latin America and the Caribbean and, by the late 1970s, to Asia.

ans in the country. What immigration there was, in other words, would heavily favor northwestern Europeans—people of "Nordic" or "Teutonic" stock. The 1924 act cut the yearly flow almost in half, to 164,000. Five years later, a further restriction set a rigid limit of 150,000 immigrants a year. In the years that followed, immigration officials seldom permitted even half that number actually to enter the country.

The legislative expression of nativism reflected largely the doctrines of progressivism, even if a harsh and narrow progressivism. Restricting immigration, its proponents believed, would contribute to the efficient and productive operation of society. There were, however, other expressions of nativism that reflected very different sentiments. To defenders of an older, more provincial America, the growth of large communities of foreign peoples, alien in their speech, their habits, and their values, came to seem a direct threat to their own embattled way of life. This provincial nativism took a number of forms. But the most prominent was the resurgence of the Ku Klux Klan as a major force in American life.

The Klan was originally the product of the first years after the Civil War. That early organization died in the 1870s. But in 1915, shortly after the premiere of the film *The Birth of a Nation*, which celebrated the early Klan, a new group of Southerners gathered on Stone Mountain outside Atlanta, Georgia, to establish a modern version of the society. At first, the new Klan, like the old, was largely concerned with intimidating blacks, who were, Klan leader William J. Simmons claimed, becoming dangerously insubordinate. After World War I, however, concern about blacks gradually became secondary to concern about Catholics, Jews, and foreigners. The Klan would devote itself, its leaders proclaimed, to purging American life of impure, alien influences.

It was then that the modern Klan experienced its greatest growth. Membership in the small towns and rural areas of the South soon expanded dramatically; more significantly, the Klan was now spreading northward, establishing a strong foothold particularly in the industrial states of the Midwest. By 1923, there were reportedly 3 million members; by 1924, 4 million.

In some communities, where Klan leaders came from the most "respectable" segments of society, the organization operated much like a fraternal society, engaging in nothing more dangerous than occasional political pronouncements. Often, however, the Klan also operated as a brutal, even violent, opponent of "alien" groups and as a defender of traditional, fundamentalist morality. Klansmen systematically terrorized blacks, Jews, Catholics, and foreigners: boycotting their businesses, threatening their families, and attempting to drive them out of their communities. Occasionally, they resorted to violence: public whipping, tarring and feathering, arson, and lynching. But what the Klan most deeply feared, it soon became clear, was not simply "foreign" or racially "impure" groups; it was any group that posed a challenge to their traditional values. Klansmen persecuted not only immigrants and blacks but those white Protestants they considered guilty of irreligion, sexual promiscuity, or drunkenness. The Klan worked to enforce prohibition; it attempted to institute compulsory Bible readings in schools; it worked to punish divorce. The Ku Klux Klan, in short, was fighting not just to pre-

The Ku Klux Klan Parading in Washington, D.C.
In 1926, the Ku Klux Klan was so powerful that it could march down Pennsylvania Avenue in the shadow of the Capitol. It professed to be a patriotic organization, but it was openly antiblack, anti-Catholic, anti-Semitic, antiforeigner, and antiunion. (Culver Pictures)

serve racial homogeneity but to defend a traditional culture against the values and morals of modernity. The organization itself began to decline in influence after 1925, when a series of internal power struggles and several sordid scandals discredited some of its most important leaders. The issues it had raised, however, retained strength among some Americans for many years.

Religious Fundamentalism

The third great cultural controversy of the 1920s revealed even more starkly the growing gulf between the new culture and the old. It was a bitter conflict over questions of religious doctrine and, even more, over the place of religion in contemporary society. By 1921, American Protestantism was already divided into two warring camps. On one side stood the modernists: urban, middle-class people who had attempted to adapt religion to the teachings of modern science and to the realities of their modern, secular society. On the other side stood the fundamentalists: provincial, largely, although not exclusively, rural men and women, fighting to preserve traditional faith and to maintain the centrality of religion in American life. The fundamentalists looked with horror at the new morality of the modern city. (It was they, for example, who formed the core of the defense of prohibition in the 1920s.) They expressed outrage at the abandonment of traditional beliefs in the face of scientific discoveries, insisting that the Bible was to be interpreted literally. Above all, they opposed the teachings of Charles Darwin, who had openly challenged the biblical story of the Creation. Human beings had not evolved from lower orders of animals, the fundamentalists insisted. They had been created by God, as described in Genesis.

Fundamentalism in practice assumed several forms. In most places, it involved simply an intensifying commitment to conservative theology. But it included as well a major evangelical movement, particularly in the South and parts of the West. Evangelists, among them the celebrated Billy Sunday, traveled from state to state attracting huge crowds to their revival meetings. Protestant modernists looked on much of this activity with condescending amusement, but one aspect of fundamentalism they viewed with real alarm. By the mid-1920s, fundamentalists in a number of states were gaining political strength with their demands for legislation to forbid the teaching of evolution in the public schools. To the modernists, such laws were almost unthinkable. Darwinism had to them become indisputable scientific fact; to forbid the teaching of evolution, they believed, would be like forbidding teachers to tell their students that the world was round. Yet they watched with incredulity as one state after another seriously considered the fundamentalist demands. In Tennessee in March 1925, the legislature actually adopted a measure making it illegal for any public-school teacher "to teach any theory that denies the story of the divine creation of man as taught in the Bible."

The result was one of the most celebrated events of the decade. When the American Civil Liberties Union offered free counsel to any Tennessee educator willing to defy the law and become the defendant in a test case, a twenty-four-year-old biology teacher in the town of Dayton, John T. Scopes, arranged to have himself arrested. And when the ACLU decided to send the famous attorney Clarence Darrow to defend Scopes, the aging William Jennings Bryan announced that he would travel to Dayton to assist the prosecution. Journalists from across the country, among them H. L. Mencken, flocked to Tennessee to cover the trial, which opened in an almost circus atmosphere. Scopes had, of course, clearly violated the law; and a verdict of guilty was a foregone conclusion, especially when the judge refused to permit "expert" testimony by evolution scholars. Scopes was fined $100, and the case was ultimately dismissed in a higher court because of a technicality. Nevertheless, Darrow scored an important victory for the modernists by calling Bryan himself to the stand to testify as an "expert on the Bible." In the course of the cross-examination, Darrow made Bryan's churlish defense of biblical truths appear increasingly foolish and finally tricked him into admitting the possibility that not all religious dogma was subject to only one interpretation. The Scopes trial did not resolve the conflict between fundamentalists and modernists. Indeed, four other states soon proceeded to pass antievolution laws of their own. And the issue continued to smolder for decades until it emerged in full force once again in the form of the "creationist" movement of the early 1980s. The Scopes trial did, however, expose the anguish of provincial Americans attempting to defend an embattled way of life.

The Democrats' Ordeal

That anguish proved particularly troubling to the Democratic party, which suffered a serious debilitation during the 1920s as a result of tensions between its urban and rural factions. Far more than the Republicans, the Democrats consisted of a diverse coalition of interest groups, linked more by local tradition than common commitment. Among those interest groups were prohibitionists, Klansmen, and fundamentalists on one side, and Catholics, urban workers, and immigrants on the other. In 1924, the tensions between them proved devastating. At the Democratic National Convention in New York that summer, bitter conflict broke out over the platform when the party's urban wing attempted to win approval of planks calling for the repeal of prohibition and a denunciation of the Klan. Both planks narrowly failed. Far more serious was a deadlock in the balloting for a presidential candidate. Urban Democrats supported Alfred E. Smith, the Irish Catholic Tammanyite who had risen to become a progressive governor of New York;

rural Democrats backed William McAdoo, Woodrow Wilson's treasury secretary (and son-in-law), later to become a senator from California, who had skillfully positioned himself to win the support of Southern and Western delegates suspicious of Tammany Hall and modern urban life. For 103 ballots, the convention dragged on, until finally both Smith and McAdoo withdrew and the party settled on a compromise: the corporate lawyer John W. Davis. After the humiliating spectacle in New York, Davis was an easy target for Calvin Coolidge and the Republican party in the fall.

In the years that followed, the schism between the two wings of the party continued to plague the Democrats. In 1928, Al Smith finally did manage to secure his party's nomination for president after another acrimonious but less prolonged battle. He was not, however, able to unite his divided party. He became, as a result, the first Democrat since the Civil War to fail to carry the South (he won only six of the eleven states of the former Confederacy). Elsewhere, although he did well in the large cities, he carried no states at all except Massachusetts. Smith's opponent, and the victor in the presidential election, was a man who perhaps more than any other personified the modern, prosperous, middle-class society of the New Era: Herbert Hoover. The business civilization of the 1920s, with its new institutions, fashions, and values, continued to arouse the animosity of large portions of the population; but the majority of the American people appeared to have accepted and approved it. In 1928, at least, the New Era seemed to be permanently enshrined.

SUGGESTED READINGS

Among the best general surveys of politics and society in the 1920s are William Leuchtenburg, *The Perils of Prosperity* (1958); John D. Hicks, *Republican Ascendancy* (1960); Arthur M. Schlesinger, Jr., *The Crisis of the Old Order* (1957); and John Braeman (ed.), *Change and Continuity in Twentieth Century America: The 1920s* (1968). Frederick Lewis Allen, *Only Yesterday* (1931), remains a classic popular account of the decade; while Isabel Leighton (ed.), *The Aspirin Age*

(1949), contains a series of entertaining essays on the period.

The Harding presidency is examined in Robert K. Murray, *The Politics of Normalcy* (1973) and *The Harding Era* (1969); and Eugene Trani and David Wilson, *The Presidency of Warren G. Harding* (1977). Burl Noggle, *Teapot Dome* (1962), examines the major scandal of the Harding years. James N. Giglio, *H. M. Daugherty and the Politics of Expediency* (1978), considers one of the leading figures of the Harding scandals. Francis Russell, *The Shadow of Blooming Grove* (1968), and Andrew Sinclair, *The Available Man* (1965), are popular biographies of the twenty-ninth president. A scholarly overview of the Coolidge presidency is available in Donald McCoy, *Calvin Coolidge* (1967); while journalist William Allen White has provided an engaging biography in *A Puritan in Babylon* (1940). The relationships between government and business are explored in James Gilbert, *Designing the Industrial State* (1972); John Hoff Wilson, *Herbert Hoover: Forgotten Progressive* (1975); and David Burner, *Herbert Hoover* (1979). The difficulties of progressive opponents of the administration receive attention in LeRoy Ashby, *Spearless Leader* (1972), which focuses on William Borah; Richard Lowitt, *George W. Norris*, vol. 2 (1971); and David P. Thelen, *Robert M. La Follette and the Insurgent Spirit* (1978). On Southern politics, see George B. Tindall, *The Emergence of the New South* (1967).

For the foreign policy of the 1920s, see L. Ethan Ellis, *Republican Foreign Policy, 1921–1933* (1968); Selig Adler, *The Uncertain Giant* (1965); and Merlo J. Pusey, *Charles Evans Hughes*, 2 vols. (1963). Joan Hoff Wilson, *American Business and Foreign Policy, 1920–1933* (1968) and *Ideology and Economics* (1974), discuss corporate influence on diplomacy and the relationship with the Soviet Union respectively. William Appleman Williams, *The Tragedy of American Diplomacy* (1962), is a revisionist critique of economic influences on foreign policy. For American policy in the Pacific, see Akira Iriye, *After Imperialism* (1965), and Warren Cohen, *America's Response to China* (1971). Roger Dingman, *Power in the Pacific* (1976), and Thomas Buckley, *The United States and the Washington Conference* (1970), examine the 1921–1922 naval conference; while Robert H. Ferrell, *Peace in Their Time* (1952), studies the Kellogg-Briand Pact. For the United States and Latin America, see Joseph Tulchin, *The Aftermath of War* (1971), and William Kamman, *A Search for Stability* (1968).

On the 1920s economy, see George Soule, *Prosperity Decade* (1947). Alfred Chandler, *Strategy and Structure* (1962), examines the development of several modern corporations; and Louis Galambos, *Competition and Cooperation* (1966), explores the growth of a trade association (the Cotton Textile Institute). A full account of the labor movement in the 1920s is available in Irving Bernstein, *The Lean Years* (1960). See also David Brody, *Steelworkers in America* (1960) and *Workers in Industrial America* (1980), Chapter 2; Robert Zenger, *Republicans and Labor* (1969); and Leslie Woodcock, *Wage-Earning Women* (1979). On American agriculture during the decade, consult Gilbert Fite, *George Peek and the Fight for Farm Parity* (1954), and Theodore Saloutos and John D. Hicks, *Twentieth Century Populism* (1951).

Daniel Boorstin, *The Americans: The Democratic Experience* (1973), offers an overview of American culture in the 1920s. Ed Cray, *Chrome Colossus* (1980);

Bernard A. Weisberger, *The Dream Maker* (1979); and James Flink, *The Car Culture* (1975), provide observations on the growing importance of the automobile; while Stuart Ewen, *Captains of Consciousness* (1976), examines the advertising industry. See Larry May, *Screening Out the Past* (1980), and Robert Sklar, *Movie-Made America* (1975), for discussion of the growth of the film industry and its effects on American culture. There is surprisingly little literature on the impact of radio in the 1920s; see, however, Erik Barnouw, *A Tower in Babel*, vol. 1 (1966). Robert Lynd and Helen Lynd, *Middletown* (1929), a sociological portrait of Muncie, Indiana, in the mid-1920s, is invaluable for understanding community life in the decade and particularly useful for examining middle-class religion. Paul Carter, *Another Part of the Twenties* (1977), discusses a range of popular social attitudes. Sheila Rothman, *Woman's Proper Place* (1978), is an important study of the changing roles of women. See also William Chafe, *The American Woman* (1972), and Linda Gordon, *Woman's Body, Woman's Right* (1976), on birth control. Paula Fass, *The Damned and Beautiful* (1977), examines American youth.

Malcolm Cowley, *Exiles Return* (1934), is an eloquent memoir of the Lost Generation. See also Edmund Wilson, *The Twenties* (1975), and Frederick J. Hoffman, *The Twenties* (1949). Nathan Huggins, *Harlem Renaissance* (1971), examines the outstanding black cultural movement of the decade. John Stewart, *The Burden of Time* (1965), is a study of the Southern Fugitives and Agrarians. The best critical study of William Faulkner is Cleanth Brooks, *William Faulkner: The Yoknapatawpha Country* (1963).

Norman Clark, *Deliver Us from Evil* (1976), examines the prohibition movement, tracing it back to its progressive roots. See also Joseph Gusfeld, *Symbolic Crusade* (1963); Andrew Sinclair, *The Era of Excess* (1962); and Herbert Asbury, *The Great Illusion* (1950). The best study of American nativism is John Higham, *Strangers in the Land* (1963). David Chalmers, *Hooded Americanism* (1965), and Kenneth Jackson, *The Ku Klux Klan in the City* (1965), examine the impact of the Klan. An account of the Scopes trial is available in Ray Ginger, *Six Days or Forever?* (1958); while Norman Furniss, *The Fundamentalist Controversy* (1954), and George M. Marsden, *Fundamentalism and American Culture* (1980), offer broader views of the fundamentalist movement. See also Lawrence Levine, *Defender of the Faith, William Jennings Bryan: The Last Decade, 1915–1925* (1965). The troubled history of the Democratic party in the 1920s can be examined in William Harbaugh, *Lawyer's Lawyer* (1973), a biography of John W. Davis; David Burner, *The Politics of Provincialism* (1967), a particularly useful study; Alan Lichtman, *Prejudice and the Old Politics* (1979), a pathbreaking quantitative study of the 1928 election; and Frank Freidel, *The Ordeal* (1954) and *The Triumph* (1956), volumes covering the 1920s in a four-volume (to date) biography of Franklin Roosevelt.

Depression and New Deal

25

An Apple Seller in New York City
In the fall of 1931 and 1932, a number of unemployed took to selling apples on the streets. President Hoover later wrote: "One incident of these times has persisted as the eternal damnation of Hoover. Some Oregon or Washington apple growers' association shrewdly appraised the sympathy of the public for the unemployed. They set up a system of selling apples on the street corners in many cities, thus selling their crop and raising their prices. Many persons left their jobs for the more profitable one of selling apples. When any left-winger wishes to indulge in scathing oratory, he demands, 'Do you want to return to selling apples?'"
(Culver Pictures)

Few Americans in the first months of 1929 saw any reason to question the strength and stability of the nation's economy. Most agreed with their new president that the booming prosperity of the years just past would not only continue but increase, and that dramatic social progress would follow in its wake. "We in America today," Herbert Hoover had proclaimed in August 1928, "are nearer to the final triumph over poverty than ever before in the history of any land. The poorhouse is vanishing from among us." Only fifteen months later, however, those words would return to haunt him, as the nation plunged into the severest and most prolonged economic depression in its history. It began with a stock market crash in October 1929, and it continued in one form or another for a full decade, until war finally restored prosperity.

The Great Depression not only produced widespread economic misery; it also placed great strains on the political and social fabric of the nation. And out of those strains emerged a series of fundamental reforms—most notably in the role of government in American life. Herbert Hoover was the first to expand the federal presence in the economy in response to the crisis. His innovative programs in the early 1930s made his the most activist peacetime administration in American history to that point. But Hoover's efforts, inhibited by conservative assumptions about the proper functions of government, were in the end painfully insufficient. And so, in 1932, the American people turned to the Democratic party and to its presidential candidate Franklin Delano Roosevelt to show them the way out of the Depression.

The Roosevelt administration—commonly known as the "New Deal," after a phrase in one of Roosevelt's campaign speeches—transformed American government. And it evoked popular reactions that made the new president simultaneously the most loved and the most despised man in the nation. Yet the New Deal was, in fact, neither as brilliantly progressive nor as dangerously revolutionary as its contemporaries often claimed. It was, rather, an essentially cautious, even at times conservative response to a grave national crisis, one that differed from the Hoover approach primarily in its pragmatic, experimental nature—its willingness to try new methods when old ones did not work. This experimentalism gradually took the Roosevelt administration in directions it had neither foreseen nor desired.

THE COMING OF THE DEPRESSION

The sudden financial collapse in 1929 came as an especially severe shock because it followed so closely a period in which the New Era seemed to be performing another series of economic miracles. In particular, the nation was experiencing in 1929 a spectacular boom in the stock market. In February 1928, stock prices began a steady ascent that continued, with only a few temporary lapses, for a year and a half. By the autumn of that year, the market had become a national obsession, attracting the attention not only of the wealthy but of millions of people of modest means. Many brokerage firms gave added encouragement to the speculative mania by offering absurdly easy credit to purchasers of stocks.

A few economists warned that the boom could not continue, that the prices of stocks had ceased to bear any relation to the earning power of the corporations that were issuing them. But most Americans refused to listen.

The Great Crash

In the autumn of 1929, the market began to fall apart. On October 21, stock prices dipped sharply, alarming those who had become accustomed to an uninterrupted upward progression. Two days later, after a brief recovery, an even more alarming decline began. J. P. Morgan and Company and other big bankers managed to stave off disaster for a while by conspicuously buying up stocks to restore public confidence. But on October 29, it became clear that all efforts to save the market would be to no avail.

That day—"Black Tuesday," as it became known—saw a devastating panic. Sixteen million shares of stock were traded; the industrial index dropped 43 points; stocks in many companies became virtually worthless. In the weeks that followed, the market continued to decline, with losses in October totaling $16 billion. And despite occasional hopeful signs of a turnaround, the market remained deeply depressed for more than four years and did not fully recover for more than a decade.

Popular folklore has established the stock market crash as the beginning, and even the

The stock market crash marked only the beginning of the price decline. Stocks stayed low in the 1930s and were relatively low even in the 1940s. By the time of the Korean War, the great bull market was in force, and it continued with only brief interruption until the 1960s. The stock prices shown here are based on the Dow-Jones stock averages.

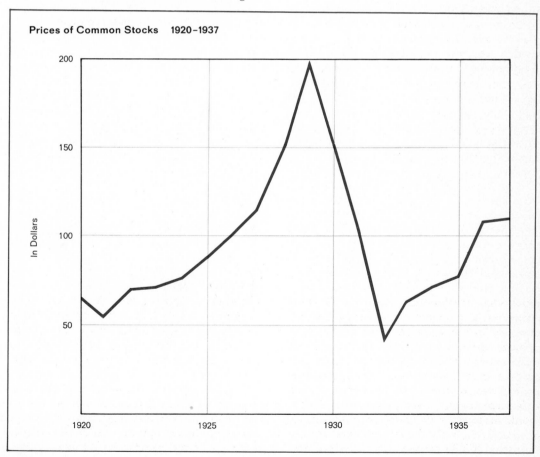

Prices of Common Stocks   1920–1937

cause, of the Great Depression. But although October 1929 might have been the first visible sign of the crisis, the Depression had earlier beginnings and more important causes.

The nation's economy had been showing some signs of distress for months before October 1929, as the two industries most responsible for prosperity began to display evidence of weakness. Construction had passed its peak and was declining rapidly; automobiles were sitting unsold in the showrooms of dealers. Business inventories of all kinds were three times as large as they had been a year before, and other signposts of economic health—freight carloads, industrial production, wholesale prices—were slipping downward. The extraordinary performance of the stock market kept most Americans from noticing these alarming signs. But the bull market was, in fact, an artificial phenomenon, flourishing at a time when the nation was already slipping into a recession.

Economists and other observers have argued for decades about what was responsible for this economic decline. They have agreed only that many factors were involved. There was, first, a serious lack of diversification in the American economy in the 1920s. Prosperity had been excessively dependent on a few basic industries, notably construction and automobiles; when those industries declined, the other sectors of the economy were not large enough or productive enough to take up the slack. More important, there was a fundamental maldistribution of purchasing power in the New Era. As production of goods increased, the proportion of the profits going to farmers, factory workers, and other potential consumers was too small to create a market for the goods they were producing. As long as corporations had continued to expand their capital facilities (their factories, warehouses, heavy equipment, and other investments), the economy had continued to flourish. By the end of the 1920s, however, capital investments had created more plant space than could profitably be used, and factories were pouring out more goods than consumers could purchase. Most Americans would happily have bought more had they been able to afford it. In 1929, only one family in six owned an automobile, only one in

five a fixed bathtub. Fewer than 24 percent of all American homes received electric power, and only 10 percent had telephones. But with farm prices and factory wages low, this potential market could not be tapped.

Government policies had contributed as well to the economic dilemma. Taxation had spared the rich and fallen disproportionately on people of modest means, increasing the inequality of incomes. Lax regulation of corporations, banks, and the securities industry had permitted egregious abuses and irresponsible speculation. High tariffs had restricted foreign trade, limiting the ability of American manufacturers to sell their surpluses overseas. Only large American loans had kept the foreign markets alive at all; and those loans were going increasingly into default, expanding the economic crisis even further.

The Depression Economy

Someone asked the British economist John Maynard Keynes in the 1930s whether he was aware of any historical era comparable to the Great Depression. "Yes," Keynes replied. "It was called the Dark Ages, and it lasted 400 years." The Depression did not last 400 years. It did, however, plunge the economy not only of the United States but of most of the Western world into a distress it had not known in the industrial era.

The collapse was so rapid and so devastating that at first it created only bewilderment among those who attempted to explain it. The American gross national product plummeted from over $104 billion in 1929 to $76.4 billion in 1932, a 25 percent decline in three years. By 1933, Americans had virtually ceased making investments in productive enterprises. In 1929, they had spent $16.2 billion to promote capital growth; in 1933, they invested only a third of a billion. The consumer price index declined 25 percent between 1929 and 1933, the wholesale price index 32 percent. Farm prices, already depressed in the 1920s, fell even more dramatically. Gross farm income dropped from $12 billion to $5 billion in four years. With economic activity contracting so sharply, it was

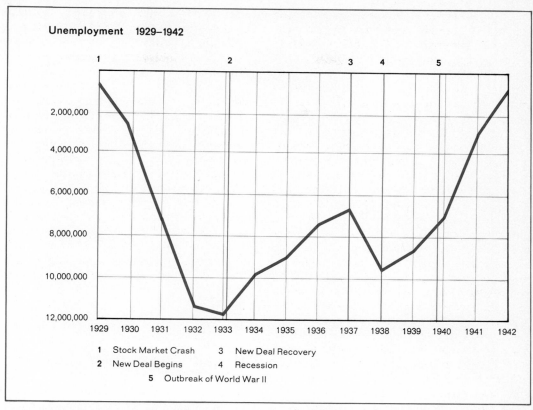

Unemployment 1929–1942

1	Stock Market Crash	3	New Deal Recovery
2	New Deal Begins	4	Recession
	5	Outbreak of World War II	

Unemployment was especially high among young people, minority groups, and residents of areas where the textile mills and coal mines had been closed. The rate of unemployment decreased drastically with the acute shortage of labor during the war years. Although the number of unemployed workers in 1942 roughly equaled the 1929 figure, the population had grown, so the rate was lower.

inevitable that industrial unemployment would greatly increase. By 1932, according to the relatively crude estimates of the time, 25 percent of the American work force was unemployed (some believed the figure was even higher). For the rest of the decade, unemployment averaged nearly 20 percent, never dropping below 15 percent.

It is hard to know whether the suffering was worse in the cities or on the farms. In the industrial Northeast and Midwest, cities were becoming virtually paralyzed by the burden of unemployment. Cleveland, Ohio, for example, had an unemployment rate of 50 percent in 1932; Akron, 60 percent; Toledo, 80 percent. To the men and women

suddenly without incomes, the situation was frightening and bewildering. Most had grown up believing that every individual was responsible for his or her own fate, that unemployment was a sign of personal failure; and even in the face of national distress, many continued to believe it. Unemployed workers walked through the streets day after day looking for jobs that did not exist. When finally they gave up, they often just sat at home, hiding their shame.

An increasing number of families were turning in humiliation to local public relief systems, just to be able to eat. But that system, which had in the 1920s served only a small number of indigents, was totally une-

Bread Line
A bread line stretches across New York City's Times Square in 1932, testimony
to the failure of government efforts to meet the escalating demands for relief.
(Wide World Photos)

quipped to handle the new demands being placed on it. In many cities, therefore, relief simply collapsed. New York, which offered among the highest relief benefits in the nation, was able to provide families an average of only $2.39 per week. Private charities attempted to supplement the public relief efforts, but the problem was far beyond their capabilities as well.

With local efforts rapidly collapsing, state governments began to feel new pressures to expand their own assistance to the unemployed. Most resisted the pressure. Tax revenues were declining, along with everything else, and state leaders balked at placing additional strains on already tight budgets. Many public figures, moreover, feared that any permanent welfare system would undermine the moral fiber of its clients.

As a result of all this, American cities were experiencing scenes that a few years earlier would have seened almost inconceivable. Bread lines stretched for blocks outside Red Cross and Salvation Army kitchens. Thousands sifted through garbage cans for scraps of food or waited outside restaurant kitchens in hopes of receiving plate scrapings. Men, women, and children suffered, and even died from, malnutrition and starvation. Nearly 2 million young men simply took to the roads, riding freight trains from city to city, living as virtual nomads.

In rural areas conditions were, in many ways, even worse, especially in a large area of the South and Middle West known as the Dust Bowl. Between 1929 and 1932, not only did farm income decline by more than 60 percent; not only did an estimated one-third of all American farmers lose their land through mortgage foreclosures or eviction. Much of the farm belt was suffering as well from a catastrophic natural disaster: one of the worst droughts in the history of the nation. Beginning in 1930, a vast area of the nation—and particularly a group of states stretching north from Texas into the Dakotas—began to experience a steady decline in rainfall and an accompanying increase in heat. The drought continued for a full decade, turning many areas that had once been fertile farm regions into virtual deserts. In Kansas, the soil in some places was devoid of moisture as far as three feet below the surface. In Nebraska, Iowa, and other states, summer temperatures were averaging over 100 degrees. Swarms of grasshoppers were moving from region to region, devouring what meager crops farmers were able to raise, often even devouring fenceposts or clothes hanging out to dry. Great dust storms—"black blizzards," as they were called—swept across the plains, blotting out the sun and suffocating livestock as well as any people unfortunate or foolish enough to stay outside.

It is a measure of how depressed the market for agricultural goods had become that even with these disastrous conditions,

Father and Sons Walking in the Face of a Dust Storm, Cimarron County, Oklahoma
Beginning late in 1933, years of extreme drought and high winds further afflicted the depression-plagued farmers of the Great Plains. The worst-hit area, centering on the panhandles of Texas and Oklahoma, eastern Colorado and New Mexico, and western Kansas, came to be known as the "Dust Bowl." "Only those who have been caught out in a 'black blizzard' can have more than a faint conception of its terrors," wrote Lawrence Svobida, a Kansas wheat farmer. "The dust begins to blow with only a slight breeze. . . . The wind increases its velocity until it is blowing at forty to fifty miles an hour. Soon everything is moving—the land is blowing, both farm land and pasture alike. The fine dirt is sweeping along at express-train speed, and when the very sun is blotted out, visibility is reduced to some fifty feet; or perhaps you cannot see at all, because the dust has blinded you and even goggles are useless to prevent the fine particles from sifting into your eyes."
—Lawrence Svobida, *An Empire of Dust* (Caldwell, Idaho: The Caxton Printers, 1940). (Library of Congress)

American farmers continued through the 1930s to produce far more than American consumers could afford to buy. With the domestic market dwindling and the international market having almost vanished, farmers were able to sell their goods only at prices so low as to make continued operations unprofitable. Thus many farmers, like many urban unemployed, left their homes and traveled to what they hoped would be better climes. Hundreds of thousands of families, from the Dust Bowl in particular (often known as "Okies," since many came from Oklahoma), packed their belongings in rickety cars or trucks and traveled to California, where they found conditions little better than those they had left. Owning no land of their own, they were forced to work as agricultural migrants, traveling from farm to farm picking fruit and other crops at starvation wages.

No nation could survive indefinitely amid such vast economic distress. No people could tolerate for long such widespread and unrelieved suffering. Increasingly, therefore, troubled Americans began to look to their government for a solution to the crisis.

The Hoover Program

Herbert Hoover entered the presidency in March 1929 believing, like most Americans, that the nation faced a bright and prosperous future. For the first six months of his administration, he attempted to expand the policies he had advocated during his eight years as secretary of commerce, policies that would, he believed, complete the stable system of cooperative individualism that he believed was the key to a successful economy. The economic crisis that began before the year was out forced the president to deal with a new set of problems; but for most of the rest of his term, he continued to rely on the principles that had always governed his public life.

Hoover's first response to the Depression was to attempt to restore public confidence in the economy. "The fundamental business of this country, that is, production and distribution of commodities," he said in 1930, "is on a sound and prosperous basis." Conse-

quently, he held a series of highly publicized meetings, summoning leaders of business, labor, and agriculture to the White House and urging upon them a program of voluntary cooperation for recovery. He persuaded businessmen not to cut production or lay off workers; he talked labor leaders into forgoing demands for higher wages or better hours. For a few brief months, the president's efforts seemed to be having some effect; but by mid-1931, economic conditions had deteriorated so badly that the structure of voluntary cooperation he had erected quickly collapsed. Frightened industrialists soon began cutting production, laying off workers, and slashing wages. Hoover was powerless to stop them.

Hoover also attempted to use government spending as a tool for fighting the Depression. Rejecting the demands of some fiscal conservatives that the government cut back its own programs to ensure a balanced budget, the president proposed to Congress an increase of $423 million—an enormous sum by the standards of the time—in federal public works programs; and he exhorted state and local governments to engage in the "energetic yet prudent pursuit" of public construction. Nevertheless, Hoover's spending programs were, in the end, no more effective than his efforts at persuasion; for he was not willing to spend enough money, or to spend it for a long enough time, to do any good. He viewed his public works program as a temporary expedient, something to promote a rapid recovery. When economic conditions worsened, he became far less willing to increase government spending, worrying instead about maintaining federal solvency. In 1932, at the depth of the Depression, he proposed a tax increase to help the government avoid a deficit.

Even before the stock market crash, Hoover had begun to construct a program to assist the troubled agricultural economy. It embodied two major initiatives, which the president proposed to a special session of Congress in April 1929. The Agricultural Marketing Act established for the first time a major government bureaucracy to help farmers maintain prices. A federally sponsored Farm Board of eight members would administer a revolving fund of $500 million, from which it could make loans to national marketing cooperatives or establish "corporations" to buy surpluses and thus raise prices. At the same time, Hoover attempted to protect American farmers from international competition by raising agricultural tariffs. The Hawley-Smoot Act of 1930 contained protective increases on seventy-five farm products and raised rates from the average of 26 percent established by the 1922 Fordney-McCumber Act to a new high of 50 percent.

Neither the Agricultural Marketing Act nor the Hawley-Smoot tariff ultimately helped American farmers in any significant way. The Marketing Act relied on voluntary cooperation among farmers and gave the government no authority to limit production. Hoover's call for a reduction of the wheat crop, for example, resulted in a drop in acreage of only 1 percent in Kansas. The Farm Board, moreover, lacked sufficient funds to deal effectively with the crisis. Prices continued to fall despite its efforts. The Hawley-Smoot Act was an unqualified disaster, as a thousand members of the American Economic Association had warned the president even before he signed it. It provoked foreign governments to enact trade restrictions of their own in reprisal, further diminishing the market for American agricultural goods. And it raised rates not only on farm products but on 925 manufactured goods as well, making industrial products more expensive for farmers.

A Change of Direction

By the spring of 1931, Herbert Hoover's political position had deteriorated considerably. Democrats had made gains in the 1930 congressional elections, winning control of the House and making substantial inroads in the Senate. Large portions of the public were beginning to hold the president personally to blame for the crisis, and Hoover's name soon became synonymous with economic distress. Shantytowns established on the outskirts of cities were known as "Hoovervilles." Progressive reformers both inside and out-

side the government urged the president to support more vigorous programs of relief and public spending. Hoover ignored the recommendation. Instead, he seized on a slight improvement in economic conditions early in 1931 as proof that his policies were working.

The international financial panic of the spring of 1931 destroyed the illusion that the economic crisis was coming to an end. Throughout much of the 1920s, the European economy had managed to survive the burden of war debts and reparations only by virtue of large loans from American banks. When those loans ceased after 1929, the financial fabric of many European nations began to unravel. In May 1931, the largest bank in Austria collapsed. Over the next several months, panic gripped the financial institutions of neighboring countries. European governments, desperate for sound assets, withdrew their gold reserves from American banks. European investors, in need of dollars to pay off their loans and protect their solvency, dumped their shares of American stocks onto the market, further depressing prices. More and more European nations were abandoning the gold standard and devaluing their currencies, leaving the United States, which remained tied to gold, at a disadvantage in international trade. American economic conditions quickly declined to new lows, and Herbert Hoover quickly adopted a new approach to the Depression.

It was not the domestic American economy that was to blame for the Depression, he now argued, but the structure of international finance. The proper response to the crisis, therefore, was not to adopt active social and economic programs at home but to work to restore international stability. Hoover's solution was to propose a moratorium—first on the payment of all war debts and reparations, then on the payment of international private debts as well. It was a sound proposal, but it came too late to halt the panic.

By the time Congress convened in December 1931, conditions had grown so desperate that Hoover finally decided to support an expanded federal role in the economy. He persuaded Congress to increase funding for federal land banks and to create a system of government home loan banks. Through them, financial institutions holding mortgages on farms, homes, and other properties could receive cash from the government for the mortgages instead of foreclosing on them—thus keeping the banks afloat and, incidentally, preventing many Americans from losing their homes and properties. Hoover also supported the Glass-Steagall Banking Act of 1932, designed to make it easier for American banks to meet the demands of overseas depositors who were withdrawing their gold from the United States. And he encouraged New York financiers to establish a $500 million fund to help troubled banks stay afloat.

The most important piece of legislation of his presidency, however, was a bill passed in January 1932 establishing the Reconstruction Finance Corporation (RFC), a government agency whose purpose was to provide federal loans to troubled banks, railroads, and other businesses. It even made funds available to local governments to support public works projects and assist relief efforts. It was an unprecedented use of federal power; and unlike many earlier Hoover programs, it operated on a large scale. In 1932, the RFC had a budget of $1.5 billion for public works alone.

Nevertheless, the new agency failed to deal directly or forcefully enough with the real problems of the economy to produce any significant recovery. Because the RFC was permitted to lend funds only to those financial institutions with sufficient collateral, much of its money went to large banks and corporations, prompting some critics to dub it a "bread line for big business." The RFC could only provide loans; it could not purchase stock or otherwise provide capital to troubled institutions, even though that was what they most desperately needed. And at Hoover's insistence, it helped finance only those public works projects that promised ultimately to pay for themselves (toll bridges, public housing, and others), thus severely limiting the scope of its efforts. Above all, the RFC did not have enough money to make any real impact on the Depression; and it did not even spend all the money it had. Of the meager $300 million available to support local relief efforts, the RFC lent out only $30

million in 1932. Of the $1.5 billion public works budget, it released only about 20 percent. Even Hoover's most vigorous and expansive program had been crippled by the cautiousness and fiscal conservatism of his administration.

Diplomatic Frustrations

After the relatively placid international climate of the 1920s, the diplomatic challenges facing the Hoover administration must have seemed ominous and bewildering. The world financial crisis was not only creating economic distress; it was producing a heightened nationalism that threatened the international agreements established during the previous decade. Above all, the Depression was toppling many existing political leaders and replacing them with powerful, belligerent governments bent on expansion as a solution to their economic problems. Hoover was confronted, therefore, with the beginning of a process that would ultimately lead to war, and he was finding himself without sufficient tools to deal with it.

In Latin America, Hoover worked studiously to repair some of the damage created by earlier American actions. He made a ten-week good-will tour through the region before his inauguration. Once in office, he attempted to abstain from intervening in the internal affairs of neighboring nations and moved to withdraw American troops from Nicaragua and Haiti. When economic distress led to the collapse of one Latin American regime after another, Hoover announced a new United States policy: America would grant diplomatic recognition to any de facto government in the region without questioning the means it had used to obtain power. He even repudiated the Roosevelt Corollary to the Monroe Doctrine by refusing to permit American intervention when several Latin American countries defaulted on debt obligations to the United States in October 1931.

In Europe, the administration fared less well. When Hoover's debt moratorium failed to produce financial stability, many economists and political leaders appealed to the president to cancel all war debts to the United States. Hoover refused, and several

European nations promptly went into default, severely damaging an already tense international climate. United States efforts to extend the disarmament agreements of the 1920s met with similar frustration. At a conference in London in January 1930, American negotiations reached agreement with European and Japanese delegates on extending the limits on naval construction established at the Washington Conference of 1921. But France and England, fearful of a resurgent Germany and an expanding Japan, insisted on so many loopholes as to make the treaty virtually meaningless. The increasing irrelevance of Hoover's idealistic commitments became even clearer at the World Disarmament Conference that opened in Geneva in January 1932. France rejected the idea of disarmament entirely and called for the creation of an international army to counter the growing power of Germany. Hoover continued to urge major reductions in armaments, including an immediate abolition of all "offensive" weapons (tanks, bombers) and a 30 percent reduction in all land and naval forces. The conference ultimately dissolved in failure.

The ineffectiveness of diplomacy in Europe was particularly troubling in view of the character of some of the new governments coming to power on the Continent. Benito Mussolini's Fascist party had been in control of Italy since the early 1920s; by the 1930s, the regime was growing highly nationalistic and militaristic, and Fascist leaders were loudly threatening an active campaign of imperial expansion. Even more ominous was the growing power of the National Socialist (or Nazi) party in Germany. The so-called Weimar Republic, which had emerged as the nation's government at the end of World War I, was by the late 1920s losing virtually all of its popular support, discredited by, among other things, a ruinous inflation. And Adolf Hitler, the stridently nationalistic leader of the Nazis, was rapidly growing in popular favor. Although he lost a 1932 election for chancellor, Hitler would sweep into power less than a year later. His belief in the racial superiority of the Aryan (German) people; his commitment to providing *Lebensraum* (living space) for his "master race"; his blatant anti-Semitism; and his passionate militarism: all posed a growing threat to European peace.

More immediately alarming to the delegates at the 1932 Geneva Conference was a major crisis in Asia—one that proved to be an early step toward World War II. The Japanese, reeling from an economic depression of their own, had developed an intense concern about the increasing power of the Soviet Union and of Chiang Kai-shek's nationalist China. In particular, they were alarmed at Chiang's insistence on expanding his government's power in Manchuria, which remained officially a part of China, but over which the Japanese had since 1905 maintained effective economic control. When the moderate government of Japan failed to take forceful steps to counter Chiang's ambitions, Japan's military leaders staged what was, in effect, a coup in the autumn of 1931—seizing control of foreign policy from the weakened liberals. Only weeks later, they launched a major invasion of northern Manchuria.

The American government had few options. For a while, Secretary of State Henry Stimson continued to hope that Japanese moderates would regain control of the Tokyo government and halt the invasion. The militarists, however, remained in command; and by the beginning of 1932, the conquest of Manchuria was complete. Hoover permitted Stimson to issue warnings to Japan and to attempt to use moral suasion to end the crisis. He forbade him, however, to cooperate with the League of Nations in imposing economic sanctions against the Japanese. Stimson's only real tool in dealing with the Manchurian invasion was a refusal to grant diplomatic recognition to the new Japanese territories. Japan was unconcerned and early in 1932 even expanded its aggression farther into China, attacking the city of Shanghai and killing thousands of civilians.

THE CRISES OF 1932

For the first several years of the Depression, most Americans were either too stunned or too confused to raise any effective protest. By the middle of 1932, however, the crisis had continued so long and had grown so severe that dissident voices began to be heard. With the administration's policies in shambles, with Hoover himself growing increasingly unpopular, and with the economy reaching new lows in almost every sector, it was easy for many Americans to believe that the nation was on the verge of collapse.

Agrarian Unrest

In the Midwest, farmers sensing themselves near economic extinction raised new and louder demands for government assistance. In particular, they called for legislation similar to the McNary-Haugen bill of the 1920s by which the government would guarantee them a return on their crops at least equal to the cost of production. Lobbyists from the larger farm organizations converged on Washington to pressure members of Congress to act. Some disgruntled farmers staged public protests in the capital. But when neither the president nor the Congress showed any signs of movement, they adopted a more drastic approach. In the summer of 1932, a group of unhappy farm owners gathered in Des Moines, Iowa, to establish a new organization: the Farm Holiday Association. Under the leadership of Milo Reno, the association endorsed the withholding of farm products from the market—in effect a farmers' strike. The strike began in August in western Iowa, spread briefly to a few neighboring areas, and succeeded in blockading several markets; but in the end it dissolved in failure. The scope of the effort was too modest to affect farm prices, and many farmers in the region refused to cooperate in any case. When clashes between strikers and local authorities resulted in several episodes of violence, Reno called off the strike. Nevertheless, the uprising created considerable consternation in state governments in the farm belt and even more in Washington, where the president and much of the Congress were facing a national election.

The Bonus March

A more celebrated protest movement emerged from a less likely quarter: American veterans. In 1924, Congress had approved the payment of a bonus to all those who had served in World War I, the money to be distributed in 1945. By 1932, however, economic distress had mobilized a widespread demand among veterans that the bonus be paid immediately. Hoover would not consider the request, fearing that acquiescence would ruin his hopes for a balanced budget; but the veterans refused to be denied. In June, more than 20,000 veterans, members of the self-proclaimed "Bonus Army," marched into Washington, built crude camps in the city and its environs, and promised to stay until Congress approved legislation to pay the bonus. A few of the veterans departed in July, after Congress had voted down their proposal. Most, however, remained where they were.

Their continued presence in Washington was an irritant and an embarrassment to Herbert Hoover, who had problems enough already and who gradually became defensive and even paranoid about the protestors. Finally, in mid-July, he ordered police to clear the marchers out of several abandoned federal buildings in which they had been staying. The police arrived; a few marchers threw rocks at them; someone opened fire; and two veterans fell dead. To Hoover, the incident seemed proof of dangerous radicalism, and he immediately ordered the United States Army to assist the police in clearing out the buildings.

General Douglas MacArthur, the army chief of staff, chose to carry out the order himself. Dressed in full battle tunic, he led the Third Cavalry (under the command of George S. Patton), two infantry regiments, a machine-gun detachment, and six tanks down Pennsylvania Avenue in pursuit of the

The Defeat of the Bonus Army
Although General Douglas MacArthur had been instructed only to dislodge Bonus Marchers from abandoned federal buildings in Washington, he pursued the fleeing veterans across the Anacostia River and burned to the ground the Hooverville they had constructed there for themselves. The general later claimed that the Bonus Marchers had themselves started the fires. (U.S. Signal Corps)

motley Bonus Army. The veterans fled in terror as the troops hurled tear gas canisters and flailed at them with their bayonets. MacArthur followed them across the Anacostia River, where he ordered the soldiers to burn their camp to the ground. More than 100 marchers were injured. One baby died.

The incident served as perhaps the final blow to Hoover's already battered political standing. To much of the public, he now stood confirmed as an aloof and insensitive figure, locked in the White House, uncomprehending of the distress around him. Hoover's own cold and gloomy personality did nothing to change the public image, and some of his embattled public statements at the time made his plight even worse "Nobody is actually starving," he assured reporters (inaccurately) in 1932. "The hoboes, for example, are better fed than they have ever

been." The Great Engineer, the personification of the optimistic days of the 1920s, had become a symbol of the nation's failure to deal effectively with its startling reversal of fortune.

The Election of 1932

Most of the American people looked to the 1932 presidential election as their most effective vehicle of protest. No one had any doubts about the outcome. The Republican party dutifully renominated Herbert Hoover for a second term in office; but the lugubrious atmosphere of their convention made it clear that few delegates believed he could carry the November election. The Democrats, in the meantime, gathered jubilantly in Chicago to nominate a candidate who, they were certain, would be the next president of the United States. Their choice was the governor of New York, Franklin Delano Roosevelt.

Roosevelt had been a well-known figure in the party for many years already. The son of a wealthy Hudson Valley railroad tycoon and a graduate of Groton, Harvard, and Columbia Law School, Roosevelt had begun his political career in 1910 in the New York State legislature. Because he was handsome, charming, and articulate, and because he was a distant cousin of Theodore Roosevelt (a connection strengthened by his marriage in 1904 to the president's niece, Eleanor), he attracted increasing attention. He served as assistant secretary of the navy under Woodrow Wilson during World War I; and in 1920, he received his party's nomination for vice president on the ill-fated ticket with James M. Cox. Less than a year later, his public career appeared to come to an end when he was stricken with polio and lost the use of his legs. But Roosevelt worked hard to return to politics; and although he was never again able to walk without the use of crutches and braces, he built up sufficient physical strength to make a courageous appearance at the 1924 Democratic convention to nominate Al Smith. In 1928, when Smith left Albany to run for president, Roosevelt succeeded him as governor; and in 1930, he easily won reelection.

Roosevelt worked no miracles in New York as the state succumbed to the rigors of the Depression. He did, however, establish enough positive programs of government assistance to provide an effective contrast to Herbert Hoover. At least as important to his political future, however, was his astute effort to win support from both the urban and rural wings of his party. By avoiding such divisive cultural issues as religion and prohibition, and by emphasizing the economic grievances that most Democrats shared, he assembled a coalition within the party that provided him with a majority of the delegates to the convention by the time it assembled. After several ballots of maneuvering, his supporters secured enough additional votes to secure him the necessary two-thirds. And the next day, in a dramatic break with tradition, he flew to Chicago to address the convention in person and accept the nomination.

In the course of his acceptance speech, Roosevelt thrilled the delegates with his ringing promise: "I pledge you, I pledge myself, to a new deal for the American people," giving his program a name that would long endure. Neither then nor in the subsequent campaign, however, did Roosevelt give much indication of what that program would be. In part, of course, it was because there was no need to be specific. Herbert Hoover's unpopularity virtually ensured Roosevelt's election; his only real concern was to avoid offending any voters unnecessarily. In part, however, it was because Roosevelt had no firm or coherent program to describe. Surrounded by advisers holding widely disparate views, the candidate seemed at times to be little more than a genial mediator—listening to everyone, disagreeing with no one.

There was also, however, evidence of important differences between Roosevelt and Hoover. Drawing from the ideas of a talented team of university professors (whom the press quickly dubbed the "Brain Trust"), Roosevelt espoused an amalgam of ideas that combined old progressive reform principles with some of the newer ideas of associationalism that had gained currency in the 1920s. Hoover continued to insist that the Depression was international in origin and that any attempt to combat it must be international as well. Roosevelt, in contrast, portrayed the crisis as a domestic (and Republican) problem and argued that the most important solutions could be found at home. Above all, perhaps, Roosevelt's style—his dazzling smile, his floppy broad-brimmed hat, his cigarette holder held at a jaunty angle between his teeth, his skillful oratory, his unfailing wit—all combined to win him a wide personal popularity only vaguely related to the specifics of his programs.

In November, to the surprise of no one, Roosevelt won by a landslide. He received 57.4 percent of the popular vote to Hoover's 39.7. The Socialist party, in this year of despair, garnered only 2.2 percent of the ballots. The communists polled a meager 103,000 votes. In the electoral college, the result was even more overwhelming. Hoover carried Pennsylvania, Connecticut, Vermont,

New Hampshire, and Maine. Roosevelt won everything else. And Democrats won majorities in both houses of Congress. It was a broad and convincing mandate, but it was not yet clear a mandate for what.

The Interregnum

The period between the election and the inauguration (which in the 1930s still lasted more than four months) was traditionally a

Roosevelt and Hoover en Route to Roosevelt's Inauguration, March 4, 1933
Roosevelt never forgot the awkwardness of his ride to the Capitol with the grim, unresponsive Hoover, exhausted from grappling with the banking crisis. No one would have guessed in the black days before the inauguration that the incoming president would set his mark on the age as few chief executives have. He alarmed even those closest to him with his amiability, his ready acceptance of suggestions, his quick "Fine, fine, fine." New Yorkers, fearful that his jaunty buoyancy, his facility at compromise, and his skill at political maneuver were a façade for weakness, had sometimes referred to him as "the Grin" or the "Boy Scout Governor." They did not yet see the energy and persistence with which he applied himself, or the cold iron sometimes not far beneath the charm. His physical courage they realized, for after his polio attack in 1921 he had indomitably stayed in politics, refusing to surrender to his infirmity. He had subordinated it so thoroughly that most people regarded him only as somewhat lame and never thought of him as using a wheelchair. He demonstrated his self-possession at Miami, in February 1933, by remaining astoundingly calm when an insane assassin missed him but mortally wounded the mayor of Chicago, sitting beside him. (UPI)

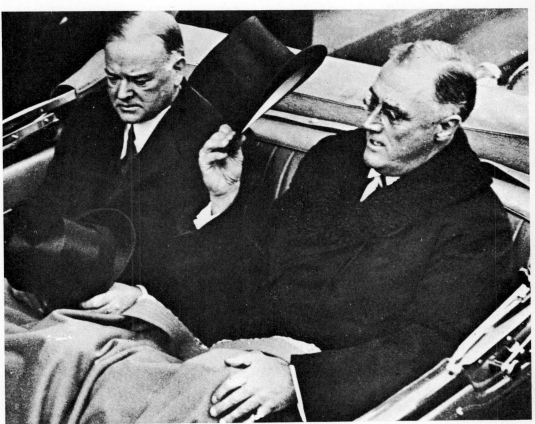

time of quiet planning and federal inaction. The winter of 1932–1933, however, was a season of growing economic crisis, and traditional patterns seemed to many Americans to be irrelevant. Among those who believed that the president-elect should act forcefully even before taking office was Herbert Hoover, who argued that international economic stability depended on a clear affirmation by the United States of the sanctity of the gold standard. He argued as well that fear of "radical" economic measures by the new administration was unsettling the domestic financial climate. In a series of brittle exchanges with Roosevelt in the months following the election, Hoover tried to exact from the president-elect a pledge to maintain policies of economic orthodoxy. Roosevelt genially refused.

In February, only a month before the inauguration, a new crisis developed. The American banking system had been in desperate trouble since the middle of 1930. By 1932, it was beginning to collapse. Public confidence in the banks was ebbing; depositors were withdrawing their money in panic; and one bank after another was closing its doors and declaring bankruptcy. The governor of Michigan, one of the states hardest hit by the panic, declared a "bank holiday" in mid-February, ordering all banks temporarily closed. Other states soon followed, and by the end of the month banking activity was restricted drastically in every state but one. Once again, Hoover wrote to Roosevelt insisting that the problem was a result of "steadily degenerating confidence" in the incoming administration. The only way to restore calm, he insisted, was for Roosevelt to give prompt public assurances that there would be no tinkering with the currency, no heavy borrowing, no unbalancing of the budget. "I realize," he wrote a Republican senator at the time, "that if these declarations be made by the president-elect, he will have ratified the whole major program of the Republican Administration." Roosevelt realized the same thing and refused to comply.

March 4, 1933, was, therefore, a day not only of economic crisis but of considerable personal bitterness. The nation waited anxiously as Herbert Hoover, convinced that the United States was headed for disaster, rode glumly down Pennsylvania Avenue with a beaming, buoyant Franklin Roosevelt, who would shortly be sworn in as the thirty-second president of the United States.

CONSTRUCTING THE NEW DEAL

Franklin Roosevelt not only served longer as president than any man in American history. He became during his years in office more central to the life of the nation than any chief executive before him. And he constructed a series of programs that permanently altered the role and structure of the federal government. Pragmatic, experimental, unwedded to any single set of social or economic beliefs, the New Deal defied easy classification or neat description. It did, however, reflect certain basic themes. It was, first, a continuation in many ways of the economic programs of the Hoover years, reflecting, in the beginning at least, the same faith in careful planning and efficient management, and sharing the same commitment to the principles of private enterprise. But it was, in addition, a set of programs that invested far stronger powers in the federal government, and that—while embracing the technocratic values of Hoover's brand of progressivism—also revived the interest in humanitarian and economic change of an earlier era of reform.

Restoring Confidence

Before Roosevelt could begin the work of rebuilding the American economy, he had to stop its decay. In particular, he had to alleviate the panic that was rapidly gripping the nation as he took office in March 1933. He did so remarkably quickly.

Part of his success was a result of his personality. Beginning with his inaugural address—in which he assured the American people that "the only thing we have to fear is fear itself"—he projected an infectious optimism that helped dispel the growing despair. He was the first president to make regular use of the radio, and his friendly "fireside chats," during which he explained his programs and plans to the people, further helped to build public confidence in the administration. Roosevelt was also a master at handling his relations with the national press. He held frequent informal press conferences, and he won both the respect and the friendship of most reporters. Their regard for the president was such that by unwritten agreement, no newsman ever photographed the president (whose legs remained completely paralyzed) being lifted into or out of his car or being wheeled in his wheelchair.

Image alone, however, could not solve the serious economic problems of March 1933; and within twenty-four hours of his inauguration, Roosevelt was moving forcefully to enact legislation that would restore at least momentary stability to the nation. With the banking crisis at a fever pitch and with Congress apparently in a mood to do virtually anything the new president suggested, Roosevelt might well have taken drastic steps, such as nationalizing the banking system. Instead, he worked to restore public confidence in existing financial institutions and to revive business's faith in the economy. On March 6, two days after taking office, he issued a proclamation closing all American banks and stopping all transactions in and all exports of gold for four days until Congress could meet in special session. Under other circumstances, the "bank holiday" might have created wide alarm. As it was, however, it produced general relief, providing a momentary hiatus in the disturbing spread of bank failures. Three days later, Roosevelt sent to Congress the Emergency Banking Act, a generally conservative bill (much of it drafted by holdovers from the Hoover administration) designed to protect the solvency of larger banks from the weakness of smaller ones. The measure authorized the Federal Reserve system to issue notes against the assets of the banks, thus increasing financial liquidity; it allowed the Reconstruction Finance Corporation to provide funds to banks by buying their stock; it forbade the hoarding and exporting of gold (thus, in effect, taking the country off the gold standard, a step that would become official on April 19). Perhaps most important to much of the public, the bill provided for Treasury Department inspection of all banks before they would be allowed to reopen. A confused and frightened Congress passed the bill within four hours of its introduction.

"I can assure you," Roosevelt told the public on March 12, in his first fireside chat, "that it is safer to keep your money in a reopened bank than under the mattress." And so it was. By his quick and confident action, Roosevelt had averted at least the immediate threat to the banking system and to the capitalist system itself. Three-quarters of the banks in the Federal Reserve system reopened within the next three days, and a billion dollars in hoarded currency and gold flowed back into them within a month. Bank failures all but disappeared in the years that followed.

On the morning after passage of the Emergency Banking Act, Roosevelt sent to Congress another measure—the Economy Act—designed to instill in the public (and especially in the business community) full confidence in the government. The act was designed to balance the federal budget by cutting the salaries of government employees and reducing pensions to veterans by as much as 15 percent. Otherwise, the president warned, the nation faced a $1 billion deficit. The bill revealed clearly what Roosevelt had always maintained: that he was at heart as much a fiscal conservative as his predecessor. And like the banking bill, it passed through Congress almost instantly.

So far, except for the gold clause in the banking bill, Roosevelt had done nothing of which Hoover and the Republicans would have disapproved. The effect, however, was the same as if he had done much more. Business confidence began to revive, and the stock market rose 15 percent in a few days. Public hopefulness quickly grew, and Roosevelt's popularity soared. Symbolic of the change in mood, perhaps, was another measure Roosevelt steered to passage during his first days in office: a bill to legalize the manufacture and sale of beer with a 3.2 percent alcohol content (an interim measure pending the repeal of prohibition, for which a constitutional amendment was already in process).

Agricultural Adjustment

Roosevelt himself was the first to recognize that these initial actions were nothing but stopgaps, that more comprehensive government programs would be necessary. The first such program was on behalf of the troubled agricultural economy, and it provided, at last, active government support for farm prices. More than that, it established an important federal role in the planning of the entire agricultural sector of the economy, a role that it would never relinquish. Farmers had long been renowned for their fierce independence; but for the most part they welcomed the new arrangements.

Within weeks of taking office, Roosevelt invited members of the various farm organizations to Washington to devise their own plan for agricultural reform. They drafted a sweeping measure that contained scraps and reworkings of many long-cherished schemes but provided most prominently for a system of crop reductions. The reforms were to be administered by the new Agricultural Adjustment Administration (AAA), which began operations in May following Congress's approval of the proposals.

Under the "domestic allotment" system of the AAA, producers of seven basic commodities (wheat, cotton, corn, hogs, rice, tobacco, and dairy products) were to receive benefit payments in return for reducing acreage or otherwise cutting production. A tax on food processing (for example, the milling of wheat) would provide the funds for the new payments; and that tax could then be added to the price of flour and other finished products and passed on to the consumer, who would thus in effect pay the farmer for growing less. Farm prices were to be subsidized up to the point of parity.

Because the 1933 agricultural season was already well under way by the time the AAA began operations, a large-scale destruction of existing crops and livestock was necessary to reduce surpluses. Six million pigs and 220,000 sows about to farrow were slaughtered. Cotton farmers plowed under a quarter of their crop. Wheat crops had been so devastated by bad weather that the AAA did not require any reductions there, but in most areas of the agricultural economy some destruction was necessary. In a society plagued by want, in which many families were suffering from malnutrition and starvation, it was difficult for the government to explain the need for destroying surpluses. The administrators of the AAA might argue that hunger in America was not a result of too little food, but of poor distribution of what food there was. They might point out that 100 million pounds of pork from the slaughtered hogs had been diverted to feed needy families. But the image of the government destroying food while poor people starved remained a powerful one and continued to fuel criticism of the Roosevelt administration for years.

The AAA had other tools at its disposal as well. It could, through the Commodity Credit Corporation, lend farmers money on the basis of their existing crops or purchase nonperishable commodities and hold them in storage against future shortages; it could lease land from farmers so as to withdraw it from production; and it could promote new marketing agreements among growers. The act creating the AAA also provided the president with power to inflate the currency by issuing greenbacks and remonetizing silver (powers he chose not to use). And the new Farm Credit Administration provided farmers with assistance in meeting mortgage payments.

The results of the AAA efforts were decidedly mixed. Prices for farm commodities did indeed rise in the years after 1933, and gross farm income increased by half in the first three years of the New Deal. The relative position of farmers in the economy, therefore, improved significantly, even though similarly rising prices for manufactured goods sharply limited their gains. But the AAA did little to help the smaller farmers, most of whom continued to languish at a competitive disadvantage in an increasingly concentrated agricultural economy. At times, even if unintentionally, the agency actually dispossessed them. In the cotton belt, for example, planters who were reducing their acreage fired many field hands and often evicted their tenants and sharecroppers.

Industrial Recovery

The industrial economy in 1933 was, as it had been for nearly three years, suffering from a vicious cycle of deflation. Production and capital investment were falling, causing workers to lose their jobs, reducing consumer demand, driving down prices, and encouraging industry to cut production and employment even further. Only by attacking all these problems simultaneously, New Deal planners believed, could American industry be revived.

Ever since 1931, leaders of the United States Chamber of Commerce had, with others, been urging upon the government an antideflation scheme that would permit trade associations to cooperate in stabilizing prices within their industries. Existing antitrust laws clearly forbade such practices, but businessmen argued that the economic emergency justified a suspension of the restrictions. Herbert Hoover had long been a supporter of the trade association movement, but he had refused to lend his assistance to the scheme.

The Roosevelt administration was far more receptive to the idea of cooperation among producers, and even to the demands of some businessmen that the government enforce trade association agreements on pricing and production. But New Dealers insisted on other provisions that would deal with the remaining economic problems as well. Businessmen would have to accept regulation of wages and hours and other concessions to labor to ensure that the incomes of workers would rise along with prices. And lest consumer buying power lag behind and defeat the scheme, the administration added another ingredient: a major program of public works spending designed to pump needed funds into the economy. For three months, the administration worked with busi-

nessmen, labor leaders, and others to construct a bill that would embody all these provisions. The result was the National Industrial Recovery Act, which Congress passed in June 1933. Roosevelt, signing the bill, called it "the most important and far-reaching legislation ever enacted by the American Congress." Businessmen hailed it as the beginning of a new era of cooperation between government and industry. Labor leaders praised it as a "magna charta" for trade unions. There was, it seemed, something in the bill for everyone.

At first, moreover, the new program appeared to be working miracles. At its center was a new federal agency, the National Recovery Administration (NRA); and to head it, Roosevelt chose the flamboyant and energetic Hugh S. Johnson, a retired general and successful businessman. Johnson envisioned himself as a kind of evangelist, generating public enthusiasm for New Deal programs. It was an appropriate image, for crucial to the success of the NRA was Johnson's ability to persuade the public to accept its provisions. He did so in two ways. First, he called on every business establishment in the nation to accept a temporary "blanket code," establishing a minimum wage of between 30 and 40 cents an hour, a maximum workweek of 35 to 40 hours, and the abolition of child labor. The result, he claimed, would be to raise consumer purchasing power, increase employment, and eliminate the infamous sweatshop. To generate enthusiasm for the blanket code, Johnson devised a symbol—the famous NRA Blue Eagle—which employers who accepted the provisions could display in their windows. Soon, Blue Eagle flags, posters, and stickers, carrying the NRA slogan "We Do Our Part," were decorating commercial establishments in every part of the country.

At the same time, Johnson was busy negotiating another, more specific set of codes with leaders of the nation's major industries—agreements designed to limit the deflationary pressures of "cutthroat competition." These industrial codes set floors below which no company would lower prices or wages in its search for a competitive advantage; and they included agreements on main-

Rallying for the NRA, 1933
The NRA emblem was a blue eagle clutching a cogwheel and a thunderbolt (symbolizing technology and energy, the cornerstones of industry). To foster compliance with the NRA codes of fair competition, merchants and householders displayed the emblem on posters, and communities staged rallies. Here, at a San Francisco demonstration in support of the NRA, 8,000 children form a giant eagle on a baseball field. (UPI)

taining employment and production. The extraordinary public support Johnson had managed to generate for the blanket code gave him substantial bargaining strength; and in a remarkably short time, he won agreements from almost every major industry in the country. A nation eager for positive action was giving the NRA its fervent support.

From the beginning, however, the New Deal's bold experiment in economic planning was plagued with serious difficulties; and ultimately, under a barrage of public criticism, the entire effort dissolved in failure. The problems were many, some of them a result of the concept of the NRA, some of them a result of its administration. Perhaps the greatest difficulty was in the structure of the industrial codes. In theory, they represented agreement among employers, work-

ers, and consumers, all of whom were represented at the bargaining table. In reality, the power lay with the businessmen themselves, and particularly with the leading figures within each industry. Often, the NRA codes were little more than rewritten versions of existing trade association agreements, strengthened now by the promise of federal enforcement. The result was, first, that most codes favored large businesses at the expense of smaller ones. Second, they often did more than simply set floors under prices; they actively and artifically raised them—often to levels higher than was necessary to ensure a profit and far higher than market forces would normally have dictated. The NRA had not been intended to promote price fixing, but in practice it did just that.

There were also serious problems in enforcement of the codes, stemming in large part from Hugh Johnson's natural affinity for the business community and his reluctance to employ forceful measures against its members. At first, most manufacturers complied happily with the new agreements, expecting a major industrial revival to result. That revivial did not come. Indeed, industrial production actually declined in the months after the establishment of the NRA—from an index of 101 in July 1933 to 71 in November—despite the rise in prices that the codes had helped to create. That failure encouraged many firms to begin cutting wages and prices once again or to violate agreements on levels of production. Johnson was not inclined to prosecute them. NRA administrators, moreover, were becoming mired in efforts to win compliance from small, local firms, spreading their energies so thin that they were unable effectively to police the large enterprises that should have been their first priority.

Another problem was that the attempts to increase consumer purchasing power did not progress as quickly as the efforts to raise prices. Section 7(a) of the charter of the NRA gave legal protection to the right of workers to form unions and engage in collective bargaining. But even though union strength increased in the ensuing months, significant wage increases were slow to follow. The public works provisions of the National Industrial Recovery Act were similarly slow to have any impact. The Public Works Administration (PWA) established by the bill to administer the spending programs was placed in the hands of Interior Secretary Harold Ickes, a self-described "curmudgeon" who only gradually allowed the $3.3 billion in public works funds to trickle out. Not until 1938 was the PWA budget pumping an appreciable amount of money into the economy.

By the spring of 1934, unsurprisingly, the NRA was besieged by criticism both from within the administration and from without. Businessmen were claiming that the wage requirements of the codes were making it impossible for them to earn adequate profits and were denouncing the provisions requiring them to bargain with unions. Economists were charging that the price fixing encouraged by the codes was undermining efforts to raise purchasing power. Reformers were complaining that the NRA was encouraging economic concentration and monopoly. Critics of all kinds were denouncing Johnson for his cozy relationship with business leaders and his increasingly erratic behavior. A national Recovery Review Board, chaired by the famous criminal lawyer Clarence Darrow, reported in the spring of 1934 that the NRA was excessively dominated by big business and unduly encouraging monopoly; and Hugh Johnson's vituperative response served only to undermine the agency's prestige even further.

Finally, in the fall of 1934, Roosevelt pressured Johnson to resign and established a new board of directors to oversee the NRA. But the agency's effectiveness failed to improve. Then in 1935, the Supreme Court intervened to bring an end to the troubled experiment. The constitutional basis for the NRA had been Congress's power to regulate commerce among the states, a power the administration had interpreted exceptionally broadly. The case before the Court involved alleged code violations by the Schechter brothers, who operated a wholesale poultry business confined to one locality: Brooklyn, New York. The Court ruled unanimously that the Schechters were not engaged in interstate commerce and, further, that Congress had unconstitutionally delegated legislative power to the president to draft the NRA codes. The legislation establishing the agency, therefore, was declared void; and the NRA was forced to cease its operations. Roosevelt expressed outrage at the so-called "sick chicken" decision and denounced the justices for their "horse-and-buggy" interpretation of the interstate commerce clause. In fact, however, the decision proved more of a blessing than a catastrophe for the New Deal, providing it with a face-saving way to abolish the decrepit NRA code system.

Regional Planning

In the AAA and even more in the NRA, those New Dealers who favored planning by private interests generally held sway. In other areas, however, those reformers who believed that the government itself should be the chief planning agent in the economy managed to establish dominance. Their most conspicuous success, and one of the most celebrated accomplishments of the New Deal as a whole, was an unprecedented experiment in regional planning: the Tennessee Valley Authority (TVA).

The TVA had its roots in a political controversy that had surfaced repeatedly in the 1920s. Throughout that decade, one of the cherished goals of the progressive reformers remaining in Congress had been public development of the nation's water resources. In particular, they had urged completion of a great dam at Muscle Shoals on the Tennessee River in Alabama, a dam begun during World War I in an effort to increase nitrate production but left unfinished when the hostilities concluded. The nation's utility companies, predictably opposed to the concept of public power in any form, had fought desperately against completion of the project, spending as much as $35 million annually in lobbying and public relations. The battle had raged on for years.

By 1933 indignation against the private power interests was intense. Monopolistic utility companies had, progressives believed, been gulling investors and overcharging customers for years. The spectacular collapse of the great Insull utility empire in the Midwest in 1932 added credence to their charges. When the public power advocates enlisted the support of Franklin Roosevelt, nothing more stood in their way.

The result was legislation enacted in May 1933 creating the Tennessee Valley Authority, a public corporation whose mandate was "national planning for a complete river watershed." The TVA was intended not only to complete the dam at Muscle Shoals and build others in the region, and not only to generate and sell electricity from them to the public at reasonable rates. It was to be the agent for a comprehensive redevelopment of the entire region: stopping the disastrous flooding that had plagued the Tennessee Valley for centuries, encouraging the development of local industries, supervising a substantial program of reforestation, and helping farmers to improve productivity. For the most part, it succeeded remarkably well. Although opposition by conservatives within the administration ultimately prevented some of the most ambitious social planning projects proposed by David Lilienthal and other TVA administrators, the project did revitalize the region in countless ways. It improved five existing dams, built twenty new ones, and constructed an extensive (and heavily trafficked) system of inland waterways. The result of all this was virtually to eliminate flooding in the region and to provide electricity to thousands who had never before had it. Indeed, the TVA soon became the greatest producer of electric power in the United States, as well as one of the cheapest suppliers. Throughout the country, largely because of the yardstick provided by the TVA, private power rates soon declined as well. The TVA also produced inexpensive phosphate fertilizers, helped farmers to prevent soil erosion, and generally raised agricultural productivity—and through it the standard of living—for the entire region. The Authority worked no miracles and made many mistakes. The Tennessee Valley remained a generally impoverished region despite its efforts. Blacks, for the most part, were excluded from employment in TVA projects and benefited only marginally from its operations. Nevertheless, most agreed that the region as a whole was enjoying significant growth and progress as a result of the government's efforts.

Financial Reforms

The primary purpose of New Deal reform, of course, was to promote recovery from the Depression. One approach, embodied in the NRA and AAA, was economic planning to regulate production. Another was to put government money into circulation through the PWA and the many relief agencies the administration established. Still another approach was to manipulate the currency so as to increase the money supply. Roosevelt's willingness to try any number of different experiments led him by the summer of 1933 to endorse that method as well.

According to some economists, the gov-

The Tennessee Valley Authority
Construction of a TVA dam in North Carolina continues under lights at night.
(TVA)

ernment could raise the prices of commodities almost automatically simply by raising the price of gold, thus inflating the currency. Federal agencies needed only to purchase large quantities of gold and cut the gold content of the dollar (measures already authorized by Congress). Acting on this advice, Roosevelt directed Henry Morgenthau, Jr., head of the Farm Credit Administration (and soon to become secretary of the treasury), to make purchases of gold each day along with his purchases of wheat, corn, and oats. A few months later, after Congress had passed the Silver Purchase Act of 1934, the president initiated a similar program for the purchase of silver. The gold- and silver-buying efforts did indeed raise the prices of the precious metals themselves. They did little or nothing, however, to raise prices in the United States; and the silver purchases, in particular, by tripling the price of the metal on the world market, wreaked havoc in nations whose currencies were on the silver standard.

Roosevelt was not an inflationist at heart, but he soon came to recognize the gold standard as a major obstacle to the restoration of adequate prices. "I have always favored sound money," he told one critical congressman, "and do now, but it is 'too darned sound' when it takes so much of farm products to buy a dollar." The Emergency Banking Act of March 1933 had been the first step toward taking the country off the gold standard; on April 18, 1933, the president made the shift official with an executive order (despite the warnings of his budget director, Lew Douglas, who had predicted the action would lead to "the end of Western civilization"). A few weeks later, Congress passed legislation confirming his decision. In January 1934, after the failure of the gold-buying experiment, the president finally established a new fixed standard for the dollar, with its gold content set at 59.09 percent of the 1932 amount. The resort to government-managed currency created an important precedent for

The New Deal

The debate among historians over the nature of the New Deal has, in many ways, mirrored the debate among Americans in the 1930s over the achievements of the Roosevelt administration. Conservatives in the 1930s denounced the New Deal as a dangerous, "socialistic" expansion of government powers, a radical threat to the most valued traditions in American life. And conservative historians writing from the perspective of later times have occasionally agreed with that assessment. Liberals in the 1930s, on the other hand, admired the New Deal as a great progressive advance toward just and sensitive government. And liberal historians have argued along much the same lines. Finally, critics from the left during the Great Depression denounced the New Deal as an inadequate response to the injustices of the era—inequitable, mired in conservatism, ineffectual. And leftist scholars have revived those charges in more recent times.

The conservative critique of the New Deal has received relatively little scholarly expression, and even less scholarly respect or attention. Edgar Robinson, writing in 1955, argued disapprovingly in *The Roosevelt Leadership* that Roosevelt had been "an eloquent proponent of revolutionary change" who moved the country toward "many of the primary leveling objectives of communism." John T. Flynn, in *The Roosevelt Myth* (1956), delivered an even more scorching attack on Roosevelt, denouncing him as both a radical and a despot.

By far the dominant view of the New Deal among scholars has been the approving, liberal interpretation—one that has appeared in various forms, but one that rests on certain basic common assumptions. First, liberals maintain, the New Deal was not a radical, socialistic, or communistic program. It was firmly within the mainstream of the American political tradition. Second, they argue, the New Deal represented a powerful (and overdue) response by the government to glaring social needs that had long gone unmet.

And third, it marked a decisive repudiation of old orthodoxies about the proper role of government, business, labor, and other groups in society.

The leading voice in this liberal chorus has long been Arthur M. Schlesinger, Jr., who argued in the three volumes of *The Age of Roosevelt* (1957–1960)—a work still to be completed—that the New Deal marked a continuation of the long struggle between public power and private interests, but that Roosevelt had moved that struggle to a new level. The unrestrained power of the business community was finally confronted with an effective challenge, and what emerged was a system of reformed capitalism, with far more protection for workers, farmers, consumers, and others than in the past.

Other liberals have gone even further in applauding the accomplishments of the New Deal. Carl Degler, in *Out of Our Past* (1959), called the Roosevelt years a "Third American Revolution" (the first two being the Revolution of 1776 and the Civil War). It marked, he claimed, "the crossing of a divide from which, it would seem, there could be no turning back." Eric Goldman, in *Rendezvous with Destiny* (1952) and later works, called the New Deal the culmination of a "Half-Century of Revolution." Although Roosevelt drew heavily on the traditions of the progressive past, "there was something more to New Deal liberalism" because it included unprecedented new departures such as social security. And Richard Hofstadter, although in many ways critical of the New Deal, made much the same argument in *The Age of Reform* (1955), admitting the continuities with the past but insisting that, as a whole, the Roosevelt program was a "drastic new departure . . . different from anything that had yet happened in the United States"—a program that even many old progressives found alarming, and opposed. The crucial change, Hofstadter argued, was in the conception of the role of government that the New Deal represented. In the past, the government had exer-

future federal policies and permanently altered the relationship between the public and private sectors. It did not, however, have any immediate impact on the depressed American economy.

Through other legislation, the early New Deal advanced even further the shift of financial power from private institutions to the federal government. The Glass-Steagall Act of June 1933 gave the government authority

cised a largely negative power—challenging inequities and excessive concentrations of influence, and attacking special privilege. Now it became as well a positive force—taking active responsibility for the welfare of American citizens, and becoming directly and continually involved in national life.

By the 1960s, however, new voices were making themselves heard, questioning both the conservative and the liberal views of the New Deal. Richard Hofstadter had offered some early criticisms, beginning in 1948, charging that the New Deal's fragmented, "pragmatic" approach had lacked a central, guiding philosophy. James MacGregor Burns, in *Roosevelt: The Lion and the Fox* (1956), raised other objections: that Roosevelt's wily political methods had often led him away from the proper goals of reform. But the first systematic "revisionist" interpretation of the New Deal came in 1963, in William Leuchtenburg's *Franklin D. Roosevelt and the New Deal.* Leuchtenburg was a generally sympathetic critic, arguing that most of the limitations of the New Deal were a result of the restrictions imposed on Roosevelt by the political and ideological realities of his time— that the New Deal probably could not have done much more than it did. Nevertheless, Leuchtenburg openly challenged earlier views of the New Deal as a revolution in social policy. He was able to muster only enough enthusiasm to call it a "halfway revolution," one that enhanced the positions of some previously disadvantaged groups (notably farmers and workers) but did little or nothing for many others (including blacks, sharecroppers, and the urban poor). Ellis Hawley augmented these moderate criticisms of the Roosevelt record in *The New Deal and the Problem of Monopoly* (1966). In examining 1930s economic policies, Hawley challenged liberal assumptions that the New Deal acted as the foe of private business interests. On the contrary, he argued, New Deal efforts were in many cases designed to enhance the position of private entrepreneurs—even, at times, at the expense of some of the liberal, reform goals that administration officials espoused.

It was, finally, historians writing from the perspective of the New Left of the 1960s who gave voice to some of the harshest criticisms of the New Deal that had appeared in the 1930s. Barton Bernstein, in a 1968 essay, compiled a dreary chronicle of missed opportunities, inadequate responses to problems, and damaging New Deal initiatives. The Roosevelt administration may have saved capitalism, Bernstein charged, but it failed to help— and in many ways actually harmed—those groups most in need of assistance. Paul Conkin, in *The New Deal* (1967), similarly chastised the government of the 1930s for its policies toward marginal farmers, its failure to institute meaningful tax reform, and its excessive generosity toward certain business interests. Even the most important progressive measures of the New Deal—the Social Security Act, for example—were marked by inadequate and regressive funding. And Howard Zinn, in an essay in 1966, harshly criticized the New Deal for working actively to preserve the worst evils of capitalism. "Many millions—businessmen, professionals, unionized workingmen, commercial farmers—had been given substantial help," he wrote. "Many millions more—sharecroppers, slumdwellers, Negroes of North and South, the unemployed—still awaited a genuine 'new deal.'"

At the time of the centennial of Franklin Roosevelt's birth in 1982, the left-wing criticisms of Bernstein, Conkin, and others had advanced little beyond these preliminary statements. Instead, most historians seemed to have reached a vague agreement that the New Deal had been an important and valuable chapter in the history of reform, even if it had worked within rigid, occasionally crippling limits. But given the volatile political mood of modern America, it seemed unlikely that many years would pass before a new interpretation—and thus a new historiographical dispute—would emerge.

---

to curb irresponsible speculation by banks. More important, in the public mind at least, it established the Federal Deposit Insurance Corporation, which guaranteed all bank deposits up to $2,500. In other words, even should a bank fail, small depositors would be able to recover their deposits. Roosevelt opposed the FDIC during congressional debate over the bill, but once in operation it proved so successful that he later approved a gradual raising of the limit on guaranteed deposits, which by the end of the decade had reached $15,000.

It was a more difficult task to work out a comprehensive overhaul of the Federal Reserve system so as to remedy the serious financial defects that had appeared during the Depression. Finally, in 1935, Congress passed a major banking act that established American finance on a stable footing with constant government supervision. The 1935 act transferred much of the authority once wielded by the regional reserve banks to the Federal Reserve Board in Washington, whose seven members now exercised direct control over interest rates. By lowering the rates, the board could make it easier to borrow money from banks and thus, in most cases, encourage prices to rise.

To protect investors in the once popular and now mistrusted stock market, Congress passed the so-called Truth in Securities Act of 1933, requiring corporations issuing new securities to register them with the Federal Trade Commission and provide full and accurate information about them to the public. In June 1934, Congress went even further and established the Securities and Exchange Commission (SEC) to police the stock market. Among other things, the establishment of the SEC was an indication of how far the financial establishment had fallen in the estimation of the public. In earlier years, J. P. Morgan and other important financiers could have wielded enough influence to stop such government interference in the financial world. Now, Morgan could not even get a respectful hearing on Capitol Hill. The criminal trials of a number of once-respected Wall Street figures for larceny and fraud (including the conviction and imprisonment of Richard Whitney, one-time head of the New York Stock Exchange and the man whose influence had briefly quelled the panic in October 1929) eroded the public stature of the financial community still further.

The Growth of Federal Relief

The most important purpose of the New Deal, Franklin Roosevelt and his colleagues believed, was to reform the economy—to restore stability and enhance productivity so that prosperity would return. In the meantime, however, millions of Americans were in desperate need of assistance, and the administration quickly recognized the necessity of providing them with relief.

Like his predecessor, Roosevelt believed that aid to the indigent was primarily a local responsibility and should remain so. But he also recognized that under the circumstances of the Depression, localities were unable to fulfill that responsibility. Among his first acts as president, therefore, was the establishment of the Federal Emergency Relief Administration, which provided cash grants to states (rather than loans, as the Hoover administration had favored) to prop up bankrupt relief agencies. To administer the program, he chose the director of the New York State relief agency, Harry Hopkins, who was ultimately to become the most important member of his administration. Hopkins, unlike Harold Ickes, realized the importance of speed in distributing government funds and disbursed the FERA grants widely and rapidly. Even he, however, shared Roosevelt's basic misgivings about establishing a government dole. "It is probably going to undermine the independence of hundreds of thousands of families," he once lamented.

Both Roosevelt and Hopkins felt somewhat more comfortable with another form of government assistance: work relief. Unlike the dole, Hopkins believed, work relief "preserves a man's morale. It saves his skill. It gives him a chance to do something socially useful." Thus when it became clear that the FERA would not be sufficient to pull the country through the winter, the administration established a second program: the Civil Works Administration. Between November and April, it put more than 4 million people to work on temporary projects: some of them of real value, such as the construction of roads, schools, and parks; others little more than make-work, such as raking leaves or supervising playgrounds. The important thing, however, was that the 400,000 CWA projects (with a budget of $1 billion) were pumping money into an economy badly in need of it and were providing assistance to people with nowhere else to turn.

Like the FERA, the CWA was intended to be a temporary expedient only. Thus as the winter continued, not only congressional critics but Roosevelt himself became increasingly uncomfortable with the program. The FERA, at least, was working through the states and localities. The CWA, even with its work provisions, was too much like a federal dole. By the spring of 1934, therefore, the president began to dismantle the agency, and he ultimately disbanded it altogether.

Of all the New Deal relief projects, the one closest to Roosevelt's own heart, and the one he had the least difficulty reconciling with his conservative beliefs, was the Civilian Conservation Corps (CCC). Established in the first weeks of the new administration, the CCC was designed to provide employment to the millions of urban youths who could find no jobs in the cities and who, in many cases, were moving restlessly from one region of the country to another in search of work. At the same time, it was to advance the work of conservation and reforestation—goals Roosevelt had long cherished. The CCC created a series of camps in national parks and forests and in other rural and wilderness settings. There, young men worked in a semimilitary environment on such projects as planting trees, building reservoirs, developing parks, and improving agricultural irrigation. As with the CWA, many of the CCC projects were of only marginal value. But the president nevertheless took great pride in the success of the corps in providing jobs to over 500,000 young men, offering them not only incomes but an opportunity to work in a "healthy and wholesome" atmosphere.

Mortgage relief was a pressing need of millions of farm owners and homeowners. Roosevelt had provided some assistance to farmers in danger of losing their land, through the AAA and particularly through the Farm Credit Administration, which within two years refinanced one-fifth of all farm mortgages in the United States. The Frazier-Lemke Farm Bankruptcy Act of 1933

went even further, enabling some farmers to regain their land even after the foreclosure of mortgages. Despite such efforts, however, small farmers continued to lose their property in many regions; by 1934, 25 percent of all American farmers had lost their land.

Homeowners were similarly troubled, and in June 1933 the administration established the Home Owners' Loan Corporation, which in a three-year period loaned out more than $3 billion to refinance the mortgages of more than a million householders. Altogether, it carried about one-sixth of the nation's urban mortgage burden. A year later, Congress established the Federal Housing Administration to insure mortgages for new construction and home repairs—a measure that combined an effort to provide relief with a program to stimulate lasting recovery of the construction industry.

The Reconstruction Finance Corporation continued, under the New Deal, to provide loans to troubled businesses. Democrats in Congress, unhappy with the RFC's tendency during the Hoover administration to make most of its loans to large banks and corporations, broadened the agency's authority so as to allow it to lend funds to smaller enterprises. The effort was only partially successful. Some small businesses did benefit from the reforms; but under the conservative management of Jesse Jones, the RFC continued to make loans only to those enterprises it believed likely to repay them. In the eyes of the agency, that meant, for the most part, large organizations.

The relief efforts of the first two years of the New Deal were intended to be limited and temporary. Few things so alarmed most New Dealers as the prospect of establishing a permanent, federal welfare state. Yet despite their efforts to limit the programs, a national policy of social welfare was beginning to emerge as a permanent element of the modern state.

SUGGESTED READINGS

Robert Sobel, *The Great Bull Market* (1968), chronicles the Wall Street boom of the 1920s; while John Kenneth Galbraith, *The Great Crash* (1954), examines the bust. Conflicting interpretations of the causes of the Depression are available in Milton Friedman and Anna Schwartz, *The Great Contraction* (1965), a reprint of Chapter 7 of their classic *Monetary History of the United States* (1963), and in Peter Temin, *Did Mone-*

tary Forces Cause the Great Depression? (1976). Friedman and Schwartz's answer to Temin's question is yes; Temin's is no. Overviews of the Depression economy include Broadus Mitchell, *Depression Decade* (1947), and Charles Kindelberger, *The World in Depression* (1973). Susan E. Kennedy, *The Banking Crisis of 1933* (1973), examines one of the Depression's low moments. Irving Bernstein, *The Lean Years* (1960), provides a compelling picture of the impact of the Depression on workers in the first years after the crash; and Arthur M. Schlesinger, Jr., *The Crisis of the Old Order* (1957), offers a picture of the broader impact of the crisis. Valuable oral histories of the impact of the Depression are available in Studs Terkel, *Hard Times* (1970), a series of interviews conducted years after the 1930s. Drawing from interviews conducted in the 1930s are Federal Writers' Project, *These Are Our Lives* (1939); Tom Terrill and Jerrold Hirsch, *Such as Us* (1978); and Ann Banks, *First-Person America* (1980). Donald Worster, *Dust Bowl* (1979), and Walter Stein, *California and the Dust Bowl Migration* (1973), offer differing views of the agricultural crisis in the Southern plains.

Important studies of the Hoover presidency include Albert Romasco, *The Poverty of Abundance* (1965); Joan Hoff Wilson, *Herbert Hoover* (1975); David Burner, *Herbert Hoover* (1978); Harris Warren, *Herbert Hoover and the Great Depression* (1959); Jordan Schwarz, *The Interregnum of Despair* (1970); and Hoover's own *Memoirs: The Great Depression* (1952). James Olson, *Herbert Hoover and the Reconstruction Finance Corporation* (1977), considers the administration's major economic innovation. Martin Fausold and George Mazuzun (eds.), *The Hoover Presidency* (1974), examines the Hoover years in a series of essays. For the foreign policy of the Hoover years, see Robert H. Ferrell, *American Diplomacy in the Great Depression* (1970); Elting Morison, *Turmoil and Tradition* (1960), a biography of Henry Stimson; Alexander DeConde, *Hoover's Latin American Policy* (1951); Raymond O'Connor, *Perilous Equilibrium* (1962), a study of the 1930 London Naval Conference; and Armin Rappaport, *Stimson and Japan* (1963).

John Shover, *Cornbelt Rebellion* (1965), studies the Farm Holiday movement; and Roger Daniels, *The Bonus March* (1971), and Donald Lisio, *The President and Protest* (1974), examine the veterans' efforts in Washington, D.C., in 1932. The emergence of Franklin Roosevelt and the election of 1932 receive extensive treatment in Arthur M. Schlesinger, Jr., *The Crisis of the Old Order* (1957); David Burner, *The Politics of Provincialism* (1967); and Frank Freidel, *The Triumph* (1956). The interregnum of 1932–1933 is examined in Frank Freidel, *Launching the New Deal* (1973); Eliot Rosen, *Hoover, Roosevelt, and the Brains Trust* (1977); and Rexford G. Tugwell, *The Brains Trust* (1968).

The best one-volume overview of the New Deal is William E. Leuchtenburg, *Franklin D. Roosevelt and the New Deal* (1963). A more thorough account of the first years of the Roosevelt administration, and one more favorable to FDR, is Arthur M. Schlesinger, Jr., *The Coming of the New Deal* (1959). Paul Conkin, *The New Deal* (1967), is a brief revisionist view that is more skeptical of the New Deal's achievements. Edgar Robinson, *The Roosevelt Leadership* (1955), is a conservative criticism. An important study of the early Roosevelt years is James MacGregor Burns, *Roosevelt: The Lion and the Fox* (1956). Gerald Nash, *The Great Depression and World War II* (1979), is a general account. The most comprehensive study of Roosevelt himself is Frank Freidel's biography in progress, *Franklin D. Roosevelt*, 4 vols. (1952–1973), the fourth volume of which follows Roosevelt through his first hundred days in the White House. Joseph P. Lash, *Eleanor and Franklin* (1971), studies the most celebrated of all first ladies and sheds light on her relationship with her husband.

The first months of the New Deal receive intensive scrutiny in Frank Freidel, *Launching the New Deal* (1973); Raymond Moley and Eliot Rosen, *The First New Deal* (1966); and Herbert Feis, *Characters in Crisis* (1966). Otis Graham, *Encore for Reform* (1967), examines the old progressives' role in the New Deal. An invaluable study of New Deal economic policy is Ellis Hawley, *The New Deal and the Problem of Monopoly* (1966). Bernard Bellush, *The Failure of the NRA* (1975), examines the cornerstone of the early New Deal economic program; and Sidney Fine, *The Automobile Under the Blue Eagle* (1963), examines the impact of the NRA on one industry. Robert F. Himmelberg, *The Origins of the National Recovery Administration* (1976), explores precursors of the NRA in the 1920s.

New Deal agricultural policy receives attention in Van L. Perkins, *Crisis in Agriculture* (1969); Richard S. Kirkendall, *Social Scientists and Farm Politics in the Age of Roosevelt* (1966); Christina Campbell, *The Farm Bureaus* (1962); and Gilbert Fite, *George M. Peek and the Fight for Farm Parity* (1954). David Conrad, *The Forgotten Farmers* (1965), examines those who did not share in the benefits of the AAA. Thomas K. McCraw, *TVA and the Power Fight* (1970), is a valuable study of the most conspicuous social project of the New Deal. Michael Parrish, *Securities Regulation and the New Deal* (1970), and Ralph F. De Bedts, *The New Deal's SEC* (1964), analyze the most prominent of the administration's financial reforms. Searle Charles, *Minister of Relief* (1963), examines the origins of welfare policies through the career of Harry Hopkins. John Salmond, *The Civilian Conservation Corps* (1967), studies the most popular of the relief agencies. James T. Patterson, *America's Struggle Against Poverty, 1900–1980* (1981), is an examination of the growth of social welfare policies, including the New Deal. Paul Mertz, *The New Deal and Southern Rural Poverty* (1978), examines some of the limits of relief.

Domestic Woes and Foreign Dangers

26

The Unemployed, 1939
Despite the many programs of the New Deal, unemployment remained a critical problem in the United States throughout the 1930s, never falling below 15 percent and rising frequently above 20 percent. Only the stimulus provided by the outbreak of World War II finally pulled the economy out of its doldrums. Here, unemployed miners idle the day away on Main Street in Herrin, Illinois. (Library of Congress)

By the beginning of 1935—the sixth year of the Great Depression—economic hardship had come to seem almost a way of life in the United States. Conditions had improved, certainly, since the desperate days of 1932; but the crisis continued. Twenty percent of the work force—10 million people—remained unemployed. National income remained 40 percent below its 1929 levels. Capital investment continued to be virtually nonexistent. And many of those who surveyed the national landscape perceived no end in sight.

Inevitably, the long years of depression had taken their toll on the nation's political and social life. The Roosevelt administration, after its vigorous and hopeful beginning, seemed to have settled into a condition of stagnant indecision. Other political groups—both the traditional opposition and a host of newer groups outside the conventional spectrum—were raising challenges to the New Deal and threatening the president's political future. Workers, intellectuals, blacks, and others were raising strident challenges to the established order. A major national upheaval seemed to be at hand.

But no such upheaval occurred. Instead, the middle years of the Great Depression exposed both the flexibility of the American political system and the innate conservatism of the American people. Franklin Roosevelt, recognizing

the danger posed by his critics, launched a much-heralded new legislative program that restored the popularity of the New Deal and helped to destroy his opposition. American society, despite some major protests and changes in certain areas, remained generally calm and moderate—preserving traditional values and trying to reconcile the Depression with them.

Whether such stability could have survived indefinitely in the face of economic crisis is another question. By the late 1930s, the Depression had lasted nearly a decade and still, many believed, there were few signs that it would soon end. But by then other issues were arising that enabled the nation to avoid confronting the implications of yet more years of economic hardship. For throughout the world, partly as a result of the Depression, which was international in scope, threats to peace were rapidly gathering force. In Asia, a militant Japan was extending its imperialist ambitions; in Europe, belligerently nationalistic governments in Germany and Italy were threatening the fragile balance of power. The United States attempted for a time to isolate itself from the expanding world crisis. But it was soon to discover that in the modern, interdependent world, a great nation could not long remain entirely aloof from great global dangers.

THE NEW DEAL IN TRANSITION

Seldom has an American president enjoyed such remarkable popularity as Franklin Roosevelt during his first two years in office. By early 1935, however, the New Deal was faced with serious problems. The Depression continued—softened, perhaps, by government programs, but generally unabated. And as a

result, the New Deal was beginning to find itself subjected to fierce public criticism. For a time the president's political future appeared in doubt. Roosevelt himself, however, appeared unperturbed by the problems. In the spring of 1935, he launched a forceful campaign of new legislation designed to preempt his critics and move the government more forcefully into the fight against the Depression.

Popular Protest

There had been opposition to the New Deal from the beginning. At first, however, the administration's critics had difficulty finding any substantial public support for their positions. But by the time two years had passed and the economy had not revived, the situation had changed. Attacks on the New Deal were now generating a substantial response.

Some of the most strident attacks came from critics on the right. Roosevelt had for a time tried to conciliate conservatives and had allowed corporate leaders to play a major role in shaping some of his early policy initiatives—most notably the NRA. By the end of 1934, however, it was clear that the opposition from the right remained unmollified. Indeed, so intense was conservative animosity toward the New Deal's "reckless spending," "economic crackpots," and "socialist" reforms that some of Roosevelt's critics could not even bear to say the president's name. They called him, simply and bitterly, "that man in the White House." In August 1934, a group of the most fervent (and most wealthy) Roosevelt opponents formed the American Liberty League, designed specifically to arouse public opposition to the New Deal's "dictatorial" policies and its supposed attacks on free enterprise. The new organization generated wide publicity and caused some concern within the administration. In fact, however, it was never able to expand its constituency much beyond the Northern industrialists (most of them Republicans) who had founded it. At its peak, membership of the organization numbered only about 125,000.

The real impact of the Liberty League and other conservative attacks on Roosevelt was not to undermine the president's political strength. It was, rather, to convince Roosevelt that his efforts to conciliate the business community had failed. By 1936, he no longer harbored any illusions about cooperation with conservatives. The forces of "organized money," he said near the end of his campaign for reelection, "are unanimous in their hate for me—and I welcome their hatred."

Roosevelt's critics on the far left also managed to produce alarm among some supporters of the administration; but like the conservatives, they proved to have only limited strength. The Socialist party of America, now under the leadership of Norman Thomas, cited the economic crisis as evidence of the failure of capitalism and sought vigorously to win public support for its own political program. In particular, it attempted to mobilize support among the most desperate elements of society—most notably the rural poor. The Southern Tenant Farmers Union, supported by the party and organized by a young socialist, attempted to create a biracial coalition of sharecroppers, tenant farmers, and others to demand economic reform. Neither the Farmers Union nor the party itself, however, made any real progress toward establishing socialism as a major force in American politics. By 1936, in fact, membership in the Socialist party had fallen below 20,000.

Somewhat more successful in using the Depression to increase its influence was the American Communist party. It attracted some significant support from within the expanding labor movement and exercised actual control over several unions. It won the backing of some prominent intellectuals and gained a large following on college campuses. Actual party membership never rose much above 50,000, but the influence of the communists spread far wider than that. Nevertheless, communism never gained anything approaching an important foothold in America even in the worst years of the Depression. The vast majority of the population remained hostile to the party. And the communists themselves were sharply divided over tactics and goals. Many believed that the real purpose of the movement should not be to oppose American capitalism but to fight against world fascism. That sentiment was largely responsible for the decision of the party in 1936 to endorse Franklin Roosevelt for reelection—a decision that created confusion and division within party ranks. Even more damaging was the 1939 friendship pact between the Soviet Union and Nazi Germany. Membership in the party declined rapidly when the communist leadership in America voiced support for Stalin's alliance with fascism.

Far more menacing to the New Deal than either the far right or the far left was a group of dissident political movements that defied easy ideological classification. Some were marginal "crackpot" organizations with little popular following; but others gained substantial public support within particular states and regions. And three men, in particular, succeeded in mobilizing genuinely national followings. Dr. Francis E. Townsend, an elderly California physician, rose from obscurity to lead a movement of more than 5 million members with his plan for federal pensions for the elderly. According to the Townsend Plan, all Americans over the age of 60 would receive monthly government pensions of $200, providing they retired from their current employment (thus freeing jobs for younger, unemployed Americans) and spent the money in full each month (which would pump needed funds into the economy). The movement raised more than $1 million in two years and commanded a formidable block of voters, most of them older men and women.

Father Charles E. Coughlin, a Catholic priest in the small Detroit suburb of Royal Oak, Michigan, achieved even greater renown by means of his weekly sermons broadcast nationally over the radio. Drawing from the Populists and other earlier political movements, he proposed a series of monetary reforms—remonetization of silver, issuing of greenbacks, and nationalization of the banking system—that would, he claimed, restore prosperity and provide economic justice. At first a warm supporter of Franklin Roosevelt, he had by 1934 become disheartened by what he claimed was the president's failure to deal harshly enough with the "money powers." In the spring of 1935, he established his own political organization, the National Union for Social Justice, which many people believed was the first step toward the formation of a third party. He was displaying an apparently remarkable influence in Congress. (An avalanche of telegrams inspired by a Coughlin sermon was generally

The Kingfish
Few public speakers could stir up a crowd as effectively as Huey Long of Louisiana, who was known to many as the "Kingfish" (a nickname borrowed from the popular radio show *Amos 'n Andy*). It was Long's own effective use of the radio, however, that contributed most directly to his spreading national appeal in the early 1930s. (George Eastman House, Rochester, New York)

believed to have been responsible for the defeat in the Senate of a treaty admitting the United States to the World Court.) And he was attracting public support throughout much of the nation—primarily from Catholics, but from others as well.

Most alarming of all to the administration was the astounding national popularity of Senator Huey P. Long of Louisiana. Long had risen to power in his home state through his strident attacks on the banks, oil companies, and utilities, and on the conservative political oligarchy allied with them that had for decades dominated the Louisiana government. Elected governor in 1928, he launched an assault on his opposition so thorough and forceful that they were soon left with virtually no political power whatever. Long dominated the legislature, the courts, and the executive departments; and he brooked no interference. When opponents accused him of violating the Louisiana constitution, he brazenly replied, "I'm the Constitution here now." Many claimed that he had, in effect, become a dictator. If so, he was a dictator who maintained the overwhelming support of the Louisiana electorate, in part because of his flamboyant personality and in part because of his solid record of accomplishment: building roads, schools, and hospitals; revising the tax codes; distributing free textbooks; lowering utility rates; and more. Barred by law from succeeding himself as governor, he ran in 1930 for a seat in the United States Senate, won easily, and left the state government in the hands of loyal, docile allies.

Once in Washington, Long, like Coughlin, soon became harshly critical of Herbert Hoover's ineffectual policies for dealing with the Depression. And, also like Coughlin, he supported Franklin Roosevelt for president in 1932. Far more rapidly than the priest, however, Long broke with the New Deal—a break that was all but complete within six months of the inauguration. As an alternative, he advocated a drastic program of wealth redistribution, a program he ultimately named the Share-Our-Wealth Plan. According to Long, the government could end the Depression easily and quickly simply by confiscating through taxation the surplus riches of the wealthiest men and women in America, whose fortunes were, he claimed, so bloated that not enough wealth remained to satisfy the needs of the great mass of citizens. By limiting incomes to $1 million annually and by limiting capital accumulation and inheritances to $5 million, the government would soon acquire enough assets to guarantee every family a minimum "homestead" of $5,000 and an annual wage of $2,500.

Long made little effort to disguise his interest in running for president. In 1934, he established his own national organization: the Share-Our-Wealth Society, which soon attracted a large following—not only in Long's native South but in New York, Pennsylvania, parts of the Midwest, and above all California. There were no accurate figures to indicate the movement's precise size, but even Long's critics admitted it might have as many as 4 million members. A poll by the Democratic National Committee in the spring of 1935 disclosed that Long might attract more than 10 percent of the electorate running as a third-party candidate, enough to tip a close election to the Republicans.

Observers in the 1930s hotly debated the significance of these dissident movements. Some believed they represented the rise of fascism in America; others claimed they were dangerously close to socialism or communism. In fact, they were neither. They represented, rather, two competing popular sentiments: the urgent desire of many Americans for government assistance in this time of need, and their equally strong desire to protect their ability to control their own lives. Long, Coughlin, Townsend, and others spoke harshly of the "plutocrats," "international bankers," and other remote financial powers who were, they claimed, not only impoverishing the nation but exercising tyrannical power over individuals and communities. They spoke equally harshly, however, of the dangers of excessive government bureaucracy, attacking the New Deal for establishing a menacing, "dictatorial" state. They envisioned a society in which government would, through a series of simple economic reforms, guarantee prosperity to every American without exercising intrusive control over private and community activities.

However much their critics may have disagreed about the merits of these programs, they agreed on one thing: the specter of dissident politics was in 1935 becoming a genuine threat to the established political parties. An increasing number of advisers were warning the president that he would have to do something dramatic to counter their strength.

The Second New Deal

In response to the growing political pressures and the continuing economic crisis, Roosevelt embarked in 1935 on a set of new initiatives that together became known as the Second New Deal. In part, the new proposals were simply an attempt to steal the thunder of the administration's critics. But they represented, too, if not a new direction at least a change in the emphasis of New Deal policy. "We have not weeded out the overprivileged," the president told Congress in January 1935, "and we have not effectively lifted up the underprivileged." His new programs, he claimed, were designed to do both.

Perhaps the most conspicuous change in New Deal policy in 1935 was its new attitude toward big business. No longer was the president attempting to conciliate financiers and industrialists. Instead, symbolically at least, he was attacking their power. In March, for example, he proposed to Congress an act to combat the concentration of power in the great utilities holding companies. In 1935, thirteen such companies controlled three-quarters of the nation's electric power; and Roosevelt spoke harshly of the injustices inherent in their monopolistic position. The companies fought desperately against the "death-sentence" bill, one of them spending $700,000 to lobby against the measure. In the end, neither side emerged entirely victorious. Congress did indeed pass the Holding Company Act of 1935; but the bill contained amendments favored by the companies that sharply limited its effects.

Equally alarming to affluent Americans was a series of tax reforms proposed by the president in 1935, a program conservatives quickly labeled a "soak-the-rich" scheme. Clearly designed to undercut the appeal of Huey Long's Share-Our-Wealth Plan, the Roosevelt proposals called for establishing the highest and most progressive peacetime tax rates in history. Rates in the highest brackets reached 75 percent on income, 70 percent on inheritances, and 15 percent on corporate incomes. In fact, the taxes sounded far more burdensome than they were (as Huey Long quickly pointed out). Nevertheless, the measure approved by Congress shifted a sizable portion of the still modest tax load onto the wealthy.

The Supreme Court decision in 1935 to invalidate the NIRA solved some problems for the administration, but it also created others. The now defunct act had contained, among other things, an important clause guaranteeing to workers the right to organize and bargain collectively. Supporters of labor, both in the administration and in Congress, advocated quick action to restore that protection. With the president himself somewhat slow to respond, the initiative fell to a group of progressives in Congress led by Senator Robert F. Wagner of New York, who in 1935 introduced what was to become the National Labor Relations Act. The new bill, ultimately known as the Wagner Act, provided workers with far more federal protection than Section 7(a) of the NIRA had offered. It specifically outlawed a group of "unfair practices" by which employers had been fighting unionization. And it created a National Labor Relations Board (NLRB) to police employers, with power to compel them to recognize and bargain with legitimate unions. The president was not happy with the bill as it moved through Congress. But he recognized the importance of labor to his own political future, and when the measure reached his desk he signed it.

The Supreme Court soon created additional problems for the New Deal, this time in the realm of agricultural policy. In January 1936, the Court struck down those provisions of the Agricultural Adjustment Act authorizing the government to regulate farm production or to tax farmers to induce them to grow less. The administration, however, remained convinced of the importance of the crop reduction program, and within weeks it won congressional approval of a new bill (the Soil Conservation and Domestic Allotment Act) that met the Court's objections while continuing the essential functions of the AAA. Now, instead of reducing production to eliminate surpluses, which the Court had claimed was an unwarranted interference with the market, the government would pay farmers to reduce production so as allegedly to "conserve soil," prevent erosion, and accomplish other secondary goals. The new law also attempted to correct one of the most glaring injustices of the original AAA: its failure to make any provision for sharecroppers and tenant farmers. Now, landlords were required to share the payments they received for cutting back production with those who worked their land. The new requirement had, however, little impact on the problem. Tenants and sharecroppers continued to receive only a minuscule proportion of the federal aid despite the regulations.

The administration embarked on other efforts to assist farmers as well. The Resettlement Administration, established in 1935, and its successor the Farm Security Administration, created in 1937, attempted through short- and long-term loans to help farmers cultivating submarginal soil to relocate on better lands. The programs ultimately succeeded, however, in moving only a few thousand farmers. Of more importance was the Rural Electrification Administration, created in 1935, which worked to make electric power available to farmers through utilities cooperatives.

New Directions in Relief

From the first moments of the New Deal, important members of the administration, most notably Secretary of Labor Frances Perkins, had been lobbying patiently for a system of federally sponsored social insurance for the elderly and the unemployed. The popularity of the Townsend movement added strength to their cause, and in 1935, finally, Roosevelt gave public support to what became the Social Security Act. It provided for several different kinds of relief. For the elderly, there were two types of assistance. Those who were presently destitute could receive up to $15 a month in federal assistance (depending on what matching sums the state might provide). More important for the future, every working American could qualify for a pension on retirement. There were severe limits on the program. Pension payments would not begin until 1942 and even then would provide only $10 to $85 a month to recipients. And wide categories of workers (including domestic servants and agricultural laborers, many of whom were black) were excluded from the program. But it was a first step in what would become the nation's most important social program for its elderly. In addition, the Social Security Act expanded the government's activities on behalf of the unemployed and dispossessed. It provided for a system of unemployment insurance, for federal aid to the blind and crippled, and for assistance to dependent children. New Dealers did not think of Social Security as a "welfare" system; even the stongest supporters of the new program continued to oppose the idea of a "dole." They insisted, rather, that Social Security was an "insurance" system, most of whose recipients would earn their benefits. In the years to come, however, Social Security was to evolve in ways its planners neither foresaw nor desired. The old-age pension program would become far more expensive and far more redistributive in its effects than expected. And Aid to Dependent Children, envisioned as a relatively modest program to aid a small number of needy people, would in the 1950s expand to become the cornerstone of the modern welfare system.

Social security was designed primarily to fulfill long-range goals. Of more immediate concern were the millions of Americans who remained unemployed and who had not yet found relief through existing government programs. To meet their needs (and not incidentally to replace such early New Deal programs of direct relief as the FERA, with which the president had always felt uncomfortable) the administration established in 1935 the Works Progress Administration (WPA). Like the Civil Works Administration and other earlier efforts, the WPA established a system of work relief for the unemployed. It far surpassed all earlier agencies, however, both in the size of its budget ($5 billion) and in the energy and imagination of its operations. Under the direction of Harry Hopkins, who had by now emerged as the New Deal's "minister of relief," the WPA employed an average of 2.1 million workers at any given moment between 1935 and 1941. The agency was responsible ultimately for the erection or renovation of 110,000 public buildings (schools, post offices, office buildings), for the construction of almost 600 airports, more than 500,000 miles of roads, and over 100,000 bridges. More important, however, the WPA provided incomes to those it employed and helped stimulate the economy in general by increasing the flow of money into it.

The WPA also displayed remarkable flexibility and imagination in offering assistance to those whose occupations did not fit into any traditional category of relief. The Federal Writers Project of the WPA, for example, offered unemployed writers support to pursue their own creative endeavors and to work on projects initiated by the agency itself. The Federal Art Project, similarly, provided aid to painters, sculptors, and others to continue their careers. The Federal Music Project and the Federal Theater Project oversaw the production of concerts and of plays, skits, and even a controversial review of public affairs known as the "Living Newspaper," thus creating work for unemployed musicians, actors, directors, and others.

Other relief agencies emerged alongside the WPA. The National Youth Administration provided assistance to those between the ages of sixteen and twenty-five, largely in the form of scholarship assistance to high-school and college students. The Emergency Housing Division of the Public Works Administration (the agency that had been established in 1933 along with the NRA, but whose benefits were slow to be felt) began federal sponsorship of public housing. It cleared some of the nation's most notorious slums and built instead some fifty new housing developments, containing nearly 22,000 units—most of them priced too high for those who had been displaced by slum clearance. Not until 1937, when Congress approved Senator Wagner's bill creating the United States Housing Authority, did the government begin to provide a substantial amount of housing for the truly poor.

The 1936 "Referendum"

The presidential election of 1936 was, it was clear from the start, to be a national referendum on Franklin Roosevelt and the New Deal. And while in 1935, there had been reason to question the president's political prospects, by the middle of 1936 there could be little doubt that he would win a second term.

The conservative opposition to Roosevelt had always been intense but never large. In 1936, it was not even strong enough to win control of the Republican party. Ignoring the anguished pleas of Herbert Hoover and others who detested all aspects of the New Deal, the party nominated the moderate governor of Kansas, Alf M. Landon, a former Bull Mooser who had never abandoned his progressive commitments. The Republican platform promised, in effect, to continue the programs of the New Deal—but constitutionally, and without running a deficit.

As for the dissidents, their strength seemed to evaporate as quickly as it had emerged. One reason was the violent death of their most effective leader, Huey Long, who was assassinated in the corridor of the Louisiana state capitol in September 1935 by a young Baton Rouge doctor. (No one ever had a chance to discover the motives of the assailant; he was gunned down on the spot by Long's bodyguards.) Another reason was the ill-fated alliance among several of the remaining dissident leaders in 1936. Father Coughlin, Dr. Townsend, and Gerald L. K. Smith (a sycophantic henchman of Huey Long trying unsuccessfully to establish himself as Long's political heir) joined forces that summer to establish a third party—the Union party. But the incessant squabbling among them, combined with the colorlessness of their presidential candidate—a mediocre North Dakota congressman, William Lemke—made the new party a ridiculous spectacle. It polled only 890,000 votes. The most important reason for the dissidents' collapse, however, was their failure ever to turn their supporters fully against Franklin Roosevelt, who had skillfully undercut the appeal of his dissident critics by espousing many of their ideas.

The campaign was a lopsided contest. Roosevelt drew huge crowds and evoked widespread enthusiasm with his impassioned attacks on the "economic royalists." Landon's pallid rhetoric and moderate platform could not effectively compete. The result was the greatest landslide in American history, Roosevelt polling just under 61 percent of the vote to Landon's 36 percent. The Republican candidate was able to carry no state except Maine and Vermont. In addition to ensuring Roosevelt a second term, the election displayed the fundamental party realignment that the New Deal had managed to effect. The Democrats now controlled a broad coalition of Western and Southern farmers, the urban working classes, the poor and unemployed, and the black communities of the Northern cities, as well as traditional progressives and committed new liberals—a coalition that constituted a substantial majority of the electorate. It would be many years before the Republican party could again muster anything approaching a majority coalition of its own.

Roosevelt emerged from the 1936 election at the zenith of his popularity and power, it appeared. Within months, however, the New Deal began to encounter serious new difficulties—both as a result of continuing opposition and as a result of the president's own political errors. His administration would never fully recover. Throughout Roosevelt's second term, recovery from the Depression remained elusive; and the New Deal, stumbling from one policy to another, appeared unable to regain the initiative it had once held.

THE NEW DEAL IN DISARRAY

The Court Fight

If the 1936 election had been a mandate for anything, Franklin Roosevelt believed, it was a mandate to do something about the Supreme Court. No program of reform, he had become convinced, could long survive the ravages of the obstructionist justices, who had already struck down the NRA and the AAA and threatened to invalidate even more legislation. Foes of such New Deal measures as the National Labor Relations Act, the Social Security Act, and the Holding Com-

Roosevelt's Second Inaugural Address [January 20, 1937]

I see a great nation, upon a great continent, blessed with a great wealth of natural resources. . . . I see a United States which can demonstrate that, under democratic methods of government, national wealth can be translated into a spreading volume of human comforts hitherto unknown, and the lowest standard of living can be raised far above the level of mere subsistence.

But here is the challenge to our democracy: In this nation I see tens of millions of its citizens—a substantial part of its whole population—who at this very moment are denied the greater part of what the lowest standards of today call the necessities of life.

I see millions of families trying to live on incomes so meager that the pall of family disaster hangs over them day by day.

I see millions whose daily lives in city and on farm continue under conditions labeled indecent by a so-called polite society half a century ago.

I see millions denied education, recreation, and the opportunity to better their lot and the lot of their children.

I see millions lacking the means to buy the products of farm and factory and by their poverty denying work and productiveness to many other millions.

I see one third of a nation ill-housed, ill-clad, ill-nourished.

pany Act were openly flouting the new laws, confident that the Supreme Court would soon disallow them. Through its narrow interpretation of the federal power over interstate commerce and taxation, and through its broad interpretation of freedom of contract, the Court seemed to have created an economic no-man's-land within which neither the federal nor the state governments could act. Roosevelt's solution was to propose expanding the Supreme Court through the addition of new justices—justices he would appoint and whose liberal views would presumably counterbalance the conservatism of the existing justices.

It was a bold measure, but it was neither a radical nor an illegal one. The Constitution called for no specific number of Supreme Court justices, and Congress had from time to time changed the size of the Court in the past. Nevertheless, the plan aroused a great public furor, largely because Roosevelt displayed what was, for him at least, an astounding political ineptitude in proposing and promoting it. Without informing congressional leaders in advance, he sent a surprise message to Capitol Hill in February 1937 proposing a general overhaul of the federal court system and including among many provisions one to add up to six new justices to the Supreme Court. The courts were "overworked," he claimed, and needed additional manpower and younger blood to enable them to cope with their increasing burdens. The explanation fooled almost no one.

Conservatives throughout the country expressed outrage at the "court-packing plan," warning that such constitutional shortcuts were the common route by which dictators seized power. And while in the past few Americans had been disposed to heed such warnings, now, as a result of Roosevelt's heavy-handed tactics, much of the public seemed to agree. Still the president had considerable political clout at his disposal; and he might well have forced Congress to approve at least a compromise measure had not the Supreme Court itself intervened in the controversy.

Even before the court-packing fight began, the ideological balance of the Court had been a precarious one. Four conservative justices could be relied upon to oppose the New Deal on almost all occasions; three were generally inclined to support it. The remaining two tended to waver, with Chief Justice Hughes often siding with the progressives and Associate Justice Owen J. Roberts more often voting with the conservatives. Were Hughes and Roberts both to side with the liberals, there would be a 5 to 4 majority in support of the New Deal without the appointment of additional justices. And that was precisely what happened. On March 29, 1937, Roberts, Hughes, and the three progressive justices voted together to uphold a state minimum wage law—in the case of *West Coast Hotel* v. *Parrish*— thus reversing a 5 to 4 decision of the previous year invalidating a similar law. Two weeks later, again by a 5 to 4 margin, the Court upheld the Wagner Act; and in May, it validated the Social Security Act. The necessity for Roosevelt's judicial reform bill had vanished. The Supreme Court had prudently moderated its position in order to avert what it considered a disastrous precedent. "You may have saved the country," Hughes jubilantly told Owen Roberts after the first decision favorable to the New Deal in March.

On one level, the affair was a significant victory for Franklin Roosevelt. No longer would the Court serve as an obstruction to New Deal reforms, particularly after a group of older justices began retiring in the following months, to be replaced by Roosevelt appointees. On another level, however, the court-packing episode was a serious defeat for the president, and one that did lasting damage to his administration. By generating public suspicion of his motives, he had reinvigorated the conservative opposition, which only months before had been in disarray. By giving members of his own party an excuse to oppose him, he had helped destroy his congressional coalition. From 1937 on, Southern Democrats and other conservatives voted against his measures with alarming consistency; never again would the president enjoy the freedom of legislative action he had had during his first years in office. Roosevelt was not even able to spare himself the embarrassment of having his Court plan publicly voted down by Congress.

"Nine Old Men"
President Roosevelt justified his plan to enlarge the Supreme Court on the grounds that too many of its members were old men who resisted progress and acted as if they were still living in the "horse-and-buggy" days. This cartoon endorsing Roosevelt's view appeared in the radical magazine *New Masses* in March 1937. (Brown Brothers)

A year later, the president's political situation deteriorated further. Determined to regain the initiative in his legislative battles, Roosevelt launched an ill-considered effort to "purge" Congress of some of its most conservative members. In Democratic primaries that spring, he openly campaigned against members of his own party who had opposed his programs. The effort was a humiliating failure. Not only was Roosevelt unable to unseat any of the five Democratic senators against whom he campaigned, but his "purge" efforts drove an even deeper wedge between the administration and its conservative opponents, ensuring that Roosevelt would suffer more legislative frustrations in the future.

Retrenchment and Recession

Hard on the heels of the court-packing fiasco came another economic crisis: a severe recession that began in the fall of 1937, continued for more than nine months, and plunged the nation into its worst suffering since 1932. It was a bitter pill for a society that was just beginning to believe that true recovery was under way; and it was a particularly bitter pill for Franklin Roosevelt, whose policies had helped to create the new collapse.

The origins of the 1937–1938 recession lay in the impressive economic progress that had preceded it. By the summer of 1937, it no longer seemed fanciful to believe that prosperity was about to return. The national income, which had dropped from $82 billion in 1929 to $40 billion in 1932, had risen to nearly $72 billion. Other economic indices showed similar improvements. To the president, therefore, the time seemed ripe for a retrenchment in government spending, for allowing the business community, as Roosevelt put it, to stand once again on its own two feet. Not incidentally, it also seemed to be a good time to balance the federal budget, whose mounting deficits had never ceased to trouble the president. And there were even arguments that the real danger now was no longer depression but inflation.

As a result, the administration moved on several fronts to cut back its recovery programs. Roosevelt persuaded the Federal Reserve Board to tighten credit by raising interest rates. More important, he drastically reduced government spending by slashing the budget for one relief program after another. Between January and August 1937, for example, he cut the WPA in half, sending 1.5 million relief workers on unpaid "vacations." The result was disaster. The fragile boom collapsed; and the private sector, left to its own devices, proved unable to revive it. The index of industrial production dropped from 117 in August 1937 to 76 in May 1938. Four million additional workers lost their jobs.

In retrospect, it is easy to discern the reasons for the collapse. The "boom" of 1937 had never been a stable or self-sustaining one even at its height. What recovery there had been was almost entirely a result of government spending. When the administration began to remove these sources of economic stimulation in 1937, recession quickly followed.

The new crisis forced yet another reevaluation of policies by the president and his advisers and produced yet another shift of emphasis within the New Deal. The advocates of government spending as an antidote to the Depression had always had to struggle for the president's favor against those who believed in more conservative fiscal policies. Now, it seemed, they stood vindicated; and the notion of using government deficits to stimulate the economy—an idea associated with the great British economist John Maynard Keynes—had established its first, timid foothold in American public policy. In April 1938, the president asked Congress for an emergency appropriation of $5 billion for public works and relief programs, and government funds soon began pouring into the economy once again. Within a few months, another tentative recovery seemed to be under way.

At the same time, another group of theorists began to win Franklin Roosevelt's ear: those who feared economic concentration and wanted the government to move forcefully to restore competition. They had been present in New Deal circles from the

beginning, but until now their position had been a weak one. By 1937, however, the president was sufficiently disillusioned with the American business community (a disillusionment only strengthened by the 1937 recession, which he tried to blame on "selfish interests") that he was willing to experiment with their approach. In April 1938, Roosevelt sent a stinging message to Congress, vehemently denouncing what he called an unjustifiable concentration of economic power. The remedy was to embark on a thorough examination of concentration with an eye to major reforms in the antitrust laws. In response, Congress established the Temporary National Economic Committee (TNEC), including representatives of both houses of Congress and of several executive agencies. At about the same time, Roosevelt appointed a new head of the antitrust division of the Justice Department: Thurman Arnold, a Yale Law School professor who soon proved to be the most vigorous trust buster to serve in that office in the nation's history. Making new and sophisticated use of the Sherman and Clayton acts, he launched more than 200 investigations over the next two years and filed 92 test cases.

Despite all this, however, the administration's commitment to restoring competition was never a wholehearted one; and the results of its antitrust efforts were ultimately of little lasting importance. The TNEC investigation ran on for nearly three years and produced volumes of testimony, but in the end it made no important recommendations for action. Nor did Thurman Arnold's vigorous tenure in the Justice Department result in any major changes in the nation's economic structure. By the time many of his cases were beginning to reach trial, World War II had begun, persuading the president that the time for antitrust activity was over. Arnold was quietly eased out of office, and the New Deal's brief experiment in trust busting sputtered to a close.

By the end of 1938, therefore, the New Deal had essentially come to an end. Not only did congressional opposition now make it difficult for the president to enact any major new programs; he had, it seemed, no new programs to propose. More important, perhaps, the threat of world crisis hung heavy in the political atmosphere, and Roosevelt was growing more concerned with persuading a reluctant nation to prepare for war than with pursuing any new avenues of reform.

THE AMERICAN PEOPLE IN HARD TIMES

Prolonged economic hardship was a new experience for most twentieth-century Americans, and as a result the Great Depression had widespread effects on the way people thought and behaved. Not only politics and government changed in the 1930s but values and cultural institutions as well. Nevertheless, hard times also revealed how strongly many traditional patterns and attitudes persisted.

Social Values

No assumption would seem to have been more vulnerable to assault during the Depression than the belief that the individual was in control of his or her own fate, that anyone displaying sufficient talent and industry could become a success. And in many ways, the economic crisis did work to erode the traditional "success ethic" in America. People became during the 1930s more accustomed to looking to their government for assistance; they learned to blame corporate moguls, international bankers, economic royalists, and others for their distress. Yet the Depression fell far short of destroying the success ethic.

The survival of the ideals of work and individual advancement was evident in many ways, not least in the reactions of those most traumatized by the Depression: responsible, conscientious working people of all economic levels who suddenly, bewilderingly found themselves without employment. Some expressed anger and struck out at the economic system. More, however, blamed themselves, if not openly, at least subconsciously. Nothing so surprised foreign observers of America in the 1930s than the apparent passivity of the unemployed, many of whom were so ashamed of their joblessness that they refused to leave their homes.

At the same time, millions responded eagerly to reassurances that they could, through their own efforts, restore themselves to prosperity and success. Dale Carnegie's *How to Win Friends and Influence People* (1936), a self-help manual preaching individual initiative, was one of the best-selling books of the decade. Harry Emerson Fosdick, a Protestant theologian who similarly preached the virtues of positive thinking and individual initiative, attracted large audiences with his radio addresses. Although many of the great financial moguls fell into wide disrepute after 1929, the public continued to revere such "self-made men" as Thomas Edison and even, to some extent, Henry Ford.

Women in the 1930s

In some respects, the 1930s were years of important change in the position of women in American society. Just as the 1920s had brought many women for the first time into business and the professions, so the 1930s brought an unprecedented number of women into government. The change was most evident within the New Deal, where Franklin Roosevelt not only appointed the first female member of the cabinet in the nation's history—Secretary of Labor Frances Perkins—but more than a hundred other women to positions throughout the federal bureaucracy. He was responding in part to pressure from his wife, Eleanor Roosevelt. A committed advocate of women's rights, she herself, through courageous work on behalf of humanitarian causes, served as an example to countless other members of her sex of the possibilities for public service. Mary Dewson, head of the Women's Division of the Democratic National Committee, was also influential in securing federal appointments for women, as well as in increasing their role within the Democratic party. Several women received appointments to the federal judiciary. And one, Hattie Caraway of Arkansas, became the first woman ever elected to a full term in the United States Senate (running to succeed her husband, who had died in office).

Symbolically important as these political gains may have been, they had little impact on the vast majority of American women, who continued to perform traditional roles as wives and mothers. Indeed, the Depression in many ways reinforced popular assumptions that the woman's place was in the home. With jobs scarce and applicants many, an increasing number of men and women alike began to advocate that what positions there were should go to unemployed men. Some, including Frances Perkins, went so far as to argue that women who had jobs should leave them so that men could take their places. Those who continued to work generally earned less than men performing comparable jobs, even on some government projects. Women in the 1930s were, perhaps, less likely to marry young (the average marriage age rose during the decade) or to bear children (the birth rate declined considerably); but neither American men nor even most American women themselves were ready to abandon their traditional views about the proper role of women.

Ethnicity

One longstanding American attitude, at least, changed considerably during the 1930s: nativism. Hostility to immigrants and their alien cultures had been a powerful force since the nineteenth century; and it had reached special intensity in the early 1920s. It did not disappear during the Great Depression, but it did abate. In part, the lessening of hostility was because of the almost complete absence of new immigrants. The restriction laws of the 1920s had stemmed the flow, and the Depression reduced it even further. Earlier generations of immigrants, at the same time, were becoming more fully assimilated; and the conspicuously alien cultures in which they had lived were becoming increasingly Americanized. There were, moreover, a number of representatives of previously unpopular immigrant groups whose public prominence in the 1930s helped win wider acceptance for their fellow ethnics. Popular heroes in entertainment (where many Jews were becoming prominent), sports (where such idols as Joe DiMaggio were emerging), and even politics (where such men as Mayor Fiorello La Guardia of New York were bringing respectability to the idea of ethnics in public office) had a substantial impact.

At the same time, American intellectuals were abandoning the supposedly scientific doctrines of the 1920s which had suggested that ethnic differences were inherited and immutable and that certain cultures, therefore, were superior to others. Instead, a series of new theories, based on scientific observation rather than speculation, was changing the academic approach to ethnicity. Anthropologists such as Franz Boas and Ruth Benedict, for example, were arguing for what came to be known as "cultural relativism." Cultural differences were not inherited, they claimed, but learned through the influence of environment. Moreover, no one culture was intrinsically superior to any other; each should be considered on its own terms. Such beliefs did not, of course, win universal or even wide public acceptance. They did, however, help to reinforce the general decline in nativist sentiment. Ethnic prejudice would continue in America, but for the most part in less strident and less vicious form than in the past.

The Racial Issue

The same could not be said, however, for racism. The Depression was a time of important changes in the lives and outlooks of American blacks, and a time of some improvements in their position in society. But it was not a time in which racism and the discrimination based on it declined in any significant way.

For the first time in American history, supporters of racial equality had, during the Great Depression, an ally in the White

Marian Anderson in Washington, 1939
Many historians refer to Marian Anderson's concert on the steps of the Lincoln Memorial in April 1939 as the first modern civil-rights demonstration. Anderson, a renowned opera singer, had been denied permission to perform in the auditorium of the Daughters of the American Revolution because of her race. Through the efforts of Eleanor Roosevelt and Secretary of the Interior Harold Ickes, a free public concert was arranged on Easter Sunday. It drew a large interracial crowd and attracted nationwide publicity. (UPI)

House. It was not the president, however, but Eleanor Roosevelt. Throughout the 1930s she exerted continuing pressure on her husband and on others in the federal government to ease discrimination against blacks. She was also responsible for what was, symbolically at least, one of the most important events of the decade for American blacks. When the black opera singer Marian Anderson was refused permission in the spring of 1939 to give a concert in the auditorium of the Daughters of the American Revolution (Washington's only concert hall), Eleanor Roosevelt secured government permission for her to sing on the steps of the Lincoln Memorial. Her Easter Sunday concert attracted 75,000 people and became, in effect, one of the first modern civil-rights demonstrations.

The president, although basically sympathetic to the plight of blacks, believed that other problems were far more pressing and was unwilling to risk losing the support of Southern Democrats by becoming too much identified with the race issue. Typical of his equivocal attitude was his harsh denunciation of lynching combined with his refusal to support legislation making lynching a federal crime. Still, Roosevelt, unlike his Democratic predecessor Woodrow Wilson, did not move to increase government discrimination against blacks; and in many ways, he gave active support to combating racism within the federal government. He appointed a number of blacks to important (if second-level) positions in his administration, creating in the process a network of officeholders that became known as the "Black Cabinet." Roosevelt appointees such as Robert Weaver, William Hastie, and Mary McLeod Bethune consulted with one another frequently and served as an active lobby for the interests of their race.

Perhaps more important, blacks benefited in significant, if limited, ways from New Deal relief programs (in large part because Eleanor Roosevelt, a close friend of relief administrator Harry Hopkins, and Harold Ickes worked hard to ensure that the programs did not exclude blacks). By 1935, according to some estimates, nearly 30 percent of all blacks were receiving some form of government assistance. Some New Deal programs, however, discriminated against blacks: the CCC, which established separate black camps; the NRA, whose codes often indirectly permitted blacks to be paid less than whites; and the AAA, whose policies led to the eviction of thousands of black farmers from their lands. But on the whole, the Roosevelt administration offered important, indeed essential, assistance to blacks to an extent unmatched by any of its predecessors.

The result was, among other things, a historic change in black electoral behavior. In 1928, the vast majority of black voters had voted Republican; by 1936, more than 90 percent of them were voting for Franklin Roosevelt. That pattern would continue in the future. "Turn Lincoln's picture to the wall," a black leader in the South said at the time. "That debt has been paid in full."

The Depression was a time, too, of important changes in the role and behavior of the leading black organizations. The NAACP, for example, began to work diligently to win a favored position for blacks within the emerging labor movement, supporting the formation of the Congress of Industrial Organizations and helping to erode racial barriers within labor unions. Walter White, secretary of the NAACP, once even made a personal appearance at an auto plant to implore blacks not to work as strikebreakers. Partly as a result of such efforts, more than half a million blacks were able to join the labor movement. In the Steelworkers Union, for example, blacks constituted about 20 percent of the membership.

At the same time, many black leaders were beginning to question their traditional belief that patient lobbying in Congress and through the courts would ultimately produce racial equality. The economic distress of American blacks, combined with adverse judicial decisions and the continuing disinterest of Congress and state legislatures in their problems, caused many to contemplate more direct forms of protest. For despite the benefits they received from the New Deal, blacks continued to languish in almost universal poverty and continued to be the victims of brutal racial discrimination. However much whites were suffering from the Great Depression, blacks were suffering worse. They were victimized, first, by the general pattern by which blacks were the "last hired and first fired"—a pattern that resulted in blacks losing their jobs far more quickly than whites when hard times arrived. Because a disproportionate number of black farmers were tenants and sharecroppers in the South, they suffered disproportionately from the crisis in Southern agriculture. Two-thirds of black cotton farmers in the 1930s made no money at all from their crops and survived only by hunting, scavenging, begging, or moving to the cities. And in the cities, both North and South, things were little better. In the past, urban blacks had had access at least to certain menial jobs unattractive to whites—such jobs as street cleaning, garbage collection, and domestic service; now even those jobs were in high demand, and most of them were going to whites. In Atlanta in 1930, an organization called the Black Shirts (consisting largely of unemployed whites) adopted the slogan "No Jobs for Niggers Until Every White Man Has a Job." In New York, department stores, insurance companies, banks, and other institutions simply refused to hire blacks for any position, no matter how modest. Moreover, local relief agencies often provided far more meager benefits to blacks than to whites.

And in addition to the continuing pattern of segregation and economic discrimination, blacks continued to suffer from random violence at the hands of whites and continued to lack effective means of legal redress. In some areas of the country, in fact, the legal system itself became an instrument of oppression. One of the most celebrated racial episodes of the 1930s was the trial and conviction of nine black youths falsely accused of raping two white women on a freight train passing through Alabama. The Scottsboro case, as it was called, attracted wide attention to the racism within the Southern judicial system. Even when the authorities received almost incontrovertible proof that the "Scottsboro boys" were innocent, the nine youths remained imprisoned; several of them were not released for years. Few could doubt that similar examples of racism were occurring elsewhere, outside the glare of publicity.

Hispanics and Indians

America's Hispanic population had been growing steadily since early in the century, largely in California and in the Southwest, through massive immigration from Mexico (which was specifically excluded from the restriction laws of the 1920s). Mexican-Americans in the Southwest filled many of the same menial jobs that blacks had traditionally occupied in other regions. Others began to farm on small, marginal tracts. Still more became agricultural migrants, traveling from region to region harvesting fruit, lettuce, and other crops. Even during the prosperous 1920s, it had been a precarious existence. The Depression made things significantly worse. In some parts of the Southwest, and particularly in Texas, public and official pressure combined to force thousands of Mexican immigrants out of the country. In California, local police occasionally raided the *barrios* (Hispanic neighborhoods), rounding up Mexican-Americans and forcing them to return to Mexico. More than half a million Hispanics left the country in response to such pressures.

For those who remained, there were both economic hardships and increasing social discrimination. A few New Deal programs offered assistance to Mexican-Americans; in Texas, the head of the state branch of the National Youth Administration, Lyndon Baines Johnson, worked to ensure that some of the agency's benefits were distributed to Hispanics. More often, however, local administrators excluded Mexicans from the relief rolls or offered them benefits far lower than those available to whites. Mexican-Americans often had no access to schools, and many hospitals refused them admission. Unlike American blacks, who had in response to discrimination established certain educational and social facilities of their own, Hispanics had nowhere to turn. Even those of them who possessed American citizenship found themselves treated like unwelcome foreigners. There were, occasionally, signs of organized resistance by Mexican-Americans themselves, most notably in California, where they attempted to form a union of migrant farm workers. But harsh repression by local growers and the public authorities allied with them prevented such organizations from making significant progress. Like black farm workers, many Hispanics began as a result to migrate to Western cities, where they lived in a poverty comparable to that of urban blacks in the South and Northeast.

For the most tragically exploited of all American minorities—Indians—the 1930s were years of several important changes. The Indian Reorganization Act of 1934 reversed the longstanding government policy of encouraging the assimilation of Native Americans into the mainstream of the nation's culture, a policy that had generally served as an excuse for robbing Indians of their tribal lands and reducing them to indigence. The act returned significant authority to the tribes to govern themselves, provided government funds to support education and cultural activities, and perhaps most important, restored the right of tribes to own land as collective entities. Previously, the government had required all Indian land to be owned by individuals. Other New Deal policies also assisted Indians. The Soil Conservation Service, for example, helped the Navajos improve their range lands and offered needed employment to many Indians on soil conservation and erosion prevention projects.

Nevertheless, American Indians remained through the 1930s what they had been for many years: an impoverished and isolated minority. Even with the redistribution of lands under the 1934 act, Indians continued to possess, for the most part, only territory that whites did not want—much of it arid, some of it desert. They continued to lack real authority to govern their own economic and social relationships, even inside their reservations. And they continued to lose property to white encroachment. Most of all, they continued to live in desperate poverty. In 1934, the average income of an American Indian was $48 a year.

Labor Militancy

American labor in the 1930s took a giant stride toward establishing itself as a powerful interest group, capable at last of challenging the power of industrialists and of winning important new benefits. During the 1920s, workers had displayed little militancy in challenging employers or demanding recognition of their unions. They had faced a powerful and highly popular business establishment. They were often coopted by the system of "welfare capitalism," which provided them with increased wages and benefits in return for their general passivity. And they had been saddled with conservative labor organizations, unwilling to risk the modest gains already won.

In the 1930s, these inhibiting factors quickly vanished. Businessmen and industrialists lost (if only temporarily) the high public standing they had enjoyed in the New Era; and on matters of labor policy at least, they lost the support of the government. Through Section 7(a) of the National Industrial Recovery Act of 1933 and, more importantly, through the Wagner Act of 1935, labor won legal guarantees of their right to organize and bargain collectively, as well as enforcement mechanisms to protect those rights. At the same time, the "welfare capitalism" of the 1920s vanished almost overnight. With the economy in sharp decline, employers quickly rescinded most of the gains they had offered labor in the preceding years. Those workers who kept their jobs often did so only by accepting reduced wages and fewer benefits. Finally, as the decade progressed, new labor organizations emerged to challenge the established, conservative unions. The result was, among other things, an important change in the outlook of many workers: a growing resentment of conditions as they were, and an increasing commitment to the idea of organizing to rectify them.

Even though the American Federation of Labor, under the leadership now of William Green, increased its activities in response to the Depression, it proved painfully inadequate for the task at hand. The A.F. of L. remained committed to the idea of the craft union: the idea of organizing workers on the basis of their skills. As a result, the Federation offered little hope to unskilled laborers, even though it was the unskilled who now constituted the bulk of the industrial work force.

During the 1930s, therefore, another concept of labor organization emerged to challenge the traditional craft union ideal: the concept of industrial unionism. Advocates of this approach argued that all the workers in a particular industry should be organized in a single union, regardless of what functions the workers performed. All auto workers should be in a single automobile union; all steel workers should be in a single steel union. Workers divided into many small unions would, many labor leaders were beginning to claim, lack the strength to deal successfully with the great corporations. United into a single great union, however, they would wield considerable power.

Leaders of the A.F. of L. for the most part opposed the new concept. But industrial unionism found a number of important spokesmen, most prominent among them John L. Lewis. Lewis was the talented, flamboyant, and eloquent leader of the United Mine Workers—the oldest major union in the country organized along industrial rather than craft lines. He was also a charismatic public figure, whose personal magnetism alone helped win thousands of recruits to his cause.

At first, Lewis and his allies attempted to work within the A.F. of L., but friction between the new industrial organizations and the older craft unions grew rapidly as a result. At the 1935 A.F. of L. convention, Lewis became embroiled in a series of angry confrontations (and one celebrated fistfight) with craft union leaders before finally walking out. A few weeks later, he created the Committee on Industrial Organization—a body officially within the A.F. of L. but unsanctioned by its leadership. After a series of bitter jurisdictional conflicts, the A.F. of L. finally expelled the new committee from its ranks, and along with it all the industrial unions it represented. In response, Lewis simply renamed the committee the Congress of Industrial Organizations (CIO), established it in 1936 as an organization directly rivaling the A.F. of L., and became its first president. The schism clearly weakened the labor movement as a whole in many ways. But by freeing the advocates of industrial unionism from the restrictive rules of the Federation, it gave important impetus to the creation of powerful new organizations.

Organizing Battles

Those new organizations had been struggling for recognition even before the schism of

John L. Lewis in Washington
John L. Lewis (*left*), president of the United Mine Workers, emerges from a meeting in Washington with Secretary of Labor James J. Davis, who served in the Harding, Coolidge, and Hoover administrations. Only a few years later, Lewis would become the most dynamic and effective labor leader in American history, serving as the guiding force behind the creation of the Congress of Industrial Organizations. (Library of Congress)

1936. Major battles were under way, in particular, in the automobile and steel industries. Out of a myriad of competing auto unions, the United Auto Workers (UAW) was, during the early and mid-1930s, gradually emerging preeminent. But through 1936, although steadily gaining recruits, it was making little progress in winning recognition from the corporations.

In December 1936, however, workers introduced a new and dramatically effective technique for challenging corporate opposi-

tion: the sit-down strike. Employees in several GM plants in Detroit simply sat down inside the plants, refusing either to work or to leave, thus preventing the company from making use of strikebreakers. The tactic quickly spread to other locations, so that by February 1937 strikers had occupied seventeen General Motors plants. The strikers ignored court orders to vacate the buildings, and they successfully resisted sporadic efforts by local police to remove them. When Michigan's governor Frank Murphy, a liberal

Democrat, refused to call out the National Guard to clear out the strikers, the company had little choice but to relent. General Motors became in February 1937 the first major manufacturer to recognize the UAW; other automobile companies soon did the same. (The sit-down strike proved effective in rubber and other industries as well; but it survived only briefly as a labor technique. It was clearly illegal, and it aroused widespread public outrage and alarm; so labor leaders ultimately abandoned it.)

In the steel industry, the battle for unionization was less easily won. In 1936, the CIO had voted a $500,000 fund to support the Steel Workers' Organizing Committee (later United Steelworkers of America) in a major campaign. Over the next few months, the on-slaught began, with the SWOC quickly recruiting tens of thousands of workers and staging a series of prolonged and often bitter strikes. In March 1937, to the amazement of almost everyone, United States Steel, the giant of the industry, relented. Rather than risk a costly strike at a time when it sensed itself on the verge of recovery from the Depression, the company signed a contract with the SWOC, the new organization's first important victory.

The lesser companies (known as "Little Steel") were, however, far less ready to surrender. On Memorial Day 1937, a group of striking workers from Republic Steel gathered with their families for a picnic and demonstration in South Chicago; and when they attempted to march peacefully (and legally)

Police Battling Strikers, 1937
A newsreel photographer took pictures of the "Memorial Day Massacre," in which policemen wielding guns and billy clubs attacked strikers at the Republic Steel plant in South Chicago. The police killed ten CIO pickets and seriously injured many other demonstrators. (Wide World)

toward the steel plant, police opened fire on them. Ten demonstrators were killed; another ninety were wounded. Despite a public outcry against the "Memorial Day Massacre," the harsh tactics of "Little Steel" ultimately proved successful. The 1937 strike failed.

But the victory of "Little Steel" was the exception rather than the rule; it was, in fact, one of the last gasps of the kind of brutal, naked strikebreaking that had proved so effective in the past. In the course of 1937, one of the most turbulent years in the history of American labor, there were 4,720 strikes—over 80 percent of them settled favorably to the unions. By the end of the year, more than 8 million workers were members of unions (as compared with 3 million in 1932). By 1941, that number had expanded to 10 million and included the workers of "Little Steel," which had finally relented. Workers were somewhat slower to win major new wage increases and benefits than they were to achieve union recognition. But the organizing battles of the 1930s had established the labor movement as a powerful force in the American economy.

Depression Culture

Just as many progressives had become alarmed when, early in the twentieth century, they "discovered" the existence of widespread poverty in the cities, so many Americans were shocked during the 1930s at their discovery of debilitating rural poverty. The plight of the farmer—and particularly of the Southern tenant farmer and sharecropper—became one of the leading themes of Depression intellectual life.

Perhaps most effective in conveying the dimensions of rural poverty was a group of documentary photographers, many of them employed by the Farm Security Administration in the late 1930s, who traveled through the South recording the nature of agricultural life. Men such as Roy Stryker, Walker Evans, Arthur Rothstein, and Ben Shahn and women such as Margaret Bourke-White and Dorothea Lange produced memorable studies of farm families and their surroundings,

studies designed to show the savage impact of a hostile environment on its victims. Through their work, not only did the problems of poverty receive wider public attention but the art of photography earned new stature.

Writers, similarly, turned away from the personal concerns of the 1920s and, in many cases, devoted themselves to searing exposés of social injustice. Erskine Caldwell exposed many of the same injustices that the FSA photographers had studied, in *Tobacco Road* (1932)—a novel about life in the rural South, which later became a long-running play. James Agee produced one of the most powerful portraits of the lives of sharecroppers, in *Let Us Now Praise Famous Men* (1941)—a careful, nonjudgmental description of the lives of three Southern families, illustrated with photographs by Walker Evans. Other writers and artists turned their gaze on social injustice in other settings. Richard Wright, a major black novelist, exposed the plight of residents of the urban ghetto, in *Native Son* (1940). James T. Farrell, in *Studs Lonigan* (1936), depicted the savage world of urban, lower-class white youths.

An even larger number of artists and intellectuals moved beyond social realism, combining an effort to expose social problems with a commitment to political solutions. Some were successful novelists of the 1920s who now turned to new themes. Ernest Hemingway, in *To Have and Have Not* (1937), displayed for the first time a concern with social issues by portraying a bitter labor struggle and advocating a collective solution; in *For Whom the Bell Tolls* (1940), he used the Spanish Civil War as a setting through which to illustrate the importance of solidarity in the face of oppression. Other, newer writers were discussing similar themes. John Steinbeck's *The Grapes of Wrath* (1939) portrayed the trials of a migrant family in California, concluding with an open call for collective social action against injustice. John Dos Passos's *U.S.A.* trilogy (1930–1937) explicitly attacked modern capitalism. Playwright Clifford Odets provided a particularly explicit demonstration of the appeal of political radicalism in *Waiting for Lefty* (1935).

For the most part, however, the cultural

products of the 1930s that attracted wide popular audiences were those that were more effective in diverting attention away from the Depression than in illuminating its problems. The two most powerful instruments of popular culture in the 1930s—radio and the movies—were particularly careful to provide mostly light and diverting entertainment. The radio industry, still fearful of the possibility of nationalization (as was occurring in other countries just establishing broadcasting systems), made every effort to avoid controversy. Although many stations carried inflammatory programs, among them Father Coughlin's sermons, the staple of broadcasting was escapism: comedies such as *Amos 'n Andy;* adventures of the *Superman* or *Dick Tracy* type; and other programs of pure entertainment. Hollywood continued to exercise tight control over its products through its resident censor Will Hays, who, in response

to growing pressure from the Catholic church's Legion of Decency, founded in 1934, redoubled his efforts to ensure that movies carried only banal, conventional messages. There were some pictures—for example, the film version of *The Grapes of Wrath*—that provided a muted political message. Far more frequent, however, were such movies as the "screwball" comedies of Frank Capra, in which evidence of economic hardship was only occasionally visible.

Popular literature, similarly, offered Americans an escape from the Depression rather than an investigation of it. Two of the best-selling novels of the decade, for example, were romantic sagas set in bygone eras: Margaret Mitchell's *Gone with the Wind* (1936), which became the source of one of the most celebrated films of all time; and Hervey Allen's *Anthony Adverse* (1933). Leading magazines, and particularly such popular

Astaire and Rogers
Although some 1930s films tried to portray the misery and social turmoil created by the Great Depression, far more typical were movies that offered pure entertainment—such as *Top Hat* (1935), starring the famous and popular dancing team of Fred Astaire and Ginger Rogers. (Culver Pictures)

new photographic journals as *Life*, did offer occasional glimpses of the ravages of the Depression. But for the most part, they concentrated on fashions, stunts, and eye-catching scenery. Even the newsreels distributed to movie theaters across the country tended to give more attention to beauty contests and ship launchings than to the Depression itself. The American people had not only prevented the Great Depression from destroying their traditional values and institutions; they had, apparently, decided to try to keep from even being reminded of it.

AMERICA AND THE WORLD CRISIS

Even as the United States was struggling to extricate itself from the worst economic crisis in its history, the nation was beginning to feel the effects of the decaying of the international structure, which would ultimately produce a catastrophic war. The two problems were not unrelated. The worldwide depression of the 1930s was producing political chaos throughout the globe; and in response to the economic problems were emerging a series of highly nationalistic, dangerously belligerent governments: most notably in Japan, Italy, and Germany.

Through most of the 1930s, however, the United States was unwilling to make more than the faintest of gestures toward restoring stability to the world. Like many other peoples suffering economic hardship, Americans were turning inward. Yet the realities of world affairs were not to allow the nation to remain isolated for very long—as Franklin Roosevelt realized earlier than most of his countrymen.

Depression Diplomacy

From Herbert Hoover, Roosevelt inherited a foreign policy less concerned with issues of war and peace than with matters of economic policy. And although the New Deal rejected some of the initiatives the Republicans had begun, it continued for several years to base its foreign policy almost entirely on the nation's immediate economic needs.

Perhaps Roosevelt's sharpest break with the policies of his predecessor was on the question of American economic relations with Europe. Hoover had argued that only by resolving the question of war debts and rein-forcing the gold standard could the American economy hope to recover. He had, therefore, agreed to participate in the World Economic Conference, to be held in London in June 1933, to attempt to resolve these issues. By the time the conference assembled, however, Roosevelt had already become convinced that the gold value of the dollar had to be allowed to fall in order for American goods to be able to compete in world markets. Shortly after the conference convened, Roosevelt released a famous "bombshell" message repudiating the orthodox views of most of the delegates and rejecting any agreement on currency stabilization. The conference quickly dissolved without reaching agreement; and not until 1936 did the administration finally agree to new negotiations to stabilize Western currencies.

At the same time, Roosevelt was moving to abandon the commitments of the Hoover administration to settle the issue of war debts through international agreement. In effect, he simply let the issue die. Not only did he decline to negotiate a solution at the London Conference, but in April 1934 he signed a bill to forbid American banks from making loans to any nation in default on its debts. The result was to stop the old, circular system by which debt payments continued only by virtue of increasing American loans; within months, war-debt payments from every nation except Finland stopped for good.

If the new administration had no interest in international currency stabilization or settlement of war debts, it did have an active interest in improving America's position in world trade. Roosevelt approved the Reciprocal Trade Agreement Act of 1934, authorizing the administration to negotiate treaties lowering tariffs by as much as 50 percent in return for reciprocal reductions by other nations. The immediate effect of the reciprocal trade agreements negotiated as a result of the act was not impressive. Most agreements in the 1930s were carefully drafted to admit only products not competitive with American industry and agriculture; and although by 1939 Secretary of State Cordell Hull had succeeded in negotiating new treaties with twenty-one countries (increasing American exports to them by nearly 40 percent), imports into the United States continued to lag. As a result, other nations were not obtaining the American currency needed to buy American products, and foreign debts to the United States increased considerably.

American hopes of expanding its foreign trade produced particular efforts by the administration to improve its diplomatic posture in two areas: the Soviet Union and Latin America. The United States and Russia had viewed each other with mistrust and even hostility since the Bolshevik Revolution of 1917, and the American government still had not officially recognized the Soviet regime by 1933. But powerful voices within the United States were urging a change in policy—less because the revulsion with which most Americans viewed communism had diminished than because the Soviet Union appeared to be a possible source of important trade. The Russians, too, were eager for a new relationship. They were hoping for American cooperation in containing the power of Japan on Russia's southeastern flank. In November 1933, therefore, Soviet Foreign Minister Maxim Litvinov reached an agreement with the president in Washington. The Soviets would cease their propaganda efforts in the United States and protect American citizens in Russia; in return, the United States would recognize the communist regime.

Despite this promising beginning, however, relations with the Soviet Union soon soured once again. American trade failed to establish a foothold in Russia, disappointing hopes in the United States; and the American government did little to reassure the Soviets

that it was interested in stopping Japanese expansion in Asia, dousing expectations in Russia. By the end of 1934, the Soviet Union and the United States were once again viewing each other with considerable mistrust. And Stalin, having abandoned whatever hopes he might once have held of cooperation with America, was beginning to consider making agreements of his own with the fascist governments of Japan and Germany.

Somewhat more successful were American efforts to enhance both diplomatic and economic relations with Latin America through what became known as the "Good Neighbor Policy." Latin America was one of the most important targets of the new policy of trade reciprocity, and the United States succeeded during the 1930s in increasing both exports to and imports from the other nations of the Western Hemisphere by over 100 percent. Closely tied to these new economic relationships was a new American attitude toward intervention in Latin America. The Hoover administration had unofficially abandoned the earlier American practice of using military force to compel Latin American governments to repay debts, respect foreign investments, or otherwise behave "responsibly." The Roosevelt administration went even further. At the Inter-American Conference in Montevideo in December 1933, Secretary of State Hull signed a formal convention declaring: "No state has the right to intervene in the internal or external affairs of another." Roosevelt respected that pledge throughout his years in office, refusing to use force against Latin American governments even in the face of strong domestic pressure.

The Good Neighbor Policy did not mean, however, that the United States had abandoned its influence in Latin America. On the contrary, it had simply replaced one form of leverage with another. Instead of military force, Americans would now use economic influence. The new reliance on economic pressures eased tensions between the United States and its neighbors considerably, eliminating the most abrasive and conspicuous irritants in the relationship. It did little, however, to stem the growing American domination of the Latin American economy.

The Rise of Isolationism

The first years of the Roosevelt administration marked not only the death of Hoover's hopes for international economic agreements. They marked, too, the end of any hopes for world peace through treaties and disarmament. That the international arrangements of the 1920s were no longer suitable for the world of the 1930s became obvious in the first months of the Roosevelt presidency, when the new administration attempted to stimulate movement toward world disarmament. An arms control conference in Geneva had been meeting, without result, since 1932; and in May 1933, Roosevelt attempted to spur it to action by submitting a new American proposal for arms reductions. Negotiations stalled and then broke down on the Roosevelt proposal; and only a few months later, first Hitler and then Mussolini withdrew from the talks altogether. The Geneva Conference, it was clear, was a failure. Two years later, Japan withdrew from the London Naval Conference, which was attempting to draw up an agreement to continue the limitations on naval armaments negotiated at the Washington Conference of 1921.

The deteriorating international situation presented the United States with a choice between more active efforts to stabilize the world or more energetic attempts to isolate the nation from it. Almost without hesitating, Americans chose the latter. Support for isolationism emerged from many quarters. Old Wilsonian internationalists had grown disillusioned with the League of Nations and its inability to stop Japanese aggression in Asia; internationalism, they were beginning to argue, had failed. Other Americans were listening to the argument that powerful business interests—Wall Street, munitions makers, and others—had tricked the United States into participating in World War I. An investigation by a Senate committee chaired by Senator Gerald Nye of Colorado revealed exorbitant profiteering and blatant tax evasion by many corporations during the war, and it suggested that bankers had pressured Wilson to intervene so as to protect their loans abroad.

Roosevelt himself shared some of the suspicions of the isolationists and claimed to be impressed by the findings of the Nye investigation. Nevertheless, he continued to hope for at least a modest American role in maintaining world peace. In 1935, he proposed to the Senate a treaty to make the United States a member of the World Court—a treaty that would have expanded America's symbolic commitment to internationalism without increasing its actual responsibilities in any important way. Nevertheless, isolationist opposition (spurred by a passionate broadcast by Father Coughlin on the eve of the Senate vote) resulted in the defeat of the treaty. It was a devastating political blow to the president, and he would not soon again attempt to challenge the isolationist tide.

That tide was growing stronger with every passing month. Through the summer of 1935, it became clear to the world that Mussolini's Italy was preparing to invade Ethiopia in an effort to expand its colonial holdings in Africa. Fearing that a general European war would ensue, American legislators began to design legislative safeguards to prevent the United States from being dragged into the conflict. The result was the Neutrality Act of 1935.

The 1935 act, and the Neutrality Acts of 1936 and 1937 that followed, were designed to prevent a recurrence of the events that many Americans now believed had pressured the United States into World War I. The 1935 law established a mandatory arms embargo against both victim and aggressor in any military conflict and empowered the president to warn American citizens that they might travel on the ships of warring nations only at their own risk. Thus, isolationists believed, the "protection of neutral rights" could not again become an excuse for American intervention in war. The 1936 Neutrality Act renewed these provisions. And in 1937, with world conditions growing even more precarious, Congress passed a yet more stringent measure. The new Neutrality Act established the so-called cash-and-carry policy, by which belligerents could purchase nonmilitary goods from the United States only by paying cash and shipping their pur-

Hitler at Nuremberg
The rising power of Nazi Germany provided an ominous backdrop to American foreign policy during the 1930s. Here, Hitler passes before troops and ardent followers during one of the Nazi party's enormous, highly disciplined rallies at Nuremberg. (Photoworld)

chases themselves. Critics ridiculed the measures as laws "to keep the United States out of World War I." But the isolationists were undeterred.

The American stance of militant neutrality was reinforced in October 1935 when Mussolini finally launched his long-anticipated attack on Ethiopia. When the League of Nations protested, Italy simply resigned from the organization, completed its conquest of Ethiopia, and formed an alliance (or "axis") with Nazi Germany. Americans responded to the news with renewed determination to isolate themselves from European instability. Two-thirds of those responding to public opinion polls at the time opposed any American action to deter aggression.

Isolationist sentiment showed its strength once again in 1936 and 1937 in response to a

civil war in Spain. The Falangists of General Francisco Franco, a group much like the Italian fascists, revolted in July 1936 against the existing government, a moderate constitutional monarchy. Hitler and Mussolini supported Franco, both vocally and with weapons and supplies. The United States joined with Britain and France in an agreement to offer no assistance to either side. Since all three nations were more sympathetic to the Loyalists than to the Falangists, the result of the agreement was to deny what might otherwise have been crucial aid to the anti-Franco forces.

Growing Dangers

Franklin Roosevelt was viewing the events of 1935 and 1936 with alarm. Slowly, cautiously, he attempted to challenge the grip of the isolationists on the nation's foreign policy; yet for a time, it seemed to be a hopeless cause. The United States appeared unable to do more than watch as a series of new dangers emerged that brought the world closer to war.

Particularly disturbing was the decaying situation in Asia, where the growth of Japanese power was becoming a direct threat to international stability. Japan's aggressive designs against China had been clear since the invasion of Manchuria in 1931. In the summer of 1937, Tokyo launched an even more devastating assault, attacking China's five northern provinces. The United States could not, Roosevelt believed, allow the Japanese aggression to go unremarked or unpunished. In October 1937, therefore, the president set out to arouse public support for a policy of containment in the Pacific. In a speech in Chicago, he warned forcefully of the dangers that Japanese aggression posed to world peace. Aggressors, he proclaimed, should be "quarantined" by the international community to prevent the contagion of war from spreading.

The president was deliberately vague about what such a "quarantine" would mean; and there is evidence that he was contemplating nothing more drastic than a break in diplomatic relations with Japan, that he was not considering economic or military sanctions. Nevertheless, public response to the speech was disturbingly hostile. As a result, Roosevelt drew back. Although his strong words had encouraged the British government to call a conference in Brussels to discuss the crisis in Asia, the United States now refused to make any commitments to collective action; and the conference produced no agreement.

Only months later, another episode gave renewed evidence of how formidable the obstacles to Roosevelt's efforts remained. On December 12, 1937, Japanese aviators bombed and sank the United States gunboat *Panay* as it sailed the Yangtze River in China. The attack was almost undoubtedly deliberate. It occurred in broad daylight, with clear visibility; and a large American flag had been painted conspicuously on the *Panay*'s deck. Even so, the American public seized eagerly on Japanese protestations that the bombing had been an accident and pressured the administration to accept Japan's apologies and overlook the attack.

The Failure of Munich

In the meantime, Roosevelt was unable to find any politically acceptable way to increase American influence in Europe. It was not yet clear, moreover, that he believed the United States should become involved there in any case, even though the forces of war were rapidly gathering momentum. In 1936, Hitler had moved the now powerful German army into the Rhineland, rearming an area that France had, in effect, controlled since World War I. In March 1938, German forces marched into Austria; and Hitler proclaimed a union (or *Anschluss*) between Austria, his native land, and Germany, his adopted one. Neither in America nor in Europe was there much more than a murmur of opposition.

The Austrian invasion, however, soon created another crisis; for Hitler had by now occupied territory surrounding three sides of western Czechoslovakia, a region he dreamed of annexing to provide Germany with the *Lebensraum* (living space) he believed it needed. In September 1938, he demanded that Czechoslovakia cede to him part of that region, the Sudetenland, an area on the Austro-German border in which many ethnic Germans lived. Czechoslovakia, which possessed substantial military power of its own, was prepared to fight rather than submit. But it realized it could not hope for success without assistance from other European nations. That assistance it did not receive. Most Western nations, including the United States, were appalled at the prospect of another war and were willing to pay almost any price to settle the crisis peacefully. Finally, on September 29, Hitler met with the leaders of France and Great Britain at Munich in an effort to resolve the crisis. The French and British agreed to accept the German demands in Czechoslovakia in return for Hitler's promise to expand no farther. "This is the last territorial claim I have to make in Europe," the Führer solemnly declared. And Prime Minister Neville Chamberlain returned to England

Lindbergh's Isolationist Argument [1941]

I know I will be severely criticized by the interventionists in America when I say we should not enter a war unless we have a reasonable chance of winning. . . . But I do not believe that our American ideals, and our way of life, will gain through an unsuccessful war. And I know that the United States is not prepared to wage war in Europe successfully at this time. . . .

There is a policy open to this nation that will lead to success—a policy that leaves us free to follow our own way of life, and to develop our own civilization. It is not a new and untried idea. . . .

It is based upon the belief that the security of a nation lies in the strength and character of its own people. It recommends the maintenance of armed forces sufficient to defend this hemisphere from attack by any combination of foreign powers. It demands faith in an independent American destiny. This is the policy of the America First Committee today. It is a policy not of isolation, but of independence; not of defeat, but of courage. —*The New York Times*, April 24, 1941.

to a hero's welcome, assuring his people that the agreement ensured "peace in our time." Among those who had cabled him encouragement at Munich was Franklin Roosevelt.

The Munich accords were the most prominent elements of a policy that came to be known as "appeasement" and came to be identified (not altogether fairly) almost exclusively with Chamberlain. Whoever was to blame, however, it became clear almost immediately that the policy was a failure. In March 1939, Hitler occupied the remaining areas of Czechoslovakia, violating the Munich agreement unashamedly. And in April, he began issuing threats against Poland. At that point, both Britain and France decided to stand firm. They quickly gave assurances to the Polish government that they would come to its assistance in case of an invasion; and they even flirted, too late, with the Stalinist regime in Russia, attempting to draw it into a mutual defense agreement. Stalin, however, had already decided that he could expect no protection from the West; he had, after all, not even been invited to attend the Munich Conference. Accordingly, he signed a nonaggression pact with Hitler in August 1939, freeing the Germans for the moment from the danger of a two-front war. For a few months, Hitler continued to try to frighten

the Poles into submitting to German rule. When that failed, he staged an incident on the border to allow him to claim that Germany had been attacked; and on September 1, 1939, he launched a full-scale invasion of Poland. Britain and France, true to their pledges, declared war on Germany two days later. World War II had begun.

Neutrality Tested

"This nation will remain a neutral nation," the president declared shortly after the hostilities began in Europe, "but I cannot ask that every American remain neutral in thought as well." It was a statement that stood in stark and deliberate contrast to Woodrow Wilson's 1914 plea that the nation remain neutral in both deed and thought; and it was clear from the start that among those whose opinions were decidedly unneutral in 1939 was the president himself. There was never any question that both he and the majority of the American people favored Britain, France, and the other Allied nations in the contest. The question was how much the United States was prepared to do to assist them.

At the very least, Roosevelt believed, the

"Stop Hitler Now!" [1940]

We Americans have naturally wished to keep out of this war—to take no steps which might lead us in. But—

We now know that every step the French and British fall back brings war and world revolution closer to US—our country, our institutions, our homes, our hopes for peace.

Hitler is striking with all the terrible force at his command. His is a desperate gamble, and the stakes are nothing less than domination of the whole human race. . . .

WE CAN HELP—IF WE ACT NOW—before it is forever too late.

We can help by sending planes, guns, munitions, food. We can help to end the fear that American boys will fight and die in another Flanders, closer to home. . . .

The United States of America is still the most powerful nation on earth—and the United States of America is YOU!—*Advertisement written by Robert Sherwood for the Committee to Defend America by Aiding the Allies and widely published in June 1940.*

United States should make armaments available to the Allied armies to help them counteract the remarkably productive German munitions industry. As a result, in September 1939, he asked Congress for a revision of the Neutrality Acts. The original measures had forbidden the sale of American weapons to any nation engaged in war; Roosevelt wanted the arms embargo lifted. Powerful isolationist opposition forced him to accept a weaker revision than he would have liked; as passed by Congress, the 1939 measure maintained the prohibition on American ships entering war zones. It did, however, permit belligerents to purchase arms on the same "cash-and-carry" basis that the earlier Neutrality Acts had established for the sale of nonmilitary materials.

For a time, it was possible to believe that little more would be necessary. After the German armies had quickly subdued Poland, the war in Europe settled into a long, quiet lull that lasted through the winter and spring—a "phony war," as it was beginning to be termed. The only real fighting during this period occurred not between the Allies and the Axis, but between Russia and its neighbors. Taking advantage of the situation in the West, the Soviet Union overran first the small Baltic republics of Latvia, Estonia, and Lithuania, and then, in late November,

Finland. Americans were, for the most part, outraged; but neither Congress nor the president was willing to do more than impose a "moral embargo" on the shipment of armaments to Russia. By March 1940, the Soviet advance was complete. The American sanctions had had no effect.

Whatever illusions Americans had harbored about the war in western Europe were shattered in the spring of 1940 when Germany launched an invasion to the west—first attacking Denmark and Norway, sweeping next across the Netherlands and Belgium, and driving finally deep into the heart of France. Allied efforts proved futile against the Nazi "blitzkrieg," and Americans watched in horror as one stronghold after another fell into German hands. On June 10, Mussolini brought Italy into the war, invading France from the south as Hitler was attacking from the north, and prompting Roosevelt to declare angrily: "The hand that held the dagger has struck it into the back of its neighbor." On June 22, finally, France fell to the German onslaught. Nazi troops marched into Paris; a new collaborationist regime began to assemble in Vichy; and in all Europe, only the shattered remnants of the British army, which had been miraculously rescued from the beaches of Dunkirk, remained to oppose the Axis forces.

Roosevelt had already begun to expand both aid to the Allies and, more importantly, preparations for a possible Nazi invasion of the United States. On May 16, he asked Congress for an additional billion dollars for defense (much of it for the construction of an enormous new fleet of warplanes) and received it quickly. With France tottering a few weeks later, he proclaimed that the United States would "extend to the opponents of force the material resources of this nation." But words, of course, were not enough, as the new British prime minister, Winston Churchill, quickly reminded him. On May 15, Churchill sent Roosevelt the first of many long lists of requests for ships, armaments, and other assistance without which, he insisted, England could not long survive. Many Americans believed that the British plight was already hopeless, that any aid to the English was a wasted effort. The president, however, disagreed and made the bold and dangerous decision to "scrape the bottom of the barrel" to make war materials available to Winston Churchill. He even circumvented the "cash-and-carry" provisions of the Neutrality Act by trading fifty American destroyers (most of them left over from World War I) to England in return for the right to build American bases on British territory in the Western Hemisphere; and he returned to the factories a number of new airplanes purchased by the American government so that the British could buy them instead.

Roosevelt was able to take such steps in part because of a major shift in American public opinion. Before the invasion of France, most Americans had believed that a German victory in the war would not be a threat to the United States. In July, with France defeated and Britain threatened, opinion had changed dramatically. More than 66 percent of those polled now claimed to believe that Germany posed a direct threat to the United States. Congress was aware of the change and was becoming willing, therefore, to permit expanded American assistance to the Allies. It was even willing to consider the need for internal preparations for war, approving in September the Burke-Wadsworth Act inaugurating the first peacetime military conscriptions in American history.

But while the forces of isolation may have weakened, they were far from dead. On the contrary, there began in the summer of 1940 a spirited and often vicious debate between those who advocated expanded American involvement in the war (who were often termed, not entirely accurately, "interventionists") and those who continued to insist on neutrality. The celebrated journalist William Allen White served as chairman of a new Committee to Defend America, whose members lobbied actively for increased American assistance to the Allies; some of them went so far as to urge an immediate declaration of war (a position that as yet had little public support) and in April created an organization of their own, the Fight for Freedom Committee. Opposing them was a powerful new lobby entitled the America First Committee, which attracted some of America's most prominent leaders. Its chairman was General Robert E. Wood, until recently the president of Sears Roebuck; and its membership included Charles Lindbergh, General Hugh Johnson, Senator Gerald Nye, and Senator Burton Wheeler. It won the editorial support of the Hearst chain and other influential newspapers; and it had at least the indirect support of a large proportion of the Republican party. (It also, inevitably, attracted a small fringe of Nazi sympathizers and anti-Semites.) The debate between the two sides was loud and bitter. Through the summer and fall of 1940, moreover, it was complicated by a presidential campaign.

The Third-Term Campaign

Much of the political drama of 1940 revolved around the question of Franklin Roosevelt's intentions. Would he break with tradition and run for an unprecedented third term? The president himself was deliberately coy and never publicly revealed his own wishes. But by refusing to withdraw from the contest, he made it impossible for any rival Democrats to establish a foothold within the party. And when, just before the Democratic Convention in July, he let it be known that he would accept a "draft" from his party, the issue was settled. The Democrats quickly renominated him and even swallowed his choice for vice president: Agriculture Secretary Henry A. Wallace, a man too liberal for the taste of many party leaders.

The Republicans, again, faced a far more difficult task. With Roosevelt effectively straddling the center of the defense debate, favoring neither the extreme isolationists nor the extreme interventionists, the Republicans had few viable alternatives. Their solution was to compete with the president on his own ground. Succumbing to the carefully orchestrated pressure of a remarkable grass-roots movement, they nominated for president a politically inexperienced businessman, Wendell Willkie. Both the candidate and the party platform took positions little different from Roosevelt's: they would keep the country out of war but would extend generous assistance to the allies. Willkie was left, therefore, with the unenviable task of defeating Roosevelt by outmatching him in personal magnetism and by trying to arouse public fears of the dangers of an unprecedented third term. An appealing figure and a vigorous campaigner, he managed to evoke more public enthusiasm than any Republican candidate in decades. In the end, however, he was no match for Franklin Roosevelt.

The president tried to give the appearance of not campaigning at all, explaining that he had to devote his full energies to mobilizing the nation's defenses. In the process, however, he managed to make frequent visits to defense plants, army bases, and shipyards across the nation, traveling through major cities at almost every stop. More important, he managed to undercut the only effective issue Willkie was able to muster. The Republican candidate began to argue that if Roosevelt's promise to stay out of war was no better than his promise to balance the budget, then American soldiers were "already almost on the transports." Roosevelt responded in a speech in Boston with his most ringing promise to date: "I have said this before, but I shall say it again and again and again: Your boys are not going to be sent into any foreign wars." (Privately, he had made the mental reservation that if the United States were attacked, the war would no longer be "foreign.")

THE ELECTION OF 1940

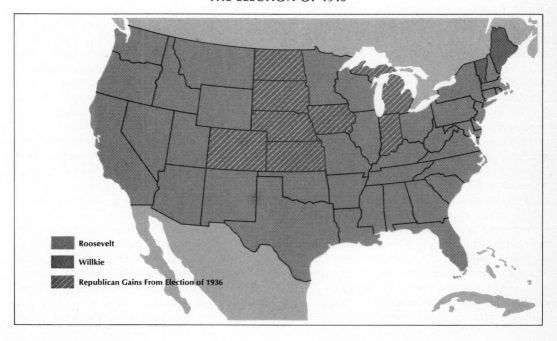

Roosevelt

Willkie

Republican Gains From Election of 1936

Although Willkie scrupulously refrained from attacking the president for assisting the Allies, he received the votes of most of those who disapproved of Roosevelt's aid policies. They were not enough. The election was closer than either the 1932 or 1936 contest, but Roosevelt nevertheless won decisively. He received 55 percent of the popular vote to Willkie's 45 percent; and he won 449 electoral votes to Willkie's 82.

Neutrality Abandoned

With the election behind him and with the situation in Europe deteriorating, Roosevelt began in the last months of 1940 to make subtle but profound changes in the American role in the war. To the public, he claimed that he was simply continuing the now established policy of providing aid to the embattled Allies. In fact, that aid was taking new and far more decisive forms.

In December 1940, Great Britain was virtually bankrupt. No longer could the British meet the "cash-and-carry" requirements imposed by the Neutrality Acts; yet England's needs, Churchill insisted, were greater than ever. The president, therefore, began to consider ways to provide continued assistance without arousing intense isolationist opposition. He might have asked for the repeal of neutrality legislation forbidding war loans, but he rejected that idea for fear of reawakening old negative feelings about the unpaid debts of World War I. Instead, he suggested a method that would "eliminate the dollar sign" from all arms transactions while still, he hoped, pacifying those who opposed blatant American intervention in the war. The new system was labeled "lend-lease." It would allow the president not only to sell but to lend or lease armaments to any nation deemed "vital to the defense of the United States." In other words, America could funnel weapons to England on the basis of no more than Britain's promise to return them when the war was over. The system would allow the United States to serve, Roosevelt declared, as an "arsenal of democracy." Isolationists attacked the measure bitterly, arguing (correctly) that it was simply a device

to tie the United States more closely to the Allies. But public opinion was on the side of the president, and Congress enacted the bill by wide margins. It empowered the president to spend $7 billion to provide supplies to the Allies, a sum as large as all the controversial loans of World War I combined.

With lend-lease formally established, Roosevelt soon faced another serious problem: ensuring that the American supplies would actually reach Great Britain. Shipping lanes in the Atlantic had become extremely dangerous as German submarines roved the waters destroying as much as a half-million tons of shipping each month. British vessels, of course, were the major victims; and the Royal Navy was losing ships far more rapidly than it could replace them and was finding it difficult to convoy materials across the Atlantic from America. Secretary of War Stimson argued that the United States should itself convoy vessels to England; but Roosevelt continued to fear isolationist opposition and relied instead on the concept of "hemispheric defense." By July 1941, arguing that the western Atlantic was a neutral zone and the responsibility of the American nations, he was patrolling the ocean as far east as Iceland, escorting convoys of merchant ships, and radioing information to British vessels about the location of Nazi submarines.

At first, Germany did little to challenge these obviously hostile American actions. By September 1941, however, the situation had changed. Nazi forces had invaded the Soviet Union in June of that year, driving quickly and forcefully deep into Russian territory. When the Soviets did not surrender, as many had predicted, Roosevelt persuaded Congress to extend lend-lease privileges to them. Now, American industry was providing the lifeblood to Hitler's foes on two fronts, and the American navy was playing a more active role than ever in protecting the flow of goods to Europe. In September, Nazi submarines began a concerted campaign against American vessels. Early that month, a German U-boat fired on the American destroyer *Greer* (which was radioing the U-boat's position to the British at the time). Roosevelt responded by ordering American ships to fire on German submarines "on sight." In October, Nazi submarines actually hit two destroyers and sank one of them, the *Reuben James,* killing many American sailors in the process. An enraged Congress now voted approval of a measure allowing the United States to arm its merchant vessels and to sail all the way into belligerent ports. The United States had, in effect, launched a naval war against Germany, as the chief of naval operations privately admitted. Hitler "has every excuse in the world to declare war on us now," he wrote in his diary at the time.

Among those excuses was a series of meetings, some private and one public, that tied the United States and Great Britain ever more closely together. In April 1941, senior military officers of the two nations had met in secret and agreed on a joint strategy to be followed were the United States to enter the war. In August, Roosevelt met publicly with Winston Churchill aboard a British vessel anchored off the coast of Newfoundland. The president made no military commitments, but he did join with Churchill in releasing a document that became known as the Atlantic Charter, in which the two nations set out "certain common principles" on which to base "a better future for the world." It was, in only vaguely disguised form, a statement of war aims, among which was a commitment to establishing a "wider and permanent system of general security" when the hostilities ceased. More significantly, perhaps, the document called openly for "the final destruction of the Nazi tyranny."

By the fall of 1941, therefore, it seemed only a matter of time before the United States became an official belligerent. Roosevelt remained convinced that he could ask for a declaration of war only in the event of an actual enemy attack. As late as November, polls disclosed that only 20 percent of the people favored entering the war. But an attack seemed certain to come, if not in the Atlantic, then in the Pacific.

The Road to Pearl Harbor

The Japanese had not sat idle during the crisis in Europe. With Great Britain preoccupied with Germany, and with Soviet attention diverted to the west, Japan sensed an unparalleled opportunity to extend its empire in the Pacific. And in September 1940, Japan signed the Tripartite pact, a defensive alliance with Germany and Italy that extended the Axis into Asia.

Roosevelt had already displayed his animosity toward the Japanese by harshly denouncing their continuing assault on China and by terminating a long-standing American commercial treaty with the Tokyo government. Still, the Japanese drive continued. In July 1941, Imperial troops moved into Indochina and seized the capital of Vietnam. The United States, having broken Japanese codes, knew that their next target was the Dutch East Indies; and when Tokyo failed to respond to Roosevelt's stern warnings, the president froze all Japanese assets in the United States, severely limiting Japan's ability to purchase needed American supplies.

Tokyo now faced a choice. It would either have to repair relations with the United States to restore the flow of supplies, or it would have to find those supplies elsewhere, most notably by seizing British and Dutch possessions in the Pacific. At first, the Tokyo government seemed willing to compromise. The Japanese prime minister, Prince Konoye, had begun negotiations with the United States even before the freezing of his country's assets; and in August he increased the pace by requesting a personal meeting with President Roosevelt. On the advice of Secretary Hull, who feared that Konoye lacked sufficient power within his own government to be able to enforce any agreement, Roosevelt replied that he would meet with the prime minister only if Japan would give guarantees in advance that it would respect the territorial integrity of China. Konoye could give no such assurances, and the negotiations collapsed. In October, the militants in Tokyo forced Konoye out of office and replaced him with the leader of the war party, General Hideki Tojo. There seemed little alternative now to war.

The Tojo government maintained for several weeks a pretense of wanting to continue negotiations. On November 20, 1941, Tokyo proposed a "modus vivendi" highly favorable to itself and sent its diplomats in Wash-

The Question of Pearl Harbor

The phrase "Remember Pearl Harbor" became a rallying cry during World War II—reminding Americans of the treachery and savagery of the surprise Japanese attack on the American naval base in Hawaii, arousing the nation to even greater efforts to exact revenge. But within a few years of the close of hostilities, the official version of the attack on December 7, 1941, began to be questioned, sparking a debate that has never entirely subsided. Was the Japanese attack on Pearl Harbor unprovoked, and did it come without warning, as the Roosevelt administration claimed at the time? Or was it part of a deliberate plan by the president to have the Japanese force a reluctant United States into the war? And, most controversial of all, did the administration know of the attack in advance? Did Roosevelt deliberately refrain from warning the commanders in Hawaii so that the air raid's effect on the American public would be more profound?

Among the first to challenge the official version of Pearl Harbor was the famous historian Charles A. Beard, who maintained in *President Roosevelt and the Coming of the War, 1941* (1948) that the United States had deliberately forced the Japanese into a position where they had no choice but to attack. By cutting off Japan's access to the raw materials it needed for its military adventure in China, by refusing stubbornly to compromise, the United States ensured that the Japanese would strike out into the southwest Pacific to take the needed supplies by force—even at the risk of war with the United States. Not only was American policy provocative in effect, Beard suggested. It was also *deliberately* provocative. And more than that, the administration, which had some time before cracked the Japanese code, must have known weeks in advance of Japan's plans to attack. Beard supported his argument by citing Secretary of War Henry Stimson's comment in his diary: "The question was how we should maneuver them into the position of firing the first shot."

A partial refutation of the Beard argument appeared in 1950 in Basil Rauch's *Roosevelt from Munich to Pearl Harbor*. The administration did not know in advance of the planned attack on Pearl Harbor, he argued. It did, however, expect an attack somewhere; and it had made subtle efforts to "maneuver" Japan into firing the first shot in the conflict. But Richard N. Current, in *Secretary Stimson: A Study in Statecraft* (1954), offered an even stronger challenge to Beard. Stimson did indeed anticipate an attack, Current argued, but not an attack on American territory; he anticipated, rather, an assault on British or

ington to the State Department to discuss it. But the effort was merely a charade. Tokyo had already decided that it would not yield on the question of China; and Washington had made it clear that it would accept nothing less than a reversal of that policy. Hull rejected the Japanese overtures out of hand; and on November 27, he told Secretary of War Henry Stimson, "I have washed my hands of the Japanese situation, and it is now in the hands of you and [Secretary of the Navy Frank] Knox, the Army and Navy." He was not merely speculating. American intelligence had already decoded Japanese messages that made clear that war was imminent, that after November 29 an attack would be only a matter of days.

What Washington did not know was where the attack would take place. Most officials were convinced that the Japanese would move first not against American territory but against British or Dutch possessions to the south. American intelligence took note of a Japanese naval task force that began sailing east from the Kuriles toward Hawaii on November 25; and a routine warning was sent to the United States naval facility at Pearl Harbor. Officials were paying far more attention, however, to a large Japanese convoy moving southward through the China

Dutch possessions in the Pacific. The problem confronting the administration was not how to maneuver the Japanese into attacking the United States, but how to find a way to make a Japanese attack on British or Dutch territory *appear* to be an attack on America. Only thus, he believed, could Congress be persuaded to approve a declaration of war.

Roberta Wohlstetter took a different approach to the question, in *Pearl Harbor: Warning and Decision* (1962), the most thorough scholarly study to appear to that point. De-emphasizing the question of whether the American government *wanted* a Japanese attack, she undertook to answer the question of whether the administration *knew* of the attack in advance. Wohlstetter concluded that the United States had ample warning of Japanese intentions and should have realized that the Pearl Harbor raid was imminent. But government officials failed to interpret the evidence correctly—largely because their preconceptions about Japanese intentions were at odds with the evidence they confronted.

Perhaps the definitive study of Pearl Harbor appeared in 1981 in the form of Gordon W. Prange's *At Dawn We Slept*. Like Wohlstetter, Prange concluded that the Roosevelt administration was guilty of a series of disastrous blunders in anticipating Japanese strategy; but he dismissed the arguments of

the "revisionists" (Beard and his successors) that the president had deliberately maneuvered the nation into the war by permitting the Japanese to attack. Yet despite the overwhelming evidence produced by Wohlstetter, Prange, and others, the revisionist claims have not been laid to rest. John Toland revived the charge of a Roosevelt betrayal in 1982, in *Infamy: Pearl Harbor and Its Aftermath*, claiming to have discovered new evidence (the testimony of an unidentified seaman) that proves the navy knew at least five days in advance that Japanese aircraft carriers were heading toward Hawaii. From that, Toland concluded that Roosevelt must have known that an attack was forthcoming and that he allowed it to occur in the belief that a surprise attack would arouse the nation. Warning the commanders in Hawaii in advance, Roosevelt feared, might cause the Japanese to cancel their plans. The president was gambling that American defenses would be sufficient to repel the attack; but his gamble failed—and resulted in the deaths of over 2,000 people and the crippling of the American Pacific fleet. But like the many previous writers who have preferred the same argument, Toland was unable to produce any direct evidence of Roosevelt's knowledge of the planned attack.

Sea. A combination of confusion and miscalculation caused the government to overlook clear indications that Japan intended a direct attack on American forces. (See "Where Historians Disagree," above.)

At 7:55 A.M. on Sunday, December 7, 1941, a wave of Japanese bombers attacked the United States naval base at Pearl Harbor. A second wave came an hour later. Because the military commanders in Hawaii had taken no precautions against such an attack, allowing ships to remain bunched up defenselessly in the harbor, the results of the air raid were catastrophic. Within two hours, the United States lost 8 battleships, 3 cruisers, 4

other vessels, 188 airplanes, and several vital shore installations. More than 2,000 men died, and another thousand were injured. The Japanese suffered only light losses.

America was suddenly rendered almost impotent in the Pacific; and the nation remained unprepared for war in almost every other respect as well. Nevertheless, the raid on Pearl Harbor did overnight what more than two years of effort by Franklin Roosevelt had been unable to do: it unified the American people in a fervent commitment to war. On December 8, the president traveled to Capitol Hill, where he grimly addressed a joint session of Congress: "Yesterday, De-

The Magazine of the U.S.S. *Shaw* Exploding During the Japanese Raid on Pearl Harbor
The destroyer *Shaw*, in a new floating drydock, went through the first attack unscathed.
One of the second wave of bombers at 9:12 A.M. hit her badly, and fire spread to her
forward magazine, which at about 9:30 went up spectacularly, blowing off her bow and
sinking the dock. From the bridge aft the damage was so slight that the *Shaw* was refloated
and a month later put in the same repaired dock to be fitted with a temporary bow. She
steamed to the mainland to be rebuilt and later rejoined the fleet. (Official U.S. Navy photo)

cember 7, 1941—a date which will live in infamy—the United States of America was
suddenly and deliberately attacked by the
naval and air forces of the Empire of Japan."
Within four hours, the Senate unanimously
and the House 388 to 1 approved a declaration of war against Japan. Three days later,

Germany and Italy, Japan's European allies,
declared war on the United States; and on the
same day, December 11, Congress recipro-
cated without a dissenting vote. For the second time in less than twenty-five years, the
United States had joined in an awesome international conflagration.

SUGGESTED READINGS

A sweeping account of dissident opposition to the
New Deal and of the administration's response is
Arthur M. Schlesinger, Jr., *The Politics of Upheaval*
(1960). George Wolfskill, *Revolt of the Conservatives*
(1962), examines the challenge from the Liberty
League. Irving Howe and Lewis Coser, *The American
Communist Party* (1957), and David Shannon, *The Socialist Party of America* (1955), chronicle challenges to
the New Deal from the left; Donald Grubbs, *Cry from
the Cotton* (1971), is an important study of the Southern Tenant Farmers Union. Opposition to the New
Deal from less radical groups is examined in Donald

McCoy, *Angry Voices* (1958); in R. Alan Lawson, *The
Failure of Independent Liberalism* (1971), which deals
with the political efforts of disaffected intellectuals;
in Alan Brinkley, *Voices of Protest: Huey Long, Father
Coughlin, and the Great Depression* (1982), which examines the rise of the leading dissident movements; and
in David H. Bennett, *Demagogues in the Depression*
(1969), which chronicles their decline. Individual
studies of the most prominent insurgents include
Abraham Holzman, *The Townsend Movement* (1963);
Charles J. Tull, *Father Coughlin and the New Deal*
(1965); and T. Harry Williams, *Huey Long* (1969), a

highly praised definitive biography. Robert Penn Warren, *All the King's Men* (1946), one of the greatest political novels in American literature, is the story of a Southern leader reminiscent of Huey Long.

Most of the general accounts of the New Deal cited after Chapter 25 contain extensive treatment of the 1935 reforms. In addition, see J. Joseph Huthmacher, *Senator Robert Wagner and the Rise of Urban Liberalism* (1968), especially for labor and housing legislation; W. D. Rowley, *M. L. Wilson and the Campaign for Domestic Allotment* (1970), and Sidney Baldwin, *Poverty and Politics: The Farm Security Administration* (1968), for changes in agricultural policy; Roy Lubove, *The Struggle for Social Security* (1968), for the major welfare innovation of the later New Deal; and Paul Conkin, *Tomorrow a New World* (1971), for the government's experimental community program. The WPA has spawned a large literature of its own, much of it focusing on the innovative art and literature programs. See, especially, Jane deHart Matthews, *The Federal Theater* (1967); Jerre Mangione, *The Dream and the Deal* (1972), on the Federal Writers Project; and William F. McDonald, *Federal Relief Administration and the Arts* (1968). For the 1936 election (and the general issue of electoral realignments in the 1930s), see Samuel Lubell, *The Future of American Politics* (1952), and John Allswang, *The New Deal in American Politics* (1978). An anthology examining the ideological currents in the Roosevelt administration is Howard Zinn, *New Deal Thought* (1966), which includes an introduction hostile to Roosevelt.

The troubled years after 1936 have received less attention from historians, but several important works are available. On the rise of conservative opposition, see James T. Patterson, *Congressional Conservatism and the New Deal* (1967); Frank Freidel, *FDR and the South* (1965); and George Wolfskill and John Hudson, *All But the People* (1969). On the court-packing fight, consult Leonard Baker, *Back to Back* (1967), and William Leuchtenburg, "The Origins of Franklin D. Roosevelt's 'Court-Packing' Plan," in Philip B. Kurland (ed)., *The Supreme Court Review* (1966). Richard Polenberg, *Reorganizing Roosevelt's Government* (1966), and Barry Karl, *Executive Reorganization and Reform in the New Deal* (1963), examine the bureaucratic reform efforts of the second term. James T. Patterson, *The New Deal and the States* (1969), explores the relationship between federal and local governments; and Charles Trout, *Boston: The Great Depression and the New Deal* (1977), examines that relationship in a single city.

Many of the secondary works and oral histories cited after Chapter 25 for descriptions of the economic impact of the Depression are also useful for the question of changing values. In addition, see Robert Lynd and Helen Merrell Lynd, *Middletown in Transition* (1935), which examines the impact of the Depression on Muncie, Indiana, and Frederick Lewis Allen, *Since Yesterday* (1940), a contemporary view of social mores. On the issue of women during the Depression, see Joseph Lash, *Eleanor and Franklin* (1971); Susan Ware, *Beyond Suffrage* (1981); and William Chafe, *The American Woman* (1972). For changing

views of ethnicity, consult Richard Krickus, *Pursuing the American Dream* (1976), and Gilman Ostrander, *American Civilization in the First Machine Age* (1970). The most comprehensive study of the experience of blacks during the Depression is Harvard Sitkoff, *A New Deal for Blacks* (1978). Also useful are Raymond Wolters, *Negroes and the Great Depression* (1970); Nancy Weiss, *The National Urban League* (1974); and Ralph Bunche, *The Political Status of the Negro in the Age of FDR* (1973), a reissue of a study originally published during World War II. John Dollard, *Caste and Class in a Southern Town*, 3rd ed. (1957), is a classic study, originally published in 1937, of racial relationships in a Southern community. Dan T. Carter, *Scottsboro* (1969), is a compelling account of one of the most celebrated racial issues of the decade. The Hispanic experience during the Depression is considered in Abraham Hoffman, *Unwanted Mexican Americans in the Great Depression* (1974), and in the appropriate chapters of Rodolfo Acuña, *Occupied America* (rev. 1981). Carey McWilliams, *Factories in the Field* (1939), studies the plight of migrant farm workers in California. Donald L. Parman, *The Navajos and the New Deal* (1976), considers the Native American response to the Roosevelt Indian policy.

The most thorough account of the labor movement during the Depression is Irving Bernstein, *Turbulent Years* (1970). See also Melvyn Dubofsky and Warren Van Tine, *John L. Lewis* (1977); David Brody, *Workers in Industrial America* (1980); Jerold Auerbach, *Labor and Liberty* (1966); Sidney Fine, *Sit-Down* (1969), on the 1936–1937 GM strike; Bert Cochran, *Labor and Communism* (1977); and Peter Friedlander, *The Emergence of a UAW Local* (1975).

William Stott, *Documentary Expression and Thirties America* (1973), offers a powerful examination of Depression photography and other forms of documentary expression. Richard Pells, *Radical Visions and American Dreams* (1973), is the most thorough study of artistic responses to the Depression. Robert Sklar, *Movie-Made America* (1975), and Andrew Bergman, *We're in the Money* (1971), explore the films of the era. Daniel Aaron, *Writers on the Left* (1961), is an important study of the interaction between literature and politics.

The best and most thorough account of the foreign policy of the Roosevelt administration is Robert Dallek, *Franklin D. Roosevelt and American Foreign Policy, 1932–1945* (1979). New Deal international economic policy is examined in Lloyd Gardner, *Economic Aspects of New Deal Diplomacy* (1964). Frank Freidel, *Launching the New Deal* (1973), examines the London Economic Conference. Beatrice Farnsworth, *William C. Bullitt and the Soviet Union* (1967); Robert Browder, *The Origins of Soviet-American Diplomacy* (1953); Edward E. Bennett, *Recognition of Russia* (1970); Bryce Wood, *The Making of the Good Neighbor Policy* (1961); and David Green, *The Containment of Latin America* (1971), examines two areas that received special diplomatic attention during the first years of the New Deal. Dorothy Borg, *The United States and the Far Eastern Crisis of 1933–1938* (1964), examines New Deal diplomacy in Asia.

Overviews of the origins of American involvement in World War II include Selig Adler, *The Uncertain Giant* (1966), and Robert Divine, *The Reluctant Belligerent* (1965). William Langer and S. Everett Gleason, *The Challenge to Isolation* (1952) and *The Undeclared War* (1953), are thorough, standard accounts. The rise of isolationist sentiment is chronicled in Selig Adler, *The Isolationist Impulse* (1957), and in Manfred Jonas, *Isolationism in America* (1966). Wayne S. Cole, *Charles A. Lindbergh and the Battle Against American Intervention in World War II* (1974), is a valuable specialized study. See also John K. Nelson, *The Peace Prophets* (1967), and Wayne S. Cole, *Senator Gerald P. Nye and American Foreign Relations* (1962). The 1940 campaign receives attention in Bernard F. Donahoe, *Private Plans and Public Dangers* (1965).

The final steps toward war are chronicled in James Leutze, *Bargaining for Supremacy* (1977), a valuable study of Anglo-American cooperation; Joseph Lash, *Roosevelt and Churchill* (1976); Warren Kimball, *The Most Unsordid Act* (1970), a study of lend-lease; Herbert Feis, *The Road to Pearl Harbor* (1950); and James MacGregor Burns, *Roosevelt: The Soldier of Freedom* (1970). Roberta Wohlstetter, *Pearl Harbor: Warning and Decision* (1962), is an invaluable study of the American handling of the 1941 fiasco. Gordon Prange, *At Dawn We Slept* (1981), is a remarkable study of Pearl Harbor, much of it from the Japanese perspective.

Total War and the Modern Nation

27

Mushroom Cloud, Nagasaki
When the atomic bomb exploded over Nagasaki, Japan, on August 9, 1945, people in the city saw an "intense flash," heard a "tremendous roaring sound," and felt a "crushing blast wave and intense heat," according to an official Japanese report. The "whole city suffered damage such as would have resulted from direct hits everywhere by ordinary bombs."
(Official U.S. Air Force photo)

"**W**ar is no longer simply a battle between armed forces in the field," an American government report of 1939 concluded. "It is a struggle in which each side strives to bring to bear against the enemy the coordinated power of every individual and of every material resource at its command. The conflict extends from the soldier in the front line to the citizen in the remotest hamlet in the rear."

The United States had experienced the demands of "total war" before. The American Civil War had mobilized a vast proportion of the nation's civilian as well as military resources. World War I had made unprecedented demands on the American economy as well as on the American armies. But never had the nation experienced so consuming a military experience as World War II. American armed forces engaged in combat around the globe— not just for a few months, as during World War I, but for nearly four years. And American society experienced changes and distortions that reached into virtually every corner of the nation.

In many respects, America moved quickly and effectively to become the united, "coordinated" society that this "total war" demanded. Having lagged far behind the rest of the world in military preparedness, the nation rapidly mobilized a great fighting force, which became one of the decisive factors in the gradual turning of the tide of war in favor of the Allies. And having experienced nearly ten years of economic sluggishness, the United States now moved to perform prodigious feats of productivity in arming itself and its allies, and in meeting the needs of its people and of much of the world. The Allied victory in 1945 left the United States in a position of undisputed world supremacy—both militarily and economically.

In other respects, however, World War II not only failed to eliminate but actually accentuated the deep divisions that remained in American society. Political battles raged furiously throughout the conflict. Racial and ethnic tensions often surfaced. And those who had spent the years of the Great Depression working for social and economic reform had to watch helplessly as conservatives took advantage of the war to halt and even dismantle their efforts.

Both in the unity it imposed and in the divisions it accentuated, World War II had a major impact on the United States. And while some of the changes it wrought proved ultimately to be temporary aberrations, others were permanent and fundamental. Americans emerged from the war having experienced lasting transformations in some of their most basic assumptions and institutions: in the role of government, in the structure of the economy, and in the expectations of the populace regarding their own society and the world.

OUTPRODUCING THE AXIS

Well before Pearl Harbor, Franklin Roosevelt had begun to mobilize both the armed forces and the nation's productive facilities for war. By December 1941, however, the United States was still not fully prepared to fight. Preparedness efforts had met consistent opposition from isolationists within Congress and without, forcing the president to moderate his efforts.

In June 1940, the fall of France spurred the administration to new endeavors. The president first reestablished and then disbanded a body that had been created in 1939: the Advisory Commission of the Council of

National Defense; and in January 1941, after further bureaucratic problems, he replaced it with the Office of Production Management, under former General Motors executive William Knudsen. Three months later, he created the Office of Price Administration and Civilian Supply, under Leon Henderson, to supervise the civilian economy. Still, because of the bureaucratic reshuffling and conflicting lines of authority of the prewar agencies, the nation continued to lack a coherent administrative structure to supervise the economic demands of war. And since so much of the military output of American factories had been shipped to England, the nation's armed forces continued to lack the weapons and equipment they needed.

Nevertheless, America entered World War II far better prepared than it had entered World War I. The United States was by the end of 1941 producing more combat munitions than any nation in the world—almost as much as Germany and Japan combined. Airplane production had risen to a rate of almost 25,000 a year. Shipyards were gearing up for a remarkable surge of construction. More than 2 million men had already been inducted into the armed forces (through a draft instituted in the fall of 1940), and new training camps were under construction to permit the induction of many more. Serious problems and shortages remained, but the groundwork had been laid for the rapid and successful mobilization that was to come.

Mobilizing Production

The attack on Pearl Harbor and the declarations of war that followed suddenly placed intolerable strains on the already struggling defense bureaucracy. Without efficient central direction, the agencies responded to the emergency by ordering tremendous quantities—indeed far too much—of everything. The result was an impossible burden on American industry—which was already far behind in existing war orders and struggling for access to scarce materials—and a bureaucratic crisis in Washington.

Roosevelt responded in January 1942 by disbanding the Office of Production Management and creating a new "super agency": the War Production Board. It was to be under the direction of Donald Nelson, formerly an executive in Sears Roebuck; and it was to have greatly expanded powers over the economy—although it was always significantly weaker than the War Industries Board had been during World War I. The task of the WPB was an arduous one. Perhaps its most difficult task was to mediate between the military and civilian sectors of the economy, determining how to allot limited materials between the two. Bureaucratic warfare and personality clashes were inevitable.

Donald Nelson, a dedicated, personable, and competent administrator, nevertheless proved unable to withstand the assaults on his authority. The WPB charter required him to distribute contracts equitably among large and small manufacturers alike; but in the end, most orders went to the larger, more influential corporations. Nelson was also charged with exercising strict civilian control over purchases and materials allotments; as the war progressed, however, the military came to exert increasing authority over such matters. And it was Nelson's responsibility to create a well-balanced production plan for the entire economy; but conflicting interest groups hampered him continually in that task. By late 1942, the war bureaucracy was once again in crisis. Although Roosevelt allowed the WPB to survive and Nelson to remain as its director, he diminished its powers considerably by persuading Associate Justice James F. Byrnes to resign from the Supreme Court and become a sort of assistant president in charge of war production. Byrnes headed first the Office of Economic Stabilization and then, after 1943, the Office of War Mobilization, which finally provided the relatively efficient war administration the president had long been seeking.

Despite all these problems, the WPB in 1942 did manage gradually to impose a measure of order on the confusion. The first step was a major reduction in the construction of war plants. Nelson and others believed that the remarkable construction boom of 1940 and 1941 had provided the nation with enough plant capacity already, that resources and manpower would be better spent utilizing existing facilities. By late 1942, construction of new war plants had virtually ceased.

There remained the problem of coordinating war production, which continued as late as the summer of 1942 to suffer from crippling bottlenecks. The vital shipbuilding program, for example, had to be cut back because of scarcities of such raw materials as steel plate and glass and of such components as valves, turbines, and engines. The WPB eventually broke most of these bottlenecks by establishing effective authority—through the Controlled Materials Plan—over the allocation of raw materials to each manufacturer.

The shortage of rubber became so critical in 1942 that it required special attention. After the WPB had failed to solve the problem, Roosevelt appointed a committee under Bernard Baruch to make a special report. This recommended sharp restrictions on the use of motor vehicles, to be accomplished through gasoline rationing and a national speed limit of thirty-five miles per hour, as well as immediate construction of enormous synthetic rubber plants. By the end of 1943, the synthetic rubber industry was producing one-third again as much rubber as the country had normally used before the war.

An indispensable adjunct of the war agencies was the Senate War Investigating Committee, headed by Harry S Truman, a previously little-known senator from Missouri. The senators ferreted out incompetence and corruption in the war-production and military-construction programs, thus preventing hundreds of millions of dollars of waste. In the wartime expenditure of $400 billion there was remarkably little corruption.

By the beginning of 1944, American war production had proved so successful that factories were more than fulfilling the nation's military needs. Their output was twice that of all the Axis countries combined; and there were even charges that military production was becoming excessive, that a resumption of civilian production should now be encouraged. (The military staunchly and successfully opposed such demands.)

Science and the War

The United States government had generally neglected scientific research in the period between the two wars. Germany, in the meantime, had made rapid strides. It was now the task of American science to close the gap. At the urging of Vannevar Bush, a noted scientist, Roosevelt agreed in 1940 to create a committee for scientific research. A year later, he expanded it into the Office of Scientific Research and Development, under the direction of Bush, which helped produce some of the most important products of the war.

The Naval Research Laboratory in Washington had discovered the principle of radar in the 1920s by bouncing a radio beam off a ship on the Potomac River. The British had improved the system and had made effective use of it during the air blitz of 1940–1941. Now, Allied scientists developed radar even further, enabling it not only to detect enemy ships and aircraft but to help direct shells against them. American rocket research, similarly, produced weapons that enormously increased the fire power of airplanes, ships, and tanks (although the Allies never matched the Germans, who by the end of the war were blasting London with enormous V-1 and V-2 rockets).

The most important scientific undertaking of the war years, however, was one conducted in almost total secrecy: the development of the atomic bomb. Reports had reached the United States in 1939, through the Italian physicist Enrico Fermi and the German mathematician Albert Einstein (then living in exile in America), that Nazi scientists had achieved atomic fission in uranium. Next, they warned, might come a bomb more powerful than any weapon ever devised. What had long been theoretically possible now seemed on the verge of accomplishment; and the United States immediately began a race in the dark to develop the weapon before the Germans did.

In December 1942, American physicists produced a controlled chain reaction in an atomic pile at the University of Chicago, solving the first great problem in producing an atomic weapon. There remained the enormous technical problems of achieving the release of this power in a bomb. Over the next three years, the government secretly poured nearly $2 billion into the so-called Manhattan Project—a massive scientific effort conducted at hidden laboratories in Oak Ridge, Tennessee, Los Alamos, New Mexico, and other sites. Hundreds of scientists worked for months on end, many of them not fully aware of what they were working on, to complete two complementary projects. One was the production of fissionable plutonium, the fuel for an atomic explosion; the other, under the supervision of J. Robert Oppenheimer, was the construction of a bomb that could employ the fuel. Frantic to complete the weapon before the Germans and worried that the device might not work when completed, the scientists pushed ahead far faster than anyone had predicted. Even so, the war in Europe had ended by the time they were ready to test the first bomb. (Only later did they discover that the Germans had never come close to constructing a usable atomic device.)

On July 16, 1945, the Manhattan Project scientists stood on a hill near Los Alamos, New Mexico, watching a tower several miles away on which was suspended the fruits of their labor. And just before dawn, they witnessed the first atomic explosion in history: a blinding flash of light brighter than any ever seen on earth, and a huge, billowing mushroom cloud. Some were exhilarated by their success. Others, among them J. Robert Oppenheimer, were already troubled by the implications of what they had done. Standing on the New Mexico desert watching the terrible explosion, Oppenheimer thought grimly of the words from Hindu scripture: "Now I am become death, the destroyer of worlds."

Economic Expansion

The industrial boom created by the war not only produced a remarkable amount of munitions for the American military. It also ended at last the Great Depression. By the middle of 1941, the economic problems of the 1930s—unemployment, deflation, industrial sluggishness—had been replaced with new problems—labor shortages, inflation, and a scarcity of consumer goods. Prosperity had returned; but because of the war, it was a prosperity with unusual characteristics.

The most important agent of the new prosperity was federal spending, which within months was pumping far more money into the economy than all the New Deal relief agencies combined. In 1939, the federal budget had been $9 billion; by 1945, it had risen to $100 billion. And the gross national product had soared as a result: from $91 billion in 1939 to $166 billion in 1945. The index of industrial production had doubled. Seventeen million new jobs had been created. Perhaps most striking was the increase in personal income. In New York, the average family income in 1938 had been $2,760; by 1942, it had risen to $4,044. In Boston, the increase was from $2,455 to $3,618; in Washington, D.C., from $2,227 to $5,316. Not everyone shared in the new prosperity. Government economists reported in 1943 that 10 million families still received less than the $1,675 per year requisite for a minimum standard of living. Most Americans, however, were relatively more affluent than they had been.

There were, of course, limits on what the recipients of these expanded incomes could do with their money. Many consumer goods—automobiles, radios, and appliances, even many types of food and clothing—were in short supply. On the whole, however, the American economy managed to meet the demands of both the military and the civilian sectors simultaneously. While the variety of goods and services available to consumers diminished during the war, the quantity actually increased.

The most persistent and debilitating feature of the Great Depression had been continuing, substantial unemployment—a condition that many people had begun to assume was a permanent feature of American life. The war ended that problem almost overnight and replaced it with another one: a serious labor shortage. The armed forces had first call on men through the Selective Service System, which had been in operation

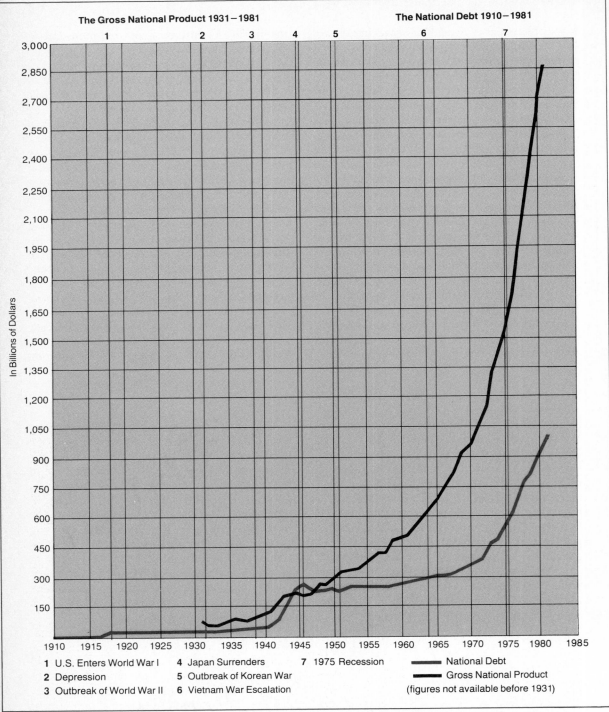

The Gross National Product 1931–1981   **The National Debt 1910–1981**

1   U.S. Enters World War I   4   Japan Surrenders   7   1975 Recession   ▬▬▬ National Debt
2   Depression   5   Outbreak of Korean War   ▬▬▬ Gross National Product
3   Outbreak of World War II   6   Vietnam War Escalation   (figures not available before 1931)

Taken by itself, the growth of the national debt since the 1930s has been tremendous. It seems less striking in comparison with the even more rapid growth of the economy, as measured by the increase in the gross national product. The GNP for a given year represents the total value, at current prices, of all goods and services produced in the country during that year. The growth of the GNP reflects a rising price level as well as an increasing output of goods and services. The actual increase in output has been much less, therefore, than the graph seems to indicate.

since the autumn of 1940. Altogether, draft boards registered 31 million men. Including volunteers, over 15 million men and women served in the armed forces during the war. Nevertheless, the working force jumped from 46.5 million to over 53 million as the 7 million unemployed and many previously considered unemployable—the very young and the elderly—and several million women went to work to fill the void.

Union membership rose with the rise in the working force, from about 10.5 million workers in 1941 to over 13 million in 1945. Keeping these workers satisfied was no easy matter. The administration was determined to prevent strikes and to restrain the formidable pressure of the labor unions from forcing wages, and thus all prices, upward. President Roosevelt followed the procedure of World War I by establishing a National Defense Mediation Board in March 1941, made

up of representatives of management, labor, and the public. In November 1941, it broke down when the CIO members resigned over the refusal of the board to recommend a union shop (that is, one in which all new workers hired must join the union) in coal mines. In January 1942, Roosevelt replaced it with the National War Labor Board, similarly constituted but much stronger. This board could set wages, hours, and working conditions, and through the war powers of the president it could enforce these by government seizure and operation of plants.

Despite the no-strike pledges of the major unions, there were nearly 15,000 work stoppages during the war. When the United Mine Workers defied the government by striking in May 1943, Congress reacted by passing a month later, over Roosevelt's veto, the Smith-Connally Act (War Labor Disputes Act). This act required unions to wait

Women in War Work
"Rosie the Riveter" was the subject of a popular song during World War II. Here women riveters engage in the production of planes for the army. (Library of Congress)

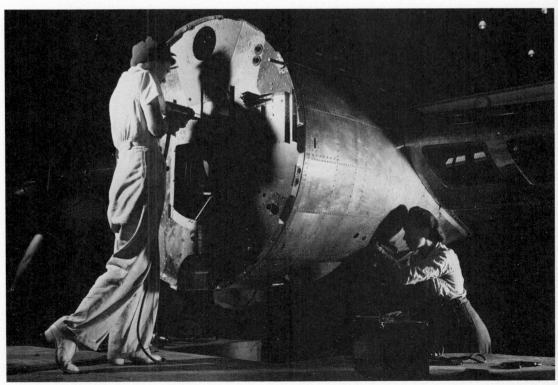

thirty days before striking and empowered the president to seize a struck war plant. In practice, the law did little to limit the power of unions. It simply gave them an additional weapon: the power to threaten a strike, which now carried with it the possibility of government control of the company. But if the federal government remained cautious in curbing union power, public animosity continued to rise. Many states passed laws to discipline the unions; and by the end of the war, pressure was growing for federal action to limit their influence.

Stabilizing the Boom

Union power was not the only factor that threatened to create economic instability. There were other challenges as well, all of which produced increasing government activity. By the middle of the war, Washington was exercising a power over the American economy far greater than anything the New Deal had ever attempted or envisioned.

Pressures from business, farmers, and labor, combined with the scarcity of consumer goods and the burgeoning of buying power, created an almost irresistible trend toward inflation. During the prewar period, the Office of Price Administration (OPA), under a vigorous New Dealer, Leon Henderson, lacked real coercive power and failed to halt inflation. Between the invasion of Poland and the attack on Pearl Harbor, prices of twenty-eight basic commodities rose by nearly 25 percent. Immediately thereafter, pressures became so acute that prices went up 2 percent per month.

In April 1942, the OPA issued a General Maximum Price Regulation that froze prices of consumer goods and of rents in defense areas only, at their March 1942 level. But the rise of uncontrolled farm prices toward 110 percent of parity forced an upward revision of food prices. This gave ammunition to the labor unions' barrage against fixed wages. In October 1942, Congress, grudgingly responding to the president's demand, passed the Anti-Inflation Act. Under its authority, Roosevelt immediately froze agricultural prices, wages, salaries, and rents throughout the country.

In July 1943, Roosevelt appointed a former advertising executive with remarkable administrative talents, Chester Bowles, to head the OPA. With a small enforcement staff, Bowles braved general unpopularity to hold the increase in living costs during the next two years to 1.4 percent. Altogether, the price level went up less than 29 percent from 1939 to the end of the war, compared with 63 percent between 1914 and the armistice.

Consumers nonetheless suffered numerous irritations and discomforts. The OPA, through unpaid local volunteers manning 5,600 price and rationing boards, administered the rationing of canned goods, coffee, sugar, meat, butter and other fats, shoes, tires, gasoline, and fuel oil. The OPA could not, however, control deterioration of qual-

Fuel Oil Ration Stamps
During and immediately after World War II, the Office of Price Administration not only set price ceilings but also issued rationing stamps, which entitled each consumer to buy certain amounts of rationed commodities. Rationing was intended to ensure an equitable distribution of scarce goods and also to help hold prices down by limiting the demand. (Courtesy of G. Litton)

ity. Black-marketing and overcharging grew in proportions far beyond OPA policing capacity.

One of the most important inflationary controls was the sale of war bonds and stamps to channel off some of the excess purchasing power, which for the single year 1945 mounted to nearly $60 billion. Throughout most of the war, personal incomes were at least one-third greater than the value of available civilian goods and services. The Treasury Department, through eight war bond drives and its payroll deduction plans was able to sell $100 billion worth of bonds.

Taxes did much more to drain off surplus purchasing power. The government raised 41 percent of its war costs through taxation, compared with 33 percent during World War I. The Revenue Act of 1942, which Roosevelt hailed as "the greatest tax bill in American history," levied a 94 percent tax on the highest incomes; the president had suggested that no one should net more than $25,000 per year during the war. Also, for the first time, the income tax fell on those in lower income brackets. To simplify payment for these new millions, Congress enacted a withholding system of payroll deductions in 1943. Corporation taxes reached a maximum of 40 percent on the largest incomes.

From 1941 to 1945, the federal government spent twice as much as it had spent in the entire 150 years of its existence to that point, and ten times as much as the cost of World War I—a total of $321 billion. The national debt rose from $49 billion in 1941 to $259 billion in 1945, yet the black warnings of national bankruptcy that had punctuated the New Deal years all but disappeared.

POLITICS AND SOCIETY

The greatest effects of the war on American politics and society were generally indirect ones: the restoration of prosperity and full employment, the redistribution of wealth through greatly increased progressive taxation, and the drawing of women into the workplace to compensate for men inducted into the armed forces. But the war had other effects on the American people that were both direct and deliberate, as various groups used the conflict to justify active efforts to shape society according to their desires.

Selling the War

Perhaps the most serious such effort was by the government itself, which found itself faced with the task of rallying an entire society behind a war being fought thousands of miles from American shores. After the early fear of a Japanese invasion of California or a German invasion of the East Coast subsided, the government realized that it would need to find new methods for making the public feel involved with the conflict. At the same time, the administration felt the need to prevent the publication or broadcast of information that might damage the war effort. The result was a pair of agencies designed to control the flow of public information.

The first was the Office of Censorship, under the direction of former Associated Press executive Byron Price. From Pearl Harbor on, Price attempted to tread the narrow line between concealing information that might be damaging to the war effort (evidence of troop movements, for example) and suppressing information that simply exposed incompetence or corruption. He faced constant and at times legitimate charges of attempting to "manage" the news. On the whole, however, the nation's press was left relatively free to criticize the administration and reveal the truth about the progress of the war. The real censorship came not from the government but from the press itself. War correspondents came to think of themselves almost as members of the military and tended not to disclose discouraging or embarrassing information. Publishers and editors, fearful of public outrage, similarly suppressed material that might sound pessimistic or denigrating.

The second agency controlling the flow of information was established in June 1942: the Office of War Information (OWI), under the direction of a well-known radio commentator, Elmer Davis. Both at home and overseas, the OWI was, in fact, the official propaganda ministry of the United States, proselytizing on behalf of the war. The domestic branch of the agency attempted to persuade Americans that they were fighting not only for a just but for a prosperous future. Official publications, films, and radio broadcasts stressed not only the "four freedoms" (freedom of speech and worship, freedom from want and fear) that the president had enunciated in 1941 but a glittering vision of postwar society. Americans were encouraged to look ahead to an era in which every man would sit behind the wheel of a new, chromium-trimmed automobile and every woman would stand enthroned in a gleaming kitchen filled with modern appliances. Only the successful completion of the war, the government implied, stood in the way of this shining future. In 1943, Congress cut funds for the domestic branch of the OWI so drastically that it had to stop producing propaganda. But other war agencies expanded their output proportionately, continuing to flood the public with arguments explaining the need for rationing, the importance of economizing, and the value of hard work.

A particularly important propaganda tool was the war bond drives. Although the drives served a legitimate economic purpose—raising money for the war and dampening inflation—they served an important social goal as well. They gave the ordinary citizen, who might have had trouble identifying with a war in which he or she was not directly involved, a way to play a part in the struggle.

Overseas, the OWI projected an idealistic view of American war aims and of the nation's aspirations for a peaceful postwar world. Through Voice of America broadcasts, begun in 1941, and through other programs, the agency made Roosevelt himself an international symbol of these ideals. By the end of the war, the president was more of a hero overseas than he was at home. To the world at large, the OWI presented an image of a nation fighting only for ideals. To

Americans at home, that image vied with an equally alluring promise of future prosperity. Still, Americans did emerge from World War II far more committed to the idea of international efforts to preserve the peace than they had from World War I.

The Retreat from Reform

Late in 1943, Franklin Roosevelt publicly suggested that "Dr. New Deal," as he called it, had served its purpose and should now give way to "Dr. Win-the-War." The statement reflected the president's own genuine shift in concern: that victory was now more important than reform. But it reflected, too, the political reality that had emerged during the first two years of war. Liberals in government were finding themselves unable to enact new programs. They were even finding it difficult to protect existing ones from conservative assault.

Many liberals had expected the war to be an opportunity for progressive national planning, for reforming the economy along the lines they had long advocated. They were sorely disappointed. The managers of the wartime economy were not reformers but corporate businessmen. William Knudsen and Donald Nelson had both been recruited from major corporations. Other administrators of wartime economic controls came largely from businesses or from conservative Wall Street law firms. Washington was flooded with so-called dollar-a-year men—administrators wealthy enough to work in the war agencies for no salary—and it was they who supervised many of the programs in which reformers had once placed such great hopes.

Unsurprisingly, perhaps, economic agencies dominated by men from the corporate world tended to favor that world when distributing contracts. An overwhelming proportion of the orders for armaments and other government purchases went to large corporations, rather than to the many smaller firms vying for a share of the bounty. There were sporadic efforts to reverse the trend. In 1942, the Murray-Patman Act created a Smaller War Plants Corporation within the

WPB, whose purpose was to spread government business more widely. In the end, however, it had little effect. Opposition from conservatives in the war agencies and even more from the military, which had little faith in the ability of small companies to perform needed tasks, frustrated such goals.

Much the same thing happened to efforts within the government to curb the growth of the great corporations through antitrust efforts. In the last years before the war, the head of the antitrust division of the Justice Department, Thurman Arnold, had launched a major campaign against economic concentration. During the war, he received continuing support from reformers in Congress and from many of the findings of the Truman committee. Nevertheless, Arnold found himself by the end of 1942 with virtually no power to pursue antitrust activity. His support from within the administration had all but vanished. Many of the corporations he was investigating were ones with which the government was doing war business and whose cooperation the military considered essential (duPont, Standard Oil, and others). Secretary of War Stimson began calling him a "self-seeking fanatic" whose efforts were frightening business and "making a very great deterrent effect upon our munitions production." Finally, in 1943, the president removed Arnold from office.

The greatest asault on liberal reform, however, came not from within the administration but from Congress. The war provided conservatives there with the excuse for which they had been waiting to dismantle many of the achievements of the New Deal, which they had always mistrusted. By the end of 1943, Congress had eliminated the Civilian Conservation Corps, the National Youth Administration, and the Works Progress Administration. With budget deficits mounting because of war costs, liberals made no headway in their efforts to increase social security benefits and otherwise extend social welfare programs. Congress cut back substantially on the one agency committed to helping perhaps the most distressed sector of the economy: poor farmers. The Farm Security Administration was soon virtually impotent.

Even had Roosevelt had the inclination to resist this conservative trend, his awareness of political realities would have been enough to stop him from trying very hard. In the congressional elections of 1942, Republicans gained 47 seats in the House and 10 in the Senate. Increasingly, the president quietly accepted the defeat or erosion of New Deal measures in order to win support for his war policies and peace plans. He also accepted the changes, however, because he realized that his chances for reelection in 1944 depended on his ability to identify himself less with domestic issues than with world peace.

The Fourth Term

Republicans approached the 1944 election determined to exploit what they believed was a smoldering national resentment of wartime regimentation and privation and a general unhappiness with the pattern of Democratic reform. They also hoped to play on concerns about the deteriorating health of the president; and they nominated as their candidate the young and vigorous governor of New York, Thomas E. Dewey. Roosevelt faced no opposition for the Democratic nomination for president; but because he was so visibly in poor health, there was great pressure on him to abandon Vice President Henry Wallace, an advanced New Dealer and hero of the CIO, and replace him with a more moderate figure, acceptable to conservative party bosses and Southern Democrats. Roosevelt reluctantly succumbed to the pressure. He refused to select the candidate most favored by party conservatives, James F. Byrnes of South Carolina, who had been a central figure in the administration for two years. But he did finally replace Wallace on the ticket with Senator Harry S Truman of Missouri, whose work as chairman of the Senate War Investigating Committee had won him national attention.

Republican and Democratic leaders agreed in advance that the conduct of the war and the plans for the peace would not be an issue in the campaign. The two parties adopted almost identical planks on those issues in their platforms. Instead, the campaign revolved around domestic economic issues and, indirectly, the president's health. Public doubts about his capacity to campaign seemed to provide a shot of adrenalin to Roosevelt. At the end of September, he addressed a raucously appreciative audience of members of the Teamsters Union and was at his sardonic best. He followed this triumph with strenuous campaign appearances in Chicago and with a day-long drive in an open car through New York City in a soaking rain.

Roosevelt's apparent capacity to serve four more years, his international leadership, and his promise to workers to revive the New Deal after the war combined to ensure him a substantial victory. He captured 53.5 percent of the popular vote to Dewey's 46 percent; and he won 432 electoral votes to Dewey's 99. Democrats lost 1 seat in the Senate, gained 20 in the House, and maintained control of both.

Blacks and the War

It was not only labor unions, mounting deficits, and economic regimentation that aroused conservative ire during the war. It was a growing fear that American blacks would use the conflict to challenge the system of segregation. The fears were well justified, for black leaders approached World War II with a newly militant outlook.

During World War I, many American blacks had eagerly seized the chance to serve in the armed forces, believing that their patriotic efforts would win them an enhanced position in postwar society. They had been cruelly disappointed. As World War II approached, blacks were again determined to use the conflict to improve the position of their race—this time, however, not by currying favor but by making demands. In the summer of 1941, with preparedness efforts at their height, A. Philip Randolph, president of the Brotherhood of Sleeping Car Porters, a black union, began to insist that the government require those companies receiving defense contracts to integrate their work forces. To mobilize support for the demand, Randolph planned a massive march on Washington, which threatened to bring more than 100,000 protesting blacks into the capital.

Roosevelt, fearful of both the possibility of violence and the certainty of political embarrassment, finally persuaded Randolph to cancel the march in return for a promise to establish a Fair Employment Practices Commission. Its purpose was to investigate discrimination against blacks in war industries; and although its enforcement powers, and thus its effectiveness, were limited, it did mark an important step toward a government commitment to racial equality.

The economic realities of the war years greatly increased the migration of blacks from the rural areas of the South into the industrial cities, where there were suddenly factory jobs available in war plants. In the South, the migration produced white resentment and suspicion, including the false rumor among white homeowners that blacks were engaged in a conspiracy to deprive the region of domestic servants. Whites pointed to the purported existence of "Eleanor Clubs," named after Eleanor Roosevelt, a champion of racial justice. The alleged purpose of the clubs (which in fact did not exist) was to "get a white woman in every kitchen in 1943." In the North, the migration produced much more severe tensions. In Detroit in 1943, a violent race riot erupted when black families began moving into a new housing project near a Polish neighborhood. Thirty-four people died in the rioting, twenty-five of them blacks.

Despite such tensions, the leading black organizations redoubled their efforts during the war to challenge the system of segregation. The Congress of Racial Equality (CORE), organized in 1943 by Randolph, mobilized mass popular resistance to discrimination in a way that the older, more conservative organizations had never done. Randolph, Bayard Rustin, James Farmer, and other, younger black leaders helped organize sit-ins and demonstrations in theaters and restaurants. In 1944, they won a much-publicized victory by forcing a Washington, D.C., restaurant to agree to serve blacks. In other areas, their victories were few. Nevertheless, the war years aroused a defiant public spirit among many blacks that would survive into the 1950s and help produce the civil-rights movement.

Racial agitation was most pronounced in civilian institutions, but the winds of change were blowing within the military as well. At first, the armed forces maintained their traditional practice of limiting blacks to the most menial assignments, keeping them in segregated training camps and units, and barring them entirely from the Marine Corps and the army air force. Gradually, however, military leaders were forced to make adjustments—in part because of public and political pressures, but largely because they recognized that these forms of segregation were wasting manpower. By the end of the war, the number of black servicemen had increased sevenfold, to 700,000; training camps were being integrated, blacks were being allowed to serve on ships with white sailors, and more black units were being sent into combat. But tensions remained. In some of the integrated army bases—Fort Dix, New Jersey, for example—riots occasionally broke out when blacks protested having to serve in segregated divisions. Substantial discrimination survived in all the services until well after the war. But within the military, as within the society at large, the traditional pattern of race relations was slowly but substantially eroding.

The Internment of the Japanese-Americans

World War I had produced in America a virtual orgy of hatred, vindictiveness, and hysteria, as well as widespread and flagrant violations of civil liberties. World War II did not. A few papers, among them Father Coughlin's *Social Justice,* were barred from the mails as seditious; but there was no general censorship of dissident publications. A few Nazi agents and American fascists were jailed; but there was no major assault on those suspected of sympathizing with the Axis. Indeed, the most ambitious effort to punish domestic fascists, a sedition trial of twenty-eight people, ended in a mistrial, and the defendants went free. Unlike World War I, socialists and communists (who generally supported the war effort) were left unpunished and unpersecuted.

Nor was there much of the ethnic or cultural animosity that had characterized World War I. Americans continued to eat sauerkraut without calling it "liberty cabbage." They continued to listen to German and Italian music. They displayed little hostility toward German- and Italian-Americans. Instead, they seemed to share the view of government propaganda that the enemy was less the German and Italian people than the vicious political systems to which they had been subjected.

But there was a glaring exception to the general rule of tolerance: the treatment of the small, politically powerless group of Japanese-Americans. From the beginning, Americans adopted a different attitude toward the Japanese enemy than they did toward their European foes. They attributed to the Japanese people certain racial and cultural characteristics that made it easier to hold them in contempt. Popular portrayals of the "Japs," as they were routinely labeled, stressed unattractive racial characteristics: a leering grin; narrow, slitted eyes; sallow, yellow skin. The Japanese, both government and private propaganda encouraged Americans to believe, were a devious, malign, and cruel people. They had, after all, launched an infamous attack on Pearl Harbor without warning.

It should not have been surprising, therefore, that this racial animosity soon extended to Americans of Japanese descent. There were not many Japanese-Americans in the United States—only about 127,000 (not counting those in Hawaii), most of them concentrated in a few areas in California. And because they generally kept to themselves and preserved traditional Japanese cultural patterns, it was easy for their neighbors to imagine that they were engaged in conspiracies on behalf of their ancestral homeland. Wild stories circulated about sabotage at Pearl Harbor and plots to aid a Japanese landing on the coast of California—all later shown to be entirely without foundation. Public pressure to remove the "threat" grew steadily.

Finally, in February 1942, the president authorized the army to "intern" the Japanese-Americans. More than 100,000 people,

Relocation of Japanese-Americans Americans of Japanese birth or ancestry living on the Pacific Coast were forced to move to camps in the interior of the country, where they were to stay for the duration of the war. The American Civil Liberties Union called the evacuation "the worst single wholesale violation of civil liberties of American citizens in our history." In this news photo of September 21, 1942, the first group departs from Los Angeles for an Arkansas camp. (ACM)

two-thirds of them American citizens, were rounded up, told to dispose of their property however they could (which often meant simply abandoning it), and taken to what the government euphemistically termed "relocation centers" in the "interior." In fact, they were facilities little different from prisons, many of them located in the desert. Conditions in the internment camps were not, for the most part, inhumane. Neither, however, were they especially comfortable. More important, a large group of loyal, hard-working American citizens were forced to spend up to three years in grim, debilitating isolation, barred from lucrative employment, provided with only minimal medical care, and deprived of decent schools for their children. The Supreme Court upheld the evacuation in a 1944 decision; and although most of the Japanese-Americans were released later that year (after the reelection of the president),

they were usually unable to win any compensation for their losses.

The experience of the Japanese-Americans was notable because it represented an indefensible violation of civil rights. But it was notable, too, because it stood in such sharp contrast to the experience of most Americans during the war. In the midst of the greatest military conflict in the history of the world, the American people were, to a remarkable extent, able to live as they had always lived—indeed, in many cases to live much better than before. They enjoyed a remarkable level of personal freedom for a people engaged in a "total war." They suffered strikingly few material privations. The ability of the American economy and of American society to absorb the strains of World War II without serious suffering or distortion was a clear augury of the remarkable era of growth and abundance that would follow.

FIGHTING A GLOBAL WAR

Whatever political disagreements and social tensions the war may have produced among the American people, there was from the beginning, a remarkable unity of opinion about

the conflict itself, "a unity," as one member of Congress proclaimed shortly after Pearl Harbor, "never before witnessed in this country." But that unity and confidence were severely tested in the first, troubled months of 1942. For despite the impressive display of patriotism and the dramatic flurry of activity, the war was going very badly. Britain appeared ready to collapse. The Soviet Union was staggering. One after another, Allied strongholds in the Pacific were falling to the forces of Japan. Slowly, however, the full might of American factories and American armies made their presence felt in both the European and Pacific theaters. And the Soviet Union, in the meantime, staved off the Nazi advance, at staggering cost to both the Germans and itself, to strengthen the Allied cause still further. By 1944, it had become clear that the momentum had shifted, that Allied forces were gradually but steadily breaking down the Axis resistance and heading toward final victory.

Organizing the Military

Neither the army nor the navy was particularly well prepared for combat in December 1941, as the fiasco at Pearl Harbor seemed clearly to illustrate. Enormous industrial production alone could not win the war. The military leaders needed to know what to order, and where and how to use it, on a scale they had not envisioned in their prewar planning. The vast increases in personnel and equipment thus forced rapid changes in planning and organization.

General George C. Marshall, chief of staff of the army, reorganized the army high command in March 1942. That same month, Admiral Ernest J. King became chief of naval operations. Together with General H. H. Arnold of the army air force, these men met with a personal representative of the president, Admiral William D. Leahy, to constitute the Joint Chiefs of Staff. They functioned as the overall command and represented the United States in combined planning with the British and occasional negotiations with the Russians. Over the Joint Chiefs of Staff was the president, who bore final responsibility for the conduct of the war. He depended heavily on the advice of the Joint Chiefs of Staff and, once major policy had been decided, seldom interfered with their strategy.

The first of the great policy decisions had come in 1940, when the Americans decided that, even if Japan entered the war, their first goal would be to defeat Germany. The United States confirmed this priority in the initial wartime conference with the British at the end of December 1941. This decision did not mean ignoring the war against Japan. But in the early years at least, the war against Germany was to be offensive, while that against Japan was to be defensive.

During the first chaotic months of shocking reverses, the armed forces allotted their men and supplies piecemeal to try to meet each new Axis threat. Top strategists emphatically warned against such dissipation of effort. No one was more insistent than

---

In the seventy-five years beginning with the Spanish-American War, the United States was engaged in five major confrontations, yet the total deaths in these conflicts were fewer than those in the Civil War alone, due largely to improvements in military medicine and handling of casualties.

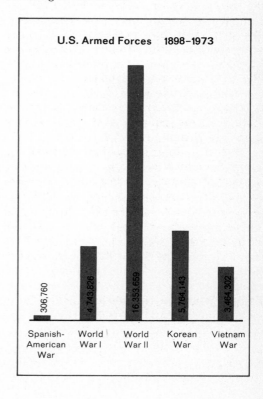

Dwight D. Eisenhower, who had been brought to Washington after Pearl Harbor as a Far Eastern expert and, by the spring of 1942, was head of the Operations Planning Division under General Marshall. In emphatic memoranda, Eisenhower hammered away at the need to build up men and supplies in Europe for the invasion of North Africa that Roosevelt and Churchill had decided on in their December 1941 meeting. Because of his vigor and his important role in developing an invasion plan, Eisenhower became the logical man to send to England (in June 1942) as commanding general in the European theater.

The Bleak Months, 1941–1942

Ten hours after the strike at Pearl Harbor, Japanese airplanes hit the airfields at Manila, destroying half the American bombers and two-thirds of the fighter planes. That same day the Japanese sank two British warships off Malaya, the only Allied warships in the Far East. Three days later Guam fell; then, in the weeks that followed, Wake Island and Hong Kong. The great British fortress of Singapore in Malaya surrendered in February 1942, the Dutch East Indies in March, and Burma in April. In the Philippines on May 6, the exhausted Philippine and American troops, having made brave withdrawals to the Bataan peninsula and the island of Corregidor in Manila Bay, ran down the last American flag in the Far East.

Only one weak outpost, Port Moresby in southern New Guinea, stood as a bulwark against the invasion of Australia. At first, it seemed likely to fall, but containment began there through the efforts of Australian and American troops on land and of American aircraft carriers on the sea. In the Battle of Coral Sea on May 6–7, 1942, the Americans turned back Japanese invasion forces threatening Port Moresby. Under General MacArthur, who had escaped from the Philippines, American and Australian troops began clearing the Japanese from New Guinea.

After the Battle of Coral Sea, the navy, having intercepted Japanese messages, knew the next move and rushed every available plane and vessel into the central Pacific. Near Midway Island, June 3–6, 1942, these forces inflicted heavy damage on a Japanese invasion fleet and headed off a drive to capture the island and neutralize Hawaii. The United States had achieved its goal of containment in the Pacific, and as men and supplies could be spared from the operations against the Nazis, it could assume the offensive against Japan.

In the Atlantic during the early months of 1942, the Nazis tried by means of submarines to confine the Americans to the Western Hemisphere. By mid-January the Germans had moved so many submarines to the Atlantic coast, where at night they torpedoed tankers silhouetted against the lights of cities, that they created a critical oil shortage. Against convoys bound for Europe they made attacks with devastating success. In the first eleven months they sank more than 8 million tons of shipping—1.2 million more than the Allies meanwhile built—and threatened to delay indefinitely the large-scale shipment of supplies and men to Europe. Gradually the United States countered by developing effective antisubmarine vessels, air patrols, detecting devices, and weapons.

The submarines made it difficult to send assistance to the British and Russians in the summer of 1942, when they needed it most. The German Afrika Korps had raced to El Alamein, only seventy-five miles from Alexandria, Egypt, threatening the Suez Canal and the Middle East. At the same time, German armies in Russia were plunging toward the Caucasus. In May the Russian foreign minister, Vyacheslav Molotov, visited Washington to demand an immediate second front that would divert at least forty German divisions from Russia; the alternative might be Russian collapse. Roosevelt promised to do everything possible to divert the Germans by invading France. But Churchill arrived the next month, when the Germans were threatening Egypt, and he strongly urged an invasion of North Africa instead.

The Mediterranean Offensive

The overwhelming losses in an August 1942 raid on Dieppe, France, undertaken by experienced Canadian troops, indicated the wisdom of making the first American landing on a relatively unprotected flank. Through advance negotiations with officials of the Vichy government of defeated France, the Americans hoped to make a bloodless landing in French North Africa. At the end of October 1942, the British opened a counteroffensive at El Alamein which sent the Afrika Korps reeling back. On November 8, Anglo-American forces landed at Oran, Algiers, and Casablanca, Morocco, with few losses. They met determined Vichy French resistance only at Casablanca.

Admiral Jean Darlan, earlier one of the most notorious collaborators with the Nazis, signed an armistice with the Allies on November 12. He ordered a cease-fire and promised the aid of 50,000 French colonial troops. Outraged American liberals protested against the deal with the Vichyites, as opposed to the French resistance forces under General Charles de Gaulle. The critics quieted somewhat a few weeks later when Darlan was assassinated.

The Germans tried to counter the invasion by ferrying troops from Sicily into Tunisia at the rate of a thousand a day. Early in 1943 the Afrika Korps, which had retreated westward across Tripoli, joined them and threw the full weight of its armor against the green American troops. The Americans lost heavily but with the aid of the British held onto their bases. Allied air power and the British navy so seriously harassed the Axis supply line from Sicily that Germany decided not to make a major stand in Tunisia. From March into May, the British army in the east and the armies in the west under Eisenhower gradually closed a vise on the German and Italian troops. On May 12, 1943, the last Axis troops in North Africa surrendered. The Mediterranean had been reopened.

That invasion, despite the continued clamoring of the Russians, was not to take place immediately. The fighting in Tunisia had tied up too large a part of the Allied combat resources for too long. Nazi submarines were still taking too heavy a toll of the Allies' inadequate shipping. Some of the ships and production had to be diverted to the antisubmarine war, and others to the

THE NORTH AFRICAN AND SICILIAN CAMPAIGNS

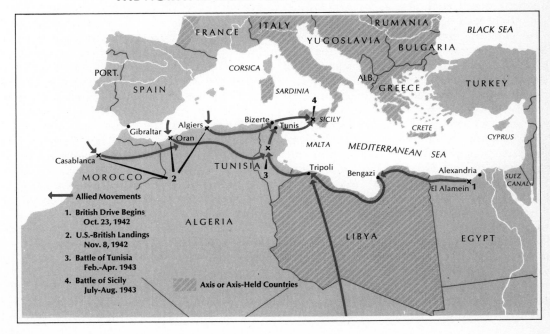

prosecution of the Pacific campaigns. Also, the planners in London had come to recognize that an enormous build-up was necessary for a successful cross-channel invasion. Fortunately for the Allies, the tide turned for the Russians also during the winter of 1942–1943, when they successfully held the Germans at Stalingrad in southern Russia, eliminating an army of 250,000 men.

As early as mid-January 1943, Roosevelt and Churchill and their staffs, while conferring at Casablanca, looked ahead to the next move. This was to be an invasion of Sicily, even though General Marshall feared it might delay the invasion of France. Churchill argued persuasively that the operation in Sicily might knock Italy out of the war and lead the Germans to tie up many divisions in defense of Italy and the Balkans.

On the night of July 9, 1943, American and British armies landed in the extreme southeast of Sicily, where defenses were comparatively light. The Americans made grievous errors, the worst being to shoot down twenty-three planeloads of their own paratroops. But in thirty-eight days the Allies conquered the island and looked toward the Italian mainland. Mussolini now fell from power, to be replaced by the pro-Allied Marshal Pietro Badoglio. At once Badoglio opened complicated negotiations to switch Italy to the side of the Allies. As the negotiations went on, the Nazis moved eight strong divisions into northern Italy, concentrated other troops near Rome, and turned the country into an occupied defense bastion.

A limited but long and punishing campaign opened on the Italian peninsula on September 3, 1943. It started with the greatest optimism, for that same day the Italian government signed an armistice agreement, and the Allies quickly seized bases and airfields in southern Italy. But the Nazi defenders fought so fiercely from hillside fortifications that by early 1944 they had stopped the slow and deliberately moving Allies at Monte Cassino. When the Allies tried to break behind the line by landing at Anzio, south of Rome, they were almost thrown back into the sea. With relatively few divisions, the Nazis were tying down the Allies while concentrating their main effort on Rus-

sia. Finally, in May 1944, the Allies captured Cassino, pressed on from the Anzio beachhead, and on June 4 captured Rome, just before the cross-channel invasion of France began.

The Liberation of France

In the fall of 1943, Germany was already reeling under incessant blows from the growing Allied air power. Great Britain had begun its mass bombing of German industrial centers in the late spring of 1942 with a thousand-plane night raid on Cologne. In August, the Americans made their first experimental daytime raids on the Continent. Bombing almost around the clock began on a gigantic scale in February 1944. Especially in the last year of the war, the bombing drastically cut production and impeded transportation. As early as the winter of 1944, it had seriously demoralized the German people.

The bombing attacks, first on the aviation industry, then on transportation, did much to clear the way for the invasion in the late spring. By May 1944, the Luftwaffe was incapable of beating off the Allied air cover for an invasion. As D-Day (invasion day) approached, the invasion was postponed from the beginning of May until early June despite the likelihood of worsening weather, in order to obtain an additional month's production of special landing craft. A sudden storm delayed the operation for a day, but on the morning of June 6, 1944, the invasion came, not at the narrowest part of the English Channel, where the Nazis expected it, but along sixty miles of the Cotentin peninsula on the Normandy coast. While airplanes and battleships offshore incessantly bombarded the Nazi defenses, 4,000 vessels, stretching as far as the eye could see, brought in troops and supplies.

Within two weeks after the initial landings, the Allies had put ashore a million men and the equipment for them. They had also captured Cherbourg, only to find that the Germans had blocked its harbor so skillfully that it could not be used until August.

Well into July, the Allies fought mile by

mile through the Normandy hedgerows. The breakthrough came on July 25, 1944, when General Omar Bradley's First Army, using its armor as cavalry had been used in earlier wars, smashed the German lines in an enormous sweep southward, then eastward. An invasion on the Mediterranean coast, beginning on August 15, quickly seized new ports (also seriously blocked) and opened new supply lines for the Allies. On August 25 French forces rode into a Paris jammed with cheering throngs. By mid-September the Allied armies had driven the Germans from almost all of France and Belgium and had come to a halt against a firm line of German defenses.

Cold weather, rain, and floods aided the Germans. In December they struck in desperation along fifty miles of front in the Ardennes Forest, driving fifty-five miles toward Antwerp before they were stopped (in the Battle of the Bulge) at Bastogne.

While the Allies were fighting their way through France to the Westwall (German defense line) and up the Italian peninsula, the Russian armies had been sweeping westward into Central Europe and the Balkans. The Russian armies advanced more rapidly than had been expected and, in late January 1945, launched an offensive of more than 150 divisions toward the Oder River, far inside Germany.

After liquidating the German thrust into the Ardennes, which had almost exhausted

The Invasion of Normandy
A Coast Guard combat photographer, climbing beyond the Nazi trench in the foreground to the top of the cliff, looked out at this panorama of Channel waters crowded with ships while landing craft were putting ashore men and supplies. The barrage balloons floated overhead to protect the ships from low-flying enemy strafers. One of them is resting on the deck of an LST (landing barge). Long lines of trucks were heading inland, carrying reinforcements for the battle for the Cotentin peninsula. (Official U.S. Coast Guard photo)

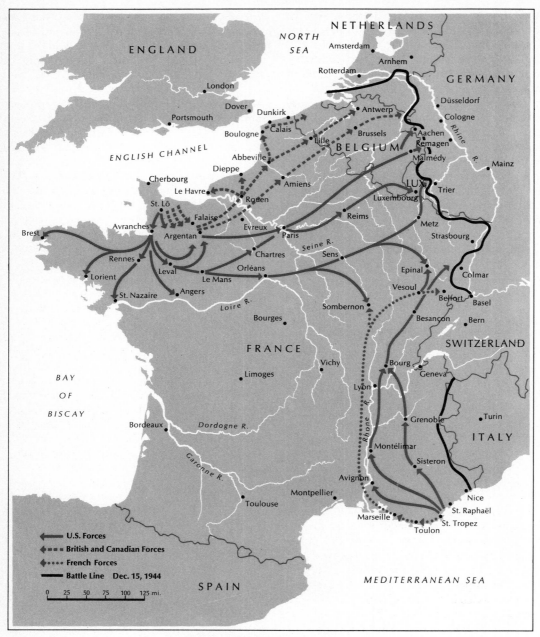

THE LIBERATION OF FRANCE

the Nazi fighting capacity, the Allied armies pushed on to the Rhine. The Americans captured Cologne on the west bank March 6, 1945, and on the next day, through remarkable luck, captured a bridge across the Rhine at Remagen. Troops poured across it. By the end of March the last great drives were under way as the British commander Montgomery with a million troops pushed across the north while Bradley's army, sweeping through central Germany, completed the encirclement and trapping of 300,000 German soldiers in the Ruhr. Russian troops were about to mount a spring offensive only thirty-five miles from Berlin.

There were fears that the Nazis were preparing for a last stand in an Alpine redoubt centering on Berchtesgaden, near the Austrian border. In fact, however, the German western front had been demolished. The only real questions were where the Americans would drive next and where they would join the Russians. The Americans, capable of moving much farther eastward than had been anticipated, could have beaten the Russians to Berlin and Prague. This would have cost American lives but would have reaped political gain in Europe. General Eisenhower decided, instead, to send American troops to capture the Alpine redoubt and then halt along the Elbe River in central Germany to meet the Russians.

On May 8, 1945, the remaining German forces surrendered unconditionally. V-E (Victory in Europe) Day arrived amidst great celebrations in Western Europe and in the United States. The rejoicing was tempered only by the knowledge of the continuing war against Japan.

The Pacific Offensive

The southern Solomon Islands, to the east of New Guinea, were being developed as a Japanese base for air raids against American communications with Australia. In August 1942, the navy and marines opened an offensive against three of these islands, Gavutu, Tulagi, and Guadalcanal. Around and on Guadalcanal a struggle of unprecedented ferocity developed as the United States and Japanese navies battled for control in a series of large-scale engagements. By the time the struggle was over, the United States and its allies had lost heavily in cruisers, carriers, and destroyers but had sunk forty-seven Japanese vessels. The Japanese navy had lost its offensive strength and thereafter concentrated on defensive operations.

During the months when the great naval battles had been going against the United States, the Americans had gained control of the air and thus were able to sustain the ma-

rines, and subsequently the army, in their precarious jungle onslaught. By February 1943, Guadalcanal had been won. Through the year the island-hopping continued all around the enormous Japanese-held perimeter: in the South Pacific through the northern Solomons to New Georgia, and in November to Bougainville; in the central Pacific, also in November, to Makin and Tarawa in the Gilberts; in the northern Pacific, to Kiska and Attu in the Aleutians.

Victories in the Marshall Islands in February 1944 cracked the Japanese outer perimeter, and before the month was out the navy had plunged far within it to wreck the bastion at Truk and raid Saipan in the Marianas. American submarines were increasingly harassing Japanese shipping and thus hampering the economy. In 1943, the Americans sank 284 ships; in 1944, they sank 492—necessitating by summer a cut of nearly a quarter in skimpy Japanese food rations and creating a crucial gasoline shortage. The inner empire of Japan was coming under relentless siege.

Meanwhile, in 1942, the Japanese forced General Joseph H. Stilwell out of Burma and brought their troops as far west as the mountains bordering on India. China was so isolated that the United States could send in meager supplies only through an aerial ferry over the "hump" of the Himalayas. On the return trip, the planes brought Chinese troops for Stilwell to train and arm. Through 1943, Stilwell with Chinese, Indian, and a few American troops fought back through northern Burma, constructing a road and parallel pipeline across the rugged mountains into Yunnan province, China. The Ledo or Stilwell Road was not open until the fall of 1944, but meanwhile the Air Transport Command managed to fly in sufficient supplies to enable the Fourteenth Air Force (before Pearl Harbor, the "Flying Tigers") to harass the Japanese. The command undertook a still larger task when B-29 bombers struck the Yawata steel mills in Japan from Chinese bases (June 1944). The Japanese retaliated in the next few months by overrunning the bases from which the bombers operated, and clearing the coastal area so they could bring supplies northward from Southeast Asia by

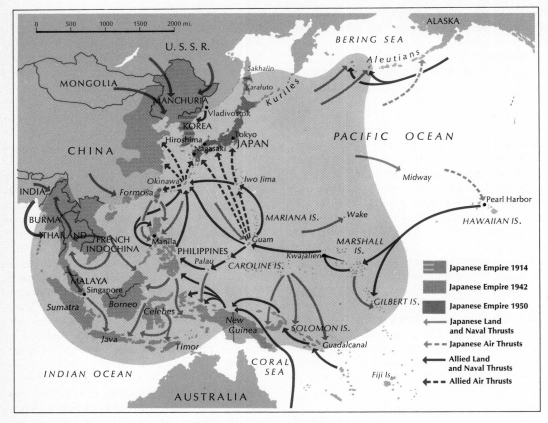

THE WAR IN THE PACIFIC

rail or road. They drove so far into the interior that they threatened the Chinese terminus of the Ledo Road, and perhaps even the center of government at Chungking.

The great Japanese offensive precipitated a long-simmering crisis in Chinese-American affairs, centering on the relations between General Stilwell and Chiang Kai-shek. Stilwell was indignant because Chiang was using many of his troops to maintain an armed frontier against the Chinese communists and would not deploy them against the Japanese. In order to meet Chiang's demands the United States would have had to send such substantial immediate support that the campaigns against Germany and directly against Japan might have to be slowed or postponed.

During 1944, Japan came under heavy blockade from the sea and bombardment

from the air. American submarines firing torpedoes and laying mines continued to make heavy inroads in the dwindling Japanese merchant marine.

In mid-June an enormous American armada struck the heavily fortified Mariana Islands, capturing Tinian, Guam, and Saipan, 1,350 miles from Tokyo. These were among the bloodiest operations of the war. In September, the Americans landed on the western Carolines. The way was being prepared for the return to the Philippines. For weeks in advance, navy craft swept the central Pacific, and airplanes ranged over the Philippines and Formosa. Finally, on October 20, General MacArthur's troops landed on Leyte Island in the Philippines. The Japanese, threatened with being fatally cut off from their new empire in Southeast Asia, threw their remaining fleets against the invaders in three major encounters—together comprising the decisive Battle of Leyte Gulf, the largest naval engagement in history—and lost almost all their remaining sea power.

The Final Victory

With remarkable speed but grievous losses, the American forces cut still deeper into the Japanese Empire during the early months of 1945. While fighting continued in the Philippines, the marines landed in February on the tiny volcanic island of Iwo Jima, only 750 miles from Tokyo. The Americans needed Iwo Jima to provide fighter cover for Japan-bound bombers and a landing place for crippled ones. The Japanese defended the island so grimly that the marines suffered over 20,000 casualties. It was the bloodiest battle in the history of the Marine Corps.

The battle for Okinawa, an island sixty-five miles long, beginning on April 1, 1945, was even bloodier. This island lies 370 miles south of Japan, and its conquest clearly would be a prelude to an invasion of the main islands. On land and from the air, the Japanese fought with a desperate fury. Week after week they sent Kamikaze suicide planes against the American and British ships, sacrificing 3,500 of them while inflicting great damage. Ashore at night, Japanese troops launched equally desperate attacks on the American lines. The United States and its allies suffered nearly 50,000 casualties on land and sea before the battle came to an end in late June 1945. The Japanese lost 110,000 killed and 7,800 taken prisoner.

The same kind of bitter fighting seemed to await the Americans when they invaded Japan. But there were signs early in 1945 that such an invasion might not be necessary. The Japanese by now had almost no ships or airplanes with which to fight; and when American forces challenged them, there was little resistance. In July 1945, for example, American warships stood off the shore of Japan and shelled industrial targets (many already in ruins from aerial bombings) with impunity. Moderate Japanese leaders, who had long since decided that the war was lost, were in the meantime increasing their power within the government. After the invasion of Okinawa, Emperor Hirohito appointed a new premier and gave him instructions to sue for peace. Although the new leader could not persuade military leaders to give up the fight, he did try, along with the emperor himself, to obtain mediation through the Soviet Union.

The Russians showed little interest in playing the role of arbitrator, perhaps because they had already decided to enter the Pacific war themselves as soon as the fighting in Europe concluded. In any case, other developments made their participation, either as peacemaker or as warrior, superfluous. At a meeting of Allied leaders in Potsdam, Germany, in mid-July 1945, President Harry S Truman (who had succeeded to the office on the death of Franklin Roosevelt three months earlier) received word that the first test of an atomic weapon had been successful. (See p. 801.) In response, he issued an ultimatum to the Japanese (signed jointly by the British) demanding that they surrender immediately or face utter devastation. The deadline was August 3. The Japanese premier wished to accept the Allied demand, but by the time the deadline arrived he had not yet been able to persuade the military leaders to surrender. With that, Truman ordered the air force to drop an atomic bomb on one of four previously selected Japanese cities.

Controversy has raged for decades over whether Truman's decision was justified and what his motives were for agreeing to use the weapon. Some people have argued that the atomic attack was unnecessary, that had the United States waited only a few more weeks the Japanese would have surrendered without it. Others, including many of the scientists involved in the Manhattan Project, have argued that whatever Japanese intentions, the United States, as a matter of moral conviction, should not have used the terrible new weapon. One horrified physicist wrote the president shortly before the attack: "This thing must not be permitted to exist on this earth. We must not be the most hated and feared people in the world." The nation's leaders, however, showed little concern about such matters. Truman, through no fault of his own, had not even been aware of the bomb's existence until a few weeks before he was called on to decide whether to use it. And knowing so little about it, he could hardly have been expected to recognize the full implications of its power. He was, apparently, making what he believed to be a simple military decision. A weapon was available that would end the war quickly; he could see no reason not to use it.

Still more controversy has existed over whether there were other motives at work in Truman's decision as well. With the Soviet Union poised to enter the war in the Pacific, did the United States want to end the conflict quickly to forestall an expanded communist presence in Asia? Did Truman use the bomb as a weapon to intimidate Stalin, with whom he was engaged in difficult negotiations, so the Soviet leader would accept American demands? Little direct evidence is available to support either of these accusations, but historians continue to disagree on the issue.

Whatever the reasons, the decision was made. On August 6, 1945, an American B-29, the *Enola Gay*, dropped an atomic weapon on the Japanese industrial city of Hiroshima. With a single bomb, the United States succeeded in destroying most of the hitherto undamaged city. Thousands of civilians died— 80,000 according to American estimates, 200,000 according to the Japanese. Many more survived to suffer the painful and crippling effects of radioactive fallout or to pass those effects on to their children in the form of serious birth defects.

Even after the horror of Hiroshima, the Japanese army refused to accept defeat. On August 9, Russia declared war on Japan. And on that same day, another American plane dropped another atomic weapon—this time on the city of Nagasaki—inflicting horrible damage on yet another unfortunate community. Finally, the Japanese relented. Some military leaders still resisted surrender; but after personal intervention by the emperor, the government announced on August 14 that it was ready to give up. On September 2, 1945, on board the American battleship *Missouri*, anchored in Tokyo Bay, the articles of surrender were signed.

World War II had come to an end, and the United States had emerged victorious. But it was a victory in which few could take lasting comfort. Fourteen million men under arms had died in the struggle. Many more civilians had perished. The United States had suffered only light casualties in comparison with some other nations, but the totals were frightful nevertheless: 322,000 dead, another 800,000 injured. And in spite of having paid so high a price for peace, the world continued to face an uncertain future. The menace of nuclear warfare, which the United States had introduced to the globe, hung like a dark cloud on the horizon. And already the world's two strongest nations—the United States and the Soviet Union—were developing suspicions of and antagonisms toward each other that would threaten the peace for decades to come.

SUGGESTED READINGS

General studies of the effects of the war on American society include John Morton Blum, *V Was for Victory* (1976), and Richard Polenberg, *War and Society* (1972). For the story of the war production effort specifically, see Donald Nelson, *Arsenal of Democracy* (1946), the WPB director's personal memoirs; Bruce Catton, *War Lords of Washington* (1946); and Eliot Janeway, *Struggle for Survival* (1951). Joel Seidman, *American Labor from Defense to Reconversion* (1953), examines the experience of workers. Leslie R. Groves, *Now It Can Be Told* (1962), is an account of the development of the atomic bomb by the general who commanded the Manhattan Project; Oscar E. Anderson, Jr., *The New World* (1962), is another valuable study of the subject. Chester Bowles, *Promises to Keep* (1971), and Lester V. Chandler, *Inflation in the United States, 1940–1948* (1951), are studies of price controls. Alan Winkler, *The Politics of Propaganda* (1978), and Philip Knightley, *The First Casualty* (1975), examine the effects of war on the press and vice versa.

James MacGregor Burns, *Roosevelt: The Soldier of Freedom* (1970), includes information about domestic politics and the 1944 election. Ellsworth Barnard, *Wendell Willkie* (1966), sheds light on the activities of the Republicans during the war. For wartime civil-rights activities, see Louis Ruchames, *Race, Jobs, and Politics* (1953), a study of the establishment of the FEPC; Neil Wynn, *The Afro-American and the Second World War* (1976); and Herbert Garfinkel, *When Negroes March* (1959). Richard M. Dalfiume, *Desegregation of the U.S. Armed Forces* (1969), examines the racial situation within the military; and August Meier and Elliott Rudwick, *CORE* (1973), studies the emergence of an important civil-rights organization. Roger Daniels, *The Politics of Prejudice* (1962) and *Concentration Camps, USA* (1971); Audrie Girdner and Anne Loftis, *The Great Betrayal* (1969); and Bill Hosokawa, *Nisei* (1969), study the internment of Japanese-Americans.

James MacGregor Burns, *Roosevelt: The Soldier of Freedom* (1970), recounts the military struggle through the experiences of the president. See also Robert Divine, *Roosevelt and World War II* (1969) and *Second Chance* (1967). Albert Russell Buchanan, *The United States and World War II*, 2 vols. (1962), is an extensive survey of both the domestic and the military experience. Briefer accounts include Fletcher Pratt, *War for the World* (1951); Margaret Hoyle, *A World in Flames* (1970); and Kenneth Greenfield, *American Strategy in World War II* (1963). See also Samuel Eliot Morison, *Strategy and Compromise* (1958), an analysis of strategic decision making, and *History of United States Naval Operations in World War II*, 14 vols. (1947–1960). A summary of this massive work is *The Two Ocean War* (1963). Winston S. Churchill, *The Second World War*, 6 vols. (1948–1953), is an invaluable account, written from a British perspective. Chester Wilmot, *The Struggle for Europe* (1952), and Charles B. McDonald, *The Mighty Endeavor* (1969), examine the American effort in Europe. See also Stephen Ambrose, *The Supreme Commander* (1970), an examination of Eisenhower's wartime command; Michael Howard, *The Mediterranean Strategy in World War II* (1968); and Dwight D. Eisenhower, *Crusade in Europe* (1948). Forrest Pogue, *George C. Marshall*, 2 vols. (1963–1966), examines the chief American strategist. Cornelius Ryan, *The Last Battle* (1966), and John Toland, *The Last Hundred Days* (1966), recount the end of the war in Europe. For the war in the Pacific, see E. J. Kind and W. M. Whitehill, *Fleet Admiral King* (1952); Barbara Tuchman, *Stilwell and the American Experience in China* (1971); John Toland, *The Rising Sun* (1970); and William Manchester, *American Caesar* (1979), a biography of Douglas MacArthur. On the use of the atomic bomb in Japan (and the diplomatic implications of the weapon), see Martin Sherwin, *A World Destroyed* (1975); Gar Alperovitz, *Atomic Diplomacy* (1965); Robert Jungk, *Brighter Than a Thousand Suns* (1958); Nuel Davis, *Lawrence and Oppenheimer* (1969); Gregg Herken, *The Winning Weapon* (1980); and W. S. Schoenberger, *Decision of Destiny* (1969). Robert Donovan, *Conflict and Crisis* (1977), an account of the first years of Truman's presidency, examines the new president's decision to use the nuclear weapon. John Hersey, *Hiroshima* (1946), describes the horrible effects of the first atomic attack.

PART SEVEN

The American Century, Since 1945

"What can we say and foresee about an American Century?" the publisher Henry Luce asked in 1941. "How shall it be created?" It was a question that many Americans were asking in the aftermath of World War II. Having emerged from the conflict not only victorious but the most admired and powerful nation in the world, the United States in 1945 viewed its future with high and fervent hopes. To predict that the coming years would constitute an "American Century" did not seem presumptuous.

To Henry Luce and to many others, America's destiny seemed clear. "It must be a sharing with all peoples of our Bill of Rights, our Declaration of Independence, our Constitution, our magnificent industrial products, our technological skills." The United States must serve as "the dynamic center of ever-widening spheres of enterprise . . . as the training center of the skilled servants of mankind—as the Good Samaritan, really believing again that it is more blessed to give than to receive." Out of these elements, Luce predicted, "surely can be fashioned a vision of the 20th Century to which we can and will devote ourselves in joy and gladness and vigor and enthusiasm."

It was a heady vision—a vision of a peaceful world united by bonds of mutual cooperation. But it was more than that. It was a vision of a world molded in the American image, a world in which the United States would reign unchallenged as the preeminent military, economic, and moral force. And it was a vision that would enchant the American people for more than two decades.

This sense of America's special virtues was in some respects a defensive reaction to a pervasive unease in the postwar years. For shortly after the end of World War II, the United States found itself embroiled in a new world struggle—a long, grim, and dangerous competition with the Soviet

Union for international supremacy. The world had moved from the horrors of "total war" to the tensions of another type of conflict: what the columnist Walter Lippmann christened the "Cold War." And although only intermittently did the Cold War produce actual military conflict, it maintained an unbroken, icy grip on the world, and on American society, for many years.

But the exuberant vision of an "American Century" was a result, too, of the remarkable growth and prosperity of American society in the postwar years. The nation's economy, having revived from the Great Depression during the war, continued in the following decades to perform remarkable feats. Indeed, never in the history of the world had a nation enjoyed such astounding economic progress as did the United States in the twenty years after 1945. For a time, it was possible to believe that America had found the secret of permanent, uninterrupted prosperity.

In both foreign and domestic affairs, therefore, the United States behaved in the postwar years with remarkable assertiveness. Having abandoned the last vestiges of isolationism, the nation now used its influence in the world in ways that earlier generations had never contemplated. The struggle against communism seemed to require constant vigilance and constant activism. No area of the globe was outside the range of American concerns; and in large ways and small, the United States found itself involved— economically, politically, and at times militarily—throughout the world in an apparently ceaseless effort to protect its own vision of the future.

At home, Americans were similarly expansive in their vision of their obligations and capabilities. By the late 1950s, in particular, a vigorous, crusading liberalism was emerging as the dominant force in American politics. And in response to that spirit, the nation embarked on a series of ambitious efforts to solve its remaining social problems. Because the economy was creating such enormous wealth, it did not seem unreasonable to assume that society could be purged at last of poverty and injustice. And it was the federal government, most liberals believed, that would be the essential agent of change.

For a time, it all seemed to work. The Cold War was not won, certainly; but America's aggressive foreign policy seemed to be the proper response to the communist challenge. Social problems were not eliminated, but impressive progress appeared to have been made. In the mid-1960s, however, the dream of an "American Century" began to encounter powerful obstacles. The commitment to combating communism throughout the world led the United States into a disastrous military venture in Vietnam—a war that dragged on inconclusively for more than seven years, eroding America's stature in the world and poisoning the political and social atmosphere at home. And the commitment to solving domestic social problems propelled Americans into an ambitious assault on the deepest national injustice of all: oppression of the nation's black citizens. That assault produced important and long-overdue improvements in the status of blacks in America. But like the war in Vietnam, it proved to be a far more difficult and costly commitment than most Americans had at first envisioned. And it helped to produce widespread social conflict and bitterness.

Together, these twin crises—war and race—led the United States into a period of wrenching national turbulence in the late 1960s, a crisis that for a time appeared to threaten the very foundations of American society. The turmoil ultimately subsided; but in its aftermath nothing was quite the same. No longer did Americans feel confident of their ability to shape the destiny of the world. No longer were they certain that their domestic problems were capable of solution. Instead, the nation embarked on a search for stability and order that would produce problems and frustrations of its own.

Cold War America

28

Berlin, 1949
In the summer of 1948, the Soviet Union established a land blockade of the city of West Berlin, an enclave of pro-Western democracy completely surrounded by communist East Germany. The Western response, a dramatic airlift that lasted 328 days, transformed Berlin into a symbol of resistance to communism and marked the institutionalization of the Cold War. Here, cheering crowds greet the first convoy of trucks (bearing CARE packages) to enter Berlin upon the lifting of the blockade on May 12, 1949. (UPI)

The immediate aftermath of World War II was a trying time for the United States. Having emerged from the struggle indisputably the greatest power in the world, America assumed that the peace would take a form to its liking. It did not. Almost immediately, it became clear that another great power—a nation not yet as strong as the United States, but strong enough to make its influence felt—had a very different vision of the postwar order. Even before the war ended, there were signs of tension between the United States and the Soviet Union, who had fought together so effectively as allies. Once the hostilities were over, those tensions quickly grew to create an enduring "Cold War" between the two nations that would cast its shadow over the entire course of international affairs for decades.

At the same time, the American people were experiencing the predictable upheavals of readjustment to civilian life. The economy was undergoing a difficult transformation in preparation for the remarkable growth that was soon to follow. Politics was in some confusion, a result of the death of Franklin Roosevelt in April 1945. And the specter of the Cold War was having profound effects on American domestic life, ultimately producing the most corrosive outbreak of antiradical hysteria of the century. America in the postwar years was both powerful and prosperous; but it was also for a time troubled and uncertain about its future.

ORIGINS OF THE COLD WAR

No issue in twentieth-century American history has aroused more debate than the question of the origins of the Cold War. Two questions, in particular, have provoked controversy: When did it begin? Who was to blame? Some have argued that the Cold War could have been avoided as late as 1947 or 1948, others that it was virtually inevitable long before the end of World War II. Some have claimed that Soviet duplicity and expansionism created the international tensions, others that American provocations and imperial ambitions were at least equally to blame. On virtually every aspect of the history of the Cold War, disagreement remains rampant. (See "Where Historians Disagree," pp. 830–831.)

But if historians have reached no general accord on these questions, they have gradually arrived at something approaching a consensus on some of the outlines of the debate. Most would agree that the origins of the Cold War can be understood only by looking at both the historic background of Soviet-American relations and the specific events of 1945 through 1948. And most would also agree that wherever the preponderance of blame may lie, both the United States and the Soviet Union contributed greatly to the atmosphere of hostility and suspicion that quickly clouded the peace.

A Legacy of Mistrust

The wartime alliance between the United States and the Soviet Union was an aberration from the normal tenor of Soviet-American relations. Ever since the Bolshevik Revolution of 1917, the two nations had viewed each other with deep mutual mistrust.

The reasons for American hostility toward the Soviet Union were both obvious and many. There was, of course, the fundamental American animosity toward communism, which had strong roots in the nation's past and had been a powerful force in society since well before the Russian Revolution. But there were more specific reasons as well.

Americans never forgot the separate peace that the Soviet government had negotiated with Germany in 1917, leaving the West to fight the Central Powers alone. They had chafed at the strident attacks emanating from Moscow on the American capitalist system, attacks that proved particularly grating during the 1930s, when that system was under duress. They had long been concerned about the Soviet regime's open avowal of the need for world revolution. They had felt a deep and understandable revulsion at the bloody Stalinist purges of the 1930s. And they had been deeply embittered in 1938 when Stalin and Hitler agreed to the short-lived Nazi–Soviet Pact.

But Soviet hostility toward the United States had deep roots as well. Russian leaders were well aware of the American opposition to their revolution in 1917, and they never forgot that the United States had sent troops into the Soviet Union at the end of World War I to work, the Russians believed, to overthrow their new government. They resented their exclusion from the international community throughout the 1920s and 1930s; Russia had been invited to participate in neither the Versailles Conference in 1919 nor the Munich Conference in 1938. The Stalin regime remembered, too, the long delay by the United States in recognizing the Soviet government; the two nations did not exchange ambassadors until 1933, sixteen years after the Revolution. And just as most Americans viewed communism with foreboding and contempt, so did most Russian communists harbor deep suspicions of and a genuine distaste for industrial capitalism. There was, in short, a powerful legacy of mistrust on both sides.

In some respects, the wartime experience helped to abate that mistrust. Both the United States and the Soviet Union tended to focus during the war less on the traditional image of a dangerous potential foe and more on the image of a brave and dauntless ally. Americans expressed open admiration for the courage of Soviet forces in withstanding the Nazi onslaught and began to depict Stalin less as the bloody ogre of the purges than as the wise and persevering "Uncle Joe." The Soviet government, similarly, praised both the American fighting forces and the wisdom and courage of Franklin Roosevelt. In other respects, however, the war deepened the gulf between the two nations. Americans did not forget the Soviet invasion of Finland and the Baltic states late in 1939, once the war with Germany had begun in the west. Nor were they unaware, as the war continued, of Soviet brutality—not only toward the fascist enemies but toward supposedly friendly forces: for example, the Polish resistance fighters. Stalin had even greater cause to resent the American approach to the war. Despite repeated assurances from Roosevelt that the United States and Britain would soon open a second front on the European continent, thus drawing German strength away from the assault on Russia, the Allied invasion did not finally occur until June 1944, more than two years after Stalin had first demanded it. In the meantime, the Russians had suffered appalling casualties—some estimates put them as high as 20 million; and it was easy for Stalin to believe that the West had deliberately delayed the invasion in order to weaken the Soviet Union. So although in most respects the wartime alliance worked well, with both sides making serious efforts to play down their differences, an undercurrent of tension and hostility remained.

Two Visions of the World

At least as important as these deep-seated suspicions was a fundamental difference in the ways the great powers envisioned the postwar world—a difference that was not at first immediately obvious, but one that ultimately shattered any hope for international amity. The first vision was that of the United States, one perhaps best expressed by the title of a famous book by Wendell Willkie, *One World* (1943), and first openly outlined in the Atlantic Charter, drafted by Roosevelt and Churchill in 1941. It was a vision of a world in which nations abandoned their traditional belief in military alliances and spheres of influence. Instead, the world would govern itself through democratic processes, with an international organization serving as the arbiter of disputes and the

Origins of the Cold War

No issue in recent American history has produced more controversy than that of the origins of the Cold War between the United States and the Soviet Union. In particular, historians have disagreed over the question of who was responsible for the breakdown of American–Soviet relations, and on whether the conflict between the two superpowers was inevitable or could have been avoided.

For more than a decade after the end of World War II, few historians saw any reason to challenge the official American interpretation of the beginnings of the Cold War. Thomas A. Bailey spoke for most students of the conflict when he argued, in *America Faces Russia* (1950), that the breakdown of relations was a direct result of aggressive Soviet policies of expansion in the immediate postwar years. Stalin's government violated its solemn promises in the Yalta Accords, imposed Soviet-dominated governments on the unwilling nations of Eastern Europe, and schemed to spread communism throughout the world. American policy was the logical and necessary response: a firm commitment to oppose Soviet expansionism and to retain its armed forces in a continual state of preparedness.

It was the American involvement in Vietnam that finally disillusioned many historians with the premises of the containment policy and, thus, with the traditional view of the origins of the Cold War. But even before the conflict in Asia had reached major proportions, the first works in what would become known as the "revisionist" interpretation began to appear. William Appleman Williams began to challenge the accepted wisdom as early as 1952; and in 1959 he published *The Tragedy of American Diplomacy*, which studied the Cold War in the context of American foreign policy throughout the twentieth century. The United States had operated in world affairs, Williams argued, in response to one overriding concern: its commitment to maintaining an "open door" for American trade in world markets. The confrontation with the Soviet Union, therefore, was less a response to Russian aggressive designs than an expression of the American belief in the necessity of capitalist expansion.

Later revisionists modified many of Williams's claims, but most accepted some of the basic outlines of his thesis: that the United States had been primarily to blame for the Cold War; that the Soviet Union had displayed no aggressive designs toward the West (and was so weak and exhausted at the end of World War II as to be unable to pose any serious threat to America in any case); that the United States had used its nuclear monopoly to attempt to threaten and intimidate Stalin; that Harry Truman had recklessly abandoned the conciliatory policies of Franklin Roosevelt and taken a provocative hard line against the Russians; and that the Soviet response had reflected a legitimate fear of capitalist encirclement. Walter LaFeber, in *America, Russia, and the Cold War, 1945–1967* (1967), maintained that America's supposedly idealistic internationalism at the close of the war—its vision of "One World," with every nation in control of its own destiny—was in reality an effort to ensure a world shaped in the American image, with every nation open

protector of the peace. No nation would control any other. Every people would have the right "to choose the form of government under which they will live."

The other vision was that of the Soviet Union and to some extent, it gradually became clear, of Great Britain. Both Stalin and Churchill had agreed to sign the Atlantic Charter espousing the "One World" principles. But neither man truly shared them. Britain had always been uneasy about the implications of the self-determination ideal for its own empire, which remained at the close of World War II the largest in the history of the world. The Soviet Union was determined to create a secure sphere for itself in Eastern Europe as protection against future aggression from the West. Both Churchill and Stalin, therefore, tended to envision a postwar structure in which the great powers would control areas of strategic interest to them, in which something vaguely similar to the trato American influence (and to American trade).

Crucial to many revisionist arguments has been the American decision to use atomic weapons against Japan in the closing days of World War II. As early as 1948, a British physicist, P. M. S. Blackett, wrote in *Fear, War, and the Bomb* that the destruction of Hiroshima and Nagasaki was "not so much the last military act of the second World War as the first major operation of the cold diplomatic war with Russia." Gar Alperovitz expanded that idea in *Atomic Diplomacy* (1965), in which he claimed that American decision makers used the bombs on an already defeated Japan not to win the war (for the war was already won) but to impress and intimidate the Soviets, to make them more "manageable." In fact, Alperovitz argued, this atomic diplomacy had the opposite effect: it convinced the Soviet Union of America's hostile intentions and helped speed the beginning of the Cold War.

Ultimately, the revisionist interpretation began to produce a reaction of its own, what some have called the "counterrevisionist" view of the conflict. Some manifestations of this reaction have consisted of little more than a reaffirmation of the traditional view of the Cold War. Herbert Feis, for example, argued in *The Atomic Bomb and the End of World War II* (1966) that the revisionist claim that the use of nuclear weapons on Japan was a tactic to intimidate the Soviets was unfounded, that Truman had made his decision on purely military grounds—to ensure a speedy American victory and eliminate the need for what was expected to be a long and costly invasion of Japan. Others challenged the revisionists by accepting some of their findings but rejecting their most important claims. Arthur M. Schlesinger, Jr., admitted in a 1967 article that the Soviets may not have been committed to world conquest, as most earlier accounts had claimed. Nevertheless, the Soviets (and Stalin in particular) were motivated by a deep-seated paranoia about the West, which made them insistent on dominating Eastern Europe and rendered any amicable relationship between them and the United States impossible.

But the dominant works of counterrevisionist scholarship have attempted to strike a balance between the two camps, to identify areas of blame and misconception on both sides of the conflict. Thomas G. Paterson, in *Soviet–American Confrontation* (1973), viewed Russian hostility and American efforts to dominate the postwar world as equally responsible for the Cold War. John Lewis Gaddis, in *The United States and the Origins of the Cold War, 1941–1947* (1972), similarly maintained that "neither side can bear sole responsibility for the onset of the Cold War." American policymakers, he argued, had only limited options because of the pressures of domestic politics. And Stalin was immobilized by his obsessive concern with maintaining his own power and ensuring absolute security for the Soviet Union. But if neither side is entirely to blame, Gaddis concluded, the Soviets must be held at least slightly more accountable for the problems; for Stalin was in a much better position to compromise, given his broader power within his own government than the politically hamstrung Truman.

ditional European balance of power would reemerge.

This difference of opinion was particularly serious because the internationalist vision of Roosevelt had, by the end of the war, become a fervent commitment among many Americans. It was a vision composed equally of expansive idealism and national self-interest. Roosevelt had never forgotten the excitement with which he had greeted the principles of Wilsonian idealism during World War I, and he saw his mission in the 1940s as one of bringing lasting peace and genuine democracy to the world. But it was clear, too, that the "One World" vision would enhance the position of the United States in particular. As the world's greatest industrial power, and as one of the few nations unravaged by the war, America stood to gain more than any other country from opening the entire world to unfettered trade. The United States would have a global market for its exports, and it would have unrestricted access to vital raw materials. Determined to avoid another economic catastrophe like that of the 1930s, Roosevelt saw the creation of the postwar order as a way to ensure continuing American prosperity.

Thus when Britain and the Soviet Union began to balk at some of the provisions the United States was advocating, the debate seemed to become more than a simple difference of opinion. It became an ideological struggle for the future of the world. And on that rock the hope for a genuine peace would ultimately founder. Roosevelt was by the end of the war able to win at least the partial consent of Winston Churchill to his principles; but although he believed at times that Stalin would similarly relent, he never managed to steer the Soviets from their determination to control Eastern Europe, from their vision of a postwar order in which each of the great powers would dominate its own sphere. Gradually, the irreconcilable differences between these two positions would turn the peacemaking process into a form of warfare.

Wartime Diplomacy

Almost from the moment of Pearl Harbor, the Roosevelt administration devoted nearly as much attention to planning the peace as it did to winning the war. Indeed, the president himself realized that the conduct of the war—the relationships among the Allies in coordinating their efforts—would go far toward determining the shape of the postwar world.

Throughout 1942, Roosevelt had engaged in inconclusive discussions with the Soviet Union, and particularly with Foreign Minister Vyacheslav Molotov, about how best to implement the principles of the Atlantic Charter, to which all the Allies had in theory subscribed. Until 1943, however, neither nation was ready for any specific commitments. In the meantime, serious strains in the alliance were beginning to appear as a result of Stalin's irritation at delays in opening the second front and his resentment of the

Anglo-American decision to invade North Africa before Europe.

It was in this deteriorating atmosphere that the president called for a meeting of the "Big Three"—Roosevelt, Churchill, and Stalin—in Casablanca, Morocco, in January 1943. Stalin declined the invitation, but Churchill and Roosevelt met nevertheless. Because the two leaders agreed that they could not accept Stalin's most important demand—the immediate opening of a second front—they reached another decision designed to reassure the Soviet Union. The Allies, Roosevelt announced, would accept nothing less than the unconditional surrender of the Axis powers. The announcement was a signal to Stalin that the Americans and British would not negotiate a separate peace with Hitler and leave the Soviets to fight on alone.

In November 1943, Roosevelt and Churchill traveled to Teheran, Iran, for their first meeting with Stalin. By now, however, Roosevelt's most effective bargaining tool—Stalin's need for American assistance in his struggle against Germany—had been removed. The German advance against Russia had been halted; Soviet forces were now launching their own westward offensive. New tensions had emerged in the alliance, moreover, as a result of the refusal by the British and Americans to allow any Soviet participation in the creation of a new Italian government following the fall of Mussolini. To Stalin, at least, the "One World" doctrine was already embodying a double standard: America and Britain expected to have a voice in the future of Eastern Europe, but the Soviet Union was to have no voice in the future of the West.

Nevertheless, the Teheran Conference seemed in most respects a success. Roosevelt and Stalin established a cordial relationship, one that the president hoped would eventually produce the same personal intimacy he enjoyed with Churchill. Stalin agreed to an American request that the Soviet Union enter the war in the Pacific soon after the end of hostilities in Europe. Roosevelt, in turn, promised that an Anglo-American second front would be established within six months.

Stalin, Roosevelt, and Churchill at Teheran
"We—the President of the United States, the Prime Minister of Great Britain, and the Premier of the Soviet Union—have met these four days past, in this, the Capital of our Ally, Iran, and have shaped and confirmed our common policy.

"We express our determination that our nations shall work together in war and in the peace that will follow. . . .

"Emerging from these cordial conferences we look with confidence to the day when all peoples of the world may live free lives, untouched by tyranny, and according to their varying desires and their own consciences.

"We came here with hope and determination. We leave here, friends in fact, in spirit and in purpose."—From a joint statement issued December 1, 1943. (National Archives)

More important to Roosevelt, all three leaders agreed in principle to a postwar international organization and to efforts to prevent a resurgence of German expansionism.

On other matters, however, the origins of future disagreements could already be discerned. Most important was the question of the future of Poland. Roosevelt and Churchill were willing to agree to a movement of the Soviet border westward, thus allowing Stalin to annex some historically Polish territory. But on the nature of the postwar government in the portion of Poland that would remain independent, there were sharp differences. Roosevelt and Churchill supported the claims of the Polish government-in-exile that had been functioning in London since 1940; Stalin wished to install another, procommunist exiled government that had spent the war in the Soviet Union. The three leaders avoided a bitter conclusion to the Teheran Conference only by leaving the issue unresolved. There had, however, been little evidence to support hopes that an amicable settlement of the Polish question would be possible.

Yalta

For more than a year, during which the Soviet Union began finally to destroy German resistance and the British and Americans launched their successful invasion of France, the Grand Alliance among the United States, Britain, and the Soviet Union alternated between high tension and warm amicability. In the fall of 1944, Churchill flew by himself to Moscow for a meeting with Stalin to resolve issues arising from a civil war in Greece. In return for a Soviet agreement to cease assisting Greek communists, who were challenging the British-supported monarchical government, Churchill consented to a proposal whereby control of Eastern Europe would be divided between Britain and the Soviet Union. "This memorable meeting," Churchill wrote Stalin after its close, "has shown that there are no matters that cannot be adjusted between us when we meet together in frank and intimate discussion." To Roosevelt, however, the Moscow agreement was evidence of how little the Atlantic Charter principles seemed to mean to his two most important allies.

It was in an atmosphere of some gloom, therefore, that Roosevelt and Churchill joined Stalin for a great peace conference in the Soviet city of Yalta in February 1945. The American president sensed resistance to his internationalist dreams. The British prime minister was already becoming disillusioned about Stalin's willingness to make concessions and compromises, warning even before the conference met that "I think the end of this war may well prove to be more disappointing than was the last." Stalin, whose armies were now only miles from Berlin and who was well aware of how much the United States still wanted his assistance in the Pacific, was confident and determined.

On a number of issues, the Big Three reached amicable and mutually satisfactory agreements. In return for Stalin's promise to enter the war against Japan, Roosevelt agreed that the Soviet Union should receive the Kurile Islands north of Japan, should regain southern Sakhalin Island and Port Arthur, both of which Russia had lost in the 1904

Russo-Japanese War, and could exercise some influence (along with the government of China) in Manchuria.

The negotiators agreed as well on a plan for a new international organization: the United Nations. Tentative plans for the UN had been hammered out the previous summer at a conference in Washington, D.C., at the Dumbarton Oaks estate. At Yalta, the leaders ratified the Dumbarton plan to create a General Assembly, in which every member should be represented, and a Security Council, on which would sit permanent representatives of the five major powers (the United States, Britain, France, the Soviet Union, and China), along with temporary delegates from several other nations. They accepted, too, the provision giving each of the major powers a veto over all Security Council decisions. These agreements became the basis for the drafting of the United Nations charter at a conference of fifty nations beginning April 25, 1945, in San Francisco. The United States Senate ratified the charter in July by a vote of 80 to 2 (a striking contrast to the slow and painful defeat it had administered to the charter of the League of Nations twenty-five years before).

On other issues, however, the Yalta Conference produced no real agreement, either leaving fundamental differences unresolved or papering them over with weak and unstable compromises. As in Teheran, the most important stumbling block remained Poland. Fundamental disagreement remained about the postwar Polish government, with each side continuing to insist on the rights of its own government-in-exile. Stalin, whose armies had by now occupied Poland, had already installed a government composed of the procommunist "Lublin" Poles, to the chagrin of the British and Americans.

Roosevelt and Churchill protested strongly at Yalta against Stalin's unilateral establishment of a new Polish government, insisting that the pro-Western "London" Poles must be allowed a place in the Warsaw regime. Roosevelt envisioned a complete restructuring of the Soviet-controlled government, based on free, democratic elections—which both he and Stalin recognized the pro-

Western forces would win. Stalin agreed only to a vague compromise by which an unspecified number of pro-Western Poles would be granted a place in the government. Although he reluctantly consented to hold "free and unfettered elections" in Poland, he made no firm commitment to a date for them. They never took place.

Nor was there agreement about one of the touchiest issues facing the three leaders: the future of Germany. All three leaders were determined to ensure that Germany could not soon again become a major military power, but there were wide differences in their views of how to accomplish that goal. Stalin wanted to impose $20 billion in reparations on the Germans, of which Russia would receive half. Churchill protested, arguing that the result would be that Britain and America would have to feed the German people. Roosevelt finally accepted the $20 billion figure as a "basis for discussion" but left final settlement to a future reparations commission. To Stalin, whose hopes for the reconstruction of Russia rested in part on tribute from Germany, it was an unsatisfactory compromise.

Roosevelt was uncertain at first about how he wished to resolve the German question. In 1944, he and Churchill had met in Quebec and agreed on what became known as the Morgenthau Plan—a plan for the pastoralization of Germany. But by accepting the principle of reparations at Yalta, he was clearly abandoning the idea of destroying German industry; without it, the Germans would have no means by which to pay. Instead, he seemed to be hoping for a reconstructed and reunited Germany, one that would be permitted to develop a prosperous, modern economy, but one that would remain under the careful supervision of the Allies. Stalin, by contrast, wanted a permanent dismemberment of Germany, a proposal the British and Americans firmly rejected. The final agreement was, like the Polish agreement, a vague and unstable one. The United States, Great Britain, France, and the Soviet Union would each control their own "zones of occupation" in Germany, zones determined by the position of troops at the time

when the war would end. (Berlin, the German capital, was already well inside the Soviet zone, but because of its symbolic importance it would itself be divided into four sectors, one for each nation to occupy.) At an unspecified date, the nation would be reunited; but no specific agreement was reached on how the reunification would occur.

As for the rest of Europe, the conference produced a murky accord on the establishment of interim governments "broadly representative of all democratic elements." They would be replaced ultimately by permanent governments "responsible to the will of the people" and created through free elections. Once again, no specific provisions or timetables accompanied the agreements.

The Yalta Accords, in other words, were less a settlement of postwar issues than a general set of loose principles that sidestepped the most divisive issues. Roosevelt, Churchill, and Stalin returned home from the conference each apparently convinced that he had signed an important agreement. But the Soviet interpretation of the accords differed so sharply from the Anglo-American interpretation that the illusion endured only briefly. Stalin continued to believe that Soviet control of Eastern Europe was essential and considered the Yalta Accords little more than a set of small concessions to Western punctiliousness. Roosevelt, in contrast, thought the agreements represented a mutual acceptance of the idea of an "open" Europe, under the direct control of no single nation. In the weeks following the Yalta Conference, therefore, he watched with horror as the Soviet Union moved systematically to establish procommunist governments in one Eastern European nation after another and as Stalin refused to make the changes in Poland that the president believed he had promised.

Still, Roosevelt refused to abandon hope. His personal relationship with Stalin was such, he believed, that a settlement of these issues remained possible. Continuing to work to secure his vision of the future, he left Washington early in the spring for a vacation at his private retreat in Warm Springs, Georgia. There, on April 12, 1945, he suffered a sudden, massive stroke and died.

THE COLLAPSE OF THE PEACE

Harry S Truman, who succeeded Roosevelt in the presidency, inherited an international predicament that would have taxed the most experienced and patient statesman. He did not, however, inherit Roosevelt's familiarity with the world situation. (He had served in the administration only three months and had received few substantive briefings on foreign policy.) Nor did he share Roosevelt's belief in the flexibility of the Soviet Union. Roosevelt had insisted until the end that the Russians could be bargained with, that Stalin was, essentially, a reasonable man with whom an ultimate accord could be reached. Truman, in contrast, sided with those in the government (and there were many) who considered the Soviet Union fundamentally untrustworthy and viewed Stalin himself with deep suspicion and basic dislike.

There was also a significant contrast between the personalities of the two men. Roosevelt had always been a wily, even devious public figure, using his surface geniality to disguise his intentions. He had, as a result, been an unusually effective negotiator. Truman, on the other hand, was a sharp, direct, and impatient leader, a man who said what he thought and seldom wavered from decisions once he had made them. They were qualities that would win him the admiration of many of his contemporaries and of an even larger proportion of later generations of Americans. They were not, however, qualities well suited to patient negotiation.

The Failure of Potsdam

Truman had been in office only a few days before he decided on his approach to the Soviet Union. He would "get tough." Stalin had made what the new president interpreted as solemn agreements with the United States at Yalta. The United States, therefore, would insist that he honor them. Dismissing the advice of Secretary of War Stimson that the Polish question was a lost cause and not worth a world crisis, Truman met on April 23 with Soviet Foreign Minister Molotov and sharply chastised him for violations of the Yalta Accords. "I have never been talked to like that in my life," a shocked Molotov reportedly replied. "Carry out your agreements and you won't get talked to like that," said the president.

In fact, however, Truman had only limited leverage by which to compel the Soviet Union to carry out what he considered to be its agreements. Russian forces already occupied Poland and much of the rest of eastern Europe. Germany was already divided among the conquering nations. The United States was still engaged in a war in the Pacific and was neither able nor willing to engage in a second conflict in Europe. Despite Truman's professed belief that the United States should be able to get "85 percent" of what it wanted, he was ultimately forced to settle for much less.

He conceded first on Poland. When Stalin made a few minor concessions to the pro-Western exiles, Truman recognized the Warsaw government, hoping that noncommunist forces might gradually expand their influence there. Other questions remained, and to settle them Truman met in July with Churchill (who was replaced in the midst of the negotiations by Clement Atlee, who had ousted him as prime minister) and Stalin at Potsdam, near Berlin, in Russian-occupied Germany. The British and Americans hoped to use the Potsdam Conference to resolve the question of Germany, and in one sense they succeeded. But the resolution was not, ultimately, to the liking of the Western leaders. Truman reluctantly accepted the adjustments of the Polish–German border that Stalin had long demanded; he refused, however, to permit the Russians to claim any reparations from the American and British zones of western Germany. The result, in effect, was to confirm that Germany would remain divided, with the western zones united into one nation, friendly to the United States, and the Russian zone surviving as another nation, with a pro-Soviet, communist government. Stalin had failed to receive the reparations he wanted, and he had been unable to secure other forms of financial assistance from the West (a failure symbolized by the abrupt ter-

Mao with American Soldiers

In later years, Mao Zedong would seem to many Americans to be a symbol of evil incarnate. During World War II, however, he on occasion fought alongside American soldiers in their common battle against Japan. Even then, though, Mao's communist forces were engaged in the long, bitter civil war against Chiang Kai-shek that would, in 1949, result in Chiang's defeat and exile to Taiwan and the creation of a Marxist state in mainland China.
(© Bruno Barbey/Magnum)

mination by the Truman administration in May of all lend-lease assistance). He would, therefore, use eastern Germany to help rebuild the shattered Russian economy. Soon, the Soviet Union was siphoning between $1.5 and $3 billion a year out of its zone of occupation.

A Dilemma in Asia

Throughout the frustrating course of its negotiations over the future of Europe, the United States was facing an equally troubling dilemma in Asia. Central to American hopes for an open, peaceful world "policed" by the great powers was a strong, independent China. But even before the war had ended, the American government was aware that those hopes faced a major, perhaps insurmountable obstacle: the Chinese government of Chiang Kai-shek. Chiang was generally friendly to the United States, but he had few other virtues. His government was hopelessly corrupt and incompetent. His popular legitimacy was feeble. And Chiang himself lived

in a world of surreal isolation, unable or unwilling to face the problems that were threatening to engulf him. Ever since 1927, the nationalist government he headed had been engaged in a prolonged and bitter rivalry with the communist armies of Mao Zedong (Mao Tse-tung).* So successful had the communist challenge grown that Mao was in control of one-fourth of the population by 1945.

Truman had managed at Potsdam to win Stalin's agreement that Chiang would be recognized as the legitimate ruler of China; but Chiang himself was rapidly losing his grip on his country. Some Americans urged the government to try to find a third faction to support as an alternative to either Chiang or Mao. A few argued that America should try to reach some accommodation with Mao. Truman, however, decided reluctantly that he had no choice but to continue supporting Chiang, despite the weakness of his position.

* Spellings of most Chinese names appear here in the new "Pinyin" form adopted by the Chinese government in the 1970s. The old spellings appear in parentheses.

American forces in the last months of the war diverted attention from the Japanese long enough to assist Chiang against the communists in Manchuria. For the next several years, as the long struggle between the nationalists and the communists erupted into a full-scale civil war, the United States continued to pump money and weapons to Chiang. By late 1947, however, it was clear to the president that the cause was lost. Although he did not abandon China entirely or immediately, he was not prepared to intervene to save the nationalist regime.

Instead, the American government was beginning to consider an alternative to China as the strong, pro-Western force in Asia: a revived Japan. During the first years of American occupation of Japan after the war, the United States commander, Douglas MacArthur, provided a firm and restrictive administration of the island. A series of purges removed what remained of the warlord government of the Japanese Empire. Americans insisted, too, on dismantling the nation's munitions industry. But after two years of occupation, American policy toward Japan shifted. It lifted all limitations on industrial development and encouraged rapid economic growth. As in Europe, the vision of an open, united Asia had been replaced with an acceptance of the necessity of developing a strong, pro-American sphere of influence.

The Containment Doctrine

By the end of 1945, the Grand Alliance was in shambles, and with it any realistic hope of a postwar world constructed along the lines Americans had urged. Although few policymakers were willing to admit openly that the United States must abandon its "One World" ideals, a new American policy was slowly emerging to replace them. Rather than attempt to create a unified, "open" world, the West would work to "contain" the threat of further Soviet expansion. The United States would be the leading force in that effort.

The new doctrine received one test before it was even fully formulated. When Stalin refused in March 1946 to follow the British and American lead in pulling his occupation forces out of Iran, the Truman administration issued a strong and threatening ultimatum. Stalin relented and withdrew. But new crises were emerging—in Turkey, where Stalin was exerting heavy pressure to win some control over the vital straits to the Mediterranean, and in Greece, where once again communist forces were threatening the pro-Western government and where the British had announced they could no longer provide assistance. Faced with these challenges, the president finally decided to enunciate a firm new policy.

For some time, Truman had been convinced that the Soviet Union, like Nazi Germany before it, was an aggressor nation bent on world conquest. He had accepted the arguments of the influential American diplomat George F. Kennan, who warned that the United States faced "a political force committed fanatically to the belief that with the U.S. there can be no permanent *modus vivendi*," and that the only answer was "a long-term, patient but firm and vigilant containment of Russian expansive tendencies." On March 12, 1947, Truman appeared before Congress and used Kennan's warnings as the basis of what became known as the Truman Doctrine. "I believe," he argued, "that it must be the policy of the United States to support free peoples who are resisting attempted subjugation by armed minorities or by outside pressures." In the same speech he requested $400 million—part of it to bolster the armed forces of Greece and Turkey, another part to provide economic assistance to Greece. Congress quickly approved the measure.

The American commitment ultimately eased Soviet pressure on Turkey and helped the Greek government to defeat the communist insurgents. More important, it established a fundamental new doctrine that would become the basis of American foreign policy for more than two decades. Communism, Truman claimed, was an ideological threat; it was indivisible; its expansion anywhere was a threat to democracy because, as Secretary of State Dean Acheson had argued, the fall of one nation to communism would have a "domino effect" on surrounding nations. It was, therefore, the policy of the

Kennan on Containment [1947]

The Soviet pressure against the free institutions of the Western world is something that can be contained by the adroit and vigilant application of counterforce at a series of constantly shifting geographical and political points, corresponding to the shifts and maneuvers of Soviet policy, but which cannot be charmed or talked out of existence. The Russians look forward to a duel of infinite duration, and they see that already they have scored great successes. . . .

But in actuality the possibilities for American policy are by no means limited to holding the line and hoping for the best. It is entirely possible for the United States to influence by its actions the internal developments, both within Russia and throughout the international Communist movement, by which Russian policy is largely determined. . . . It is . . . a question of the degree to which the United States can create among the peoples of the world generally the impression of a country which knows what it wants, which is coping successfully with the problems of its internal life and with the responsibilities of a World Power, and which has a spiritual vitality capable of holding its own among the major ideological currents of the time.— "X" [George F. Kennan], *Foreign Affairs*, July 1947.

United States to assist pro-Western forces in any struggle against communism anywhere in the world, whether that struggle directly involved the Soviet Union or not. The Truman Doctrine marked the final American abandonment of the "One World" vision of a generation of idealists. But it replaced it with another, equally unrealistic vision—a vision of two worlds, one enslaved and one free, in which every rivalry and every conflict could be defined as a struggle between the United States and the Soviet Union. In the years to come, the ideology of the Truman Doctrine would often blind Americans to local or regional particularities, with the result that the United States would on more than one occasion interpret an internal revolution as an expression of Soviet expansionism.

The Marshall Plan

The Truman Doctrine was only one half—the military half—of the new containment doctrine. The second, and more effective, part of the new American policy was a proposal to aid in the economic reconstruction of Western Europe. There were a number of motives for the assistance. One was a simple, humanitarian concern for the European peoples, whose economies lay in ruins and whose future appeared bleak. Another was practical necessity: until Europe could support itself economically, it would remain a drain on the United States, which was endeavoring in the meantime to feed it. But there was powerful self-interest at work as well. Without a strong European market for American goods, most policymakers believed, the United States economy would be unable to sustain the prosperity it had achieved during the war. And above all, unless something could be done to strengthen the perilous position of the pro-American governments in Western Europe, they might well fall to communism, which was gaining strength as a result of the economic misery.

In June 1947, therefore, Secretary of State George C. Marshall spoke before a commencement gathering at Harvard University and announced a plan to provide economic assistance to all European nations (including the Soviet Union) that would join in drafting a program for recovery. Although Russia and its eastern satellites quickly rejected the plan, claiming (with some justification) that it represented an American attempt to reshape Europe in its own image, sixteen Western European nations eagerly participated. There was substantial opposition at first to Truman's request for an enormous appropriation to fund the effort; but congressional opponents lost power quickly, embarrassed by the unwelcome support of the American Communist party and shocked by a sudden seizure of power by communists in Czechoslovakia, which had hitherto remained at least nominally free of Soviet control. In April 1948, the president signed a bill establishing the Economic Cooperation Administration and providing an initial budget of $4 billion. Over the next three years, the Marshall Plan, as it soon became known, channeled over $12 billion of American aid into Europe, sparking what many viewed as a miraculous economic revival. By the end of 1950, European industrial production had risen 64 percent, communist strength in the member nations was declining, and the opportunities for American trade had been fully revived.

Mobilization at Home

That the United States had fully accepted a continuing commitment to the containment policy became clear in 1947 and 1948 through a series of measures designed to maintain American military power at near wartime levels. Although the government had moved rapidly in 1945 to release almost 7 million men from the armed forces in the space of a few months, it was not long before the president began to demand a renewal of universal military training through a continuing draft. Congress finally restored the Selective Service System in 1948. The United States had announced shortly after the surrender of Japan that it was prepared to accept an international agreement banning nuclear weapons (through a proposal known as the Baruch Plan). The Soviet Union, arguing that since only America had developed a bomb, America alone should abandon it, resisted any system of international inspection and controls. In response, the United States simply redoubled its own efforts in atomic research, elevating nuclear warfare to a central place in its military arsenal. The Atomic Energy Commission, established in 1946, became the supervisory body charged with overseeing all nuclear research, civilian and military alike.

Perhaps the clearest indication of America's continuing concern with military power, however, came through the National Security Act of 1947. It created a new Department of Defense, whose secretary would combine the traditional functions of the secretary of war and the secretary of the navy and preside over all branches of the armed services. The National Security Council (NSC), operating out of the White House and including the president, members of his cabinet, and others, would govern foreign and military policy. The Central Intelligence Agency (CIA) would be responsible for collecting information through both open and covert methods and, as the Cold War continued, for engaging secretly in active political and military operations on behalf of American goals.

Despite some problems of administration, the National Security Act effected important changes in the nation's ability to conduct a cold war. It transferred to the president expanded powers over all defense activities, centralizing in the White House control that had once been widely dispersed. It enabled the administration to take warlike actions without an open declaration of war; and it created vehicles by which the government could act politically and militarily overseas behind a veil of secrecy.

The Road to NATO

At about the same time, the United States was moving to strengthen the military capabilities of Western Europe. Convinced that only a reconstructed Germany could serve as the necessary bulwark against communist expansion, Truman abandoned earlier policies designed to restrain German power and forged an agreement with England and France to merge the three western zones of occupation into a new West German republic (which would include the American, British, and French sectors of Berlin, even though that city lay well within the Soviet zone). Stalin interpreted the move (correctly) as a direct challenge to his hopes for a subdued Germany and a docile Europe. At almost the same moment, he was facing a challenge from inside what he considered his own sphere. The government of Yugoslavia, under the leadership of Marshall Josip Broz Tito, broke openly with the Soviet Union and declared the nation an unaligned communist state. The United States offered Tito assistance.

Stalin's response came quickly. On June 24, 1948, taking advantage of the lack of a written guarantee of Western transit through eastern Germany, he imposed a tight blockade around the western sectors of Berlin. If Germany was to be officially divided, he was implying, then the country's Western government would have to abandon its outpost in the heart of the Soviet-controlled eastern zone. The United States was being given a choice between dropping its plan for a united West Germany or surrendering Berlin. Truman refused to do either. Although he was unwilling to risk war by responding militarily to the blockade, he ordered a massive airlift to supply the city with food, fuel, and supplies. The airlift continued for more than ten months, transporting nearly 2.5 million tons of material, keeping alive a city of 2 million people, and transforming West Berlin into a symbol of the West's resolve to resist communist expansion. Finally, late in the spring of 1949, Stalin lifted the now ineffective blockade. And in October, the division of Germany into two nations—the Federal Republic in the west and the Democratic Republic in the east—became official.

The crisis in Berlin accelerated the consolidation of what was already in effect an alliance of the United States and the countries of Western Europe. On April 4, 1949, twelve nations signed an agreement establishing the North Atlantic Treaty Organization (NATO) and declaring that an armed attack against one member would be considered an attack against all. The NATO countries would, moreover, create a joint military force in Europe to defend against what many believed was the threat of a Soviet invasion. The American Senate quickly ratified this first peacetime alliance between the United States and Europe since the eighteenth century. The

NATO alliance did more than create a powerful military force in Western Europe. It greatly increased American influence there as well. The United States quickly became the most important supplier of the NATO military forces; and an American officer, General Dwight D. Eisenhower, assumed the powerful position of supreme commander of Allied forces in Europe.

The Enduring Crisis

The Berlin blockade, the offer of aid to Yugoslavia, the creation of NATO—all had in most respects been expressions of American confidence. Truman had believed, along with most other policymakers, that the United States was easily the more powerful of the two great rivals, that the Soviet Union would not dare provoke war because of the certainty of defeat. For a time, it had seemed that the battle against communism was being won.

But a series of events in 1949 began seriously to erode that confidence and launched the Cold War into a new and more enduring phase. An announcement in September that the Soviet Union had successfully exploded its first atomic weapon, years before most Americans had considered it possible, came as a severe shock to the nation. So did the collapse of Chiang Kai-shek's nationalist government in China, which occurred with startling speed in the last months of 1949. Chiang fled with his political allies and the remnants of his army to the offshore island of Formosa (Taiwan), and the entire Chinese mainland came under the control of a communist government that many Americans believed to be a mere extension of the Soviet Union. The United States, powerless to stop the communists without a major military commitment that virtually no one wanted, had no choice but to watch the collapse of its ill-chosen ally. Few policymakers shared the belief of the so-called China lobby that the United States should now commit itself to the rearming of Chiang Kai-shek. But neither would the administration recognize the new communist regime, particularly after the Maoist government began expropriating American property, expelling American businessmen, and strengthening its ties to the Soviet Union. The Chinese mainland would remain almost entirely closed to the West for a full generation. The United States, in the meantime, would devote increased attention to the revitalization of Japan as a buffer against Asian communism, ending the American occupation of the island, finally, in 1952.

With the containment policy in apparent disarray, and with political opposition mounting at home, Truman called for a thorough review of American foreign policy. The result was an important National Security Council report, commonly known as NSC-68, which outlined a significant shift in the American position. The April 1950 document argued that the United States could no longer rely on other nations to take the initiative in resisting communism. It must itself establish firm and active leadership of the noncommunist world. Among other things, the report called for a major expansion of American military power, with a defense budget almost four times the previously projected figure. It also reinforced what was already a strong sense of mission in the formation of American foreign policy. Upon the United States, the report maintained, lay the sole responsibility of defending freedom in the world. America had, its citizens were beginning to believe, embarked on a moral crusade. That conviction would help to produce three decades of international frustration.

POSTWAR ADJUSTMENTS

The increasing dangers overseas were only a part of the frustrations facing the United States after the war. The nation also encountered serious difficulties in adapting its complex economy to the new demands of peace; and the instability that resulted contributed to the creation of a heated political climate.

The Problems of Reconversion

The bombs that destroyed Hiroshima and Nagasaki ended the war months earlier than almost anyone had predicted and propelled the nation precipitously into a process of reconversion. The lack of planning was soon compounded by a growing popular impatience, as civilians clamored to buy the consumer goods denied them during the preceding four years and as returning veterans began to demand jobs, housing, and services. Under intense public pressure, the Truman administration attempted to hasten the "return to normal," despite dire warnings by some planners and economists. The result was a period of severe economic problems.

They were not, however, the problems that most Americans had feared. There had been many predictions that peace would bring a return of Depression unemployment, as war production ceased and returning soldiers flooded the labor market. But there was no general economic collapse in 1946—for several reasons. Government spending dropped sharply and abruptly to be sure; $35 billion of war contracts were canceled at a stroke within weeks of the Japanese surrender. But increased consumer demand soon compensated. Consumer goods had been generally unavailable during the war, so many workers had saved a substantial portion of their wages and were now ready to spend them. A $6 billion tax cut pumped additional money into general circulation. The Servicemen's Readjustment Act of 1944, better known as the GI Bill of Rights, provided substantial economic and educational assistance to veterans, increasing spending even further.

But while the sudden flood of consumer demand ensured that there would be no new depression, it also created rampant, debilitating inflation. For more than two years inflation continued, with prices rising at rates of 14 or 15 percent. In the summer of 1946, the president vetoed an extension of the authority of the wartime Office of Price Administration because Congress had weakened the agency's authority. In so doing, he permitted government price controls, which were already having difficulty holding down price increases, to be removed altogether. A month later, he relented and signed a bill little different from the one he had rejected. But in the meantime inflation had soared briefly to 25 percent.

Compounding the economic difficulties was a sharp rise in labor unrest. Unions had accepted government-imposed restraint on their demands during the war, but now they were willing to wait no longer, particularly as inflation cut into the existing wage scales with painful force. By the end of 1945, there had already been major strikes in the automobile, electrical, and steel industries. Government intervention had helped settle the strikes relatively quickly, but the agreements fueled inflation even further.

In April 1946, a fresh crisis emerged when John L. Lewis led the United Mine Workers out on strike, shutting down the coal fields for forty days. The economic impact was devastating. Freight and shipping activity declined by 75 percent; the steel industry made plans to shut down operations; fears grew that without vital coal supplies, the entire nation might virtually grind to a halt. Truman finally forced coal production to resume by ordering government seizure of the mines, but at the cost of conceding to the union most of its demands, which he had earlier denounced as inflationary. Almost simultaneously, the nation's railroads suffered a total shutdown—the first in the nation's history—as two major unions walked out on strike. By threatening to use the army to run the trains, Truman pressured the workers back to work after only a few days. Once again, however, the nation had stared economic chaos in the face.

The Fair Deal Rejected

On September 16, 1945, only four days after the formal Japanese surrender, Truman submitted to Congress a twenty-one point domestic program outlining what he later termed the "Fair Deal." It called for expansion of social security benefits, the raising of the legal minimum wage from 40 to 65 cents an hour, a program to ensure full employment, a permanent Fair Employment Prac-

tices Act, public housing and slum clearance, long-range environmental and public works planning, and government promotion of scientific research. Weeks later he added other proposals: federal aid to education, government health insurance, prepaid medical care, funding for the St. Lawrence Seaway, and nationalization of atomic energy. The president was, it was clear, declaring an end to the wartime moratorium on reform and creating an impressive new liberal agenda. The announcement of the Fair Deal, he later wrote, "symbolizes for me my assumption of the office of President in my own right."

Truman's proposals greatly heartened Democratic liberals, who had continued to wonder whether the new president would prove a satisfactory successor to Franklin Roosevelt. But the Fair Deal made little progress in Congress. Truman's programs fell victim to the same general public and

---

Under the friendly Roosevelt administration, union membership soared during the New Deal and World War II. From 1955 on, the chart indicates the combined A.F. of L. and CIO membership.

Organized Labor 1900–1980

[1]Data unavailable for 1948–1950.
[2]1980 data are preliminary.
[3]The sharp increase in independent union membership between 1978 and 1980 is due to the fact that the Bureau of Labor Statistics began to include professional and state employees' unions in this category.

"Weather Clear, Track Fast"
A cartoon by D. R. Fitzpatrick for the *St. Louis Post-Dispatch* expresses the widespread national concern about soaring postwar inflation. President Truman's vacillating economic policies and his mishandling of the repeal of wage and price controls helped exaggerate what would have been a serious problem in any case. The inflation contributed to the dramatic Republican victory in the 1946 congressional elections.

---

congressional conservatism that had crippled the last years of the New Deal and had increased during the war. The economic problems and labor unrest of 1946 only intensified congressional resistance to further spending and reform. And what little hope there had been for legislative progress died in November 1946, when the Republican party—making use of the simple but devastating slogan "Had Enough?"—won control of both houses of Congress.

With the new Congress in place, the retreat from reform rapidly became a stampede. The president bowed to what he claimed was the popular mandate to lift most remaining wage and price controls, and Congress moved further to deregulate the economy. Inflation rapidly increased. When a public outcry arose over the soaring prices for meat, Senator Robert Taft, perhaps the

most influential Republican conservative in Congress, advised consumers to "Eat less," and added, "We have got to break with the corrupting idea that we can legislate prosperity, legislate equality, legislate opportunity." True to the spirit of Taft's words, the Republican Congress quickly applied what one congressman described as a "meat-axe to government frills." It refused to appropriate funds to aid education, increase social security, or support reclamation and power projects in the West. It defeated a proposal to raise the minimum wage. It passed tax measures that cut rates dramatically for high-income families and only moderately for those with lower incomes. Only vetoes by the president finally forced a more equitable bill.

The most notable action of the Eightieth Congress was an open assault on one of the cornerstones of Depression reform: the Wagner Act of 1935. Conservatives had always resented the enormous powers the legislation granted unions; and in the light of the labor difficulties following the war, such resentments intensified sharply. The result was the Labor-Management Relations Act of 1947, better known as the Taft-Hartley Act, which loosened several of the earlier restrictions on employers and added some important new prohibitions against the unions. The act made illegal the so-called closed shop (a workplace in which no one could be hired without first being a member of a union). And although it continued to permit the creation of so-called union shops (in which workers must join a union after being hired), it permitted states to pass "right-to-work" laws prohibiting even that. This provision, the controversial Section 14(b), remained a target of the labor movement for decades. The act also empowered the president to call for a "cooling-off" period before a strike by issuing an injunction against any work stoppage that endangered national safety or health. These and other provisions delighted conservatives, who viewed union power as one of the nation's greatest social evils. But they outraged workers and union leaders, who denounced the measure as a "slave labor bill" and called on the president to veto it. Truman needed little persuading. He had opposed the Taft-Hartley Act from the beginning and, on June 20, 1947, returned it to Congress with a stinging veto message. Both houses easily overruled him the same day.

The Taft-Hartley Act did not destroy the labor movement, as many union leaders had predicted. But it did seriously damage the position of weaker unions in relatively lightly organized industries such as chemicals and textiles; and it made far more difficult the organizing of workers who had never been union members at all, especially in the South. Powerful unions remained powerful, for the most part; but unorganized or loosely organized workers now faced serious obstacles. Equally important in the short run, the passage of Taft-Hartley served as a symbol of the repudiation of New Deal reform by the Republican party and its Congress, a warning that government innovations that many had come to take for granted were now in jeopardy. "Victories fought and won years ago were suddenly in doubt," a columnist for the *New Republic* wrote at the time. "Everything was debatable again."

The Election of 1948

Truman and his advisers were convinced that the American public was not ready to abandon the achievements of the New Deal, that the 1946 election had not been a mandate for a surrender to conservatism. As they planned strategy for the 1948 campaign, therefore, they placed their hopes in an appeal to enduring Democratic liberalism. Throughout 1948, Truman proposed one reform measure after another (including, on February 2, the first major civil-rights bill of the century). Congress, of course, ignored or defeated them all; but the president was effectively building a campaign issue for the fall.

There remained, however, the serious problem of Truman's personal unpopularity—the assumption among a vast segment of the electorate that he lacked stature, that his administration was weak and inept. Many of the qualities that made him such an admired figure in later years—his outspokenness, his impatience, his "common-man" demeanor—seemed at the time to be evidence of his unfitness to fill the shoes of Franklin Roosevelt. Liberals within his own

party were actively looking for an alternative candidate. Conservatives were regarding the president with disgust.

All of these tensions came to a head at the Democratic Convention that summer. Two factions abandoned the party altogether. Southern conservatives were angered by Truman's proposed civil-rights bill and outraged by the approval at the convention of a civil-rights plank in the platform (engineered by Hubert Humphrey, the mayor of Minneapolis). They walked out and formed the States' Rights (or "Dixiecrat") party, with Governor Strom Thurmond of South Carolina as its nominee. At the same time, the party's left wing formed a new Progressive party, with Henry A. Wallace as its candidate. The Wallace supporters objected to what they considered the slow and ineffective domestic policies of the Truman administration; but they resented even more the president's confrontational stance toward the Soviet Union.

In addition, many Democrats unwilling to leave the party attempted to dump the president in 1948. The Americans for Democratic Action (ADA), a coalition of liberals formed shortly after the war, tried to entice Dwight D. Eisenhower, the popular war hero, to contest the nomination, certain that he could win the November election while Truman could not. Only after Eisenhower had refused did the party bow to the inevitable and, in near despair, give the nomination to Truman. The Republicans, in the meantime, had once again nominated Governor Thomas E. Dewey of New York, whose substantial reelection victory in 1946 had made him one of the nation's leading political figures. Austere, dignified, and competent, he seemed to offer an unbeatable alternative to the president. That his views on most issues were only marginally different from Truman's appeared further to strengthen his chances of victory.

Nothing, it seemed, could save the president from certain defeat. His party was seriously splintered. Polls showed him trailing so far behind Dewey that late in September public opinion analysts stopped taking surveys. Dewey was conducting a quiet, statesmanlike campaign, behaving much as if

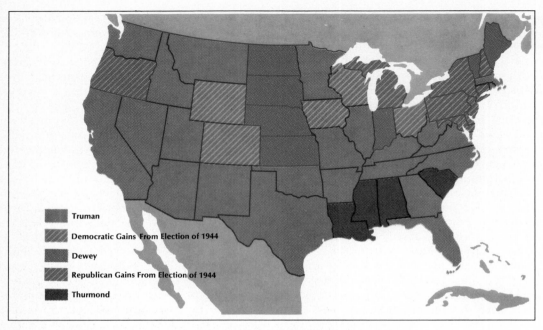

Truman

Democratic Gains From Election of 1944

Dewey

Republican Gains From Election of 1944

Thurmond

THE ELECTION OF 1948

he were already president. Only Truman, it seemed, believed he could win. He had provided a foretaste of what was to come in his speech accepting the Democratic nomination, a blistering attack on the Republican party. As the campaign gathered momentum, he became still more aggressive, turning his fire not on Dewey but on the "do-nothing, good-for-nothing" Republican Congress, which was, he told the voters, responsible for fueling inflation and abandoning the workers and the common people. To dramatize his point, he called Congress into special session in July to give it a chance, he said, to enact the liberal measures the Republicans had recently written into their platform. Congress met for two weeks and, predictably, did almost nothing. Truman was delighted.

Before the campaign was over, the president had traveled nearly 32,000 miles and made 356 speeches, delivering blunt, extemporaneous attacks. He had told Alben Barkley, his running mate, "I'm going to fight hard. I'm going to give them hell." He called for repeal of the Taft-Hartley Act, increased price supports for farmers, and strong civil-rights protection for blacks (he was the first president to campaign in Harlem). He sought, in short, to re-create much of Franklin Roosevelt's New Deal coalition. And to the surprise of virtually everyone, he succeeded. When the returns came in, the nation was stunned to learn that Harry Truman had won a narrow but decisive victory: 49.5 percent of the popular vote to Dewey's 45 percent (with the two splinter parties dividing the small remainder between them), and an electoral margin of 303 to 189. Democrats, in the meantime, had regained both houses of Congress by substantial margins. It was the most dramatic upset in the history of presidential elections.

COLD WAR REFORM AND LIMITED WAR

Truman interpreted the 1948 election as a mandate for the revival of liberal reform. But

while he enjoyed a few legislative successes in the ensuing months, most of his domestic

President Harry S Truman
As a campaigner, President Truman apparently had no chance in 1948, but he was remarkably successful in his extemporaneous speaking at whistle-stops, which together with his
policies had rallied behind him much of the farm and labor vote. On the morning after
the election, he gleefully displayed a newspaper that had underestimated him—as indeed
had much of the American public. (UPI)

programs quickly fell victim to his own and
the nation's preoccupation with the Cold
War. In competition with international concerns, the Fair Deal generally suffered. And it
faded almost entirely from view when, beginning in 1950, the United States found itself embroiled in a difficult and frustrating
war in Korea.

The Fair Deal Revived

Despite the Democratic victory in 1948, it
often seemed that the Eighty-first Congress
was no more hospitable to reform than its
Republican predecessor. Truman failed once
again to win approval of such major new reforms as aid to education and national health

insurance. Nevertheless, his administration managed in the first two years of its second term to consolidate and extend a number of already established New Deal reforms that before the election had seemed to be in jeopardy.

On three issues, in particular, Truman won important victories. Congress raised the legal minimum wage from 40 cents to 75 cents an hour. It approved an expansion of the Social Security System, increasing benefits by 75 percent and extending them to 10 million additional people. And it strengthened the federal commitment to public housing. The National Housing Act of 1949 provided for the construction of 810,000 units of low-income housing over six years, to be accompanied by long-term rent subsidies.

While many of the other initiatives Truman had sponsored before 1948 gradually faded from view, he continued to press strenuously on what was perhaps the most controversial domestic issue of all: civil rights. The president had little luck persuading Congress to accept the civil-rights legislation he proposed in 1949, legislation that would have made lynching a federal crime, provided federal protection of black voting rights, abolished the poll tax, and established a Fair Employment Practices Commission to limit discrimination in hiring. Although a majority of the Senate appeared ready to support at least some aspects of this package, a vigorous filibuster by Southern Democrats (who also controlled crucial committees) managed to block the legislation. Nevertheless, Truman proceeded on his own to battle several forms of racial discrimination. He had appointed a federal Civil Rights Commission in 1946, whose 1947 report became the first important government call for the total elimination of segregation. Truman publicly approved its recommendations, although he was as yet unable to implement them. He ordered an end to discrimination in the hiring of government employees. He began to dismantle segregation within the armed forces. And he allowed the Justice Department to become actively involved in court battles against discriminatory statutes. The Supreme Court, in the meantime, sig-

naled its own growing awareness of the issue by ruling, in *Shelley* v. *Kraemer* (1948), that the courts could not be used to enforce private "covenants" meant to restrict blacks from residential neighborhoods. The Truman record, and the judicial decisions that accompanied it, made only minor dents in the structure of segregation. They did, however, signal the beginning of a commitment by liberal Democrats—and by the federal government as a whole—finally to confront the problem of race.

War in Korea

Truman's domestic policies had had a difficult time from the beginning competing against the nation's obsession with the Soviet threat in Europe. In 1950, a new and more dangerous element of the Cold War emerged and all but killed hopes for further Fair Deal reform. On June 24, 1950, the armies of communist North Korea swept across their southern border and began a major invasion of the pro-Western half of the Korean peninsula to the south. Suddenly, the United States found itself embroiled in a new kind of conflict. The nation was neither fully at war nor fully at peace. It had, rather, discovered the peculiar demands of "limited war."

Korea had long been a source of international controversy. A peninsula of great strategic importance in Asia, it offered easy access to the Soviet Union, Japan, and China. At the end of World War II, therefore, neither the United States nor the Soviet Union—both of which had sent troops into Korea against the Japanese—was willing to leave. As a result, the nation had been divided, supposedly temporarily, along the thirty-eighth parallel. The Russians departed in 1949, leaving behind a communist government in the north with a strong, Soviet-equipped army. The Americans left only months later, handing control to the pro-Western government of Syngman Rhee, a ruthless and only nominally democratic leader and an ardent nationalist. He possessed a far less imposing army than his northern counterparts, and he used it primarily to strengthen his own position against internal political opposition.

In the Trenches in Korea
The conflict in Korea was America's first experience with a distinctly modern phenomenon: "limited war," a war in which the military must observe strict political constraints in its conduct of the fighting. The restrictions placed upon the military were one of the reasons for the rising frustration with the war in the early 1950s; but a more important one was the long stalemate in the fighting. (Wide World Photos)

The situation proved a strong temptation to the Soviet leadership. The communist government of the north, recognizing its military superiority, was eager to invade the south to reunite the nation. The Russians would not, Stalin believed, have to play any direct role themselves. The unification of Korea under a sympathetic communist regime, moreover, would be an important strategic gain to the Soviets, who were looking with concern at American efforts to make Japan an American stronghold in Asia. With much to gain and little, he believed, to lose, Stalin gave his approval to the invasion.

The Truman administration was quick to respond. On June 27, the president ordered American air and naval forces to assist the South Korean army against the invaders; and on the same day he appealed to the United Nations to intervene. Because the Soviet Union was boycotting the Security Council at the time (to protest the council's refusal to recognize the new communist government of China), American delegates were able to win UN agreement to a resolution calling for international assistance to the embattled Rhee government. On June 30, the United States ordered its own ground forces into Korea, and Truman appointed General Douglas MacArthur to command the UN operations there. (Several other nations offered minor assistance to the effort, but the "UN" armies were, in fact, overwhelmingly American.)

The intervention in Korea was the first expression of the newly militant American foreign policy outlined in NSC-68. Very quickly, the administration decided that the war would not simply be an effort at containment, but also at "liberation." After a surprise American invasion at Inchon in September had routed the North Korean forces from the south and sent them fleeing back across the thirty-eighth parallel, Truman gave MacArthur permission to pursue the communists into their own territory. His aim, as an American-sponsored UN resolution proclaimed in October, was to create "a unified, independent and democratic Korea." (Paralleling this decision came new American initiatives in other areas: efforts to strengthen the Chiang regime in Taiwan for a possible future assault on the Chinese mainland; and assistance to the French, who were attempting to rout communist forces from Vietnam and Laos.)

From Invasion to Stalemate

For several weeks, MacArthur's invasion of North Korea proceeded smoothly. On October 19, the capital, Pyongyang, fell to the UN forces. At the same time, parachutists managed to trap and immobilize much of the rest of the North Korean army. Victory seemed near. Slowly, however, the United States was becoming aware of the growing presence of forces from communist China; and by November 4, it was clear that eight Chinese divisions had entered the war. Suddenly, the UN offensive stalled and then collapsed. Through December 1950, American forces fought a bitter, losing battle against far more numerous Chinese divisions, retreating at almost every juncture. Within weeks, communist forces had pushed the Americans back below the thirty-eighth parallel once again and had captured the South Korean capital of Seoul. By March, the rout had ceased, and the UN armies had managed to regain much of the territory they had so recently lost, taking back Seoul and pushing the communists north of the thirty-eighth parallel for the second time. But with that, the war degenerated into a protracted, brutal stalemate.

It was then that the nation first began to experience the true dilemmas of "limited war." Truman had been determined from the beginning to avoid embroiling the nation in a direct conflict with China, a conflict that would, he believed, lead to a world conflagration. As early as December 1950, he had begun seeking a negotiated solution to the struggle; and he continued through the next two years to insist that there would be no wider war. He faced, however, a formidable opponent in General MacArthur, a soldier of

the old school who could not accept the idea of any limits on a military endeavor. The United States was fighting the Chinese, he argued. It should, therefore, attack China itself, if not through an actual invasion, then at least by bombing communist forces massing north of the Chinese border. In March 1951 he gave a public indication of his unhappiness with the administration's policy, sending to House Republican leader Joseph W. Martin a message that concluded: "There is no substitute for victory." His position quickly won wide popular support from a nation frustrated by the long, inconclusive war.

For nine months, Truman had chafed at MacArthur's resistance to his decisions about the conduct of the war. More than once, he had warned him to keep his objections to himself. The release of the Martin letter, therefore, struck the president as intolerable insubordination. On April 11, 1951, he relieved MacArthur of his command.

The result was a virtual firestorm of public outrage. Sixty-nine percent of the American people supported MacArthur in the controversy, a Gallup Poll reported. When the general returned to the United States in 1951, the first time he had set foot in the country since 1935, he was greeted with hysterical enthusiasm. His televised farewell appearance before a joint session of Congress attracted an audience of millions. Public criticism abated somewhat when a number of prominent military figures, including General Omar Bradley, publicly supported the president's decision. But the controversy had cast in sharp relief the dilemmas of limited war.

In the meantime, the Korean stalemate continued for what seemed interminable months. In July 1951, negotiations began between the opposing forces at Panmunjom, near the thirty-eighth parallel; but they produced no swift resolution. Instead, the talks—and the war—dragged on until 1953.

Limited Mobilization

Just as the war in Korea produced only a limited American military commitment abroad, so it created only a limited economic mobili-

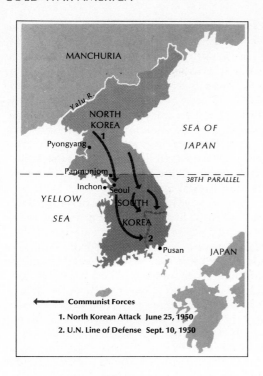

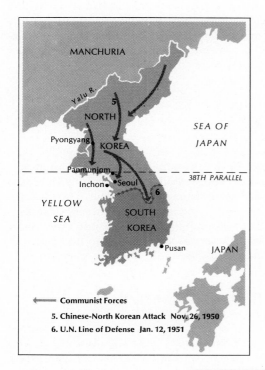

THE KOREAN WAR, 1950–1953

zation at home. Although the Truman administration drew heavily on the experiences of World War II in meeting the demands for armaments and supplies, never was it necessary to create the enormous bureaucracy and pervasive controls that had been required a decade earlier. Nevertheless, the Korean War did place pressure on the government to control the economy in several important ways. First, Truman attempted to halt a new wave of inflation by setting up the Office of Defense Mobilization to hold down prices and discourage high union wage demands. Then, confronted with the failure of these cautious regulatory efforts, the president took more drastic action. When railroad workers walked off the job in 1951, Truman ordered the government to seize control of the railroads. But the dramatic gesture had little impact; workers ultimately got most of what they had demanded before the railroads were returned to their owners. In 1952, a nationwide steel strike threatened to interrupt vital war production; and again, Truman moved to seize the steel mills, citing his powers as commander in chief. This time, however, the courts intervened. In a 6-to-3 decision, the Supreme Court ruled that the president had exceeded his authority, and Truman was forced to relent. A lengthy and costly strike ensued.

There were, however, important positive results of the military commitment in Korea, most notably the significant boost it gave to national prosperity. Just at the point when some economists believed the postwar consumer demand was about to decline, a new surge of funds was being pumped into the economy by the federal government, which increased military expenditures more than fourfold, to $60 billion in 1953. Unemployment declined. Industry embarked on a new wave of capital expansion.

But the war had other, less healthy effects on American life. Coming at a time of rising insecurity about the position of the United States in the world, it intensified anxiety about communism. As the long stalemate continued, producing 140,000 American casualties (and more than 1 million South Korean dead and wounded), frustration increasingly turned to anger. The United States, which had recently won the greatest war in history, seemed unable to conclude what many Americans considered a minor border skirmish in an unimportant country. Many began to believe that something must be deeply wrong—not only in Korea but within the United States as well. Such fears became one of many factors contributing to the rise of the second major campaign of the century against domestic communism.

THE CRUSADE AGAINST SUBVERSION

There has never been a single, satisfactory explanation of why, in the years following World War II, the American people developed a growing fear of internal communist subversion that by the early 1950s had reached the point of near hysteria. Only by looking at the convergence of many factors at once is it possible to understand the era of the "great fear."

One factor was obvious. Communism was not an imagined enemy in the 1950s; it had tangible shape, in the person of Joseph Stalin and the Soviet Union, which had become a dark and menacing threat to America's hopes for the world. The continuing setbacks overseas, the frustrations in

Korea, the "loss" of China, the shocking realization that Russia had developed an atomic bomb—all created a sense of unease and a need to find someone to blame. The idea of a communist conspiracy within American borders was a natural outlet. But there were other factors as well, rooted in domestic political rivalries.

HUAC and Alger Hiss

Much of the anticommunist furor emerged out of the search by the Republican party for an issue with which to attack the Democrats, and out of the efforts of the Democrats to take that issue away. Beginning in 1947, the House Un-American Activities Committee (HUAC), established by the Democrats in 1938 to uncover malign foreign influences in the United States and now under the control of Republicans, launched a series of widely publicized and highly inflammatory investigations to prove that, under Democratic rule, the nation had allowed communist subversion to reach alarming levels. The committee turned first to the movie industry, arguing that communists had so infiltrated Hollywood that American films were being tainted with Soviet propaganda. A parade of writers and producers was summoned to testify; and when some of them refused to answer questions about their political beliefs, they were sent to jail for contempt. Others were barred from employment in the industry when Hollywood, attempting to protect its public image, adopted a blacklist consisting of those of "suspicious loyalty."

Far more frightening to much of the public, however, was HUAC's investigation into charges of disloyalty leveled against a former high-ranking member of the State Department: Alger Hiss. Whittaker Chambers, a self-avowed former communist agent, told the committee in 1948 that Hiss had passed classified documents to him in 1937 and 1938. When Hiss sued him for slander, Chambers produced microfilms of the documents (called the "pumpkin papers," because Chambers had kept them hidden in a pumpkin in his garden). Hiss could not be tried for espionage because of the statute of limitations. But as a result of the committee's efforts (and particularly because of the relentless pursuit of the case by Richard M. Nixon, a freshman Republican congressman from California), Hiss was charged with lying to the HUAC inquisitors. After a sensational trial, in which a number of leading Democratic liberals—including Adlai Stevenson, Felix Frankfurter, and Dean Acheson—testified as character witnesses for Hiss, the jury was unable to reach a verdict. A second trial produced a conviction for perjury, and Hiss served several years in prison, still proclaiming his innocence. The Hiss case not only discredited a talented young diplomat; it cast suspicion on an entire generation of liberal

Democrats and made it possible for the public to believe that communists had actually infiltrated the government.

The Federal Loyalty Program

The Truman administration, in the meantime, was making its own contribution to increasing the popular fear. Partly to protect itself against Republican attacks, partly to encourage support for the president's foreign policy initiatives, the executive branch in 1947 initiated a widely publicized program to review the "loyalty" of federal employees. A series of "loyalty boards" undertook a sweeping investigation of the government; and in August 1950, the president authorized the dismissal in sensitive departments of even those deemed no more than "bad security risks." The faintest suspicion of disloyalty could cause a federal employee to lose his or her job. By 1951, more than 2,000 government employees had resigned and 212 had been dismissed.

Not only was the Employee Loyalty Program itself being abused; the program also served as a signal throughout the executive branch to launch a major assault on subversion. The attorney general established a list of dissident organizations and, in 1948, obtained indictments of eleven American communists for "conspiring to teach the violent overthrow of the government." The Federal Bureau of Investigation (FBI), whose director, J. Edgar Hoover, had been obsessed with the issue of communism for years, launched major crusades to investigate and harass alleged radicals. Federal information and education programs began to become tainted with strident anticommunist propaganda.

By now, the anticommunist frenzy was growing so intense that even a Democratic Congress was becoming obsessed with it. In 1950, over the objections of the Department of Defense, the Department of Justice, and the CIA, it enacted the McCarran Internal Security Act. The bill required all communist organizations to register with the government and to publish their records. Americans were liable for prosecution on grounds as vague as "fomenting revolution." Communists were barred from working in defense plants and denied passports. Members of overseas "subversive organizations" were denied visas to enter the country. Truman vetoed the bill. Congress easily overrode his veto.

Of particular importance in fanning public fears were the efforts of the FBI and the Justice Department to prove a communist conspiracy to steal America's atomic secrets for the Soviet Union. The early explosion of a Russian nuclear weapon made such charges credible. And the testimony in 1950 of Klaus Fuchs, a young British scientist, that he had delivered to the Russians full details of the manufacture of the bomb gave the charges substance. Through an arcane series of connections, the case ultimately settled on an obscure New York couple, Julius and Ethel

Rosenberg, whom the government claimed had been the masterminds of the conspiracy. The Rosenbergs had allegedly received the information from Ethel's brother, a machinist who had worked on the Manhattan Project, and passed it on to the Soviet Union. Several witnesses corroborated the story; although the Rosenbergs vehemently denied any guilt, they were found guilty and, on April 5, 1951, sentenced to death. A rising chorus of public protests and a long string of appeals failed to save them. On June 19, 1953, they died in the electric chair.

All these factors—the HUAC investigations, the Hiss trial, the loyalty investigations, the McCarran Act, the Rosenberg case, and more—combined, by the early 1950s, to create a paranoia about communist subver-

Demonstrating for the Rosenbergs
Ministers and others march in front of the White House to plead with President Eisenhower to grant clemency to Julius and Ethel Rosenberg, who awaited execution on charges of delivering atomic secrets to the Soviet Union. Their pleas were to no avail. On June 19, 1953, the Rosenbergs died in a New York electric chair—to some, a symbol of communist infiltration of American life; to others, a symbol of the corrosiveness of the Red Scare of the early 1950s. (UPI)

sion that seemed to grip the entire country. State and local governments launched loyalty programs of their own, dismissing thousands of employees. Local courts began handing down extraordinarily harsh sentences to defendants convicted of anything resembling subversion. Schools and universities rooted out teachers suspected of teaching "un-American" ideas. Unions found themselves under continuing assault for suspected (and occasionally real) communist leanings. And a pervasive fear settled on the country—not only fear of communist infiltration but the fear of being suspected of communism. It was a climate that made possible the rise of an extraordinary public figure, whose behavior at any other time would have been dismissed as preposterous.

McCarthyism

Joseph McCarthy was an undistinguished, first-term, Republican senator from Wisconsin when, in February 1950, he suddenly burst into national prominence. In the midst of a speech in Wheeling, West Virginia, he raised a sheet of paper into the air and claimed to "hold in my hand" a list of 205 known communists currently working in the American State Department. No person of comparable stature had ever made so bold a charge against the federal government; and in the weeks to come, as McCarthy repeated and expanded on accusations, he emerged as the nation's preeminent leader of the crusade against communism.

He had seized on anticommunism not out of any real concern but because he needed an issue with which to run for reelection in 1952. And he continued to exploit the issue for the next four years because, to his surprise, it won him fame and notoriety beyond his wildest dreams. His rise was meteoric. Within weeks of his charges against the State Department he was expanding his accusations to other agencies. After 1952, with the Republicans in control of the Senate and McCarthy the chairman of a special subcommittee, he conducted highly publicized investigations of subversion—investigations

that probed virtually every area of the government. His unprincipled assistants, Roy Cohn and David Schine, sauntered arrogantly through federal offices and American embassies overseas looking for evidence of communist influence. One hapless government official after another found himself summoned before McCarthy's subcommittee, where the senator belligerently and often cruelly badgered witnesses and destroyed public careers.

In the course of this extraordinary crusade, not once did McCarthy produce conclusive evidence that any federal employee had communist ties. But the public seemed not to care. A growing constituency adored him for his coarse, "fearless" assaults on a government establishment that many considered arrogant, effete, even effeminate. They admired his efforts to expose the "traitors" who had, he claimed, riddled the Truman administration. They even tolerated his attacks on public figures who earlier would have been considered unassailable, men such as General George C. Marshall and Governor Adlai Stevenson. Republicans, in particular, rallied to his claims that the Democrats had been responsible for "twenty years of treason," that only a change of parties could rid the country of subversion. McCarthy, in short, provided his followers with an issue into which they could channel a wide range of resentments: fear of communism, animosity toward the country's "Eastern establishment," and frustrated partisan ambitions.

For several years, McCarthy terrorized American public life, intimidating all but a very few from speaking out in opposition to him. In 1952, when some Democratic senators dared to denounce him, McCarthy openly campaigned against their reelection, and several went down to defeat. Journalists and intellectuals, with some notable exceptions, drew back from challenging him for fear of being themselves discredited by his attack. Even the highly popular Dwight D. Eisenhower, running for president in 1952, did not dare to oppose him. Outraged at McCarthy's attacks on General Marshall, Eisenhower briefly considered issuing a public protest. In the end, however, he remained silent.

The Republican Revival

Public frustration over the stalemate in Korea and popular fears of internal subversion combined to make 1952 an inhospitable year for the Democratic party. Truman, whose own popularity had diminished almost to the vanishing point, wisely withdrew from that year's presidential contest, creating the first open battle for the nomination since 1932. Senator Estes Kefauver of Tennessee launched a spirited campaign, performing well in the primaries. But party leaders ultimately settled on Governor Adlai E. Stevenson of Illinois, whose early reluctance to run seemed only to enhance his attractiveness.

Stevenson's dignity, wit, and eloquence quickly made him a beloved figure to many liberals and intellectuals, who developed a devotion to him that they had never offered Harry Truman. But those same qualities seemed only to fuel Republican charges that Stevenson lacked the strength or the will to combat communism sufficiently. McCarthy described him as "soft" and took delight in deliberately confusing him with Alger Hiss.

Stevenson's greatest problem, however, was the candidate the Republicans chose to oppose him. Rejecting the efforts of conservatives to nominate either Robert Taft or Douglas MacArthur, the Republicans turned to a man who had had so little previous identification with the party that liberal Democrats had tried to draft him four years earlier. Their choice was General Dwight D. Eisenhower, military hero, former commander of NATO, now president of Columbia University in New York. Despite a vigorous struggle by the Taft forces, Eisenhower won nomination on the first ballot. He chose as his running mate the young Californian senator who had won national prominence through his crusade against Alger Hiss: Richard M. Nixon.

Eisenhower and Nixon proved to be a powerful combination in the autumn campaign. While Eisenhower attracted support by virtue of his geniality and his statesmanlike pledges to settle the Korean conflict (at one point dramatically promising to "go to Korea" himself), Nixon effectively exploited the issue of domestic anticommunism. After

THE ELECTION OF 1952

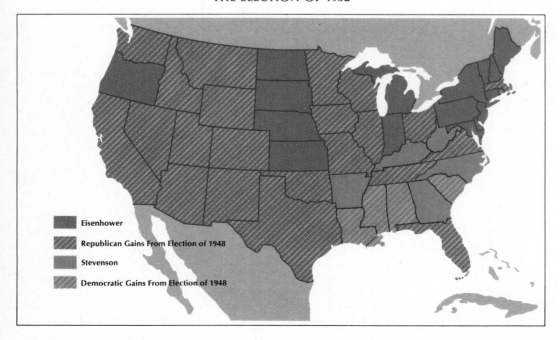

Eisenhower

Republican Gains From Election of 1948

Stevenson

Democratic Gains From Election of 1948

surviving early accusations of financial improprieties (which he effectively neutralized in a famous television speech), Nixon went on to launch harsh attacks on Democratic "cowardice," "appeasement," and "treason." He spoke derisively of "Adlai the appeaser" and ridiculed Secretary of State Dean Acheson for running a "cowardly college of communist containment." And he missed no opportunity to publicize Stevenson's early support for Alger Hiss as opposed to Nixon's role in exposing Hiss's misdeeds. Eisenhower and Nixon both made effective use of allegations of corruption in the Truman administration and pledged repeatedly to "clean up the mess in Washington."

The response at the polls was overwhelming. Eisenhower won both a popular and an electoral landslide: 55 percent of the popular vote to Stevenson's 44 percent, 442 electoral votes to Stevenson's 89. Republicans gained marginal control of both houses of Congress; but it was clear that their presidential candidate was far more popular than the party as a whole. Nevertheless, the election of 1952 ended twenty uninterrupted years of Democratic control of the federal government. And while it might not have seemed so at the time, it also helped signal the end of the turbulent postwar era and the beginning of a period marked by a search for cohesion and stability.

SUGGESTED READINGS

A good introduction to the vast literature on the Cold War is Walter LaFeber, *America, Russia, and the Cold War* (1967; rev. 1980), which carries the story to 1980. Wartime relations between the United States and the Soviet Union are analyzed in John L. Snell, *Illusion and Necessity* (1967); Gaddis Smith, *American Diplomacy During the Second World War* (1965); Herbert Feis, *Churchill, Roosevelt, and Stalin* (1957); and William McNeill, *America, Britain and Russia* (1953). On the wartime accords, see Diane Clemens, *Yalta* (1970); Herbert Feis, *Between War and Peace: The Potsdam Conference* (1960); Athan G. Theoharis, *The Yalta Myths* (1970); and W. L. Neumann, *After Victory* (1969). Broader studies of the origins of the Cold War include John L. Gaddis, *The United States and the Origins of the Cold War* (1972); George C. Herring, Jr., *Aid to Russia* (1973); Daniel Yergin, *Shattered Peace* (1977); Thomas Paterson, *Soviet-American Confrontation* (1974); Gregg Herken, *The Winning Weapon* (1980); and Martin Sherwin, *A World Destroyed* (1975).

The foreign policies of the Truman administration receive particular attention in Robert Donovan, *Conflict and Crisis* (1977); Lloyd Gardner, *Architects of Illusion* (1970); and Richard Freeland, *The Truman Doctrine and the Origins of McCarthyism* (1971). George F. Kennan, *American Diplomacy: 1900–1950* (1952) and *Memoirs, 1925–1950* (1967), are invaluable works by one of the architects of the containment doctrine; Dean Acheson's *Present at the Creation* (1970) is another useful memoir. Joyce Kolko and Gabriel Kolko, *The Limits of Power* (1970), is a highly critical study. Hadley Arkes, *Bureaucracy, the Marshall Plan and National Interest* (1973), examines the European recovery plan.

Akira Iriye, *The Cold War in Asia* (1974), is a valuable overview. John K. Fairbank, *The United States and China*, 3rd ed. (1971), and Edwin O. Reischauer, *The United States and Japan*, 3rd ed. (1965), are both standard works, with chapters on the postwar years. Michael Schaller, *The U.S. Crusade in China* (1979), and Kenneth F. Shewmaker, *Americans and the Chinese Communists* (1971), provide background to the events of 1949. Lisle Rose, *Roots of Tragedy* (1976), is an overview of American policy in Asia in the postwar years. Godfrey Hodgson, *America in Our Time* (1976), is a valuable survey of the development of Cold War ideology. Harry S Truman, *Memoirs*, 2 vols. (1955–1956), is an important document of the time. Ronald Radosh, *Prophets on the Right* (1975), explores some of the domestic pressures on foreign policy.

On the policies and problems of the Truman administration, see Alonzo Hamby, *Beyond the New Deal* (1973); Cabell Phillips, *The Truman Presidency* (1966); Robert Donovan, *Conflict and Crisis* (1977); Barton Bernstein (ed.), *Politics and Policies of the Truman Administration* (1970); and Bert Cochran, *Truman and the Crisis Presidency* (1973). Eric Goldman, *The Crucial Decade—And After* (1960), is a breezy account of the era. William Berman, *The Politics of Civil Rights in the Truman Administration* (1970), and Donald McCoy and Richard Ruetten, *Quest and Response* (1973), examine the record on race. R. Alton Lee, *Truman and Taft-Hartley* (1967), explores one of the president's most prominent disputes; and James T. Patterson, *Mr. Republican* (1972), a biography of Senator Robert Taft, examines the career of one of his leading conservative opponents. Maeva Marcus, *Truman and the Steel Seizure* (1977), is a study of one of the administration's flamboyant but unsuccessful attempts to quell instability. On the dramatic election of 1948, see Irwin Ross, *The Loneliest Campaign* (1968); Norman

Markowitz, *The Rise and Fall of the People's Century* (1973), a study of the campaign of Henry Wallace; and Allen Yarnell, *Democrats and Progressives* (1974).

For the Korean War, consult Joseph C. Goulden, *Korea: The Untold Story of the War* (1982); Allen Whiting, *China Crosses the Yalu* (1960); Robert Leckie, *Conflict* (1962); Bruce Cummings, *The Origins of the Korean War* (1980); John Spanier, *The Truman-MacArthur Controversy* (1959); Carl Berger, *The Korean Knot* (1957); and Glenn Paige, *The Korean Decision* (1968); Ronald Caridi, *The Korean War and American Politics* (1969), is an analysis of the domestic impact. A survey of the anticommunist frenzy of the era is David Caute, *The Great Fear* (1978). Edward Shils, *The Torment of Secrecy* (1956), is an attempt to explain the origins of anticommunist hysteria. On the Hiss case, see Allen Weinstein, *Perjury* (1978), which argues that Hiss was guilty. Robert and Michael Meeropol, the children of Julius and Ethel Rosenberg, argue the innocence of their parents in *We Are Your Sons* (1975). Richard Freeland, *The Truman Doctrine and the Origins of McCarthyism* (1971); Athan Theoharis, *Seeds of Repression* (1971); and Alan Harper, *The Politics of Loyalty* (1969), discuss the impact of Truman administration policies on the anticommunist frenzy. On McCarthy, see Richard Rovere, *Senator Joe McCarthy* (1959); Richard Fried, *Men Against McCarthy* (1976); Robert Griffith, *The Politics of Fear* (1970); Michael Rogin, *The Intellectuals and McCarthy* (1967); and Thomas C. Reeves, *The Life and Times of Joe McCarthy* (1982), the first major biography. Victor Navasky, *Naming Names* (1980), discusses the sensitive issue of informers during the Red Scare. Joseph Starobin, *American Communism in Crisis* (1972), discusses the plight of the embattled party.

The Affluent Society

29

Freeways
The rapid construction of interstate highways in the 1950s and 1960s changed the face of the American landscape. It also altered the fabric of American life, both by providing a stimulus to the booming economy and by encouraging the rapid exodus of middle-class families from city to suburb. The Los Angeles freeway system, pictured here, is perhaps the ultimate expression of the nation's fascination with and dependence on the automobile. (UPI)

In later decades, Americans tended to look back on the 1950s and early 1960s as something of a golden age: an era of boundless prosperity, of social stability, of national optimism and confidence. To some extent, that image was simply a result of the nostalgia with which most generations view earlier, apparently happier times. But to a remarkable degree, it was also the image that many Americans of the 1950s held of their own society. Seldom before had the United States experienced an era of such pride and self-satisfaction.

Two fundamental realities shaped the mood of the decade. There was, first, a booming national prosperity. And there was, second, the continuing struggle against communism, a struggle that created an undercurrent of anxiety but that also encouraged Americans to look even more approvingly at their own society. The combination produced what many observers at the time, and many historians later, described as a broad consensus—a wide agreement on the basic purposes and values of national life. Only in limited ways did American politics express real differences of opinion about the country's goals. A moderate, unadventurous Republican administration seemed to satisfy most Americans in both its foreign and its domestic policies.

But this apparent consensus often blinded Americans to the serious problems that continued to plague their society. Prosperity, real as it was, did not extend to everyone. More than 30 million Americans, according to some estimates, continued to live in poverty in the 1950s. And despite the smug belief in the essential virtuousness of American life, large minorities within the population—most prominently the 15 percent of the American people who were black—continued to suffer from a vicious system of social, political, and economic discrimination. Gunnar Myrdal, a Swedish sociologist well acquainted with life in the United States, wrote at the time: "American affluence is heavily mortgaged. America carries a tremendous burden of debt to its poor people." The efforts to pay that debt would ultimately help move the nation out of the complacency of the 1950s and into a far more turbulent era in the 1960s.

THE IMPACT OF PROSPERITY

Perhaps the most striking feature of American life in the 1950s and early 1960s, and one that virtually no observer could ignore, was prosperity—a booming, almost miraculous economic growth that made even the heady 1920s seem pale by comparison. It was, moreover, a prosperity far better balanced and far more widely distributed than that of thirty years earlier. It was not, however, as universal as Americans liked to believe.

Economic Growth

By 1949, despite the continuing problems of postwar reconversion, what some called the "miracle" of American economic expansion had begun. It would continue with only minor interruptions for almost twenty years. The gross national product, the most basic indicator of economic growth, alone provides ample evidence of the prosperity of the era. Between 1945 and 1960, the American GNP grew by 250 percent, from $200 billion to $500 billion. That growth appears even more remarkable in view of public expectations in 1945 that the GNP would soon decline, once the extraordinary demands of war production subsided. Unemployment, which during the Depression had averaged between 15 and 25 percent, remained throughout the 1950s and early 1960s at about 5 percent or lower. Inflation, in the meantime, hovered at about 3 percent a year or less.

There was no single cause. Government spending, which had ended the Depression in the 1940s, continued to stimulate growth. There was increasing public funding of schools, housing, veterans' benefits, welfare, and interstate highways (for which the government spent over $100 billion beginning in 1956)—all helping to sustain prosperity. Above all, there was military spending, which continued at almost wartime levels. The Korean War, in particular, helped to spark the economic boom. During the first half of the 1950s, when military spending was at its peak, the annual growth rate was 4.7 percent. For the second half of the decade, with the Korean War concluded and spending on armaments in decline, the rate of growth was only 2.25 percent.

Technological progress also contributed to the boom. Because of advances in production techniques and mechanical efficiency, worker productivity increased more than 35 percent in the first decade after the war, a rate far higher than that of any previous era. The development of electronic computers, which first became commercially available in the mid-1950s, helped improve the performance of many American corporations. And technological research and development itself became an important new sector of the economy, expanding the demand for scientists, engineers, and other highly trained experts.

The national birth rate reversed a long pattern of decline, sparking the so-called postwar baby boom, which peaked in 1957. The nation's population rose almost 20 percent in the decade, from 150 million in 1950 to 179 million in 1960. This growth mirrored a worldwide demographic explosion that would ultimately place great strains on the resources of the planet. In the United States of the 1950s, however, the baby boom meant increased consumer demand and expanding economic growth.

The rapid expansion of suburbs—whose population grew 47 percent in the 1950s, more than twice as fast as the population of the nation as a whole—helped stimulate growth in several important sectors of the economy. The automobile industry experienced the greatest boom in its history, as the number of privately owned cars more than doubled in a decade. The demand for new homes helped sustain a vigorous housing industry. The construction of roads, which was both a cause and a result of the growth of suburbs, stimulated the economy even further.

Economic Consolidation

The prosperity of the 1920s had been accompanied by a rapid increase in economic centralization and concentration. The prosperity of the 1950s brought with it a similar consolidation. There were more than 4,000 corporate mergers in the course of the 1950s; and more than ever, a few large corporations were controlling an enormous proportion of the nation's economic activity. This was particularly true in industries benefiting from government defense spending. As during World War II, the federal government tended to award military contracts to large corporations. In 1959, for example, half of all defense contracts went to only twenty firms. But the pattern repeated itself in almost all areas of the economy, as corporations moved from being single-industry firms to becoming diversified conglomerates. By the end of the decade, half of the net corporate income in the nation was going to only slightly more than 500 firms, or one-tenth of 1 percent of the total number of corporations.

Unlike the 1920s, this increase in corporate consolidation was accompanied by a rise in the power of labor organizations. Corporations enjoying such remarkable growth were reluctant to allow strikes to interfere with their operations; and since the most important unions were now so large and entrenched that they could not easily be suppressed or intimidated, business leaders made important concessions to them. As early as 1948, Walter Reuther, president of the United Automobile Workers, obtained from General Motors a contract that included a built-in "escalator clause"—an automatic cost-of-living increase pegged to the consumer price index. The provision set a crucial precedent—not only for the rest of the automobile industry but for the economy at large. In 1955, Reuther received a guarantee from Ford Motor Company of continuing wages to auto workers even during layoffs (although not the guaranteed annual wage he had demanded). A few months later, steelworkers in several corporations did receive guarantees of an annual salary. By the mid-1950s, factory wages in all industries had risen substantially, to a healthy average of $80 per week.

Not all laborers shared in such gains. The labor movement enjoyed great success in winning new benefits for workers already organized in strong unions. For the majority of laborers who were as yet unorganized, there were fewer advances. Total union membership remained relatively stable at about 16 million throughout the 1950s; and while this was in part a result of a shift in the work force from blue-collar to white-collar jobs, it was at least as much a result of new obstacles to organization. The Taft-Hartley Act and the state right-to-work laws that it spawned made it more difficult to create new unions that would be powerful enough to demand recognition from employers.

The economic successes of the entrenched unions in the 1950s helped pave the way for the reunification of the labor movement. In December 1955, the American Federation of Labor and the Congress of Industrial Organizations ended their twenty-year rivalry and merged to create a giant new federation, the AFL-CIO, under the leadership of George Meany. But the climate of the era produced other, less welcome changes in the nature of the labor movement. Some unions, no longer required to engage in the militant crusades against corporate resistance that had dominated the 1930s, were themselves becoming wealthy, powerful bureaucracies. Most continued to operate responsibly and effectively; but some of the most important unions began to face accusations of corruption and indifference.

The powerful Teamsters Union became in 1957 the focal point of a congressional investigation, which charged president David Beck with the misappropriation of over $320,000 in union funds. Beck ultimately stepped down from his office to be replaced by Jimmy Hoffa, who was widely believed to have close ties to underworld crime. Government investigators pursued Hoffa for nearly a decade before finally winning a conviction against him in 1967. After his release from prison in 1971 (on a pardon from President Richard Nixon), he attempted to regain his position in the union. But before he could succeed, he disappeared and was generally presumed to have been murdered. The United Mine Workers, the union that had spearheaded the industrial movement in the 1930s, similarly became tainted by suspicions of corruption and by violence. John L. Lewis's last years as head of the union were plagued with scandals and dissent within the organization. His successor, Tony Boyle, was ultimately convicted of complicity in the 1969 murder of Joseph Yablonski, the leader of a dissident faction within the union. Even more troubling, perhaps, was the growing belief among many union members that the leaders of these and other labor organizations had lost touch with the rank and file. They often appeared to have grown more involved with the internal bureaucratic and political struggles of the union organization itself than with the welfare of the members.

Economic Dislocations

Americans in the 1950s liked to believe that their growing prosperity was reaching virtually every area of the society. It was not. Important groups continued to struggle on the fringes of the economic boom, unable to share in the abundance. Between 1948 and 1956, while national income increased 50 percent, farm prices dropped 33 percent, a victim of enormous surpluses in basic staples. In 1948, farmers had received 8.9 percent of the national income; in 1956, they received only 4.1 percent. In part, this decline reflected the steadily shrinking farm population; in 1956 alone, one out of every eleven rural residents moved into or was absorbed by a city. But it also reflected the deteriorating economic condition of those farmers who remained. They experienced not only a decline in their own income but a steady increase in the prices they paid for consumer goods.

Farmers, at least, were able to attract some public attention to their plight. Other, poorer groups languished in virtual obscurity. As middle-class Americans left the cities for the suburbs, it became easy to ignore the existence of severe poverty in the heart of the major industrial metropolises. Black ghettoes were expanding rapidly in the 1950s, as black farmers joined the general exodus from country to city and as the black population in general expanded rapidly. Continuing racial discrimination helped doom these communities to unmitigated, ever increasing, poverty. In New York City and elsewhere, growing Puerto Rican and other Hispanic communities were earning less than what the government considered the minimum necessary for "adequate" living. Urban ghettoes were becoming so isolated from the eco-nomic mainstream that their residents were finding it almost impossible to obtain employment. Thus some "inner cities" were turning into virtual prisons for poor people, who had neither the resources to move to areas where jobs were more plentiful nor the political power to force development of their own communities. A similar predicament faced residents of several particularly destitute rural regions—most notably the Appalachian areas of the Southern and border states, which were experiencing an almost total economic collapse. Lacking adequate schools, health care, and services, the residents of Appalachia, like the residents of the urban ghettoes, were almost entirely shut off from the mainstream of American economic life. Not until the 1960s, when such exposés as Michael Harrington's *The Other America* (1962) began drawing attention to the continuing existence of poverty in the nation, did the middle class begin to recognize the seriousness of the problem.

The Honeymooners
One of the most popular television comedies of the 1950s—*The Honeymooners*, starring Jackie Gleason and Art Carney—was also one of the least typical. Its working-class characters (a bus driver, a sewer worker, and their wives) contrasted sharply with the suburban, middle-class families of most television series. (UPI)

The Consumer Culture

The process of cultural consolidation, like
the process of economic consolidation, gathered momentum in the 1950s. Middle-class
Americans, at least, found themselves living
in a society growing more alike from one region and one community to the next.

At the center of middle-class culture was
a rampant, at times almost obsessive, consumerism. It was a result of many things: the
spread of affluence, the increasing variety
and availability of products, and the adeptness of advertisers in creating a demand for
those products. It was also a result of the
growth of consumer credit, which increased
by 800 percent between 1945 and 1957. Easily available credit cards, revolving charge
accounts, and easy-payment plans made immediate gratification of consumer yearnings
not only desirable but possible. Affluent
Americans in the 1950s and 1960s showed renewed interest in such longtime consumer
crazes as the automobile, and Detroit responded to the boom with ever-flashier styl-
ing and accessories. Consumers also responded eagerly to the development of such
new products as dishwashers, garbage dis-
posals, televisions, and "hi-fis" and stereos.

Suburbs, similarly, helped create an
American life style that differed little from
one region to another. Since suburban housing developments were usually new and constructed all at once, they tended to be far
more similar to one another than older
neighborhoods, which had grown up more
slowly. The general (and deliberate) isolation
of suburbs from congested urban areas made
regional variations even fewer. And within
the suburbs themselves, homes were often
almost indistinguishable from one another.
Among the popular symbols of American
society in the 1950s were the Levittowns—
huge, mass-produced suburban towns,
created by developer Arthur Levitt, where
street after street was lined with identical
single-family houses. Builders across the
country followed Levitt's lead and adopted
standardized building methods. Separated
from urban institutions and surrounded by
uniformity, residents of suburbia developed
an increasingly homogenized life style. And
because there was so little that was distinctive about most suburban communities, there
was also little to discourage families from
moving elsewhere as economic opportunities
appeared. The conformity of suburban life
was accompanied, therefore, by an increasing
rootlessness among members of the middle
class, who often developed no permanent ties
to any one region but identified instead with
the larger, national culture.

The Media

The postwar era witnessed as well the birth
of the most important agent of cultural ho-
mogenization of all: television. Television did
not even exist as a commercial medium until
after World War II. In 1946, there had been
only 17,000 sets in the entire country. By
1953, two-thirds of all American homes had
televisions. By 1957, there were 40 million
television sets in use—almost as many sets as
there were families. More people had television sets, according to one report, than had
refrigerators.

The impact of television on American life
was rapid, pervasive, and profound. Television news had by the end of the 1950s replaced newspapers, magazines, and radios as
the nation's most important vehicle of information. A small group of anchormen, producers, and reporters, almost all based on the
East Coast, exercised substantial control over
how the vast majority of Americans viewed
public events. Television advertising exposed
the entire nation to new fashions and products. Television entertainment programming,
almost all of it controlled by three national
networks, created a common image of
American life—an image that was predominantly white, middle-class, and suburban.
Even those unable to share in the affluence of
the era could, through television, acquire a
vivid picture of how the rest of their society
lived.

The Allure of Science

In 1961, *Time* magazine chose as its "man of
the year" not a specific person but the

"American Scientist." It was an indication of the widespread fascination with which Americans in the age of atomic weapons viewed science and technology. Major medical advances—for example, Jonas Salk's discovery of a vaccine to prevent polio—seemed to confirm the important role that scientific research would play in promoting progress. So did such technological innovations as the jet airplane, the computer, synthetics, and new types of commercially prepared foods. Nothing, however, better illustrated the nation's veneration of scientific expertise than the popular enthusiasm for the American space program.

Reaching the Moon

Edwin "Buzz" Aldrin stands on the lunar surface in July 1969, as he and *Apollo XI* commander Neil Armstrong become the first men ever to set foot on the moon. Reflected in Aldrin's visor are Armstrong, who is taking the photograph, and the lunar module *Eagle*, in which the astronauts landed and in which they would later rejoin the mother ship, *Columbia*, for the return to earth. Although the moon landing created wide excitement, it represented in fact the tail end of America's fascination with the space program. It was in the late 1950s and early 1960s that the romance of space had captured the nation's imagination most completely—in part because in those years Americans had viewed themselves as engaged in an important contest with the Soviet Union in the "space race." Moon landings after 1969 attracted a decreasing level of public interest; and by the late 1970s, the space program was in rapid decline. Enthusiasm seemed to revive early in 1981 with the successful flight of the first reusable "space shuttle," but NASA remained plagued by limited funding. (NASA)

The program began, in large part, because of the Cold War. When the Soviet Union announced in 1957 that it had launched a satellite—*Sputnik*—into outer space, the United States reacted with shock and alarm. Strenuous efforts began to improve scientific education in the schools, to develop more research laboratories, and, above all, to speed the development of America's own exploration of outer space. The centerpiece of that exploration was the manned space program, established in 1958 with the selection of the first American space pilots. In the years that followed, these seven "astronauts" became the nation's most widely revered heroes. The entire country watched on May 5, 1961, as Alan Shepard became the first American launched into space (several months after a Soviet "cosmonaut," Yuri Gagarin, had made a similar flight). John Glenn, who on February 2, 1962, became the first American to orbit the globe (again, only after Gagarin had already done so), was soon an even more celebrated national idol. Yet Americans marveling at space exploration were reacting less to the individual men involved than to the enormous scientific effort that lay behind their exploits.

Ultimately, the nation would tire of the space program, which never managed to convince the public that it offered any practical benefits. But interest remained high as late as the summer of 1969, when Neil Armstrong and Edwin Aldrin became the first men to walk on the surface of the moon. Not long after that, the enthusiasm began to subside, and the government began to cut the funding for future missions. The broader faith in science and technology, however, proved more enduring.

Organized Society and Its Detractors

Even more than in the 1920s, Americans in the 1950s and 1960s were aware of the importance of organizations and bureaucracies in their lives. White-collar workers, who in the 1950s came to outnumber blue-collar laborers for the first time, found employment predominantly in corporate settings with rigid hierarchical structures. Industrial workers confronted ponderous bureaucracies in their own unions. Consumers discovered the frustrations of bureaucracy in dealing with the large, national companies from whom they bought goods and services. It was becoming clear to all Americans that the key to a successful future lay in acquiring the specialized training and skills necessary for work in large organizations, where every worker performed a particular, well-defined function.

As in earlier eras, Americans reacted to these developments with ambivalence, often hostility. The debilitating impact of bureaucratic life on the individual was slowly becoming one of the central themes of popular and scholarly analyses of national life. William H. Whyte, Jr., produced one of the most widely discussed books of the decade: *The Organization Man* (1956), which attempted to describe the special mentality of the worker in a large, bureaucratic setting. Self-reliance, Whyte claimed, was losing place to the ability to "get along" and "work as a team" as the most valuable trait in modern character. Sociologist David Riesman made similar observations in *The Lonely Crowd* (1950), in which he argued that the traditional "inner-directed" man, who judged himself on the basis of his own values and the esteem of his family, was giving way to a new "other-directed" man, more concerned with winning the approval of the larger organization or community. Even those who lived and worked outside bureaucratic settings, some critics argued, were subjected to the homogenizing pressures of a "mass culture," dominated by television and designed to appeal to the "lowest common denominator."

The most decisive critics of the culture of the affluent society were a number of young poets and writers generally known as the "beats" (or, by derisive critics, as "beatniks"). To them, the conventional society of the American middle class was an object of contempt, a world to be avoided and despised. They wrote harsh critiques of the sterility and conformity of American life, the meaningless of American politics, and the banality of popular culture. Allen Ginsberg, one of the most celebrated of the beats, attracted wide acclaim with his dark, bitter poem *Howl* (1955), decrying the "Robot apartments! invincible suburbs! skeleton treasuries! blind capitals! demonic industries!" of modern life. Jack Kerouac, a talented novelist whose severe alcoholism and early death sharply limited his creative output, nevertheless produced what may have been the leading document of the Beat Generation: *On the Road* (1957), an account of a cross-country automobile trip that depicted the rootless, iconoclastic life style of Kerouac and his friends.

Other, gentler writers also used their work to express misgivings about the enormity and impersonality of modern society. Saul Bellow produced a series of novels—*The Adventures of Augie March* (1953), *Seize the Day* (1956), *Herzog* (1964), and others—that chronicled the difficulties of modern, urban Jews in finding fulfillment in the dehumanizing environment in which they were forced to live. J. D. Salinger, one of the most popular writers of the era, wrote in *The Catcher in the Rye* (1951), of the crushing impact of modern life on vulnerable, sensitive individuals. The novel described the dilemma of prep-school student Holden Caulfield, unable to find any area of society—school, family, friends, city—in which he could feel secure or committed. Salinger's series of short stories and novelettes about the Glass family likewise described the assaults of contemporary society on people of intelligence and sensitivity. In the 1950s and early 1960s, such warnings remained relatively muted, as in the writings of Bellow and Salinger, or had only a limited impact on the culture at large, as with the work of Ginsberg and Kerouac. By the late 1960s, however, these concerns were becoming crucial to the creation of a widespread and influential "counterculture."

The New Economics

Among the many phenomena that made the "age of affluence" an extraordinary period in American life was the confident, exhilarating, at times even arrogant tone of the nation's political climate. Americans continued to differ sharply on any number of political issues; but most did so within a framework of agreement about the essential righteousness of American values and about the strength and stability of the American political and economic system.

Basic to this sense of national confidence was the exciting (and to some surprising) discovery of the power of the American economic system. During the Depression, some had questioned the viability of capitalism. In the 1950s, such doubts all but disappeared. Two features in particular made the postwar economy a source of national pride and confidence.

First was the belief that Keynesian economics made it possible for government to regulate and stabilize the economy without intruding directly into the private sector. The British economist John Maynard Keynes had argued as early as the 1920s that by varying the flow of government spending and managing the supply of currency, the state could stimulate the economy to cure recession and dampen growth to prevent inflation. The experience of the last years of the Depression and the first years of the war had seemed to confirm this argument. And by the mid-1950s, Keynesian theory was rapidly becoming a fundamental article of faith—not only among professional economists but among much of the public at large. The most popular economics textbook of the 1950s and 1960s, Paul Samuelson's *Economics*, imbued generations of college students with Keynesian dogma. Armed with these fiscal and monetary tools, economists now believed, it was possible for the government to maintain a permanent prosperity. The dispiriting boom-and-bust cycle that many had long believed to be a permanent feature of industrial capitalism could now be banished forever. Never again would it be necessary for the nation to experience another Depression.

If any doubters remained, they found ample evidence to dispel their misgivings during the brief recessions the economy experienced during the era. When the economy slackened in late 1953, Secretary of the Treasury George M. Humphrey and the Federal Reserve Board worked to ease credit and make money more readily available. The economy quickly recovered, helping to confirm the value of Keynesian tactics. A far more serious recession began late in 1957 and continued for more than a year. This time, the Eisenhower administration ignored the Keynesians and adopted such deflationary tactics as cutting the budget. The slow, halting nature of the recovery, in contrast with the rapid revival in 1954, seemed further to support the Keynesian philosophy. The new economics finally won full acceptance in 1963, when John Kennedy proposed a tax cut to stimulate economic growth. Although it took Kennedy's death and the political skills of Lyndon Johnson finally to win passage of the measure in 1964, the result was all that the Keynesians had predicted: an increase in private demand, which stimulated economic growth and reduced unemployment.

In addition to the belief in the possibility of permanent economic stability was the equally exhilarating belief in permanent economic growth. As the economy continued to expand far beyond what any observer had predicted was possible only a few years before, more and more Americans assumed that such growth was now without bounds—that there were few effective limits on the abundance available to the nation. This was not only a comforting thought in itself; it also provided a new outlook on social and economic problems. In the 1930s, many Americans had argued that the elimination of poverty and injustice would require a redistribution of wealth—a limitation on the fortunes of the rich and a distribution of this wealth to the poor. By the mid-1950s, reformers concerned about economic depriva-

tion were arguing that the solution lay in increased production. The affluent would not have to sacrifice in order to eliminate poverty. The nation would simply have to produce more abundance, thus raising the quality of life of even the poorest citizens to a level of comfort and decency.

EISENHOWER AND THE "MIDDLE OF THE ROAD"

It was appropriate, perhaps, that Dwight D. Eisenhower, a man who had risen to prominence as a great military leader, should preside over an era in which the American people were preoccupied with international tensions. And it was fitting, too, that this essentially conservative man, who enjoyed the company of wealthy businessmen, should serve as president in a period when Americans wanted nothing so much as a lasting stabilization of their newly prosperous economy. It should not have been surprising, therefore, that Eisenhower, the least experienced politician to serve in the White House in the twentieth century, was nevertheless the most politically successful president of the postwar era. At home, he pursued essentially moderate policies, avoiding most new initiatives but accepting the work of earlier reformers. Abroad, he continued and even intensified American commitments to oppose communism but brought to some of those commitments a measure of restraint that his successors could not always match.

A Business Government

The first Republican administration in twenty years staffed itself with men drawn from the same quarter as those who had staffed Republican administrations in the 1920s: the business community. To his cabinet the president appointed a leading corporation lawyer (Secretary of State John Foster Dulles), the president of General Motors (Defense Secretary Charles E. Wilson), the head of a major financial firm (Treasury Secretary George Humphrey), a New England manufacturer, two automobile distributors, a

farm marketing executive, and other wealthy corporate figures. Only Secretary of Labor Martin P. Durkin, president of the plumbers' union, stood apart. "Eight millionaires and a plumber," the New Republic caustically remarked. Within eight months, Durkin resigned, to be replaced by yet another businessman. Members of the new administration were not apologetic about their backgrounds. Charles Wilson assured senators considering his confirmation that he foresaw no conflict of interest because he was certain that "what was good for our country was good for General Motors, and vice versa."

The inclination of the Eisenhower government to limit federal activities and encourage private enterprise received clear illustration in its policies toward government power development. The president, who referred to the Tennessee Valley Authority in 1953 as an example of "creeping socialism" and once talked wistfully of selling "the whole thing," supported the private rather than public development of natural resources. Throughout his administration, he opposed federal public-works projects in favor of private ventures.

Eisenhower moved in other areas as well to limit government involvement in the economy. To the chagrin of farmers, he lowered federal support for farm prices. He also removed the last limited wage and price controls maintained by the Truman administration. He opposed the creation of new social service programs such as national health insurance (although he did support a bill to underwrite private insurance programs, a bill that never passed). He strove constantly to reduce federal expenditures (even during the recession of 1958) and balance the budget.

He ended 1960, his last full year in office, with a $1 billion surplus.

The Survival of Social Welfare

Eisenhower's philosophy of "dynamic conservatism," as he termed it, may not have been hospitable to new social programs. But it did permit the survival, and even on occasion the expansion, of some existing ones. The president resisted pressure from the right wing of his party to dismantle those welfare policies of the New Deal that had survived the conservative assaults of the war years and after. During his term, a Republican Congress agreed to extend the Social Security System to an additional 10 million new people and unemployment compensation to an additional 4 million people. The minimum hourly wage increased from 75 cents to $1. And the administration did support one positive new government program of great importance: interstate highway construction. The Federal Highway Act of 1956 authorized $25 billion for a ten-year building effort; the cost would ultimately expand far beyond that figure.

That Eisenhower did not launch a stronger assault on existing social programs and that he actually supported some liberal reforms was partly a result of political realities. During his first two years in office, although Congress was nominally under Republican control, a coalition of Democrats and liberal Republicans limited the freedom of conservatives to act. And from 1954 to the end of Eisenhower's years in office (indeed until 1980), both houses of Congress remained securely in Democratic hands.

Not even Eisenhower's personal popularity was sufficient to bring his party back to power in Congress. In 1956, Eisenhower ran for a second term, even though he had suffered a serious heart attack the previous year. With Adlai Stevenson opposing him once again, he won by another, even greater landslide, receiving nearly 57 percent of the popular vote and 442 electoral votes to Stevenson's 89. Still, Democrats retained control of both houses of Congress. And in 1958, they increased that control by substantial margins.

The nation had endorsed Eisenhower's inclination to moderate the reforming zeal of earlier years, to "hold the line." They were not, however, ready to accept the belief of others in his party that the nation should adopt an even more militantly conservative policy.

The Decline of McCarthyism

The Eisenhower administration did little in its first years in office to discourage the anticommunist furor that had gripped the nation. Indeed, it helped to sustain it. The president actually intensified the already much-abused hunt for subversives in the government, which Truman had begun several years earlier. More than 2,220 federal employees resigned or were dismissed as a result of security investigations. Among them were most of the leading Asian experts in the State Department, who were harried from office because they had shown inadequate enthusiasm for the now exiled regime of Chiang Kai-shek. Their absence was later to prove costly, as the government expanded its commitments in Asia without sufficient knowledge of the political realities within the region.

Among the most celebrated episodes of the first year of the new administration was the case of J. Robert Oppenheimer, director of the Manhattan Project during the war and one of the nation's most distinguished and admired physicists. Although Oppenheimer was now out of government service, he continued as a consultant to the Atomic Energy Commission. But he had angered some officials by his public opposition to development of the new, more powerful, hydrogen bomb. In 1953, the FBI distributed a dossier within the administration detailing Oppenheimer's prewar association with various left-wing groups. And the president responded by ordering a "blank wall" to be placed between Oppenheimer and government secrets. A federal investigation, requested by Oppenheimer himself and conducted in an inflamed and confused atmosphere, confirmed the decision to deny him a security clearance. The episode deeply embittered much of the scientific community and caused a major public outcry.

The Army-McCarthy Hearings
During the 1954 televised hearings on alleged Communist influence in the army, Senator Joseph McCarthy of Wisconsin uses a map to show the supposed distribution of Communists throughout the country, while the chief counsel for the army, Joseph Welch, remains conspicuously unimpressed. (UPI)

The strong opposition to the persecution of Oppenheimer was one indication that the anticommunist hysteria of the early 1950s was beginning to abate. A more important signal of the change was the political demise of Senator Joseph McCarthy. McCarthy continued during the first year of the Eisenhower administration to operate with almost total impunity. The president, who privately loathed him, nevertheless refused to speak out in public. "I will not get into the gutter with that guy," he reportedly explained. But McCarthy finally overreached himself in January 1954 when he began launching oblique attacks against the president and a direct assault on Secretary of the Army Robert Stevens and the armed services in general. In the face of these outrageous charges, Congress decided it had no choice but to stage a series of special meetings, the Army–McCarthy hearings as they became known. They were among the first such hearings to be nationally televised, and the result was devastating to McCarthy. Day after day, the public watched McCarthy in action—bullying witnesses, hurling groundless (and often cruel) accusations, evading issues, and offering churlish objections at every point. He began to appear less a hero than a villain, and ultimately less that than a mere buffoon. In December 1954, the Senate voted 67 to 22 to condemn him for "conduct unbecoming a senator." And three years later, with little public support left, he died—a victim of complications arising from serious alcoholism.

The Supreme Court, in the meantime, was also beginning to restrict the official harassment of suspected "subversives." Many people had expected the Court to become more conservative once the new president began to appoint new members. In fact, quite the opposite occurred. In 1953, Eisenhower nominated the former Republican governor of California, Earl Warren, to be the new chief justice. And to the surprise of many, including Eisenhower, Warren became the moving force behind the most strenuous judicial effort to protect and expand civil liberties in the nation's history. In 1957, the Warren Court limited the FBI's latitude in using secret evidence against an opponent. More important, that same year it struck down the Smith Act, ruling that urging the overthrow of the government was not a crime unless it involved the direct incitement of illegal actions. The following year, the Court forbade the State Department to deny passports to members of the Communist party.

THE RISE OF THE CIVIL-RIGHTS MOVEMENT

The Eisenhower years may have represented a national mood of cautious moderation in many areas. On one issue, however, they were a time in which a major social revolution finally commenced. After decades of skirmishes, there began in the 1950s an open battle against racial segregation and discrimination, a battle that would prove to be one of the longest and most difficult of the century.

The *Brown* Decision

In 1954, years of patient legal efforts by the NAACP and other black reformers finally bore fruit when, on May 17, the Supreme Court announced its decision in the case of *Brown* v. *Board of Education of Topeka*. In considering the legal segregation of a Kansas public school system, the Court finally rejected the doctrine of the 1896 *Plessy* v. *Ferguson* decision, which had established that communities could provide blacks with separate facilities as long as the facilities were equal to those of whites. Explaining the unanimous opinion of his colleagues, Chief Justice Warren declared: "We conclude that in the field of public education the doctrine of 'separate but equal' has no place. Separate educational

Brown et al. v. Board of Education of Topeka et al. [1954]

In approaching this problem, we cannot turn the clock back to 1868 when the [Fourteenth] Amendment was adopted, or even to 1896 when *Plessy* v. *Ferguson* was written. We must consider public education in the light of its full development and its present place in American life throughout the Nation. Only in this way can it be determined if segregation in public schools deprives these plaintiffs of the equal protection of the laws.

Today, education is perhaps the most important function of state and local governments. Compulsory school attendance laws and the great expenditures for education both demonstrate our recognition of the importance of education to our democratic society. It is required in the performance of our most basic public responsibilities, even service in the armed forces. It is the very foundation of good citizenship. Today it is a principal instru-

ment in awakening the child to cultural values, in preparing him for later professional training, and in helping him to adjust normally to his environment. In these days it is doubtful that any child may reasonably be expected to succeed in life if he is denied the opportunity of an education. Such an opportunity where the state has undertaken to provide it, is a right which must be made available to all on equal terms.

We come then to the question presented: Does segregation of children in public schools solely on the basis of race, even though the physical facilities and other "tangible" factors may be equal, deprive the children of the minority group of equal educational opportunities? We believe that it does.—*Excerpt of opinion of the Supreme Court delivered by Chief Justice Earl Warren.*

facilities are inherently unequal." Communities must work to desegregate their schools, the Court ordered, "with all deliberate speed."

It was not to be so easy. In some communities, compliance came relatively quickly and relatively painlessly, as in Washington, D.C. Far more often, however, strong local resistance produced long delays. Some school districts attempted to circumvent the ruling with purely token efforts to integrate. Others simply ignored the ruling altogether. By the fall of 1957, only 684 of 3,000 affected school districts in the South had even begun to desegregate their schools. In those that had complied, white resistance often produced angry mob actions and other violence. An increasing number of white parents simply withdrew their children from the public schools and enrolled them in all-white "segregation academies," many of them poorly staffed and equipped. The *Brown* decision, far from ending segregation, launched a prolonged battle between federal authority and state and local governments. In the years to come, federal courts would have to play an ever-increasing role in public education to ensure compliance with the desegregation rulings. And the executive branch, whose responsibility it was to enforce the decisions of the courts, found itself frequently pitted against local authorities attempting to defy the law.

The first of such confrontations occurred in September 1957 in Little Rock, Arkansas. The courts had ordered the desegregation of that city's Central High School. Governor Orval Faubus, a rabid and ambitious segregationist, ordered the National Guard to intervene to stop it. Faubus finally called off the Guard in response to the orders of a federal judge; but an angry mob quickly took its place in blocking integration of the school. Faced with this open defiance of federal authority (and with real danger to the safety of the black students involved), Eisenhower finally responded by sending federal troops to Little Rock to restore order and ensure that the court orders would be obeyed. Central High School admitted its first black students; but controversy continued to plague the Little Rock school system for several years.

The Expanding Movement

The legal assault on school segregation was only one part of the war against racial discrimination in the 1950s. The *Brown* decision seemed also to spark a growing number of popular challenges to segregation by blacks in one community after another. The first and most celebrated occurred in Montgom-

State of South Carolina, Resolution on Desegregation [1956]

For almost sixty years, beginning in 1896, an unbroken line of decisions of the [Supreme] Court interpreted the Fourteenth Amendment as recognizing the right of the States to maintain racially separate public facilities for their people. If the Court in the interpretation of the Constitution is to depart from the sanctity of past decisions and to rely on the current political and social philosophy of its members to unsettle the great constitutional principles so clearly established, the rights of individuals are not secure and government under a written Constitution has no stability. . . .

The educational opportunities of white and colored children in the public schools of South Carolina have been substantially improved during recent years and highly satisfactory results are being obtained in our segregated schools. If enforced, the decision of the Court will seriously impair and retard the education of the children of both races, will nullify these recent advances and will cause untold friction between the races.—*Excerpt from Joint Resolution, February 14, 1956.*

ery, Alabama. There, in December 1955, a black woman, Rosa Parks, was arrested when she refused to give up her seat on a city bus to a white passenger. The incident produced outrage in the city's black community, which organized a successful black boycott of the bus system to demand an end to segregated seating. One year later, the Supreme Court ordered the bus company to change its policy, and the boycott ended.

The real accomplishment of the Montgomery boycott, however, was less in changing the seating policies of the bus system than in establishing a new form of racial protest and in elevating to prominence a new figure in the movement for civil rights. The leader of the boycott was a local Baptist pastor, Martin Luther King, Jr., son of a prominent Atlanta minister and the possessor of a charismatic leadership ability that even he had not suspected. King won national attention with his doctrine of "nonviolence"—that is, of passive resistance even in the face of direct assaults by white segregationists. King drew from the teachings of Mahatma Gandhi, the legendary Indian nationalist leader, whose life he had studied while a student in Boston. He urged blacks to engage in peaceful demonstrations; to allow themselves to be arrested, even beaten, if necessary; and to respond to hate with love. King's unparalleled oratorical talents ensured that his message would be widely heard. And for the next thirteen years, he would serve as the most influential and widely admired black leader of the century.

Pressure from the courts, from Northern liberals, and from blacks themselves also speeded the pace of racial change in other areas. As early as 1947, one important color line had been breached when the Brooklyn Dodgers signed Jackie Robinson as the first black to play major league baseball. By the mid-1950s, blacks had established themselves as a major force in almost all professional sports. Within the government, President Eisenhower completed the integration of the armed forces, attempted to desegregate the federal work force, and in 1957 signed a civil-rights act providing federal protection for blacks who wished to register to vote. It was a weak bill, with few mechanisms for enforcement; but it was a signal that the executive and legislative branches were beginning to join the judiciary in the federal commitment to the "Second Reconstruction."

A BALANCE OF TERROR

An undercurrent of anxiety tinged the domestic events of the Eisenhower years, for Americans were well aware throughout the affluent 1950s how dangerous was the world in which they lived. Above all, they were aware of the horrors of a possible nuclear war, as both the United States and the Soviet Union began to make atomic weapons more and more central to their foreign policies. Yet the nuclear threat had another effect as well. With the costs of war now so enormous, both of the superpowers began to edge away from direct confrontations. And increasingly, the attention of the United States began to turn to the rapidly escalating change and instability in the nations of the Third World.

Dulles and Massive Retaliation

Eisenhower's secretary of state, and indisputably the dominant figure in the nation's foreign policy in the 1950s, was John Foster Dulles, an aristocratic corporate lawyer with a stern moral revulsion toward communism. As a deeply religious man, Dulles detested the atheistic dogmas of Marxism. As a man closely tied to the nation's financial establishment, he feared the communist challenge to world free enterprise. He entered office denouncing the containment policies of the Truman years as excessively passive, arguing that the United States should pursue instead an active program of "liberation," which would lead to a "rollback" of communist expansion. Once in power, however, he had to defer to the far more moderate views of the president himself. And Dulles began, instead, to develop a new set of doctrines that reflected the impact of nuclear weapons on the world.

The most prominent of those doctrines was the policy of "massive retaliation,"

Secretary of State John Foster Dulles Reporting to President Eisenhower, May 17, 1955
The Eisenhower administration made extensive use of television to dramatize its actions to
the American people. For the first time, the president's press conferences were televised,
and on several occasions such as this, Secretary Dulles reported to the president in front of
the television cameras. He had just returned from Europe, where he had signed the treaty
restoring sovereignty to Austria. (U.S. Department of State)

which Dulles announced early in 1954. The
United States would, he explained, respond
to communist threats to its allies not by using
conventional forces in local conflicts (a policy
that had led to such frustration in Korea) but
by relying on "the deterrent of massive retaliatory power . . . a great capacity to retaliate
instantly, by means and at times of our own
choosing." He left no doubt that the retaliation he was envisioning was a nuclear one.
The new doctrine reflected in part Dulles's
inclination for tense confrontations, an approach he once defined as "brinksman-
ship"—pushing the Soviet Union to the
brink of war in order to exact concessions.
But the real force behind the massive retaliation policy was an economic one. With
pressure growing both in and out of government for a reduction in American military
expenditures, an increasing reliance on

atomic weapons seemed to promise, as some
advocates put it, "more bang for a buck."
Many argued further that smaller, so-called
tactical nuclear weapons could replace conventional forces even in limited wars.

The "new look" in American defense
policy seemed at first to please almost everyone. It maintained the national commitment (and, its advocates argued, the national
ability) to counter communist expansion
throughout the world. Yet it did so at greatly
reduced cost, satisfying those who were demanding new efforts to balance the budget.

At the same time, Dulles intensified the
efforts of Truman and Acheson to "integrate" the entire noncommunist world into a
system of mutual defense pacts. During his
years in office, he logged almost 500,000
miles in foreign travels to cement new alliances that were modeled on NATO but were,

without exception, far weaker than the European pact. By the end of the decade, the United States had become a party to almost a dozen such treaties in all areas of the world. In Southeast Asia, there was the SEATO alliance, which included Thailand and the Philippines but few other Asian nations. In the Middle East, there was the Baghdad Pact, soon renamed the CENTO alliance, which tied the United States to Turkey, Pakistan, Iraq, and Iran. Other, smaller agreements pledged American aid to additional areas.

Dilemmas in Asia

What had been the most troubling foreign policy concern of the Truman years—the war in Korea—plagued the Eisenhower administration only briefly. The new president did indeed "go to Korea" as he had promised in his campaign—visiting briefly in the months between the election and his inauguration. But peace came as a result of other things, primarily a softening of both the American and communist positions. On July 27, 1953, negotiators at Panmunjom finally signed an agreement ending the hostilities. Each antagonist was to withdraw its troops a mile and a half from the existing battle line, which ran roughly along the thirty-eighth parallel, the prewar border between North and South Korea. A conference in Geneva was to consider means by which to reunite the nation peacefully, although in fact the 1954 meeting produced no agreement and left the cease-fire line as the permanent border between the two countries.

In the meantime, however, American attention was being drawn to problems in other parts of Asia. There was, first, the continuing pressure on the administration from the so-called China lobby, or "Asia-firsters," who insisted on active American efforts to restore Chiang Kai-shek to the Chinese mainland. Such demands were wholly unrealistic. Chiang had nothing approaching sufficient military strength to launch an effective invasion. Even had he been able to muster the forces, he would have found virtually no popular following within China itself. Nevertheless, the administration continued to supply him with weapons and other assistance.

Almost simultaneously, the United States was becoming drawn into a long, bitter struggle in Southeast Asia. Ever since the end of World War II, France had been attempting to restore its authority over its one-time colony, Vietnam, which it had had to abandon to the Japanese during World War II. Opposing the French, however, were the powerful nationalist forces of Ho Chi Minh, which were determined to win independence for their nation. Ho had appealed on several occasions to the United States for support in the first years after the war but had received no reply. By 1954, he was accepting substantial aid from communist China and the Soviet Union. America, in the meantime, had been paying more than 70 percent of French war costs since 1950. A crisis emerged in early 1954 when 12,000 French troops became surrounded in a disastrous siege at the city of Dienbienphu, which they were incapable of defending. Only American intervention, it was clear, could prevent the total collapse of the French military effort.

Eisenhower spoke out strongly about the importance of preserving a "free" Vietnam, using the analogy once employed by Acheson of a row of dominoes. If Vietnam fell, he implied, the rest of Asia would soon follow. Yet despite the urgings of Secretary of State Dulles, Vice President Nixon, and others, Eisenhower refused to permit direct American military intervention in Vietnam, claiming that neither the Congress nor America's other allies would support such action. In fact, Eisenhower seemed to sense how difficult and costly such intervention would be.

Without American aid, the French defense of Dienbienphu finally collapsed on May 7, 1954; and France quickly agreed to a settlement of the conflict at a conference in Geneva that summer. The Geneva Accords of July 1954, to which the United States was not a party, established a temporary division of Vietnam along the seventeenth parallel. The north would be governed by Ho Chi Minh, the south by a pro-Western regime. Democratic elections would serve as the basis for uniting the nation in 1956. The agreement marked the effective end of the French commitment to Vietnam, but it became the basis for an expanded American presence. Realizing that Ho Chi Minh would win any election in Vietnam, Eisenhower and Dulles decided almost immediately that they could not accept the agreement. Instead, they helped establish a pro-American government in the south, headed by Ngo Dinh Diem, a wealthy, corrupt member of his country's Roman Catholic minority. Diem, it was clear from the start, would not permit elections. He felt secure in his refusal because the United States had promised to provide him with ample military assistance against any attack from the north.

Crises in the Middle East

However effective nuclear weapons may have been as a deterrent against direct Soviet aggression, they were—as the events in Asia suggested—less useful in enabling the United States to control local uprisings in the Third World. Yet it was just such uprisings, American policymakers were coming to believe, that now constituted the greatest danger of communist expansion. The dilemma of the 1950s, therefore, became how best to respond to insurgency in remoter, less-developed regions. (Few policymakers pondered seriously the question of *whether* the United States should always attempt to counter that insurgency; nor did America make much of an effort to distinguish between purely indigenous local uprisings and those engineered by the Soviet Union. The assumptions of the containment policy—that communism was unacceptable anywhere outside its existing borders—not only survived virtually unchallenged but blinded the United States to the distinctions among different forms of radicalism.) Such problems arose in many parts of the globe, but nowhere more acutely than in the Middle East. The region was a volatile and important one for two reasons: Israel and oil.

The establishment of a Jewish state in Palestine had been the dream of Zionists in many parts of the world for more than half a century. The plight of the hundreds of thousands of homeless Jews uprooted by World War II, and the international outrage that followed revelations of the Nazi holocaust, gave new strength to Zionist demands in the late 1940s. Palestine had been a British pro-

tectorate since the end of World War I; and in deference to local Arab opposition, the British after 1945 had attempted to limit Jewish immigration there. But despite such efforts, Jews came to Palestine in such enormous numbers that they could not be ignored. Finally, Britain brought the problem to the United Nations, which responded by recommending a partition of Palestine into a Jewish and an Arab state. On May 14, 1948, the British mandate ended, and Jews proclaimed the existence of the nation of Israel. President Truman recognized the new government the following day, thus effectively blocking a UN proposal to keep the area under a temporary trusteeship. But the creation of Israel was only the beginning of the battle for a Jewish homeland. Palestinian Arabs, unwilling to accept being displaced in what they considered their own country, fought determinedly against the new state in 1948—the first of many Arab-Israeli wars. And the United States found itself with a new ally whose survival would require years of extensive American aid.

The interest of the United States in preventing the Islamic areas of the Middle East from becoming communist went far beyond the abstract imperatives of the containment doctrine. The region contained the richest oil reserves in the world, reserves in which American companies had already invested heavily. Thus the United States reacted with alarm as it watched Mohammed Mossadegh, the nationalist prime minister of Iran, begin to resist the presence of Western corporations in his nation. In 1951, he ordered the seizure of Iran's oil wells from the British companies that had been developing them. During the next two years, American observers grew convinced that Mossadegh was becoming friendly with the Soviet Union. In 1953, as a result, the American Central Intelligence Agency (CIA) joined forces with conservative Iranian military leaders to engineer a coup that drove Mossadegh from office. To replace him, the United States favored elevating the young Shah of Iran, Mohammed Reza Pahlevi, from his position as a token constitutional monarch to that of a virtual absolute ruler. In return, the Shah allowed American companies to share in the development of Iranian oil reserves; and he remained closely tied to the United States for the next twenty-five years, even as his regime was becoming increasingly despotic and unpopular.

American policy was less effective in dealing with the nationalist government of Egypt, under the leadership of General Gamal Abdel Nasser. Nasser pressured the British in 1954 to remove their remaining troops from his country, an effort the United States accepted and even assisted. But Dulles and other policymakers were less willing to tolerate Nasser's flirtations with the Soviet Union, which took the form of Soviet shipments of armaments in return for Egyptian cotton. To punish Nasser for his transgressions, Dulles suddenly withdrew American offers of assistance in building the great Aswan Dam across the Nile. A week later, Nasser retaliated by seizing from the British control of the Suez Canal, saying that he would use the income from it to build the dam himself.

During the tedious negotiations that followed, Britain, France, and Israel all began to grow impatient with the pace of American efforts to effect a settlement. Control of the Suez Canal was of vital strategic importance; and Nasser's growing military strength made further delay costly. Thus on October 29, 1956, Israeli forces struck a preemptive blow against Egypt; and the British and French followed the next day by landing troops to drive the Egyptians from the canal. Dulles and Eisenhower reacted with horror, fearing that the Suez crisis would drive the Arab states toward the Soviet Union and precipitate a new world war. By refusing to support the invasion, and by joining in a United Nations denunciation of it, the United States helped pressure the French and British to withdraw. Egypt and Israel agreed to a cease-fire, and a precarious truce was in place. In the following years, just as Dulles had feared, the government of Egypt turned to the Soviet Union for assistance, accepting Russian financing of the Aswan Dam and making the Soviets an important force in the Middle East.

In Washington, the president responded in 1957 by enunciating the so-called Eisenhower Doctrine, by which the United States would offer economic and military aid "to secure and protect the territorial independence" of Middle Eastern nations "against overt armed aggression from any nation controlled by international communism." In practice, that meant more than simply opposing Soviet aggression. It meant working to prevent the spread of pan-Arab nationalism: Nasser's efforts to unite all the Arab states into a single nation, in which he would be the dominant force. Egypt and Syria merged to form the United Arab Republic in February 1958, causing modest concern in Washington. But that concern soon turned to alarm as pan-Arab forces began to challenge the pro-Western governments of Lebanon, Jordan, and Iraq. The United States could do little about Iraq, which fell under the control of a pro-Nasser military government in July (although only temporarily). But in Lebanon and Jordan, the situation was different. At the request of the embattled Beirut government, Eisenhower ordered 5,000 American marines to land on the beaches of Lebanon in mid-July; British troops entered Jordan at about the same time. The effect of the interventions was negligible. The governments of both countries managed to stabilize their positions on their own, and within months both the American and the British forces withdrew.

Throughout the troubled course of American intervention in the Middle East, the Soviet Union was never more than an indirect presence. It provided aid to countries that would accept it. It attempted to increase its influence, just as the United States was doing. It did not, however, make any overt efforts to supplant existing governments. The real concern of the United States in the Middle East was one Americans did not fully understand. It was not communism but nationalism. American policymakers were becoming convinced that they must oppose not only Soviet aggression but internal challenges to the authority of pro-American governments, even if those challenges reflected nationalist far more than communist aspirations.

Latin America and "Yankee Imperialism"

Similar difficulties were arising in an area important to, but generally neglected by, American foreign policy: Latin America. American economic interests in the region

Peruvians Threaten Nixon
On his goodwill tour of South America in 1958, Vice President Nixon was the target of violent anti-American demonstrations. When, on May 8, he appeared at San Marcos University in Lima, Peru, local police had difficulty in restraining the mob. The demonstrators threw stones, one of which grazed the vice president's neck. (UPI)

were vast; in some countries, United States corporations were the dominant force in the economy. Yet in many Latin American nations, the American interests were supporting conservative, despotic governments whose members enriched themselves and permitted little wealth to filter down to the mass of the desperately poor and rapidly expanding populations. The United States government, in the meantime, had all but abandoned even the limited initiatives of Roosevelt's Good Neighbor Policy, sending most of its foreign aid to Europe and Asia rather than to Latin America.

Animosity toward the United States, therefore, grew steadily during the 1950s, as many Latin Americans began to regard the influence of United States business in their countries as an insidious form of imperialism. Some nationalists in the region had once

believed that the United States would support popular efforts to overthrow undemocratic governments. But in 1954, the Eisenhower administration suggested otherwise when it helped topple a new, leftist government in Guatemala that Secretary Dulles believed was potentially communist. Four years later, the depths of anti-American sentiment became clear when Vice President Richard Nixon visited the region, to be greeted in city after city by angry, hostile, occasionally dangerous mobs.

Americans were shocked by the outburst of animosity, and the administration began hasty, belated efforts to improve relations with its neighbors. But the legacy of more than fifty years of casual exploitation of Latin America was too strong to prevent the rise of other nationalist movements hostile to the United States. No nation in the region had been more closely tied to America than Cuba. Its leader, Fulgencio Batista, had ruled as a military dictator since 1952, when with American assistance, he had toppled a more moderate government. Cuba's economy had become a virtual fiefdom of American corporations, which controlled almost all the island's natural resources and had cornered over half of the vital sugar crop. Beginning in 1957, a popular movement of resistance to the Batista regime began to gather power under the leadership of Fidel Castro. By late 1958, the Batista forces were in almost total disarray. And on January 1, 1959, with Batista now in exile in Spain (having taken millions of dollars in government funds along with him), Castro marched into Havana and established a new government.

Despite its long support of the Batista government, the United States had long been vaguely embarrassed by its ties to that corrupt regime. At first, therefore, Americans reacted warmly to Castro, particularly since there was little evidence that he was tied to any communist elements. But as Castro began implementing drastic policies of land reform and expropriation of foreign-owned businesses and resources, Cuban–American relations rapidly deteriorated. The new government was outraging American businessmen by its assaults on their interests. It was, moreover, causing concern to Eisenhower and Dulles by its growing interest in communist ideas and tactics. When Castro began accepting assistance from the Soviet Union in 1960, the United States cut back the "quota" by which Cuba could export sugar to America at a favored price. Early in 1961, as one of its last acts, the Eisenhower administration severed diplomatic relations with Castro. The American CIA had already begun secretly training Cuban expatriates for an invasion of the island to topple the new regime. Totally isolated by the United States, Castro soon cemented a close and lasting alliance with the Soviet Union.

Europe and the Soviet Union

The problems of the Third World would soon become the central focus of American foreign policy. Through most of the 1950s, however, the United States remained chiefly concerned with its direct relationship with the Soviet Union and with the possibility of communist expansion in Europe. The "massive retaliation" doctrine was the first American effort to deter such expansion. The rearming of West Germany was another. Beginning in 1954, the West German government began, within strict guidelines imposed by the United States, Britain, and France, to develop its first armed forces since the end of World War II. In 1957, the first German forces joined NATO, making the nation a full military ally of the United States.

In the meantime, however, many Americans continued to hope that the United States and the Soviet Union would be able to negotiate solutions to some of their remaining problems. Such hopes were buoyed when, after the death of Stalin in 1953, signs began to emerge of a new Russian attitude of conciliation. The Soviet Union extended a peace overture to the rebellious Tito government in Yugoslavia; it returned a military base to Finland; it signed a peace treaty with Japan; and, above all, it agreed to terminate its long military occupation of Austria, making that nation a neutral state. Pressure for negotiation intensified when, between 1953 and 1954, both the United States and the Soviet Union successfully tested the new hydrogen bomb, a nuclear device of vastly greater power than those developed during the war. These factors seemed briefly to bear fruit in 1955, when Eisenhower and other NATO leaders met with the Soviet premier, Nicolai Bulganin, at a cordial summit conference in Geneva. But when a subsequent conference of foreign ministers met to try to resolve specific issues, the "spirit of Geneva" quickly dissolved, as neither side could agree to the terms of the other.

The failure of conciliation brought renewed vigor to the Cold War, not only helping to produce tensions between the superpowers in the Third World but spurring a vastly increased Soviet–American arms race. Both nations engaged in extensive nuclear testing in the atmosphere, causing alarm among many scientists and environmentalists. Both nations redoubled efforts to develop effective intercontinental ballistic missiles, which could deliver atomic warheads directly from one continent to another. The apparent Russian lead in such development caused wide alarm in the United States. The American military, in the meantime, developed a new breed of atomic-powered submarines, capable of launching missiles from anywhere in the world.

The arms race not only increased tensions between the United States and Russia; it increased tensions within each nation as well. In America, public concern about nuclear war was becoming an obsessive national nightmare, a preoccupation never far from popular thought. Movies, television programs, books, popular songs: all expressed the pervasive fear. Government studies began to appear outlining the hideous casualties that a nuclear war would inflict on the nation. Schools, local governments, and individual families built a huge network of bomb shelters for protection against atomic blasts and radioactive fallout. Fear of communism, therefore, combined with fear of atomic war to create a widespread national unease.

Khrushchev and Berlin

In this tense and fearful atmosphere, new Soviet provocations in Berlin in 1958 created a particularly troubling crisis. The linking of West Germany first to NATO and then to the new European Common Market, establishing that nation as a full partner of the West, made the continuing existence of an anticommunist West Berlin a particularly galling irritation to the Soviets. In November 1958, therefore, Nikita Khrushchev, who succeeded Bulganin as Soviet premier and Communist party chief in 1958, renewed the demands of his predecessors that the NATO powers abandon the city, threatening vaguely to cut its ties to the West if they did not. The United States and its allies refused, and America and Russia were locked in another tense confrontation.

Khrushchev declined to force the issue when it became apparent that the West was unwilling to budge. Instead, he suggested that he and Eisenhower engage in personal discussions, both by visiting each other's countries and by conferring at a summit meeting in Paris in 1960. The United States eagerly agreed. Khrushchev's 1959 visit to America produced a cool but cordial response; and plans proceeded for the summit conference and for Eisenhower's visit to Moscow shortly thereafter. Only days before the scheduled beginning of the Paris meeting, however, the Soviet Union announced that it had shot down an American U-2, a high-altitude spy plane, over Russian territory. Its pilot, Gary Powers, was in captivity. The Eisenhower administration responded clumsily, at first denying the allegations and then, when confronted with incontrovertible proof, awkwardly admitting the circumstances of Powers's mission and attempting to explain them. Khrushchev lashed back in anger, breaking up the Paris summit almost before it could begin and withdrawing his invitation to Eisenhower to visit the Soviet Union. But the U-2 incident was really only a pretext. By the spring of 1960, both Khrushchev and Eisenhower were aware that no agreement was possible on the Berlin issue; and Khrushchev, therefore, was eager for an excuse to avoid what he believed would be fruitless negotiations.

Eisenhower's Farewell

The events of 1960 provided a somber backdrop for the end of the Eisenhower administration. After eight years in office, Eisenhower had failed to eliminate the tensions between the United States and the Soviet Union. He had failed to end the costly and dangerous armaments race. And he had presided over a transformation of the Cold War from a relatively limited confrontation with the Soviet Union in Europe to a global effort to resist communist subversion.

Yet Eisenhower had brought to these matters his own sense of the limits of American power. He had refused to commit American troops to anticommunist crusades except in carefully limited and generally low-risk situations, such as Guatemala and Lebanon. He had resisted pressures from the British, from the French, and from hardliners in his own government to place American force behind efforts to maintain colonial power in Vietnam and in the Suez. He had placed a certain measure of restraint on those who urged the creation of an enormous American military establishment, warning in his farewell address in January 1961 of the "unwarranted influence" of a vast "military-industrial complex." His caution, both in domestic and in international affairs, stood in marked contrast to the attitudes of his successors, who argued that the United States must act far more boldly and aggressively on behalf of its goals at home and abroad.

SUGGESTED READINGS

Broad studies of the society of the 1950s include William Leuchtenburg, *A Troubled Feast* (1979); Carl Degler, *Affluence and Anxiety* (1968); John Brooks, *The Great Leap* (1966); and Godfrey Hodgson, *America in Our Time* (1976). On the economy, consult John K. Galbraith, *The Affluent Society* (1958) and *The New Industrial State* (1967); C. Wright Mills, *The Power Elite* (1956); Harold G. Vatter, *The U.S. Economy in the 1950s* (1963); and Robert Heilbroner, *The Limits of American Capitalism* (1965). Joel Seidman, *American Labor from Defense to Reconversion* (1953), and John Hutchinson, *The Imperfect Union* (1970), examine changes in the labor movement. A sociological examination of suburban society can be found in Herbert Gans, *The Levittowners* (1967). The rise of mass media receives attention in Edward J. Epstein, *News from Nowhere* (1973), and David Halberstam, *The Powers That Be* (1979). Tom Wolfe, *The Right Stuff* (1979), is an engaging and perceptive discussion of the origins of the space program. More conventional studies include R. L. Rosholt, *An Administrative History of NASA* (1966), and Walter Sullivan (ed.), *America's Race for the Moon* (1962).

Among the many books examining the effects of modern, organized society on the individual, several are of particular value. See David Riesman, *The Lonely Crowd* (1950); William Whyte, *The Organization Man* (1956); and C. Wright Mills, *White Collar* (1956). On the beats, see Bruce Cook, *The Beat Generation* (1971), and John Tytell, *Naked Angels* (1976). For Jack Kerouac, see Ann Charters, *Kerouac* (1973), and Dennis McNally, *Desolate Angel* (1979). Good examples of the political and intellectual climate of the era include Arthur M. Schlesinger, Jr., *The Vital Center* (1949); Daniel Bell, *The End of Ideology* (1960); and Richard Hofstadter, *The Age of Reform* (1954). Mary Sperling McAuliffe, *Crisis on the Left* (1978), is a fine account of the split among liberals and the origins of the "consensus." Daniel Bell (ed.), *The Radical Right* (1963), is a collection of hostile studies of the survival of extreme conservatism.

General studies of the Eisenhower administration include Charles C. Alexander, *Holding the Line* (1975); Herbert S. Parmet, *Eisenhower and the American Crusade* (1972); Peter Lyon, *Eisenhower: Portrait of a Hero* (1974); and Eisenhower's own memoirs, *The White House Years*, 2 vols. (1963–1965). Other memoirs by important figures in the administration include Emmet John Hughes, *The Ordeal of Power* (1963); Sherman Adams, *Firsthand Report* (1961); and Richard Nixon, *Six Crises* (1962). The foreign policy of the Eisenhower years is discussed in Robert Divine, *Eisenhower and the Cold War* (1981). On Dulles, see Townsend Hoopes, *The Devil and John Foster Dulles* (1973), a generally critical study; and Louis Gerson, *John Foster Dulles* (1967), a more favorable view. On the early stages of American involvement in Vietnam, see Chester Cooper, *Lost Crusade* (1970); Frances Fitzgerald, *Fire in the Lake* (1972); John T. McAlister, Jr., *Vietnam: The Origins of Revolution* (1969); and George Herring, *America's Longest War* (1979). Chester Cooper, *The Lion's Last Roar* (1978), and Hugh Thomas, *Suez* (1967), examine the major Middle Eastern crisis of the era. Mira Wilkins, *The Maturing of Multinational Enterprise* (1974), examines a major source of change in American foreign policy. Kermit Roosevelt, *Counter-coup* (1980), is a firsthand account by the CIA operative who organized the 1954 coup in Iran; and Burton Kaufman, *The Oil Cartel Case* (1978), provides additional insights into United States involvement in Iranian affairs. Robert A. Divine, *Foreign Policy and U.S. Presidential Elections*, 2 vols. (1974), and *Blowing in the Wind: The Nuclear Test Ban Debate, 1954–1960* (1978), are also useful.

Philip Stern, *The Oppenheimer Case* (1969), examines one of the outstanding internal security controversies of the era. Michael Straight, *Trial by Television* (1954), discusses the decline of McCarthy, as do many of the books on McCarthy cited after Chapter 28. On the Warren Court, see Paul Murphy, *The Constitution in Crisis Times* (1972); Alexander Bickel, *Politics and the Warren Court* (1965) and *The Supreme Court and the Idea of Progress* (1970); Philip Kurland, *Politics, the Constitution, and the Warren Court* (1970); and John Weaver, *Earl Warren* (1967). A thorough and rewarding study of the *Brown* decision is Richard Kluger, *Simple Justice* (1975). On the emergence of the civil-rights movement, see Anthony Lewis, *Portrait of a Decade* (1964); Martin Luther King, Jr., *Stride Toward Freedom* (1958), a personal account of the Montgomery bus boycott; and William Chafe, *Civilities and Civil Rights* (1980), a fine study of the origins of the movement in Greensboro, North Carolina.

The Ordeal of Liberalism

The War at Home, 1970
This 1970 demonstration in New York City was emblematic of a widespread national revulsion, which peaked in the late 1960s and early 1970s, against American involvement in the war in Vietnam. Protesters here make use of a slogan derived from a popular song by John Lennon and Yoko Ono.
(© Harvey Stein 1970)

The calm, reassuring presence of Eisenhower seemed perfectly to match the political mood of the 1950s—a mood that combined a desire for domestic stability with a concern for international security. By the end of the decade, however, many Americans were beginning to clamor for a more active and assertive approach to public policy. The nation had, liberals complained, been allowed to "drift." It was time for an energetic assault on both domestic and world problems. Such sentiments helped produce two presidents whose activism transformed the nature of their office and the thrust of American politics.

Those same sentiments helped to make the 1960s one of the most turbulent eras of the twentieth century. For several years after the inauguration of John F. Kennedy as president, the nation seemed to move firmly and confidently to combat the expansion of communism; and it seemed to act decisively to confront its most serious social prob-lem: racial inequality. By 1968, however, the United States was embroiled in a major social, cultural, and political crisis. In extending the historic containment doctrine to dictate a deepening American involvement in the civil war in Vietnam, the United States was embroiling itself in a conflict it did not understand and could not resolve. And in assaulting the problem of racial injustice, the nation was undertaking a far more difficult and wrenching task than most reformers at first realized. These and other pressures produced not only political turmoil but cultural changes so profound that those who described them as a "revolution" exaggerated only slightly.

By the end of the 1960s, the confident assumptions that had fueled the liberal crusades of the first half of the decade lay in ruins. Instead, American society found itself searching for ways to restore stability and unity to the nation.

EXPANDING THE LIBERAL STATE

The presidency had been growing steadily more important in American public life throughout the twentieth century, and the development of atomic weapons—weapons that came under the personal control of the president—added a new dimension to the powers of the office in the 1950s. By 1960, more and more Americans were looking to the presidency as the source of all initiatives and were calling for more assertive leadership. Such exhortations found a receptive audience in the two men who served in the White House from 1961 until 1969: John F. Kennedy and Lyndon B. Johnson.

John F. Kennedy

The campaign of 1960 produced two young candidates who claimed to offer the nation active leadership. The Republican nomination went almost uncontested to Vice President Richard Nixon, who for the occasion abandoned the strident anticommunism that had characterized his earlier career and adopted a centrist position in favor of moderate reform. The Democrats, in the meantime, emerged from a spirited primary campaign united, somewhat uneasily, behind John F. Kennedy, an attractive and articulate senator from Massachusetts who had narrowly missed being the party's vice-presidential candidate in 1956. He had premised his campaign, he said, "on the single assumption that the American people are uneasy at the present drift in our national course." He was, wrote *New Republic* columnist TRB, "a young man offering positive leadership and presidential power to the uttermost."

Two Presidential Candidates Debate on Television
Before an estimated audience of 70 million viewers, the 1960 Republican nominee, Vice
President Richard M. Nixon, and the Democratic nominee, Senator John F. Kennedy, participated in an unprecedented series of televised debates. Until then, the lesser-known Kennedy had seemed the underdog. "It was the sight of the two men side by side that carried
the punch," Theodore H. White has written. "There was, first and above all, the crude,
overwhelming impression that side by side the two seemed evenly matched—and this even
matching in the popular imagination was for Kennedy a major victory. Until the cameras
opened on the Senator and the Vice President, Kennedy had been the boy under assault
and attack by the Vice President as immature, young, inexperienced. Now, obviously, in
flesh and behavior he was the Vice President's equal."—*The Making of the President 1960*
(New York: Atheneum, 1961), p. 288. (NBC)

He was also a Catholic, a political liability
that had almost cost him the nomination
and that continued to dog him throughout
the campaign. Kennedy compensated for
that with his remarkably appealing public
image—one that seemed perfectly suited for
television—and with an unusually sophisticated and capable campaign. The crucial moment, perhaps, came when he met Vice President Nixon in a series of televised debates.
Cool, poised, and relaxed, Kennedy stood in
marked contrast to the haggard and somewhat nervous Nixon, who was, during the
first debate at least, recovering from an illness. The favorable response Kennedy received from the debates helped propel him to
victory.

It was, however, one of the narrowest
victories in the history of presidential elections. A vigorous effort on behalf of Nixon
by President Eisenhower in the closing days
of the campaign, combined with continuing
doubts about Kennedy's youth (he turned
forty-three years old in 1960) and religion,
almost enabled the Republicans to close what
had at one time been a substantial Democratic lead. But in the end, Kennedy held on
to win a tiny plurality of the popular vote—
49.7 percent to Nixon's 49.5 percent—and
only a slightly more comfortable electoral
majority—303 to 219. If a few thousand
voters in Illinois and Texas had voted differently, Nixon would have won the election.
The narrowness of Kennedy's victory

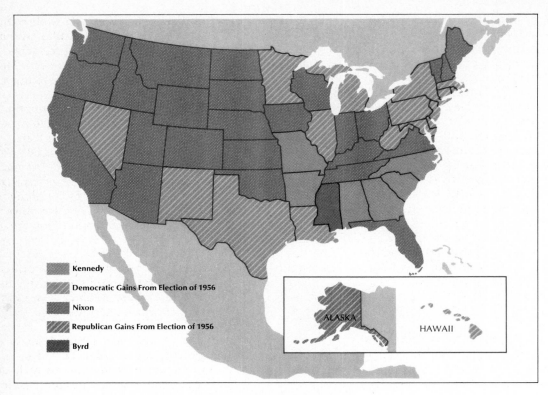

Kennedy

Democratic Gains From Election of 1956

Nixon

Republican Gains From Election of 1956

Byrd

ALASKA

HAWAII

THE ELECTION OF 1960

placed a serious constraint on his ability to accomplish his goals. His brief administration, therefore, was less an occasion for dynamic reform than a lesson to the young president in the limits of his office. Kennedy had campaigned promising a program of domestic legislation more ambitious than any since the New Deal, a program he described as the "New Frontier." He was able to steer little of it to completion during his presidency.

Kennedy's most serious problem from the beginning was the Congress. Although Democrats remained in control of both houses, they owed little to the new president, whose "coattails" in 1960 had been exceedingly short. Nor did the presence of Democratic majorities ensure a sympathetic reception for reform proposals; those majorities rested in large part on conservative Southerners far more likely to vote with the Republicans than with Kennedy. Moreover,

many of those same Southerners maintained control, by virtue of their seniority, of the most important congressional committees. One after another of Kennedy's legislative proposals, therefore, found themselves hopelessly stalled long before they reached the floor of the House or Senate.

As a result, the president had to look elsewhere for opportunities to display forceful, positive leadership. One such area was the economy, which from the beginning of his administration had been his primary concern. Economic growth was sluggish in 1961 when Kennedy entered the White House. Unemployment was hovering at about 6 percent of the work force. In addition to such legislative initiatives as requesting tax credits for businesses investing in capital growth, Kennedy attempted to use his executive powers unilaterally to improve the economy. With congressional approval, he initiated a series of tariff negotiations with foreign governments—the "Kennedy Round"—to reduce barriers to international trade, in an effort to stimulate American exports. He began to consider the use of Keynesian fiscal and monetary tools in more direct and positive ways than those used by any previous administration. He even put his personal prestige on the line in a battle to curb inflation. In 1962, several steel companies, led by United States Steel, announced that they were raising their prices by $6 a ton, a move certain to trigger similar action by the rest of the steel industry. Angrily denouncing the steel companies both publicly and privately, the president exerted enormous pressure on United States Steel to rescind its decision—threatening the company with lawsuits and cancellations of government contracts. He even called the president of U.S. Steel, Roger Blough, to the White House for an impassioned tongue-lashing. Finally, the steel companies relented and abandoned the price rise. But the president had won only a fleeting victory. His relationship with the business community was a strained one from that moment on, and a few months later the steel companies quietly raised prices again. The president did not protest.

Where Kennedy found the greatest opportunities to display his vision of presidential leadership was in two areas: foreign policy and style. In his capacity as a world leader, he discovered—like other presidents both before and after him—that he could act without the constraints that hampered his domestic initiatives. And in adopting a new presidential style, he was able to employ his own most effective political skills. More than any other president of the century (excepting perhaps the two Roosevelts), Kennedy made his own personality an integral part of his presidency and a central focus of national attention.

Nothing more clearly illustrates how important Kennedy and the presidency had become to the American people than the tragedy of November 22, 1963, and the popular reaction to it. Already, the president was beginning to campaign for reelection the following year; and in November, he traveled to Texas with his wife and Vice President Lyndon Johnson for a series of political appearances. While the presidential motorcade rode slowly through the streets of Dallas, shots rang out. Two bullets struck the president—one in the throat, the other in the head. He was sped to a nearby hospital, where minutes later he was pronounced dead.

The circumstances of the assassination seemed clearer at the time than they did from the vantage point of later years. Lee Harvey Oswald, who appeared to be a confused and embittered Marxist, was arrested for the crime later that day, on the basis of strong circumstantial evidence. (Among other things, Oswald had shot and killed a police officer who had tried to apprehend him.) Two days later, as Oswald was being moved from one jail to another, Jack Ruby, a Dallas nightclub owner, stepped from a crowd of reporters and fired a pistol into Oswald's abdomen, an event that was broadcast graphically around the world on television. Oswald died only hours later. The popular assumption at the time was that Oswald had acted alone, expressing through the murder his personal frustration and anger, and that Ruby had acted out of grief and out of a desire to make himself a popular hero. These assumptions received what seemed to be conclusive confirmation by a federal commission, chaired by Chief Justice Earl Warren, that was appointed to review the events surrounding the assassination. In later years, however, more and more questions and doubts arose about the circumstances of the shooting; and an increasing number of Americans became convinced that the Warren Commission report had not revealed the full story.

The death of President Kennedy was one of those traumatic episodes in national history that have left a permanent mark on all who experienced it. The entire nation seemed to suspend its normal activities for four days to watch the televised activities surrounding the presidential funeral. Images of Kennedy's widow, his small children, his funeral procession, his dramatic grave site at Arlington Cemetery with its symbolic eternal flame—all became deeply embedded in the public mind. For months thereafter, the American people displayed an almost obsessive interest in the martyred president and his family. For years, they continued to ven-

President Johnson Takes the Oath of Office
With Mrs. Johnson (*left center*) and Mrs. Kennedy at his side, Lyndon Baines Johnson took his oath of office as president on the afternoon of November 22, 1963, before Judge Sarah T. Hughes aboard the presidential airplane at Dallas, Texas. Johnson, born on a cattle ranch near Stonewall, Texas, on August 27, 1908, was of Confederate forebears, but considered himself more a Westerner than a Southerner. He had to bear the handicap of being regarded as a Southerner in national politics, even though he pointed with pride to his grandfather, who had been a Populist member of the Texas legislature, and his father, who had also served in the legislature and had been a firm opponent of the Ku Klux Klan. Johnson taught elementary school for a year after graduating from Southwest Texas State Teachers College, then became secretary to a Texas congressman. An ardent New Dealer, he was Texas director of the National Youth Administration and, after his election to the House of Representatives in 1937, a protégé of President Roosevelt. When Roosevelt died, Johnson said: "He was just like a daddy to me always." After an initial defeat, Johnson won election to the United States Senate in 1948 by a primary margin of eighty-seven votes. As senator from a state in which new business and industrial interests were increasingly powerful, Johnson came to be known less for his liberalism (which he continued to avow) than for his moderation. He liked to quote, as had his father, the words of the prophet Isaiah: "Come, let us reason together." An unparalleled master of the arts of political persuasion, Johnson rose to the position of Senate majority leader. Again and again he managed to bring together and to compromise the differences among Democratic senators from South and North. As vice president, Johnson lacked the opportunity to practice these arts: he spent much of his time on missions outside the United States. When he was suddenly elevated to the presidency, he pointed out to the Congress that he had taken the leadership in obtaining the civil rights acts of 1957 and 1960. Once again he undertook to bridge divisions of opinion in order to obtain constructive legislation. (Wide World)

erate him in a way reserved in the past for only a very few public figures. When in later times Americans would look back at the optimistic days of the 1950s and early 1960s and wonder how everything had seemed to unravel, many would think of November 22, 1963, as the beginning of the end.

Lyndon B. Johnson

At the time, however, the American public seemed to take comfort in the personality and performance of Kennedy's successor in the White House, Lyndon B. Johnson. A native of Texas, Johnson had entered public life in the 1930s, first as an administrator of the New Deal's National Youth Administration, then as a young congressman with personal ties to Franklin Roosevelt. After twelve years in the House, he won election in 1948 to the United States Senate. And there, by carefully cultivating the favor of party leaders, he rose steadily in influence to become the Senate majority leader. He brought to that post, as he would bring to the presidency, a remarkable level of energy and a legendary ability to persuade and cajole his colleagues into following his lead. He had failed in 1960 to win the Democratic nomination for president; but he had surprised many who knew him by agreeing to accept the second position on the ticket with Kennedy. The events in Dallas thrust him into the White House.

Johnson's personality could hardly have been more different from Kennedy's. Tall, gawky, inelegant in his public speech, he was the antithesis of the modern media politician. Where Kennedy had been smooth and urbane, Johnson was coarse, even crude. Where Kennedy had been personally reticent and almost unfailingly polite, Johnson was effusive, garrulous, and at times viciously cruel. But like Kennedy, Johnson was a man who believed in the active use of power. And he proved, in the end, far more effective than his predecessor in translating his goals into reality.

Johnson's ability to manage the Congress provided perhaps the most vivid contrast with Kennedy. Between 1963 and 1966, he compiled the most impressive legislative record of any president since Franklin Roosevelt. He was aided by the tidal wave of emotion that followed the death of President Kennedy, which helped win passage of many New Frontier proposals as a memorial to the slain leader. But Johnson also constructed a remarkable reform program of his own, one that he ultimately labeled the "Great Society." And he won approval of much of it through the same sort of skillful lobbying that had made him an effective majority leader.

Johnson envisioned himself, as well, as a great "coalition builder," drawing into the Democratic fold as many different constituencies as possible. Even more than Kennedy, he tried to avoid the politics of conflict—that is, of winning the support of one group by attacking another. Johnson wanted the support of everyone, and for a time he very nearly got it. His first year in office was, by necessity, dominated by the campaign for reelection. And from the beginning, there seemed to be very little doubt that he would win. As a Democrat in an era of wide support for liberal reform, as the successor of a beloved and martyred president, and as a personification of the same energetic activism that had helped make Kennedy so popular, he was an almost unbeatable candidate. He was further aided by the Republican party, which in 1964 fell under the sway of its right wing and nominated the conservative Senator Barry Goldwater of Arizona. Liberal Republicans abandoned Goldwater and openly supported Johnson.

In the fall campaign, Johnson avoided specific, detailed promises, concentrating instead on attracting support from as wide a range of voters as possible and letting Goldwater's stubborn conservatism drive even more Americans into the Democratic fold. The strategy worked. Johnson received more votes, over 42 million, and a larger plurality, over 61 percent, than any candidate in history. Goldwater managed to carry only his home state of Arizona and five states in the deep South. Record Democratic majorities in both houses of Congress, many of whose members had been swept into office only because of the margin of Johnson's victory, ensured that the president would be able to fulfill many of his goals. On election night, Johnson told the nation that he regarded his victory as a "mandate for unity." For a time, that unity seemed to survive; and Johnson seemed well on his way to achieving his own most cherished aim: becoming the most successful reform president of the century.

The Assault on Poverty

The domestic programs of Kennedy and Johnson shared two fundamental goals: maintaining the strength of the American economy and expanding the responsibilities of the federal government for the general social welfare. In the first, the two presidents were simply continuing a commitment that had been central to virtually every administration since early in the century. In the second, however, they were responding to a marked change in public assumptions. In particular, they were responding to what some described as the "discovery of poverty" in the late 1950s and early 1960s, the rather sudden realization by Americans who had been glorying in prosperity that there remained substantial portions of the population who remained destitute.

For the first time since the 1930s, therefore, the federal government in the 1960s took steps not only to strengthen and expand existing social welfare programs but to create a host of important new ones. The effort began in the Kennedy administration, although at first without great result. Kennedy did manage to win approval of important changes in existing welfare programs. A revision of the minimum wage law extended coverage to an additional 3.6 million workers and raised the minimum hourly wage from $1.00 to $1.25. Another measure increased social security benefits. Kennedy's most ambitious proposals, however, remained unfulfilled until after his death.

The most important of these, perhaps, was Medicare: a program to provide federal aid to the elderly for medical expenses. Its enactment in 1965 came at the end of a bitter, twenty-year debate between those who believed in the concept of national health assistance and those who denounced it as "social-

ized medicine." But the program as it went into effect removed many objections. Doctors serving Medicare patients continued to practice privately and to charge their normal fees; Medicare simply shifted responsibility for paying a large proportion of those fees from the patient to the government. With that barrier now hurdled, advocates of national health insurance pushed for even more extensive coverage; and in 1966, President Johnson finally steered to passage the Medicaid program, which extended federal medical assistance to welfare recipients too young to qualify for Medicare. Criticism of both programs continued from all sides. National health insurance advocates continued to insist that coverage be extended to all Americans. Others spoke harshly of the bureaucratic problems Medicare and Medicaid created, and of the corruption these programs seemed to encourage. Still more complained bitterly of the tremendous costs the reforms were imposing on the government and the taxpayer; beginning in 1969, as a result, the government began attempting to limit eligibility for assistance in order to reduce expenses.

Medicare and Medicaid were the first steps in a comprehensive assault on poverty—one that Kennedy had been contemplating in the last months of his life, and one that Johnson brought to fruition on his own. Determined to eradicate the "pockets of poverty" that were receiving wide public attention, Johnson announced to Congress only weeks after taking office the declaration of an "unconditional war on poverty." The Economic Opportunity Act he then steered to passage provided for, among other things, the establishment of an Office of Economic Opportunity—the centerpiece in Johnson's vision of the Great Society. From the OEO stemmed a vast array of educational programs: vocational training, remedial education, college work-study grants, and others. The office funneled government money as well into programs to provide employment for unemployed youths—through the Job Corps, the Neighborhood Youth Corps, and other agencies. And it established VISTA (Volunteers in Service to America), a program reminiscent of the paternal reform efforts of the progressive era. VISTA volunteers moved out across the country into troubled communities to provide educational and social services. Other OEO programs financed housing assistance, health care, neighborhood improvements, and many more antipoverty efforts.

The war on poverty was designed to encourage communities themselves to take the initiative in planning reforms, and almost half its funds were disbursed to various Community Action programs. But the reality was often far from the ideal. The nearly $3 billion that the OEO spent during its first two years of existence did much to assist those who managed to qualify for funds. It helped significantly to reduce poverty in certain areas. It fell far short, however, of its goal of eliminating poverty altogether. The job-training programs that formed so important a part of the war on poverty produced generally disappointing results, particularly among the urban black unemployed; blacks continued, once trained, to be barred from many jobs because of racial discrimination, or because the jobs simply did not exist in their communities. Community Action programs often fell victim either to local mismanagement or to cumbersome federal supervision, and in either case frequently resulted in a substantial waste of funds. Above all, however, the war on poverty never really approached the dimensions necessary to achieve its goals. From the beginning, funds were inadequate. And as the years passed and a costly war in Southeast Asia became the nation's first priority, even those limited funds began to dwindle. Nearly 17 percent of the American people continued to live in poverty by the late 1960s despite the efforts of the OEO—an improvement over the more than 20 percent who had qualified as poor in 1959, but far from Johnson's hopes.

Cities and Schools

Closely tied to the antipoverty program were federal efforts to promote the revitalization of decaying cities and to strengthen the nation's schools. Again, many such programs had received support from the Kennedy administration but won passage under Johnson. President Kennedy himself had managed to steer through Congress the Housing Act of 1961, which offered $4.9 billion in federal grants to cities for the preservation of open spaces, the development of mass-transit systems, and the subsidization of middle-income housing. Johnson went further. He established the Department of Housing and Urban Development, as if to symbolize the government's commitment to the cities. (The first secretary of this department, Robert Weaver, became the first black ever to serve in the cabinet.) And Johnson also inaugurated the Model Cities program, which offered federal subsidies for urban redevelopment.

Kennedy had fought long and in vain to win congressional passage of a program to provide federal aid to public education. Like the idea of federal health insurance, the concept of aid to education aroused deep suspicion in many Americans, who saw it as the first wedge in a federal effort to take control of the schools from localities. Conservatives argued forcefully that once the government began paying for education, it would begin telling the schools how and what they must teach. Opposition arose from another quarter as well: Catholics insisted that aid to education must extend to parochial as well as public schools, something that President Kennedy had refused to consider and that many Americans believed was unconstitutional. Johnson managed to circumvent both objections with the Elementary and Secondary Education Act of 1965 and a series of subsequent measures. Such bills extended aid to both private and parochial schools—aid that was based on the economic conditions of their students, not the needs of the schools themselves. The formula met criteria earlier established by the Supreme Court, and it satisfied some, although not all, conservatives. Total federal expenditures for education and technical training rose from $5 billion to $12 billion between 1964 and 1967.

The great surge of reform of the Kennedy-Johnson years reflected not only a new awareness of the nation's social problems but the boundless confidence of a society that believed its resources and abilities were limitless. By the time Johnson left office, legislation had been either enacted or initiated to deal with almost every imaginable social problem: poverty, health, education, cities, transportation, the environment, the consumer, agriculture, science, the arts.

The reforms meant, of course, a radical increase in federal spending. For a time, rising tax revenues from the growing economy nearly compensated for the new expenditures. In 1964, Lyndon Johnson managed to win passage of the $11.5 billion tax cut that Kennedy had first proposed in 1962. Although the cut increased an already sizable federal deficit, it produced substantial economic growth over the next several years that made up for much of the revenue initially lost. But as the Great Society programs began to multiply, and particularly as they began

to compete with the escalating costs of America's military ventures, the federal budget rapidly began to outpace increases in revenues. In 1961, the federal government had spent $94.4 billion. By 1970, that sum had more than doubled, to $196.6 billon. And except for 1969, when there was a modest surplus, the budget throughout the decade showed a deficit, which in 1968 rose to $25.1 billion—the highest in history to that point. (By the early 1980s, it would seem a modest gap, as Congress and the president struggled without success to keep deficits below $100 billion.) By 1973, the budget had risen again, to over $246 billion; by 1980, it was in excess of $600 billion. The national debt, in the meantime, had risen from $286.3 billion in 1960 to $458 billion in 1973. By 1982, it had exceeded $1 trillion.

THE BATTLE FOR RACIAL EQUALITY

By far the most important commitment to reform in the 1960s was the effort to ensure justice and equality for American blacks. It was also the most difficult commitment, the one that produced the severest strains on American society. Yet despite the initial reluctance of many whites, including even many liberals, to confront the problem, it was an issue that could no longer be ignored. Black Americans were themselves ensuring that the nation would have to deal with the problem of race.

The Expanding Protests

John Kennedy had long been sympathetic to the cause of racial justice, but he was hardly a committed crusader. His intervention during the 1960 campaign to help win the release of Martin Luther King, Jr., from a Georgia prison won him a large plurality of the black vote. Once in office, however, he was reluctant to jeopardize his legislative program by openly committing himself to racial reform, fearing that he would alienate key Democratic senators. Resisting the arguments of those who urged new civil-rights legislation, the Kennedy administration worked instead

to expand the enforcement of existing laws and to support litigation to overturn existing segregation statutes. Both efforts produced only limited results. Still, the administration hoped to contain the issue of race and resisted pressure to do more.

But that pressure was rapidly growing too powerful to ignore. In February 1960, black college students in Greensboro, North Carolina, staged a sit-in at a segregated Woolworth's lunch counter—an event that received wide national attention. In the following months, such demonstrations spread throughout the South, forcing many merchants to integrate their facilities. Of almost equal significance, the sit-in movement aroused the support of a substantial number of northern whites, particularly on college campuses; and in 1961, students of both races began what they called "freedom rides." Traveling by bus throughout the South, they went from city to city attempting to force the desegregation of bus stations. They were met in some places with such savage violence on the part of whites that the president finally dispatched federal marshals to help keep the peace and ordered the integration of all bus and train stations.

Continuing judicial efforts to enforce the

Martin Luther King, Jr., 1963
Martin Luther King, Jr., speaks from the steps of the Lincoln Memorial during the great March on Washington, August 28, 1963. His famous "I Have a Dream" speech of that day was not only the greatest triumph of his career, but one of the great oratorical moments of modern American history. (© Bob Adelman/ Magnum)

integration of public education produced an even greater test of the president's resolve. In October 1962, a federal court ordered the University of Mississippi to enroll its first black student, James Meredith; and Governor Ross Barnett, a rabid segregationist, refused to enforce the order. When angry whites in Oxford, Mississippi, began rioting to protest the court decree, Kennedy sent federal troops to the city to restore order and protect Meredith's right to attend the university. Events in Alabama the following year proved even more influential. In April 1963, Martin Luther King, Jr., launched a series of extensive nonviolent demonstrations in Birmingham, Alabama, a city unsurpassed in the strength of its commitment to segregation. Local officials responded brutally. Police Commissioner Eugene "Bull" Connor personally supervised measures to prevent King's peaceful marches, using attack dogs, tear gas, electric cattle prods, and fire hoses—at times even against small children. Hundreds of demonstrators were arrested, as much of the nation watched televised reports of the conflicts in horror. Two months later, Governor George Wallace stood in the doorway of a building at the University of Alabama to prevent the court-ordered enrollment of several black students. Only the arrival of federal marshals forced him to give

way. The same night, NAACP official Medgar Evers was murdered in Mississippi.

A National Commitment

The events in Alabama and Mississippi were both a personal shock and a political warning to the president. He could not, he realized, any longer avoid the issue of race. In a historic television address the night of the University of Alabama confrontation, Kennedy spoke eloquently of the "moral issue" facing the nation. "If an American," he asked, "because his skin is dark, . . . cannot enjoy the full and free life which all of us want, then who among us would be content to have the color of his skin changed and stand in his place? Who among us would then be content with the counsels of patience and delay?" Days later, he introduced a series of new legislative proposals prohibiting segregation in "public accommodations" (stores, restaurants, theaters, hotels, and so on), barring discrimination in employment, and increasing the power of the government to file suit on behalf of school integration.

Congressional opposition to the new proposals was strong, and it was clear from the start that only a long and arduous battle would win passage of the legislation. But once again, it was black Americans them- selves who made clear that there would be no retreat from the effort. In August 1963, more than 200,000 demonstrators marched down the Mall in Washington, D.C., and gathered before the Lincoln Memorial for the greatest civil-rights demonstration in the nation's his- tory. President Kennedy, who had at first op- posed the idea of the march, in the end gave it his open support. And the peaceful gath- ering, therefore, seemed at the time to denote less the existence of a bitter racial struggle than the birth of a new national commitment to civil rights. Martin Luther King, Jr., in one of the greatest speeches of his career, indeed one of the most memorable of any public fig- ure of the century, aroused the crowd with a litany of images prefaced again and again by the phrase "I have a dream." The march was the high water mark of the peaceful, interra- cial civil-rights movement—and one of the high points of liberal optimism as well. Darker days were soon to come.

Johnson and Civil Rights

The assassination of President Kennedy gave new impetus to the battle for civil-rights leg- islation. The ambitious measure that Ken- nedy had proposed in June 1963 had passed through the House of Representatives with relative ease; but it seemed hopelessly stalled

in the Senate, where a determined filibuster by Southern conservatives continued to pre- vent a vote. Early in 1964, after Johnson had applied both public and private pressure, supporters of the measure finally mustered the two-thirds majority necessary to close debate; and the Senate passed the most com- prehensive civil-rights bill in the history of the nation.

At the very moment of passage of the Civil Rights Act of 1964, however, new ef- forts were under way in the South to win even greater gains for blacks. And during the "freedom summer" of that year, thousands of civil-rights workers, black and white, Northern and Southern, spread out through the South, establishing "freedom schools," staging demonstrations, and demanding not only an end to segregation but the inclusion of blacks in the political process. Like earlier civil-rights activists, they met a hostile and, in some cases at least, a murderous response. Three of the first freedom workers to arrive in the South disappeared; several weeks later, the FBI found their bodies buried under an earthen dam.

Black demands continued to escalate during 1965, and government efforts to sat- isfy them continued to intensify. In Selma, Alabama, in March, Martin Luther King, Jr., helped organize a major demonstration by blacks demanding the right to register to

Confrontation in Selma
Televised pictures of the often brutal confronta- tions between civil-rights demonstrators and police in Selma, Alabama, shocked much of the na- tion in 1965 and helped spur action on the Civil Rights Act of that year, which provided federal protection for black vot- ing rights. (© Bob Adel- man/Magnum)

vote. Confronted with official resistance, the demonstrators attempted a peaceful protest march; but Selma sheriff Jim Clark led local police in a brutal attack on the demonstrators that horrified the nation. Two Northern whites participating in the Selma march were murdered in the course of the effort there— one, a minister, beaten to death in the streets of the town; the other, a Detroit housewife, shot as she drove along a highway at night. The national outrage that followed the events in Alabama helped Lyndon Johnson win passage of the Civil Rights Act of 1965, which guaranteed federal protection to blacks attempting to exercise their right to vote. The traditional criteria for limiting the franchise to whites—literacy tests, knowledge of the Constitution, "good character," and others— were now illegal. (Another, similar device— the poll tax—had been abolished by constitutional amendment in 1964.)

But the civil-rights acts, the Supreme Court decisions, the new social welfare programs designed to help poor blacks, and other government efforts—all were insufficient. Important as such gains were, they failed to satisfy the rapidly rising expectations of American blacks, whose vision of equality included not only an end to segregation but access to economic prosperity. What had once seemed to many liberals a simple moral commitment was becoming a far more complex and demanding issue. Gradually, the generally peaceful, largely optimistic civil-rights movement of the early 1960s was evolving into what would become a major racial crisis.

The Changing Context

It was inevitable, perhaps, that the focus of the racial struggle would shift away from the issue of segregation to the far broader demands of poor urban blacks. For decades, the nation's black population had been undergoing a major demographic shift; and by the 1960s, the problem of race was no longer a primarily Southern or rural one, as it had been earlier in the century. In 1910, only about 25 percent of all blacks had lived in cities and only 10 percent outside the South.

By 1966, 69 percent were living in metropolitan areas and 45 percent were outside the South. In several of the largest cities, the proportion of blacks at least doubled between 1950 and 1968. Blacks constituted 30 percent or more of the population of seven of those cities and nearly 70 percent of the population of Washington, D.C. Conditions in the black ghettoes of most cities were abysmal; and while the economic condition of much of American society was improving, in many poor urban communities—which were experiencing both a rapidly growing population and the flight of white businesses— things were getting worse. More than half of all American nonwhites lived in poverty in the early 1960s. Black unemployment was twice that of whites. Black ghetto residents were far more likely than whites to be victimized by crime, to be enticed into drug addiction, and to be subjected to substandard housing at exploitive prices. They were far less likely than whites to receive an adequate education or to have access to skilled employment.

As the battle against legal segregation progressed in the early 1960s with the passage of the landmark Civil Rights Acts of 1964 and 1965, even such relatively moderate black leaders as Martin Luther King, Jr., began to turn their attention to the deeper problems of racial injustice. By the mid-1960s, the legal battle against school desegregation had moved beyond the initial assault on de jure segregation (segregation by law) to an attack on de facto segregation (segregation by practice, as through residential patterns), thus carrying the fight into Northern cities. The nation was taking its first steps toward the busing of students from one school district to another to achieve integration, an issue that would prove as deeply divisive as any social question of its time. Many black leaders (and their white supporters) were demanding, similarly, that the battle against job discrimination move beyond the prohibition of overtly racist practices. Employers should not only abandon negative measures to deny jobs to blacks; they should adopt positive measures to recruit minorities, thus compensating for past injustices. Regulations adopted by the federal government in 1968, and strengthened in later rulings, required all institutions doing business with or receiving funds from the federal government (including schools and universities) to conform to so-called Affirmative Action guidelines. Thus yet another issue had arisen that would soon anger and alienate many whites.

The most important problem, however, remained a far more basic one: urban poverty. Beginning in 1964, moreover, it thrust itself into public prominence when residents of black ghettoes in major cities participated in a series of riots that shocked and terrified much of the nation's white population. There were a few scattered disturbances in the summer of 1964, most notably in New York City's Harlem. But the first major race riot occurred the following summer in the Watts section of Los Angeles. In the midst of a more or less routine traffic arrest, a white police officer struck a protesting black bystander with his club; and the apparently minor incident unleashed a storm of pent-up anger and bitterness that resulted in a full week of mounting violence. As many as 10,000 rioters were estimated to have participated, attacking white motorists, burning buildings, looting stores, and sniping at policemen. As in most race riots, it was the blacks themselves who suffered most; of the thirty-four people who died during the Watts uprising, which was eventually quelled by the National Guard, most were black. In the summer of 1966, there were forty-three additional outbreaks, the most serious of them in Chicago and Cleveland. And in the summer of 1967, there were eight major riots, including the most serious of them all—a racial clash in Detroit in which forty-three people (thirty-three of them black) died.

Televised reports of the violence horrified the nation. After the Detroit uprising, President Johnson expressed the ambivalence of many white liberals about the riots, calling sternly on the one hand for a restoration of law and order, and appealing simultaneously for an attack on the social problems that were causing despair and violence. A special Commission on Civil Disorders echoed the latter impulse. Its celebrated report, issued in the spring of 1968, recommended massive spending to eliminate the abysmal conditions of the ghettoes. "Only a commitment to national action on an unprecedented scale," the commission concluded, "can shape a future compatible with the historic ideals of American society." To much of the nation, however, the lesson of the riots was that racial change was moving too quickly and that stern, coercive measures were necessary to stop violence and lawlessness.

Black Power

Disillusioned with the ideal of peaceful change in cooperation with whites, an increasing number of blacks were turning to a new approach to the racial issue: the philosophy of "black power." Black power could mean many different things. In its most moderate form, it was simply a belief in the importance of black self-reliance. In its more extreme guises, black power could mean complete separatism and even violent revolution. In all its forms, however, black power suggested a move away from interracial cooperation and toward increased black racial awareness.

The most important and lasting impact of the black-power ideology was a social and psychological one: the instilling of racial pride in black Americans who had long been under pressure from their nation's dominant culture to think of themselves as somehow inferior to whites. But black power had political manifestations as well, most notably in creating a deep schism within the civil-rights movement. Traditional black organizations that had emphasized cooperation with sympathetic whites—groups such as the NAACP, the Urban League, and King's Southern Christian Leadership Conference—now faced competition from younger, more radical groups—the Student Nonviolent Coordinating Committee (SNCC), the Congress of Racial Equality (CORE), and others—calling for more radical and occasionally even violent action against the "racism" of white society. New groups were emerging entirely outside the civil-rights movement as well. Particularly alarming to whites were such overtly revolutionary organizations as the Black Panthers, based in Oakland, California; and the

Black Power: Commission's Report

What is new about "Black Power" is phraseology rather than substance.... The decade after World War I—which saw the militant, race-proud "new negro," the relatively wide-spread theory of retaliatory violence, and the high tide of the Negro-support-of-Negro-business ideology—exhibits striking parallels with the 1960's....

Black Power rhetoric and ideology actually express a lack of power. The slogan emerged when the Negro protest movement was slowing down, when it was finding increasing resistance to its changing goals, when it discovered that nonviolent direct action was no more a panacea than legal action.... This combination of circumstances provoked anger deepened by impotence. Powerless to make any fundamental changes in the life of the masses—powerless, that is, to compel white America to make those changes—many advocates of Black Power have retreated into an unreal world, where they see an outnumbered and poverty-stricken minority organizing itself independently of whites and creating sufficient power to force white America to grant its demands....

The Black Power advocates of today consciously feel that they are the most militant group in the Negro protest movement. Yet they have retreated from a direct confrontation with American society on the issue of integration and, by preaching separatism, unconsciously function as an accommodation to white racism.—*Report of the National Advisory Commission on Civil Disorders, 1968.*

Black Power: SNCC Paper

If we are to proceed toward true liberation, we must cut ourselves off from white people. We must form our own institutions, credit unions, coops, political parties, write our own histories ...

... on whatever level of contact ... blacks and whites come together, that meeting or confrontation is not on the level of the blacks but always on the level of the whites. This only means that our everday contact with whites is a reinforcement of the myth of white supremacy. Whites are the ones who must try to raise themselves to our humanistic level. We are not, after all, the ones who are responsible for a genocidal war in Vietnam; we are not the ones who are responsible for neocolonialism in Africa and Latin America; we are not the ones who held a people in animalistic bondage over 400 years. We reject the American dream as defined by white people and must work to construct an American reality defined by Afro-Americans.—*Position paper by members of the Student Nonviolent Coordinating Committee, 1966.*

separatist group, the Nation of Islam, which denounced all whites as "devils" and appealed to blacks to embrace the Islamic faith and work for complete racial separation. The most celebrated of the Black Muslims, as whites often termed them, was Malcolm Little, who adopted the name Malcolm X ("X" to denote his lost African surname). His celebrated *Autobiography* (1965)—written in collaboration with Alex Haley—became one of the most influential documents of the 1960s. Malcolm X himself died shortly before publication of his book when black gunmen, presumably under orders from rivals within the Nation of Islam, burst into a meeting he was addressing and assassinated him.

LIBERAL ACTIVISM, THE WORLD, AND VIETNAM

In international affairs as much as in domestic reform, the optimistic liberalism of the Kennedy and Johnson administrations dictated a more positive, more active approach to dealing with the nation's problems than in the past. Just as social difficulties at home required a search for new solutions, so the threat of communism overseas seemed to call for new methods and strategies. And just as the new activism in domestic reform ultimately produced frustration and disorder, so did the new activism overseas gradually pull the nation toward disaster.

Diversifying Foreign Policy

John Kennedy's stirring inaugural address was a clear indication of how central to his and to the nation's thinking was opposition to communism. "In the long history of the world," he proclaimed, "only a few generations have been granted the role of defending freedom in its hour of maximum danger. I do not shrink from this responsibility; I welcome it." Yet the speech, which significantly made no mention whatsoever of domestic affairs, was also an indication of Kennedy's belief that the United States had not done enough to counter Soviet expansion. The defense policies of the new administration, therefore, emphasized not only strengthening existing implements of warfare but developing new ones.

Kennedy had charged repeatedly during his campaign that the United States was suffering from a "missile gap," that the Soviet Union had moved ahead of America in the number of missiles and warheads it could deploy. Even before the election, Kennedy received information indicating that whatever missile gap there was favored the United States. Nevertheless, once in office, he insisted on substantial increases in the nation's nuclear armaments. The Soviet Union, which had several years earlier decided to slow the growth of its atomic arsenal, responded with a new missile-building program of its own.

At the same time, however, Kennedy was not satisfied with the nation's ability to meet communist threats in "emerging areas" of the Third World—the areas in which, Kennedy believed, the real struggle against communism would be waged in the future. A nuclear deterrent might prevent a Soviet invasion of Western Europe; but in the Middle East, in Africa, in Latin America, in Asia, where insurgent forces had learned to employ methods of jungle and guerrilla warfare, different methods would be necessary. Kennedy gave enthusiastic support to the development of new counterinsurgency forces—a million soldiers trained specifically to fight modern, limited wars. He even chose their uniforms, which included the distinctive green beret from which the Special Forces derived their nickname.

Along with military diversification, Kennedy favored the development of methods for expanding American influence through peaceful means. To repair the badly deteriorating relationship with Latin America, he proposed an Alliance for Progress: a series of projects undertaken cooperatively by the United States and Latin American governments for peaceful development and stabilization of the nations of that region. Its purpose was both to spur social and economic development and to inhibit the rise of Castro-like movements in other Central or South American countries. Poor coordination and inadequate funding sharply limited the impact of the program, but relations between the United States and some Latin American countries did improve. Kennedy also inaugurated the Agency for International Development (AID) to coordinate foreign aid. And he established what became one of his most popular innovations: the Peace Corps, which trained and sent abroad young volunteers to work in developing areas.

Fiasco in Cuba

Kennedy's efforts to improve relations with developing countries were not aided by a hopelessly bungled act of aggression against the Castro government in Cuba. Convinced that "communist domination in this hemisphere can never be negotiated" and that Castro represented a threat to the stability of other Latin American nations, Kennedy agreed in the first weeks of his presidency to continue a project the Eisenhower administration had begun. For months, the CIA had been helping secretly to train a small army of anti-Castro Cuban exiles in Central America. On April 17, 1961, with the approval of the president, 2,000 of the armed exiles landed at the Bay of Pigs in Cuba, expecting first American air support and then a spontaneous uprising by the Cuban people on their behalf. They received neither. At the last minute, Kennedy withdrew the air support, fearful of involving the United States too directly in the invasion. And the expected uprising did not occur. Instead, well-armed Castro forces easily crushed the invaders; and within two days the entire mission had collapsed.

A somber President Kennedy took full responsibility for the fiasco. Governments around the world—not only communist but neutral and pro-Western as well—joined in condemning the United States. But despite the humiliation, Kennedy refused to abandon the principle of overthrowing Castro by force. "We do not intend to abandon Cuba to the Communists," he said only three days after the Bay of Pigs. On the contrary, the failure only redoubled his determination to display American power in the world.

Confrontations with the Soviet Union

In the grim aftermath of the Bay of Pigs, Kennedy traveled to Vienna in June 1961 for his first meeting with Soviet Premier Nikita Khrushchev. Their frosty exchange of views did little to reduce tensions between the two nations. Nor did Khrushchev's continuing irritation over the existence of a noncommunist West Berlin in the heart of East Germany. Particularly embarrassing to the communists was the mass exodus of residents of East Germany to the West through the easily traversed border in the center of Berlin. Before dawn on August 13, 1961, the Soviet Union stopped the exodus by directing East Germany to construct a wall between East and West Berlin. Guards fired on those who continued to try to escape.

The rising tensions culminated the following October in the most dangerous and dramatic crisis of the Cold War. During the summer of 1962, American intelligence agencies had become aware of the arrival of Soviet technicians and equipment in Cuba and of military construction in progress. At first, the administration assumed that the new weapons system was purely defensive. On October 14, however, aerial reconaissance photos produced clear evidence that in fact the Soviets were constructing missile sites on the island. The reasons for the Russian effort were not difficult to discern. The existence of offensive nuclear missiles in Cuba would go far toward compensating for the American lead in deployable atomic weapons, giving the Soviet Union the same easy access to enemy territory that the United States had long possessed by virtue of its missile sites in Europe and the Middle East. The weapons would, moreover, serve as an effective deterrent against any future American invasion of Cuba—a possibility that seemed very real both to Castro and to the Soviet leadership.

To Kennedy, however, the missile sites represented an unconscionable act of aggression by the Soviets toward the United States. Almost immediately, he decided that the weapons could not be allowed to remain. On October 22, after nearly a week of tense deliberations by a special task force in the White House, the president announced on television that he was establishing a naval and air blockade around Cuba, a "quarantine" against all offensive weapons. Soviet ships bound for the island slowed course or stopped before reaching the point of confrontation. But work on the missile sites continued at full speed. Preparations were under way for an American air attack on the missile sites when, late in the evening of October 26, Kennedy received a message from Khrushchev implying that the Soviet Union would remove the missile bases in exchange for an American pledge not to invade Cuba. Ignoring other, tougher Soviet messages, the president agreed; privately, moreover, he gave assurances that the United States would remove its missiles from Turkey (a decision he had already reached months before but had not yet implemented). On October 27, the agreement became public. The crisis was over.

The Cuban missile crisis brought the world closer to nuclear war than at any time since World War II. It exposed in dangerous fashion the perils that both the Soviet Union and the United States were creating by allowing their own rivalry to extend into Third World countries. But it also, ironically, helped produce a significant alleviation of Cold War tensions. Both the United States and the Soviet Union had been forced to confront the momentous consequences of war; and both seemed ready in the following months to move toward a new accommodation. In June 1963, President Kennedy addressed a commencement audience at American University in Washington, D.C., with a message starkly different from those of his earlier speeches. The United States did not, he claimed, seek a "Pax Americana enforced on the world by American weapons of war." And he seemed for the first time to offer hope for a peaceful rapprochement with the Soviet Union. "If we cannot now end our differences," he said, "at least we can help make the world safe for diversity." That same summer, the United States and the Soviet Union concluded years of negotiation by agreeing to a treaty to ban the testing of nuclear weapons in the atmosphere. It was the first step toward mutual arms reduction since the beginning of the Cold War—a small step, but one that seemed to augur a new era of international relations.

Johnson and the World

Lyndon Johnson entered the presidency lacking even John Kennedy's limited experience with international affairs. He had traveled widely while vice president, but he had been included in few important decisions. He was eager, therefore, not only to continue the policies of his predecessor but to prove quickly that he too was a strong and forceful leader. To his misfortune, however, he quickly became dependent on those members of the Kennedy administration with the most assertive, even arrogant, view of the proper uses of American power.

Johnson was even less adept than his predecessor—who had displayed little sensitivity on the subject—at distinguishing between nationalist insurgency and communist expansion. His response to an internal rebellion in the Dominican Republic was a clear illustration. A 1961 assassination had toppled the repressive dictatorship of General Rafael Trujillo, and for the next four years various factions in the country had struggled for dominance. In the spring of 1965, a conservative military regime began to collapse in the face of a revolt by a broad range of groups (including some younger military leaders) on behalf of the left-wing nationalist Juan Bosch. For Johnson, the situation seemed an ideal opportunity to display the effectiveness of American force. Arguing (falsely) that Bosch threatened to establish a pro-Castro, communist regime, he dispatched 30,000 American troops to quell the disorder. The troops remained—although later they came under the auspices of the Organization of American States—until the Johnson administration had assurances that the Dominican Republic would establish a pro-American, anticommunist regime. Only after a conservative candidate defeated Bosch in a 1966 election were the forces withdrawn.

From Johnson's first moments in office, however, his foreign policy was almost totally dominated by a bitter civil war in Vietnam and by the expanding involvement of the United States there. That involvement had been growing slowly for more than a decade by the time Johnson assumed the presidency. In many respects, therefore, he was simply the unfortunate legatee of commitments initiated by his predecessors. But the determination of the new president, and of others within his administration, to prove their worthiness in the battle against communism led to the final, decisive steps toward a full-scale and catastrophic commitment.

Guns and Advisers

The American involvement in Vietnam had developed so slowly and imperceptibly that when it began spectacularly to expand, in 1964 and 1965, few could remember how it had originated. The first steps toward intervention, certainly, had seemed at the time to be little more than minor events on the periphery of the larger Cold War. American aid to French forces in Indochina before 1954 had been limited and indirect; the nation's involvement with the Diem regime thereafter, while more substantial, seemed for several years no greater than its involvement with many other Third World governments. But as Diem began to face growing internal opposition, and as the threat from the communists to the north appeared to grow, the United States found itself drawn ever deeper into what would ultimately become widely known as the "quagmire."

Ngo Dinh Diem had been an unfortunate choice as the basis of American hopes for a noncommunist Vietnam. Autocratic, aristocratic, and corrupt, he staunchly resisted any economic reforms that would weaken the position of the Vietnamese upper class and the power of his own family. A belligerent Roman Catholic in a nation whose citizens were overwhelmingly Buddhist, he invited dissent through his efforts to limit the influence of Vietnam's traditional religion. By

1958, he was embroiled in an intense civil war in the south. Two years later, that war intensified, as communist guerrillas (or Viet Cong) organized the National Front for the Liberation of South Vietnam (NLF). The NLF had close ties to the government of Ho Chi Minh and, as the war expanded in the following years, received increasing assistance from the north.

Faced with a steadily deteriorating political and military position, Diem appealed to the United States for assistance. The Eisenhower administration increased the flow of weapons and ammunition to South Vietnam during its last years in office and introduced the first few American military advisers to the area—about 650 in all. But it was the Kennedy administration, with its fervent belief in the importance of fighting communism in emerging areas, that expanded that assistance into a major commitment. Despite misgivings about the reliability of Diem, Kennedy substantially increased the flow of munitions into South Vietnam. More important, he raised the number of American military personnel to 15,500.

But the real depth of the American commitment to the war became clear in 1963, when the Diem regime stood on the brink of

American Advisers in Vietnam
The introduction of military "advisers" to train South Vietnamese troops was the first step toward the long and disastrous American involvement in the war in Vietnam. In this photograph, American officers instruct Vietnamese soldiers on how to counter guerrilla warfare. Behind them is one of the American helicopters that were to become the primary means of transport in the conduct of the war. (U.S. Army photo)

collapse. The military struggle against the Viet Cong was going badly. And Diem's brutal tactics in dispersing Buddhist demonstrators in Saigon had produced a religious crisis as well. Several Buddhist monks burned themselves to death in the streets of the capital, arousing further popular resistance to the government and horrifying the American public, which witnessed the immolations on television. Early in November, after receiving tacit assurances of support from the United States, South Vietnamese military leaders seized control of the government from Diem, executing the deposed president, his brother, and other associates. The Americans had not sanctioned the killings, but they had been instrumental in instigating the coup. Faced with what he considered a choice between allowing South Vietnam to fall or expanding the American involvement, John Kennedy had chosen the latter. Before he could indicate what further steps he was prepared to take, he himself fell victim to an assassin on November 22.

From Aid to Intervention

Lyndon Johnson, therefore, inherited what was already a substantial American commitment to the survival of an anticommunist South Vietnam. During his first two years in office, he expanded that commitment into a full-scale American war. Why he did so has long been a subject of debate.

Many factors played a role in Johnson's fateful decision. But the most obvious explanation is that the new president faced many pressures to expand the American involvement and only a very few to limit it. As the untested successor to a revered and martyred president, he felt obliged to prove his worthiness for the office by continuing the policies of his predecessor. Aid to South Vietnam had been one of the most prominent of those policies. Johnson also felt it necessary to retain in his administration many of the important figures of the Kennedy years. In doing so, he surrounded himself with a group of foreign policy advisers—Secretary of State Dean Rusk, Secretary of Defense Robert McNamara, National Security Adviser McGeorge

Bundy—who strongly believed not only that the United States had an important obligation to resist communism in Vietnam, but that it possessed the ability and resources to make that resistance successful. As a result, Johnson seldom had access to information making clear how difficult the new commitment might become. A compliant Congress raised little protest to, and indeed at one point openly endorsed, Johnson's use of executive powers to lead the nation into war. And for several years at least, public opinion remained firmly behind him—in part because Barry Goldwater's bellicose remarks about the war during the 1964 campaign made Johnson seem by comparison to be a moderate on the issue. Above all, intervention in South Vietnam was fully consistent with nearly twenty years of American foreign policy. An anticommunist ally was appealing to the United States for assistance; all the assumptions of the containment doctrine seemed to require the nation to oblige. Johnson seemed unconcerned that the government of South Vietnam existed only because the United States had put it there, and that the regime had never succeeded in acquiring the loyalty of its people. Vietnam, he believed, provided a test of American willingness to fight communist aggression, a test he was determined not to fail.

During his first months in office, Johnson expanded the American involvement in Vietnam only slightly, introducing an additional 5,000 military advisers there and preparing to send 5,000 more. Then, early in August 1964, the president announced that American destroyers on patrol in international waters in the Gulf of Tonkin had been attacked by North Vietnamese torpedo boats. Later information raised serious doubts as to whether the attack had actually occurred or, if it had, whether it had been, as the president insisted, "unprovoked." At the time, however, virtually no one questioned Johnson's portrayal of the incident as a serious act of aggression or his insistence that the United States must respond. By a vote of 416 to 0 in the House and 88 to 2 in the Senate (with only Wayne Morse of Oregon and Ernest Gruening of Alaska dissenting), Congress hurriedly passed the Gulf of Tonkin Resolution, which authorized the president to "take all necessary measures" to protect American forces and "prevent further aggression" in Southeast Asia. The resolution became, in Johnson's view at least, an open-ended legal authorization for escalation of the conflict.

Publicly committed now to the defense of what the United States liked to term an independent, democratic government in the south, the administration had to confront the failure of any faction to establish a stable regime there to replace Diem. With the South Vietnamese leadership in disarray, more and more of the burden of opposition to the Viet Cong fell on the United States. In February 1965, seven Americans died when communist forces attacked a military base at Pleiku. Johnson retaliated by ordering the first United States bombings of the north, attempting to destroy the depots and transportation lines that were responsible for the flow of North Vietnamese soldiers and supplies into South Vietnam. The bombing continued until 1972, even though there was little evidence that it was effective in limiting North Vietnamese assistance to the NLF.

A month later, in March 1965, two battalions of American marines landed at Da Nang in South Vietnam. Although Johnson continued to insist that he was not leading the United States into a "ground war" in Southeast Asia, there were now more than 100,000 American troops in Vietnam. The following July, finally, the president publicly admitted that the character of the war had changed. American soldiers would now, he admitted, begin playing an active role in the conduct of the war. By the end of the year, there were more than 180,000 American combat troops in Vietnam; in 1966, that number doubled; and by the end of 1967, there were nearly 500,000 American soldiers fighting on the ground, while the air war had intensified until the tonnage of bombs dropped ultimately exceeded that in Europe during World War II. Meanwhile, American casualties were mounting. In 1961, 14 Americans had died in Vietnam; in 1963, the toll was 489. By the spring of 1966, more than 4,000 Americans had been killed; and they were continuing to die at a faster rate than soldiers in the ineffective South Vietnamese army.

Yet the gains resulting from the carnage had been negligible. The United States had finally succeeded in 1965 in creating a reasonably stable government in the south under General Nguyen Van Thieu. But the new regime was a corrupt and brutal dictatorship, unable to maintain control over a vast proportion of its own countryside. The Viet Cong, not the Thieu regime, controlled the majority of South Vietnam's villages and hamlets.

The Quagmire

For more than seven years, therefore, American combat forces remained bogged down in a war that the United States was never able either to win or fully to understand. Combating a foe whose strength lay not in weaponry but in a pervasive infiltration of the population, the United States responded with the kind of heavy-handed technological warfare designed for conventional battles against conventional armies. American forces succeeded in winning most of the major battles in which they became engaged, routing the Viet Cong and their North Vietnamese allies from such strongholds as Dak To, Con Thien, and later, Khe Sanh. There were astounding (if not always reliable) casualty figures showing that far more communists than Americans were dying in combat—statistics that the United States military referred to as a "favorable kill ratio." There was a continuing stream of optimistic reports, from American military commanders, civilian officials, and others, that the war was progressing—including the famous words of Secretary of Defense McNamara that he could "see the light at the end of the tunnel." But if the war was not actually being lost, it certainly was not being won. It was, moreover, becoming clear to some observers that it was a war that perhaps could not be won.

At the heart of the problem was the fact that the United States was not fighting an army as much as a popular movement. The Viet Cong derived their strength in part from the aid they received from North Vietnam and, indirectly, from the Soviet Union and China. Far more important, however, was

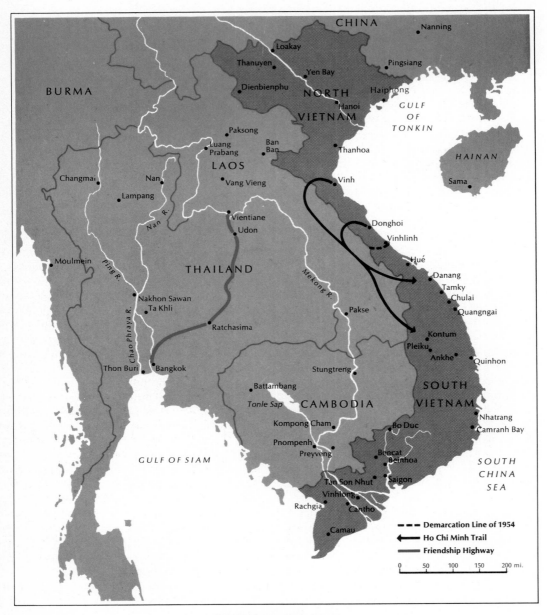

VIETNAM, 1954–1975

their success in mobilizing members of the native population—men, women, and even children—who were indistinguishable from their neighbors and who fought not only openly in major battles, but covertly through sabotage, ambush, and terror. American troops might drive Viet Cong forces from a particular village or city; but as soon as the Americans left, the NLF forces would return. The frustrations of this kind of warfare mounted steadily, until the United States found itself involved in a series of desperate strategies.

Central to the American war effort was

the much-heralded "pacification" program, designed in part by General William Westmoreland, whose purpose was to rout the Viet Cong from particular regions and then "pacify" those regions by winning the "hearts and minds" of the people. Routing the Viet Cong was often possible, but the subsequent pacification was not. American forces were incapable of establishing the same kind of rapport with members of an ancient, provincial culture that the highly nationalistic Viet Cong forces were able to achieve. Gradually, therefore, the pacification program gave way to the more desperate "relocation" strategy. Instead of attempting to win the loyalty of the peasants in areas in which the Viet Cong were operating, American troops would uproot the villagers from their homes, send them fleeing to refugee camps or into the cities (producing by 1967 more than 3 million refugees), and then destroy the vacated villages and surrounding countryside. Saturation bombing, bulldozing of settlements, chemical defoliation of fields and jungles—all were designed to eliminate possible Viet Cong sanctuaries. But the Viet Cong responded simply by moving to new sanctuaries elsewhere. The futility of the United States effort was suggested by the statement of an American officer after flattening one such hamlet that it had been "necessary to destroy the town in order to save it."

As the war dragged on and victory remained elusive, some American officers and officials began to argue that the United States should expand its efforts in Indochina. Some argued for heavier bombing and increased troop strength; others insisted that the United States attack communist enclaves in surrounding countries; a few began to urge the use of nuclear weapons. The Johnson administration, however, resisted. Unwilling to abandon its commitment to South Vietnam for fear of destroying American "credibility" in the world, the government was also unwilling to expand the war too far, for fear of provoking direct intervention by the Chinese, the Soviets, or both. Caught in a trap of his own making, the president began to encounter additional obstacles and frustrations at home.

The War at Home

Few Americans, and even fewer influential ones, had protested the American involvement in Vietnam as late as the end of 1965. But as the war dragged on and its futility began to become apparent, political support for it began to erode. At first, the attack emerged from the perimeters of government: from intellectuals, from students, and from the press. By the end of 1967, the debate over the war had moved fully into the mainstream of national politics.

Many of the earliest objections to the war emerged on college and university campuses. Political scientists, historians, Asian experts, and others began in 1965 to raise questions about both the wisdom and the morality of the Vietnam adventure, arguing that it reflected, among other things, a fundamental American misunderstanding of politics and society in Southeast Asia. A series of "teach-ins" on university campuses, beginning at the University of Michigan in 1965, sparked a national debate over the war, long before such debate developed inside the government. By the end of 1967, American students opposed to the war had grown so numerous and so vocal as to form a major political force. Enormous peace marches in New York, Washington, D.C., and other cities drew increasing public attention to the antiwar movement. Campus demonstrations occurred almost daily. A growing number of journalists, particularly reporters who had spent time in Vietnam, helped sustain the movement with their frank revelations about the brutality and futility of the war.

The chorus of popular protest soon began to stimulate opposition to the war from within the government itself. Senator J. William Fulbright of Arkansas, chairman of the powerful Senate Foreign Relations Committee, became one of the earliest influential public figures to turn against the war. Beginning in January 1966, he began to stage highly publicized and occasionally televised congressional hearings to air criticisms of the war, summoning as witnesses such distinguished public figures as George F. Kennan and General James Gavin. Other prominent members of Congress joined Fulbright in op-

The Debate on Vietnam: The Opposition [1965]

A great debate on the Vietnamese conflict is now raging all over the United States. It goes from the White House, Congress and the Pentagon to every home, office, factory, and farm. It is unresolved because the Government has not yet decided on its policy or, if it has, President Johnson is not telling the American people. The debate's subject, in its simplest form, is whether to fight a big war in Vietnam or to seek a way out through a combination of continuing defense and diplomatic negotiation.

The case for a vastly stepped-up American military commitment—as set forth . . . by military analyst Hanson W. Baldwin—is that the "Communist strategy of creeping aggression" must be stopped in Vietnam before it swallows all of Asia and the world. Under this theory, the United States should undertake saturation bombing of North Vietnam and send as many as a million American soldiers, sailors and fliers into a "war to win."

Such an approach discards any pretense that our objective in Vietnam is to protect the Vietnamese people; it turns the conflict into a naked ideological struggle that ignores all the deep cleavages recent years have brought in both the Communist and free worlds. Not one of our major allies in the West could be expected to endorse, much less actively assist, an American involvement so massive it would amount to a military occupation of leaderless South Vietnam. America's efforts to demonstrate the superiority of its social system by abolishing poverty and building a Great Society would vanish under the necessity for pouring our youth and treasure into a limitless solo adventure.—*The New York Times*, February 21, 1965.

The Debate on Vietnam: The Defense [1965]

Speaking at the Johns Hopkins University on April 7, 1965, shortly after deciding to send combat troops to South Vietnam, President Johnson said that the "deepening shadow of Communist China" was falling over Asia and that the trouble in Vietnam was "part of a wider pattern of aggressive purpose." He continued:

Why are we in South Vietnam?

We are there because we have a promise to keep. Since 1954 every American President has offered to support the people of South Vietnam. We have helped to build and we have helped to defend. Thus, over many years, we have made a national pledge to help South Vietnam defend its independence.

I intend to keep our promise.

To dishonor that pledge, to abandon this small and brave nation to its enemy—and to the terror that must follow—would be an unforgivable wrong.

We are there to strengthen world order. Around the globe—from Berlin to Thailand—are people whose well-being rests, in part, on the belief they can count on us if they are attacked. To leave Vietnam to its fate would shake the confidence of all these people in the value of American commitment. The result would be increased unrest and instability, or even war.

posing Johnson's policies—including, in 1967, Robert F. Kennedy, brother of the slain president, then a senator from New York. Even within the administration, the consensus seemed to be crumbling. Secretary of State Rusk remained a true believer until the end; but McGeorge Bundy and Robert McNamara, both of whom had used their political and intellectual talents brilliantly (if dubiously) to extend the American involvement in Vietnam, quietly left the government in 1967 and 1968. Bundy's successor, Walt W. Rostow, was if anything even more committed to the war than his predecessor and one-time mentor. But the new secretary of defense, Clark Clifford, became a powerful voice within the administration on behalf of a cautious scaling down of the commitment.

Other factors weakened the position of supporters of the war as well. America's most important allies—Great Britain, France, West Germany, and Japan—all began to criticize the Vietnam involvement. Of more immediate concern, the American economy was beginning to suffer. Johnson's commitment to fighting the war while continuing his Great Society reforms—his promise of "guns and butter"—proved impossible to maintain. The inflation rate, which had remained at 2 percent through most of the early 1960s, rose to 3 percent in 1967, 4 percent in 1968, and 6 percent in 1969. In August 1967, President Johnson asked Congress for a tax increase—a 10 percent surcharge that was widely labeled a "war tax"—which he knew was necessary if the nation was to avoid even more ruinous inflation. In return, congressional conservatives demanded and received a $6 billion reduction in the funding for Great Society programs. The war in Vietnam, in other words, was now not only a source of concern for its own sake. It had also become a direct threat to liberal efforts to redress social injustices at home.

THE TRAUMAS OF 1968

By the end of 1967, the twin crises of the war in Vietnam and the deteriorating racial situation at home, crises that fed upon and exaggerated each other, had helped to create deep social tensions in America. In the course of 1968, those tensions seemed suddenly to burst to the surface and threaten national chaos. Not since World War II had the United States experienced so profound a sense of crisis. Perhaps never before in its history had the nation suffered as many traumatic shocks in such short order.

The Tet Offensive

On January 31, 1968, the first day of the Vietnamese New Year (Tet), Viet Cong forces launched an enormous, concerted attack on American strongholds throughout South Vietnam. The attack displayed a strength that American commanders had long insisted the Viet Cong did not possess. Some major cities, most notably Hue, fell to the communists. Others suffered major disruptions. But what made the Tet offensive genuinely shocking to the American people, who saw vivid reports of it on television, was what happened in Saigon. If any place in South Vietnam had seemed secure from enemy attack, it was the capital city. Now, suddenly, Viet Cong forces were in the heart of Saigon, setting off bombs, shooting down South Vietnamese officials and troops, and holding down fortified areas.

Even more chilling was the evidence the Tet offensive gave of the brutality of the fighting in Vietnam, of the savagery it seemed to have aroused in those who became involved in it. In the midst of the Tet offensive, television cameras recorded the sight of a captured Viet Cong guerrilla being led up to a South Vietnamese officer in the streets of Saigon. Without a word, the officer pulled out his pistol and shot the young guerrilla through the head, leaving him lying dead with his blood pouring onto the street. No single event did more to undermine support in the United States for the war. That American forces soon dislodged the Viet Cong from most of the positions they had seized, and that the Tet offensive in the end cost the communists such appalling casualties that they were significantly weakened for months to come, had little impact on American opinion.

In the weeks that followed, many of the pillars of American public opinion finally began to move into opposition to the war. Leading newspapers began taking editorial stands in favor of deescalation of the conflict. *Time* and *Newsweek* began running searing exposés and urging American withdrawal. Network commentators began voicing open doubts about the wisdom of American policies. Within weeks of the Tet offensive, public opposition to the war had almost doubled. And Johnson's personal popularity had slid to 35 percent, the lowest of any president since the darkest days of the Truman administration.

The Political Challenge

As early as the summer of 1967, dissident Democrats had been attempting to mobilize support behind an antiwar candidate who would challenge Lyndon Johnson in the 1968 primaries. For many months, they tried to enlist Senator Robert Kennedy, the most widely known critic of the war. But mindful of the difficulties in challenging an incumbent president, Kennedy declined. In his stead, the dissidents recruited Senator Eugene McCarthy of Minnesota, a subdued, cerebral candidate who avoided heated rhetoric in favor of carefully reasoned argument and attracted a particularly devoted following among college students. A brilliantly orchestrated campaign by young volunteers in the New Hampshire primary produced a startling triumph for McCarthy in March; he came within 1 percentage point of outpolling the president.

A few days later, Robert Kennedy finally entered the campaign, deeply embittering many of those who had dedicated themselves to the cause of McCarthy, but bringing his own substantial strength among blacks, poor people, and workers to the antiwar cause. Polls showed the president trailing badly in the next scheduled primary, in Wisconsin. Public animosity toward Johnson was such that he did not dare venture from the White House to campaign. On March 31, Johnson went on television to announce a limited halt in the bombing of North Vietnam—his first major concession to the antiwar forces—and, far more surprising, his withdrawal from the presidential contest.

For a moment, it seemed as though the antiwar forces had won—that nothing could stop them from seizing the Democratic presidential nomination and even the presidency itself. Robert Kennedy quickly established himself as the champion of the Democratic primaries, winning one election after another. In the meantime, however, Vice President Hubert Humphrey, with the support of President Johnson, entered the contest and began to attract the support of party leaders and of the many delegations that were selected not by popular primaries but by state party organizations. He soon appeared to be the front runner in the race.

The King Assassination

In the midst of this bitter political battle, in which the war had been the dominant issue, the attention of the nation suddenly turned again to the matter of race in response to a shocking tragedy. On April 4, Martin Luther King, Jr., who had traveled to Memphis, Tennessee, to lend his support to a strike by black sanitation workers in the city, was shot and killed while standing on the balcony of his motel. The assassin, James Earl Ray, who was captured days later in London, had no apparent motive. Speculation was rampant that he had been hired by others to do the killing, but if so he never revealed the identity of his employers.

The tragic death of King, who had remained the most widely admired black leader among both blacks and whites, deeply affected Americans of all races, producing an outpouring of grief matched in recent memory only by the reaction to the death of John Kennedy. Among blacks, however, it also produced widespread anger. In the days after the assassination, major riots broke out in more than sixty American cities. Forty-three people died; more than 3,000 suffered injuries; as many as 27,000 people were arrested. No one of these riots was as intense as some earlier uprisings, but together the disorders were the greatest manifestation of racial unrest in the nation's history.

The Kennedy Assassination and Chicago

Robert Kennedy continued his campaign for the presidential nomination. Late in the night of June 6, he appeared in the ballroom of a Los Angeles hotel to acknowledge the cheers of his supporters for his victory in that day's California primary. Waiting for him in a nearby corridor, in the meantime, was Sirhan Sirhan, a young Palestinian who had become enraged, apparently, by pro-Israeli remarks Kennedy had made several days earlier in a televised debate with Eugene McCarthy. As Kennedy was leaving the ballroom after his victory statement, Sirhan emerged from a crowd and shot him in the head. Early the next morning, Kennedy died. In reality, he had been the victim of a single, apparently crazed individual. But to much of the nation, stunned and bewildered by yet another public tragedy, Kennedy seemed to have been a victim of national social chaos.

The presidential campaign continued desultorily during the last weeks before the convention. Hubert Humphrey, who had seemed likely to win the nomination even before Robert Kennedy's death, now faced only minor opposition. Despite the embittered claims of many Democrats that Humphrey would simply continue the bankrupt policies of the Johnson administration, there seemed no possibility of stopping him. The approaching Democratic Convention, therefore, began to take on the appearance of an exercise in futility; and antiwar activists, despairing of winning any victories within the convention, began to plan major demonstrations outside it.

When the Democrats finally gathered in Chicago in August, even the most optimistic observers were predicting a turbulent convention. Inside the hall, carefully sealed off from all demonstrators by Mayor Richard Daley, delegates engaged in a long, bitter debate over an antiwar plank that both Kennedy and McCarthy supporters wanted to insert in the platform. Miles away, in a downtown park, thousands of students and other antiwar protesters had set up camps and were staging demonstrations. On the third night of the convention, as the delegates were beginning their balloting on the now

Chicago, 1968
Helmeted Chicago police charge antiwar demonstrators in Grant Park during the 1968 Democratic Convention. Despite the efforts of Mayor Richard J. Daley to limit television coverage of the confrontations, the networks carried extensive pictures of the violence. Aware of the cameras, many of the demonstrators defiantly chanted, "The whole world is watching!" (UPI)

virtually inevitable nomination of Hubert Humphrey, demonstrators and police clashed in a bloody riot in the streets of Chicago. Miraculously, no one was killed; but hundreds of protesters were injured as police attempted to disperse them with tear gas and billy clubs. Aware that the violence was being televised to the nation, the demonstrators taunted the authorities with the chant, "The whole world is watching!" And Hubert Humphrey, who had spent years dreaming of becoming his party's candidate for president, received a nomination that night that appeared at the time to be almost worthless.

The Conservative Response

The turbulent events of 1968 persuaded many observers that American society was on the verge of a fundamental social upheaval. Newspapers, magazines, the press— all helped create the impression of a nation in the throes of revolutionary change. In fact, however, the prevailing response of the American people to the turmoil was a conservative one.

The most visible sign of the conservative "backlash" was the surprising success of the campaign of George Wallace for the presidency. Wallace had established himself in 1963 as one of the leading spokesmen for the defense of segregation when, as governor of Alabama, he had attempted to block the admission of black students to the University of Alabama. In 1968, he became a third-party candidate for president, basing his campaign on a host of conservative grievances. Although he tempered some of his earlier positions on the race issue, he continued to appeal to those who resented the intrusion of the federal government into local affairs. He denounced the forced busing of students, the proliferation of government regulations and social programs, and the permissiveness of authorities toward race riots and antiwar demonstrations. He chose as his running mate retired Air Force General Curtis LeMay, a bellicose advocate of expanding the war in Vietnam. There was never any serious chance that Wallace would win the election; but his remarkable standing in the polls over many months—rising at times to over 20

George Wallace
Analysts were hard put to explain the remarkable popularity of Governor George C. Wallace, who ran an effective, even if ultimately unsuccessful, third-party campaign for the presidency in 1968. Some believed his appeal rested almost entirely on white resentment of the civil-rights movement; but it was clear that he was also tapping a wide range of frustrations growing out of the social and political instability of the 1960s. Whatever the reasons, Wallace provided powerful evidence of the depths of popular resentment of the liberal state. (UPI)

percent of those interviewed—was a clear indication that he had struck a responsive chord.

A far more skillful effort to mobilize the "silent majority" in favor of order and stability was under way within the Republican party. Richard Nixon, whose political career had seemed at an end after his losses in the presidential race of 1960 and in a California gubernatorial campaign two years later, reemerged as the preeminent spokesman for

"Middle America." Although he avoided the crudeness and stridency of the Wallace campaign, he skillfully exploited many of the same concerns that were sustaining the Alabama governor. Nixon was far more perceptive than other leaders of public opinion in realizing that many Americans were now tired of hearing about their obligations to the poor, tired of hearing about the sacrifices necessary to achieve racial justice, tired of reforms that seemed designed to help criminals. By offering a vision of stability, law and order, government retrenchment, and "peace with honor" in Vietnam, he easily captured the nomination of his party for the presidency. And after the spectacle of the Democratic Convention, he and his running mate, Governor Spiro Agnew of Maryland, enjoyed a commanding lead in the polls as the November election approached.

That lead diminished greatly in the last weeks before the voting. Old doubts about Nixon's character, doubts based in part on the often vicious anticommunism of his ear-

lier career, continued to haunt the Republican candidate. A skillful last-minute surge by Hubert Humphrey, who somehow managed to restore at least a tenuous unity to the Democratic party, narrowed the gap further. And the continuing appeal of George Wallace appeared to be hurting the Republicans more than the Democrats. In the end, however, Nixon eked out a victory almost as narrow as his defeat in 1960. He received 43.4 percent of the popular vote to Humphrey's 42.7 percent (a margin of only about 500,000 votes), and 301 electoral votes to Humphrey's 219. George Wallace, who like most third-party candidates faded in the last weeks of the campaign, still managed to poll 13.5 percent of the popular vote and to carry five Southern states with a total of 46 electoral ballots. Nixon had hardly won a decisive mandate. But the election had made one thing clear. The majority of the American people were more interested in the restoration of stability than in fundamental social change.

THE ELECTION OF 1968

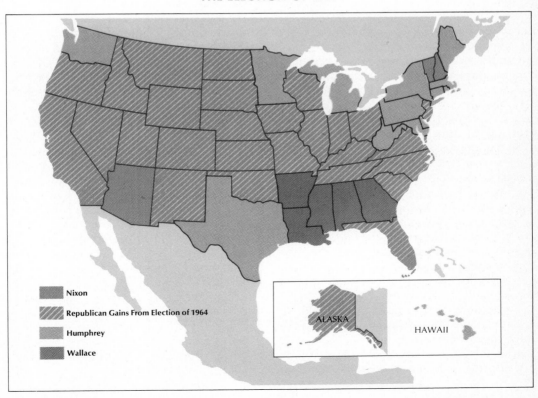

Nixon

Republican Gains From Election of 1964

Humphrey

Wallace

ALASKA

HAWAII

THE TURBULENT SOCIETY

The conservative reaction was a response not only to the political turmoil of the 1960s, but to the social and cultural changes that accompanied it. The political crises and the cultural transformations were not unrelated. Indeed, in some respects they were almost indistinguishable from one another, for few eras in American history have seen the nation's culture so pervasively politicized.

The New Left

Among the products of the civil-rights movement and the war in Vietnam was a radicalization of many American students, who in the course of the 1960s formed what became known as the New Left. The New Left emerged from many things, but from nothing so much as the civil-rights movement, in which many idealistic young Americans had become involved in the early 1960s. Exposed as a result to evidence of social injustice, enraged by the violence and racism they encountered at the hands of segregationists and others, some civil-rights activists were by the mid-1960s beginning to consider far more radical political commitments than they once had embraced. As early as 1962, a group of students gathered in Michigan, formed an organization, Students for a Democratic Society (SDS), and issued a creed, the Port Huron Statement, which signaled much of what was to come. "Many of us began maturing in complacency," the statement (most of it the work of student activist Tom Hayden) declared. "As we grew, however, our comfort was penetrated by events too troubling to dismiss." In the following years, as the racial crisis grew more intense and as the war in Vietnam expanded, members of SDS became even more troubled, expanding the scope of their demands and the range of their activities until they had become the cutting edge of student radicalism.

For a time, that radicalism centered on issues related to the modern university, with which most members of the New Left were associated. A 1964 dispute at the University of California at Berkeley over the rights of students to distribute political leaflets on campus was the first outburst of nearly a decade of campus turmoil. The tumultuous Berkeley Free Speech Movement soon moved beyond the immediate issue of pamphlet distribution and produced far more fundamental protests against the depersonalized nature of the modern "multiversity" and against the role of educational institutions in sustaining corrupt or immoral public policies. The antiwar movement greatly inflamed and expanded the challenge to the universities; and beginning in 1968, campus demonstrations, riots, and building seizures became almost commonplace. At Columbia University in New York, students seized the offices of the president and other members of the administration, occupying them for days until local police forcibly ejected them. At Harvard University a year later, the seizure of administrative offices resulted in an even more violent confrontation with police. Over the next several years, hardly any major university was immune to some level of disruption from radicals and activists among its own student body. Occasionally, there were more serious episodes. Small groups of particularly fervent radicals—most notably the "Weathermen," an offshoot of SDS—were responsible for instances of arson and bombing that destroyed some campus buildings and claimed several lives.

The New Left never succeeded in attracting the support of more than a few students to its most radical tactics and demands. It succeeded brilliantly, however, in elevating the antiwar movement to a major national crusade. Among other things, student activists were instrumental in organizing some of the largest political demonstrations in American history to protest the war in Vietnam. The march on the Pentagon of October 1967, where demonstrators were met by a solid line of armed troops; the "Spring Mobilization" of April 1968, which attracted hundreds of thousands of demonstrators in cities around the country; the Vietnam "Moratorium" of the fall of 1969, during which millions of opponents of the war gathered in major rallies across the nation; and countless other demonstrations, large and small—all helped thrust the issue of the war into the center of America's politics.

Closely related to opposition to the war—and another issue that helped to fuel the New Left—was opposition to military conscription. The government had relied on the draft to staff its peacetime army since the early 1950s, generally without controversy. But when in the 1960s draftees began to be called on to fight in a stalemated, unpopular war, dissent grew quickly. The gradual abolition of many traditional deferments—for students, teachers, husbands, fathers, and others—swelled the ranks of those faced with conscription (and thus likely to oppose it). And the high-handed and often illegal manner in which the draft was being administered by General Lewis Hershey spawned even greater bitterness. The shadow of the draft—the possibility of actually being compelled to join a despised military and fight in a hated war—loomed large over an entire generation of American youth. Draft card burnings became common features of antiwar rallies on college campuses. Many draft-age Americans simply refused induction, accepting what were occasionally long terms in jail as a result. Thousands of others fled to Canada, Sweden, and elsewhere (where they were joined by many deserters from the armed forces) to escape conscription, even though they realized it might be years before they could return home without facing prosecution. Not until 1977, when President Jimmy Carter issued a general pardon to draft resisters and a far more limited pardon to deserters, did the Vietnam exiles begin to return to the country in substantial numbers.

The Counterculture

Closely allied to the emergence of the New Left was the growth of a new youth culture openly scornful of the values and conventions of middle-class society. The most visible characteristic of the counterculture, as it became known, and the one that seemed to have the widest influence, was a change in life style. As if to display their contempt for conventional standards, young Americans flaunted long hair, shabby or flamboyant clothing, and a rebellious disdain for traditional speech and decorum. Central to the counterculture were drugs: marijuana smoking—which from 1966 began to become as common a youthful diversion as beer drinking had once been—and the use of other, more potent hallucinogens, such as LSD. There was as well among members of the counterculture a new and more permissive view of sex.

It was these open challenges to traditional life styles that parents and others found most disturbing about the counterculture; and there was a temptation among many in the older generation to dismiss such youths simply as iconoclasts and hedonists. That was no doubt true of many. But the counterculture also encompassed a clear philosophy, one that offered a far more fundamental challenge to the American mainstream than the changes in appearance and social behavior. Like the New Left, with which it was often closely allied, the counterculture challenged the very structure of modern American society, attacking its banality, its hollowness, its artificiality, its isolation from nature.

The most committed adherents of the counterculture—the so-called hippies, who came to dominate the Haight-Ashbury neighborhood of San Francisco and whose influence spread to many other areas, and the "drop-outs," who retreated to rural communes in Colorado, New Hampshire, and elsewhere—rejected modern society altogether and attempted to find refuge in a simpler, more natural existence. But even those whose commitment to the counterculture was less dramatic shared a pervasive commitment to the idea of personal fulfillment. Such popular phrases as "Do your own thing" and "If it feels good, do it," which became banalized through repetition over time, nevertheless seemed to capture much of the spirit of the counterculture. In a corrupt and alienating society, the new creed seemed to suggest, the first responsibility of the individual is cultivation of the self, the unleashing of one's own full potential for pleasure and fulfillment.

Theodore Roszak, whose book *The Mak-*

ing of a Counter Culture (1969) became a central document of the era, captured much of the spirit of the movement in his frank admission that "the primary project of our counter culture is to proclaim a new heaven and a new earth so vast, so marvelous that the inordinate claims of technical expertise must of necessity withdraw to a subordinate and marginal status in the lives of men." Charles Reich, in *The Greening of America* (1970), was even more explicit, arguing that the individual should strive for a new form of consciousness—"Consciousness III," as he called it—in which the self would be the only reality.

The effects of the counterculture were not restricted to rebellious youths. They reached out as well to the society at large and provided a set of social norms that many young people (and some adults) chose to imitate. Long hair and freakish clothing became the badge not only of hippies and radicals but of an entire generation. The use of marijuana, the freer attitudes toward sex, the iconoclastic (and often obscene) language: all spread far beyond the realm of the true devotees of the counterculture. And perhaps the most pervasive element of the new youth society was one that even the least radical members of the generation embraced: rock music.

Rock-'n'-roll had first achieved wide popularity in the 1950s, on the strength of such early performers as Buddy Holly and, above all, Elvis Presley. Early in the 1960s, its influence began to spread, a result in large part of the phenomenal popularity of the Beatles, whose music was first heard in the United States in 1964. For a time, most rock musicians—like most popular musicians before them—concentrated largely on uncontroversial romantic themes. But rock's driving rhythms, its undisguised sensuality, its often harsh and angry tone—all made it an appropriate vehicle for expressing the themes of social and political unrest of the late 1960s. By the end of the decade, therefore, rock had begun to reflect many of the new iconoclastic values of its time. Once again, the Beatles helped lead the way by abandoning their once simple and seemingly innocent style for a new, experimental, even mystical approach that reflected the growing popular fascination with drugs and Eastern religions. Others, such as Bob Dylan and the Rolling Stones, turned even more openly to themes of anger, frustration, and rebelliousness. Many popular musicians used their music to express explicit political radicalism as well.

Even those Americans who had no interest in rock music or other aspects of the counterculture could not avoid evidence of how rapidly the norms of their society were changing. Those who attended movies saw a gradual disappearance of the banal, conventional messages that had dominated films since the 1920s. Instead, they saw explorations of political issues, of new sexual mores, of violence, of social conflict. And the most influential entertainment medium of all, television, began similarly to turn away from its evocation of the stable, middle-class, suburban family. Beginning in the early 1970s, it started to offer programming imbued with social conflict—as exemplified by the enormously popular *All in the Family*, whose hero, Archie Bunker, was a lower-middle-class bigot.

Indian Militancy

The 1960s saw the emergence as well of powerful "liberation" movements among racial, ethnic, and other minority groups. The emergence of black self-awareness and black political power was, of course, the most obvious manifestation of the new spirit. But other groups, too, became engaged in a search for liberation.

Few minorities had deeper or more justifiable grievances against the prevailing culture than American Indians—or Native Americans, as they began to call themselves in the 1960s. Ever since the 1890s, Indians had lived in unalleviated poverty as wards of the federal government, which subjected them to a series of fluctuating and often brutal policies. By the 1960s, not only had the Indian population grown much faster than that of the rest of the nation (nearly doubling between 1950 and 1970 to a total of about 800,000), but Indians had established themselves as the least prosperous, least healthy, and least stable group in the society. Annual family income for Indians was $1,000 less than that for blacks. The Native American unemployment rate was ten times the national rate; joblessness was particularly high on the reservations, where nearly half the Indians lived and where few industries or other sources of employment existed. Life expectancy was more than twenty years lower than the national average. Suicides among Indian youths were a hundred times more frequent than among white youths. And while black Americans attracted the attention (for good or for ill) of many whites, Indians remained all but totally ignored.

Although the Kennedy administration attempted to restore government support for tribal autonomy—a policy maintained by succeeding administrations as well—Indian grievances were, like the grievances of other minorities, soon receiving open expression. In 1961, more than 400 members of 67 tribes gathered in Chicago to discuss ways of bringing all Indians together in an effort to redress common wrongs. The manifesto they issued, the Declaration of Indian Purpose, reflected the same impulse toward cultural liberation that other segments of the population would soon adopt. It stressed the "right to choose our own way of life" and the "responsibility of preserving our precious heritage." In succeeding years, younger and more militant Indians formed their own organizations—modeled on the new black-power groups—of which the most prominent was the American Indian Movement (AIM), established in 1968 and drawing its greatest support from those Indians who lived in urban areas. The new activism succeeded in winning some attention from the government to the plight of the tribes. Congress included Indians in the benefits of the Economic Opportunity Act; and Lyndon Johnson promised in 1968 a "new goal" for Indian programs that "stresses self-determination" and "erases old attitudes of paternalism." The results, however, were negligible.

Leaders of AIM and other insurgent groups soon turned instead to direct action. In 1968, Indian fishermen, seeking to exercise old treaty rights on the Columbia River and in Puget Sound, clashed with officials of the state of Washington. The following year,

members of several tribes occupied the abandoned federal prison on Alcatraz Island in San Francisco Bay, claiming the site "by right of discovery." In response to the growing pressure, the new Nixon administration appointed a Mohawk-Sioux to the position of Commissioner of Indian Affairs in 1969; and in 1970, the president promised both increased tribal self-determination and an increase in federal aid. The promises were not fulfilled.

Indian frustration finally produced the most forceful protests in decades in the winter of 1972–1973. In November 1972, nearly one thousand protesters forcibly occupied the building of the Bureau of Indian Affairs in Washington for six days. The most celebrated protest occurred later that winter at Wounded Knee, South Dakota, the site of the 1890 massacre of Sioux Indians by federal troops. In the early 1970s, Wounded Knee was part of a vast Sioux reservation, two-thirds of which was in the control of white ranchers. Conditions for the Indian residents were desperate and alone might have been sufficient to spark resistance. Passions among younger and more militant tribal members were aroused further after the 1972 murder of a Sioux by a group of whites, who were not, many Indians believed, adequately punished. In February 1973, members of AIM seized and occupied for two months the town of Wounded Knee, demanding radical changes in the administration of the reservation and insisting that the government honor its long-forgotten treaty obligations. A brief clash between the occupiers and federal forces left one Indian dead and another wounded. Shortly thereafter the siege came to an end.

Far more effective than these militant protests were the victories that various tribes were achieving in the 1970s in a wave of lawsuits in the federal courts. Citing violations by the federal government of ancient treaty obligations, Native Americans began winning judicial approval of their demands for restitution. Beginning with a case in Alaska in 1969, the legal actions spread quickly across the country, establishing a possible basis for a major change in the economic status of many tribes.

Hispanic Americans

Far more numerous and far more visible than the Indian minority were Hispanic Americans, the fastest-growing minority group in the nation. In 1960, Hispanics had numbered only slightly over 3 million; in 1970, they had increased to more than 9 million; by 1980, most estimates placed their numbers at nearly 20 million, making them the second largest minority (after blacks) in the country. They were also among the poorest.

Hispanics were not, of course, a single, undifferentiated group. There were large numbers of people of Puerto Rican background, concentrated in New York City. A substantial Cuban population was settled in Florida, largely the result of a wave of middle-class refugees who had fled the Castro regime in the early 1960s. (A second flood, of poorer immigrants, arrived in 1980, when Castro temporarily lifted exit restrictions.) The most numerous group—Mexican-Americans—lived in California, Texas, and other states of the Southwest. An uncounted number of them, as many as 7 million according to some estimates, were illegal immigrants (*mojados*, or "wetbacks"). Others were temporary migrant workers (*braceros*). Many, however, were descendants of families who had been living in Mexican territory when it was incorporated into the United States in the nineteenth century.

Like blacks and Indians, Hispanic Americans responded to the highly charged climate of the 1960s by developing their own sense of ethnic identification and by organizing for political and economic power. Their successes were impressive. Affluent Hispanics became an important force in Miami, where they operated major businesses and filled influential positions in the professions; in Los Angeles, where they organized as an influential political group; and in the Southwest, where they elected Mexican-Americans to seats in Congress and to several governorships.

For the majority of Hispanics, however, the path to economic and political power was more arduous. In New York, Puerto Rican immigrants were crammed into the city's worst slums, including the notorious South Bronx, which became in the 1970s a national symbol of urban decay. In other cities, Hispanics suffered economic deprivation and overt discrimination; in many areas, they became involved in bitter and violent rivalries with blacks.

One Hispanic group, at least, brought the power of organization and political action strongly to bear against problems of poverty and oppression. In California, an Arizona-born Mexican-American farm worker, César Chávez, succeeded where generations of migrants before him had tried and failed: he created an effective union of itinerant farm workers. His United Farm Workers (UFW), a largely Hispanic organization, launched a prolonged strike in 1965 against growers to demand, first, recognition of their union and, second, increased wages and benefits. When employers resisted, Chávez enlisted the cooperation of college students, churches, and civil-rights groups (including CORE and SNCC) and organized a nationwide boycott, first of table grapes and then of lettuce. In 1968, Chávez campaigned openly for Robert Kennedy, bringing his farm workers into the coalition of the dispossessed that the senator was attempting to establish and, more important, winning national recognition of the UFW's cause. Two years later, Chávez won a substantial victory when the growers of half of California's table grapes signed contracts with his union. In the ensuing years, his union suffered less from the opposition of growers than from competition with the powerful Teamsters Union, which attempted to entice farm workers into its own vast labor network.

Hispanic Americans also became the focus of another dispute that was to prove divisive in the 1970s: the issue of bilingualism. It was a question that aroused the opposition not only of many whites but of some Hispanics as well. Supporters of bilingualism in education argued that Spanish-speaking Americans were entitled to schooling in their own language, that only thus could they achieve an equal footing with English-speaking students. Opponents cited not only the cost and difficulty of bilingualism but the dangers it posed to the ability of Spanish-speaking students to become assimilated into

César Chávez
Evident in this picture is the magnetism of César Chávez, the labor organizer who rose to be an outstanding hero of Mexican-Americans in the 1960s. He is shown talking with grape workers at a California vineyard. (Paul Fusco from Magnum)

the mainstream of American culture. Even many Hispanics feared that bilingualism would isolate their communities further from the rest of America and increase resentments toward the minority.

The New Feminism

American women in the 1960s were hardly a minority. They constituted 51 percent of the population. In the course of the decade, however, many women began to identify with members of other oppressed groups and to demand a liberation of their own. Sexual discrimination was so deeply embedded in the fabric of society that when feminists first began to denounce it, many Americans responded with bafflement and anger. By the 1970s, however, public awareness of the issue had increased dramatically; and the role of women in American life had changed

more radically than that of any other group in the nation.

Betty Friedan's book *The Feminine Mystique* (1963) is often cited as the first major document of contemporary women's liberation. A sharp denunciation of the position of the suburban housewife and of the "comfortable concentration camp" of the suburban home, it attacked traditional views of women's proper role, arguing that for many women, being a housewife and mother was not sufficiently rewarding to provide a sense of fulfillment. Three years later, Friedan joined with other feminists to create the National Organization for Women (NOW), which was to become the nation's largest and most influential feminist organization. "The time has come," the founders of NOW maintained, "to confront with concrete action the conditions which now prevent women from enjoying the equality of opportunity and freedom of choice which is their right as individual Americans and as human beings." Like other movements for liberation, feminism drew much of its inspiration from the black struggle for freedom. "There is no civil rights movement to speak for women," the NOW organizers claimed, "as there has been for Negroes and other victims of discrimination."

The complaints of the feminists were many. They were, they argued, barred from educational institutions, from professions, from politics, and from countless other areas of American life because of ancient male prejudices about the proper role of women. They faced innumerable forms of legal and economic discrimination, including the widespread practice of paying women less than men even when they were doing equal work. Underlying all these problems were male assumptions that women were somehow intellectually and emotionally unfit for male occupations, that their biologically determined role was to serve as wives and mothers.

By the late 1960s, such resentments had attracted a large following among middleclass women, and the feminist movement had gained substantial strength. Already, women had won important new legal protections and substantial economic and political advances. In 1964, for example, Congress in-

corporated into the Civil Rights Act an amendment—Title VII—that extended to women the protection of the law in the struggle against discrimination. It had been introduced as a joke by Southern Democrats attempting to discredit the entire civil-rights package; but it survived the legislative debate and became the basis for a major federal assault on sexual discrimination in later years. In 1971, the government extended its Affirmative Action guidelines to include women—linking sexism with racism as an officially acknowledged social problem.

Women were making rapid progress, in the meantime, in their efforts to move into the economic and political mainstream. The nation's major educational institutions began in the late 1960s to open their doors to women for the first time. Princeton and Yale, two of the most prestigious all-male colleges, accepted women undergraduates in 1969. Within a few years, all but a few major academic institutions had done the same. Many women's colleges, in the meantime, began accepting male students. Women were becoming an important force in business and in the professions. Nearly half of all married women held jobs by the mid-1970s, and almost nine-tenths of all women with college degrees worked. Two-career families, in

Feminists in New York, 1970
The movement on behalf of women's rights emerged somewhat later than some of the other liberation movements of the 1960s, but it had an impact at least equal to any of the others. By the time of this demonstration in 1970, the cause of feminism had become deeply embedded in the national consciousness—and it had begun to produce a powerful counterreaction.
(© Harvey Stein)

which both the husband and the wife maintained active professional lives, were becoming a widely accepted norm. So were such symbolic changes as the refusal of many women to adopt their husbands' names when they married, and the use of the term "Ms." in place of "Mrs." or "Miss"—the latter change intended to denote the irrelevance of a woman's marital status in the professional world.

Women were also advancing in some of the most visible areas of American life. In politics, they were by the early 1970s beginning to compete effectively with men for both elected and appointive positions. In 1980, two women won seats in the United States Senate—both elected in their own right rather than, like all woman senators before them, to succeed their husbands. A substantial number of women served in the United States House of Representatives throughout the 1970s, and two won election to state governorships. The number of female appointments in the executive branch rose steadily; two women held cabinet positions in the Carter administration. And the first female justice of the Supreme Court—Sandra Day O'Connor—took her seat in 1981.

In professional athletics, in the meantime, women were beginning to compete with men both for attention and for an equal share of prize money. Billie Jean King spearheaded the most effective female challenge to male domination of sports. Under her leadership, professional women tennis players established their own, successful tours and demanded equal financial incentives when they played in the same tournaments as men. By the late 1970s, the federal government was pressuring colleges and universities to provide women with athletic programs equal to those available to men.

Of all the feminist crusades of the 1960s and 1970s, none united more women from more different backgrounds than the campaign for passage of the Equal Rights Amendment (ERA) to the Constitution. Congress approved the amendment in 1972 and sent it to the states; and for a while it seemed that eventual ratification was only a matter of time. By the end of the 1970s, however, the

momentum behind the amendment had died. Approval of the ERA remained several states short of the three-quarters necessary for enactment; and some state legislatures that had earlier voted in favor were trying to rescind their approval. In 1979, Congress granted a three-year extension of the time permitted for ratification. Far more indicative of public sentiment on the issue, however, was the rising chorus of objections to the amendment from those who feared that it would create a major disruption of traditional social patterns. In 1980, the Republican party—after forty years of support for the idea of the ERA—wrote into its platform a new plank opposing the amendment. And two years later, the amendment finally died when the time allotted for ratification expired. The Equal Rights Amendment had been the central demand of American feminism since it was first proposed in 1923. In 1982, it was a hope still far from realization.

Another vital element of the women's movement since the 1920s had been the effort to win for women greater control of their own physical and sexual lives. In its least controversial form, this impulse helped produce an increasing awareness in the 1960s and 1970s of the problems of rape, sexual abuse, and wife beating. Far more divisive, however, was the desire of many women to control their reproductive function in new ways. There continued to be some controversy over the dissemination of contraceptives and birth-control information; but that issue, at least, seemed to have lost much of the explosive character it had possessed in the 1920s, when Margaret Sanger had become a figure of public scorn for her efforts on its behalf. A related issue, however, stimulated as much popular passion as any question of its time: abortion. Until the 1960s, abortion had been illegal in all but a few states, although it was often performed quietly (and at times dangerously) out of sight of the law. But the growing strength of the women's movement increased pressure on behalf of the legalization of abortion. Several states had abandoned restrictions on abortion by the end of the 1960s. And in 1973, the Supreme Court invalidated all laws prohibiting abortion during the "first trimester," the first three months of pregnancy. The issue, it seemed, had been settled.

In the following years, however, opposition to abortion revived, growing by the early 1980s into one of the nation's most powerful political forces. The right-to-life movement, as it called itself, managed first to persuade Congress to ban all federal Medicaid funding for abortions; many state legislatures imposed similar bans. At the same time, pressure was growing for a "human life" amendment to the Constitution, prohibiting abortion even for those women who could afford it. The moral and religious fervor that the abortion issue had aroused, among American Catholics and fundamentalist Protestants in particular, seemed certain to keep it a focus of controversy for many years.

The women's movement was at once the most potent symbol and the most glaring exception to the general impulse toward politi-

cal and cultural "liberation" of the late 1960s. Feminism expressed both a desire to win social justice through collective political action—a desire that characterized the New Left—and a concern for individual fulfillment and personal freedom—a concern that typified much of the counterculture. But it differed from both in one fundamental respect: its success. The women's movement may not have fulfilled all its goals by the early 1980s. But it had achieved fundamental and permanent changes in the position of women in American life; and it had itself become a lasting political and social force. Most of the other liberation movements of the 1960s, however, suffered a far different fate. Because of either decay from within or, more often, growing opposition from without, the crusades for social justice, cultural liberation, and economic reform seemed to fade almost as rapidly as they had emerged.

SUGGESTED READINGS

On the election of 1960, see Theodore H. White, *The Making of the President, 1960* (1961), a now classic study. On Kennedy himself, see Arthur M. Schlesinger, Jr., *A Thousand Days* (1965), and Theodore Sorensen, *Kennedy* (1965), for admiring portraits by administration insiders; Herbert Parmet, *Jack* (1980); Henry Fairlie, *The Kennedy Promise* (1973); Lewis Paper, *The Promise and the Performance* (1975); and Bruce Miroff, *Pragmatic Illusions* (1976). Garry Wills, *The Kennedy Imprisonment* (1982), is a devastatingly critical reassessment, which examines the entire Kennedy family. On the Kennedy assassination, see *The Report of the Warren Commission* (1964), for the official investigation; William Manchester, *The Death of a President* (1967), for an emotional portrait of the days following the slaying; and Anthony Summers, *Conspiracy* (1980), and E. J. Epstein, *Inquest* (1966), for a discussion of the continuing controversies surrounding the event. Studies of Lyndon Johnson include Doris Kearns, *Lyndon Johnson and the American Dream* (1976), and Eric Goldman, *The Tragedy of Lyndon Johnson* (1968). Ronnie Dugger, *The Politician* (1982), examines Johnson's prepresidential career. Johnson's memoirs, *Vantage Point* (1971), offer a defense of his record. George Reedy, *The Twilight of the Presidency* (1970), offers valuable reflections by Johnson's press secretary. Jim Heath, *Decade of Disillusionment* (1975), is an overview of the Kennedy–Johnson years.

On the domestic programs of the Kennedy–Johnson era, see Tom Wicker, *JFK and LBJ* (1968), for a study of congressional politics and the presidency; Jim Heath, *John F. Kennedy and the Business Community* (1969); Victor Navasky, *Kennedy Justice* (1971); James Sundquist, *Politics and Policy* (1968); Sar Levitan, *The Great Society's Poor Law* (1969); Sar Levitan and Robert Taggart, *The Promise of Greatness* (1976); and Daniel Knapp and Kenneth Polk, *Scouting the War on Poverty* (1971). For the maturing of the civil-rights movement, see David Lewis, *King* (1970); Carl Brauer, *John F. Kennedy and the Second Reconstruction* (1977); Martin Luther King, Jr., *Why We Can't Wait* (1964); David Garrow, *Protest at Selma* (1978); William Chafe, *Civilities and Civil Rights* (1980); and Harris Wofford, *Of Kennedy and Kings* (1980). Stephen Oates, *Let the Trumpet Sound* (1982) is a major biography of King.

On the foreign policy of the Kennedy–Johnson years, see Richard Walton, *Cold War and Counterrevolution* (1972); Louise Fitzsimmons, *The Kennedy Doctrine* (1972); Godfrey Hodgson, *America in Our Time* (1976), which is also valuable for its study of the domestic climate of the era; Roger Hilsman, *To Move a Nation* (1965); Philip Geyelin, *Lyndon B. Johnson and the World* (1966); and Richard Barnet, *Intervention and Revolution* (1968), which examines American policies toward the Third World. On the disastrous 1961 invasion of Cuba, consult Haynes Johnson, *The Bay of*

Pigs (1964), and Peter Wyden, *Bay of Pigs* (1969). Elie Abel, *The Missile Crisis* (1966); Graham Allison, *Essence of Decision* (1971), an innovative examination of decision making; Robert Kennedy, *Thirteen Days* (1969), a personal memoir; and Herbert Dinerstein, *The Making of a Missile Crisis* (1976), which considers the Soviet position, examine the Cuban missile crisis. Dan Kurzman, *Santo Domingo* (1966), and Jerome Slater, *Intervention and Negotiation* (1970), discuss the American intervention in the Dominican Republic in 1964. Warren Cohen, *Dean Rusk* (1980), examines the secretary of state.

The one indispensable source on the Vietnam War is the Defense Department studies published as *The Pentagon Papers*, of which several editions are available. One of the most complete is the four-volume Senator Gravel edition (1975). Other books on Vietnam, in addition to those cited after Chapter 29, include David Halberstam, *The Best and the Brightest* (1972), a study of the decision makers who engineered the commitment; Guenter Lewy, *America in Vietnam* (1978), a controversial defense of the commitment; John Galloway, *The Gulf of Tonkin Resolution* (1970); and Alexander Kendrick, *The Wound Within* (1974). Norman Podhoretz, *Why We Were in Vietnam* (1982), makes a case for the American commitment. Leslie Gelb and Richard Betts, *The Irony of Vietnam: The System Worked* (1979), is a fatalistic view. Michael Herr, *Dispatches* (1977), is a collection of essays by a war correspondent expressing the agony of the military experience. Lawrence Baskir and William Strauss, *Chance and Circumstance* (1978), examines the draft during the Vietnam War. Gloria Emerson, *Winners and Losers* (1976), assesses the wide-reaching impact of the war. Thomas Powers, *The War at Home* (1973), and Irwin Unger, *The Movement* (1974), discuss the domestic opposition.

On the rise of black power, see Stokely Carmichael and Charles Hamilton, *Black Power* (1967), the book that gave the phenomenon its name; *The Autobiography of Malcolm X* (1966), which was ghostwritten by Alex Haley; Benjamin Muse, *The American Negro Revolution* (1969); and Archie Epps, *Malcolm X and the American Negro Revolution* (1969). On the urban riots, consult Robert Fogelson, *Violence as Protest* (1971); Joe R. Feagin and Harlan Hahn, *Ghetto Revolts* (1973); and the *Report of the National Advisory Commission on Civil Disorders* (1968).

The traumas of 1968 are brilliantly examined in Lewis Chester, Godfrey Hodgson, and Lewis Page, *American Melodrama* (1969), as well as in Godfrey Hodgson's important general study of modern America, *America in Our Time* (1976). Arthur M. Schlesinger, Jr., *Robert Kennedy and His Times* (1978), is a thorough and sympathetic biography. Norman Mailer, *Miami and the Siege of Chicago* (1968), is a personalized examination of the political conventions. Ben Stavis, *We Were the Campaign* (1969), is a study of the McCarthy crusade. Marshall Frady, *Wallace*, (rev., 1976), is a portrait of the conservative challenger. Theodore White, *The Making of the President, 1968* (1969), is a sober view of the Nixon election.

For an overview of social and cultural aspects of the 1960s, see William O'Neill, *Coming Apart* (1971); Ronald Berman, *America in the Sixties* (1968); Milton Viorst, *Fire in the Streets* (1979); and Morris Dickstein, *Gates of Eden* (1977). Todd Gitlin, *The Whole World Is Watching* (1981); Irwin Unger, *The Movement* (1974); Lawrence Lader, *Power on the Left* (1979); Kirkpatrick Sale, *SDS* (1973); and Peter Clecak, *Radical Paradoxes* (1973), examine the New Left. Kenneth Keniston, *Young Radicals* (1968), and Lewis Feuer, *The Conflict of Generations* (1969), are also useful. Sources for examining the counterculture include Paul Goodman, *Growing Up Absurd* (1960), one of the early statements of its philosophy; Theodore Roszak, *The Making of a Counter Culture* (1969), a ringing defense; Charles Reich, *The Greening of America* (1970), an influential contemporary work; and Ronald Berman, *America in the Sixties* (1968), a hostile view. Joan Didion, *Slouching Towards Bethlehem* (1967) and *The White Album* (1979), offer provocative reflections on the mood of the counterculture. Other important works on the political and cultural climate of the era include John Diggins, *The American Left in the Twentieth Century* (1973), and Richard Flacks, *Youth and Social Change* (1971).

On the issue of American Indians, see Wilcomb Washburn, *Red Man's Land/White Man's Land* (1971); Vine Deloria, Jr., *Behind the Trail of Broken Treaties* (1974) and *Custer Died for Your Sins* (1969); D'Arcy McNickle, *Native American Tribalism* (1973); and Stan Steiner, *The New Indians* (1968). A survey of the history of Hispanic Americans is Rodolfo Acuña, *Occupied America*, 2nd ed. (1981). See also Julian Samora, *Los Mojados* (1971); Oscar Lewis, *La Vida* (1969); and Matt Meier and Feliciano Rivera, *The Chicanos* (1972). Ronald Taylor, *Chavez and the Farm Workers* (1975), considers the labor struggles of Mexican-Americans.

Literature on the contemporary women's movement includes William Chafe, *The American Woman* (1972), which traces feminism back to the 1920s; Sheila Rothman, *Woman's Proper Place* (1978), which examines women's roles since the turn of the century; Jo Freeman, *The Politics of Women's Liberation* (1975); Sara Evans, *Personal Politics* (1979); and Gayle Yates, *What Women Want* (1975). The book that helped launch the movement is Betty Friedan, *The Feminine Mystique* (1963).

The Crisis of Authority

31

Nixon's Farewell, 1974 Only two years before, Richard Nixon had won reelection by one of the greatest majorities in American history. Now, on August 9, 1974, he bids a crowd on the White House lawn farewell as he boards a helicopter— the first stage of a flight to California— following his resignation from the presidency. The Watergate scandals, which culminated in Nixon's departure, were the most prominent of many developments in the 1970s that raised questions in the minds of many Americans about the quality and integrity of the nation's leadership. (UPI)

The election of Richard Nixon in 1968 was the result of more than the unpopularity of Lyndon Johnson's policies and the divisions within the Democratic party. It was the result, too, of a changing national mood. A growing number of Americans—a clear majority, it seemed, on the basis of the election returns—were tired of the social turmoil of the 1960s and resentful of the attention directed toward minorities and the poor. The sober, middle-class values of thrift, hard work, and self-reliance were, they believed, under assault.

Federal social programs were funneling billions of dollars into the inner cities to help the poor and unemployed, increasing the tax burden on the middle class. Government regulations and court rulings were launching open attacks on traditional community values and institutions. Hippies and radicals were dominating public discourse with their bitter critiques of everything middle-class Americans held dear. It was time, such men and women believed, for a restoration of stability.

In Richard Nixon they found a man who seemed perfectly to match their mood. Himself a product of a hardworking, middle-class family, he had risen to prominence on the basis of his own unrelenting efforts. His public demeanor displayed nothing of the flashiness of the Kennedys or the stridency of the Democratic left. He projected instead an image of stern dedication to traditional values. The extraordinary narrowness of his margin of victory in 1968 suggested that many Americans continued to consider him sanctimonious, "tricky," and generally unappealing. To much of the nation, however, he was the embodiment of the search for a new, more placid, social order.

Yet the presidency of Richard Nixon, far from returning calm and stability to American politics, produced an unparalleled national crisis. The new president inherited many problems from his predecessor that would have plagued any leader. The war in Vietnam, the social conflicts of the 1960s, the failure of major institutions to perform as the public had come to expect—all had combined by 1969 to make Americans suspicious of their leaders and mistrustful of their government. Yet it was the performance of Nixon's own administration that caused the most rapid erosion of that public respect for authority. By the early 1970s, the once vigorous American economy had begun a long descent into crisis; and the failure of government to reverse its course raised serious questions about the ability of elected officials to govern. Of more immediate importance, beginning in 1972, the administration found itself embroiled in a series of scandals that not only resulted in Nixon's untimely departure from office but further increased public cynicism about the nation's leadership.

NIXON, KISSINGER, AND THE WAR

Central to the search for stability, Richard Nixon believed as he took office in 1969, was a resolution of the stalemate in Vietnam. Yet the new president felt no freer than his predecessor to abandon the American commitment in Indochina. On the one hand, he realized that the endless war was undermining both the nation's domestic stability and its position in the world. On the other hand, he feared that a precipitous retreat would destroy American honor and "credibility."

During the 1968 campaign, Nixon

claimed to have formulated a plan to bring "peace with honor" in Vietnam. He had refused to disclose its details. Once in office, however, he soon made clear that the plan consisted of little more than a vague set of general principles, not of any concrete measures to extricate the United States from the quagmire. American involvement in Indochina continued for four more years, during which the war expanded both in its geographic scope and in its bloodiness. And when a settlement finally emerged early in 1973, it produced neither peace nor honor. It succeeded only in removing the United States from the wreckage.

Vietnamization

Nixon had long been far more interested in foreign than domestic affairs. He considered himself an expert on international relations, having read and traveled widely during his years as a private citizen. And like other presidents, he enjoyed the freedom from legislative and political obstacles that the conduct of foreign policy, unlike domestic policy, provided. Yet despite Nixon's own passionate interest in diplomacy, he brought with him into government a public figure who ultimately seemed to overshadow the president himself in the conduct of international affairs: Henry Kissinger.

Kissinger was a respected and prolific professor of international politics at Harvard when Nixon tapped him to serve as his special assistant for national security affairs. Both Secretary of State William Rogers, who had served as Eisenhower's attorney general, and Secretary of Defense Melvin Laird, who had been an influential member of Congress, were far more experienced in public life. But Kissinger quickly outshone them both. Nixon's passion for concentrating decision making in the White House was in large measure responsible; but Kissinger's own remarkable adeptness both in fighting for bureaucratic influence and in currying favor with the press was at least equally important. Together, Nixon and Kissinger set out to find an acceptable solution to the stalemate in Vietnam.

The new Vietnam policy moved along several fronts. Nixon repeatedly insisted that he would not consider a policy of surrender. At the same time, he sought to limit domestic opposition to the war. In the course of 1969, therefore, he initiated several new policies designed to weaken the antiwar movement without ending the fighting. Aware that the military draft was one of the most visible targets of dissent, the administration devised a new "lottery" system, through which only a limited group of nineteen-year-olds—those with low lottery numbers—would be eligible for the draft. The new system would continue to supply the military with its manpower needs while removing millions of potential critics from the danger of conscription. Later, the president urged the creation of an all-volunteer army that would permit the abolition of the draft altogether. By 1973, the Selective Service System was on its way to at least temporary extinction.

Far more important in stifling dissent, however, was the new policy of "Vietnamization" of the war—that is, the training and equipping of the South Vietnamese military to assume the burden of combat in place of American forces. In the fall of 1969, Nixon announced the withdrawal of 60,000 American ground troops from Vietnam, the first reduction in United States troop strength since the beginning of the war. The withdrawals continued steadily for more than three years, so that by the fall of 1972 relatively few American soldiers remained in Indochina. From a peak of more than 540,000 in 1969, the number had dwindled to about 60,000.

Yet the Vietnamization process was not only painfully slow, it also did little to reduce the level of fighting in Vietnam. One reason was the persistent inability of American and Vietnamese negotiators to make any discernible progress at the interminable peace talks that had begun in Paris in 1968. The United States continued to insist on the withdrawal of all communist forces from South Vietnam and the preservation of the Thieu regime as prerequisites to any settlement. The North Vietnamese and the Viet Cong refused to abandon their commitment to reunification of their nation. There was, it seemed, no common ground.

Vietnamese Children Flee Napalm
Terrified children with napalm burns run from the village of Trang Ban, southwest of Saigon in South Vietnam, after South Vietnamese government planes mistakenly drop fire bombs on the village, June 8, 1972. (UPI)

Escalation

To Nixon and Kissinger, therefore, the most effective strategy for settling the conflict seemed to be the strengthening of the South Vietnamese military position through an expansion of the war. That required, they believed, new military efforts to destroy the "staging areas" in Cambodia from which the North Vietnamese had been launching many of their attacks. Very early in his presidency, Nixon ordered the air force to begin a series of secret bombings of Cambodian territory to destroy the enemy sanctuaries. He withheld information about the raids from Congress and the public. In the spring of 1970, with what some have claimed was American encouragement and support, conservative military leaders overthrew the neutral government of Prince Norodom Sihanouk, Cambodia's leader for two decades, and established a new, pro-American regime under General Lon Nol. Lon Nol quickly gave his approval to American incursions into his territory; and on April 30, Nixon went on television to announce that he was ordering United States troops across the border into Cambodia to "clean out" the bases that the enemy had been using for its "increased military aggression."

So successful had Nixon been in seeming to deescalate the war that the once-powerful peace movement had by mid-1970 begun to lose much of its strength. The Cambodian invasion, however, restored it to life, giving it a more determined spirit than ever before. The first days of May saw the most widespread and vocal antiwar demonstrations ever. Hundreds of thousands of protesters gathered in Washington to denounce the president's policies. Millions, perhaps, participated in countless smaller demonstrations on campuses nationwide. Antiwar frenzy was reaching so high a level that it became possible briefly to believe that a genuine revolution was imminent.

The mood of crisis intensified on May 4, when the nation heard the appalling news that four students had been killed and nine others injured when members of the National Guard had opened fire on an antiwar rally at Kent State University in Ohio. A decade of investigations failed to provide any clear explanation for the tragedy, although it seems clear that Governor James Rhodes and the commanders of the Guard had needlessly (and some charged deliberately) inflamed the situation on campus with their heavy-handed tactics. At the time, the incident seemed to many young Americans to confirm their worst suspicions of their government and their society. Ten days later, police killed two black students at Jackson State University in Mississippi during a demonstration there.

The intensity of the public outcry against the use of troops in Cambodia clearly startled the president, and he quickly announced that the American forces would be through with their work there within weeks and would not return. But the clamor against the war continued. Congress angrily repealed the Gulf of Tonkin Resolution in December, stripping the president of what had long served as the legal basis for the war. Nixon ignored the action, claiming that he had the authority to continue military efforts in Vietnam to protect American troops already there.

Then, in June 1971, first the *New York Times* and later other newspapers began publishing excerpts from a secret study of the war prepared by the Defense Department during the Johnson administration. The so-called Pentagon Papers, leaked to the press by former Defense official Daniel Ellsberg, provided shocking confirmation of what many had long believed: that the government had been consistently dishonest, both in reporting the military progress of the war and in explaining its own motives for American involvement. The administration went to

Four Dead in Ohio
Kent State University students react with horror to the killing of four demonstrators by the Ohio National Guard on May 4, 1970. The burning of a decrepit National Guard armory on campus had provided Governor James Rhodes with a pretext for sending in the guard, even though university officials had urged him to close down the campus instead. Two days of escalating tensions between students and guardsmen culminated in the shootings. (UPI)

court to suppress the documents, but to no avail. The Supreme Court ruled that the press had the right to publish them.

Particularly troubling, both to the public and to the government itself, were signs of decay within the American military. Morale and discipline among United States troops in Vietnam, who had been fighting a savage and inconclusive war for more than five years, was rapidly deteriorating. The trial and conviction in 1971 of Lieutenant William Calley, who was charged with overseeing a massacre of more than a hundred unarmed South Vietnamese civilians, attracted wide public attention to the dehumanizing impact of the war on those who fought it. Less publicized were other, more widespread problems among American troops in Vietnam: desertion, drug addiction, refusal to obey orders, even the occasional killing of unpopular officers by enlisted men. Among the disenchanted—deserters, draft resisters, and others—were not simply the radical college students so unpopular with most Americans but many otherwise conventional sons of middle- and lower-class families.

The continuing carnage, the increasing savagery, and the social distress at home were drawing an ever-larger proportion of the population into opposition to the war. By 1971, nearly two-thirds of those interviewed in public-opinion polls were urging American withdrawal from Vietnam. From Richard Nixon, however, there came no sign of retreat. On the contrary, the events of the spring of 1970 left him more convinced than ever of the importance of resisting what he called the "bums" who opposed his military policies. With the approval of the White House, both the FBI and the CIA intensified their surveillance and infiltration of antiwar and radical groups, often resorting to blatant illegalities in the process. Administration officials sought to discredit prominent critics of the war by leaking damaging personal information about them. At one point, White House agents broke into the office of a psychiatrist in an unsuccessful effort to steal files on Daniel Ellsberg. During the congressional campaign of 1970, Vice President Spiro Agnew, using the acid rhetoric that had already made him the hero of many conserva-

tives, stepped up his attack on the "effete" and "impudent" critics of the administration. The president himself once climbed on top of an automobile to taunt a crowd of angry demonstrators.

In Indochina, meanwhile, the fighting raged on. In February 1971, Nixon ordered the air force to assist the South Vietnamese army in an invasion of Laos—a test, as he saw it, of his Vietnamization program. Within weeks, the badly mauled South Vietnamese scrambled back across the border in defeat. American bombing in Vietnam and Cambodia continued to increase, despite its demonstrated ineffectiveness, so that by the end of 1971 the Nixon administration had dropped more explosives on the region than the Johnson administration had done in five years. When in March 1972 the North Vietnamese mounted their biggest offensive since 1968, Nixon responded by escalating the bombing once again, ordering attacks on targets near Hanoi, the capital of North Vietnam, and Haiphong. He called as well for the mining of seven North Vietnamese harbors (including Haiphong) to stop the flow of supplies from China and the Soviet Union.

"Peace with Honor"

The approach of the 1972 presidential election, in which the war promised to be the leading issue, finally did what years of military frustration and escalating public protests had failed to do; it convinced the administration that it must alter its terms for the withdrawal of American forces. In April 1972, the president dropped his longtime insistence on a removal of North Vietnamese troops from the south before any American withdrawal. In July, word leaked out that Henry Kissinger had been meeting privately in Paris with the North Vietnamese foreign secretary, Le Duc Tho, and rumors abounded that a cease-fire was near. On October 26, only days before the presidential election, Kissinger announced that "Peace is at hand."

Several weeks later, however, negotiations broke down once again. Although both the American and North Vietnamese governments were ready to accept the Kissinger–Tho plan for a cease-fire, the Thieu regime balked, still insisting that the full withdrawal of North Vietnamese forces from the south be a prerequisite to any agreement. Kissinger tried to win additional concessions from the communists to meet Thieu's objections, but on December 16—despite the American insistence that the agreement was "99 percent complete"—talks broke off.

The next day, December 17, American planes began to bomb North Vietnamese cities in the heaviest and most destructive raids of the entire war. In the past, the United States had made at least token efforts to spare civilian targets from aerial attacks. But the saturation bombing of Hanoi, Haiphong, and other cities allowed of no such distinctions. The Pentagon announced that it was attempting to destroy docks, airfields, railyards, power plants, and the like; but such targets were, of course, located in the middle of heavily populated areas. For twelve days, American B-52s rained terror on the North Vietnamese people. (Fifteen of the giant bombers were shot down, fourteen more than had been lost in the entire course of the war to that point.) Then, on December 30, Nixon terminated the "Christmas bombing" as quickly as he had begun it. The United States and the North Vietnamese returned to the conference table. And on January 27, 1973, representatives of the four interested parties (the governments of the United States, North Vietnam, and South Vietnam, together with the "Provisional Republican Government" of the south—the Viet Cong) signed an "agreement on ending the war and restoring peace in Vietnam." Nixon and Kissinger were fond of claiming that the Christmas bombing had forced the North Vietnamese to relent. In fact, a far more important factor was the increasing American pressure on Thieu to accept the cease-fire and Nixon's promise to him that the United States would respond "with full force" to any violation of the agreement.

The terms of the Paris Accords were little different from those that Kissinger and Tho had accepted in principle the previous fall. The two most prominent components were the establishment of an immediate cease-fire and the return by the North Vietnamese of several hundred American prisoners of war, whose fate had become an emotional issue of great importance within the United States. After that, the agreement descended quickly into murky and plainly unworkable political arrangements. The Thieu regime would survive for the moment—perhaps the only major concession Kissinger was able to wrest from Tho. But there would be no withdrawal of North Vietnamese forces from the south and no abandonment of the communist commitment to a reunified Vietnam. What Nixon boastfully described as a "peace with honor" was really little more than a formula for allowing the United States to extricate itself from the quagmire before the South Vietnamese regime collapsed, a recipe for providing what some officials caustically described as a "decent interval." No knowledgeable military observer believed that the South Vietnamese military could hold off the communists without continuing American support.

The American forces were hardly out of Indochina and the prisoners of war barely reunited with their families before the Paris Accords collapsed. During the first year after the cease-fire, the contending Vietnamese armies suffered greater battle losses than the Americans had endured during ten years of fighting. In Laos, fighting came to an end only after communist forces had established control of more than half the country. In Cambodia, the war raged on, and American planes continued to bomb communist installations in that country until Congress compelled the president to desist in August 1973. In March 1975, finally, the North Vietnamese launched a full-scale offensive against the now hopelessly weakened forces of the south. Thieu appealed to Washington for assistance; Nixon appealed to Congress for additional funding; and Congress, unwilling to pour additional money into what seemed a hopeless cause, refused. Late in April 1975, communist forces marched into Saigon, shortly after officials of the Thieu regime and the American embassy had fled the country in humiliating disarray. At about the same time, the Lon Nol regime in Cambodia fell to the Khmer Rouge, the Cambodian equivalent of the Viet Cong.

The Fall of Saigon
One of the most humiliating spectacles in recent American history was the
chaotic evacuation of Saigon in the spring of 1975. With Viet Cong troops
only miles away, desperate South Vietnamese officials and others fought with
American soldiers and diplomats for space on the few airplanes and helicopters available for the evacuation. (UPI)

Still, the war in Indochina did not end.
Although Vietnam was soon reunited after
more than thirty years of civil war, conflict
continued in the surrounding nations. In
Cambodia, the new communist government
of Pol Pot (who renamed the country Kam-
puchea) launched a reign of terror perhaps
unparalleled in modern history, forcing virtually the entire population to uproot itself
and causing the death—by murder, exhaustion, or starvation—of more than a third of
the country's residents. Conditions grew
even worse in 1978 when the new communist
government of Vietnam invaded Cambodia
(with the support of the Soviet Union) and
drove Pol Pot and the Khmer Rouge from
power. Not only did the Cambodians suffer
from the war itself; but the conflict created a
severe famine that threatened to exterminate

the population. Massive, if belated, relief efforts from the United States and many other
countries alleviated some of the suffering by
the end of 1979; but the future of Cambodia
remained bleak and uncertain.

Vietnam, in the meantime, faced an invasion of its territory by the forces of communist China, which supported Pol Pot and
feared the extension of Russian influence in
the region. The two sides established an uneasy truce after several weeks of fighting; but
there remained no stable peace between the
ancient adversaries. American officials had
claimed for years that the collapse of South
Vietnam would lead quickly to coordinated
communist domination of all of Southeast
Asia. In fact, the new regimes were soon
fighting each other as bitterly as they had
once fought against the West.

Such were the dismal results of more than a decade of direct American military involvement in Vietnam. They had come at a staggering cost. The greatest burden, of course, had been borne by the people of Indochina. More than 1.2 million Vietnamese soldiers had died in combat, along with countless civilians throughout the region. A beautiful land had been ravaged; an ancient culture had been all but destroyed. The agrarian economy of much of Indochina lay in ruins, and the social fabric of the region would, it seemed clear, take many years to be restored.

But the United States had paid a heavy price as well. The war had cost the nation almost $150 billion in direct costs and incalculably more indirectly. It had resulted in the deaths of over 55,000 young men and the injury of 300,000 more, many of whom were permanently maimed or crippled. Countless other Vietnam veterans suffered severe psychological and emotional damage. American domestic life had been racked by dissent for more than five years. Pressing social problems had gone unaddressed. Members of an entire generation had been scarred by the experience, many of them cruelly disillusioned, some of them deeply and permanently embittered toward their government and their political system. And the nation at large had suffered a heavy blow to its confidence and self-esteem. Only a decade before, Americans had believed that they could create a great society at home and maintain peace and freedom in the world. Now they harbored serious doubts about their ability to do either.

NIXON, KISSINGER, AND THE WORLD

The continuing war in Vietnam provided a dismal backdrop to what Nixon considered his larger mission in world affairs: the construction of a new international order. The president had become convinced that old assumptions of a "bipolar" world—in which the United States and the Soviet Union were the only truly great powers—were now obsolete. The rise of China, Japan, and Western Europe, the increasing nationalism of the Third World, the growing disunity within the communist alliance—all augured a new, "multipolar" international structure. To deal with this changing world, Nixon drew on the theories of Henry Kissinger, a longtime student of the nineteenth-century European balance of power. The United States must, Nixon and Kissinger believed, work for a new equilibrium. "It will be a safer world and a better world," the president proclaimed in 1971, "if we have a strong, healthy United States, Europe, Soviet Union, China, Japan—each balancing the other, not playing one against the other, an even balance."

The China Initiative

For more than twenty years, ever since the fall of Chiang Kai-shek in 1949, the United States had treated China, the second largest nation on earth, as if it did not exist. There were no official contacts between the two countries. Only a tiny handful of Americans had visited the mainland. News of developments within China was available only in brief and unreliable fragments. One of the world's greatest powers, a nation now in possession of nuclear weapons, was living in almost total isolation from the West, while the United States continued to recognize the decaying exile regime on Taiwan as the legitimate government of China.

Nixon and Kissinger, however, believed that there were now good reasons for forging a new relationship with the Chinese communists. A rapprochement would not only be a belated recognition of reality. It might, in addition, aid the efforts to win a settlement of the war in Vietnam; and it would strengthen China's position as a counterbalance to the Soviet Union, thus inducing the Russians to adopt a more conciliatory attitude toward the United States. The Chinese, for their part, were at least equally eager for a new relationship with the United States. Their own dispute with the Soviet Union—a reflection of the historic antagonism between the two countries, which their mutual commitment to

Nixon in China
The first American president to visit China while in office, Nixon received a carefully staged welcome from the Chinese Communist leaders. On the day of his arrival, February 21, 1972, he was invited to review an honor guard of the Chinese army in company with Premier Chou En-lai. (UPI)

communism had only briefly suppressed—had grown far more bitter than any rivalry with the West. By 1970, Soviet and Chinese forces were massed along both sides of the border, poised, it seemed, for a war between the two communist powers. The Beijing (Peking)* government was eager, therefore, both to forestall the possibility of a Soviet–American alliance against China and to end China's own isolation from the international arena.

Early in 1971, Nixon hinted at a change in American policy when, in a public statement, he made official use for the first time of the

legitimate name of the Chinese government: the People's Republic of China. In July, he sent Henry Kissinger on a secret mission to Beijing. And when Kissinger returned, the president made the startling announcement that he would visit China himself within the next few months. That fall, the United States dropped its long opposition to the admission of communist China to the United States; in October, as a result, the UN admitted the communist delegation and expelled the representatives of the Taiwan regime. Finally, in February 1972, Nixon arrived in China for a week-long visit. American television broadcast vivid pictures of presidential tours of famous Chinese landmarks, which had been

* Reformed spelling. See footnote, page 837.

invisible to much of the West for more than two decades, of meetings with Zhou Enlai (Chou En-lai) and Mao Zedong, and of gracious and friendly exchanges of toasts during elaborate state dinners. In a single stroke, Nixon managed to erase much of the deep animosity toward China that the American people had developed over the course of a generation.

The diplomatic results of the summit meeting were similarly important. The United States and China agreed to scientific, cultural, journalistic, and other exchanges and to a series of steps toward the resumption of trade. More significant, Nixon agreed to accept the principle of eventual reunification of Taiwan with the mainland; and he offered vague assurances that American troops would ultimately withdraw from Taiwan and leave the two Chinese regimes to settle the future of the island between themselves. The United States and China did not agree on establishing formal diplomatic relations. Nixon was not yet prepared openly to repudiate the Chiang regime, which the United States had supported for so long. But a year after the Nixon visit, the two countries set up "liaison offices" in Washington and Beijing that served as embassies in all but name.

Détente

The initiatives in China helped pave the way as well for a new relationship with the Soviet Union, which was as eager to prevent a Chinese–American alliance as Beijing was determined to prevent a Soviet–American one. The Russians also hoped to win technological assistance from the United States and to develop trade ties that might enable them to purchase badly needed grain from American farmers. The Soviet leadership had finally decided, moreover, that it had achieved something approaching nuclear parity with the United States; party chief Leonid Brezhnev and others were interested, therefore, in moving to decelerate the costly arms race. The Nixon administration shared the hopes for progress toward arms limitation, and it was hopeful as well that it could win Soviet assistance in settling the war in Vietnam and

stabilizing the explosive situation in the Middle East.

The road to what soon became known as "détente" had actually begun in 1968, the last year of the Johnson administration, when the United States and the Soviet Union signed a treaty agreeing to discourage the further proliferation of nuclear weapons in the world. More important, however, was the beginning of talks between American and Russian diplomats in Helsinki in 1969 on a strategic arms limitation treaty (SALT). The negotiations continued for two and a half years, and the result was the conclusion in 1972 of the first phase of a new arms control accord: the so-called SALT I. In May of that year, the president traveled to Moscow for a cordial meeting with the Soviet leadership and a glittering ceremony to sign the agreement. The Moscow summit produced as well a series of accords establishing new trade and other exchanges between the two nations—including the soon to be infamous Soviet–American wheat deal, by which the United States sold nearly one-quarter of the total American grain supply to the Russians at a cost far below the world market price. The federal government made up the price difference through subsidies to American farmers.

Nixon returned from Moscow in triumph, boasting of dramatic progress toward bringing the arms race to an end. In fact, SALT I did not end the arms race or even slow it to any great extent. It simply moved it in a different direction. The two nations agreed to limit themselves to their existing number of intercontinental ballistic missiles (ICBMs), thus institutionalizing Soviet superiority in total missile strength. But the United States continued to possess a substantial lead in the total number of its warheads, largely because it had almost twice as many submarines equipped with nuclear missiles as the Soviets. Each country would, in addition, sharply limit its construction of antiballistic missile systems (ABMs). The treaty thus limited the quantity of certain weapons on both sides. It said nothing, however, about limiting quality or about forestalling the creation of entirely new weapons systems. In the following years, the contest for increased sophistication in weapons systems continued unabated. Both nations spent vast sums developing new forms of armaments not restricted by the treaty: the Soviet backfire bomber and the American cruise missile, among others.

SALT I had always been intended as the first step in a far more comprehensive arms control agreement. In June 1973, during a visit by Brezhnev to Washington, the Soviet and American governments pledged renewed efforts to speed the completion of the next phase of the negotiations. Nixon and Brezhnev agreed in principle to abstain from nuclear war, to work for a permanent freeze on offensive nuclear weapons, and to extend Soviet–American cooperation in other areas as well.

The Problems of Multipolarity

The policies of rapprochement with communist China and détente with the Soviet Union reflected several basic assumptions of the Nixon–Kissinger foreign policy. The communist world was no longer a monolithic bloc, the administration now believed, and it required a far more flexible and varied diplomatic approach than it had in the 1950s. The Soviet threat to Western Europe, American officials were convinced, was much abated, removing the most serious source of tension from the Cold War. Above all, the new policies reflected a belief that world stability depended primarily on the relationships among the great powers, that the pervasive concern of previous administrations with "emerging areas" had diverted American policy from pursuit of its most important goals. By the last years of the Nixon administration, however, it had become clear that it was the Third World that remained the most volatile and dangerous source of world instability; that tensions in developing countries had the capacity not only to produce local turmoil but to erode the new relationships among the superpowers.

Central to the Nixon–Kissinger policy toward the Third World was the effort to maintain a stable status quo without involving the United States too deeply in local disputes. The so-called Nixon Doctrine, which

the president announced in 1969 and 1970, displayed both the extent and the limits of the administration's concerns in the developing regions. The United States would, the president declared, "participate in the defense and development of allies and friends," but it would leave the "basic responsibility" for the future of those "friends" to the nations themselves. In practice, the Nixon Doctrine meant a declining American interest in contributing to Third World development; a growing contempt for the United Nations, where underdeveloped nations were gaining influence through their sheer numbers; and increasing support to authoritarian regimes attempting to withstand radical challenges from within. In 1970, for example, the CIA poured substantial funds into Chile to help support the established government against a communist challenge. When the Marxist candidate for president, Salvador Allende, came to power through an honest, open election, the United States began funneling more money to opposition forces in Chile to help "destabilize" the new government. In 1973, a military junta seized power from Allende, who was subsequently murdered under mysterious circumstances. There was good reason to believe that the CIA had played a direct role in the coup; undoubtedly, American policies had contributed to creating the circumstances under which the coup became possible. The new regime of General Augusto Pinochet was as brutally repressive as any in the Western Hemisphere. It received warm approval and increased military and economic assistance from the United States.

Far more troubling than Latin America, however, was the Middle East. Long an area of interest to the United States because of its strategic position between the Soviet Union and the Mediterranean, the region was now also of vital economic importance to the West, which beginning in the 1960s had become highly dependent on the purchase of oil from the Arab states. For the United States, this energy dependence presented special problems. As the most important ally and defender of Israel, America was standing squarely in opposition to the Islamic states, which were unanimous in their condemnation of Zionism.

Hostility toward Israel had grown particularly intense after the humiliating Arab defeat in the Six-Day War of 1967, in which Israeli forces had routed the armies of Egypt, Jordan, and Syria and had seized territory from all three nations. In the following years, Israel remained adamant in its refusal to relinquish the newly occupied territories. The situation grew even more volatile as a result of the desperate plight of hundreds of thousands of Palestinian Arab refugees, some of whom had been virtually homeless since 1948 and whose numbers had drastically increased after the 1967 war. Many of them lived in Jordan, whose ruler, King Hussein, was eager to maintain stable relations with the United States. Disturbed by the activities of the new Palestinian Liberation Organization (PLO) and other radical or terrorist groups, Hussein used his own armies to attack the Palestinians and expel them from Jordan after a series of uprisings in 1970, almost precipitating another general war in the region. Many of the exiled Palestinians moved to Lebanon, helping to precipitate more than a decade of instability and civil war there.

In the meantime, the United States was working quietly to repair its relations with the Islamic states and create the framework for a general settlement of the Middle Eastern dilemma, a task the Nixon administration hoped would be eased as a result of its policies of détente with the Soviet Union. Such efforts suffered a serious setback in October 1973 when, on the Jewish high holy day of Yom Kippur, Egyptian and Syrian forces suddenly attacked Israel. The ensuing conflict was far different from the 1967 war, during which Israel had quickly and decisively overwhelmed its opponents. For ten days, the Israelis struggled to recover from the surprise attack; finally, they launched an effective counteroffensive against Egyptian forces in the Sinai. Only then did the United States and the Soviet Union intervene to bring an end to the fighting in the region. Under heavy American pressure, the government of Israel agreed not to press its advantage and accepted a cease-fire.

The imposed settlement of the Yom Kippur War reflected a significant change in the American position in the Middle East. It displayed, first, a new sensitivity to Soviet inter-

Peacemaking in the Middle East
In the spring of 1974, after repeated visits to Egypt, Israel, and Syria, Secretary of State Kissinger succeeded in working out a cease-fire between Egypt and Israel and then between Syria and Israel. After accepting his plan for troop disengagements along the Syrian border, Israeli leaders gave him their thanks at a farewell party in Jerusalem on May 29. He was photographed at the party with Israeli Premier Golda Meir and Religious Affairs Minister Yitzhak Rafael. (Wide World Photos)

ests in the region. So worried had the Nixon administration become about Russian intervention in the conflict that at one point the president had ordered American nuclear forces onto a full, worldwide alert. Later, making use of their newly cordial relationship, the two superpowers tacitly agreed to restrain their allies and work for an armistice. The war gave clear evidence, however, of an even more important new reality: the growing dependence of the United States and its allies on Arab oil. Permitting Israel to continue its drive into Egypt would not only have invited Soviet retaliation; it would have jeopardized the ability of the United States to purchase needed petroleum from the Arab states. A brief but painful embargo by the Islamic governments on the sale of oil to America in 1973 provided an ominous warning. The lesson of the Yom Kippur War, therefore, was that the United States could

no longer ignore the interests of the Arab nations in its efforts on behalf of Israel.

A larger lesson of 1973 was even more disturbing. The Yom Kippur War and the oil embargo had given clear evidence of the new limits facing the United States in its effort to construct a stable world order. The nations of the Third World could no longer be depended on to act as passive, cooperative "client states." The easy access to raw materials on which the American economy had come to depend was becoming a thing of the past. The United States could not even rely any longer on the automatic support of its NATO allies. None of the principal nations of Western Europe had joined the United States in providing military support for Israel in the 1973 war, and most had complained bitterly when American policies had resulted in their own temporary loss of access to vital Middle Eastern oil.

THE NEW FEDERALISM

For a time in the 1960s, it had seemed to many Americans that the forces of chaos and radicalism were taking control of the nation. Seldom had society been so fraught with conflict; seldom had middle-class Americans found themselves under such unrelenting assault. The growing fear of disorder had aroused a growing antagonism toward student radicals, black militants, hippies, and other dissidents. It had also produced deep resentment of the federal government, which some Americans believed had become the exclusive preserve of those minorities and social activists and whose policies, many claimed, were becoming disruptive and intrusive. The domestic policy of the Nixon administration, therefore, was an attempt to restore balance: between the needs of the poor and the desires of the middle class, between the power of the federal government and the interests of local communities. The president himself described the effort as the "New Federalism"—a series of programs to "reverse the flow of power and resources from the states and communities to Washington and start power and resources flowing back . . . to the people."

The New Balance

Almost immediately on taking office, Nixon began to give voice to the resentments of what he liked to call the "Middle Americans" or the "silent majority." In particular, Nixon played to their grievances against the federal government and to the conservative fear of social decay. Skillfully and effectively, he established himself, in the public mind at least, as the defender of traditional values and local customs. Through his "Southern strategy," he began to limit federal efforts to impose integration on reluctant communities. He tried, unsuccessfully, to persuade Congress to pass legislation prohibiting school desegregation through the use of forced busing. And he forbade the Department of Health, Education, and Welfare to cut off federal funds from school districts that had failed to comply with court orders to integrate (precipitating the resignation of Secretary Robert Finch and other HEW officials).

At the same time, he worked to reduce or dismantle many of the social programs of the Great Society and the New Frontier. He cut off hundreds of federal grants for urban renewal, social welfare, job training, and educational assistance. He attempted to reduce funding for dozens of other social programs, only to be blocked by the Democratic Congress; on occasion, he attempted to defy congressional opposition by simply impounding funds for programs he considered unnecessary. In 1973, he abolished the Office of Economic Opportunity, the centerpiece of the antipoverty program of the Johnson years. And at the same time, he was working to decentralize control of other social programs—both by transferring authority to state and local governments and by establishing a program of "revenue sharing," through which the federal government would return some of its tax revenues to localities.

One of the administration's boldest efforts was an attempt to overhaul the nation's enormous welfare system. The cumbersome, expensive, and inefficient welfare bureaucracy was the most glaring symbol of what Nixon and his supporters considered the excessive intrusiveness of the federal government. The primary vehicle for federal relief—Aid to Families with Dependent Children—was not only costly; it required a large, awkward infrastructure of caseworkers, administrators, and others, and it extended the authority of the federal government directly into the daily lives of families and communities. As an alternative, Nixon proposed what he called the Family Assistance Plan. Designed in large part by the president's urban adviser, Daniel Patrick Moynihan, the FAP established what was in effect a guaranteed annual income for all Americans: $1,600 in federal grants, which could be supplemented by outside earnings up to $4,000. Even many liberals applauded the proposal as an important step toward expanding federal responsibility for the poor. To Nixon, however, the appeal of the plan was its simplicity. It would reduce the supervisory functions of the federal government and transfer to welfare recipients themselves daily responsibility for their own lives. Although the FAP won approval in the House in 1970, concerted attacks by welfare recipients (who considered the benefits inadequate) and members of the welfare bureaucracy (whose own influence stood to be

sharply diminished by the bill) helped kill it in the Senate. It was never revived.

Nixon appealed to conservative and provincial sentiments in other ways as well. He issued strident denunciations of protesters and radicals, ordered the Justice Department to arrest demonstrators and dissidents, and unleashed Vice President Spiro Agnew to attack not only youthful critics of the administration but the liberal news media and the "biased" television networks. He rejected as "morally bankrupt" the recommendations of a special commission on pornography, which saw no reason for the government to suppress the distribution of obscene materials. He expressed sympathy for those who opposed abortion. He refused to consider extending amnesty to draft resisters. He issued strong denunciations of those who encouraged the use of drugs. He was, in short, establishing a new stance for the federal government: one that balanced its commitments to helping the poor and minorities against a larger concern for preserving traditional values and protecting the status of the middle class. As campus protests and race riots began to subside after the traumas of 1968 and 1970, his policies seemed to be succeeding.

In fact, however, it was in large part an illusory success; for despite Nixon's efforts, government responsibility for social welfare and federal intrusion into local communities increased dramatically during his administration. The steady growth in the size of the urban "underclass"—impoverished inner-city residents totally and permanently dependent on welfare—by itself mandated a major expansion in federal assistance. So did the inexorable momentum of a government bureaucracy whose major thrust for decades had been the extension of its own authority. A steady stream of new regulations—on school desegregation, on Affirmative Action, on agricultural practices, and on many other issues—flowed from Washington despite the president's commitment to decentralized power. Nixon succeeded in changing many public assumptions about the proper role of the federal government. It remained for others, however, to attempt to translate the new assumptions into reality.

The Nixon Court

One of the loudest cheers during Richard Nixon's acceptance speech at the 1968 Republican Convention greeted his pledge to change the composition of the Supreme Court. The reaction was unsurprising. Of all the liberal institutions that had aroused the enmity of the "silent majority" in the 1950s and 1960s, none had evoked more anger and bitterness than the Warren Court. Not only had its rulings on racial matters disrupted traditional social patterns in both the North and the South, but its staunch defense of civil liberties had, in the eyes of many Americans, contributed directly to the increase in crime, disorder, and moral decay. One after another landmark decision seemed to tread on the sensibilities of provincial and conservative Americans. In *Engel* v. *Vitale* (1962), the Court had ruled that prayers in public schools were unconstitutional, sparking outrage among religious fundamentalists and others, who would spend more than two decades fighting the edict. In *Roth* v. *United States* (1957), the Court had sharply limited the authority of local governments to curb pornography. In *Gideon* v. *Wainwright* (1963), the Court had ruled that every felony defendant was entitled to a lawyer regardless of his or her ability to pay; in *Escobedo* v. *Illinois* (1964), the Court had declared that a defendant must be allowed access to a lawyer before questioning by police; above all, in *Miranda* v. *Arizona* (1966), the Court had confirmed the obligation of authorities to inform a criminal suspect of his or her rights. In these and other cases, the Court had greatly strengthened the civil rights of criminal defendants and had, in the eyes of many Americans, greatly weakened the power of law-enforcement officials to do their jobs.

Other examples of "judicial activism" had antagonized both local and national political leaders. In *Baker* v. *Carr* (1962), the Warren Court, in its most influential decision since *Brown* v. *Board of Education*, had ordered state legislatures to apportion representation so that the votes of all citizens would carry equal weight. In dozens of states, systems of legislative districting that had given disproportionate representation to rural areas were thus rendered invalid. The reapportionment that resulted greatly increased the political voice of blacks, Hispanics, and other poor urban residents. By 1968, in short, the Warren Court had become the target of Americans of all kinds who felt that the balance of power in the United States had shifted too far toward the poor and dispossessed at the expense of the middle class.

Richard Nixon shared such sentiments, and he was determined to use his judicial appointments to give the Court a more conservative cast. His first opportunity came almost as soon as he entered office. Chief Justice Earl Warren, who had tried to resign during the last months of the Johnson administration only to be stymied by the refusal of Congress to approve the appointment of liberal Associate Justice Abe Fortas as his successor, announced his resignation early in 1969. Nixon replaced him with a federal appeals court judge of known conservative leanings, Warren Burger.

The president had less success in filling the next Court opening to become available. In May 1969, Abe Fortas resigned his seat after the disclosure of a series of alleged financial improprieties. To replace him, Nixon named Clement F. Haynsworth, a federal circuit court judge from South Carolina. Although Haynsworth received the endorsement of the American Bar Association and had the respect of much of the judicial community, he came under fire from Senate liberals, black organizations, and labor unions for his conservative record on civil rights. The damaging discovery that he had sat on cases involving corporations in which he himself had a financial interest created even more opposition; and the Senate finally rejected him.

Nixon's next choice was a particularly unfortunate one, motivated some believed by the president's desire to punish the liberals who had scuttled the Haynsworth nomination. G. Harold Carswell, a judge of the Florida federal appeals court, was almost entirely lacking in distinction. Critics quickly pointed out that an inordinate number of his cases had been reversed by a higher court. Others uncovered evidence of racist statements that Carswell had made in the past. Most damaging of all, however, was the widely held belief that the new appointee was simply unfit for the Supreme Court—a mediocre man being elevated to a position for which he was unqualified. Nixon supporter Roman Hruska, a conservative senator from Nebraska, did not help matters by arguing publicly that even if Carswell was mediocre, he should be approved to give mediocre people "a little representation" too. "We can't have all Brandeises and Frankfurters and Cardozos," Hruska explained. The Senate rejected the Carswell nomination.

An enraged President Nixon, ignoring the real reasons for these unprecedented congressional defeats, announced that the votes had been a result of prejudice against the South. But he was careful thereafter to choose men of standing within the legal community to fill vacancies on the Supreme Court. Harry Blackmun, a moderate jurist from Minnesota; Lewis F. Powell, Jr., a respected judge from Virginia; and William Rehnquist, a member of the Nixon Justice Department—all met with little opposition from the Senate. And the Warren Court gradually gave way to what many observers came to describe as the "Burger Court," but which others termed the "Nixon Court."

The new Court, however, fell short of what the president and many conservatives had hoped. Far from retreating from its commitment to social reform, the Court in many areas actually extended its reach. In *Swann* v. *Charlotte-Mecklenburg Board of Education* (1971), it ruled in favor of the use of forced busing to achieve racial balance in schools. Not even the intense and occasionally violent opposition of local communities as diverse as Boston and Louisville, Kentucky, was able to weaken the judicial commitment to integration. In *Furman* v. *Georgia* (1972), the Court overturned existing capital punishment statutes and established strict new guidelines for such laws in the future. In *Roe* v. *Wade* (1972), it struck down laws forbidding women to have abortions.

In other decisions, however, the Burger Court did signal a marked withdrawal from its crusading commitment to civil liberties and reform. It attempted instead to create a moderate balance. Although the justices approved busing as a tool for achieving integration, they rejected, in *Milliken* v. *Bradley* (1974), a plan to transfer students across district lines (in this case, between Detroit and its suburbs) to achieve racial balance. While the Court upheld the principle of Affirmative Action in its celebrated 1978 decision *Bakke* v. *Board of Regents of California*, it established restrictive new guidelines for such programs in the future. In other rulings, it confirmed the right of the press to publish free from government restraints (as in the 1971 Pentagon Papers decision) but limited the right of reporters to withhold information about their sources from the courts. The justices were slower to retreat from the unpopular Warren Court rulings expanding the protections available to criminal defendants, but they showed signs of retrenchment there as well. In *Stone* v. *Powell* (1976), for example, the Court agreed to certain limits on the right of a defendant to appeal a state conviction to the federal judiciary.

The Election of 1972

However unsuccessful the Nixon administration may have been in achieving some of its specific goals, it had by 1972 scored a series of triumphs in enlisting the loyalties of the electorate. The "real majority"—what a 1970 book of that name by Richard Scammon and Ben Wattenberg called the "unyoung, unblack, and unpoor"—responded enthusiastically to the president's attacks on liberal court decisions; his denunciation of radicals, hippies, and the liberal press; his opposition to busing, abortion, and pornography; his support for traditional moral and religious values; and his appeal for new efforts to combat crime. They approved his call for retrenchment in social welfare programs, and they applauded his restraint—or, as Daniel Moynihan described it, "benign neglect"—in advancing the cause of civil rights. Although the unpopularity of the war in Vietnam continued to plague him as the reelection campaign approached, Nixon's dramatic initiatives in the Soviet Union and China increased public confidence in his ability to end the fighting.

Nixon entered the presidential race in 1972, therefore, with a substantial reserve of strength. The events of that year improved his position immeasurably. His energetic re-election committee collected enormous sums of money to support the campaign. The president himself made full use of the powers of incumbency, refraining from campaigning in the primaries (in which he faced, in any case, only token opposition) and concentrating on highly publicized international decisions and state visits. And agencies of the federal government dispensed funds and favors to communities around the country in a concerted effort to strengthen Nixon's political standing in questionable areas.

Nixon was most fortunate in 1972, however, in his opposition. The return of George Wallace to the presidential fray caused some early concern, for Nixon's own reelection strategy rested on the same appeals to the troubled middle class that Wallace was so skillfully expressing. But although Wallace showed remarkable strength in the early Democratic primaries, the possibility of another third-party campaign in the fall vanished in May, when a would-be assassin shot the Alabama governor during a rally at a Maryland shopping center. Paralyzed from the waist down, Wallace was unable to continue campaigning.

The Democrats, in the meantime, were making the greatest contribution to the Nixon cause by nominating for president a representative of their most liberal faction: Senator George S. McGovern of South Dakota. An outspoken critic of the war, a forceful advocate of liberal positions on virtually every social and economic issue, McGovern seemed to embody those aspects of the turbulent 1960s that middle-class Americans were most eager to reject. McGovern profited greatly from party reforms (which he himself had helped to draft) that gave increased influence to women, blacks, and young people in the selection of the Democratic ticket. But those same reforms helped make the Democratic Convention of 1972 an unappealing spectacle to much of the public. The party's left wing, flushed with triumph, ran roughshod over Democratic conservatives—among other things, ousting the delegation of Mayor Richard Daley of Chicago from the convention. To many voters watching on television, the proceedings supported an already growing impression that McGovern was the candidate of hippies, aggressive women, and blacks. The candidate then disillusioned even some of his own supporters by his confused response to revelations that his running mate, Senator Thomas Eagleton of Missouri, had undergone treatment for an emotional disturbance. McGovern first announced that he supported Eagleton "1,000 percent," then suddenly dropped him from the ticket. The remainder of the Democratic presidential campaign was an exercise in futility.

For Nixon, by contrast, the fall campaign was an uninterrupted triumphal procession. After a Republican Convention utterly devoid of controversy, the president made a few, carefully planned appearances in strategic areas of the country. Most of his time, however, he devoted to highly publicized work on behalf of "world peace." And in October, although by then it was clearly unnecessary politically, he sealed the victory with a skillfully orchestrated demonstration that a settlement of the war in Vietnam was near. On election day, as a result, Nixon won reelection by one of the largest margins in history: 60.8 percent of the popular vote compared with 37.5 percent for the forlorn McGovern, an electoral margin of 520 to 17. The Democratic candidate had carried only Massachusetts and the District of Columbia. The new commitments that Nixon had so effectively expressed—to restraint in social reform, to decentralization of political power, to the defense of traditional values, and to a new balance in international relations—had clearly won the approval of the American people. But other problems, some beyond the president's control and some of his own making, were already lurking in the wings.

THE TROUBLED ECONOMY

Although it was political scandal that would ultimately destroy the Nixon presidency, an even more serious national crisis was emerging in the early 1970s: the decline of the American economy. Rising inflation, eroding productivity, and a weakening position in international trade all contributed to a serious deterioration in the nation's once robust economic health. Americans had grown accustomed to boundless prosperity and uninterrupted growth, and they looked to their government to restore both when things began to turn sour. The inability of the government to do so greatly intensified public unhappiness about the quality of leadership.

Sources of Decline

For more than twenty years, the American economy had been the envy of the world. The United States had been responsible for as much as a third of the world's industrial production and had dominated international trade. The American dollar had been the strongest currency in the world, the yardstick by which other nations measured their own monetary health. The American standard of living, already high at the end of World War II, had improved dramatically in the years since. Personal incomes had doubled, and spending both on major investments and on consumer goods had soared. Most Americans had begun to assume that this remarkable prosperity was the normal condition of their society. In fact, however, it had rested in large part on several artificial conditions that were by the late 1960s rapidly disappearing.

The most disturbing economic problem, one that was symptomatic of all the others, was inflation, which had been creeping upward for several years when Richard Nixon took office and which shortly thereafter began to soar. Its most visible cause was the performance of the federal government in the mid-1960s. At the same time that President Johnson had persuaded Congress to accept a tax cut in 1964, he was rapidly increasing spending both for domestic social programs and for the war in Vietnam. The result was a major expansion of the money supply, resting largely on government deficits, that pushed prices rapidly upward.

But there were other, more fundamental causes of the inflation and of the economic problems that lay behind it. Much of America's economic strength in the 1950s and 1960s had rested on the nation's unquestioned supremacy in international trade. American industrial goods were in high demand around the world; and the United States had easy access to raw materials, unconstrained by competition from other, weaker industrial nations. By the late 1960s, however, the world economic picture had changed. No longer were American factories unchallenged in pursuit of world markets. They faced stiff competition from West Germany, Japan, and other emerging economic powers. No more did the United States have exclusive access to cheap raw materials around the globe; not only were other industrial nations now competing for increasingly scarce raw materials, but Third World suppliers of those materials were beginning to realize their value and demand higher prices for them.

Central to the problem, it gradually became clear, was access to sources of energy. More than any nation on earth, the United States had based its economy on the easy availability of cheap and plentiful fuels. No society was more dependent on the automobile; none was more profligate in its use of oil and gas in its homes, schools, and factories. As the economy expanded in the 1960s, an already high demand for energy soared much higher. And with domestic petroleum reserves beginning to dwindle, the nation increased its dependence on imports from the Middle East and Africa.

For many years, the Organization of Petroleum Exporting Countries (OPEC) had operated as an informal bargaining unit for the sale of oil by Third World nations. Not until the early 1970s, however, did it begin to display its strength. Aware of the growing dependence of Western economies on the resources of its member nations, OPEC was

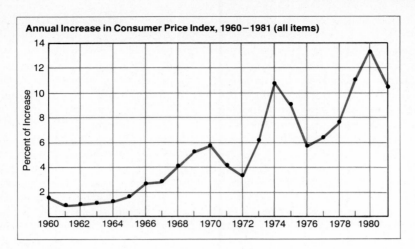

Annual Increase in Consumer Price Index, 1960–1981 (all items)

no longer willing to follow the direction of American and European oil companies. Instead, it began to use its oil both as an economic tool and as a political weapon. In 1973, in the midst of the Yom Kippur War, Arab members of OPEC announced that they would no longer ship petroleum to nations supporting Israel—that is, to the United States and its allies in Western Europe. At about the same time, the OPEC nations agreed to raise their prices 400 percent. These twin shocks produced momentary chaos in the West. The United States suffered its first fuel shortage since World War II, and the disruptive effects were a painful reminder to the American people of their dependence on plentiful energy. Motorists faced long lines at gas stations; schools and offices closed down to save on heating oil; factories cut production and laid off workers for lack of sufficient fuel. A few months later, the crisis eased. But the price of energy continued to skyrocket in the following years, both because of OPEC's new militant policies and because of the weakening competitive position of the dollar in world markets. No single factor did more to produce the soaring inflation of the 1970s.

The Nixon Response

Richard Nixon, therefore, inherited an economy in which growth was already sluggish, in which inflation was already troubling, and

in which even greater new problems lurked. Within weeks of taking office, he announced a "game plan" for dealing with these various woes. He would, he promised, spend less and tax more. But such policies were easier announced than implemented, evoking as they did both congressional and popular protest. As a result, Nixon turned increasingly to an economic tool more readily available to him: control of the currency. Placing conservative economists at the head of the Federal Reserve Board, he ensured sharply higher interest rates and a contraction of the money supply. But the "tight money" policy did little to curb inflation. The cost of living rose nearly 15 percent during Nixon's first two and a half years in office. In 1971, moreover, the United States recorded its first balance-of-trade deficit (an excess of imports over exports) in nearly eighty years. With inflation unabated and economic growth in decline, the United States was encountering a new and puzzling dilemma: "stagflation," a combination of rising prices and general economic stagnation.

By the summer of 1971, therefore, the president was under strong public pressure to act decisively to reverse the economic tide. First, he released the dollar from the fluctuating gold standard that had controlled its worth since the end of World War II, allowing its value to fall in world markets. The devaluation helped stimulate exports, but it also made it more expensive for America to purchase vital raw materials abroad. At the

Energy Crisis
Gasoline shortages in 1973 and again in 1979 introduced Americans to the reality of the worldwide energy crisis. Long lines at gas stations tried the patience of the public, producing complaints, arguments, and occasionally violence. (UPI)

same time, the president announced an even bolder and more startling new policy. For years, he had denounced the idea of using government controls to curb inflation. His experience as an employee of the Office of Price Administration during World War II had left him with a deep distaste for wage and price regulation; and as late as June 1970, he had insisted: "I will not take this nation down the road of wage and price controls." On August 15, 1971, however, he reversed himself. Under the provisions of the Economic Stabilization Act of 1970, the president imposed a ninety-day freeze on all wages and prices at their existing levels. Then, in November, he launched Phase II of his economic plan: mandatory guidelines for wage and price increases, to be administered by a federal agency. Inflation subsided tem-

porarily, but the recession continued. The unemployment rate for 1971 was 6 percent, compared with 4 percent two years earlier.

Fearful that the recession would be more damaging than inflation in an election year, the administration reversed itself once again late in 1971: interest rates dropped sharply; government spending increased—producing the largest budget deficit since World War II. The new tactics served their purpose. By election day, personal incomes were up and unemployment was down. But there were disastrous side effects. Even though wage and price controls managed to hold down inflation in some areas, consumers were soon paying drastically higher prices for food and other basic goods. At this critical moment, with both domestic and world inflation on the verge of skyrocketing, Nixon abandoned the strict Phase II controls and replaced them with a set of flexible, largely voluntary, and almost entirely ineffective guidelines—Phase III of the administration's economic program.

With the end of wage and price controls, inflation quickly resumed its upward course. The rate for 1973 rose to 9 percent; in 1974, after the Arab oil embargo and the OPEC price increases, it soared to 12 percent, the highest rate since shortly after the end of World War II. The value of the dollar continued to slide, and the nation's international trade continued to decline. Nixon now turned his attention to solving the new "energy crisis," which had become America's most pressing preoccupation. But the administration seemed to have no clearer idea of how to deal with that problem than it had of how to deal with the general inflation. The president spoke vaguely of conservation, of increasing production, of restoring "energy independence." But there were few concrete proposals for accomplishing them. And Nixon, in the meantime, was becoming so embroiled in his own political problems that he would have had great difficulty winning approval of a major new program in any case.

The stumbling and erratic economic programs of the Nixon administration were indicative of a broader national confusion about the future prospects for American prosperity. With little understanding of the international forces creating the economic problems, both the government and the people focused on immediate issues and short-range solutions. The Nixon pattern—of lurching from a tight money policy to curb inflation at one moment to a spending policy to cure recession at the next—repeated itself during the two administrations that followed. Such policies had little effect, ultimately, either on inflation or on the general economic stagnation.

WATERGATE AND THE PRESIDENCY

Although economic problems greatly concerned the American people in the 1970s, a stunning political development almost entirely preoccupied the nation beginning early in 1973: the fall of Richard Nixon. The president's political demise was a result in part of his own personality. Defensive, secretive, resentful of his critics, he brought to his office an element of mean-spiritedness that helped undermine even his most important accomplishments. But the larger explanation lay in Nixon's view of American society and the world, and of his own role in both. Far more than most of his compatriots, the president was convinced that the United States faced grave dangers from the radicals and dissidents who were challenging his policies. Obsessed with what he considered his mission to create a new "structure of peace" in the world, he came increasingly to consider any challenge to his policies a threat to "national security." By identifying his own political fortunes with those of the nation, in other words, Nixon was creating a climate in which he and those who served him could justify virtually any means to stifle dissent and undermine opposition.

The White House Autocracy

Nixon's outlook was in part a culmination of decades of changes in the nature of the presidency. Public expectations of the president had increased dramatically in the years since World War II; yet the constraints on the authority of the office had grown as well. Congress had become more difficult to control; the bureaucracy had become cumbersome and unmanageable; the press, particularly in light of the war in Vietnam, had become suspicious and increasingly hostile. In response, a succession of presidents had sought out new methods for the exercise of power, often stretching the law, occasionally breaking it.

Nixon not only continued, but greatly accelerated these trends. Facing a Democratic Congress hostile to his goals, he attempted to find ways to circumvent the legislature whenever possible. Saddled with a federal bureaucracy unresponsive to his wishes, he constructed a hierarchy of command in which virtually all executive power became concentrated in the White House. A few cabinet members retained direct access to the president, among them Attorney General John Mitchell, a longtime personal friend, and Henry Kissinger, who became secretary of state in 1973 but had already established himself as the dominant figure in American foreign policy. For the most part, however, Nixon isolated himself almost completely, relying on a few trusted advisers through whom he exercised his power. At the head of what critics sometimes called the "palace guard" stood two particularly influential aides: H. R. Haldeman, the president's chief of staff, and John Ehrlichman, his chief domestic adviser. Operating within this rigid, autocratic structure, the president became a solitary, brooding figure, whose contempt for his opponents and impatience with obstacles to his policies festered and grew. Insulated from criticism, surrounded by flatterers, he became increasingly blatant in his defiance of the normal constraints on his office. Unknown to all but a few intimates, he also became mired in a pattern of illegalities and abuses of power that late in 1972 began to burst to the surface.

The Spreading Scandals

Early in the morning of June 17, 1972, police arrested five men who had broken into the offices of the Democratic National Committee, located in the Watergate Office Building in Washington, D.C. Two others were seized a short time later and charged with supervising the break-in. And when reporters for the *Washington Post* began researching the backgrounds of the culprits, they discovered a series of startling facts. Among those involved in the burglary were former employees of the Committee for the Re-Election of the President (CRP). One of them had worked in the White House itself. They had, moreover, been paid for the break-in from a secret fund of the reelection committee, a fund controlled by members of the White House staff. The further the reporters looked, the more

evidence they found that the burglary had been part of a larger pattern of illegalities, planned and financed by the president's closest associates.

Public interest in the disclosures grew only slowly in the last months of 1972. Few Americans, apparently, chose to question the president's assurances that neither he nor his staff had any connection with what he called "this very bizarre incident." Early in 1973, however, the Watergate burglars went on trial; and under relentless prodding from federal judge John J. Sirica, one of the defendants, James W. McCord, agreed to cooperate both with the grand jury and with a special Senate investigating committee recently established under Senator Sam J. Ervin of North Carolina. McCord's testimony opened a floodgate of confessions, and for months a parade of White House and campaign officials exposed one illegality after another. Foremost among them was a member of the inner circle of the White House, Counsel to the President John Dean, who leveled allegations against Nixon himself.

There were, in effect, two separate scandals emerging from the investigations. One was a general pattern of abuses of power involving both the White House and the Nixon campaign committee. Every week, it seemed, there was a new, even more damaging revelation. White House "plumbers," under the direction of John Ehrlichman, had established illegal wiretaps, intercepted mail, and engaged in burglaries (including the attempt to steal files from Daniel Ellsberg's psychiatrist) in an effort to prevent leaks of sensitive or politically embarrassing information, or, as in Ellsberg's case, to discredit critics of the administration. Members of the reelection committee had solicited illegal contributions, "laundered" the money through accounts in Mexico, and used the funds to support a variety of "dirty tricks" against Democratic presidential candidates and other maneuvers to sabotage the campaigns of Nixon's opponents. And associates of the president had created devious opportunities for Nixon to increase his personal wealth, including several real-estate transactions and income-tax dodges of dubious legality.

The Watergate burglary, was, therefore,

only a small part of a larger pattern. But it was the break-in itself that became the major focus of public attention for nearly two years. There was never any conclusive evidence that the president had planned or approved the burglary in advance. John Dean and others testified that it had been the responsibility of then Attorney General Mitchell, who had hoped to plant electronic bugs in and steal copies of files from the Democratic offices. (Mitchell had subsequently resigned from the Justice Department to head the president's reelection committee; then, after the scandals began to break, he resigned from CRP as well, citing "personal problems.") But if there was no proof that Nixon had planned the break-in, there was mounting suspicion that he had been involved in what became known as the "cover-up"—illegal efforts to obstruct investigations of and to withhold information about the episode. Testimony before the Ervin Committee provided evidence of the complicity not only of Dean and Mitchell, but of Haldeman, Ehrlichman, and other key White House figures. As interest in the case grew to something approaching a national obsession, only one question remained: in the words of Senator Howard Baker of Tennessee, a member of the Ervin Committee, "What did the President know and when did he know it?"

Nixon, in the meantime, steadfastly denied knowing anything. One by one, he accepted the departure of those members of his administration implicated in the scandals: first a string of lower-level aides; then, with great reluctance, Haldeman and Ehrlichman, who resigned on the same day that Nixon dismissed John Dean. But the president himself remained adamant, declaring at one news conference: "I am not a crook."

There the matter might have rested had it not been for the disclosure during the Senate hearings of a White House taping system that had recorded virtually every conversation in the president's office during the period in question. All the various groups investigating the scandals sought access to the tapes; Nixon, pleading "executive privilege," refused to release them. A special prosecutor appointed by the president to handle the Watergate cases, Harvard law professor Ar-

chibald Cox, took Nixon to court in October 1973 in an effort to force him to relinquish the recordings. Nixon, now clearly growing desperate, fired Cox and suffered the humiliation of watching both Attorney General Elliot Richardson (who had succeeded Mitchell) and his deputy resign in protest. This "Saturday night massacre" made the president's predicament infinitely worse. Not only did public pressure force him to appoint a new special prosecutor, Texas attorney Leon Jaworski, who proved just as determined as Cox to subpoena the tapes; but the episode precipitated an investigation by the House of Representatives into the possibility of impeachment.

The Fall of Richard Nixon

Nixon's situation deteriorated further in the following months. Late in 1973, Vice President Spiro Agnew became embroiled in a scandal of his own when evidence surfaced that he had accepted bribes and kickbacks while serving as governor of Maryland. In return for a Justice Department agreement not to press the case, Agnew pleaded *nolo contendere* (no contest) to a lesser charge, of income-tax evasion, and resigned from the government. With the controversial Agnew no longer in line to succeed to the presidency, the prospect of removing Nixon from the White House suddenly became far less worrisome to Democrats. The new vice president was House Minority Leader Gerald Ford, an amiable and popular Michigan congressman whom Democrats considered more acceptable. The impeachment investigation quickly gathered pace. In April 1974, in an effort to head off further subpoenas of the tapes, the president released transcripts of a number of relevant conversations, claiming that they proved his innocence. Investigators and much of the public felt otherwise. Even these edited tapes seemed to suggest not only appalling ill will on Nixon's part but also his complicity in the cover-up.

In July, finally, the crisis came to a boil. First the Supreme Court ruled unanimously, in *United States* v. *Richard M. Nixon,* that the president must relinquish the tapes to Special Prosecutor Jaworski. Days later, the House Judiciary Committee voted to recommend three articles of impeachment, charging that Nixon had, first, obstructed justice in the Watergate cover-up; second, misused federal agencies to violate the rights of citizens; and third, defied the authority of Congress by refusing to deliver tapes and other materials subpoenaed by the committee. Even without additional evidence, Nixon might well have been impeached by the full House and convicted by the Senate. Early in August, however, he provided at last the "smoking gun," the concrete proof of his guilt that his defenders had long contended was missing from the case against him. Among the tapes that the Supreme Court compelled Nixon to relinquish were several that offered incontrovertible evidence of his involvement in the Watergate cover-up. Only days after the burglary, the recordings disclosed, the president had ordered the FBI to stop investigating the break-in. Impeachment and conviction now loomed inevitable.

For several days, Nixon brooded in the White House, on the verge, some claimed, of a mental breakdown. Many of the normal operations of the government ground to a virtual halt as the nation waited tensely for a resolution of the greatest constitutional crisis since Reconstruction. Finally, on August 8, 1974, Nixon addressed the nation and announced his resignation—the first president in American history ever to do so. At noon the next day, while Nixon and his family were flying west to their home in California, Gerald Ford took the oath of office as president.

Americans expressed both relief and exhilaration that, as the new president put it, "Our long national nightmare is over." They were relieved to be rid of Richard Nixon, who had lost virtually all of the wide popularity that had won him his landslide re-election victory only two years before. And they were exhilarated that, as some boasted, "the system had worked." A president had been held accountable to the law; and the transfer of power had been smooth and orderly. But the wave of good feeling could not obscure the deeper and more lasting damage of the Watergate crisis. In a society in which distrust of leaders and of institutions of authority was already widespread, the fall of Richard Nixon seemed to confirm the most cynical assumptions about the character of American public life. The depths of that cynicism were evident in the widespread belief, which public-opinion polls documented, that what Nixon had done, bad as it was, was little worse than what other presidents had done undetected before him.

SUGGESTED READINGS

A fascinating examination of Richard Nixon, written early in his presidency, is Garry Wills, *Nixon Agonistes* (1970). Jonathan Schell, *The Time of Illusion* (1975), is the best general analysis of the Nixon administration. See also William Safire, *Before the Fall* (1975), for an insider's view; and Nixon's own account, *RN: The Memoirs of Richard Nixon* (1978). Fawn Brodie, *Richard Nixon* (1981), and Bruce Mazlish, *In Search of Nixon* (1972), are psychological portraits. On the Nixon–Kissinger policies in Southeast Asia, see Kissinger's memoirs, *White House Years* (1979), for a defense. More hostile are Gareth Porter, *A Peace Denied* (1975), and William Shawcross, *Nixon, Kissinger, and the Destruction of Cambodia* (1978), a devastating attack. General studies of the Nixon–Kissinger foreign policy, in addition to Kissinger's memoirs, include Roger Morris, *Uncertain Greatness* (1977), and Seyom Brown, *The Crises of Power* (1979). On Kissinger himself, see David Landau, *Kissinger: The Uses* *of Power* (1972); Marvin Kalb and Bernard Kalb, *Kissinger* (1974). Kissinger's second volume of memoirs, *Years of Upheaval* (1982), discusses the period 1973–1975. Other useful works include Tad Szulc, *The Illusion of Peace* (1978), and Roger Hilsman, *The Crouching Future* (1975). On arms control and détente, see Harland Moulton, *From Superiority to Parity* (1973). John Stockwell, *In Search of Enemies* (1977), and Thomas Powers, *The Man Who Kept the Secrets* (1979), examine the CIA. Michel Oksenberg and Robert Oxnam (eds.), *Dragon and Eagle* (1978), discusses the changing Sino-American relationship. William Quandt, *Decade of Decision* (1977), and Robert Stookey, *America and the Arab States* (1975), discuss the United States and the Middle East.

On Nixon's domestic policies, in addition to the general studies mentioned above, see Daniel P. Moynihan, *The Politics of a Guaranteed Income* (1973), and Vincent Burke and Vee Burke, *Nixon's Good Deed*

(1974), on welfare reform; and R. L. Miller, *The New Economics of Richard Nixon* (1972), and R. P. Nathan et al., *Monitoring Revenue Sharing* (1975), for economic policy and the New Federalism. Bob Woodward and Scott Armstrong, *The Brethren* (1980), is a gossipy but revealing picture of the Nixon Court. Theodore H. White, *The Making of the President, 1972* (1973), is an admiring account of Nixon's triumphant reelection. The changing economic climate is examined in Richard Barnet, *The Lean Years* (1980), a controversial study of scarcity, and in Joan Edelman Spero, *The Politics of International Economic Relations* (1977). J. C. Hurewitz (ed.), *Oil, the Arab-Israeli Dispute, and the Industrial World* (1976), examines the energy crisis. The Watergate affair has already spawned a vast literature. In addition to the general studies of the Nixon administration cited above, see Theodore H. White, *Breach of Faith* (1975), and Anthony Lukas, *Nightmare* (1976). Bob Woodward and Carl Bernstein, *All the President's Men* (1974), is a personal account by the reporters who first broke the Watergate story. *The Final Days* (1976), by the same authors, chronicles Nixon's last days in the White House. John Dean, *Blind Ambition* (1976), is the most revealing of the many Watergate memoirs by members of the Nixon administration. Its veracity is challenged by John Ehrlichman, *Witness to Power* (1982). Richard Cohen and Jules Witcover, *A Heartbeat Away* (1974), chronicles the fall of Spiro T. Agnew. A broad study of the expanding powers of the presidency, culminating in a review of Watergate, is Arthur M. Schlesinger, Jr., *The Imperial Presidency* (1973).

A Search for Answers

32

The Hostages Return, 1981
The fifty-one Americans who had been held in captivity for more than a year by militants in Iran step off a plane at an American air force base in West Germany, completing the first leg of their trip home to the United States. Their return to America produced an outpouring of national celebration unequaled since the end of World War II. But their long captivity had been a painful and humiliating lesson to the nation in the limits of its power in the world. (UPI)

America by the mid-1970s was a nation in search of its future. But as to what that future could or should be there was little agreement. A decade before, the country had been engaged in a debate over how best to distribute the fruits of its abundant economy. Now it was facing serious questions about whether that economy could be prevented from collapsing. In the 1960s, Americans had argued over how best to use their awesome international power. Now the nation wondered how much of that power still existed. The United States was, in short, mired in a bewildering search for answers to what was coming to be known as the "question of limits." Harsh new realities, both at home and in the world, were requiring major adjustments in virtually every area of American life.

One such adjustment occurred in the fabric of the nation's society and culture. In the 1960s, many Americans had dreamed of a country able and willing to solve virtually all its problems. That vision of perfection had fueled the liberal reforms of the early part of the decade and, in somewhat different form, the radicalism of the second half. In the 1970s, the yearning for fundamental social change faded. In its place emerged a new cultural outlook that focused less on the direction of society than on the plight of the individual. Journalist Tom Wolfe, in an influential magazine essay, christened the 1970s the "Me Decade." Whether or not that label was entirely fair, it was clear that many Americans were growing more cautious, more conservative, and more inward-looking.

A similar narrowing of expectations was affecting national politics. The election of Richard Nixon in 1968 (and again in 1972) had been a first signal of the nation's turn to the right. After Nixon's fall, the political climate continued to grow more conservative. Under Gerald Ford (Nixon's immediate successor), under Jimmy Carter, and above all under Ronald Reagan, the government seemed to be turning even further away from the expansive liberal visions of the 1960s.

THE FORD CUSTODIANSHIP

Gerald Ford inherited the presidency under unenviable circumstances. He faced both the public cynicism that had emerged from the Watergate scandals and the popular fears that were developing as a result of economic decay and social disorder. His task, therefore, was to restore confidence in the presidency and to revive a stable prosperity in the nation at large. He enjoyed modest success in the first of these efforts but very little in the second.

Restoring Confidence

Few Americans considered Ford a brilliant or an overwhelmingly skillful leader. (Jokes about presidential clumsiness and ineptitude abounded.) But the public admired his candor and his obvious integrity. Polls showed that nearly three-quarters of the nation approved his performance during his first months in office.

At first, Ford worked largely through the White House staff and cabinet he had inherited from Richard Nixon. Slowly, however, he began to fill his administration with officials of his own choosing; and in the process he showed signs of trying to pull together the two wings of the Republican party. To fill the vacant post of vice president, he appointed former New York governor Nelson Rockefeller, who had for years been the most conspicuous Republican liberal. In his

The Transfer of Power
Only moments before this picture was taken, Richard Nixon had delivered an emotional, tearful farewell to the White House staff as he prepared to fly home to California after resigning his office. Here, Gerald Ford—who would later that day take the oath of office as president—walks Nixon to a waiting helicopter. Between the two presidents are their wives, Betty Ford and Pat Nixon. (UPI)

cabinet, he sought to give representation to a far wider spectrum of the population than his predecessor; among his nominees were a university president, a college professor, a woman, and a black.

The president's effort to establish himself as a symbol of candor and integrity suffered a severe setback only a month after he took office when he suddenly granted Richard Nixon "a full, free, and absolute pardon . . . for all offenses against the United States" during his presidency. Ford explained that he was attempting to spare the nation the ordeal of years of litigation and to spare Nixon himself any further suffering. It was, he insisted, an act of "compassion," an effort "to firmly shut and seal this book." To much of the public, however, it was evidence of bad judgment at best and a secret deal with the former president at worst. Resentment of Nixon remained particularly high because the former president still refused to admit his guilt; many Americans believed that until he did, he should continue to suffer the consequences of his actions. Ford defended the pardon decision vigorously, even appearing before a congressional committee to explain it. But his action caused a decline in his popularity from which he never fully recovered.

Seeking International Stability

With the resignation of Nixon, the attention of the nation quickly returned to the more lasting problems confronting the United States, among them America's changing role in the world. At first, it seemed that the foreign policy of the Ford years would differ little from that of the Nixon administration. The new president retained Henry Kissinger as secretary of state and continued the general policies of seeking rapprochement with China, détente with the Soviet Union, and stability in the Middle East. For a time, there were signs of progress in all these areas.

In particular, there appeared to be major progress in the effort to produce another arms control agreement with the Soviet Union. Ford met with Leonid Brezhnev late in 1974 at Vladivostok in Siberia and signed a new accord that was to serve as the basis for SALT II. The following summer, a European security conference in Helsinki, Finland, produced an agreement that seemed to advance détente even further. The Soviet Union and Western nations agreed, at last, to ratify the borders that had divided Europe since the end of World War II; and, particularly important in American eyes, the Russians accepted the so-called Basket Three clause, which pledged increased respect for human rights.

In the Middle East, in the meantime, the tireless efforts of Henry Kissinger were producing some important results. After months of shuttling back and forth between Cairo and Tel Aviv, Kissinger announced a major new accord by which Israel agreed to return large portions of the occupied Sinai to Egypt, and the two nations pledged not to resolve future differences by force. In China, finally, the death of Mao Zedong in 1976 brought to power a new, more moderate government, eager to expand its ties with the United States.

But these successes were, in the end, only minor triumphs within a larger setting of frustration. For the Ford years witnessed a series of major setbacks in America's efforts to create a stable "structure of peace." The new relationship with the Soviet Union was already showing signs of wear by 1975. Critics argued that the Vladivostok accords had set such high ceilings on the construction of armaments that they were virtually meaningless. Members of Congress were raising an outcry over Soviet internal policies of repression toward dissidents and Jews. And there was growing concern as well about alleged Soviet interference in revolutions in Africa and Latin America. Ford and Kissinger continued to defend the idea of détente, but support for the policy was rapidly eroding.

Equally disturbing was what many Americans viewed as a pattern of defeats and embarrassments in all areas of the world. Vietnam and Cambodia fell to the communists in 1975, underscoring the futility of years of American effort. Arab nations that had once treated the United States with deference were now gleefully raising oil prices and threatening to reduce production. And Third World nations were becoming increasingly vocal in attacking the United States; the United Nations seemed at times to have become little more than a gallery for those who wished to denounce American policies. Humiliation piled on humiliation, until the government felt obliged to respond.

When members of the Cambodian Khmer Rouge (the communist organization now governing the nation) captured an unarmed American merchant ship, the *Mayaguez*, in the spring of 1975, the administration's patience seemed finally to snap. Ford sent in the marines to rescue the crew, even though the captors had by then already agreed to release them. This display of American force appealed to the nation's wounded sense of pride; but the result was the unnecessary deaths of several dozen American soldiers. At about the same time, the new American ambassador to the United Nations, Daniel Patrick Moynihan, launched his own campaign to restore American pride. His shrill counterattack against Third World delegates and his strident denunciations of the United Nations itself won him great popularity (and, in 1976, a United States Senate seat from New York); but his confrontational tactics, critics charged, eroded further the nation's already troubled relationship with emerging areas and damaged the already declining viability of the United Nations.

Energy and Inflation

The Ford administration enjoyed little more success than its predecessor in devising a workable approach to the nation's economic problems. Rejecting the idea of wage and price controls, the president called instead for voluntary efforts to curb inflation. He appeared at one press conference wearing a large button with the word "WIN" emblazoned across it—a symbol, he said, of his new campaign to "Whip Inflation Now." The WIN campaign had no discernible effect on the economy and invited wide public ridicule. Of somewhat greater impact was Ford's pursuit of the now familiar path of tightening the money supply to curb inflation, and then struggling to deal with the recession that resulted. By supporting high interest rates, opposing increased federal spending (largely by use of presidential vetoes), and resisting pressures for a tax reduction, Ford helped produce in 1974 and 1975 the severest recession since the 1930s. Production declined more than 10 percent in the first months of 1975, and unemployment rose to nearly 9 percent of the labor force. There was a temporary abatement of inflation, which dropped briefly below 5 percent in 1976; but by then, the administration was already beginning to reverse its course and support new measures to stimulate the economy.

Complicating these problems was the expanding energy crisis. Despite the rising cost of imported oil, American dependence on OPEC supplies continued to grow. And the nation's use of energy remained the highest in the world. The United States was responsible for nearly a third of the world's energy consumption every year, and it was by 1976 importing almost a third of its energy supply from the OPEC countries. The Ford administration imposed a few new regulations to force energy conservation, but to little effect. More important to the president's strategy was the proposed deregulation of the petroleum industry, which would have allowed the oil companies to charge more for their energy so as to encourage increased produc-

tion. The Democratic Congress resisted such proposals.

The Election of 1976

As the 1976 presidential election approached, Ford continued to enjoy a wide personal popularity, but his policies were coming under attack from both the right and the left. Conservative critics charged that the president was showing insufficient strength in dealing with America's declining position in the world. Liberals charged that he was attempting to fight inflation at the expense of the poor. In the Republican primary campaign, Ford faced a powerful challenge from former California governor Ronald Reagan, leader of the party's conservative wing. He only barely survived the assault, in part because he had agreed to abandon Nelson Rockefeller and choose another candidate, Senator Robert Dole of Kansas, for vice president.

THE ELECTION OF 1976

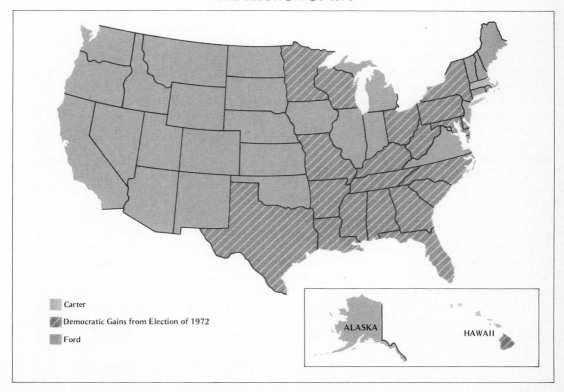

Carter

Democratic Gains from Election of 1972

Ford

ALASKA

HAWAII

The Democrats, in the meantime, were experiencing problems of their own. The fiasco of 1972 had left the party numb and confused, and there was little agreement in 1976 about who could best appeal to the troubled electorate. From this disarray emerged a new candidate almost entirely unknown to the nation at large: Jimmy Carter, a former governor of Georgia, who organized a brilliant primary campaign and appealed to the general unhappiness with government by promising to combat the "bloated bureaucracy." Capitalizing on the momentum of his early primary victories, Carter secured the Democratic nomination before most Americans had developed any very distinct impression of him. His campaign continued after the convention to emphasize "themes" —integrity, compassion, morality, and skepticism of government—rather than issues. And while the tentativeness of Carter's support became clear when his early, mammoth lead dwindled to almost nothing by election day, unhappiness with the economy and a general disenchantment with Ford enabled the Democrat to hold on for a narrow victory. Despite an unusually low voter turnout, which most observers believed was helpful to the Republicans, Carter emerged with 50 percent of the popular vote to Ford's 47.9 percent and 297 electoral votes to Ford's 240. Most Americans welcomed the prospect of a new political regime after eight years of Republican government characterized by frustration and crisis. But there were as yet few indications that Carter had any better ideas of how to deal with the mounting problems than the man he had defeated.

THE TRIALS OF JIMMY CARTER

It was Jimmy Carter's misfortune to assume the presidency at a moment when the nation faced problems of staggering complexity and difficulty. No leader could have avoided antagonizing much of the public under such inhospitable circumstances. But Carter made his predicament worse by a style of leadership that seemed to invite hostility and derision. And he left office in 1981 as one of the least popular presidents of the century.

The Outsider in Washington

Carter had campaigned for the presidency as an "outsider," a representative of ordinary Americans who was, like them, deeply suspicious of the entrenched bureaucracies and complacent officials who had dominated American government for decades. He carried much of that suspiciousness with him to Washington. Surrounding himself in the White House with a group of close-knit associates from Georgia, he seemed deliberately to spurn assistance from more experienced political figures. His first weeks in office abounded with stories of insulting behavior by the White House staff toward leaders of Congress. Cordiality was soon restored to most administration actions, but the president continued throughout his term in office to be plagued by his own inexperience and that of members of his staff. When his popularity began to slide, as it soon did, those who repudiated him numbered among their greatest complaints that he displayed little competence as a leader.

In fact, Carter was among the most intelligent and quick-witted men ever to serve in the White House. His greatest problem was less one of ability than of vision. Supporters in 1976 had dismissed the "fuzziness" of Carter's campaign as an effective electoral strategy. In the following years, however, they began to question whether it had not also been a reflection of Carter's real view of public policy. Never in the course of his presidency did he succeed in conveying to the public any coherent sense of purpose or overall direction. While he took firm and often courageous stands on individual issues, he failed to demonstrate any recognition of how such issues were linked together. His was, as a disenchanted member of his own White House staff later described it, a peculiarly "passionless presidency."

In the absence of any coherent guiding principles (beyond a strong and openly expressed Christian piety), Carter seemed at times to be governing almost exclusively through the use of symbols. On inauguration day, he spurned the traditional limousine and walked with his family down Pennsylvania Avenue from the Capitol to the White House. In the following months, he missed no opportunity to demonstrate his "closeness" to the people. To explain a new policy, he arranged a televised "fireside chat"; dressed informally in a cardigan sweater, the president spoke to the nation while seated in a wing chair beside a blazing fire (which burned out in the course of the broadcast). On several occasions, he visited "average" communities for "town meetings" with common citizens. And from time to time he participated in radio programs during which members of the public could telephone the White House and speak directly with the president. For a while, such tactics attracted wide popular approval. Gradually, however, much of the public began to look skeptically on the symbols, wondering if they were not serving as a substitute for policy.

Doubts about Carter's leadership grew particularly strong in response to a widespread perception that he was subordinating public policy to immediate political interests. His was the first administration to make extensive, almost daily use of public-opinion polls in the formulation of decisions. And the result, it often seemed, was a disturbing lack of consistency in direction, a tendency, as some critics put it, for Carter to "lurch from crisis to crisis." This perceived lack of purpose helped as well to make the president the target of criticism from almost every quarter. No political faction could be certain that Carter was its ally. Liberals, who had believed him in 1976 to be an authentic "populist," soon began to complain that he was more conservative than his Republican predecessors. Conservatives, who had taken heart at Carter's antigovernment campaign rhetoric, expressed scorn for his failure adequately to "tame" the federal bureaucracy. Even when Carter adopted a policy to the liking of a particular group, there was always an uneasy sense that the policy might soon be abandoned if political pressures dictated a different approach. Ultimately the president, who had won election by a narrow margin to begin with, lost almost all leverage in his dealings with Congress. So low was his popularity with the public through most of his term that few legislators feared the political costs of opposing him.

In spite of these problems, Carter did achieve a measure of success in his effort to reform and reorganize the federal government. As governor of Georgia, he had taken great pride in his creation of a more rationally organized bureaucracy. He attempted to do the same in Washington. He instituted a series of important reforms in the civil service, in an effort to make permanent government employees more responsive to the needs of the public and to give administrators more control over their staffs. He reshuffled many of the offices and agencies that had been springing up, often chaotically, for nearly two decades; and he created two new executive departments: the Department of Energy and the Department of Education. He also sponsored a reform of the Social Security System that provided it with at least a temporary reprieve from bankruptcy.

In other areas, Carter made genuine efforts to pursue reform, only to fall victim to congressional opposition. He proposed a major restructuring of the federal welfare system during his first year in office, only to see it die quietly in Congress. He introduced measures to reform the tax system, one of his most conspicuous campaign promises, but proved powerless to keep them from being gutted by special interest groups fighting to preserve or expand their favored status. The president's lack of political clout was, of course, one reason for these failures. So was his tendency to cave in to political pressures without serious resistance. But there is room for doubt as to whether any leader, working in the confused political climate in which Carter was operating, could have moved more rapidly.

Energy and the Economy

Like his two immediate predecessors, Carter was from the beginning of his administration required to devote the bulk of his domestic effort to the problems of the economy, which were becoming increasingly linked to the problems of energy. And like Nixon and Ford before him, Carter followed the familiar pattern of fighting inflation through tight money and fighting recession through economic stimulants. In his case, however, the order was reversed. Entering office in the midst of a severe recession, Carter moved first to reduce unemployment through an increase in public spending for public works and public services and a substantial cut in federal taxes. Unemployment soon began to decline—from nearly 8 percent late in 1976 to only slightly above 5 percent by the end of 1978. But inflation, predictably, soared. The Ford administration had left behind an inflation rate of slightly under 5 percent. In 1977, it rose to 7 percent, and in 1978 to nearly 10 percent. During Carter's last two years in office, things grew even worse, with inflation averaging well over 10 percent ("double-digit inflation," it began to be called) and at one point in 1980 reaching as high as 18 percent.

Carter responded in now traditional fashion. Appointing first G. William Miller and then Paul Volcker, conservative economists both, to head the Federal Reserve Board, he ensured a policy of high interest rates and reduced currency supplies. By 1980, interest rates had risen to the highest levels in American history, several times exceeding 20 percent. He began to cut back on government spending, vetoing some of the same public works and welfare proposals he had supported during his first year in office. He reduced and delayed the tax reductions he had earlier proposed. And although he introduced nothing as laughable as Gerald Ford's WIN program, he too created a voluntary and generally ineffective system of wage–price "restraint," to be administered through the Council on Wage and Price Stability. Its director, Alfred Kahn, became an energetic and articulate spokesman for fiscal caution, helping to elevate public awareness of the inflation problem. But neither Kahn's efforts nor any other aspects of the administration's policy succeeded in stopping the inflationary spiral. By 1980, the president was making frantic efforts to balance the federal budget.

Some economists claimed that a balanced budget was a prerequisite to price stability, others that it would only marginally reduce inflation. But the argument was never resolved because the president never managed to eliminate the deficits. The tight money policy, in the meantime, was by 1980 pushing the economy into another severe recession.

Inextricably tied to the problem of inflation was the problem of energy, which grew steadily more troublesome in the course of the Carter years. One of the president's first acts was to present to the public what he called a "comprehensive energy program," whose success, he insisted, was vital to the nation's future. Solving the energy problem, he claimed (in words borrowed from William James), was "the moral equivalent of war." The specific features of the Carter plan were less dramatic than the rhetoric. Central to the program was a major commitment to energy conservation, which most Democrats applauded. But the policy of encouraging conservation through a system of tax levies, tax incentives, and rebates antagonized countless interest groups. When Congress finally passed the president's energy bill in August 1978, little was left of the original proposals.

A particularly fierce battle had raged over the issue of deregulating the price of natural gas and domestic oil reserves. Carter urged dropping regulations so as to increase prices, which would, he claimed, both encourage conservation and increase production. But he insisted on coupling deregulation with a "windfall profits tax" on the oil and gas companies that many conservatives opposed. Liberals, in the meantime, wanted no price increases at all, fearful of the effect on the poor. They urged retention of controls. The final bill called for a gradual phasing out of many regulations, to be accompanied by a windfall profits tax far weaker than the president had requested.

In the summer of 1979, the energy battle moved into a new and more desperate phase. Increasing instability in the Middle East produced a second major fuel shortage, forcing American motorists to wait in long gasoline lines once again and creating problems for businesses, industries, and homeowners. In the midst of the crisis, OPEC announced another major price increase, clouding the economic picture still further. Faced with increasing pressure to act (and with public-opinion polls showing his approval rating at a dismal 26 percent, lower than Richard Nixon in his worst moments), Carter went to the presidential retreat Camp David in the Maryland mountains and invited a string of visitors to advise him—not only on a new energy program but on the revitalization of his administration.

Ten days later, he emerged to deliver a remarkable television address. Speaking with unusual fervor, the president complained of a "crisis of the American spirit" and a "national malaise" that had reduced the nation to confusion and despair. As a solution, he proposed a major new commitment to a "positive" energy program. His new proposals included the expansion and strengthening of some of his earlier ones: greater tax incentives for conservation and production, punitive taxes on "gas-guzzling" automobiles, increased use of coal, and research into solar and wind power. The heart of the program, however, was a major federal commitment to the development of new "synthetic fuels." Carter requested Congress to establish a federal corporation with a budget of nearly $90 billion to supervise the creation of the new industry. A scaled-down version of the president's proposals passed the Congress in 1980.

Human Rights and National Interests

Among Jimmy Carter's most fervent campaign promises was a pledge to build a new basis for American foreign policy, one in which the defense of "human rights" would replace the pursuit of "selfish interests" as the cornerstone of America's role in the world. Rhetorically, at least, Carter maintained that commitment during his first months in office, speaking out sharply and often about violations of human rights in many countries (including, most prominently, the Soviet Union) and establishing an Office of Human Rights in the State Department.

Beyond the general commitment to establishing a new "tone" for American foreign policy, the Carter administration focused on several areas of particular concern—the same areas, essentially, that had been the focus of the Kissinger era. (As efforts on behalf of these specific goals began to conflict at numerous points with the emphasis on human rights, the president quietly retreated from his concern with the rights issue.) Carter's first major diplomatic accomplishment was the completion of negotiations on a pair of treaties that would turn over control of the Panama Canal to the government of Panama. In exchange for Panamanian agreements to maintain the neutrality of the canal, the United States would gradually withdraw most of its troops and supervisory personnel from the Canal Zone, which it had controlled since Theodore Roosevelt's bold maneuvers at the beginning of the century. Domestic opposition to the treaties was intense, inflamed by conservative critics who viewed the new arrangements as part of a general retreat from international power. Such arguments were not without foundation. Carter and his predecessors had supported relinquishing the canal because they recognized that in Panama, as elsewhere, the United States could no longer expect passive acceptance of its wishes. Control of the canal by the United States had become the source of deep resentment in Central America. Relinquishing it was thus the best way to improve relations with the region and avoid the possibility of years of violence. After an acrimonious debate, the Senate ratified the treaties by a vote of 68 to 32, marshaling only one vote more than the necessary two-thirds.

Far less controversial, within the United States at least, was Carter's dramatic success in arranging a peace treaty between Egypt and Israel—the crowning diplomatic accomplishment of his presidency. Inheriting from Henry Kissinger a negotiating process that seemed hopelessly stalled, Carter tried at first to arouse support for a "comprehensive" settlement of the Middle Eastern crisis through an international conference in Geneva. The response from the nations involved was not heartening. It fell to the Egyptian president, Anwar Sadat, and the Is-

The Principals of Camp David
The crowning diplomatic accomplishment of Jimmy Carter's presidency was the signing of the
Egyptian-Israeli peace treaty on March 26, 1979. Here, Carter stands on the White House lawn
shortly before the signing ceremony, flanked by Egyptian President Anwar Sadat and Israeli
Prime Minister Menachem Begin. In succeeding years, the framework for peace established by
the treaty began to seem increasingly shaky. Israel's reluctance to deal with the Palestinian
refugee problem to Egypt's satisfaction contributed to the growing problems. So did the
assassination by Arab fundamentalists of President Sadat in 1981. Sadat's successor, Hosni
Mubarak, showed signs during his first months in office of moving toward a renewed
accommodation with the other Arab states. (UPI)

raeli prime minister, Menachem Begin,
therefore, to initiate the first great breakthrough. In November 1977, accepting a formal invitation from Begin, Sadat flew to the
Israeli capital of Tel Aviv for a dramatic state
visit, declaring in the course of it that Egypt
was now willing to accept the state of Israel
as a legitimate political entity. With that, the
greatest single obstacle to peace between the
two nations—the obstacle that had frustrated
nearly thirty years of diplomatic efforts—
was removed.

There remained, however, the tortuous
task of translating these good feelings into a
concrete treaty of peace. When talks between
Israeli and Egyptian negotiators stalled,
Carter invited Sadat and Begin to a summit
conference at Camp David in September
1978, holding them there for two weeks

while he, Secretary of State Cyrus Vance,
and others mediated the disputes between
them. On September 17, Carter escorted the
two leaders into the White House to announce agreement on a "framework" for an
Egyptian–Israeli peace treaty. Final agreement, the two sides promised, would be
completed within three months.

In the months that followed, the euphoria
of the Camp David summit faded as new obstacles to the treaty seemed to emerge almost
daily, a result in large part of the insistence of
the Begin government that Israel continue to
establish new settlements in the disputed territory of the West Bank of the Jordan River
(which Israel had seized during the 1967 war
and which some Palestinian Arabs hoped
might become a new homeland for them).
Only after Carter himself had intervened

again, persuading Sadat to agree to a post-
ponement of resolution of the sensitive Palestinian refugee issue, did the negotiations finally bear fruit. On March 26, 1979, Begin
and Sadat returned together to the White
House to sign a formal peace treaty between
their two nations. Jimmy Carter, whose personal diplomacy had been largely responsible for the moment, looked on proudly.

The Middle East agreement was a tremendous personal triumph for the president.
It was also, however, a symbol of America's
new problems in the world; and it became,
ultimately, the source of still further difficulties. Like his predecessors, Carter was
acutely aware of how desperately dependent
the United States had become on the resources of the Middle East. Another
Arab-Israeli war, accompanied by another
oil embargo, could well destroy the American economy. Carter's efforts to produce a
settlement were an expression, in some respects, of American strength. But they were
also a sign of American weakness, for peace
in the Middle East was as important to the
United States as it was to the nations of the
region. Nor was the treaty a final solution to
the problems of the area. Other Arab nations
reacted with hostility—not only toward
Egypt and Israel but toward the United States
as well.

In the first years after the signing of the
treaty, tensions in the region escalated further. The assassination of Anwar Sadat by
dissident Egyptian fundamentalists in 1981
added a new obstacle to the peace process,
for Sadat's successor, Hosni Mubarak, almost immediately gave signs of renewed interest in restoring Egypt's ties to the rest of
the Arab world. The increasing recalcitrance
of the Israeli government—which officially
annexed several disputed territories in 1981
and which continued to refuse to make any
important concessions to the Palestinians—
further fueled antagonisms in the region. Although Israel lived up to its treaty agreement
and in April 1982 returned to Egypt the
territories of the Sinai, which Israel had captured in 1967, the exchange seemed at the
time less the culmination of a successful peace
process than its dying gasp. And several
months later, Israel launched a major in-

vasion of Lebanon, designed to drive the militant Palestinian Liberation Organization
from its strongholds there. The invasion's
success further clouded the chances for a
wider Arab-Israeli agreement.

Great Power Diplomacy

In the meantime, Carter attempted to continue progress toward improving relations
with China and the Soviet Union and toward
completing a new arms control agreement.
Although he did not share Kissinger's belief
in the importance of creating a new great
power balance, he did share the concerns of
his predecessors for reducing international
tensions and dealing more realistically with
old adversaries.

The new relationship with China progressed rapidly during 1978, as Chinese
leader Deng Xiaoping began concerted efforts to change the rigid policies of the late
Mao Zedong and turn his nation toward the
outside world. In particular, Deng wanted at
least indirect support from the West for
China's increasingly tense "cold war" with
the Soviet Union. Carter responded eagerly
to Deng's overtures; and on December 15,
1978, Washington and Beijing issued a joint
communiqué announcing the restoration of
formal diplomatic relations between the two
nations on January 1, 1979. Carter faced
strong domestic conservative opposition to
the agreement, largely because it required
the United States to break relations and
abandon its alliance with the Nationalist regime on Taiwan. Once again, critics charged,
the United States was displaying weakness
and unreliability in its foreign policy. But
Carter responded to such criticisms much as
he had responded to attacks on the canal
treaties, claiming that the new policy represented an intelligent recognition of international realities. In March 1979, America and
China exchanged ambassadors.

Only a few months later, Carter traveled
to Vienna to meet with a visibly ailing Leonid
Brezhnev to complete the final steps in the
drafting of the new SALT II arms control
agreement. Lower-level negotiators had been

working for months to resolve remaining differences; and in Vienna, the Soviet and American leaders took the final step—settling the last details, signing the documents, and clasping each other in a warm embrace. The treaty set new limits on the number of long-range missiles, bombers, and nuclear warheads on each side—limits that some critics denounced as far too high to constitute meaningful disarmament, but that supporters claimed marked an important first step in limiting the construction of new weapons. Future negotiations, the two sides agreed, would work toward actually reducing the existing arsenals. Like SALT I, the new treaty represented no major breakthrough and would, if ratified, limit the future arms race only slightly, if at all. Nevertheless, it attracted the support of most Democratic liberals and most supporters of détente.

Almost immediately, however, SALT II met with fierce conservative opposition. A powerful group of Senate Republicans denounced the treaty as excessively favorable to the Soviet Union, citing in particular provisions that restricted development of the American cruise missile while leaving the Soviets free to proceed with their new backfire bomber. Conservative critics took little comfort from Brezhnev's pledge to limit the rate of production of the new aircraft. Others denounced concessions permitting increases in certain Soviet missile systems that would, some charged, increase an already large Russian advantage in that area. Central to the arguments of the opposition, however, was a larger issue: a fundamental distrust of the Soviet Union that nearly a decade of détente had failed to destroy. Pointing to Soviet activities in Third World countries in Africa, to increasing Russian influence among the radical governments of the Middle East, and to allegations of Soviet support of international terrorism, conservatives argued that ratification of SALT II would represent an unjustifiable endorsement of aggression and subversion. By the fall of 1979, with the Senate scheduled to begin debate over the treaty shortly, ratification was already unlikely. Events in the ensuing months would provide the final blow—both to the treaty and to the larger framework of détente.

THE YEAR OF THE HOSTAGES

The accumulated frustrations of more than a decade seemed to culminate in the events of the last months of 1979 and the full year that followed. Not since 1968 had the United States experienced such a sense of cascading crisis. If the events of 1979 and 1980 were not as wrenching and disruptive as those of twelve years before, they were at least equally debilitating to the nation's pride and self-confidence. Both at home and abroad, it seemed, America was facing evidence of accelerating decline.

Crisis in Iran

For more than thirty years, the United States had provided political support and, more recently, massive military assistance to the government of the Shah of Iran, depending on that nation as a bulwark against Soviet expansion in the Middle East. By 1979, however, the Shah was in deep trouble with his own people, reaping the harvest of years of unpopular policies. Iranians resented the repressive, authoritarian tactics through which the Shah had maintained his autocratic rule. The SAVAK, the monarch's secret police, which had long made use of torture and arbitrary imprisonment to stifle dissent, aroused particular hatred. At the same time, the Shah was earning the animosity of the Islamic clergy through his rapid efforts to modernize and Westernize his fundamentalist society. The combination of resentments produced a powerful revolutionary movement; and in January 1979, finally, the Shah fled the country for an uncertain exile.

The United States, which had supported the Shah unswervingly until very near the end, was caught unawares by his fall from power. The Carter administration was even

Teheran, 1979
Iranian militants stand atop the wall surrounding the United States embassy
and burn an American flag for the benefit of thousands of demonstrators
(and cameramen) on the street below. Inside the embassy, American diplomats and soldiers are held hostage in an effort to compel the United States to
return the deposed Shah to Iran. Fifty-two of the hostages remained in captivity for fourteen months, until January 20, 1981—the day of Ronald Reagan's
inauguration as president of the United States. (UPI)

less aware, apparently, of the deep resentments that the Iranian people continued to
harbor toward America, which had become a
hated symbol of Western intrusion into their
society. The president made cautious efforts
in the first months after the Shah's abdication
to establish cordial relations with the succession of increasingly militant regimes that
followed. By late 1979, however, such efforts
were beginning to appear futile. Not only did
revolutionary chaos in the nation make any
normal relationships impossible, but what
power there was in Iran resided with a zeal-
ous religious leader, the Ayatollah Ruhollah
Khomeini, whose hatred of the West in general and the United States in particular was
deep, abiding, and intense.

The Shah spent most of his first months

of exile living in Mexico, having been quietly
informed that the American government
would not welcome his presence in the
United States. Late in October, however, the
president succumbed to the urgings of several friends of the Shah and admitted the
monarch to New York, where he entered a
hospital for treatment of cancer. Days later,
on November 4, 1979, an armed mob invaded the American embassy in Teheran,
seized the diplomats and military personnel
inside, and held them as hostages—demanding the return of the Shah to Iran in exchange
for their freedom. Although the militants released a few of the hostages within days,
fifty-three Americans remained prisoners in
the embassy.

American citizens had been held hostage

by foreign governments in the past. In 1968, eighty-two members of the crew of the *Pueblo*, a navy intelligence-gathering ship, were captured and held prisoner by the government of North Korea. It took eleven months for the Johnson administration to win their release, during which time the American public all but forgot about the problem. But the reaction of the nation to the events in Teheran was radically different. Coming after years of what Americans considered international humiliations and defeats, the hostage seizure released a surprising well of anger and emotion. President Carter, facing a difficult reelection battle, did his best to sustain the sense of crisis. But even without his efforts, it was clear, the American people would have reacted strongly. Television newscasts relayed daily pictures of angry anti-American mobs outside the embassy, the faces of many demonstrators contorted with hatred as they chanted such slogans as "Death to America" and "Death to Carter." Contemptuous statements by the militants guarding the hostages that "The U.S. can do nothing" further inflamed American passions. The nation responded not only with anger but with remarkable displays of emotional patriotism. The surprising victory of the United States Olympic hockey team, which defeated a highly favored Soviet squad and won the gold medal at the 1980 winter Olympics in upstate New York, produced a national celebration of remarkable fervor. It was, clearly, an expression of far more than simple enthusiasm about hockey.

Russia and Afghanistan

Only weeks after the hostage seizure, the nation suffered another dispiriting shock when it learned that Soviet troops had invaded Afghanistan, the mountainous nation lying between Russia and Iran. The Soviet Union had, in fact, been a power in Afghanistan for years, and the dominant force since April 1978, when a coup had established a Marxist government there with close ties to the Kremlin. The invasion, many Soviet experts argued, was Moscow's response to the failure of the new Afghan government to restore stability to the nation. The Soviets were particularly concerned about the activities of Islamic insurgents, whose presence raised the possibility of a fundamentalist revolution in Afghanistan (and perhaps even in Islamic areas of the Soviet Union itself) similar to the one in progress in Iran. But while some observers claimed that the Soviet invasion was simply a Russian attempt to secure the status quo, others—most notably the president—viewed the situation differently. The invasion of Afghanistan, Carter claimed, was a Russian "stepping stone to their possible control over much of the world's oil supplies." It was also the "gravest threat to world peace since World War II." Dire warnings began issuing from the White House about the possibility of a Soviet attack on Iran or other Middle Eastern nations.

Whatever the reasons for the Soviet invasion, the situation in Afghanistan became the final blow to the already badly weakened structure of détente. Carter angrily imposed a series of economic sanctions on the Russians, called for an American boycott of the 1980 summer Olympic Games in Moscow, and announced the withdrawal of SALT II from Senate consideration. He also announced a new American policy—what some called the "Carter Doctrine"—by which the United States pledged to oppose, by force if necessary, any further aggression in the Persian Gulf. Critics reacted contemptuously, asserting that the United States lacked the military capacity to defend the Persian Gulf from a Soviet invasion, even if such an invasion were in the offing. But the president persevered, resolved it seemed, to reassert American determination after so many humiliating international setbacks.

The Campaign of 1980

By the time of the crises in Iran and Afghanistan, Jimmy Carter was in desperate political trouble. His standing in popularity polls was lower than that of any president in history. His economic policies were in shambles. Senator Edward Kennedy, one of the most magnetic figures in the Democratic party, was preparing to challenge him in the primaries. Nothing, it seemed, could save the president. But the seizure of the hostages and the stern American response to the Soviet invasion did wonders for Carter's candidacy. His standing in the polls improved dramatically, and his moribund campaign suddenly revived and produced for the president a series of impressive victories in the early primaries.

Carter's troubles were, however, far from over. As month followed month without any discernible progress in efforts to secure the release of the hostages in Iran, public clamor began to build. In April, after the collapse of one round of negotiations, the president ordered a rescue attempt by American commandos. It ended in abject failure when several military helicopters failed in the desert. Eight commandos died when two aircraft collided during the hasty retreat. Secretary of State Cyrus Vance, who had opposed both the rescue mission and much of the new belligerence in the nation's foreign policy, resigned in protest—the first secretary of state to do so since William Jennings Bryan in 1916. And the president began to suffer a series of damaging defeats in the primaries. Carter, however, continued to benefit greatly from the many personal controversies surrounding Edward Kennedy (most notably a 1969 automobile accident at Chappaquiddick Island in Massachusetts that had left a young woman dead), and he managed in the end to stave off the challenge and win his party's nomination. But it was an unhappy convention that listened to the president's listless call to arms; and Carter's campaign aroused little enthusiasm from the public at large as he prepared to face a powerful challenge.

The Republican party had, in the meantime, rallied enthusiastically behind a man whom, not many years before, many Americans had considered a frightening reactionary. Ronald Reagan, a one-time film actor, a former California governor, and a poised and articulate campaigner, seemed in 1980 to be a man in tune with his times. Like Carter before him, he was a strident critic of the excesses of the federal government. More important, he championed a restoration of American "strength" and "pride" in the world. Although he refrained from discussing the issue of the hostages, Reagan clearly benefited from the continuing popular frustration at Carter's inability to resolve the crisis. In a larger sense, he benefited as well from the accumulated frustrations of more than a decade of domestic and international disappointments.

Election day was the anniversary of the seizure of the hostages in Iran, a fact that was not lost on much of the press and the public. It was also the day on which the conservative forces that had been gathering strength in American life for more than a decade finally seized control of the nation's political life. By a startlingly wide margin, Ronald Reagan swept to victory in the presidential election. His popular margin was decisive: 51 percent of the ballots cast, to 41 percent for Jimmy Carter, and 7 percent for John Anderson—a moderate Republican congressman who had mounted an independent campaign. Reagan's electoral margin was overwhelming. He swept not only the western half of the nation, which had been Republican territory for years, but virtually all of the traditional bastions of Democratic strength: the South, the industrial states of the Midwest and Northeast, even such traditionally liberal strongholds as Massachusetts and New York. Carter carried only five states and the District of Columbia, for a total of 49 votes to Reagan's 489. Even more startling was the tidal wave of Republican victories in the congressional races. The party won control of the Senate for the first time since the 1950s; and although the Democrats retained a diminished majority in the House, the lower chamber too seemed firmly in the hands of conservatives.

Celebration

Almost at the very moment of Reagan's inauguration, the fifty-two hostages remaining in Iran (one had been released several months before, after he fell ill) were boarding an airplane en route to freedom after their 444-day ordeal. Jimmy Carter, in the last hours of his presidency, had concluded months of negotiations by agreeing to release

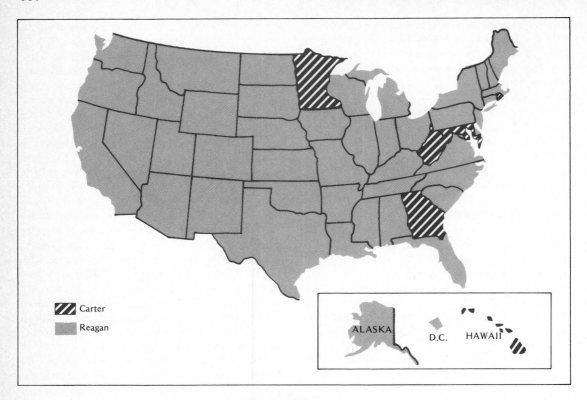

Carter

Reagan

ALASKA   D.C.   HAWAII

THE ELECTION OF 1980

several billion dollars in Iranian assets that he had frozen in American banks shortly after the seizure of the embassy. The government of Iran, desperate for funds to support a losing war effort against neighboring Iraq, had ordered that the hostages be freed in return. The next few days produced a virtual orgy of national emotion, as Americans welcomed the hostages home with mingled relief, joy, and anger. Not since the end of World War II had there been such demonstrations of patriotism and celebration. But while the joy in 1945 had marked a great American triumph, the euphoria in 1981 marked something quite different—a troubled nation grasping for reassurance.

THE "REAGAN REVOLUTION"

Ronald Reagan assumed the presidency in January 1981 promising a change in government more fundamental than any since the New Deal of fifty years before. And he had at his disposal enviable political strength with which to make those proposals reality. He had his own undoubted skills as a communicator, born of his years of work as an actor. He had a clear mandate from the American people, as evidenced by his overwhelming victory in the 1980 election. He had a Congress more susceptible to his requests than any President had enjoyed since the mid-1960s: a Republican Senate and a House of Representatives that, though controlled by the Democrats, was of a conservative bent.

During most of Reagan's first year in office, these formidable assets served the new president well as he enjoyed a period of legislative success that invited comparison with those of some of his most effective liberal predecessors. By the beginning of his second year in office, however, Reagan, like the four presidents before him, started to encounter the failures and frustrations that seemed to have become the inevitable accompaniments to power.

"Supply-Side" Economics

Reagan's campaign for the presidency had centered around several goals. It had promised to end the drift in American foreign policy and restore the nation's military strength. It had promised to reduce the intrusive influence of government upon American life. And it had promised to restore the economy to health by a bold experiment in what became known as "supply-side" economics. It was this last pledge that the new administration attempted to fulfill first and that, initially at least, became the source of its most conspicuous triumphs.

Supply-side economics operated from the assumption that the woes of the American economy were in large part a result of government interference and of excessive taxation, which left inadequate capital available to investors to stimulate growth. The solution, therefore, was to reduce taxes, with particularly generous benefits to corporations and wealthy individuals, in order to encourage new investments. The result would be a general economic revival that would affect all levels of the population. But cutting taxes was only one part of the supply-side program. Because a tax cut would reduce government revenues, it would be necessary also to reduce government expenses. Otherwise, large federal deficits might negate the effects of the tax cut by requiring the government to borrow in the marketplace, thus raising interest rates and drying up capital for investment once again. A cornerstone of the Reagan economic program, therefore, was a drastic cut in the federal budget, one intended to produce—within four years—a balance between government revenues and expenditures for the first time since 1969.

In his first months in office, therefore, Reagan hastily assembled a legislative program that would enact the basic features of the supply-side program. He proposed a major revision in the 1982 federal budget (which had been prepared by the Carter ad-

---

Reaganomics
By late 1981, the Reagan economic program—which had been launched with such impressive popular and congressional support early in the year—was encountering substantial opposition. But, as cartoonist Dan Wasserman suggests, the president himself remained firmly and, it seemed, serenely committed to what had become known as "Reaganomics." (© 1981 Los Angeles Times Syndicate)

YOU CUT MY WELFARE BENEFITS

TO END YOUR DEPENDENCY ON THE GOVERNMENT

YOU AXED SAFETY REGULATIONS

TO IMPROVE YOUR PRODUCTIVITY

YOUR INTEREST RATES COST ME MY JOB

TO SAVE YOU FROM INFLATION

REAGANOMICS IS NEVER HAVING TO SAY YOU'RE SORRY

WASSERMAN © 1981 LOS ANGELES TIMES SYNDICATE

ministration in its last months). His energetic budget director, David Stockman, proposed new reductions that would cut expenditures by some $40 billion; and despite grumbling by special-interest groups and liberals and impassioned pleas by constituencies threatened by the loss of social services, the new budget cuts passed through Congress with relative ease, almost in the form the administration had proposed. In addition, the president proposed a bold, three-year rate reduction on both individual and corporate taxes. The tax cut encountered more serious opposition in Congress and was subjected to numerous amendments. But in the summer of 1981, it too was passed, generally in the form the administration had proposed. No president since Lyndon Johnson had compiled so impressive a legislative record in his first months in office.

By early 1982, however, the Reagan economic program was beset with difficulties. The nation had entered into the worst recession since the Great Depression of the 1930s, with national unemployment approaching 10 percent of the work force. A number of major industries—steel, automobiles, and others—had been experiencing difficulties for some time and were now faced with virtual collapse. In some regions of the country, most notably the industrial Midwest, the economy seemed to have de-

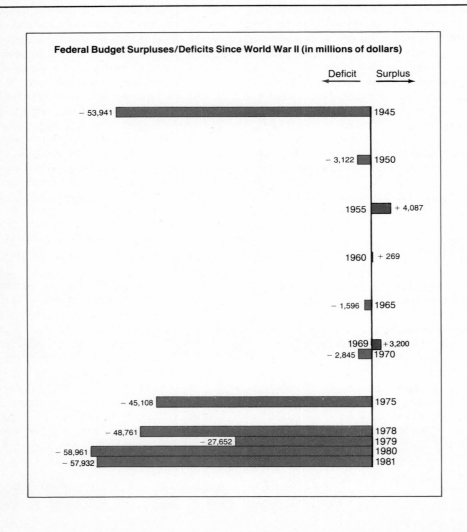

Federal Budget Surpluses/Deficits Since World War II (in millions of dollars)

scended into virtual depression conditions. The Reagan economic program was not entirely to blame for the problems; the causes of the recession stretched well back into the Carter years and before. But a growing number of critics were claiming in 1982 that the administration's policies were doing nothing to improve the situation and were promising ultimately to make things worse.

Central to the complaints were the staggering budget deficits that the Reagan administration was now projecting. Having entered office promising a balanced budget within four years, Reagan proposed a budget early in 1982 that would entail a deficit of between $96 billion (the administration's projection) and more than $180 billion (the estimate of the Congressional Budget Office). Reduced revenues as a result of the tax cut, the failure of the depressed economy to perform as the administration had predicted, and huge increases in the defense budget (which more than offset the reductions in domestic spending the president had proposed) were responsible for the shortfall. Even more alarming, future deficits were projected to be far larger. By 1985, according to the most optimistic 1982 predictions, there would be a $171 billion gap between revenues and expenditures. Critics warned that the real figure would be much higher. The Reagan administration tried to downplay the importance of the deficits and continued to insist that its basic economic plan would work and should not be tampered with. Critics in Congress, Republicans and Democrats alike, disagreed and engaged in a long and difficult struggle to find ways to reduce the deficit.

In the meantime, the continuation of high interest rates for borrowed money (a policy that the enormous federal deficits seemed certain to encourage further) made recovery from the recession extraordinarily difficult. The high rates were most directly discouraging to the markets for homes, automobiles, and other major items generally purchased on credit. But the drying up of those markets created a ripple effect throughout the economy, diminishing demand for other goods as well.

Reagan and the World

The Reagan administration encountered similar difficulties in its international dealings. Although the United States encountered no major international crises during the first year of the new presidency, it met a number of serious setbacks.

Relations with the Soviet Union, which had been steadily deteriorating in the last years of the Carter administration, grew still more chilly after Reagan took office. Both the president and his secretary of state, Alexander Haig, spoke harshly of the Soviet regime, accusing it of sponsoring world terrorism and declaring that any armaments negotiations must be "linked" to negotiations about Soviet behavior in other areas. Relations with the Russians deteriorated further after the government of Poland (presumably under pressure from Moscow) imposed martial law on the country in the winter of 1981. For nearly a year before that, much of the West had watched with admiration as Polish workers challenged the hegemony of the communist regime by forming an independent union (Solidarity) and demanding wide-ranging reforms. But as those reforms began to include a major reduction in the power of the party leadership in Poland, both the communist hierarchy and the Soviet government upon which it relied grew increasingly concerned. The declaration of martial law was widely viewed as an effort not only to quell Solidarity, but to forestall a Soviet invasion.

The events in Poland served as a reminder to the United States of its longstanding distaste for Soviet domination of Eastern Europe, a distaste that had first emerged in the immediate aftermath of World War II and had continued, with varying degrees of intensity, ever since. To the Reagan administration, however, the Polish crisis came to symbolize something more: the aggressive, expansionist designs of the Soviet Union, which had to be countered wherever and whenever possible. Although there was little the United States could do to reverse the course of events in Poland (beyond imposition of symbolic and largely ineffective

Reagan and the Queen
During his June 1982 visit to Western Europe, President Ronald Reagan joined Queen Elizabeth II of Great Britain at Windsor Castle in one of his (and her) favorite activities: horseback riding. Reagan's trip had been designed to improve America's troubled relations with its NATO allies. But only days after his return to the United States, the president angered many European leaders by announcing harsh new measures intended to prevent completion of a natural-gas pipeline from the Soviet Union to the West. (UPI)

economic sanctions), the episode renewed the administration's determination to reshape American foreign policy elsewhere in the world.

By early 1982, American foreign policy had begun to embrace once again many of the assumptions that had fueled its international activities in the 1950s. The nation's most important mission in the world, American leaders now maintained, was to counter Soviet power. This meant that the United States should increase its military strength in many places around the globe; more important, it should strengthen its alliances with anticommunist regimes, regardless of the attractiveness or stability of those regimes. And the United States should once again involve itself in efforts to stem the tide of revolution in Third World nations. The most conspicuous example of the new activism was in the Central American nation of El Salvador, where a repressive military regime was engaged in a hideously murderous struggle with communist revolutionaries, supported, according to the Reagan administration, by Cuba and the Soviet Union. Despite strong opposition from many groups within the United States, the president committed himself to increased military and economic assistance to the Salvadoran regime—although he insisted that this assistance would not extend to the introduction of American forces into the region.

Defenders of the Reagan foreign policy

argued that the United States was at last beginning to take its responsibilities as a world power seriously again, after the debilitating traumas of the war in Vietnam. Fuzzy liberal idealism, they claimed, was being replaced with a realistic view of American interests. Critics replied that the administration was demonstrating a hopeless nostalgia for an earlier era, when American power and prestige had been far greater and when the world had seemed far less complicated. By focusing single-mindedly on the threat from the Soviet Union, such analysts claimed, the United States was ignoring the importance of local interests and the complexity of world affairs. Others made more serious charges: that the Reagan administration's bellicosity was pushing the world into a new and dangerous arms race and increasing the dangers of a nuclear holocaust.

These last criticisms, strengthened by a growing popular outcry against nuclear weapons, began in 1982 to force the administration to moderate some of its more bellicose anti-Soviet positions. That summer, the United States and the Soviet Union opened new arms-control negotiations for the first time in four years, although prospects for an early agreement seemed dim. The Reagan foreign policy, which many claimed was sadly confused and inconsistent, suffered another blow in June 1982, when Secretary of State Haig suddenly and unexpectedly resigned, making clear his unhappiness with the president's performance. (Evidence soon emerged that he had been pressured to leave by adversaries in the White House.) Reagan chose George Shultz, who had served in the Nixon cabinet, to succeed Haig.

CONFUSION AND CONSERVATISM

Not only the political climate was turning more conservative in the late 1970s and early 1980s; the social and cultural climates were as well. In a society plagued with disorder and uncertainty, an increasing number of men and women were retreating into a defensive conservatism. Others were choosing to ignore social and political issues altogether and were looking instead to the enrichment of their own lives. The crusading, optimistic liberalism of earlier years was giving way to a narrowing of vision and goals. This new conservatism was often less an expression of confidence in old truths than a reflection of bewilderment—of a search for stable values that might provide a rudder for an apparently aimless society.

The New Demography

One of the most fundamental changes in American life in the postliberal era was the new profile of the American population. After decades of steady growth, the nation's birthrate began to decline in the 1970s, leading some to predict a leveling off of the population by the end of the century. A more immediate result was a significant increase in the proportion of elderly citizens. More than 10 percent of the population in 1980 was more than sixty-five years old, as compared with 8 percent a decade earlier. The median age was steadily rising.

Even more striking was the change in the geographic distribution of the American population. The most widely discussed demographic phenomenon of the 1970s was the rise of what became known as the "Sunbelt" or "Southern Rim"—the Southeast, the Southwest, and above all, California, which became the nation's most populous state (surpassing New York) in 1964 and continued to grow in the years that followed. By the end of the 1970s, the population of the Sun-

belt had risen to exceed that of the industrial regions of the North and East, which were experiencing not only a relative, but in many cases an absolute, decline in their numbers. In addition to shifting the nation's economic focus from one region to another, the rise of the Sunbelt was, for the moment at least, producing a change in the political climate. The South and the West had always been more conservative than many other regions of the country. The changes in both areas during the 1960s and 1970s seemed, if anything, to strengthen that conservatism. In particular, the boom mentality of this growing region conflicted sharply with the concerns of the Northeast, which—saddled with a declining economic base, highly congested, and home to large, impoverished minority groups—remained far more committed to social programs and far more interested in regulated growth than the more wide-open areas of the Sunbelt.

Acutely affected by the changing distribution of population were the major industrial cities, particularly those in the Northeast and Midwest (the so-called "Frostbelt"), which continued to confront the specter of social and financial decay. As more and more industries and corporate headquarters moved from the older urban centers to the suburbs or to the beckoning Sunbelt, many cities experienced a major contraction of their economic bases. Unemployment increased. Tax bases declined, as municipalities lost the revenues from those enterprises that had departed. And the demand for social services increased, as members of minorities found it ever more difficult to find even menial employment.

Under the twin burdens of shrinking economic bases and expanding demands for social services, one city after another encountered fiscal crises. New York City barely averted bankruptcy in 1975—and then only after federal assistance and an unprecedented arrangement to finance municipal loans. Cleveland, Ohio, became, in late 1978, the first major metropolis in the nation to go into receivership since the Great Depression.

The crusading liberal urban leaders of the 1960s—men such as New York's Mayor John Lindsay, who served from 1966 to 1974—had no place in the cities of the late 1970s. Successful urban politicians were now far more likely to be men such as Edward I. Koch, who became mayor of New York in 1978 and who was overwhelmingly reelected (almost without opposition) four years later. Koch openly subordinated concern for the poor to a commitment to fiscal stability and to the welfare of the middle class.

By the late 1970s, many observers were pointing to signs of an urban renaissance. Affluent men and women were beginning to abandon the suburbs (which were developing urban problems of their own) and return to downtown areas, where they often bought up declining real estate, refurbished it, and created prosperous new communities: a process that became known as gentrification. The phenomenon had many obvious benefits for cities. It helped restore a viable tax base. It attracted new businesses. And it meant that the community's most affluent members would now have a direct stake in the well-being of the city. But gentrification was far from a panacea to the woes of cities. The return of affluent, middle-class people to urban neighborhoods usually meant a displacement of poorer residents, who found it increasingly difficult and expensive to find decent housing. And the gentrification process increased the social stratification within many cities. The economic profile of some cities was one of a large group of the least affluent members of society, a growing group of the most affluent, and often little in between.

Despite the positive effects of gentrification on some neighborhoods, moreover, urban dwellers continued to struggle with a gradual decay of services and a rise in social disorder. Urban public schools suffered an increase in violence, drug addiction, and truancy; and the white middle class looked upon the school system as a virtually hopeless morass and showed little inclination to improve it. High-school graduates in some major cities were found to be virtually illiterate. City streets became zones of increasing danger. The rate of violent crime nearly quadrupled between 1960 and 1980 (not only in the declining cities of the North, but in the boom towns of the Sunbelt; Houston, by the early 1980s, had the highest murder rate in the country).

The most basic demographic fact of America in the 1970s, however, was its sheer size. The United States suffered far less from overpopulation than much of the rest of the world; but it was, nevertheless, becoming an ever more crowded society. The American population of 226 million (according to the 1980 census) was more than twice as large as that of sixty years before. Of equal significance, some groups in the population were growing faster than others. While the white population increased relatively modestly in the 1970s—from about 177 million to about 188 million, or by 6 percent—the nonwhite population (mostly blacks and Hispanics) grew at a staggering rate—by 52 percent, from 25 million to 38 million. The fastest-growing element was the nation's Hispanic population, whose numbers increased both by natural growth and by massive immigration, legal and illegal. Even the census takers admitted that their numbers were probably larger than the 14.6 million (nearly 8 percent of the population) that the survey results suggested. It was, in other words, the less affluent groups in society that were experiencing the greatest increase in numbers.

Nonwhites in the Postliberal Era

In the aftermath of the civil-rights movement and the other liberal efforts of the 1960s, America's nonwhites experienced two conflicting processes. On the one hand, there were increased opportunities for advancement available to those who were in position to take advantage of them. On the other hand, as the economy declined and government services dwindled, there was a growing sense of helplessness and despair among the larger groups of nonwhites who continued to find themselves barred from upward mobility.

For the black middle class, which by the late 1970s constituted nearly a third of the entire black population of America, the progress was at times astonishing. Economic disparities between black and white professionals did not vanish, but they diminished substantially. Black families moved into more affluent urban communities and, in many cases, into suburbs—at times as neighbors of whites, more often into predominantly black suburban communities. The number of blacks attending college nearly quadrupled in the decade following the passage of the civil-rights acts; and by 1980 the percentage of black high-school graduates going on to college was virtually the same as that of white high-school graduates (although a far smaller proportion of blacks than whites managed to complete high school). Middle-class blacks, in other words, had realized great gains from the legislation of the 1960s, from the changing national mood on race, and from the creation of controversial Affirmative Action programs. But they had also, according to many studies, begun to lose touch with other members of their race who remained trapped in poverty and whom many of the liberal programs of the 1960s never reached.

This growing "underclass"—made up not only of blacks, but in increasing measure of Hispanics—felt the impact of the economic troubles of the 1970s and 1980s with special force. By the late 1970s, more than one-fourth of all black families lived in poverty, 20 percent more than had done so a decade earlier. More than one-fifth of all the Hispanic families counted by the government likewise lived in poverty (as well as many more who remained out of the reach of the census). At the same time, fewer than 7 percent of white families could be officially classified as poor. To whatever degree economic troubles might harm the nation as a whole, it harmed these impoverished nonwhites with greater power. Black and Hispanic unemployment was consistently higher than white joblessness; and among black teenagers, unemployment in some cities exceeded 50 percent. The black family structure suffered as well from the dislocations of urban poverty. There was a radical increase in the number of single-parent, female-headed black house-

holds in the 1960s and 1970s, a growth of more than 150 percent.

Nonwhites were victimized by many things in the contracting economy of the 1970s. They suffered, as they always had, from white racism and from a growing impatience with Affirmative Action and other programs designed to advance their fortunes. They suffered from a steady decline in the number of unskilled jobs in the economy. They suffered from the deterioration of public education and of other social services, which made it more difficult for them to find opportunities for advancement. And they suffered, in some cases, from a sense of futility and despair, born of years of entrapment in brutal urban ghettoes. By the 1980s, whole generations of nonwhites had grown to maturity living in destitute neighborhoods where welfare and crime were virtually the only means of support for many people.

The New Religion and the New Right

Throughout human history, a constant feature of rapidly changing societies has been the search for stability, the quest for a haven from uncertainty and confusion. So it was in the United States as its people faced the new realities of a troubled world. Americans flocked in growing numbers to movements and creeds that seemed to offer refuge from the perils of modern life.

Above all, it seemed, they flocked to religion. Many social critics had in the 1960s predicted the virtual extinction of religious influence in American life. *Time* magazine had reflected such assumptions in 1966 with a celebrated cover emblazoned with the question "Is God Dead?" Nevertheless, America in the 1970s entered the throes of a major religious revival, the most powerful since the Second Great Awakening of the early nineteenth century.

Some of the new religious enthusiasm found expression in the rise of various cults and pseudofaiths: the Church of Scientology; the Unification Church of the Reverend Sun Myung Moon; even the tragic People's Temple, whose members committed mass suicide in their jungle retreat in Guyana in 1978. But the most important impulse of the revival of religion was the rise of evangelical Christianity. It was not a sudden phenomenon. It had, in fact, been in progress at least since the 1950s, when the Reverend Billy Graham had begun to attract a huge national following for his energetic revivalism. For many years, however, the new religion had gone unnoted by much of the media, which had dismissed it as a limited, provincial phenomenon. By the 1970s, they could no longer do so. More than 70 million Americans now described themselves as "born-again" Christians—men and women who had established a "direct personal relationship with Jesus." Christian evangelicals owned their own newspapers, magazines, radio stations, and television networks. They operated their own schools and universities. They occupied positions of eminence in the worlds of entertainment and professional sports. And one of their number ultimately occupied the White House itself—Jimmy Carter, who during the 1976 campaign, had talked proudly of his own "conversion experience" and who continued openly to proclaim his "born-again" Christian faith during his years in office.

For Jimmy Carter, evangelical Christianity had served as a prod to social commitment and public service; it had formed the basis for his commitment to racial and economic justice and to world peace. To many others, the message of the new religion was very different—but no less political. Christian revivalism had by the 1970s become closely tied to deep political and social conservatism. Such organizations as the Reverend Jerry Falwell's "Moral Majority" expressed the dominant political sentiments of fundamentalist evangelicals. They opposed federal interference in local affairs, denounced abortion, defended unrestricted free enterprise, and supported a strong American posture in the world. Some even reopened issues that had long seemed closed. For example, many fundamentalist Christians questioned the scientific doctrine of evolution and urged the teaching in schools of the biblical story of the Creation instead. Others drew criticism from defenders of civil liberties by demanding stricter censorship of television, movies, and printed materials.

Defenders of the new religion praised it for providing a "moral compass" for many troubled Americans; and they cited its success in redeeming young people, in particular, from crime, drug addiction, and despair. Critics charged that evangelical Christianity too often produced among its members a dogmatic self-righteousness and a dangerous moral absolutism. The religious revival, they warned, threatened to create a climate of oppressive political and social intolerance.

Closely tied to the new religion was a new political right, many of whose members were themselves evangelical Christians. The New Right drew heavily on the conservative dogmas of earlier eras; but in addition to doctrinal enthusiasm, it displayed a remarkable organizing zeal. While earlier right-wing political groups, such as the John Birch Society, had stumbled along in administrative chaos, the new organizations marshaled their influence with awesome skill and effectiveness. Mass mailing campaigns of staggering size raised great sums of money to support conservative efforts. The National Conservative Political Action Committee, for example, spent millions of dollars in support of its chosen political candidates in 1980 and claimed credit for the defeat of many liberal senators and congressmen.

The power of the New Right in the early 1980s represented the culmination of many decades of steadily growing conservative sentiment. Such sentiment had surfaced occasionally in the 1950s in the form of militantly anticommunist political organizations; it had shown itself in 1964, when it helped to engineer the Republican nomination of Barry Goldwater for president. And it had triumphed, finally, in 1980, when it became a central force in propelling Ronald Reagan into the White House. But the phenomenon was, despite its conspicuous strength, difficult to define with any precision. The most active groups within the New Right were not conservatives of traditional stripe—people associated with and supportive of the business community, defending the position of established economic and social elites. They were, rather, middle-class and lower-middle-class people, whose political demands centered more around social and cultural issues than economic ones, who seemed to exhibit not so much a staid conservatism as a right-wing populism.

Most expressive of this cultural thrust

The Supreme Court, 1981
The eight male justices of the Supreme Court pose for a photograph with their newest colleague: Justice Sandra Day O'Connor, the first woman ever to sit on the nation's highest bench. O'Connor's appointment pleased feminists, but it strengthened the Court's conservative faction, which had been gaining control of decisions since the early 1970s. (UPI)

within the New Right was its emphasis upon what became known as "family" issues. In effect, the new conservative groups were waging a frontal attack upon feminism. Leaders of the New Right campaigned fervently (and successfully) against the proposed Equal Rights Amendment to the Constitution. Even more powerful was the movement to prevent women from aborting unwanted pregnancies (see p. 920). Other issues dear to the New Right were similarly cultural in focus: the restoration of prayer in the public schools; opposition to gun-control legislation; an end to busing as a tool for achieving school desegregation. And running throughout the ideology of the New Right was a broader theme: the effort of men and women with traditional, usually fundamentalist, values to defend their communities and their life styles from the incursions of a new, secular, and—as they saw it—immoral culture. Animosity toward the federal government, a basic element of the New Right, rested on the belief that the nation's leadership had become the agent of these new, radical forces in American life.

The Changing Left

The New Left of the 1960s did not disappear after the end of the war in Vietnam, but it faded rapidly as an important influence in American political life. Students who had fought in its battles grew up, left school, and entered conventional careers. Radical leaders, disillusioned by the unresponsiveness of American society to their demands, resignedly gave up the struggle and chose instead to work "within the system." Although Marxist critiques continued to flourish in academic circles, to much of the public they came to appear dated and irrelevant. Yet a left of sorts did survive through the 1970s, giving evidence in the process of how greatly the nation's political climate had changed. Instead of promoting radical change, activists more often fought for preservation and restraint.

Nothing better symbolized the concerns of the changing left than its commitment to protection of the environment. Where 1960s activists had rallied to protest racism, poverty, and war, their 1970s counterparts fought to save the wilderness, protect endangered species, and limit reckless economic development. Above all, they mobilized themselves to confront the danger of nuclear power and, ultimately, nuclear war. The spread of atomic power plants in the 1950s and 1960s had aroused little controversy at the time; but by the mid-1970s, a well-organized and often militant antinuclear movement had emerged in almost every region of the country to oppose new plant construction and to warn of the dangers of existing facilities. A frightening accident in 1979 at a nuclear power plant at Three Mile Island in Pennsylvania seemed to expose serious deficiencies in the safety mechanisms that both government and private industry had assured the public were in place; and the result was an intensification of antinuclear activity.

Of even greater potential significance was a related movement that seemed to surface almost overnight in 1981 and 1982: a movement to stop the spread of nuclear weapons and to promote world disarmament. Opposition to atomic weapons had never entirely vanished in America; no rational person, of course, had ever hoped for a nuclear war, and small groups of scientists and others had attempted for years to produce public pressure for an end to the arms race. But for most of the first thirty-five years after the detonation of atomic bombs in New Mexico and Japan in 1945, such protests had remained muted and isolated. Then, beginning in the late 1970s, a powerful antinuclear movement emerged in Europe, gaining in numbers and intensity so rapidly that by 1980 it had become a formidable political force. And in 1981, partly in response to the European movement, partly in response to the deteriorating international climate, and partly, it seemed, in response to bellicose statements by officials of the federal government, the antinuclear movement gained force in the United States as well.

It took many forms. Some advocated a return to the disarmament negotiations that

Disarmament Day, June 12, 1982
A Vermont contingent marches down 42nd Street in New York en route to Central Park for an enormous demonstration on behalf of nuclear-arms control. The rally, which attracted more than half a million people, was one of the largest expressions of a movement against nuclear weapons that was rapidly gaining force in the early 1980s. (UPI)

had produced the SALT II treaty, which the Senate had never ratified. Others called for an American commitment to "no-first-use" of atomic weapons. Still others agitated for a "nuclear freeze," for halting production of any new weapons or weapons systems (a position that the Reagan administration opposed because it would, they claimed, leave the United States in a position of military inferiority toward the Soviet Union). By mid-1982, the nuclear-freeze movement, in particular, had attracted wide support. State and local governments in widely scattered areas of the country (including parts of the supposedly conservative South) were going on record in support of the idea. Influential members of Congress (among them Senator Edward M. Kennedy) were publicly endorsing the idea. Referendum questions on the issue were being placed on ballots in several states.

The concern for the environment, the opposition to nuclear power, the fear of nuclear war—all were reflections of a far more fundamental assumption of the post-Vietnam left. In a sharp break from the nation's long commitment to growth and progress, the new dissidents argued that only by limiting growth and curbing traditional forms of progress could society hope to survive. Industrial society had, they claimed, created a desperate threat to the planet's ecological balance. Continued growth would place intolerable strains on the world's finite resources. Some of these critics of the "idea of progress" expressed a gloomy resignation, urging a lowering of social expectations and foreseeing an inevitable deterioration in the quality of life. It was not surprising, perhaps, that they evoked hostility from conservative Americans seeking to restore the nation's fading glory. Other advocates of restraint believed that change did not require decline: human beings could live more comfortably and more happily if they simply learned to respect the limits imposed on them by their environment.

Turning Inward

For many Americans, however, the answer to the dilemmas of living in uncertain times lay not in religion or politics but in the cultivation of the self. No aspect of the era aroused more comment than this tendency of individuals to "turn inward," that is, to replace social concerns with personal ones.

Among affluent Americans, at least, there emerged a pervasive concern with personal "life styles." Newspapers introduced special sections devoted to such newly popular pursuits as gourmet cooking, physical fitness, and home decorating. Magazines specialized in helping Americans achieve personal fulfillment through a satisfying life style; among the new periodicals was one with the frank and revealing title *Self*. Along with the inter-

est in life style came a growing concern for self-expression—for "getting in touch with one's feelings." Such pseudoscientific theories as EST, Esalen, and Lifespring encouraged their followers to drop traditional social inhibitions against displaying anger, hatred, or jealousy. The key to emotional stability, they claimed, was the open expression of personal emotions. Nor did economic life remain immune from the new spirit. Books such as Robert Ringer's *Looking Out for Number One* (1978) became national best sellers by urging individuals to behave selfishly in the marketplace.

The commitment to self-cultivation and individual fulfillment was not new in American life, of course. It had roots in the "self-made man" ethos of the turn of the century, in the creed of "Lost Generation" intellectuals of the 1920s, in the philosophy of the "beats" of the 1950s, and in the counterculture of the 1960s. But by the 1970s, the impulse seemed to be taking a new and, in the eyes of some observers, alarming form: emphasizing less the idea of personal liberation than the drive for a bland, elitist conformity; placing less value on creative accomplishment than on material comfort. Defenders of the phenomenon described it as the expression of healthy self-respect. Critics denounced it as a defensive reaction to the ominous and bewildering course of contemporary society. It was, they claimed, a retreat from social commitment born of a thinly concealed sense of hopelessness.

The American people had suffered many trials and disappointments since the heady days at the end of World War II when an "American Century" seemed about to dawn, when the United States appeared poised for a prolonged era of domestic tranquility and international preeminence. By the 1980s, America, like much of the rest of the world, was faced with the problems of a faltering international economy, an increasing world population, a domestic social fabric showing signs of strain, and a nuclear threat to the survival of mankind that showed few signs of abating.

There were no clear answers available for the problems of the nation and the world in these newly troubled times; and it seemed likely that Americans would, in the years to come, find it necessary to adjust to the idea that there were limits to their powers and abilities, that certain problems and frustrations would have to be accepted as the inevitable accompaniment of the structure of the modern world. Yet Americans had reason for optimism as well as they viewed the years before them. Time and time again in their history—in the first perilous years of settlement in the seventeenth century, in the uncertain struggle for independence in the eighteenth century, in the dark days of the Civil War in the nineteenth century, and in two world wars and a great depression in the twentieth—the American people had faced perils that threatened to destroy the civilization they had so painfully built. In each such crisis, however, the nation had shown its capacity to adjust to its problems and, if not always to solve them, at least to endure. The dream of an "American Century" may have been irretrievably lost by the 1980s. But the larger, more powerful dream of America—of a nation founded on democratic principles, struggling constantly to make those principles a reality even if frequently failing in the attempt—continued to survive.

SUGGESTED READINGS

The new demographic patterns that had emerged in American society by the 1970s are examined in Kirkpatrick Sale, *Power Shift* (1975), which considers the rise of the so-called Sunbelt. Douglas Glasgow, *The Black Underclass* (1980), studies the plight of inner-city ghetto residents. On the new evangelicism, see John Woodridge, *The Evangelicals* (1975), and Marshall Frady, *Billy Graham* (1979). Peter Steinfels, *The Neo-conservatives* (1979), discusses an increasingly important element of the New Right. Jonathan Schell, *The Fate of the Earth* (1982), is a passionate document of the antinuclear movement. Christopher Lasch, *The Culture of Narcissism* (1978), is a gloomy view of America in the 1970s.

The Ford administration has not spawned a large literature, but see Gerald Ter Horst, *Gerald Ford* (1975); Richard Reeves, *A Ford Not a Lincoln* (1976); and Ford's own memoirs, *A Time to Heal* (1979).

Several useful studies of the Carter presidency have already appeared. The most insightful is the series of articles "The Passionless Presidency" by James Fallows, a former Carter speech writer, in the *Atlantic Monthly* (1979). Fallows has also published an excellent analysis of the controversial state of the American military, *National Defense* (1981). Jimmy Carter's campaign autobiography, *Why Not the Best* (1975), is an unusually revealing example of the genre. Jules Witcover, *Marathon* (1977), and James Wooten, *Dasher* (1978), examine the remarkable Carter campaign of 1976. Clark Mollenhoff, *The President Who Failed* (1980), is a hostile account. Roy Blount, Jr., *Crackers* (1980), offers humorous reflections by a Southerner about Carter and his region. Jack Bass and Walter Devries, *The Transformation of Southern Politics* (1976), is a more serious examination of the changing South.

Theodore H. White, *America in Search of Itself* (1982), includes an account of the 1980 campaign within a somber discussion of the nation's social and political plight. William Boyarsky, *The Rise of Ronald Reagan* (1968), is an early view of the fortieth president; while Hedrick Smith et al., *Reagan: The Man, the President* (1980), is a more recent study. Rowland Evans and Robert Novack, *The Reagan Revolution* (1981), is an admiring analysis, which discusses the first months of the new administration. George Gilder, *Wealth and Poverty* (1981), is a statement of the controversial economic ideology of the Republican administration. Burton Yale Pines, *Back to Basics* (1982), is an admiring description of the "traditionalist" revival.

THE DECLARATION OF INDEPENDENCE

In Congress, July 4, 1776,

THE UNANIMOUS DECLARATION OF THE THIRTEEN
UNITED STATES OF AMERICA

When, in the course of human events, it becomes necessary for one people to dissolve the political bands which have connected them with another, and to assume, among the powers of the earth, the separate and equal station to which the laws of nature and of nature's God entitle them, a decent respect to the opinions of mankind requires that they should declare the causes which impel them to the separation.

We hold these truths to be self-evident, that all men are created equal; that they are endowed by their Creator with certain unalienable rights; that among these, are life, liberty, and the pursuit of happiness. That, to secure these rights, governments are instituted among men, deriving their just powers from the consent of the governed; that, whenever any form of government becomes destructive of these ends, it is the right of the people to alter or to abolish it, and to institute a new government, laying its foundation on such principles, and organizing its powers in such form, as to them shall seem most likely to effect their safety and happiness. Prudence, indeed, will dictate that governments long established, should not be changed for light and transient causes; and, accordingly, all experience hath shown, that mankind are more disposed to suffer, while evils are sufferable, than to right themselves by abolishing the forms to which they are accustomed. But, when a long train of abuses and usurpations, pursuing invariably the same object, evinces a design to reduce them under absolute despotism, it is their right, it is their duty, to throw off such government and to provide new guards for their future security. Such has been the patient sufferance of these colonies, and such is now the necessity which constrains them to alter their former systems of government. The history of the present King of Great Britain is a history of repeated injuries and usurpations, all having, in direct object, the establishment of an absolute tyranny over these States. To prove this, let facts be submitted to a candid world:

He has refused his assent to laws the most wholesome and necessary for the public good.

He has forbidden his governors to pass laws of immediate and pressing importance, unless suspended in their operation till his assent should be obtained; and, when so suspended, he has utterly neglected to attend to them.

He has refused to pass other laws for the accommodation of large districts of people, unless those people would relinquish the right of representation in the legislature; a right inestimable to them, and formidable to tyrants only.

He has called together legislative bodies at places unusual, uncomfortable, and distant from the depository of their public records, for the sole purpose of fatiguing them into compliance with his measures.

He has dissolved representative houses repeatedly for opposing, with manly firmness, his invasions on the rights of the people.

He has refused, for a long time after such dissolutions, to cause others to be elected; whereby the legislative powers, incapable of annihilation, have returned to the people at large for their exercise; the state remaining, in the meantime, exposed to all the danger of invasion from without, and convulsions within.

He has endeavored to prevent the population of these States; for that purpose, obstructing the laws for naturalization of foreigners, refusing to pass others to encourage their migration hither, and raising the conditions of new appropriations of lands.

He has obstructed the administration of justice, by refusing his assent to laws for establishing judiciary powers.

He has made judges dependent on his will alone, for the tenure of their offices, and the amount and payment of their salaries.

He has erected a multitude of new offices, and sent hither swarms of officers to harass our people, and eat out their substance.

He has kept among us, in time of peace, standing armies, without the consent of our legislatures.

He has affected to render the military independent of, and superior to, the civil power.

He has combined, with others, to subject us to a jurisdiction foreign to our Constitution, and unacknowledged by our laws; giving his assent to their acts of pretended legislation:

For quartering large bodies of armed troops among us:

For protecting them by a mock trial, from punishment, for any murders which they should commit on the inhabitants of these States:

For cutting off our trade with all parts of the world:

For imposing taxes on us without our consent:

For depriving us, in many cases, of the benefit of trial by jury:

For transporting us beyond seas to be tried for pretended offences:

For abolishing the free system of English laws in a neighboring province, establishing therein an arbitrary government, and enlarging its boundaries, so as to render it at once an example and fit instrument for introducing the same absolute rule into these colonies:

For taking away our charters, abolishing our most valuable laws, and altering, fundamentally, the powers of our governments:

For suspending our own legislatures, and declaring themselves invested with power to legislate for us in all cases whatsoever.

He has abdicated government here, by declaring us out of his protection, and waging war against us.

He has plundered our seas, ravaged our coasts, burnt our towns, and destroyed the lives of our people.

He is, at this time, transporting large armies of foreign mercenaries to complete the works of death, desolation, and tyranny, already begun, with circumstances of cruelty and perfidy scarcely paralleled in the most barbarous ages, and totally unworthy the head of a civilized nation.

He has constrained our fellow citizens, taken captive on the high seas, to bear arms against their country, to become the executioners of their friends, and brethren, or to fall themselves by their hands.

He has excited domestic insurrections amongst us, and has endeavored to bring on the inhabitants of our frontiers, the merciless Indian savages, whose known rule of warfare is an undistinguished destruction of all ages, sexes, and conditions.

In every stage of these oppressions, we have petitioned for redress, in the most humble terms; our repeated petitions have been answered only by repeated injury. A prince, whose character is thus marked by every act which may define a tyrant, is unfit to be the ruler of a free people.

Nor have we been wanting in attention to our British brethren. We have warned them, from time to time, of attempts made by their legislature to extend an unwarrantable jurisdiction over us. We have reminded them of the circumstances of our emigration and settlement here. We have appealed to their native justice and magnanimity, and we have conjured them, by the ties of our common kindred, to disavow these usurpations, which would inevitably interrupt our connections and correspondence. They, too, have been deaf to the voice of justice and consanguinity. We must, therefore, acquiesce in the necessity which denounces our separation, and hold them as we hold the rest of mankind, enemies in war, in peace, friends.

We, therefore, the representatives of the United States of America, in general Congress assembled, appealing to the Supreme Judge of the world for the rectitude of our intentions, do, in the name, and by the authority of the good people of these colonies, solemnly publish and declare, that these united colonies are, and of right ought to be, free and independent states: that they are absolved from all allegiance to the British Crown, and that all political connection between them and the state of Great Britain is, and ought to be, totally dissolved; and that, as free and independent states, they have full power to levy war, conclude peace, contract alliances, establish commerce, and to do all other acts and things which independent states may of right do. And, for the support of this declaration, with a firm reliance on the protection of Divine Providence, we mutually pledge to each other our lives, our fortunes, and our sacred honor.

The foregoing Declaration was, by order of Congress, engrossed, and signed by the following members:

JOHN HANCOCK

New Hampshire
Josiah Bartlett
William Whipple
Matthew Thornton

Massachusetts Bay
Samuel Adams
John Adams
Robert Treat Paine
Elbridge Gerry

Rhode Island
Stephen Hopkins
William Ellery

Connecticut
Roger Sherman
Samuel Huntington
William Williams
Oliver Wolcott

New York
William Floyd
Philip Livingston
Francis Lewis
Lewis Morris

New Jersey
Richard Stockton
John Witherspoon
Francis Hopkinson
John Hart
Abraham Clark

Pennsylvania
Robert Morris
Benjamin Rush
Benjamin Franklin
John Morton
George Clymer
James Smith
George Taylor
James Wilson
George Ross

Delaware
Caesar Rodney
George Reed
Thomas M'Kean

Maryland
Samuel Chase
William Paca
Thomas Stone
Charles Carroll,
    of Carrollton

Virginia
George Wythe
Richard Henry Lee
Thomas Jefferson
Benjamin Harrison
Thomas Nelson, Jr.
Francis Lightfoot Lee
Carter Braxton

North Carolina
William Hooper
Joseph Hewes
John Penn

South Carolina
Edward Rutledge
Thomas Heyward, Jr.
Thomas Lynch, Jr.
Arthur Middleton

Georgia
Button Gwinnett
Lyman Hall
George Walton

Resolved, That copies of the Declaration be sent to the several assemblies, conventions, and committees, or councils of safety, and to the several commanding officers of the continental troops; that it be proclaimed in each of the United States, at the head of the army.

THE CONSTITUTION OF THE UNITED STATES OF AMERICA[1]

We the People of the United States, in Order to form a more perfect Union, establish Justice, insure domestic Tranquility, provide for the common defence, promote the general Welfare, and secure the Blessings of Liberty to ourselves and our Posterity, do ordain and establish this CONSTITUTION for the United States of America.

Article I

SECTION 1.
All legislative Powers herein granted shall be vested in a Congress of the United States, which shall consist of a Senate and House of Representatives.

SECTION 2.
The House of Representatives shall be composed of Members chosen every second Year by the People of the several States, and the Electors in each State shall have the Qualifications requisite for Electors of the most numerous Branch of the State Legislature.

No Person shall be a Representative who shall not have attained to the Age of twenty-five Years, and been seven Years a Citizen of the United States, and who shall not, when elected, be an Inhabitant of that State in which he shall be chosen.

[Representatives and direct Taxes[2] shall be apportioned among the several States which may be included within this Union, according to their respective Numbers, which shall be determined by adding to the whole Number of free Persons, including those bound to Service for a Term of Years, and excluding Indians not taxed, three fifths of all other Persons.][3] The actual Enumeration shall be made within three Years after the first Meeting of the Congress of the United States, and within every subsequent Term of ten Years, in such Manner as they shall by Law direct. The Number of Representatives shall not exceed one for every thirty Thousand, but each State shall have at Least one Representative; and until such enumeration shall be made, the State of New Hampshire shall be entitled to chuse three, Massachusetts eight, Rhode-Island and Providence Plantations one, Connecticut five, New York six, New Jersey four, Pennsylvania eight, Delaware one, Maryland six, Virginia ten, North Carolina five, South Carolina five, and Georgia three.

When vacancies happen in the Representation from any State, the Executive Authority thereof shall issue Writs of Election to fill such Vacancies.

The House of Representatives shall chuse their Speaker and other Officers; and shall have the sole Power of Impeachment.

SECTION 3.
The Senate of the United States shall be composed of two Senators from each State, chosen by the Legislature thereof, for six Years; and each Senator shall have one Vote.

Immediately after they shall be assembled in Consequence of the first Election, they shall be divided as equally as may be into three Classes. The Seats of the Senators of the first Class shall be vacated at the Expiration of the second Year, of the second Class at the Expiration of the fourth Year, and of the third Class at the Expiration of the sixth Year, so that one-third may be chosen every second Year; and if Vacancies happen by Resignation, or otherwise, during the Recess of the Legislature of any State, the Executive thereof may make temporary Appointments until the next Meeting of the Legislature, which shall then fill such Vacancies.

No Person shall be a Senator who shall not have attained to the Age of thirty Years, and been nine Years a Citizen of the United States, and who shall not, when elected, be an Inhabitant of that State for which he shall be chosen.

The Vice President of the United States shall be President of the Senate, but shall have no vote, unless they be equally divided.

---

[1] This version, which follows the original Constitution in capitalization and spelling, was published by the United States Department of the Interior, Office of Education, in 1935.

[2] Altered by the Sixteenth Amendment.

[3] Negated by the Fourteenth Amendment.

The Senate shall chuse their other Officers, and also a President pro tempore, in the absence of the Vice President, or when he shall exercise the Office of President of the United States.

The Senate shall have the sole Power to try all Impeachments. When sitting for that purpose they shall be on Oath or Affirmation. When the President of the United States is tried, the Chief Justice shall preside: And no person shall be convicted without the Concurrence of two thirds of the Members present.

Judgment in Cases of Impeachment shall not extend further than to removal from Office, and disqualification to hold and enjoy any Office of honor, Trust, or Profit under the United States: but the Party convicted shall nevertheless be liable and subject to Indictment, Trial, Judgment, and Punishment, according to Law.

SECTION 4.

The Times, Places and Manner of holding Elections for Senators and Representatives, shall be prescribed in each State by the Legislature thereof; but the Congress may at any time by Law make or alter such Regulations, except as to the Places of Chusing Senators.

The Congress shall assemble at least once in every Year, and such Meeting shall be on the first Monday in December, unless they shall by Law appoint a different Day.

SECTION 5.

Each House shall be the Judge of the Elections, Returns and Qualifications of its own Members, and a Majority of each shall constitute a Quorum to do Business; but a smaller number may adjourn from day to day, and may be authorized to compel the Attendance of absent Members, in such Manner, and under such Penalties, as each House may provide.

Each House may determine the Rules of its Proceedings, punish its Members for disorderly Behaviour, and, with the Concurrence of two thirds, expel a Member.

Each House shall keep a Journal of its Proceedings, and from time to time publish the same, excepting such Parts as may in their Judgment require Secrecy; and the Yeas and Nays of the Members of either House on any question shall, at the Desire of one fifth of those Present, be entered on the Journal.

Neither House, during the Session of Congress, shall, without the Consent of the other, adjourn for more than three days, nor to any other Place than that in which the two Houses shall be sitting.

SECTION 6.

The Senators and Representatives shall receive a Compensation for their Services, to be ascertained by Law, and paid out of the Treasury of the United States. They shall in all Cases, except Treason, Felony, and Breach of the Peace, be privileged from Arrest during their Attendance at the Session of their respective Houses, and in going to and returning from the same; and for any Speech or Debate in either House, they shall not be questioned in any other Place.

No Senator or Representative shall, during the Time for which he was elected, be appointed to any civil Office under the Authority of the United States, which shall have been created, or the Emoluments whereof shall have been increased, during such time; and no Person holding any Office under the United States shall be a Member of either House during his continuance in Office.

SECTION 7.

All Bills for raising Revenue shall originate in the House of Representatives; but the Senate may propose or concur with Amendments as on other bills.

Every Bill which shall have passed the House of Representatives and the Senate, shall, before it become a Law, be presented to the President of the United States; If he approve he shall sign it, but if not he shall return it, with his Objections, to that House in which it shall have originated, who shall enter the Objections at large on their Journal, and proceed to reconsider it. If after such Reconsideration two thirds of that House shall agree to pass the bill, it shall be sent, together with the objections, to the other House, by which it shall likewise be reconsidered, and if approved by two thirds of that House, it shall become a Law. But in all such Cases the Votes of both Houses shall be determined by Yeas and Nays, and the Names of the Persons voting for and against the Bill shall be entered on the Journal of each House respectively. If any Bill shall not be returned by the President within ten Days (Sundays excepted) after it shall have been presented to him, the Same shall be a Law, in like Manner as if he had signed it, unless the Congress by their Adjournment prevent its Return, in which Case it shall not be a Law.

Every Order, Resolution, or Vote to which the Concurrence of the Senate and House of Representatives may be necessary (except on a question of Adjournment) shall be presented to the President of the United States; and before the Same shall take Effect, shall be approved by him, or being disapproved by him, shall be repassed by two thirds of the Senate and House of Representatives, according to the Rules and Limitations prescribed in the Case of a Bill.

SECTION 8.

The Congress shall have Power To lay and collect Taxes, Duties, Imposts and Excises, to pay the Debts and provide for the common Defence and general Welfare of the United States; but all Duties, Imposts and Excises shall be uniform throughout the United States;

To borrow money on the credit of the United States;

To regulate Commerce with foreign Nations, and among the several States, and with the Indian Tribes;

To establish an uniform rule of Naturalization, and uniform Laws on the subject of Bankruptcies throughout the United States;

To coin Money, regulate the Value thereof, and of foreign Coin, and fix the Standard of Weights and Measures;

To provide for the Punishment of counterfeiting the Securities and current Coin of the United States;

To establish Post Offices and post Roads;

To promote the Progress of Science and useful Arts, by securing for limited Times to Authors and Inventors the exclusive Right to their respective Writings and Discoveries;

To constitute Tribunals inferior to the Supreme Court;

To define and punish Piracies and Felonies committed on the high Seas, and Offenses against the Law of Nations;

To declare War, grant Letters of Marque and Reprisal, and make Rules concerning Captures on Land and Water;

To raise and support Armies, but no Appropriation of Money to that Use shall be for a longer Term than two Years;

To provide and maintain a Navy;

To make Rules for the Government and Regulation of the land and naval forces;

To provide for calling forth the Militia to execute the Laws of the Union, suppress Insurrections and repel Invasions;

To provide for organizing, arming, and disciplining the Militia, and for governing such Part of them as may be employed in the Service of the United States, reserving to the States respectively, the Appointment of the Officers, and the Authority of training the Militia according to the discipline prescribed by Congress;

To exercise exclusive Legislation in all Cases whatsoever, over such District (not exceeding ten Miles square) as may, by Cession of particular States, and the acceptance of Congress, become the Seat of the Government of the United States, and to exercise like Authority over all Places purchased by the Consent of the Legislature of the State in which the Same shall be, for the Erection of Forts, Magazines, Arsenals, Dock-yards, and other needful Buildings;—And

To make all Laws which shall be necessary and proper for carrying into Execution the foregoing Powers, and all other Powers vested by this Constitution in the Government of the United States, or in any Department or Officer thereof.

SECTION 9.

The Migration or Importation of such Persons as any of the States now existing shall think proper to admit, shall not be prohibited by the Congress prior to the Year one thousand eight hundred and eight, but a tax or duty may be imposed on such Importation, not exceeding ten dollars for each Person.

The privilege of the Writ of Habeas Corpus shall not be suspended, unless when in Cases of Rebellion or Invasion the public Safety may require it.

No bill of Attainder or ex post facto Law shall be passed.

No capitation, or other direct, Tax shall be laid unless in Proportion to the Census or Enumeration herein before directed to be taken.

No Tax or Duty shall be laid on Articles exported from any State.

No Preference shall be given by any Regulation of Commerce or Revenue to the Ports of one State over those of another: nor shall Vessels bound to, or from, one State, be obliged to enter, clear, or pay Duties in another.

No Money shall be drawn from the Treasury, but in Consequence of Appropriations made by Law; and a regular Statement and Account of the Receipts and Expenditures of all public Money shall be published from time to time.

No Title of Nobility shall be granted by the United States: And no Person holding any Office of Profit or Trust under them, shall, without the Consent of the Congress, accept of any present, Emolument, Office, or Title, of any kind whatever, from any King, Prince, or foreign State.

SECTION 10.

No State shall enter into any Treaty, Alliance, or Confederation; grant Letters of Marque and Reprisal; coin Money; emit Bills of Credit; make any Thing but gold and silver Coin a Tender in Payment of Debts; pass any Bill of Attainder, ex post facto Law, or Law impairing the Obligation of Contracts, or grant any Title of Nobility.

No State shall, without the Consent of the Congress, lay any Imposts or Duties on Imports or Exports, except what may be absolutely necessary for executing its inspection Laws; and the net Produce of all Duties and Imposts, laid by any State on Imports or Exports, shall be for the Use of the Treasury of the United States; and all such Laws shall be subject to the Revision and Control of the Congress.

No state shall, without the Consent of Congress, lay any duty of Tonnage, keep Troops, or Ships of War in time of Peace, enter into any Agreement or Compact with another State, or with a foreign Power, or engage in War, unless actually invaded, or in such imminent Danger as will not admit of delay.

Article II

SECTION 1.

The executive Power shall be vested in a President of the United States of America. He shall hold his Office during the Term of four years, and, together with the Vice President, chosen for the same Term, be elected, as follows:

Each State shall appoint, in such Manner as the Legislature thereof may direct, a Number of Electors, equal to the whole Number of Senators and Representatives to which the State may be entitled in the Congress: but no Senator or Representative, or Person holding an Office of Trust or Profit under the United States, shall be appointed an Elector.

[The Electors shall meet in their respective States, and vote by Ballot for two persons, of whom one at least shall not be an Inhabitant of the same State with themselves. And they shall make a List of all the Persons voted for, and of the Number of Votes for each; which List they shall sign and certify, and transmit sealed to the Seat of the Government of the United States, directed to the President of the Senate. The President of the Senate shall, in the Presence of the Senate and House of Representatives, open all the Certificates, and the Votes shall then be counted. The Person having the greatest Number of Votes shall be the President, if such Number be a Majority of the whole Number of Electors appointed; and if there be more than one who have such Majority, and have an equal Number of Votes, then the House of Representatives shall immediately chuse by Ballot one of them for President; and if no Person have a Majority, then from the five highest on the List the said House shall in like Manner chuse the President. But in chusing the President, the Votes shall be taken by States, the Representation from each State having one Vote; a quorum for this Purpose shall consist of a Member or Members from two-thirds of the States, and a Majority of all the States shall be necessary to a Choice. In every Case, after the Choice of the President, the Person having the greatest Number of Votes of the Electors shall be the Vice President. But if there should remain two or more who have equal votes, the Senate shall chuse from them by Ballot the Vice President.][4]

The Congress may determine the Time of chusing the Electors, and the Day on which they shall give their Votes; which Day shall be the same throughout the United States.

No person except a natural-born Citizen, or a Citizen of the United States, at the time of the Adoption of this Constitution, shall be eligible to the Office of President; neither shall any Person be eligible to that Office who shall not have attained to the Age of thirty-five years, and been fourteen Years a Resident within the United States.

In Case of the Removal of the President from Office, or of his Death, Resignation, or Inability to discharge the Powers and Duties of the said Office, the same shall devolve on the Vice President, and the Congress may by Law provide for the Case of Removal, Death, Resignation, or Inability, both of the President and Vice President, declaring what Officer shall then act as President, and such Officer shall act accordingly, until the disability be removed, or a President shall be elected.

The President shall, at stated Times, receive for his Services a Compensation, which shall neither be increased nor diminished during the Period for which he shall have been elected, and he shall not receive within that Period any other Emolument from the United States, or any of them.

Before he enter on the execution of his Office, he shall take the following Oath or Affirmation:—"I do solemnly swear (or affirm) that I will faithfully execute the Office of President of the United States, and will, to the best of my Ability, preserve, protect, and defend the Constitution of the United States."

SECTION 2.

The President shall be Commander in Chief of the Army and Navy of the United States, and of the Militia of the several States, when called into the actual Service of the United States; he may require the Opinion, in writing, of the principal Officer in each of the executive Departments, upon any subject relating to the Duties of their respective Offices, and he shall have Power to Grant Reprieves and Pardons for Offenses against the United States, except in Cases of Impeachment.

He shall have Power, by and with the Advice and Consent of the Senate, to make Treaties, provided two-thirds of the Senators present concur; and he shall nominate, and by and with the Advice and Consent of the Senate, shall appoint Ambassadors, other public Ministers and Consuls, Judges of the supreme Court, and all other Officers of the United States, whose Appointments are not herein otherwise provided for, and which shall be established by Law: but the Congress may by Law vest the Appointment of such inferior Officers, as they think proper, in the President alone, in the Courts of Law, or in the Heads of Departments.

The President shall have Power to fill up all Vacancies that may happen during the Recess of the Senate, by granting Commissions which shall expire at the End of their next Session.

SECTION 3.

He shall from time to time give to the Congress Information of the State of the Union, and recommend to their Consideration such Measures as he shall judge necessary and expedient; he may, on extraordinary occasions, convene both Houses, or either of them, and in Case of Disagreement between them, with respect to the Time of Adjournment, he may adjourn them to such Time as he shall think proper; he shall receive Ambassadors and other public Ministers; he shall take care that the Laws be faithfully executed, and shall Commission all the Officers of the United States.

SECTION 4.

The President, Vice President and all civil Officers of the United States, shall be removed from Office on Impeachment for, and Conviction of, Treason, Bribery, or other high Crimes and Misdemeanors.

Article III

SECTION 1.

The judicial Power of the United States, shall be vested in one supreme Court, and in such inferior Courts as the Congress may from time to time ordain and establish. The

---

[4] Revised by the Twelfth Amendment.

Judges, both of the supreme and inferior Courts, shall hold their Offices during good Behaviour, and shall, at stated Times, receive for their Services, a Compensation, which shall not be diminished during their Continuance in Office.

SECTION 2.

The judicial Power shall extend to all Cases, in Law and Equity, arising under this Constitution, the Laws of the United States, and Treaties made, or which shall be made, under their Authority;—to all Cases affecting ambassadors, other public ministers and consuls;—to all cases of admiralty and maritime Jurisdiction;—to Controversies to which the United States shall be a Party;—to Controversies between two or more States;—between a State and Citizens of another State;[5]—between Citizens of different States,—between Citizens of the same State claiming Lands under Grants of different States, and between a State, or the Citizens thereof, and foreign States, Citizens or Subjects.

In all Cases affecting Ambassadors, other public Ministers and Consuls, and those in which a State shall be Party, the supreme Court shall have original Jurisdiction. In all the other Cases before mentioned, the supreme Court shall have appellate Jurisdiction, both as to Law and Fact, with such Exceptions, and under such Regulations as the Congress shall make.

The trial of all Crimes, except in Cases of Impeachment, shall be by Jury; and such Trial shall be held in the State where the said Crimes shall have been committed; but when not committed within any State, the Trial shall be at such Place or Places as the Congress may by Law have directed.

SECTION 3.

Treason against the United States, shall consist only in levying War against them, or in adhering to their Enemies, giving them Aid and Comfort. No Person shall be convicted of Treason unless on the Testimony of two Witnesses to the same overt Act, or on Confession in open Court.

The Congress shall have power to declare

the Punishment of Treason, but no Attainder of Treason shall work Corruption of Blood, or Forfeiture except during the Life of the Person attainted.

Article IV

SECTION 1.

Full Faith and Credit shall be given in each State to the public Acts, Records, and judicial Proceedings of every other State. And the Congress may by general Laws prescribe the Manner in which such Acts, Records and Proceedings shall be proved, and the Effect thereof.

SECTION 2.

The Citizens of each State shall be entitled to all Privileges and Immunities of Citizens in the several States.

A Person charged in any State with Treason, Felony, or other Crime, who shall flee from Justice, and be found in another State, shall on demand of the executive Authority of the State from which he fled, be delivered up, to be removed to the State having Jurisdiction of the crime.

No Person held to Service or Labour in one State, under the Laws thereof, escaping into another, shall, in Consequence of any Law or Regulation therein, be discharged from such Service or Labour, but shall be delivered up on Claim of the Party to whom such Service or Labour may be due.

SECTION 3.

New States may be admitted by the Congress into this Union; but no new State shall be formed or erected within the Jurisdiction of any other State; nor any State be formed by the Junction of two or more States, or parts of States, without the Consent of the Legislatures of the States concerned as well as of the Congress.

The Congress shall have Power to dispose of and make all needful Rules and Regulations respecting the Territory or other Property belonging to the United States; and nothing in this Constitution shall be so construed as to Prejudice any Claims of the United States, or of any particular State.

---

[5] Qualified by the Eleventh Amendment.

SECTION 4.

The United States shall guarantee to every State in this Union a Republican Form of Government, and shall protect each of them against Invasion; and on Application of the Legislature, or of the Executive (when the Legislature cannot be convened) against domestic Violence.

Article V

The Congress, whenever two-thirds of both Houses shall deem it necessary, shall propose Amendments to this Constitution, or, on the Application of the Legislatures of two-thirds of the several States, shall call a Convention for proposing Amendments, which, in either Case, shall be valid to all Intents and Purposes, as part of this Constitution, when ratified by the Legislatures of three-fourths of the several States, or by Conventions in three-fourths thereof, as the one or the other Mode of Ratification may be proposed by the Congress; Provided that no Amendment which may be made prior to the Year One thousand eight hundred and eight shall in any Manner affect the first and fourth Clauses in the Ninth Section of the first Article; and that no State, without its Consent, shall be deprived of its equal Suffrage in the Senate.

Article VI

All Debts contracted and Engagements entered into, before the Adoption of this Constitution, shall be as valid against the United States under this Constitution, as under the Confederation.

This Constitution, and the Laws of the United States which shall be made in Pursuance thereof; and all Treaties made, or which shall be made, under the Authority of the United States, shall be the supreme Law of the Land; and the Judges in every State shall be bound thereby, and Thing in the Constitution or Laws of any State to the Contrary notwithstanding.

The Senators and Representatives before mentioned, and the Members of the several State Legislatures, and all executive and judicial Officers, both of the United States and of the several States, shall be bound by Oath or Affirmation to support this Constitution; but no religious Test shall ever be required as a qualification to any Office or public Trust under the United States.

Article VII

The Ratification of the Conventions of nine States shall be sufficient for the Establishment of this Constitution between the States so ratifying the same.

Done in Convention by the Unanimous Consent of the States present the Seventeenth Day of September in the Year of our Lord one thousand seven hundred and Eighty seven, and of the Independence of the United States of America the Twelfth. In Witness whereof We have hereunto subscribed our Names.[6]

George Washington
President and deputy from Virginia

New Hampshire	New Jersey	Delaware	North Carolina
John Langdon	William Livingston	George Read	William Blount
Nicholas Gilman	David Brearley	Gunning Bedford, Jr.	Richard Dobbs
	William Paterson	John Dickinson	Spaight
	Jonathan Dayton	Richard Bassett	Hugh Williamson
		Jacob Broom	

[6] These are the full names of the signers, which in some cases are not the signatures on the document.

Massachusetts	Pennsylvania	Maryland	South Carolina
Nathaniel Gorham	Benjamin Franklin	James McHenry	John Rutledge
Rufus King	Thomas Mifflin	Daniel of	Charles Cotesworth
	Robert Morris	St. Thomas Jenifer	Pinckney
Connecticut	George Clymer	Daniel Carroll	Charles Pinckney
	Thomas FitzSimons		Pierce Butler
William Samuel	Jared Ingersoll		
Johnson	James Wilson		
Roger Sherman	Gouverneur Morris		
New York		**Virginia**	**Georgia**
Alexander Hamilton		John Blair	William Few
		James Madison, Jr.	Abraham Baldwin

Articles in Addition to, and Amendment of, the Constitution of the United States of America, Proposed by Congress, and Ratified by the Legislatures of the Several States, Pursuant to the Fifth Article of the Original Constitution[7]

[Article I]

Congress shall make no law respecting an establishment of religion, or prohibiting the free exercise thereof; or abridging the freedom of speech, or of the press; or the right of the people peaceably to assemble, and to petition the Government for a redress of grievances.

[Article II]

A well regulated Militia, being necessary to the security of a free State, the right of the people to keep and bear Arms shall not be infringed.

[Article III]

No Soldier shall, in time of peace, be quartered in any house, without the consent of the Owner, nor in time of war, but in a manner to be prescribed by law.

---

[7] This heading appears only in the joint resolution submitting the first ten amendments.

[Article IV]

The right of the people to be secure in their persons, houses, papers, and effects, against unreasonable searches and seizures, shall not be violated, and no Warrants shall issue, but upon probable cause, supported by Oath or affirmation, and particularly describing the place to be searched, and the persons or things to be seized.

[Article V]

No person shall be held to answer for a capital or otherwise infamous crime, unless on a presentment or indictment of a Grand Jury, except in cases arising in the land or naval forces, or in the Militia, when in actual service in time of War or public danger; nor shall any person be subject for the same offence to be twice put in jeopardy of life or limb; nor shall be compelled in any criminal case to be a witness against himself, nor be deprived of life, liberty, or property, without due process of law; nor shall private property be taken for public use, without just compensation.

[Article VI]

In all criminal prosecutions, the accused shall enjoy the right to a speedy and public trial, by an impartial jury of the State and district wherein the crime shall have been committed, which district shall have been previously ascertained by law, and to be informed of the nature and cause of the accusation; to be confronted with the witnesses against him; to have compulsory process for obtaining witnesses in his favour, and to have the Assistance of Counsel for his defence.

[Article VII]

In suits at common law, where the value in controversy shall exceed twenty dollars, the right of trial by jury shall be preserved, and no fact tried by a jury, shall be otherwise reexamined in any Court of the United States, than according to the rules of the common law.

[Article VIII]

Excessive bail shall not be required, nor excessive fines imposed, nor cruel and unusual punishments inflicted.

[Article IX]

The enumeration of the Constitution, of certain rights, shall not be construed to deny or disparage others retained by the people.

[Article X]

The powers not delegated to the United States by the Constitution, nor prohibited by it to the States, are reserved to the States respectively, or to the people.
     [Amendments I-X, in force 1791.]

[Article XI][8]

The Judicial power of the United States shall not be construed to extend to any suit in law or equity, commenced or prosecuted against one of the United States by Citizens of another State, or by Citizens or Subjects of any Foreign State.

[Article XII][9]

The Electors shall meet in their respective States and vote by ballot for President and Vice-President, one of whom, at least, shall not be an inhabitant of the same State with themselves; they shall name in their ballots the person voted for as President, and in distinct ballots the person voted for as Vice-President, and they shall make distinct lists of all persons voted for as President, and of all persons voted for as Vice-President, and of the number of votes for each, which lists they shall sign and certify, and transmit sealed to the seat of the government of the United States, directed to the President of the Senate;—The President of the Senate shall, in the presence of the Senate and House of Representatives, open all the certificates and the votes shall then be counted;—The person having the greatest number of votes for President, shall be the President, if such number be a majority of the whole number of Electors appointed; and if no person have such majority, then from the persons having the highest numbers not exceeding three on the list of those voted for as President, the House of Representatives shall choose immediately, by ballot, the President. But in choosing the President, the votes shall be taken by states, the representation from each state having one vote; a quorum for this purpose shall consist of a member or members from two-thirds of the states, and a majority of all the states shall be necessary to a choice. And if the House of Representatives shall not choose a President whenever the right of choice shall devolve upon them, before the fourth day of March next following, then the Vice-President shall act as President, as in the case of the death or other constitutional disability of the President.—The person having the greatest number of votes as Vice-President, shall be the Vice-President, if such number be a majority of the whole number

---

[8] Adopted in 1798.

[9] Adopted in 1804.

of Electors appointed, and if no person have a majority, then from the two highest numbers on the list, the Senate shall choose the Vice-President; a quorum for the purpose shall consist of two-thirds of the whole number of Senators, and a majority of the whole number shall be necessary to a choice. But no person constitutionally ineligible to the office of President shall be eligible to that of Vice-President of the United States.

[Article XIII][10]

SECTION 1.
Neither slavery nor involuntary servitude, except as a punishment for crime whereof the party shall have been duly convicted, shall exist within the United States, or any place subject to their jurisdiction.

SECTION 2.
Congress shall have power to enforce this article by appropriate legislation.

[Article XIV][11]

SECTION 1.
All persons born or naturalized in the United States, and subject to the jurisdiction thereof, are citizens of the United States and of the State wherein they reside. No State shall abridge the privileges or immunities of citizens of the United States; nor shall any State deprive any person of life, liberty, or property, without due process of law; nor deny to any person within its jurisdiction the equal protection of the laws.

SECTION 2.
Representatives shall be apportioned among the several States according to their respective numbers, counting the whole number of persons in each State, excluding Indians not taxed. But when the right to vote at any election for the choice of electors for President and Vice-President of the United States, Representatives in Congress, the Executive and Judicial officers of a State, or the members of the Legislature thereof, is denied to any of the male inhabitants of such State, being twenty-one years of age, and citizens of the United States, or in any way abridged, except for participation in rebellion, or other crime, the basis of representation therein shall be reduced in the proportion which the number of such male citizens shall bear to the whole number of male citizens twenty-one years of age in such State.

SECTION 3.
No person shall be a Senator or Representative in Congress, or elector of President and Vice-President, or hold any office, civil or military, under the United States, or under any State, who, having previously taken an oath, as a member of Congress, or as an officer of the United States, or as a member of any State legislature, or as an executive or judicial officer of any State, to support the Constitution of the United States, shall have engaged in insurrection or rebellion against the same, or given aid or comfort to the enemies thereof. But Congress may by a vote of two-thirds of each House, remove such disability.

SECTION 4.
The validity of the public debt of the United States, authorized by law, including debts incurred for payment of pensions and bounties for services in suppressing insurrection or rebellion, shall not be questioned. But neither the United States nor any State shall assume or pay any debts or obligation incurred in aid of insurrection or rebellion against the United States, or any claim for the loss or emancipation of any slave; but all such debts, obligations, and claims shall be held illegal and void.

SECTION 5.
The Congress shall have the power to enforce, by appropriate legislation, the provisions of this article.

[10] Adopted in 1865.
[11] Adopted in 1868.

[Article XV]^{12}

SECTION 1.
The right of citizens of the United States to vote shall not be denied or abridged by the United States or by any State on account of race, color, or previous condition of servitude—

SECTION 2.
The Congress shall have power to enforce this article by appropriate legislation.

[Article XVI]^{13}

The Congress shall have power to lay and collect taxes on incomes, from whatever source derived, without apportionment among the several States, and without regard to any census or enumeration.

[Article XVII]^{14}

The Senate of the United States shall be composed of two Senators from each State, elected by the people thereof, for six years; and each Senator shall have one vote. The electors in each State shall have the qualifications requisite for electors of the most numerous branch of the State legislatures.

When vacancies happen in the representation of any State in the Senate, the executive authority of such State shall issue writs of election to fill such vacancies: *Provided,* That the legislature of any State may empower the executive thereof to make temporary appointments until the people fill the vacancies by election as the legislature may direct.

This amendment shall not be so construed as to affect the election or term of any Senator chosen before it becomes valid as part of the Constitution.

[Article XVIII]^{15}

SECTION 1.
After one year from the ratification of this article the manufacture, sale, or transportation of intoxicating liquors within, the importation thereof into, or the exportation thereof from the United States and all territory subject to the jurisdiction thereof for beverage purposes is hereby prohibited.

SECTION 2.
The Congress and the several States shall have concurrent power to enforce this article by appropriate legislation.

SECTION 3.
This article shall be inoperative unless it shall have been ratified as an amendment to the Constitution by the legislatures of the several States, as provided in the Constitution, within seven years from the date of the submission hereof to the States by the Congress.

[Article XIX]^{16}

The right of citizens of the United States to vote shall not be denied or abridged by the United States or by any State on account of sex.

Congress shall have power to enforce this article by appropriate legislation.

[Article XX]^{17}

SECTION 1.
The terms of the President and Vice-President shall end at noon on the 20th day of January, and the terms of Senators and Representatives at noon on the 3d day of January, of the years in which such terms would have ended if this article had not been

---

^{12} Adopted in 1870.
^{13} Adopted in 1913.
^{14} Adopted in 1913.

^{15} Adopted in 1918.
^{16} Adopted in 1920.
^{17} Adopted in 1933.

ratified; and the terms of their successors shall then begin.

SECTION 2.
The Congress shall assemble at least once in every year, and such meeting shall begin at noon on the 3d day of January, unless they shall by law appoint a different day.

SECTION 3.
If, at the time fixed for the beginning of the term of the President, the President elect shall have died, the Vice-President elect shall become President. If a President shall not have been chosen before the time fixed for the beginning of his term, or if the President elect shall have failed to qualify, then the Vice-President elect shall act as President until a President shall have qualified; and the Congress may by law provide for the case wherein neither a President elect nor a Vice-President elect shall have qualified, declaring who shall then act as President, or the manner in which one who is to act shall be selected, and such person shall act accordingly until a President or Vice-President shall have qualified.

SECTION 4.
The Congress may by law provide for the case of the death of any of the persons from whom the House of Representatives may choose a President whenever the right of choice shall have devolved upon them, and for the case of the death of any of the persons from whom the Senate may choose a Vice-President whenever the right of choice shall have devolved upon them.

SECTION 5.
Sections 1 and 2 shall take effect on the 15th day of October following the ratification of this article.

SECTION 6.
This article shall be inoperative unless it shall have been ratified as an amendment to the Constitution by the legislatures of three-fourths of the several States within seven years from the date of its submission.

[Article XXI][18]

SECTION 1.
The eighteenth article of amendment to the Constitution of the United States is hereby repealed.

SECTION 2.
The transportation or importation into any State, Territory, or possession of the United States for delivery or use therein of intoxicating liquors, in violation of the laws thereof, is hereby prohibited.

SECTION 3.
This article shall be inoperative unless it shall have been ratified as an amendment to the Constitution by conventions in the several States, as provided in the Constitution, within seven years from the date of the submission hereof to the States by the Congress.

[Article XXII][19]

No person shall be elected to the office of the President more than twice, and no person who has held the office of President, or acted as President, for more than two years of a term to which some other person was elected President shall be elected to the office of the President more than once.

But this Article shall not apply to any person holding the office of President when this Article was proposed by the Congress, and shall not prevent any person who may be holding the office of President, or acting as President, during the term within which this Article becomes operative from holding the office of President or acting as President during the remainder of such term.

This article shall be inoperative unless it shall have been ratified as an amendment to the Constitution by the legislatures of three-fourths of the several states within seven years from the date of its submission to the states by the Congress.

---

[18] Adopted in 1933.
[19] Adopted in 1951.

[Article XXIII][20]

SECTION 1.

The District constituting the seat of Government of the United States shall appoint in such manner as the Congress may direct:

A number of electors of President and Vice-President equal to the whole number of Senators and Representatives in Congress to which the District would be entitled if it were a State, but in no event more than the least populous State; they shall be in addition to those appointed by the States, but they shall be considered, for the purposes of the election of President and Vice-President, to be electors appointed by a State; and they shall meet in the District and perform such duties as provided by the twelfth article of amendment.

SECTION 2.

The Congress shall have power to enforce this article by appropriate legislation.

[Article XXIV][21]

SECTION 1.

The right of citizens of the United States to vote in any primary or other election for President or Vice President, for electors for President or Vice President, or for Senator or Representative in Congress, shall not be denied or abridged by the United States or any state by reason of failure to pay any poll tax or other tax.

SECTION 2.

The Congress shall have the power to enforce this article by appropriate legislation.

[Article XXV][22]

SECTION 1.

In case of the removal of the President from office or of his death or resignation, the Vice President shall become President.

---

[20] Adopted in 1961.
[21] Adopted in 1964.
[22] Adopted in 1967.

SECTION 2.

Whenever there is a vacancy in the office of the Vice President, the President shall nominate a Vice President who shall take office upon confirmation by a majority vote of both Houses of Congress.

SECTION 3.

Whenever the President transmits to the President Pro Tempore of the Senate and the Speaker of the House of Representatives his written declaration that he is unable to discharge the powers and duties of his office, and until he transmits to them a written declaration to the contrary, such powers and duties shall be discharged by the Vice President as Acting President.

SECTION 4.

Whenever the Vice President and a majority of either the principal officers of the executive departments or of such other body as Congress may by law provide, transmit to the President Pro Tempore of the Senate and the Speaker of the House of Representatives their written declaration that the President is unable to discharge the powers and duties of his office, the Vice President shall immediately assume the powers and duties of the office as Acting President.

Thereafter, when the President transmits to the President Pro Tempore of the Senate and the Speaker of the House of Representatives his written declaration that no inability exists, he shall resume the powers and duties of his office unless the Vice President and a majority of either the principal officers of the executive departments or of such other body as Congress may by law provide, transmit within four days to the President Pro Tempore of the Senate and the Speaker of the House of Representatives their written declaration that the President is unable to discharge the powers and duties of his office. Thereupon Congress shall decide the issue, assembling within forty-eight hours for that purpose if not in session. If the Congress, within twenty-one days after receipt of the latter written declaration, or, if Congress is not in session, within twenty-one days after Congress is required to assemble, determines by two-thirds vote of both Houses that the

President is unable to discharge the powers and duties of his office, the Vice President shall continue to discharge the same as Acting President; otherwise, the President shall resume the powers and duties of his office.

[Article XXVI][23]

SECTION 1.
The right of citizens of the United States, who are eighteen years of age or older, to vote shall not be denied or abridged by the United States or by any State on account of age.

SECTION 2.
The Congress shall have power to enforce this article by appropriate legislation.

---

[23] Adopted in 1971.

ADMISSION OF STATES TO THE UNION*

1 Delaware	Dec. 7, 1787	26 Michigan	Jan. 26, 1837
2 Pennsylvania	Dec. 12, 1787	27 Florida	Mar. 3, 1845
3 New Jersey	Dec. 18, 1787	28 Texas	Dec. 29, 1845
4 Georgia	Jan. 2, 1788	29 Iowa	Dec. 28, 1846
5 Connecticut	Jan. 9, 1788	30 Wisconsin	May 29, 1848
6 Massachusetts	Feb. 6, 1788	31 California	Sept. 9, 1850
7 Maryland	Apr. 28, 1788	32 Minnesota	May 11, 1858
8 South Carolina	May 23, 1788	33 Oregon	Feb. 14, 1859
9 New Hampshire	June 21, 1788	34 Kansas	Jan. 29, 1861
10 Virginia	June 25, 1788	35 West Virginia	June 19, 1863
11 New York	July 26, 1788	36 Nevada	Oct. 31, 1864
12 North Carolina	Nov. 21, 1789	37 Nebraska	Mar. 1, 1867
13 Rhode Island	May 29, 1790	38 Colorado	Aug. 1, 1876
14 Vermont	Mar. 4, 1791	39 North Dakota	Nov. 2, 1889
15 Kentucky	June 1, 1792	40 South Dakota	Nov. 2, 1889
16 Tennessee	June 1, 1796	41 Montana	Nov. 8, 1889
17 Ohio	Mar. 1, 1803	42 Washington	Nov. 11, 1889
18 Louisiana	Apr. 30, 1812	43 Idaho	July 3, 1890
19 Indiana	Dec. 11, 1816	44 Wyoming	July 10, 1890
20 Mississippi	Dec. 10, 1817	45 Utah	Jan. 4, 1896
21 Illinois	Dec. 3, 1818	46 Oklahoma	Nov. 16, 1907
22 Alabama	Dec. 14, 1819	47 New Mexico	Jan. 6, 1912
23 Maine	Mar. 15, 1820	48 Arizona	Feb. 14, 1912
24 Missouri	Aug. 10, 1821	49 Alaska	Jan. 3, 1959
25 Arkansas	June 15, 1836	50 Hawaii	Aug. 21, 1959

* In the case of the first thirteen states, the date given is that of ratification of the Constitution.

PRESIDENTIAL ELECTIONS

Year	Candidates	Parties	Popular Vote	Percentage of Popular Vote	Electoral Vote
1789	GEORGE WASHINGTON (Va.)*				69
	John Adams				34
	Others				35
1792	GEORGE WASHINGTON (Va.)				132
	John Adams				77
	George Clinton				50
	Others				5
1796	JOHN ADAMS (Mass.)	Federalist			71
	Thomas Jefferson	Democratic-Republican			68
	Thomas Pinckney	Federalist			59
	Aaron Burr	Dem.-Rep.			30
	Others				48
1800	THOMAS JEFFERSON (Va.)	Dem.-Rep.			73
	Aaron Burr	Dem.-Rep.			73
	John Adams	Federalist			65
	C. C. Pinckney	Federalist			64
	John Jay	Federalist			1
1804	THOMAS JEFFERSON (Va.)	Dem.-Rep.			162
	C. C. Pinckney	Federalist			14
1808	JAMES MADISON (Va.)	Dem.-Rep.			122
	C. C. Pinckney	Federalist			47
	George Clinton	Dem.-Rep.			6
1812	JAMES MADISON (Va.)	Dem.-Rep.			128
	De Witt Clinton	Federalist			89
1816	JAMES MONROE (Va.)	Dem.-Rep.			183
	Rufus King	Federalist			34
1820	JAMES MONROE (Va.)	Dem.-Rep.			231
	John Quincy Adams	Dem.-Rep.			1
1824	JOHN Q. ADAMS (Mass.)	Dem.-Rep.	108,740	30.5	84
	Andrew Jackson	Dem.-Rep.	153,544	43.1	99
	William H. Crawford	Dem.-Rep.	46,618	13.1	41
	Henry Clay	Dem.-Rep.	47,136	13.2	37
1828	ANDREW JACKSON (Tenn.)	Democrat	647,286	56.0	178
	John Quincy Adams	National Republican	508,064	44.0	83
1832	ANDREW JACKSON (TENN.)	Democrat	687,502	55.0	219
	Henry Clay	National Republican ⎫	530,189	42.4	49
	John Floyd	Independent ⎬			11
	William Wirt	Anti-Mason	33,108	2.6	7
1836	MARTIN VAN BUREN (N.Y.)	Democrat	765,483	50.9	170
	W. H. Harrison	Whig ⎫			73
	Hugh L. White	Whig ⎬	739,795	49.1	26
	Daniel Webster	Whig ⎪			14
	W. P. Magnum	Independent ⎭			11

* State of residence at time of election.

Year	Candidates	Parties	Popular Vote	Percentage of Popular Vote	Electoral Vote
1840	**WILLIAM H. HARRISON (Ohio)**	Whig	1,274,624	53.1	234
	Martin Van Buren	Democrat	1,127,781	46.9	60
	J. G. Birney	Liberty	7,069		—
1844	**JAMES K. POLK (Tenn.)**	Democrat	1,338,464	49.6	170
	Henry Clay	Whig	1,300,097	48.1	105
	J. G. Birney	Liberty	62,300	2.3	—
1848	**ZACHARY TAYLOR (La.)**	Whig	1,360,967	47.4	163
	Lewis Cass	Democrat	1,222,342	42.5	127
	Martin Van Buren	Free-Soil	291,263	10.1	—
1852	**FRANKLIN PIERCE (N.H.)**	Democrat	1,601,117	50.9	254
	Winfield Scott	Whig	1,385,453	44.1	42
	John P. Hale	Free-Soil	155,825	5.0	—
1856	**JAMES BUCHANAN (Pa.)**	Democrat	1,832,955	45.3	174
	John C. Frémont	Republican	1,339,932	33.1	114
	Millard Fillmore	American	871,731	21.6	8
1860	**ABRAHAM LINCOLN (Ill.)**	Republican	1,865,593	39.8	180
	Stephen A. Douglas	Democrat	1,382,713	29.5	12
	John C. Breckinridge	Democrat	848,356	18.1	72
	John Bell	Union	592,906	12.6	39
1864	**ABRAHAM LINCOLN (Ill.)**	Republican	2,213,655	55.0	212
	George B. McClellan	Democrat	1,805,237	45.0	21
1868	**ULYSSES S. GRANT (Ill.)**	Republican	3,012,833	52.7	214
	Horatio Seymour	Democrat	2,703,249	47.3	80
1872	**ULYSSES S. GRANT (Ill.)**	Republican	3,597,132	55.6	286
	Horace Greeley	Democrat; Liberal Republican	2,834,125	43.9	66
1876	**RUTHERFORD B. HAYES (Ohio)**	Republican	4,036,298	48.0	185
	Samuel J. Tilden	Democrat	4,300,590	51.0	184
1880	**JAMES A. GARFIELD (Ohio)**	Republican	4,454,416	48.5	214
	Winfield S. Hancock	Democrat	4,444,952	48.1	155
1884	**GROVER CLEVELAND (N.Y.)**	Democrat	4,874,986	48.5	219
	James G. Blaine	Republican	4,851,981	48.2	182
1888	**BENJAMIN HARRISON (Ind.)**	Republican	5,439,853	47.9	233
	Grover Cleveland	Democrat	5,540,309	48.6	168
1892	**GROVER CLEVELAND (N.Y.)**	Democrat	5,556,918	46.1	277
	Benjamin Harrison	Republican	5,176,108	43.0	145
	James B. Weaver	People's	1,041,028	8.5	22
1896	**WILLIAM McKINLEY (Ohio)**	Republican	7,104,779	51.1	271
	William J. Bryan	Democrat-People's	6,502,925	47.7	176
1900	**WILLIAM McKINLEY (Ohio)**	Republican	7,207,923	51.7	292
	William J. Bryan	Dem.-Populist	6,358,133	45.5	155
1904	**THEODORE ROOSEVELT (N.Y.)**	Republican	7,623,486	57.9	336
	Alton B. Parker	Democrat	5,077,911	37.6	140
	Eugene V. Debs	Socialist	402,283	3.0	—
1908	**WILLIAM H. TAFT (Ohio)**	Republican	7,678,908	51.6	321
	William J. Bryan	Democrat	6,409,104	43.1	162
	Eugene V. Debs	Socialist	420,793	2.8	—

Year	Candidates	Parties	Popular Vote	Percentage of Popular Vote	Electoral Vote
1912	WOODROW WILSON (N.J.)	Democrat	6,293,454	41.9	435
	Theodore Roosevelt	Progressive	4,119,538	27.4	88
	William H. Taft	Republican	3,484,980	23.2	8
	Eugene V. Debs	Socialist	900,672	6.0	—
1916	WOODROW WILSON (N.J.)	Democrat	9,129,606	49.4	277
	Charles E. Hughes	Republican	8,538,221	46.2	254
	A. L. Benson	Socialist	585,113	3.2	—
1920	WARREN G. HARDING (Ohio)	Republican	16,152,200	60.4	404
	James M. Cox	Democrat	9,147,353	34.2	127
	Eugene V. Debs	Socialist	919,799	3.4	—
1924	CALVIN COOLIDGE (Mass.)	Republican	15,725,016	54.0	382
	John W. Davis	Democrat	8,386,503	28.8	136
	Robert M. LaFollette	Progressive	4,822,856	16.6	13
1928	HERBERT HOOVER (Calif.)	Republican	21,391,381	58.2	444
	Alfred E. Smith	Democrat	15,016,443	40.9	87
	Norman Thomas	Socialist	267,835	0.7	—
1932	FRANKLIN D. ROOSEVELT (N.Y.)	Democrat	22,821,857	57.4	472
	Herbert Hoover	Republican	15,761,841	39.7	59
	Norman Thomas	Socialist	881,951	2.2	—
1936	FRANKLIN D. ROOSEVELT (N.Y.)	Democrat	27,751,597	60.8	523
	Alfred M. Landon	Republican	16,679,583	36.5	8
	William Lemke	Union	882,479	1.9	—
1940	FRANKLIN D. ROOSEVELT (N.Y.)	Democrat	27,244,160	54.8	499
	Wendell L. Willkie	Republican	22,305,198	44.8	82
1944	FRANKLIN D. ROOSEVELT (N.Y.)	Democrat	25,602,504	53.5	432
	Thomas E. Dewey	Republican	22,006,285	46.0	99
1948	HARRY S TRUMAN (Mo.)	Democrat	24,105,695	49.5	304
	Thomas E. Dewey	Republican	21,969,170	45.1	189
	J. Strom Thurmond	State-Rights Democrat	1,169,021	2.4	38
	Henry A. Wallace	Progressive	1,156,103	2.4	—
1952	DWIGHT D. EISENHOWER (N.Y.)	Republican	33,936,252	55.1	442
	Adlai E. Stevenson	Democrat	27,314,992	44.4	89
1956	DWIGHT D. EISENHOWER (N.Y.)	Republican	35,575,420	57.6	457
	Adlai E. Stevenson	Democrat	26,033,066	42.1	73
	Other	—	—		1
1960	JOHN F. KENNEDY (Mass.)	Democrat	34,227,096	49.9	303
	Richard M. Nixon	Republican	34,108,546	49.6	219
	Other	—	—		15
1964	LYNDON B. JOHNSON (Tex.)	Democrat	43,126,506	61.1	486
	Barry M. Goldwater	Republican	27,176,799	38.5	52
1968	RICHARD M. NIXON (N.Y.)	Republican	31,770,237	43.4	301
	Hubert H. Humphrey	Democrat	31,270,533	42.7	191
	George Wallace	American Indep.	9,906,141	13.5	46

Year	Candidates	Parties	Popular Vote	Percentage of Popular Vote	Electoral Vote
1972	RICHARD M. NIXON (N.Y.)	Republican	47,169,911	60.7	520
	George S. McGovern	Democrat	29,170,383	37.5	17
	Other	—	—		1
1976	JIMMY CARTER (Ga.)	Democrat	40,828,587	50.0	297
	Gerald R. Ford	Republican	39,147,613	47.9	241
	Other	—	1,575,459	2.1	—
1980	RONALD REAGAN (Calif.)	Republican	43,901,812	50.7	489
	Jimmy Carter	Democrat	35,483,820	41.0	49
	John B. Anderson	Independent	5,719,722	6.6	—
	Ed Clark	Libertarian	921,188	1.1	—

PRESIDENTS, VICE PRESIDENTS, AND SECRETARIES OF STATE

President	Vice President	Secretary of State
1. George Washington, Federalist 1789	John Adams, Federalist 1789	T. Jefferson 1789 E. Randolph 1794 T. Pickering 1795
2. John Adams, Federalist 1797	Thomas Jefferson, Dem.-Rep. 1797	T. Pickering 1797 John Marshall 1800
3. Thomas Jefferson, Dem.-Rep. 1801	Aaron Burr, Dem.-Rep. 1801 George Clinton, Dem.-Rep. 1805	James Madison 1801
4. James Madison, Dem.-Rep. 1809	George Clinton, Dem.-Rep. 1809 Elbridge Gerry, Dem.-Rep. 1813	Robert Smith 1809 James Monroe 1811
5. James Monroe, Dem.-Rep. 1817	D. D. Tompkins, Dem.-Rep. 1817	J. Q. Adams 1817
6. John Quincy Adams, Dem.-Rep. 1825	John C. Calhoun, Dem.-Rep. 1825	Henry Clay 1825
7. Andrew Jackson, Democratic 1829	John C. Calhoun, Democratic 1829 Martin Van Buren, Democratic 1833	M. Van Buren 1829 E. Livingston 1831 Louis McLane 1833 John Forsyth 1834
8. Martin Van Buren, Democratic 1837	Richard M. Johnson, Democratic 1837	John Forsyth 1837
9. William H. Harrison, Whig 1841	John Tyler, Whig 1841	Daniel Webster 1841
10. John Tyler, Whig and Democratic 1841		Daniel Webster 1841 Hugh S. Legare 1843 Abel P. Upshur 1843 John C. Calhoun 1844
11. James K. Polk, Democratic 1845	George M. Dallas, Democratic 1845	James Buchanan 1845
12. Zachary Taylor, Whig 1849	Millard Fillmore, Whig 1848	John M. Clayton 1849
13. Millard Fillmore, Whig 1850		Daniel Webster 1850 Edward Everett 1852

President	Vice President	Secretary of State
14. Franklin Pierce, Democratic 1853	William R. D. King, Democratic 1853	W. L. Marcy 1853
15. James Buchanan, Democratic 1857	John C. Breckinridge, Democratic 1857	Lewis Cass 1857 J. S. Black 1860
16. Abraham Lincoln, Republican 1861	Hannibal Hamlin, Republican 1861 Andrew Johnson, Unionist 1865	W. H. Seward 1861
17. Andrew Johnson, Unionist 1865		W. H. Seward 1865
18. Ulysses S. Grant, Republican 1869	Schuyler Colfax, Republican 1869 Henry Wilson, Republican 1873	E. B. Washburne 1869 H. Fish 1869
19. Rutherford B. Hayes, Republican 1877	William A. Wheeler, Republican 1877	W. M. Evarts 1877
20. James A. Garfield, Republican 1881	Chester A. Arthur, Republican 1881	J. G. Blaine 1881
21. Chester A. Arthur, Republican 1881		F. T. Frelinghuysen 1881
22. Grover Cleveland, Democratic 1885	T. A. Hendricks, Democratic 1885	T. F. Bayard 1885
23. Benjamin Harrison, Republican 1889	Levi P. Morton, Republican 1889	J. G. Blaine 1889 J. W. Foster 1892
24. Grover Cleveland, Democratic 1893	Adlai E. Stevenson, Democratic 1893	W. Q. Gresham 1893 R. Olney 1895
25. William McKinley, Republican 1897	Garret A. Hobart, Republican 1897 Theodore Roosevelt, Republican 1901	J. Sherman 1897 W. R. Day 1897 J. Hay 1898
26. Theodore Roosevelt, Republican 1901	Chas. W. Fairbanks, Republican 1905	J. Hay 1901 E. Root 1905 R. Bacon 1909
27. William H. Taft, Republican 1909	James S. Sherman, Republican 1909	P. C. Knox 1909

POPULATION OF THE UNITED STATES

Division and State	1790	1800	1810	1820
UNITED STATES	3,929,214	5,308,483	7,239,881	9,638,453
GEOGRAPHIC DIVISIONS				
New England	1,009,408	1,233,011	1,471,973	1,660,071
Middle Atlantic	952,632	1,402,565	2,014,702	2,699,845
South Atlantic	1,851,806	2,286,494	2,674,891	3,061,063
East South Central	109,368	335,407	708,590	1,190,489
West South Central			77,618	167,680
East North Central		51,006	272,324	792,719
West North Central			19,783	66,586
Mountain				
Pacific				
NEW ENGLAND				
Maine	96,540	151,719	228,705	298,335
New Hampshire	141,885	183,858	214,460	244,161
Vermont	85,425	154,465	217,895	235,981
Massachusetts	378,787	422,845	472,040	523,287
Rhode Island	68,825	69,122	76,931	83,059
Connecticut	237,946	251,002	261,942	275,248

President	Vice President	Secretary of State
28. Woodrow Wilson, Democratic 1913	Thomas R. Marshall, Democratic 1913	W. J. Bryan 1913 R. Lansing 1915 B. Colby 1920
29. Warren G. Harding, Republican 1921	Calvin Coolidge, Republican 1921	C. E. Hughes 1921
30. Calvin Coolidge, Republican 1923	Charles G. Dawes, Republican 1925	C. E. Hughes 1923 F. B. Kellogg 1925
31. Herbert Hoover, Republican 1929	Charles Curtis, Republican 1929	H. L. Stimson 1929
32. Franklin D. Roosevelt, Democratic 1933	John Nance Garner, Democratic 1933 Henry A. Wallace, Democratic 1941 Harry S Truman, Democratic 1945	C. Hull 1933 E. R. Stettinius, Jr. 1944
33. Harry S Truman, Democratic 1945	Alben W. Barkley, Democratic 1949	J. F. Byrnes 1945 G. C. Marshall 1947 D. G. Acheson 1949
34. Dwight D. Eisenhower, Republican 1953	Richard M. Nixon, Republican 1953	J. F. Dulles 1953 C. A. Herter 1959
35. John F. Kennedy, Democratic 1961	Lyndon B. Johnson, Democratic 1961	D. Rusk 1961
36. Lyndon B. Johnson, Democratic 1963	Hubert H. Humphrey, Democratic 1965	D. Rusk 1963
37. Richard M. Nixon, Republican 1969	Spiro T. Agnew, Republican 1969 Gerald R. Ford, Republican 1973	W. P. Rogers 1969 H. A. Kissinger 1973
38. Gerald R. Ford, Republican 1974	Nelson Rockefeller, Republican 1974	H. A. Kissinger 1974
39. Jimmy Carter, Democratic 1977	Walter Mondale, Democratic 1977	C. Vance 1977 E. Muskie 1980
40. Ronald Reagan, Republican 1981	George Bush, Republican 1981	A. Haig 1981 G. Schultz 1982

1830	1840	1850	1860	1870	1880
12,866,020	17,069,453	23,191,876	31,443,321	39,818,449	50,155,783
1,954,717	2,234,822	2,728,116	3,135,283	3,487,924	4,010,529
3,587,664	4,526,260	5,898,735	7,458,985	8,810,806	10,496,878
3,645,752	3,925,299	4,679,090	5,364,703	5,853,610	7,597,197
1,815,969	2,575,445	3,363,271	4,020,991	4,404,445	5,585,151
246,127	449,985	940,251	1,747,667	2,029,965	3,334,220
1,470,018	2,924,728	4,523,260	6,926,884	9,124,517	11,206,668
140,455	426,814	880,335	2,169,832	3,856,594	6,157,443
		72,927	174,923	315,385	653,119
		105,871	444,053	675,125	1,114,578
399,455	501,793	583,169	628,279	626,915	648,936
269,328	284,574	317,976	326,073	318,300	346,530
280,652	291,948	314,120	315,098	330,551	332,286
610,408	737,699	994,514	1,231,066	1,457,351	1,783,085
97,199	108,830	147,545	174,620	217,353	276,531
297,675	309,978	370,792	460,147	537,454	622,700

Division and State	1790	1800	1810	1820
GEOGRAPHIC DIVISIONS				
MIDDLE ATLANTIC				
New York	340,120	589,051	959,049	1,372,812
New Jersey	184,139	211,149	245,562	277,575
Pennsylvania	434,373	602,365	810,091	1,049,458
SOUTH ATLANTIC				
Delaware	59,096	64,273	72,674	72,749
Maryland	319,728	341,548	380,546	407,350
Dist. of Columbia		14,093	24,023	33,039
Virginia	747,610	880,200	974,600	1,065,366
West Virginia				
North Carolina	393,751	478,103	555,500	638,829
South Carolina	249,073	345,591	415,115	502,741
Georgia	82,548	162,686	252,433	340,989
Florida				
EAST SOUTH CENTRAL				
Kentucky	73,677	220,955	406,511	564,317
Tennessee	35,691	105,602	261,727	422,823
Alabama				127,901
Mississippi		8,850	40,352	75,448
WEST SOUTH CENTRAL				
Arkansas			1,062	14,273
Louisiana			76,556	153,407
Texas				
EAST NORTH CENTRAL				
Ohio		45,365	230,760	581,434
Indiana		5,641	24,520	147,178
Illinois			12,282	55,211
Michigan			4,762	8,896
Wisconsin				
WEST NORTH CENTRAL				
Minnesota				
Iowa				
Missouri			19,783	66,586
North Dakota				
South Dakota				
Nebraska				
Kansas				
MOUNTAIN				
Montana				
Idaho				
Wyoming				
Colorado				
New Mexico				
Arizona				
Utah				
Nevada				
PACIFIC				
Washington				
Oregon				
California				

Division and State	1890	1900	1910	1920
UNITED STATES	62,947,714	75,994,575	91,972,266	105,710,620
GEOGRAPHIC DIVISIONS				
New England	4,700,749	5,592,017	6,552,681	7,400,909
Middle Atlantic	12,706,220	15,454,678	19,315,892	22,261,144
South Atlantic	8,857,922	10,443,480	12,194,895	13,990,272
East South Central	6,429,154	7,547,757	8,409,901	8,893,307
West South Central	4,740,983	6,532,290	8,784,534	10,242,224
East North Central	13,478,305	15,985,581	18,250,621	21,475,543
West North Central	8,932,112	10,347,423	11,637,921	12,544,249
Mountain	1,213,935	1,674,657	2,633,517	3,336,101
Pacific	1,888,334	2,416,692	4,192,304	5,566,871
Noncontiguous				

1830	1840	1850	1860	1870	1880
1,918,608	2,428,921	3,097,394	3,880,735	4,382,759	5,082,871
320,823	373,306	489,555	672,035	906,096	1,131,116
1,348,233	1,724,033	2,311,786	2,906,215	3,521,951	4,282,891
76,748	78,085	91,532	112,216	125,015	146,608
447,040	470,019	583,034	687,049	780,894	934,943
39,834	43,712	51,687	75,080	131,700	177,624
1,211,405	1,239,797	1,421,661	1,596,318	1,225,163	1,512,565
				442,014	618,457
737,987	753,419	869,039	992,622	1,071,361	1,399,750
581,185	594,398	668,507	703,708	705,606	995,577
516,823	691,392	906,185	1,057,286	1,184,109	1,542,180
34,730	54,477	87,445	140,424	187,748	269,493
687,917	779,828	982,405	1,155,684	1,321,011	1,648,690
681,904	829,210	1,002,717	1,109,801	1,258,520	1,542,359
309,527	590,756	771,623	964,201	996,992	1,262,505
136,621	375,651	606,526	791,305	827,922	1,131,597
30,388	97,574	209,897	435,450	484,471	802,525
215,739	352,411	517,762	708,002	726,915	939,946
		212,592	604,215	818,579	1,591,749
937,903	1,519,467	1,980,329	2,339,511	2,665,260	3,198,062
343,031	685,866	988,416	1,350,428	1,680,637	1,987,301
157,445	476,183	851,470	1,711,951	2,539,981	3,077,871
31,639	212,267	397,654	749,113	1,184,059	1,636,937
	30,945	305,391	775,881	1,054,670	1,315,497
		6,077	172,023	439,706	780,773
	43,112	192,214	674,913	1,194,020	1,624,615
140,455	383,702	682,044	1,182,012	1,721,295	2,168,380
				2,405	36,909
				11,776	98,268
			28,841	122,933	452,402
			107,206	364,399	996,096
				20,595	39,159
				14,999	32,610
				9,118	20,789
			34,277	39,864	194,327
		61,547	93,516	91,874	119,565
				9,658	40,440
		11,380	40,273	86,786	143,963
			6,857	42,491	62,266
			11,594	23,955	75,116
		13,294	52,465	90,923	174,768
		92,597	379,994	560,247	864,694

1930	1940	1950	1960	1970	1980
122,775,046	131,669,275	150,697,361	179,323,175	203,211,926	226,504,825
8,166,341	8,437,290	9,314,453	10,509,367	11,841,663	12,348,493
26,260,750	27,539,487	30,163,533	34,168,452	37,199,040	36,788,174
15,793,589	17,823,151	21,182,335	25,971,732	30,671,337	36,943,139
9,887,214	10,778,225	11,477,181	12,050,126	12,803,470	14,662,882
12,176,830	13,064,525	14,537,572	16,951,255	19,320,560	23,743,134
25,297,185	26,626,342	30,399,368	36,225,024	40,252,476	41,669,738
13,296,915	13,516,990	14,061,394	15,394,115	16,319,187	17,184,066
3,701,789	4,150,003	5,074,998	6,855,060	8,281,562	11,368,330
8,194,433	9,733,262	14,486,527	20,339,105	25,453,688	30,431,388
			858,939	1,068,943	1,365,481

Division and State	1890	1900	1910	1920
NEW ENGLAND				
Maine	661,086	694,466	742,371	768,014
New Hampshire	376,530	411,588	430,572	443,083
Vermont	332,422	343,641	355,956	352,428
Massachusetts	2,238,947	2,805,346	3,366,416	3,852,356
Rhode Island	345,506	428,556	542,610	604,397
Connecticut	746,258	908,420	1,114,756	1,380,631
MIDDLE ATLANTIC				
New York	6,003,174	7,268,894	9,113,614	10,385,227
New Jersey	1,444,933	1,883,669	2,537,167	3,155,900
Pennsylvania	5,258,113	6,302,115	7,665,111	8,720,017
SOUTH ATLANTIC				
Delaware	168,493	184,735	202,322	223,003
Maryland	1,042,390	1,188,044	1,295,346	1,449,661
Dist. of Columbia	230,392	278,718	331,069	437,571
Virginia	1,655,980	1,854,184	2,061,612	2,309,187
West Virginia	762,794	958,800	1,221,119	1,463,701
North Carolina	1,617,949	1,893,810	2,206,287	2,559,123
South Carolina	1,151,149	1,340,316	1,515,400	1,683,724
Georgia	1,837,353	2,216,331	2,609,121	2,895,832
Florida	391,422	528,542	752,619	968,470
EAST SOUTH CENTRAL				
Kentucky	1,858,635	2,147,174	2,289,905	2,416,630
Tennessee	1,767,518	2,020,616	2,184,789	2,337,885
Alabama	1,513,401	1,828,697	2,138,093	2,348,174
Mississippi	1,289,600	1,551,270	1,797,114	1,790,618
WEST SOUTH CENTRAL				
Arkansas	1,128,211	1,311,564	1,574,449	1,752,204
Louisiana	1,118,588	1,381,625	1,656,388	1,798,509
Oklahoma	258,657	790,391	1,657,155	2,028,283
Texas	2,235,527	3,048,710	3,896,542	4,663,228
EAST NORTH CENTRAL				
Ohio	3,672,329	4,157,545	4,767,121	5,759,394
Indiana	2,192,404	2,516,462	2,700,876	2,930,390
Illinois	3,826,352	4,821,550	5,638,591	6,485,280
Michigan	2,093,890	2,420,982	2,810,173	3,668,412
Wisconsin	1,693,330	2,069,042	2,333,860	2,632,067
WEST NORTH CENTRAL				
Minnesota	1,310,283	1,751,394	2,075,708	2,387,125
Iowa	1,912,297	2,231,853	2,224,771	2,404,021
Missouri	2,679,185	3,106,665	3,293,335	3,404,055
North Dakota	190,983	319,146	577,056	646,872
South Dakota	348,600	401,570	583,888	636,547
Nebraska	1,062,656	1,066,300	1,192,214	1,296,372
Kansas	1,428,108	1,470,495	1,690,949	1,769,257
MOUNTAIN				
Montana	142,924	243,329	376,053	548,889
Idaho	88,548	161,772	325,594	431,866
Wyoming	62,555	92,531	145,965	194,402
Colorado	413,249	539,700	799,024	939,629
New Mexico	160,282	195,310	327,301	360,350
Arizona	88,243	122,931	204,354	334,162
Utah	210,779	276,749	373,351	449,396
Nevada	47,355	42,335	81,875	77,407
PACIFIC				
Washington	357,232	518,103	1,141,990	1,356,621
Oregon	317,704	413,536	672,765	783,389
California	1,213,398	1,485,053	2,377,549	3,426,861
NONCONTIGUOUS				
Alaska				
Hawaii				

1930	1940	1950	1960	1970	1980
797,423	847,226	913,774	969,625	992,048	1,124,660
465,293	491,524	533,242	606,921	731,681	920,610
359,611	359,231	377,747	389,881	444,330	511,456
4,249,614	4,316,721	4,690,514	5,148,578	5,689,110	5,737,037
687,497	713,346	791,896	859,488	946,725	947,154
1,606,903	1,709,242	2,007,280	2,535,234	3,031,709	3,107,576
12,588,066	13,479,142	14,830,192	16,782,304	18,236,967	17,557,288
4,041,334	4,160,165	4,835,329	6,066,782	7,168,164	7,364,158
9,631,350	9,900,180	10,498,012	11,319,366	11,793,909	11,866,728
238,380	266,505	318,085	446,292	548,104	595,225
1,631,526	1,821,244	2,343,001	3,100,689	3,922,399	4,216,446
486,869	663,091	802,178	763,956	765,510	637,651
2,421,851	2,677,773	3,318,680	3,966,949	4,648,494	5,346,279
1,729,205	1,901,974	2,005,552	1,860,421	1,744,237	1,949,644
3,170,276	3,571,623	4,061,929	4,556,155	5,082,059	5,874,429
1,738,765	1,899,804	2,117,027	2,382,594	2,590,516	3,119,208
2,908,506	3,123,723	3,444,578	3,943,116	4,589,575	5,464,265
1,468,211	1,897,414	2,771,305	4,951,560	6,789,443	9,739,992
2,614,589	2,845,627	2,944,806	3,038,156	3,218,706	3,661,433
2,616,556	2,915,841	3,291,718	3,567,089	3,923,687	4,590,750
2,646,248	2,832,961	3,061,743	3,266,740	3,444,165	3,890,061
2,009,821	2,183,796	2,178,914	2,178,141	2,216,912	2,520,638
1,854,482	1,949,387	1,909,511	1,786,272	1,923,285	2,285,513
2,101,593	2,363,880	2,683,516	3,257,022	3,641,306	4,203,972
2,396,040	2,336,434	2,233,351	2,328,284	2,559,229	3,025,266
5,824,715	6,414,824	7,711,194	9,579,677	11,196,730	14,228,383
6,646,697	6,907,612	7,946,627	9,706,397	10,652,017	10,797,419
3,238,503	3,427,796	3,934,224	4,662,498	5,193,669	5,490,179
7,630,654	7,897,241	8,712,176	10,081,158	11,113,976	11,418,461
4,842,325	5,256,106	6,371,766	7,823,194	8,875,083	9,258,344
2,939,006	3,137,587	3,434,576	3,951,777	4,417,731	4,705,335
2,563,953	2,792,300	2,982,483	3,413,864	3,804,971	4,077,148
2,470,939	2,538,268	2,621,073	2,757,537	2,824,376	2,913,387
3,629,367	3,784,664	3,954,653	4,319,813	4,676,501	4,917,444
680,845	641,935	619,636	632,446	617,761	652,695
692,849	642,961	652,740	680,514	665,507	690,178
1,377,963	1,315,834	1,325,510	1,411,330	1,483,493	1,570,006
1,880,999	1,801,028	1,905,299	2,178,611	2,246,578	2,363,208
537,606	599,456	591,024	674,767	694,409	786,690
445,032	524,873	588,637	667,191	712,567	943,935
225,565	250,742	290,529	330,066	332,416	470,816
1,035,791	1,123,296	1,325,089	1,753,947	2,207,259	2,888,834
423,317	531,818	681,187	951,023	1,016,000	1,299,968
435,573	499,261	749,587	1,302,161	1,770,900	2,717,866
507,847	550,310	688,862	890,627	1,059,273	1,461,037
91,058	110,247	160,083	285,278	488,738	799,184
1,563,396	1,736,191	2,378,963	2,853,214	3,409,169	4,130,163
953,786	1,089,684	1,521,341	1,768,687	2,091,385	2,632,663
5,677,251	6,907,387	10,586,223	15,717,204	19,953,134	23,668,562
			226,167	300,382	400,481
			632,772	786,561	965,000

INDEX

Page references to illustrations, maps, and their captions appear in *italics*.

About the Authors

RICHARD N. CURRENT is University Distinguished Professor of History at the University of North Carolina at Greensboro. He is co-author of the Bancroft Prize–winning *Lincoln the President*. His books include: *Three Carpetbag Governors; The Lincoln Nobody Knows; Daniel Webster and the Rise of National Conservatism;* and *Secretary Stimson*. Professor Current has lectured on U.S. history in Europe, Asia, South America, Australia, and Antarctica. He has been a Fulbright Lecturer at the University of Munich and the University of Chile at Santiago and has served as Harmsworth Professor of American History at Oxford. He is past president of the Southern Historical Association.

T. HARRY WILLIAMS was Boyd Professor of History at Louisiana State University. He was awarded both the 1969 Pulitzer Prize and National Book Award for his biography of *Huey Long*. His books include: *Lincoln and His Generals; Lincoln and the Radicals; P. G. T. Beauregard; Americans at War; Romance and Realism in Southern Politics; Hayes of the Twenty-Third; McClellan, Sherman, and Grant; The Union Sundered;* and *The Union Restored*. Professor Williams was a Harmsworth Professor of American History at Oxford and President of both the Southern Historical Association and the Organization of American Historians.

FRANK FREIDEL is Bullitt Professor of American History at the University of Washington and Charles Warren Professor Emeritus of History at Harvard University. He is writing a six-volume biography of Franklin D. Roosevelt, four volumes of which have been published. Among his other books are: *Our Country's Presidents; F.D.R. and the South;* and *America in the Twentieth Century*. He is co-editor of the 1974 edition of the *Harvard Guide to American History* and past president of the Organization of American Historians. He is also a former president of the New England Historical Society.

ALAN BRINKLEY is Dunwalke Associate Professor of American History at Harvard University and has also taught at the Massachusetts Institute of Technology. He is a graduate of Princeton University, received his Ph.D. from Harvard, and has been awarded fellowships by the National Endowment for the Humanities and the American Council of Learned Societies. He is the author of *Voices of Protest: Huey Long, Father Coughlin, and the Great Depression*, co-author of *America in the Twentieth Century*, and the author of many articles and reviews.

A NOTE ON THE TYPE

The main text of this book was set via computer-driven cathode ray tube in Palatino, a type face designed by the noted German typographer Hermann Zapf. Named after Giovanbattista Palatino, a writing master of Renaissance Italy, Palatino was the first of Zapf's type faces to be introduced in America. The first designs for the face were made in 1948, and the fonts for the complete face were issued between 1950 and 1952. Like all Zapf-designed type faces, Palatino is beautifully balanced and exceedingly readable.

Other elements in this book were set via computer-driven cathode ray tube in Optima, a typeface designed by Hermann Zapf from 1952 to 1955 and issued in 1958. In designing Optima, Zapf created a truly new type form—a cross between the classic roman and a sans-serif face. So delicate are the stresses and balances in Optima that it rivals sans-serif faces in clarity and freshness and old-style faces in variety and interest.

Book design by Leon Bolognese

Cover design and construction by Jack Ribik

Cover photography by James McGuire

Composed by American–Stratford Graphic Services, Inc., Brattleboro, Vermont
Printed and bound by American Book–Stratford Press, Saddlebrook, N.J.